REMAKING
THE MODERN
WORLD 1900–2015

D1716274

THE BLACKWELL HISTORY OF THE WORLD

General Editor: **R. I. Moore**

A History of Latin America
Available in third edition as "A
History of Latin America to 1825"
Peter Bakewell

The Birth of the Modern World
C. A. Bayly

The Origins of Human Society
Peter Bogucki

A History of Russia, Central Asia
and Mongolia: Volume I
David Christian

A History of Russia, Central Asia
and Mongolia: Volume II
David Christian

A History of Australia, New Zealand
and the Pacific
*Donald Denoon, Philippa Mein-Smith
and Marivic Wyndham*

A History of South-East Asia
Anthony Reid

A History of China
Morris Rossabi

The Western Mediterranean and the
World
Teofilo F. Ruiz

A History of India
Second Edition
Burton Stein

A History of Japan
Second Edition
Conrad Totman

REMAKING
THE MODERN
WORLD 1900–2015

GLOBAL CONNECTIONS
AND COMPARISONS

C. A. BAYLY

WILEY Blackwell

Registered Offices
John Wiley & Sons, Inc., 111 River Street, Hoboken, NJ 07030, USA
John Wiley & Sons Ltd, The Atrium, Southern Gate, Chichester, West Sussex, PO19 8SQ, UK

Editorial Office
101 Station Landing, Medford, MA 02155, USA

For details of our global editorial offices, customer services, and more information about Wiley products visit us at www.wiley.com.

Wiley also publishes its books in a variety of electronic formats and by print-on-demand. Some content that appears in standard print versions of this book may not be available in other formats.

Library of Congress Cataloging-in-Publication data is available for this book.

ISBN 9781405187152 (hardback)
ISBN 9781405187169 (paperback)

Cover Design: Wiley
Cover Image: (front cover) © Agencia EFE/REX/Shutterstock

Set in 10/12 pt PlantinStd by Thomson Digital, Noida, India

Printed in Singapore by C.O.S. Printers Pte Ltd

10 9 8 7 6 5 4 3 2 1

CONTENTS

List of Figures and Photo Credits   vii

Series Editor's Preface   ix

Christopher Bayly and the Making of World History   xiii

Preface   xix

Introduction   1
1   The World Crisis, *c.*1900–1930: Europe and the "Middle East"   12
2   The World Crisis, *c.*1900–1930: Africa, Asia and Beyond   29
3   Authoritarianism and Dictatorship Worldwide, *c.*1900–1950   49
4   Democracies and Their Discontents, *c.*1900–1950   67
5   The Depression: State Intervention and Popular Resistance   84
6   The Second World War and its Consequences   96
7   Peripheral Conflicts and the End of Old Regimes, *c.*1945–1955   118
8   America's Hegemony and Colonialism's Finale, mid-1950s to 1970s   139
9   The "Tipping Point": World Politics and the Shock of the "Long 1980s"   162
10   The Expansion of Human Knowledge: The Twentieth-Century Person and Society   179
11   The Self and Human Society   194
12   Arts, Literature and Entertainment: Crisis and Recovery   215
13   Religion: Contestation and Revival   231
14   A Century of Killing and a Century of Crime   247
15   Internationalism and Transnationalism in Theory and Practice   263
16   The Shadow of Empire in the Modern World   270
17   The Pressure of People   287
18   Between Two Centuries: Economic Liberalisation and Political Fragmentation, *c.*1991 to 2015   298

Conclusion: Periods and Prophecy   323

Notes   333

Bibliography   363

Index   379

List of Figures and Photo Credits

Figure 1   Maori soldiers. Sir George Grey Special Collections,
            Auckland Libraries, 31-A2. Photo by Herman John
            Schmidt   14
Figure 2   The 9th Queen's Royal Lancers of the British Army
            charging German artillery, 1916. Underwood Photo
            Archives/Superstock   18
Figure 3   Nehru at Harrow, c.1906. Hulton Archive/Getty Images   35
Figure 4   Portrait of Chiang Kai-shek on the wall of the Sun Co.
            department store at the corner of Nanking Road and Yu
            Ya Ching Road. George Lacks/The LIFE Picture
            Collection/Getty Images   36
Figure 5   A young Hitler with members of the 16th Bavarian
            Reserves Infantry Regiment during the First World War.
            Roger Viollet/Agence France-Presse/Getty Images   47
Figure 6   Japanese suffragists carrying 20,000 petitions to the
            Imperial Diet requesting a women's suffrage bill, 1920s.
            George Rinhart/Bettmann/Corbis/Getty Images   116
Figure 7   President Sukarno and Marilyn Monroe at a party at the
            Beverly Hills Hotel, 1956. Bettmann/Getty Images   125
Figure 8   Yogyakarta, Indonesia, 1948. © Charles Breijer/
            Nederlands Fotomuseum   149
Figure 9   People strolling near the Berlin Wall. Bernauer Strasse,
            Berlin, 1969. Ullsteinbild/TopFoto   157
Figure 10   Fiat cars at Singapore Harbour. Singapore Press Holdings
            Ltd.   182
Figure 11   Eva Perón handing out election badges from her
            campaign train, February 1946. Juan Perón is in the
            background. Thomas D. McAvoy/The LIFE Picture
            Collection/Getty Images   201
Figure 12   Pakistan President Mohammad Ayub Khan with Jackie
            Kennedy. Tour of Pakistan, 1962. Art Rickerby/The
            LIFE Picture Collection/Getty Images   203

Figure 13   *The Peach Girl*, 1931. Ryan Lingyu and Jin Yan. Liana
             Film Co/REX/Shutterstock   221

Figure 14   Leon Trotsky and his wife with Frida Kahlo and others
             on arrival in Mexico, 1937. OFF/Agence France-Presse/
             Getty Images   223

Figure 15   The Beatles, 1967. "All you need is love". Getty Images   227

Figure 16   John Frum followers, Vanuatu. Thierry Falise/
             LightRocket/Getty Images   234

Figure 17   One of the symbols of Vietnam's Cao Dai religion of
             modernity. Xavier Rossi/StockPhoto/Getty Images   235

Figure 18   A march past performed by Bukit Panjang Government
             School pupils during the coronation of Queen Elizabeth
             II, 1953. National Archives of Singapore   277

Figure 19   Gandhi and Nehru at a Congress meeting, 1946. Ruhe/
             Ullstein Bild via Getty Images   283

SERIES EDITOR'S PREFACE

There is nothing new in the attempt to grasp history as a whole. To understand how humanity began and how it has come to its present condition is one of the oldest and most universal of human needs, expressed in the religious and philosophical systems of every civilization. But only in the last few decades has it begun to appear both necessary and possible to meet that need by means of a rational and systematic appraisal of current historical knowledge. Until the middle of the nineteenth century history itself was generally treated as a subordinate branch of other fields of thought and learning – of literature, rhetoric, law, philosophy or religion. When historians began at that time to establish its independence as a field of scholarship in its own right, with its own subject matter and its own rules and methods, they made it in practice not the attempt to achieve a comprehensive account of the human past but the history of Western Europe and of the societies created by European expansion and colonisation. In laying the scholarly foundations of their discipline they also reinforced the Enlightenment's belief in the advance of "civilization" and, more recently, of "Western civilization". In this form, with relatively minor regional variations, it became the basis of the teaching of history almost everywhere for most of the twentieth century. Research and teaching of the histories of other parts of the world developed mainly in the context of area studies like those of ancient Greece and Rome, rooted in philology, and conducted through the exposition of the canonical texts of their respective languages.

While those approaches prevailed, world history as such remained largely the province of thinkers and writers principally interested in constructing theoretical or metaphysical systems. Only towards the end of the twentieth century did the community of academic historians begin to recognise it as a proper and even urgent field for the application of their knowledge and skills. The inadequacy of the traditional parameters of the discipline is now acknowledged, and the sense is growing that a world facing a common future of headlong and potentially catastrophic transformation needs its common history. The realisation of such a history has been delayed, however, by simple ignorance on the one hand – for the history of enormous stretches of space and time has until very recently been known not at all, or so patchily and superficially as not to be worth revisiting – and on the other by the lack of a widely acceptable basis upon which to organise and discuss what is nevertheless the enormous and enormously diverse knowledge that we have.

The first of those obstacles is now being rapidly overcome. There is almost no part of the world or period of its history that is not the object of energetic and sophisticated investigation by archaeologists and historians. The expansion of the horizons of academic history since the 1980s has been dramatic. The quality and quantity of historical research and writing have risen exponentially in each decade, and the advances have been most spectacular in some of the areas previously most neglected. The academics have not failed to share the results of their labours. Reliable and accessible, often brilliant, accounts are now readily available of regions, periods and topics that even 20 years ago were obscure to everyone but a handful of specialists. In particular, collaborative publication, in the form of volumes or sets of volumes in which teams of authors set forth, in more or less detail, their expert and up-to-date conclusions in the field of their research, has been a natural and necessary response to the growth of knowledge. Only in that way can non-specialists, at any level, be kept even approximately in touch with the constantly accelerating accumulation of information about the past.

Yet the amelioration of one problem exacerbates the other. It is truer than it has ever been that knowledge is growing and perspectives multiplying more quickly than they can be assimilated and recorded in synthetic form. We can now describe a great many more trees in a great deal more detail than we could before. It does not always follow that we have a better view of the wood. Collaboration has many strengths, but clarity, still less originality, of vision is rarely prominent among them. History acquires shape, structure, relevance – becomes, in the fashionable catchphrase, something for thinking with – by advancing and debating new suggestions about what past societies were like, how they worked and why they changed over long periods of time, how they resembled and why they differed from contemporaneous societies in other parts of the world, and how they interacted with one another. Such insights, like the sympathetic understanding without which the past is dead, are almost always born of individual creativity and imagination. That is why each volume in this series embodies the work and vision of a single author. Synthesis on such a scale demands learning, resolution and, not least, intellectual and professional courage of no ordinary degree. We have been singularly fortunate in finding scholars of great distinction who are willing to undertake it.

There is a wealth of ways in which world history can be written. The oldest and simplest view, that it is best understood as the history of contacts between peoples previously isolated from one another, from which (as some think) all change arises, is now seen to be capable of application since the earliest times. An influential alternative focuses upon the tendency of economic exchange to create self-sufficient but ever-expanding "worlds" which sustain successive systems of power and culture. Another seeks to understand the differences between societies and cultures, and therefore the particular character of each, by comparing the ways in which their values, social relationships and structures of power have developed. The rapidly emerging field of ecological history returns to a very ancient tradition of seeing interaction with the physical environment, and with other animals, at the centre of the human predicament, while insisting that its understanding demands an approach which is culturally, chronologically and geographically comprehensive. More recently still "Big History", led by a contributor to this series, has begun to show how human history can be integrated with that not only of the natural but also of the cosmic environment, and better understood in consequence.

The Blackwell History of the World seeks not to embody any single approach, but to support them all, as it will use them all, by providing a modern, comprehensive and accessible account of the entire human past. Each volume offers a substantial overview of a portion of world history large enough to permit, and indeed demand, the reappraisal of customary boundaries of regions, periods and topics, and in doing so reflects the idiosyncrasies of its sources and its subjects, as well as the vision and judgement of its author. The series as a whole combines the indispensable narratives of very long-term regional development with global surveys of developments across the world, and of interaction between regions and what they have experienced in common, or visited upon one another, at particular times. Together, these volumes will provide a framework in which the history of every part of the world can be viewed, and a basis upon which most aspects of human activity can be compared across both time and space. A frame offers perspective. Comparison implies respect for difference. That is the beginning of what the past has to offer the future.

SERIES EDITOR'S ACKNOWLEDGEMENTS

The editor is grateful to all the contributors for advice and assistance on the design and contents of the series as a whole, as well as on individual volumes. Both editor and contributors wish to place on record, individually and collectively, their debt to the late John Davey, formerly of Blackwell Publishing, without whose vision and enthusiasm the series could not have been initiated, and to his successor, Tessa Harvey, without whose energy, skill and diplomacy, sustained over many years, it could not have been realised.

The author of this book, Christopher Bayly, died suddenly in April 2015, leaving it unfinished, though in effect complete. He was a historian of immense distinction, and his contribution to history in general and world history in particular is described below. To this series he gave two volumes of the highest quality and originality, and to its editor unbounded inspiration, advice and support. His loss is irreparable. In the task of bringing the manuscript he left to publication the assistance of Daniel Jacobius Morgan, who had worked closely with him in his final months, has been unstintingly generous, and indispensable. I am grateful for the judgement and advice of Michael Bentley and Christopher Clark, and for the patience of Haze Humbert through an exceptionally demanding production process. Susan Bayly has guided it at every point, and through many hazards, with seemingly inexhaustible patience, fortitude and grace. Nobody else could have ensured that this would be the book Chris meant it to be. It is hers too.

R. I. Moore

To our series editor's moving words of thanks I must add some heartfelt acknowledgements of my own. Our cherished friends and family have been tirelessly supportive as we have seen my dearest Chris's manuscript through to publication. And while I cannot mention everyone by name, I do wish to convey my appreciation to Daniel Jacobius Morgan, and to Bob Moore for his unflagging commitment and insight. Special thanks are also due to Sugata Bose, David Cannadine, Derek Davis, Richard Drayton, Tim Harper and Gordon Johnson; and to Chris Clark, whose eloquent words in our memoir below so brilliantly capture Chris's brio and profundity. I also thank Barbara Roe, who recovered the images we have been able to use as Chris wanted, especially the marvellous picture of the Spanish Civil War freedom fighter gazing into an uncertain future with a look of courage and optimism on her lovely young face, which we knew Chris intended as his cover illustration. And there are many others, both in Britain and beyond, including Chris's former students now adorning an amazing array of historical fields and subdisciplines across the world. I think of you all with affection and gratitude, greatly heartened by all you have done to ensure that we can temper our sense of abiding loss with the gift of this final, magnificent product of Chris's erudition and humanity.

Susan Bayly
Cambridge, March 2018

CHRISTOPHER BAYLY AND THE MAKING OF WORLD HISTORY

Professor Sir Christopher Bayly, LittD, FBA, the author of this volume, died in Chicago of a heart attack on 19 April 2015 at the age of 69. Bayly was the pre-eminent historian of India and the British Empire and a pioneer in the field of global history. He was also the first academic ever to be knighted "for services to history outside of Europe". Chris's distinction was international, as the long list of his appointments and honours testifies, but his career was centred on St Catharine's College, Cambridge, where he was elected in 1970 to a Fellowship and College Lectureship in History and became Director of Studies in History. In 1981, Chris Bayly was appointed to Cambridge University's Smuts Reader-ship in Commonwealth Studies, and thereafter he was appointed to a succes-sion of posts in the Faculty of History, culminating in the Vere Harmsworth Professorship of Imperial and Naval History in 1992. At the time of his death, he also held concurrently professorships at Chicago, Copenhagen and Queen Mary University of London.

Chris was born in Tunbridge Wells, Kent, to a family entangled with the recent history of Empire. He remembered childhood conversations with his London cockney grandfather, who had fought during the First World War in Egypt, Palestine and Turkey. His father had seen service all over the world as a merchant mariner, including on ships running copra from India. "So I had an early introduction to colonial and world history," he would later say. The history Chris learnt at the Skinners' School in Tunbridge Wells and as an undergraduate at Balliol, Oxford, in 1963, was broad in its intellectual horizons but strongly European in focus. The turn towards a career in Indian history came in 1965, when Chris embarked on a long vacation journey across land to India, passing through Turkey, Iran, Afghanistan and Pakistan. Forced to avoid the Indian–Pakistani warzone, he travelled south to Karachi and caught a Shia pilgrimage boat to Basra. "I got a sense of India from the other side," he recalled in a July 2014 interview. "Not dropping out of an aircraft. India in West Asia, and particularly the Muslim dimension. So that was a very formative experience."

At St Antony's, his graduate college, Sarvepalli Gopal and Albert Hourani guided his reading in the histories of India and the Middle East; the supervisor of his doctoral thesis was Jack Gallagher (also of Balliol), who was then overseeing a transformation in British imperial history. Chris came to Cambridge in 1970 at the invitation of Eric Stokes, Smuts Professor of British Commonwealth History, who had been at St Catharine's College since 1963. The transfer to Cambridge was arranged, as Chris later recalled, in the strikingly relaxed way typical of those times: "Jack phoned Eric: 'Eric, have you got a job there for this funny person called Bayly that I've got?' He said: 'Maybe we do', and that was it."

Eric Stokes was to be Chris's most important mentor. In the 1970s, Stokes was moving away from the issues of principle and ideology that had commanded the attention of his earlier work towards an approach to Indian history that stressed the importance of landholding structures and the pressures exerted on them by British systems of revenue management. An interest in the dynamic interaction between local elites and imperial governments would also be an abiding feature of Chris's work on India. Stokes's unpretentious and likeable scholarly persona was another inspiration. In a touching piece for the *Oxford Dictionary of National Biography*, Chris found words for Stokes, who had died in 1981, that one might use of Chris himself: "His influence as a historian was accomplished not with domineering patronage, but through humour, self-deprecation, and intellectual inquisitiveness."

Chris Bayly's books don't document results; they track intellectual journeys. "This book," Chris writes at the opening of *Rulers, Townsmen and Bazaars* (1983), a study that transformed historical understanding of the impact of British rule in India, "grew out of a fascination with the rich pattern of commercial life still to be found in the tangled lanes of brass-smiths' stalls and ancient merchant houses which lay behind the waterfront of the city of Benares." The stately waterfront mansions of the *ghats* of Benares were just a point of disembarkation. What interested him were the tangled lanes behind.

These steps away from the waterfront, into the recesses behind elite networks and smooth historiographical surfaces, can be traced in every book Chris wrote. Chris was acutely aware of the intricately layered quality of human societies. Again and again, he offers us vertiginous views through superimposed social textures. Nothing in what unfolds before our eyes is obvious, because everything is in motion. Clans and occupational fraternities coalesce into class-like structures; power changes hands: cosmopolitan oligarchs cede power to merchants; Nanakpanthi Khattris take over from their Islamicised caste fellows; Kannada merchants and Chettis slip into positions once occupied by Armenians and Jews. Chris saw a piece of agency, a spark of resilience and hope, in everyone who entered his field of vision.

This seething, ever-present mobility made it utterly impossible to think of India as something stagnant or passive, something to which history or empire simply happened. Chris's eye was fixed on those forces of self-organisation and self-reinvention that predated the arrival of the British and would survive their departure to shape the India of today.

Already in the earliest books on India, Chris had discerned parallels with peasant Egypt, small-town Meiji-era Japan and the striving professional classes of nineteenth-century China. These expansive reflections later fed into the two breakthrough books that shaped and deepened the new field of world history –

Imperial Meridian and *The Birth of the Modern World* – establishing Chris as one of the foremost historians of his generation worldwide. *Imperial Meridian* (1989) marked a transition from highly textured work on the Indian subcontinent to a new kind of history focused on how the interactions between great imperial power complexes shaped and were shaped by processes of change within them. The most historiographically significant work in this mode was *The Birth of the Modern World: Global Connections and Comparisons, 1780–1914* (2004), to which *Remaking the Modern World* is the sequel.

The Birth of the Modern World not only did much to establish world history as a scholarly discipline but also altered the conceptual framework of the subject by de-centring the West. It forged a new kind of world history which reflected both an appreciative engagement with the work of other historians across the widest possible span of fast-changing disciplinary specialisms and an eagerness to build bridges with neighbouring fields. Anthropology was a subject that loomed especially large on Chris's intellectual horizons. There was of course a personal dimension to this encounter. Thirty-four years of marriage to Susan, an anthropologist of India and Vietnam, took shape as a life of perpetual travel and reunion, sustained and nourished by joyfully impassioned argument, and keen enthusiasm for one another's work.

In many ways Chris took an anthropologist's as well as an historian's eye to his work in India. At a time when many other historians regarded official state archives as the only important source, Chris was searching out the privately archived north Indian collections of commercial family record books from which he derived the most important insights in *Rulers, Townsmen and Bazaars*. Once deciphered, these complex texts allowed him to reconstruct the social and religious life of the merchant networks and thus to peer into worlds whose inner life had left little trace on the grand narratives of official reportage. What Chris found most attractive in the anthropology he read was its practitioners' insistence that the intimate and the everyday are matters of profound importance for a sympathetic understanding of the world's people and places. He responded with particular keenness to the insights of those anthropologists who brought to the exploration of social and cultural life in both familiar and far-flung settings a recognition that human existence is experienced dynamically, in a world of continual flux and change. Indeed, he was an important contributor to anthropology's own debates about how to do justice to the complexities of change and transformation in a discipline once thought to be equipped only to chart the specifics of the here and now, as observed by the intensive methods of ethnographic participant-observation.

One of Chris's critical early forays into new history writing reflected precisely this excitement about the dialogue with anthropology. This was the essay on Indian cloth entitled "The origins of swadeshi (home industry)", which he published in 1986 in the ground-breaking joint volume *The Social Life of Things* edited by the anthropologist Arjun Appadurai. Still widely read within and beyond both history and anthropology, Chris's account of the remarkable array of meanings ascribed to the production and consumption of items, ranging from the sumptuous shawls ceremonially exchanged by rulers and courtiers in India's precolonial princedoms to Gandhi's famous khadi homespun cotton, charts the subtleties of Indian taste, choice and culture as matters of economic, political and moral initiative and in no sense a reflection of uncontested or inert cultural givens. His writings on Indian temple and trading cities, on the surprising involvement in early colonial economic life of north India's networks of Hindu spiritual ascetics and his explorations of Hindu and Muslim statecraft in the transition from precolonial to colonial rule have also been appreciatively read by anthropologists.

At the heart of *The Birth of the Modern World* was a narrative of convergence. The book opened with a powerful evocation of the diversity of bodily practices across the world's societies at the beginning of the modern era; the nineteenth century, Bayly argued, saw the rise of global uniformities in the structures and articulations of states, religions and economic life, visible not only in great institutions but also in modes of dress and the consumption of food. The book shrank the distance between "the West" and "the rest"; industrialisation, urbanisation, nationalism and the development of the state were for him ultimately global processes, notwithstanding local specificities. The book registered moments of heightened difference and antagonism, but for Chris, these were always subordinate phenomena. Antagonisms flourished precisely because societies were becoming more connected and more alike.

Chris's account allowed for what he described as "the brute fact of western domination", but his book also stressed the limited and temporary character of that domination and insisted on the "interdependence" of diverse processes of change. No one who reads this book can fail to be impressed by the subtlety and lucidity of the reasoning, the breadth of compass, the attention to reciprocity in political, economic and social relationships and the well-oiled analytical gears that enabled Chris to travel elegantly between the local and the global.

And even as he enlarged the scope of his attention, Chris continued to generate fresh insights into Indian history. *Empire and Information* (1996) offered a compelling account of British intelligence gathering in India between 1780 and 1870, showing how "native informants" recruited by the British actively shaped the process. In analogous fashion, *Origins of Nationality in South Asia* (1998) and *Recovering Liberties* (2011) elucidated how Indians responded as autonomous agents to Western nationalism and liberal political and economic thought.

Chris's books bore the imprint of wide and humane interests; they were also methodologically eclectic. As Richard Drayton, former Research Fellow at St Catharine's College and Rhodes Professor of Imperial History at King's College London, put it in an obituary for the *Guardian*: Chris Bayly had "an astonishing capacity to respond quickly to new perspectives and had the knack, in particular, of grafting historical ideas from one specialism to another. He read widely across the social sciences and had a magpie's eye for something brilliant in another discipline." Conversation was a crucial part of the gathering and comparing that drove Chris's historical thinking: when discussions with students or colleagues got interesting, Chris would often pull out a small crumpled notebook and start scribbling down ideas.

As these observations may suggest, Chris lived in his work. Not for it, but in it. The "Bayly mahal", as he sometimes affectionately called the home he and his wife Susan founded when they married in 1981, was a place of conversation over work and wine, a conversation anchored in shared passions, complementary interests and pride in each other's achievements. And C3 on Main Court, the room Chris occupied for decades at St Catharine's College, was much more than an office. Eloquent objects were gathered there. The model ship his father had built. The tall eighteenth-century Venetian rosewood slippers decorated in mother of pearl – witnesses to the cultural links between northern Italy, the Ottoman Empire and China. The beautiful Gandhara head of the Buddha, 1500 years old and carved by Greek and South Asian artisans in a style native to eastern Afghanistan – of all the things Chris and Susan had found together, this was his favourite.

It was in C3 that so many conversations happened, conversations that never failed to take Chris's guests to new places. And this was not just a matter of the sparks that were always falling from Chris's forge, but also his other gifts – gifts of unassuming and attentive friendship. Just a few days after his death, one of Chris's former St Catharine's graduate students, Jayeeta Sharma, wrote: "I will never forget how awkward I felt, as a provincial student from a little place in north-eastern India, how he helped me to find my moorings, with C3 as a welcoming, warm and beautiful space for talk, laughter, and hospitality." Words like this remind us of why Chris was admired and loved in equal measure.

After he had declined the offer by his former students to produce a Festschrift, a conference was organized in Varanasi (Benares) in January 2015 to honour his achievements. Here one could see Chris at ease and happy in the setting of the civilization that had absorbed and rewarded his attention for so many years. It is hard to imagine a more fitting acknowledgement: it was on the stone bathing wharves (*ghats*) of this beautiful, thronging city that the young Chris Bayly had begun his research into the mercantile elites of northern India. He was probably the first scholar to make use of the account books (*bahi khatas*) that all significant mercantile families had kept for centuries. In these, Chris found not just a meticulous record of revenues and expenditures but also entries documenting the constellation of relationships and affiliations that sustained the economic and moral life of merchant networks across much of the subcontinent. Alongside the double entry bookkeeping were salutations to various deities, lists of temple accoutrements and accounts of expenditures on worship, bathing in the Ganges and gifts to Brahmins. And what struck him most as he worked with those difficult, handwritten texts was what he saw and heard when he lifted his gaze from the faded pages and observed what the banker merchant families were doing all around him, especially the visits they hosted from the naked *sadhu* holy men still consigning their brotherhoods' assets to the trusted men of business whose forbears their own precursors had dealt with in centuries past. As Chris himself put it, "Notions of credit, piety and commercial security were closely tied together." A nexus connecting commerce and religion announced itself here that would be a central theme in his subsequent work.

Connections of this kind were the stuff that Chris's historical thinking was made of. He was personally a sceptic in religious matters. Yet, his books are striking for their integration of religious identities and forms of social mobilisation into larger narratives of transformation. He respected the Marxist tradition in historical writing for its deep interest in processes of social change, but he never allowed social, economic or political categories to occlude the agency of individuals seeking to make their way in a difficult and changing world.

Christopher Clark
Susan Bayly
March 2018

PREFACE

This volume is a companion volume to my *Birth of the Modern World 1780–1914: Global Connections and Comparisons* (2004). It adopts a roughly similar approach, that is to say it contains a series of analytical narrative chapters (1–9 and 18) enclosing more conceptual chapters on subjects such as the person, the arts and religion during the twentieth and early twenty-first centuries (10–17). The book is designed for advanced undergraduates, graduate students and academic colleagues, but I hope members of the general public interested in history will also read it. Like the earlier book, it is not so much a textbook as a reflection on world history. Much of this history has taken place during the lifetime of the author and many of his readers. This raises problems. Older readers might well respond to parts of this text by saying, "Well, we knew that; what's new?" But my impression is that many younger readers, including students, will only have the vaguest idea of historical events and arguments before their own times and outside their specialist knowledge. This is especially so for the years 1900 to 1950, except perhaps for the standard themes around Hitler and Stalin. So, I have felt it necessary to include some more basic narrative history. Fixing on a title also raised an interesting issue about historical memory. It was originally to be *The Crisis of the Modern World*, which seemed appropriate to older members of my family. But a friend from a formerly colonised country said to me, "You can't use that title. This was the century when we got our freedom!"

Obviously, too, as an author, my own knowledge and reading are limited in light of the scope of the study. I know more about South Asia than Latin America and have a better knowledge of French and Indian than German or Chinese historical literature, for instance. Nevertheless, almost everything I read in newspapers, hear on the radio, see on the TV and discuss with friends and colleagues seems only too relevant to this book. Contemporary events, as discussed in the Introduction, have also caused me constantly to rethink my view of the past, which is why I have brought the argument forward to 2015. The problem, then, even compared with a study of the nineteenth century, becomes what to leave out, rather than what to include. That is also true of references. Some authors of world histories simply list books by chapter at the end of their study. I have chosen to reference useful general studies in the text itself, but clearly this only represents a tiny proportion of all relevant publications which can now be counted in hundreds of thousands for such topics as the First World War or Nazism, or in the millions overall. Writing modern world history – and the Introduction considers some of the debates about its worth – can only be a flawed activity. But I argue that it adds value to other forms of historical writing and to public debate more generally.

I have had the enormous advantage of having access to some of the best history departments and universities in the world while writing this book: the universities of Cambridge, Chicago, Queen Mary University of London, Copenhagen and JNU, Delhi, among others. I am greatly indebted to the generosity of the government of India which established the Vivekananda Chair at the University of Chicago which I held for two quarters in 2014 and 2015. Some of what I learnt (and forgot) of British and European history at Oxford many years ago has usefully come back to mind. My personal intellectual debts are also enormous and I can only mention a few of them. Susan Bayly, historian and now anthropologist, has instructed me during an almost permanent domestic seminar. Colleagues in the various colleges, history and South Asian departments have constantly stimulated my interest: Chris Clark, Hans van de Ven, Richard Drayton, Saul Dubow, Kim Wagner, Peter Bang, Dipesh Chakrabarty, Rochona Majumdar and Muzaffar Alam, among many others. Bob Moore, the general editor, Andrew Arsan, Sunil Purushotham, Simon Layton and students at Queen Mary and Chicago made many sage suggestions. But I must particularly thank warmly my Cambridge colleague Shruti Kapila, who revivified my interest in the history of ideas. She, along with Faisal Devji, has been instrumental in creating a new form of global intellectual history. For, above all, the remaking of the modern world in the last century was brought about by ideas and human imagination.

C. A. B.
Summer 2015

INTRODUCTION[1]

The Challenges to Global History: Events and Ideas
The Challenges to Global History: Historians and their Doubts
The Motors of Change

OVER the last 20 years, world history or global history has become almost a fashion in the historical profession.[2] Even though the number of works on global connections and comparisons is still vastly outnumbered by regional, national and topic-centred histories, a series of formidable works have been published. Jürgen Osterhammel's *Transformation of the World*, dealing with the nineteenth century, and the first volume of his and Akira Iriye's series *A World Connecting 1870–1945*, edited by Emily Rosenberg, are particularly substantial versions of the genre both intellectually and physically. Among single-authored monographs, the last two volumes of the sociologist Michael Mann's *The Sources of Social Power* are notable for their historical detail and theoretical coherence. All these should be seen in light of the continuing importance of Eric Hobsbawm's four-volume work, especially his *Age of Extremes*, which, in part because of its Marxist orientation, also conveys a degree of intellectual consistency which some other contributions lack.[3] The problems of perspective, scale and time, which arise in the writing of such "connected history", have been analysed theoretically by Michael Werner and Bénédicte Zimmermann and other historians and sociologists aiming to surmount what has been called "methodological nationalism".[4]

Remaking the Modern World 1900–2015: Global Connections and Comparisons, First Edition. C. A. Bayly.
© 2018 John Wiley & Sons Ltd. Published 2018 by John Wiley & Sons Ltd.

THE CHALLENGES TO GLOBAL HISTORY: EVENTS AND IDEAS

Historians select their topics, whether knowingly or not, because of their deep connection with current events. That was as true of the radical 1960s and 1970s when the "English Revolution" of the seventeenth century was the topic of the day, as of the 1990s' interest in the Atlantic world and early globalisation. Yet, the impact of current events poses particular advantages and problems for historians of the last century, especially if they lived through much of it. The issue deserves more than a simple allusion in this preface because, as the former British prime minister Harold Macmillan told a journalist, "Events, dear boy, events!" are not only the biggest problem for politicians but also for contemporary historians. Quite apart from family memories of the First and Second World Wars, extraordinary changes in world politics and in the intellectual environment have caused me to rethink some of the assumptions on which this book is based, not once but several times. The Arab Spring has been followed by an "Arab Winter". In Egypt, for instance, the apparent resurgence of the Muslim Brotherhood, founded in 1922, has given way to a new bout of military-backed rule, not dissimilar to the governments of the 1960s to the 1990s. Meanwhile, radical Muslim extremism in the form of Hizbullah, Hamas or ISIS raises questions about the long-term moral and political formation of the modern "Middle East", particularly when the leaders of some Islamist movements specifically denounce the Sykes–Picot Agreement of 1916, which foreshadowed the division of the region.

In the same way, the overwhelming victory of the Bharatiya Janata Party in the Indian elections of 2014 challenges historians, especially perhaps in the University of Cambridge, to reassess their long-standing emphasis on regionalism and caste as the basis of Indian politics. The strength of the Christian "moral majority" in the United States and the revival of the Orthodox Church in Russia also seem, at least superficially, to support those dissenting political scientists who have long dismissed the idea that secularism is the dominant moral form of the twentieth-century Western world. Again, how far has the rise of Eurosceptic parties of both Right and Left in Europe and conflict in the Ukraine since 2010 undermined historians' assumption that the long movement of the continent since the 1950s towards peaceful economic and political union was irreversible?

These incentives to rethink an emerging standard historiography prompted by contemporary politics have been matched by intellectual developments. The centrality of the idea of globalisation and the triumph of neoliberal democracy in the 1990s, announced famously by Francis Fukuyama, was a clear outcome of the fall of the USSR.[5] Yet, globalisation theory, positing "ever-closer" global union, de-territorialisation and international governance, encountered theoretical criticism some time before the reassertion of aggressive national states and the decline in international bodies threw doubt on it.[6] Historians had meanwhile signed up to global history, before once again edging away from it.

Most recently, the public debate fuelled by Thomas Piketty's *Capital in the Twenty-First Century* reflects this more pessimistic view of recent global economic change.[7] Why, in the words of French newspapers, did this economist become "*un rock star*" or "*un bulldozer*" (note these two linguistically globalised words)? After all, Joseph Stiglitz and Paul Krugman had been pointing to the rapid growth of income equality across the Western world since the time of Margaret Thatcher and Ronald Reagan in the 1980s and even more so since the financial crash of 2007–2008. Right-wing journals queried Piketty's figures; left-wing ones argued that he was not Marxist enough. From the point of view of a modern historian, however, the importance of the book was its long historical range. When the return on capital invested in property or stocks and shares consistently outperformed the broader economic growth rate, as it had since the early nineteenth century, a privileged, inheriting elite was bound to emerge and inequality of income was bound to grow. According to Piketty, this trend was only disrupted by the dramatic effects of the two world wars and the Depression of the 1930s. To this extent, the years from 1950 to 1980 were exceptional in their deviation from the long-standing movement to social inequality, which he dated to the aftermath of the French Revolution. After 2000, indeed, the trend to inequality within rapidly developing countries, such as China, India and Brazil, seemed to be pointing in the same direction, even while inequality between nations across the world was slowly declining.

This book accepts much of Piketty's argument. Even if the actual statistical trend is less clear or universal than he argued, the discourse of inequality was itself of great social and political significance. During the belle époque before 1914, it empowered European socialists and the American Progressive Movement. After 2010, President Barack Obama similarly used the argument of growing inequality to fend off attacks by his Republican critics. I will suggest, however, that the notion of inequality has to be greatly broadened beyond income inequality to include differentials based on inherited status, ethnicity, race and so-called tribe.[8] A critical force in generating these forms of inequality was the legacy of the nineteenth-century European empires and the informal "empire" of Western commercial and ideological dominance that followed their demise.[9] Here, the twentieth century also saw a significant shift from layered inequality maintained by dominant elites to what might be called collective inequality within a state of apparent political freedom. So, for instance, black labour on the estates of the southern United States in 1850 was transformed into agglomerations of very poor, but ostensibly free, black people in its cities by 1950. The same can be said for gender inequality. In 1850, women were effectively bonded servants within extended families. By 2000, they were ostensibly free, but their access to the highest incomes, the best jobs and property was still distinctly lower than that of men and was actually declining in some areas, especially in Muslim societies.

Along with the debate about inequality another contemporary concern, pressing on historians, has been climate change and sustainability. A wide range of polemics, some proposing immediate planetary disaster, others denying the very existence of inexorable climate change, have alerted the profession to the historical conditions which, especially over the last century, have ravaged plant and animal life, polluted the air and damaged water tables across the world. This subject is treated in Chapter 17.[10]

THE CHALLENGES TO GLOBAL HISTORY: HISTORIANS AND THEIR DOUBTS

A second intellectual challenge to the writing on modern global history, apart from "Events, dear boy, events!" has come from within the profession itself. There is once again, as in the case of the debate about inequality, a deep connection with contemporary politics here. In France, the intellectual right wing opposed *histoire croisée* or "connected history", advanced by Werner and Zimmerman, among others, stressing instead French nationhood. In Britain, the then Education Secretary, Michael Gove, tried to reinstate British, or rather southern English, history in the school syllabus in place of well-meaning, if incoherent, teaching on the wider world. But it would be unfair to suggest that sceptical colleagues are no more than ivory-tower ideologues of the Front National or the UK Independence Party. Any fashion in the writing of history, whether it was the social history of the 1960s and 1970s, the postmodernist phase or the neoliberal writing of the 1980s and 1990s, or indeed the global history of the last two decades, inevitably encounters its critics. In the case of world or global history, a range of criticisms have emerged in recent years from scholars who doubt the value of the concept of networks, theories of globalisation and an emphasis on diasporas and movement. Other commentators highlight the difficulty of finding coherent "motors of change" in world history.

In these critiques, historians have been directed to consider what did not move and what did not change at a world level. World or global history has been charged either with a kind of flabby universalism or, equally, a constipated desire to assimilate every event and every fact into an unreadable jumble. Postcolonial and postmodernist historians have also represented the field of global history as a way of smuggling back Western liberal, imperialist or capitalist values into historiography or refusing to accept that "meta-narratives" of globalisation are no more than orientalising discourses of power, representing no underlying reality.

Like all critiques in the historical profession, these charges have some force and I will consider them before moving on to argue for the importance of a cautious and self-aware form of world history which does not detract from the national or the local. So, what of the objections to the current direction of world and global history? In 2013, the Princeton University historian David A. Bell wrote a pithy review in the *New Republic* of Emily Rosenberg's *A World Connecting*, entitled "This is what happens when historians overuse the idea of network."[11] In addition to ignoring the role of individuals in history, Bell argued that world historians too often failed to provide an adequate discussion of the more abstract motors of change. In the case of the Rosenberg volume he asserted that "the largest single absence is war". Elsewhere, he regretted the absence of a treatment of political ideas and of daily life that was transformed during the twentieth century. He ended his critique by suggesting that world history written in a "networking" mode had perhaps reached a point of "diminishing returns". In 2014, the intellectual historian Samuel Moyn wrote a review of Jürgen Osterhammel's massive *The Transformation of the World*, similarly arguing that the whole was less than the sum of its parts.[12] More recently, David Armitage's and Jo Guldi's *History Manifesto*,[13] arguing for *longue durée* global history, encountered strong criticism from Peter Mandler and Deborah Cohen.[14] Moyn returned to the debate, critiquing the absence of a strong theoretical base in both global and long-term histories.[15] Other historians, reflecting the anti-globalisation mood after 2008, voiced similar criticisms.

I do not believe that the global approach is in need of a Gibbonian "Vindication".[16] But in a book designed, in part, for student use, some clarification and response are needed. First, a good case can be made that modern world history is indeed "philosophy teaching by example" in Gibbon's sense. That is to say, the approach should be seen as a field of instruction as well as a branch of research. It is rather important that students and the general public arrive at some understanding of how today's connected – or often radically disconnected – world came into being, not least because the last 20 years have seen a set of profoundly new transnational links and conflicts, such as the eurozone, the al-Qaeda movement or the penetration of Chinese business into Africa. All of these have been publicly evaluated against earlier phenomena with which they may be, or are often not, connected: the League of Nations, late-nineteenth-century anarchism and European imperialism in Africa and Asia, for instance. As P. K. O'Brien eloquently points out, thinking outside national boundaries becomes a moral imperative for historians when much of the world is still consumed by warfare and poverty.[17] Perhaps a wider understanding of global comparisons can banish dangerous ignorance. Critics of global history should indeed be careful of appearing to be cheerleaders for a new and often chauvinist parochialism, especially when the humanities and the social sciences are under attack from the money-obsessed instrumentalism of many academic administrators.

Secondly, beyond the issue of public knowledge, there are very significant gains for historiography and professional historians themselves that arise from a study of comparative world or global history. Historians and public intellectuals are often unaware that themes and arguments, which seem to be purely products of their own local, national or regional debates and historical research, had emerged before, or contemporaneously, in other fields. Similarly, national and regional historians can often learn from a consideration of arguments developed for quite distant societies. One of the most important "turns" in recent world history, the Subaltern Studies movement, arose when Indian historians of the underprivileged came to read the rather different studies of the English rural labourer and working class pioneered by E. P. Thompson and his students.[18] In turn, this intellectual appropriation had a major impact on Latin American and Southeast Asian studies. Another key global debate arose from Kenneth Pomeranz's *The Great Divergence*, a book which significantly post-dated the point at which China was overtaken in economic and political vitality by the Western powers.[19] This resulted in works by numerous historians who reconsidered the "great divergence" in regard to their own societies. Notable here was J.-L. Rosenthal's work with R. Bin Wong that reconsidered the *longue durée* economic and social history, not only of China but also of France.[20] It showed how minor political and social differences between the two societies were magnified over time and contributed to the historiography of both and, by extension, to world history.

One final point that can be made about the importance of comparative world history and global history is the manner in which it makes it possible for historians to show in detail how some global networks emerged but, equally, how other ideas and practices were not really linked at all but took on fundamentally different forms in different societies. Despite recent critiques, not all world historians stress only linkages, connections and networks. Investigating them, however, is a vital tool for all, including regional, national and local historians. The results are often ambivalent, but then most historical events are ambivalent. One could mention here the concept of "local cosmopolitanism", which emerged in the work of the Southeast Asian historian Engseng Ho, for instance.[21] While the Chinese and Malay populations he studied certainly had global connections, real or spiritual, to China, Mecca and Medina, these links were appropriated to local ideologies and structures of authority that were quite different from post-Enlightenment European cosmopolitanism, if that ever existed itself. Ideas and practices were "cannibalised", to use Arjun Appadurai's word: their appropriation and consumption created totally different substances. But this is not at all at odds with the position of advocates of the methodology of comparative history, such as Werner and Zimmermann. In many cases global networks and influences were at best superficial. Yet, to reply to the various critics, and indeed to the postmodernists, it is only possible to understand such difference by contemplating the possibility of connection and the nature of appropriation.

THE MOTORS OF CHANGE

Critics of global history have additionally asked for much greater clarity in the analysis of change. A range of historians have analysed the major forces of change during the "long" twentieth century in superficially similar terms. Their vigorous debates concern not so much their character significance but the relationship between them and questions of timing. Broadly, capital and the control of labour, the modern state, imperialism, religion and secularism, war and the proliferation of communication: all these dominated discussion from 1900 to 2015. The Marxist–Leninist interpretation of capitalism, extended by Rudolf Hilferding in the 1920s, continued to inform works such as Eric Hobsbawm's four volumes, though historians of Asia, Africa and Latin America broadened the scope of this work by showing how capital "off-shored" the control of labour to non-European societies. This, in turn, supposedly made possible a leap to socialism in Mao Zedong's China or Vietnam, circumventing the need for these societies to pass through a "bourgeois" stage of economic development. Later, Michael Hardt and Antonio Negri posited a shift after the

1960s from European colonialism, once the "highest stage of capitalism", to a yet more powerful, but obscure, form of capital-powered Empire: amorphous, yet linking Western democracies, international bodies and even the centralised state capitalism of post-Mao China. This argument was another clear reaction to the collapse of Communism in Europe and the neoliberal discourse of the 1990s.

A second body of work on the expansion of the modern state after 1900, the last phase of European empires through to the 1960s, and the postcolonial states after that date, accepted much of the Marxist critique. But it often dissented from its political tone and assigned more influence to forces beyond capital itself. The self-styled "macro-sociologist" Michael Mann did much to create a more complex picture of change in his *Sources of Social Power*, tracing the interaction of ideological, economic and military power over the century.[22] Mann's final volume moved the analysis further beyond Western Europe and America, paralleling a shift in the work of imperial historians such as A. G. Hopkins from the colonial state to an analysis of globalisation.[23] This work made possible an assessment not only of the way in which power moved from the centre to the "peripheries" but also of how change in the former colonial peripheries disrupted and changed power at the centre, especially in the years after 1960. The work of Hopkins and his collaborators distinguished between periods of globalisation in the long term and also discussed the dialectical relationship in theory and practice between the global and the local.[24]

Another broad range of studies considered the expansion, decline and rise of religious belief and practice, powered by newspapers, radio, television and, later, the Internet and the blog.[25] This had proved a critical subject of debate from the time of Max Weber in the 1920s, through the work of anthropologists after 1945, to discussion in the 2000s of Islamism, Hindutva, modernised Buddhism in East Asia or Pentecostal Christianity in Africa, South Korea and Latin America. A particularly noteworthy and early example was Marshall G. S. Hodgson's *The Venture of Islam*.[26] Hodgson's studies emphasised the power of ideas rather than economic and material change which dominated historical analysis after 1950, following the work of Fernand Braudel.

While all these "motors of change" from capital to religion and communications appear in this book, the problem remains of how to configure their entanglement, conflicts and combinations over space and time. I agree with many of these historians and sociologists that warfare was, on the surface, the single most pervasive driving force throughout the twentieth and early twenty-first centuries. The impact of warfare changed its form, however, from devastating mass conflict, which killed as many as 50 million people between 1914 and 1945, to fear of global devastation and the regional conflicts of the Cold War and decolonisation between 1945 and 1990. Thereafter, and through to 2015, much of the world continued to be embroiled in what I call small wars of fragmentation, as existing autocracies and nation states disintegrated. Certainly, the demise of the nation state, widely proposed in the 1970s, was premature. Yet, by 2000, the question of the future of the state was being asked again. But it was local fragmentation as much as forces of globalisation and internationalism that were now indicted for its decline. Religious and social conflict, reflecting local struggles over resources and demands for self-respect, sparked numerous insurgencies from Syria and Iraq to Sudan, central India and upland Latin America. Tribal, ethnic and religious entities or regional groups were widely in contest with the nation state across much of the world by 2015, though in most cases their ultimate aim was to create a different form of the state, whether locally ethnic, as in the case of the Kurds, or broad and Sharia-driven, as in the case of ISIS and Boko Haram.

The consequences of the century's warfare were omnipresent in all walks of life, though not always malign. The need to mobilise resources or to erase the humiliation of defeat brought into being more rigorous national state forms in the early twentieth century, whether Communist or fascist. It also completed the process of democratisation in Western societies as working-class men and women were drawn into struggles for national survival. Advances in medical science, in transport and in communications were very widely stimulated by war and the fear of war. The obvious examples were the development of nuclear power, air and space travel and long-distance surveillance. Less obvious was the creation of medical remedies for malaria, cholera and polio, which resulted indirectly from the need to protect European and American troops fighting wars in East and South Asia. Finally, as Piketty noted, mass warfare reduced inequality for a generation and helped create the European welfare state, which was widely imitated across Asia and Africa.

The spectre of war also pushed forward the patchy development of international political and financial institutions: the League of Nations, the United Nations and the World Bank, for instance. The human and psychological sciences developed rapidly from studies focussed on the middle class to a much wider social remit, as questions about trauma and responsibility, inherited and learnt characteristics in the mass of the population reformed psychology, sociology and anthropology. Religions were both remodelled to assuage the horror of mass warfare and also recast as ideologies to promote success in supposedly righteous warfare, as with Catholic conservatives in the Spanish Civil War of the 1930s or the Islamists of the Taliban after 1980. All these dimensions of the century are treated in this book in chapters on "a century of killing", internationalism, the person, the human and social sciences and religion (Chapters 10–15).

Far more difficult to answer is the question of why warfare reached such a peak during the century and powered these fundamental changes in human life. To point to war as the single motor of change at a world level is itself too vague. In fact, some argue that the causation needs to be reversed, that it was these moral and material changes that actually powered warfare. Here historians, political scientists and sociologists remain at odds with each other. One answer that often seems to underlie political science approaches is that wars themselves created further wars as a result of the failure of the intervening arrangements for peace. This is clearly true up to a point, but it is not particularly revealing either. Evidently, the "unequal treaties" at the end of the First World War invigorated right-wing groups in Germany and Austria, leading to the rise of Nazism. The collapse of Tsarist Russia led on directly to the Bolshevik Revolution and the power struggle with the West that dominated much of the century. Again, the small wars of fragmentation after 1990 in the Middle East, Africa and elsewhere often reflected constitutional changes made in the face of wars by the former colonial powers. The legacy of French colonialism in Syria and British colonialism in Iraq for the turmoil in these two states after 1990 is only too easy to follow. Yet again, these formulations seem only to work at the higher level of political and economic interest and identity. What, then, lies beneath?

Here we should return first to those great spectres of the century, capital, empire and the nation, while noting how intertwined they were, rather than assigning either one a "sub-structural" or "super-structural" importance. None of these concepts simply represented a set of practical economic structures. Capital, nation and empire were also ideological processes. In the phase that lasted from about 1890 to 1945, competitive nationalism powered by capital brought massive and destructive conflict. If we take Vladimir Lenin's understanding of imperialism to refer to empire within Europe as well as in Africa, Asia and the Pacific, then imperialism was indeed "the highest stage of capitalism". Yet, critically, capitalism itself was impelled by and imbricated with the interests and populist ideologies of the strengthening nation state.[27] It is not difficult to see, for instance, that Cecil Rhodes's career in southern Africa, or the project of building the Berlin–Baghdad or Trans-Siberian railways, were ultimately directed by states or political actors attempting to ensure their wealth, but also their identity, rather than being simply the projects of an abstraction called capital. To take another example, the big Japanese domestic *zaibatsu* (commercial conglomerates) of the 1930s were themselves wary of war and imperialism in China. It was offshore nationalistic elements, the South Manchuria Railway Company, the Japanese Army in north China and the navy in the South China Sea that insisted on the expansion of the nation.

In all these cases capital fuelled and was fuelled by warfare, but hyperactive national and extra-national identities provided the direction of conflict. Certainly, the Communist revolutions socialised capital, as in Stalin's "socialism in one country", but democratic nationalism later re-emerged as a major driving force of historical change after 1945. This nationalism was not simply a reflection of the "tainted origin and protective function of conventional ethical beliefs".[28] For many people throughout the century the nation represented the location of social justice, equity and a concern for the good, and this was even true in Communist societies. The democratisation of politics, the state, capital and property over the century was a driving factor of change, even if it sometimes took on malign forms.

Taking the period of the Cold War of "peace" between 1945 and the late 1980s, American capitalism and military power reached a position of dominance across much of the world. Its consequences included the new welfare states of Western Europe, benign international development bodies, including UNESCO, the International Monetary Fund (IMF), the Rockefeller and Ford Foundations, but also the Latin American state, poised between oligarchic democracy and popular authoritarianism. In the East, the USSR provided another universal form of state socialism, but one ultimately overthrown by the superior ability of the American model to generate wealth and at least a sense of individual freedom if not its reality. The newly independent states of the postcolonial world tended at first to move towards the socialist model, suspicious of international flows of capital because of their experience of imperialism. In all these cases, again, capital was directed by national ideologies. Even the rallying cries of "free market" or "socialist international" represented underlying nationalisms. Yet, the wartime experience of mass slaughter and the fear generated by the nuclear arms race directed the motors of change towards international compromise.

The neoliberal moment from the early 1990s through to 2008, after what this book calls the "tipping point of 1979–1991", arguably represents the closest approximation to the all-encompassing genie of capital, feasting on international trade and production at the expense of the poorest, which Marx, Engels and Lenin had summoned up. Firms and oligarchs off-shored their wealth to the detriment of governments, former Communist Party officials built up fortunes as managers and credit and asset bubbles were created outside the control of national governments. The old Communist theorists of the nineteenth century were, perhaps, only "out" by a century. One could speak of the global growth of wealth and inequality, a position by no means at odds with the picture painted by various versions of *The Communist Manifesto* after 1848 and, latterly, by Hardt and Negri. The difference from that picture still lies, however, in the continual salience of the nation and of religion beyond the power of capital. In 2013 and 2014, there was no reason easily deducible from capital or economic interest alone for the nations bordering the South China Sea to fight over a group of unproductive islands. There was no economic reason why Sunni insurgents in Iraq and Syria should destroy cities and historical artefacts or murder productive citizens because they belonged to the Shia community or were Yazidis or Christians. Yet, none of this is to deny that capital was complicit with these conflicts. The South China Sea, for example, contained oil reserves; the Sunni insurgency in Iraq and Syria was powered by oil wealth, smuggling and the sale of artefacts to Western art dealers.

Yet, the most significant manner in which the 2010s differed from the years around Lenin's explosive publication of 1917, *The State and Revolution*, was the absence in the later period of an internationally organised anti-state and anti-capital movement, except, critically, in the populist religious sphere. It is striking that the rage of youth, the poor and the marginalised ethnicity in the early twenty-first century did not manifest itself in a single secular social movement as it had earlier in socialism, Communism or anarchism, but in a myriad of local oppositions and risings, often tinged with religion, identity politics and chauvinism. There is little sign of a worldwide "vanguard" of intellectual leaders inspired by class antagonism, though theorists such as Alain Badiou and Slavoj Žižek urge us to await, for perhaps a generation or more, the coming revolution against the new global elite.[29] For even the Islamist insurgencies were split on ethnic and doctrinal lines and capable of little more than terrorist disruption outside the Muslim world.

The intertwining of nationalism, democracy and capital in different forms over the century presented here echoes, though also at times departs from, aspects of the arguments of the historians and theorists mentioned earlier, from the founding Communists, through Hobsbawm to Mann. These were the clearest motors of change. But at the same time this book considers other, wider preconditions. Massive population growth since 1900 is clearly one. This provided a further political rationale for war and change. The Nazi demand for *lebensraum* or the Japanese imperative to settle its overcrowded northern farming population in Manchuria represented the first dimension. At the same time, mass urbanisation provided the impetus behind the development of more intensive policing, education and medical research to prevent disease. The pressure of population on land and natural resources led throughout the century to a growing awareness of the ecological problems that the human population faced, leading both to conflict and also to organisations at a national, regional and international level designed to alleviate these problems.

The exponential growth of communications, meanwhile, seemed to change the nature of human sociality, creating an invented moral world beyond the family, the community and the nation: "The medium became the message", to paraphrase Marshall McLuhan's words.[30] The cellular structure of Communisms, Zionism and Islamism in the first half of the century reflected the rapid global movement of not just people but ideas through print and the telegraph. By 1990, communication had itself become a distinct motor of change. It is no accident that the political science term "identity politics" emerged in the 1980s and 1990s as the world was increasingly closely linked by the World Wide Web. Systems of religious belief recovered from their apparent stagnation in the early part of the century, both because of their new capacity to communicate with followers and also because they could offer aid to impoverished urban and isolated poor urban or rural populations which states could not, or would not, succour. Identity politics, communication and religious radicalism contributed to the small wars of fragmentation which erupted after 1990, just as the neoliberal age exacerbated conflicts inherited from the age of empire and the aggressive nation states of the 1920s and 1930s.

Every one of these forms must be studied by historians, anthropologists and sociologists of regions, nations and smaller communities. Yet, world historians, working with the theme of globalisation, its shocks and lacunae, certainly have both a moral and also an academic case for adding to these numerous studies a broad comparative view of worldwide social networks or, equally, of describing their absence. This book is written in a spirit of cooperation, not confrontation, with national and local histories.

[1]   THE WORLD CRISIS, C. 1900–1930: EUROPE AND THE "MIDDLE EAST"

The World Before War: Idealism, Communitarianism and Radicalism

The First World War: Europe and the American Intervention

The Crucible of War: The Eastern and Western Fronts

Decentring the World Crisis: South-Eastern Europe and the "Middle East"

Reflections, Comparisons and Differences

THERE could hardly be a more deeply studied or more complex event with which to open any general history than the First World War. The vast range of writing on the conflict has recently been greatly expanded by the many publications and programmes timed to coincide with the centenary of the war's outbreak in 1914 and its course thereafter.[1] This chapter, therefore, is not intended to add further detail on the European war as such. Yet, it does attempt to put the war more firmly into a wider geographical and temporal context. It reemphasises the war's importance for the European empires and beyond, but also places it within a near 40-year span of global developments, beginning in the generation before 1914, with their consequent dramatic impact on society, economy and ideologies.

In regard to the first point – the geographical dimension – it will be useful to outline a typology of different regions and forms of conflict during the war itself, differentiating between the detailed narratives of other historians who have begun to expand its range.[2] There were, first, areas of mass warfare, mass killing and general mobilisation. Evidently, these included Western Europe, western

Remaking the Modern World 1900–2015: Global Connections and Comparisons, First Edition. C. A. Bayly.
© 2018 John Wiley & Sons Ltd. Published 2018 by John Wiley & Sons Ltd.

Russia, the Balkans and parts of the Ottoman Empire, especially its northern and southern borderlands. Next, there were areas of highly disruptive, but less sustained, conflict which did not see mass mobilisation or fundamental economic transformation, for instance much of colonial Africa, where European empires fought out the war. Then again, there were areas, colonised or semi-colonised, which saw significant military and civilian labour recruitment and consequent political turmoil, but did not themselves become the site of direct armed conflict. These included India, French Indochina, the China coast, the United States and the British dominions: Australia, Canada, New Zealand, the Pacific Islands and South Africa. Finally, there were parts of the world which felt the economic and political effects of the war, provided resources for it but did not directly contribute significant manpower to the conflict, such as Central and South America and Japan.

One striking effect of this geographical expansion of the range of warfare was the manner in which it reached small communities distant from the fronts, sometimes advantaging them, sometimes not. So, for instance, New Zealand Maori soldiers were recruited for the British Empire in significant numbers. Early conflicts with white officers gave way to a sense of ethnic and national solidarity after the Gallipoli debacle.[3] This helped the Maori communities gain a stronger voice in the country during the 1920s, whereas in the previous century their land and social cohesion had been constantly under threat. By contrast, indigenous peoples in eastern Siberia were suppressed by the White Army and then the Bolsheviks between 1917 and 1922.[4] This geographical expansion gave a great advantage to the Allied powers, which, unlike the Central Powers, could draw on agrarian as well as manpower resources from four continents.[5]

In terms of the temporal expansion of focus, this chapter emphasises the major changes that had preceded the European war, especially the conflict between Japan and Russia and the Chinese, Persian and Mexican revolutions. It is difficult to bring these conflicts into a single frame of analysis, particularly one which embraces the war itself. Yet, there were common features and connections. In all cases – and this would also extend to the post-war conflicts in North Africa, the Middle East and China – these events reflected aspects of the last phase of the "new imperialism" of the 1890s, led by an imperialist front which now included Japan. In a limited way, it also included Theodore Roosevelt's United States, which, since the early nineteenth century, had kept European empires at arm's length, but had nevertheless been an indirect supporter of their attempts to divide the world.

Lenin wrote of the war and imperialism of this period as "the highest stage of capitalism",[6] and there is, indeed, much analytical power in his argument, as noted in the Introduction. But here the idea of "gentlemanly capitalism" advanced by P. J. Cain and A. G. Hopkins, who developed earlier arguments of Joseph Schumpeter, remains significant.[7] Yet, it was older landowning and military elites, many drawn from rural and non-industrial areas of the competing states, that often sparked off these conflicts and provided atavistic ideologies to support them. These old or declining elites included the *Junker* class in Germany; the samurai of Japan, which had lost economic power after 1868;

Figure 1 Maori soldiers. Sir George Grey Special Collections, Auckland Libraries, 31-A2. Photo by Herman John Schmidt.

families of military and landholding elites from southern France and Corsica; and the imperial governors, judges and naval families of the now-ageing British Empire. Nationalism and a sense of entitlement certainly empowered the spread of intrusive finance capital across the world, but they cannot be reduced to it.

The longer-term causes – and consequences – of the world crisis should also be brought into the picture. Again, a quasi-Leninist interpretation remains useful. Ruling elites, worried by the emerging power of industrial, artisanal and even peasant labour, subjected these new and alarming forces to an "internal reconquest" through aggressive nationalist rhetoric, calls to empire and, in the final analysis, conscription and warfare. New media, mass newspaper circulation, an expanded telegraph and postal system and, later, radio were used to mobilise people for economic progress and patriotism, but also in hostility against a newfound enemy. This form of moral coercion persisted well beyond the end of the Great War itself. Colonial wars in the 1920s and the Spanish Civil War of the 1930s were pre-eminently new wars of propaganda.

In fact, nearly 30 years of conflict created a form of general traumatic psychosis on a global scale. Post-war nightmares which sparked further conflict included the "Jewish conspiracy", which allegedly brought down Germany; the threat of "Bolshevism" on the River Tyne in England in 1919; and most broadly, the mental crisis of the world's middle classes diagnosed, in their different ways, by Franz Kafka, Thomas Mann, Sigmund Freud, Carl Jung and Mohandas Gandhi. Traces of the impact of the world crisis, c.1900–1926, can be found across every subject touched in this book, from the understanding of the twentieth-century person through the trajectory of religion to the nature of modernity in art.

THE WORLD BEFORE WAR: IDEALISM, COMMUNITARIANISM AND RADICALISM

If the First World War had not been such a trauma for much of the human race, the two decades before it would now be seen as a period of radical change and rupture rather than the serene end to the Victorian era,[8] as it is often portrayed in popular literature, television and film. Unprecedented developments in communication were heralded by Louis Blériot's first air flight, the first radio connection across the Atlantic and even the creation of a new set of time zones across the world. While attention has been concentrated on the treaties which presaged the war itself, international agreements directed to reducing conflict had been implemented for Antarctica and a series of peace conferences, doomed as they later appeared, had been greeted as signs of hope in international affairs. They seemed an appropriate balance to the onward march of European empire. Democratic socialist parties flourished in Western Europe while colonial subjects invoked the spirit of the nation in an age of idealistic spirituality represented by the Chicago World Parliament of Religions of 1893.

Politics changed dramatically at a world level over these years. The so-called Progressive Era in the United States saw attempts to improve popular representation and education along with moves to cut back on the power, influence and corruption of the big corporations, which had emerged as the economy expanded rapidly after 1890.[9] Presidents Theodore Roosevelt and William Taft endorsed these moves in a period when income inequality grew very rapidly. Mexico's revolution predated the Bolshevik revolution by five years. In Britain, governments moved to introduce minimum wages. Yet more dramatic changes took place outside Europe and the Americas. The Boxer Rebellion of 1900 and the multinational intervention against it undermined the 300-year-old Qing Empire, and presaged the 1911 revolution, which plunged the country into conflict and uncertainty that lasted until 1949. The Persian revolution of the same period gave heart to liberals across the Middle East, but led in the longer term to the installation of a military autocracy. The Young Turk revolution of 1908 in the Ottoman Empire both modernised the regime and promoted Arab separatism.

Meanwhile, colonial powers viewed with alarm the rise of Pan-Islamic movements[10] heralded by the Mahdist state in the Sudan in the 1880s and 1890s. Nationalist agitation in Egypt and India passed into a more militant phase with the Wafd and the Indian National Congress divided between radicals beginning to espouse violence against the British and moderates still looking for constitutional gains from colonial policymakers. The latter sought to portray themselves as liberals but were often constrained by conservative proconsuls and the movements of events. This dilemma also faced the British in Ireland, where, after 1913, Sinn Fein and Catholic Irish nationalism was opposed by a strong counter-force in Protestant unionism. In France, a secular, anti-Catholic party took power in 1902, while the Social Democratic Party made gains in Germany. Under Theodore Roosevelt, the United States seemed to be moving towards a new phase of imperialism, if only locally in the Caribbean and Latin America.

Yet by far the most dramatic event of the period was the Japanese defeat of Russia in 1905[11] and the ensuing Russian Revolution in the same year, which, although violently suppressed, heralded a new era of leftist radical politics. The emergence of a centralist, domineering Communist Party had already been foreshadowed by the Bolshevik–Menshevik split of 1903. The year 1905, however, saw the formation of the first soviet directed by Leon Trotsky, advocate of "permanent revolution".[12] Japan's victory also signalled to Asian, Middle Eastern and African colonised people the first breach in Europe's 200 years of world dominance. Yet, the various popular uprisings of these years from Russia in 1905, through Pan-Islamic movements across the Muslim world to the radical *Swadeshi* ("home production") movement in India resulted in an imperial "counter-attack" by the major powers which attempted to impose stronger government in their borderlands, preparing the way for two generations of further conflict.[13] These moves included the reassertion of Russian control over Finland, Poland and Kirghizstan; Habsburg control over its Serbian borderlands; Anglo-Russian intrusion into Persia; and the Indian government's partition of Bengal in 1905, an attempt to divide Muslims from the Hindu radicals. In Brazil between 1898 and 1903, the central government brutally suppressed settlers and *mestizos* in the Canudos rebellion, as part of what was called, in retrospect, "the scramble for the Amazon".

One further effect of this political turmoil and the development of communications in the last two decades of fragile world peace was the speeding up of migration. The Russian crisis and rise of anti-Semitism there sent hundreds of thousands of Jewish refugees to the West and, in particular, to the United States and Canada. Here they joined migrants from crowded northern European industrial cities and impoverished rural areas such as southern Italy and Sicily, while Spanish migrants continued to move to Latin America. Elsewhere, the decisive victory of Japan attracted numbers of anticolonial activists from India and Southeast Asia, who formed cells in Tokyo and other major cities.

Groups which felt themselves oppressed in the prevailing social order grasped the opportunity of the new means of communication, notably newspapers, radio and film, to advertise their grievances. Suffragettes paraded for women's votes in Britain. Led by Gandhi, Indians and, later, Africans demanded civil rights in South Africa, where, following the Anglo-Boer War, they remained excluded from the privileges taken for granted in white society. In the United States, the black population of the South, which had drifted to northern cities as the industrial economy grew, was slowly politicised. Very widely, the monopoly of the old white ruling families was challenged by new forms of politics and new methods of communication. The four years of warfare with its unparalleled orgy of killing overshadowed, but in another sense speeded up, the radical changes which this age of idealism, conflict and migration had already unleashed.

THE FIRST WORLD WAR: EUROPE AND THE AMERICAN INTERVENTION

The First World War has long been the most studied and memorialised event in history. It was marked by economic and political turmoil on a massive scale and began what Oswald Spengler perhaps rightly saw as the "decline of the West", or at least its initial phase. The war's consequences – the emergence of mass democracy, Communist revolution and the rise of fascism – were epochal. The centenary of the outbreak of war in 2014 was heralded by a further wide range of publications, television series and reminiscences based on private papers. Among the most significant recent revisions was that proposed by Christopher Clark, who presented a more nuanced version of the crisis of July 1914 in his book *The Sleepwalkers*.[14] This partly shifted the "blame" for the outbreak of war away from Germany, showing how miscalculations by Austria–Hungary and Russia in response to the assassination of Archduke Franz Ferdinand by an aggressive Serbian nationalist cell were compounded by the complacency and fear of statesmen in London and Paris. Even the German statesman Helmuth von Moltke only urged "a preventive war . . . as long as we still have a reasonable chance in this struggle".[15] Clark demonstrated that Russia, not Germany, was the first to mobilise in an effort to protect its Serbian brothers, a fact recognised in 2014 by Vladimir Putin. This represented a significant intellectual shift, since the standard view was more a projection backwards of Germany's role in 1939 than a straightforward analysis of the July crisis. Ironically, the most vigorous proponent of the earlier view had been the German historian Fritz Fischer, who had traced the origin of Germany's war aims back to the 1890s or earlier.[16]

Clark also advanced a more difficult, sociological argument that most political and military leaders involved in the July crisis and the subsequent rush to war were gripped by a kind of "crisis of masculinity". As lower-class and non-white movements became more assertive in the two decades before 1914, the once comfortable ruling classes of gentlemanly capitalists, landowners and old military families felt the need to assert their leadership and continuing dominance by bellicose statements and actions which turned a local crisis into a conflagration. Yet, during the 2014 centenary, British participation was debated, as it had long been, along the lines of local nationalism. Conservative patriots argued that the Kaiser's Germany was a proto-fascist state, presaging the Third Reich, and therefore had to be confronted. The historian Niall Ferguson suggested that Britain should have refrained from participation in

Figure 2 The 9th Queen's Royal Lancers of the British Army charging German artillery, 1916. Underwood Photo Archives/Superstock.

the war until its forces were strong enough to defeat Germany without a long and desperate struggle. This kind of speculation is worth considering, but the more important point is that, for the previous century, France had continually fought against German domination of the Continent, while the British had also opposed any hegemonic continental power.

A broad study published before the flurry of activity connected with the 1914 centenary was Hew Strachan's monumental history, published in 2001, and his subsequent shorter history of the war as a whole, published in 2003.[17] This was followed by David Stevenson's one-volume history in 2004[18] and Adam Tooze's *The Deluge* in 2014.[19] Strachan's interest in tactics and strategy and his useful overturning of the idea that nobody expected a long war were valuable. So too was his insistence on the bellicosity of European nationalism, fuelled both by a perverted form of Christianity and Nietzschean desire for supremacy. Again, his depiction of industrial and financial mobilisation in 1914 was of great importance in broadening the field of study beyond the purely military dimension of warfare.

Strachan's and Stevenson's most significant contribution to the literature, however, was their insistence that it was Germany's global strategy on land and sea, once it had been drawn into war, that turned a European conflict into a world war. This is not to say that this was inevitable, let alone that it represented a long-term German plan for world domination. Yet, even before the end of 1914, Germany's rulers had planned to strike at the weak links in the global power of Britain, France and Russia by fostering Pan-Islamism and the aims of the Ottoman Empire, so threatening Russia's southern territories and even challenging British India by suborning the ruler of Afghanistan. The German seaborne offensive in the Atlantic and Pacific, initially announced by the voyage of the battleship SMS *Emden* into the Indian Ocean in 1914, was designed to divert British resources away from Europe. But the expansion of this policy to the Atlantic ultimately brought the United States into the conflict and so ensured Germany's defeat in the longer run. The following sections aim to follow and develop this line of argument, but also to extend the chronology of war backwards into the 1900s and forward into the 1920s.

Both world wars, indeed, are best seen as world crises in Winston Churchill's sense and their causes and consequences had exceptionally long genealogies.[20] Conservative historians in both Europe and the United States recently began to object to the moving of the focus away from the Eastern and Western fronts, and it is clearly true that the mass casualties of four years of warfare were disproportionately felt in Europe. Equally, the conflict presaged the decline of Europe's long dominance of the world scene, even though the United States did not move decisively into the military and political void until 1943. Yet, putting the European war into world context highlights a whole range of historical changes from the early victories of radical socialism, through non-European nationalism to new forms of Islamism, all of which were to shape the following century as decisively as the European war itself.

THE CRUCIBLE OF WAR: THE EASTERN AND WESTERN FRONTS

The Western European war took a path only too well known in earlier conflicts, with the invasion of Belgium and northern France. But at the Battle of the Marne on the Belgian border, Germany failed to repeat the quick success of 1870, which had inaugurated its new world power.[21] Paris was saved and Europe was enmeshed in a long war of attrition in the trenches which ran between Flanders and Switzerland. This massive conflict began to be decided in 1917, when the first tanks came onto the battlefield, but the decisive point was only reached in 1918, when American troops began to reinforce the forces of the Triple Entente against the Central Powers. On the Eastern Front, Russian troops were held at bay in 1914 by Field Marshal von Hindenburg, but the unexpectedly rapid Russian counter-attack gave an advantage to the French, as German troops were diverted east. At the same time, Germany's Ottoman ally was defeated by the Russians at the Battle of Sarikamish in 1914 and this, in turn, led to a long military standoff in the east and south, similar to that on the Western Front. The deadlock was not broken until the tsar fell in March 1917 and Russian military power disintegrated as a consequence of the ensuing revolutions.

In the meantime, the need for mass mobilisation of perhaps 60 million men, machinery and resources had undermined the old liberal political consensus in Britain and France, leading to the installation of coalition governments the like of which had not been seen before. At sea, Germany once again made early advances, but British naval power slowly recovered. The British established a naval blockade of the Continent, managed to protect trans-Atlantic shipping with difficulty and, finally, began to turn the German fleet back following the Battle of Jutland in 1916. Yet, even after the advent of US forces in early 1918, the Germans were still able to mount highly effective campaigns on the Western

Front, now drawing in resources from the east, where an armistice had been declared with Russia. As was to occur once again in the Second World War, however, Germany had too limited a resource base in Europe, especially after the country's Ottoman and Austro-Hungarian allies began to weaken and disintegrate in the Balkans.[22] German cities lacked food, the air war began to demoralise civilian populations and political radicalism spread amongst an impoverished urban working class. Still, unlike the situation in Russia, open Communist insurgency did not take place until the Spartacist revolt of 1919.

The Great War in Europe provoked huge social, economic and moral changes which were evident throughout the century. As men were called up after 1916, women were drawn into the workforce and demands for women's political rights, which had been heard before the war, particularly in Britain and France, became more insistent. Progress was set back after 1918, but the slow movement towards women's enfranchisement continued in Western Europe and the United States at least. Technical developments in air, sea and road travel counted among the more benign developments. A report announced, "The Clyde Valley emerged from the period of hostilities with its productive capacity in steel, shipbuilding and engineering greatly enhanced."[23] But air bombardment, machine gunnery and the use of chemical weapons such as chlorine and mustard gas were dramatic features of the war and these were later used across the world, particularly in the European colonies.

Perhaps, though, the moral and ideological forms which emerged during and after the conflict were its most powerful results. Mutiny was often met with execution. But the more ambivalent form of "conscientious objection" to war was the inevitable consequence of mass mobilisation. Radical hostility to all authority buoyed socialist and fascist movements across Europe. Equally, the arrival of American troops alerted Europeans to the less rigidly class-based society across the Atlantic and to its command of material resources and inventiveness. The mass slaughter of the conflict empowered new religious movements, such as the Oxford Group that would eventually become Moral Re-Armament, and the determination to establish international bodies such as the League of Nations. Yet, it also sowed the seeds of forms of more mobile warfare and created a generation of hate-filled young men which heralded the next round of politically legitimated killing.

If the collapse of the old regimes, the mobilisation of labour and the slow advance of gender equality were features of change across much of the Western European and American world as a result of the war, fragmentation on ethnic, linguistic and religious lines was equally general both inside and outside these continents. The collapse of the Austro-Hungarian and Ottoman empires created a host of minor wars, especially in the imperial borderlands, which persisted over the next century as newly empowered ethnic groups began to claim nations as their own, marginalising and expelling minority peoples. China began to fragment into regions and even in Africa, India and Southeast Asia various forms of inter-ethnic and inter-religious rivalries were reinforced.

Why was this? Economic crisis and the collapse of the legitimacy, if not force, of European rule was one common feature. At the same time, the empires and nation states in conflict had armed and empowered a whole range of middle groups, officers and subalterns (in the strict sense of the world), who took up the fight for regional and local political entities which had been only distant aspirations in the pre-war era. Outside Europe and the Americas, the war should indeed be seen as a further stage of the new imperialism which had emerged at the end of the nineteenth century. The surviving colonial powers found that playing off some of these groups against others helped to perpetuate their diminished local influence, if not dominance. The chapter goes on to assess the impact of the war in these broader arenas.

DECENTRING THE WORLD CRISIS: SOUTH-EASTERN EUROPE AND THE "MIDDLE EAST"

The most recent generation of historians of the First World War displayed much greater interest than their predecessors in the origins and consequences of conflict in the Balkans, Russia and the Caucasus. This modified the prevailing view of the central role of statesmen and soldiers in Berlin, Paris and London. The "shift to the East", however, can be taken much further and justified in terms of the longer span of world history. The conflict on the Western Front certainly gave rise to what has been called Europe's civil war, 1914–1945. But thereafter, both Eastern and Western Europe entered a new era of relative peace. In the Middle East, by contrast, the long-term consequences of the First World War in the break-up of the Ottoman Empire, the rise of Zionism, the creation of Israel and a whole range of ethnically engineered states in Iraq, Syria, Egypt and Libya were still very much in evidence in 2015. From the point of view of global Islam, the conquest of the Hijaz by Abdulaziz ibn Saud in 1925 – a direct consequence of the war – was one of the critical developments of the twentieth century, empowering a radical, puritan strain of the faith. Even in South and East Asia, which were not directly involved in the war, the conflict unleashed new forms of mass politics and, in the case of Japan, a new imperialism, with worldwide consequences in the 1930s and 1940s. Adam Tooze, in turn, brought China into the picture.[24]

Emerging ethnic and religious nationalism in the central and south-eastern territories of the Austro-Hungarian Empire, which set Slavic Orthodox subjects against their former Catholic German rulers, coloured the history of the next generation after 1914. While there was no simple teleology, the fragmentation of empire between German, Hungarian and Czech speakers, as between Bosnian Muslims and Serbs, was to reverberate through the following century. Even before the war, a related process, caused by similar moves on the part of an imperial state, had been evident in the Ottoman Empire. Istanbul had gradually centralised power, moving away from the model of ethnic plurality which had characterised the Empire of the Renaissance period and after.[25] Non-Muslims, such as Greeks, Armenians and Syrian Christians, had been weeded out of the army and the self-government previously devolved to the old religious and ethnic authorities (the millets) had been curtailed. Most significantly, after the Young Turk revolution of 1908, the state had embarked upon a policy of

"Turkification". Whereas previously, Arab and other local leaders had been slowly acculturated into the ways of Istanbul by residence and state service, now the Turkish language was increasingly imposed on the elites of outlying provinces.[26]

This was an uneven process and loyalty to the Ottoman Empire remained strong, but a reaction was inevitable. Some Arabs had long felt a sense of suppressed superiority in regard to the Turkish imperial centre.[27] The Prophet had been an Arab and Arabic was the language of the Qur'an. They felt that the Khilafat should have remained in the hands of an Arab regime and the holy places governed by Arab leaders without interference from Ottoman Turkish authorities, which had become more intrusive as the Hijaz Railway was completed towards the end of the nineteenth century. Ambivalently, the Egyptian middle and upper classes had urged "Egypt for the Egyptians", that is to say for the Arabs, against both Turks and Europeans since Colonel Urabi's rebellion of 1881. People in the Baghdad province of the empire had also called for local Arab autonomy during political crises in the 1900s. This sentiment became public during Arab conferences held in Paris and Lausanne in 1913. The later historian of the "Arab Awakening", George Antonius, noted that conservative Arabs believed that the secularising Young Turks had betrayed the faith to Western influences.[28] This was certainly the claim made by Sharif Hussein of Mecca when, with the support of the British and the French, he raised the Hijaz against the Ottoman Empire in 1916. Meanwhile, the former Christian subjects of the Ottoman Empire in Europe, buttressed by Russia, fought two precursor wars against Istanbul in 1909 and 1913, which set the scene for the widening of conflict in 1914.

In Syria and Lebanon, the Great War imposed extreme hardship on the local populations, compounded by famine, drought and infestation by locusts.[29] The Ottoman authorities came down heavily on signs of Arab disaffection, executing several leaders in 1916 and 1917. But most Arabs hedged their bets in regard to their future relations with Ottoman power, particularly as much of the Arab part of the empire remained under Istanbul's control until late in 1917. The Ottomans also retained the loyalty of significant numbers of Arab officials who had been trained in Istanbul. Yet, the existence of earlier claims to local autonomy did ensure that, when Allied armies invaded Palestine, Syria and what was to become Iraq, Britain and France could institute a "divide and rule" strategy, not only between Arabs and Turks, or more accurately "Ottomanised" leaders, but also between Sunnis and Shias, Wahhabis and Orthodox, Kurds and Arabs, Alawites, Christians, Jews, Copts and Muslims.[30] The ethnic and religious balancing acts characteristic of semi-independent new states, such as Iraq or Trans-Jordan, and imperial provinces, such as Palestine and Syria, provided a constant source of political confusion and divisions throughout the twentieth century and were transformed into revolution and warfare once again after 2011.

The Ottoman authorities had gradually become disillusioned with their old ally, Britain, following the Anglo-Russian Entente of 1907, because they felt abandoned in favour of their greatest enemy. Germany had been reaching out to the empire since the Kaiser's visit of 1900. But war was by no means inevitable before 1911, when both the British and the Young Turks began to take a more aggressive stance.[31] The main war aims of the British in the sector were the protection of the Suez Canal from an Ottoman attack through Palestine and an attempt to knock the Ottomans out of the war rapidly and expose the southern flank of the Central Powers. Secondly, a thrust through Basra and Baghdad, using the Indian Army, seemed an appropriate strategy. Basra, with a substantial Indian population and with its north-facing waterways controlled by the British firm Lynch and Company, seemed an excellent staging post. Predictably, neither of these aims was easily achieved. The Anglo-Indian army was stalled by fierce Ottoman resistance at Kut al-Amara, south of Baghdad. A landing, promoted by Winston Churchill, at Gallipoli in 1915 by British and ANZAC (Australian and New Zealand) forces intended to avoid a lengthy advance from Egypt through Palestine was overwhelmingly defeated, leading to recriminations between British and Australian leaders. Ultimately, however, British forces took Baghdad in 1917, entered Jerusalem in the same year and marched into mainland Turkey in the summer of 1918, stirring the jealousy of French leaders.

These painful military advances were accompanied by murky political and diplomatic manoeuvrings. Egypt, already a virtual British colony in 1914, was completely taken over and mobilised for the Palestine conflict once the British had declared war against the Ottoman Empire. Arthur Balfour, the British Foreign Secretary, announced the creation of a vaguely defined "national home for the Jewish people" in Palestine in 1917.[32] British hopes for rapid agrarian development pioneered by Zionist settlers blended with London's desire for a strategic bloc of pro-Western force north of the Canal. The Sykes–Picot Agreement of 1916, publicised by the USSR after the Bolshevik Revolution and formalised at the later peace conferences, gave Syria to the French and Palestine and Trans-Jordan to the British, overriding the Arab desire for independence. Iraq, like Syria, was to be technically a mandated territory under the newly formed League of Nations. But it, too, began its independence from Istanbul as a virtual British colony. Further north, the British occupied Istanbul and became complicit in a Greek invasion of Asia Minor, which was only frustrated by the fierce resistance of Turkish regular troops led by Mustafa Kemal Atatürk.

Over much of the Middle East, as in Europe, then, direct involvement in fighting had the effect of heightening tensions between ethnic and religious groups whose elites had already begun to assert stronger identities well before the First World War.[33] A related and equally powerful force was the escalation of class identities and labour conflict as a result of the political and economic pressures of the war. Returning soldiers of peasant and working-class backgrounds demanded a better livelihood and new rights to land and income. But these aspirations clashed with the economic conditions let loose by the war. After 1916, there had been a global increase in prices as the demand for commodities and labour soared. Not only soldiers but also huge numbers of labourers were drafted into the war fronts. By 1919, however, prices had collapsed, labour was dispensed with and this occurred precisely at a time when old supremacies and new states were attempting to build up their revenue bases across Africa and Eurasia. The result was a firestorm of peasants' and workers' movements which erupted in the Middle East, Asia and Africa. This coincided with industrial unrest in Britain and France, the Spartacist movement in defeated Germany and the "red" and "green" revolutions across Eastern Europe and Russia. The forces of state and empire cracked down fiercely on these movements, setting the scene for the rise of both authoritarian government and mass colonial nationalism over the next generation.

So, in the former Ottoman domains a series of major revolts against European control flared up between 1919 and 1923.[34] In Egypt, frustration that the country was unable to claim independence under the leadership of the landlord-dominated Wafd Party combined with deep social problems to create an explosion similar to that of 1879–1882. Large numbers of workers who had been critical in the logistical support for Britain's Palestine campaign were laid off. The rural community was scarified by the sudden decline in prices of basic commodities as wartime demand fell off. The ulama, the clerical class, long hostile to the growing numbers and deeper intrusion of British and other European officers after 1914, provided a degree of ideological leadership for the revolt against British control which reached its peak in 1919. Egypt, the most populous of the Arab countries, proved extraordinarily difficult for the British to control. Eventually, in 1922, they conceded a degree of local self-government to the Wafd and Egyptian local leaders, but not before the revolt had forced the British to maintain large numbers of Commonwealth and Indian troops in the country at considerable cost.[35] Further to the west, the conditions of war promoted unrest in Libya and Tripoli, conquered piecemeal by the Italians after 1911, and also in French Algeria, where wartime privation increased tensions between French settlers, the local Jewish population and the Arab majority.[36]

Meanwhile, the three provinces of Mesopotamia, now Iraq, rebelled in 1920. Former Ottoman officials, displaced by British and Indian officials in Basra and Baghdad, vented similar grievances to their peers in Damascus and the Lebanese towns where French troops and civilians were billeted on them. Ottoman loyalism played a part and there were armed interventions from Syria into western Iraq. Equally, heavy-handed British administration of the bazaars and the introduction of the "Tribal Civil and Criminal Disputes Regulation" on an Indian model offended established judicial officers. Peasant farmers rebelled across the region, affected by similar price falls to those in Egypt and India, demands for labour services by the occupying armies and also by a rise in land revenue as the British and British Indian authorities attempted to recoup the enormous costs of the Mesopotamian campaign.[37] At this point, economic and political grievances mixed with religious and ethnic ones. Shia clergy and commoners revolted around the holy cities of Karbala and Najaf, offended by the presence of infidels. Then later, in 1922–1923, when some of these insurgencies had been smothered by RAF bombing or had lost steam, there was a major revolt in the Kurdish areas to the north. British intrusion here again caused a sharp reaction.[38] The costly British determination to remain arose, in the words of the Arab specialist, Gertrude Bell, from the fear that "[i]f Mesopotamia goes Persia goes, inevitably, and then India".[39]

In Syria, the French rapidly converted a conquered territory into a mandate under the League of Nations and then into a virtual colonial province, centred on Damascus.[40] A number of impulses came together to create this new form of French imperialism towards the end of the First World War. Before 1914, the Parti colonial had been a bit player in French politics. But public opinion had been mobilised by the sight of French Senegalese, Algerian and Indochinese troops marching into battle on the Western Front.[41] The idea of colonial development (*"mise en valeur des colonies françaises"*) promoted by Albert Sarraut, Governor of Indochina before the war, appealed to a society devastated by conflict and determined to seek reparations from Germany and the repayment of pre-war Ottoman loans.[42] The occupation of Syria seemed the least that could be expected if France was not to be marginalised by the British and the country's presence there was supposedly legitimated by a history stretching back to the Crusades.

The French, like the British, were adept at playing off ethnic and religious groups against each other, again with long-term consequences for the stability of the region.[43] They sought, and largely received, the support of the Maronite Christians of Lebanon. Lebanese merchants working in French colonies in Africa, who remitted money to their homeland, also tended to support the regime. In short order after the First World War, the French suppressed rebellions by the minority Druze, also of Mount Lebanon, and the majority Sunnis of the Damascus region. Fostering political parties supposedly representing the elites of the minority groups, the French brazened out their control of the region through a further set of revolts in the early 1930s, until the onset of the next war in 1939.

Palestine provided a further example of an anticolonial insurgency which emerged out of wartime conditions and policies. Even in the last days of Ottoman administration, pressure from the great powers had forced the Ottoman administration to admit large numbers of Jewish settlers, many of them fleeing the pogroms that scarred the Russian Empire in its last two decades. The Balfour Declaration of 1917, announced as the British began to rule Palestine, encouraged a new surge of Jewish settlement, which fanned out from Haifa and the coastal towns into the interior of Palestine. This occurred at a time when Arab farmers and Bedouin herdsmen were suffering badly from the straitened circumstances of wartime and early British rule. The influx of settlers tipped the balance between the Muslim and Christian Arab inhabitants and the long-established Jewish population. This had amounted to about 10% of the total but was now swelled to more than 20% by the new arrivals. Jewish settlers brought with them firm ideas about settlement, development and a determination that "a homeland for the Jews" meant local and separate Jewish administration from a position of strength.[44] Arab protest against this culminated in riots in Jerusalem in 1920 as well as the more famous Wailing Wall riots of 1929. The conflict between Jews and Arabs over territorial control of the holy city was to continue throughout the century.[45]

Another indirect, though critical, outcome of the First World War was of importance here. In 1916, Sharif Hussein of Mecca had revolted against the Ottoman Empire, with covert British support, later dramatised in the writings of T. E. Lawrence. The Sharif, chafing since the 1900s against Ottoman interference in the Hajj and his Hijaz kingdom, invoked the Arab Khilafat against what he termed "Turkish usurpation and Westernisation". But after the end of the war, relations between the British and the Sharifian kingdom declined, while conflicts developed between the Sharifians and the purist Wahhabis of central and eastern Arabia, who, since the early 1800s, had believed themselves to be the rightful protectors of the holy places of Mecca and Medina.[46] In 1926, as noted above, supported by another British officer, Henry St John Philby, the Wahhabis annexed the Hijaz to the kingdom of Saudi Arabia, demolished many of what they regarded as impious shrines and tombs and imposed a rigid form of Islam in Mecca and Medina. Ultimately, the British came to see the Saudi dynasty as a buffer against French and other foreign interventions along the Red Sea and compromised with the new regime. This was to be a momentous development in the history of Islam, though it was not until some years later that the importance of Arabian oil resources became clear.

The fate of the Turkish rump of the Ottoman Empire was of considerable significance, for it resulted in the emergence of a new type of state: a republic dominated by Muslims yet formally secular, and ruled by a president who was supported by a powerful, modernised army, urban elites and some remaining large landholders. This was a precedent followed later as the European powers withdrew from Egypt, Iraq, Pakistan, Libya and Algeria. For much of the twentieth century, it was assumed that this form of state had effectively suppressed Islamism, and its generally neutral attitude to private property and foreign investment, particularly for oil extraction, allowed a compromise with Western powers to emerge. An outcome of this sort was, however, far from clear during the war years themselves. In the northern Ottoman lands, indeed, the war years extended from 1911 to 1923. An Italian–Ottoman war broke out in 1911, leading to the Italian occupation of Libya. This was followed in short order by the two Balkan Wars of 1911 to 1914. First, Greece and Serbia partitioned much of the remainder of "Turkey in Europe" and created an independent, but still partly Muslim, Albania. Then followed the Second Balkan War, when the victorious Christian powers fought amongst themselves, allowing a small Ottoman resurgence, but which also forced Serbia into greater dependence on Russia, a situation which led indirectly to the Great War itself.

After the Ottoman defeat by the British and French and the Arab revolt, the Western powers moved effectively to partition Turkey itself, occupying Istanbul and conspiring in a Greek invasion of Smyrna. In the capital, the last Ottoman Sultan and a hastily reconvened parliament became clients of the British. Lloyd George, the British prime minister, had long been a Hellenophile though the key continuing British concern was for the freedom of navigation along the Bosporus. But the British had overreached themselves. Indian soldiers had already mutinied in Singapore and Mesopotamia and now showed serious signs of disaffection in Istanbul and its environs. The long war and earlier patterns of Turkification, spreading down to the small towns and peasant farmers of Anatolia, had also created a powerful sense of nationality linking the army and ordinary people. A remarkable leader, Mustafa Kemal "Atatürk", turned this sentiment to his advantage as the Greeks occupied the Aegean coast.

Establishing a Grand National Assembly in the inland town of Ankara, Atatürk thrust westwards, defeating the Greeks on the coast and forcing the British, who were themselves divided on how to respond, to a stalemate.[47] War-weariness and the realisation that Atatürk would compromise on freedom of the Straits and refrain from intervention in French-controlled Syria or British-controlled Iraq ultimately led to the 1923 Peace of Lausanne which guaranteed the territorial integrity of the new Turkish Republic. Atatürk asserted, "he is a weak leader who needs religion to uphold his government." The Sultanate and Khilafat were abolished and Turkey became the first avowedly secular Muslim society.

REFLECTIONS, COMPARISONS AND DIFFERENCES

The emergence of the Turkish Republic, a linguistically and ethnically homogenous state (Kurds apart), which created a distance between religious confession and political power, was also characteristic of the effects of the War as they impacted on large parts of Europe. Here nationality was increasingly defined in ethnic terms. Whether in Poland, Czechoslovakia, Serbia or Yugoslavia, there began an attempt culturally to assimilate or drive out minority communities which culminated 20 years later with the ethnic cleansing enforced by Nazism, fascism and its Eastern European proxies. The War had created a range of militant nationalist organisations promoting a hard-edged ethnicity, fearful of "the foreigner" and often doubly enraged by the Peace Treaties of 1919. Some of these conditions applied to the remainder of the Middle East beyond Turkey which, like Europe, had been directly embroiled in military conflict. Yet, here it is important to avoid overgeneralisation – the kind of overemphasis on connection and similarity queried by some of the historians mentioned in the Introduction. In large parts of the Arab Middle East, Iran or parts of Africa discussed in the next chapter, vigorous ethnicities certainly emerged after 1914, but their purchase was much weaker than in Europe or even in the new Turkey.

In part this was because the older ideology and tactic of ethnic and class-based alliance persisted here well beyond the War and held benefits for both local elites and the colonial powers: Alavite (Shia) and other minority rulers were able to retain circumscribed power in Syria–Lebanon, Sunnis held a dominant position in a Shia majority Iraq, and landowners controlled the Wafd Party in Egypt. Representative politics and quasi-democracy, in its aggressive European form, had virtually no antecedents in much of the Middle East, where local monarchs or military strongmen tended to replace Ottoman governors, as Chapter 3 suggests. The communication of invented national traditions here was much less in evidence than in Europe and was held in check by the colonialists. Some political scientists have argued that the so-called Arab Spring of the 2010s, rather than being a democratic awakening, was an ethnic nationalist upsurge similar to that seen in Europe after the First World War. In this sense, events in the Middle East after 1916 were a mere premonition. Provided the danger of positing a straightforward modernisation theory is avoided, there seems some truth in this. Certainly, as George Antonius argued, Arab and other regional ethnicities were "awakened" by the First World War and this created historical memories which later leaders, secular and religious, could draw upon.[48] Yet, there was no simple historical progress in these regions towards a single modernity, nationalist or otherwise, over the next three generations.

[2] THE WORLD CRISIS, c. 1900–1930: AFRICA, ASIA AND BEYOND

Decentring the War Continued: Africa, Iran and Afghanistan
India and the War: The Creation of a People
Decentring the War in East Asia: China and Japan,
　　Nationalism and the New Imperialism
The British Dominions and the Americas
Converging Global Crises 1911–1926: Returning to Europe
The Social Consequences of Conflict: Governmentality and
　　Revolt

THIS chapter examines the effects of the First World War and its immediate consequences for the final three categories of the geographical typology outlined in Chapter 1: areas where relatively small-scale, but destructive, conflict rather than major campaigns took place, particularly Africa; areas subject to recruitment and major disruption, but not to direct warfare, such as India and China; and areas not centrally involved in the war, but nevertheless profoundly affected by it. This chapter, like the previous one, takes a long view of the world crisis, considering the whole period from about 1900 to the 1930s. Finally, it returns to Europe, examining the effects of the conflicts of the immediate postwar years on politics, economy and society.

Here the issue of relative historical weight arises once again. Scholars have rightly asserted the primacy of European conflict in the First World War itself and in creating the conditions for the next range of confrontations that culminated in 1939. But this weighting should not be allowed to overshadow the significance of the world crisis beyond Europe. Japan, for instance, played a small role in the war itself, but its participation nevertheless inaugurated a series

Remaking the Modern World 1900–2015: Global Connections and Comparisons, First Edition. C. A. Bayly.
© 2018 John Wiley & Sons Ltd. Published 2018 by John Wiley & Sons Ltd.

of events which led indirectly to the rise of Japanese expansionism in China, the Second World War in Asia and, ultimately, the dropping of the atomic bomb on Hiroshima and Nagasaki: the defining events of the century. Again, one historian recently denounced a world history volume for giving inordinate space to the British assault on an Indian crowd in the Amritsar Massacre of 1919 by comparison with its treatment of the Western Front. True, perhaps at most 1,000 Indians were slaughtered at Amritsar compared with the millions who died in Flanders. Yet, Amritsar was central to the emergence of what was to become the largest anticolonial movement in history. The image of the event has persisted in the memory of "the world's largest democracy" and beyond, so that both Winston Churchill and a more recent British prime minister, David Cameron, felt obliged to express regret for it. Meanwhile, Indian politicians criticised their own government for investigating recent political atrocities with even less vigour than the British investigation after Amritsar. The important challenge is to avoid complacent over generalisation and attend to detailed local differences yet, at the same time, to reject the pervasive north-west European parochialism which was so much in evidence during the centenary of the war's beginning and continues to dominate many histories.[1]

DECENTRING THE WAR CONTINUED: AFRICA, IRAN AND AFGHANISTAN

The analysis, therefore, now moves south into Africa and then to the Asian sphere, where the contest between European empires and Muslim populations was replicated in Iran, India and Malaya. In North Africa, both Arab and Berber regions were indirectly implicated in the war, since these were former Ottoman provinces now dominated by Western powers and drawn into the fighting through the conscription of troops, labourers and animals. The case of Egypt's second occupation and the 1919 revolt had some parallels to the west of North Africa in the crisis in the Sharifian sultanate of Morocco, once loosely part of the Ottoman Empire. From the age of the "new imperialism" in the 1890s onward, France and Spain pressed into Morocco's sovereignty. In the Rif territories to the south of the sultanate, local leaders and ulama increasingly adapted Islamic political language to express their hostility to what they took to be a Western puppet state. After 1918, they merged it with ideas of self-determination circulating following President Wilson's intervention in which he argued for local autonomy for the Rif. The consequent revolt of Abd el-Krim against Spanish and French invasion lasted until 1926; the atrocities it occasioned were condemned around the world.[2] Spokesmen in Spain and France claimed the uprising was a form of barbarism threatening the West and threatening a new world war. By contrast, many in Germany, now suffering under the terms of the 1919 Peace Conference, hailed Abd el-Krim as a national hero, as did newspapers in the Arab societies to the East. Bolshevik Russia, meanwhile, depicted the revolt as the response of an oppressed peasantry to colonialism and imperialism.

Africa south of the Sahara, however, was also the scene of what was effectively the last stage of the European imperialist partition of the continent, designed to further exploit its resources, particularly labour.[3] The new imperialism had gathered pace in the 1870s and 1880s and reached a climax after the Treaty of Berlin (1885) and the South African War (1899–1902). The British occupation of Kenya and the German occupation of Tanganyika had not involved direct conflict between the colonial powers, though there were contests between their local African proxies. The Maji Maji rebellion in Tanganyika (1905–1907) and the brutal German suppression of revolts in German South West Africa had also implicated British agents.[4] All this was accompanied by the uncontrolled spread of human and cattle disease.

The war of 1914–1918, however, brought on locally violent armed confrontation between the powers in Central, East and German South West Africa. The campaign in the latter territory was particularly complicated for the British. With the Anglo-Boer War fresh in their memory, Afrikaners were unwilling to fight German troops on Britain's behalf. Some actually mutinied. But equally, the British governor-general in Pretoria was unwilling to force the issue because of the danger that the position of the prime minister, Louis Botha, would be compromised by being forced into war against the wishes of his Afrikaner compatriots.[5] The conquest of German South West Africa was, therefore, undertaken not by regular troops but by volunteers of British origin.

The Belgian Congo provides a similarly complex picture. Before the war, driven by a lust for minerals and later rubber for the new motor tyres, King Leopold's agents had ruthlessly exploited what had been Crown property. In 1908, the Belgian government took over the colony and the situation improved somewhat. In 1916, with Belgium occupied by the Germans, an Anglo-Belgian force originating in Africa invaded and took it back. Government there in the interwar years was corrupt and often violent, but the boom in rubber production ensured a relatively higher standard of living for its population than over much of Africa.[6]

Large numbers of colonial troops and labourers were drafted into these conflicts from areas as far distant from the fulcrum of war as the Gold Coast. The percentage of deaths to the size of the military labour force in Africa was high, even by standards of other war fronts. Some estimates suggest that three-quarters of a million Africans, most of them non-combatants, died as a consequence of these small-scale, but vicious wars. Both sides burnt villages and destroyed crops and livestock indiscriminately. But death from disease, as African troops and labourers were brought into contact with new infections outside their regions of origin, was the most significant cause of mortality. Forced conscription for labour consequently brought about African revolts in British Nyasaland and in central Mozambique, a German territory. Even after the British and French had defeated Germany's African armies, sub-Saharan Africa suffered inordinately from the devastating influenza epidemic of 1918–1919 that swept across the enfeebled world. Another 2–5% of the population of the African colonies perished at this time.[7] Allied and German leaders were largely oblivious to this suffering. A German general stated, "The

Teutonic sense of loyalty peculiar to us Germans had kept its head high even under the conditions of war in the tropics."[8]

Africa's revolts tended to be expressed in a variety of forms, from public proto-nationalist protests in the Gold Coast and the more urban parts of East Africa to ethnic uprisings around spirit mediums and seers in rural areas. In Asia, however, Muslim and nationalist leaders legitimated anticolonial movements by drawing on longer-term aspirations to modern statehood. The pressure of the eastern war and ensuing revolt had already passed on from the provinces of the Ottoman Empire through Iran to Afghanistan and on into South Asia, the heart of Britain's empire. Even though these areas were not subject to direct warfare, the political and economic consequences were considerable.

Iran (Persia), as noted, had already been the scene of an aborted constitutional revolution against the Qajar dynasty in the years 1905–1909. This reflected a combination of changes in the politics of ethnic groups with the emergence of a new administrative and commercial middle class that had already asserted its hostility to economic and political concessions handed to the Western powers over the previous generation. Imperialist pressure was particularly clear in the Anglo-Russian agreement of 1907, an early result of the détente between the two powers, which effectively partitioned the north and the south of Iran. The Russians were concerned to prevent Muslim and insurrectionary movements spilling over their southern borders. The British, who deployed the South Persia Rifles in the region, wanted to protect newly discovered oilfields in Iran adjoining the port of Basra. They also worried, in the traditional manner, about the sea route to India. This virtual Iranian partition of 1907 set the scene for a long period when the country was under direct foreign influence: Russian, Soviet, British and ultimately American, a situation which only ended when Ayatollah Khomeini seized power in 1979.[9] This explains Iran's tetchy and suspicious relationship with the Western powers over the following half century.

During the First World War, Iran was the scene of a confusing array of ethnic rebellions and usurpations by various regional strongmen. Various "jihadist" plots by the Axis powers, along the lines of John Buchan's romantic novel *Greenmantle*, were hatched and failed. The global radical movement of Indian exiles, Ghadar ("mutiny"), also established itself in the Iranian city of Meshed, where it was violently suppressed by the British.[10] Between 1919 and 1923, however, a Russian-trained military man, Reza Shah Pahlavi, gradually got the upper hand, occupied Tehran and moved to the south. This was a period when the Soviets were establishing control over Central Asia and had little to gain by a new confrontation with the British in Iran. The British and Indian authorities, therefore, came to a tacit agreement with Reza Shah, conceding power to him, provided that he, in turn, recognised British oil interests in the south and the British presence in Iraq.[11] As a military rather than a dynastic figure, such as Emir Faisal, Reza Shah ranks along with Atatürk as one of a succession of despots with whom the British, French and Americans could do business because they neither leaned towards the Soviets overmuch nor fostered Islamist movements which posed a threat to colonial control. Like many of these figures,

Reza Shah and his successor carried out just enough development to assuage the emerging urban middle class and co-opt the major "tribal" leaders.

Further to the east, the war, and later the Bolshevik revolution, shook the fragile balance between ethnic groups (Pakhtun, or Pathan, and Azeri) living on the border between the Northwest Frontier of British India and Afghanistan. The British had long feared covert Afghan influence among the Pakhtun tribes of their northern borders, especially as this was sometimes tinged with Islamic messianism. They had fought two none-too-successful wars with these dissidents: the first and second Anglo-Afghan wars of 1838–1842 and 1878–1880. Then, in 1919–1920, a further war broke out as the Afghan regime attempted to consolidate its power among the Pakhtuns while British India was focussed on the First World War and its aftermath. This might have seemed merely one in a succession of late-imperial campaigns of little consequence. Yet, the Pakhtuns' stubborn sense of identity, mirroring that of the Kurds or Palestinians, was to have momentous consequences in later world politics through to 2015. It helped to bring down the Soviet-backed regime in the 1980s and mortally damaged the power of the Western alliance at the start of the twenty-first century. After 1923, the British managed to establish a new, but fragile modus vivendi with the Afghan government and the frontier chieftains, but this scarcely outlasted the 1930s.

INDIA AND THE WAR: THE CREATION OF A PEOPLE

Aside from these conflicts on the Northwest Frontier and the few shells that fell on Indian ports from the German battleship SMS *Emden*, the Indian subcontinent itself was not directly affected by the long period of direct conflict from 1911 to 1926. But the indirect effects on India's economy, society and politics were enormous. The Balkan wars had stirred Muslim opinion in India well before the major conflict began in Europe and the Ottoman Empire. Younger Indian Muslims had been gradually distancing themselves from their political dependence on the British government from the beginning of the century, even though it had granted them constitutional concessions in the 1909 reforms.[12] Concern for the future of the Ottoman Sultan and Khalifa, the last independent Muslim ruler, had grown as Russia, Serbia and now even Britain appeared to be eating away at the sovereignty of the empire. Muslims were mobilised through bodies such as the Red Crescent Society, which took provisions and medical supplies to the Ottoman front in the Balkan wars.

When Britain, France and Russia declared war on the Ottoman Empire and thousands of Indian troops, many of them Muslim, along with armies of labourers, were sent to Basra and Palestine, Indian Muslim religious leaders came close to declaring a holy war, something that had not happened even in the heat of the rebellion of 1857. There were mass demonstrations and boycotts of British goods and institutions, which spread beyond major cities into the countryside. In south India, it merged with a social movement of Muslim Mappila peasants against the injustices of the local land system. Indian troops in Singapore, many of them Muslims, mutinied in 1915 as Khilafatist and

Ghadarite revolutionary ideologies merged. The force of anticolonial sentiment was redoubled in 1916 when Mohandas Gandhi, recently returned from political agitation in South Africa, threw the weight of the Hindu population behind this Muslim movement in defence of the Khilafat.[13] The reaction reached its peak in 1919–1920 when British and British India troops occupied Istanbul on the defeat of the Ottoman Empire. The specifically Muslim element in this popular political unrest dwindled, however, when Kemal Atatürk and the new Turkish government abolished both the Khilafat and the Sultanate. The British government, having partly regained the political initiative, also managed to wean Muslim elites from political agitation by giving them small slices of real political influence under the constitutional changes inaugurated in 1919 by the so-called Montagu–Chelmsford Reforms.

The First World War also brought about a radical transformation of wider Indian opinion. As in the Middle East, this was in part a result of economic pressures.[14] War production resulted in a steep price rise and shortage of some materials and foodstuffs between 1914 and 1917. Labour costs also rose with the mass export of labour to the war fronts and the despatch of nearly one million troops (including some 200,000 from the princely states). One consequence of this was strenuous attempts by landlords large and small to insist on, or even revive, lapsed forms of unpaid labour services (*begar* and *rasad*). Farmers, particularly low-caste or outcaste groups, were hit hard by these pressures. But the war's end, far from ending them, added a new range of grievances. Men flowed back from the war zones, reducing the cost of labour. War production ended and demand for commodities, particularly clothing for troops, declined, thus reducing demand for labour in factories in Bombay, Gujarat and elsewhere. Meanwhile, the British government maintained land revenue and other taxes at the same level. Overall, the result was a rolling series of agrarian agitations which broadened out from organised protests by small landowners to movements amongst tenants and, ultimately, low-caste landless labourers. Most of this explosion of grievances was not organised by urban nationalist politicians. Instead, local-level rural councils (the panchayats) led the movement. This was a turning point in Indian nationalism. The young radical Jawaharlal Nehru foreswore "the petty politics of the city"[15] and ventured out into the north Indian countryside "afire with enthusiasm and full of a strange excitement". In a few cases, as in the riots in Chauri Chaura in north India in 1922, when policemen were murdered, serious violence followed.[16]

The most striking event of the war years was the emergence of Mohandas Gandhi as a leader of Indian opinion. Shrewdly assimilating his own idea of personal transformation through sacrifice to the very obvious fact that it would be difficult to drive out the British by force, Gandhi pioneered the idea of non-cooperation with a "satanic government" through the operation of "soul force" (*satyagraha*).[17] He also moved to enlist Muslim opinion in a common effort by endorsing the Khilafat movement. Non-cooperation did not fundamentally challenge the coercive might of colonial power – memorably demonstrated in the massacre of unarmed civilians in Amritsar in 1919. It did, however, permanently put the British government at a moral disadvantage and also

Figure 3 Nehru at Harrow, c.1906. Hulton Archive/Getty Images.

broadcast the anticolonial message across the empire. The new regional, religious and class alliance under the Congress began to fragment after 1922. The Raj was to survive another generation by taking advantage of regional, caste and religious divisions amongst its subjects. Yet, the myth of the Freedom Struggle was born and the idea of a people in revolt was to provide a powerful inducement to the creation of Indian democracy and anticolonial resistance worldwide over the next half-century.

DECENTRING THE WAR IN EAST ASIA: CHINA AND JAPAN, NATIONALISM AND THE NEW IMPERIALISM

In China the effects of the First World War were apparently dwarfed by two major events that took place before and after it, again diversifying the notion of the world crisis.[18] These were the foreign intervention against the Boxer Rebellion of 1900 and the May Fourth Movement of 1919, directed against foreign exploitation. In fact, though, the events of the war did provide an indirect link between these two phases of the crisis of modern China. The Boxer

Rebellion and its aftermath had left the four-centuries-old Qing government humiliated and facing a massive indemnity to the Western powers and Japan. This crisis resulted in the fall of the Qing following the rebellion of 1911, which was mainly engineered by Sun Yat-sen and overseas Chinese through Shanghai. The revolt had been supported by regional non-Manchu Chinese governors including Yuan Shikai, a military leader and protégé of Li Hongzhang, a long-standing power broker in the south. Yuan set about modernising his forces along French and German lines. During the war when the Western nations and the Nanjing government were distracted by the struggle in Europe, Yuan drove out Sun and seized power with the intention of installing himself as founder of a new imperial dynasty. This was not to be, however, as he died in 1916. But his legacy was a growing tension between Beijing and the south. In addition, Chinese governments had long been dependent on loans from Western countries, particularly Britain and the United States, but the effect of the war was to dry up this source of funds and so deepen the crisis.

In 1917, sensing the outcome of the war and hoping for US intervention to restrict European power in China, the Chinese government declared war on the Central Powers and formally entered the conflict. Though the commitment was not on the scale of the forced Indian involvement, a Chinese labour corps of around 140,000 men was despatched to the war fronts. Some of these workers played an important part in repairing the newly manufactured tanks as they began to appear on the Western Front. Yet, the Chinese were to be deeply outraged by the post-war settlement. True to its cynical character, the Paris

Figure 4 Portrait of Chiang Kai-shek on the wall of the Sun Co. department store at the corner of Nanking Road and Yu Ya Ching Road. George Lacks/The LIFE Picture Collection/Getty Images.

Peace Conference awarded the former German settlement of Shandong to the Japanese, rather than repatriating it to China. But the Chinese leadership also managed to play its hand badly.[19] In due course, too, France and Italy insisted on the revival of payments under the Boxer Indemnity of 1900, which had been suspended in 1917 in gratitude for China's declaration of war. This outrage found expression in the famous May Fourth Movement of 1919. This was one of the first mass demonstrations in Chinese history, bringing together students and the urban middle classes in a huge movement against colonialism and foreign meddling, comparable to contemporary events in India, Egypt and Iraq.[20] Mao Zedong wrote that it "marked a new stage in China's bourgeois democratic revolution against imperialism and feudalism" and a premonition of "the Great Revolution which followed."[21] Even their hopes for an end to Western and Japanese interventions, which the Chinese had felt during the Washington Naval Conference of 1921–1922, came to nothing. China lived out the 1920s divided and fractured, with key territories still under foreign control and vital interests such as the Maritime Customs Service still under allied supervision.[22]

By far the most important consequence of the First World War for the future of China, however, was the simple diffusion of the methods of warfare which had reached their temporary perfection on the Western Front. After Sun's death in 1925, Chiang Kai-shek's new government in the Canton region built up its forces and in 1926 embarked upon an assault to retrieve its northern territories from local warlords and military commanders. In the process, it deployed tanks, massed artillery and up to 80 aircraft against its enemies, the first time these sophisticated new weapons were used in China. The assault was a harbinger of the conflicts which were to flare on until the Communist government established control over the whole country in 1948–1950.

Japan's involvement with China was age old, but had taken on a distinctive form in the late nineteenth century as its newly centralised regime seized Taiwan and Korea, both formally dependencies of the Qing Empire. Japan had crushed China in the war of 1894–1895 and participated in the Allied invasion of the country during the Boxer Rebellion. Japan was owed massive sums by China as a result of the 1895 peace settlement and the Boxer indemnity. This was the major reason why its government insisted on the cession to Japan, rather than the new Chinese government, of the former German colony of Shandong in 1919. It is clear that Japan's successful military and political modernisation since the 1870s had given it vast new confidence, as had its defeat of Russia during the war of 1904–1905.[23]

Colonialism was still seen, before and after the war, as a sign of a country's modernity. Japan indulged in distant, economically driven colonial rule, but also sent many poor farmers from its own underprivileged provinces as settlers to Korea, Taiwan and then Manchuria. Indeed, the Japanese leadership imitated both the British and the French models of colonialism. It is, however, too simple to posit a straightforward teleology linking Japanese expansionism of the pre-war and wartime periods with its later assault on China and Southeast Asia during the 1930s and 1940s. Japan had done well out of its delayed belligerence during the war. Although it smarted from relative marginalisation during the debates around the Washington Naval Treaty when the United States and Britain maintained their maritime dominance, Japan's horizons had steadily expanded between 1914 and 1919. Its later aggressive policies were much more a consequence of the Depression, the rise of Chinese nationalism and the death of the older, more cautious elites of the Meiji period than they were directly a result of the First World War. Nevertheless, the deeper intervention of Japan in wider East Asian affairs between 1900 and 1929 marked out the region as an area of permanent military and political conflict.

THE BRITISH DOMINIONS AND THE AMERICAS

Of all the countries of the British and English-speaking world, it was perhaps Australia, even more than Britain itself, which was most directly affected not just by the indirect economic and political shocks of the war but by the consequences of the fighting itself. This was ironic because, along with New Zealand, which was also heavily involved, Australia was the most distant from the war fronts. Both dominions had emerged united and confidently into the twentieth century.[24] Their democratic, public health and educational systems were perhaps more advanced than anywhere else in the world and marred only by a pervasive belief in eugenics, which condemned their Aboriginal and Maori populations to marginalisation and assault. Citizens enlisted happily in defence of the "mother country" as the war began. But casualties rapidly mounted. The failed landing at Gallipoli in 1915 during the war against the Ottomans became part of a legend of ANZAC "mate-ship", bravery and sacrifice, which was increasingly contrasted with the supposed rigidity and incompetence of the British officer class. There were 14,000 Australian fatalities on the Western Front alone in 1916 and 22,000 in 1917. Consequently, Australian society was plagued in the 1920s and 1930s by the presence of inordinate numbers of wounded men. The war severely damaged the economies of both dominions, cutting off demand for wool and meat both in Britain and in continental Europe. Rural hardship at the end of the war persisted into the years of the Depression, as Chapter 5 shows. Conflicts had also emerged in Australian society over the issue of conscription (which was not ultimately implemented) and over the British connection, particularly in light of the strength of feeling aroused among Irish Australians by the 1916 uprising in Ireland itself. Later, socially conservative governments found themselves in conflict with a newly vigorous labour movement across Australia.

Even though more than 100,000 Americans died at the front, the most populous and now the richest of all the English-speaking societies, the United States, did not suffer proportionately the same level of casualties as Australia, New Zealand or the United Kingdom. The United States only entered the war in 1917 after Germany declared a strategy of unlimited U-boat warfare and began to attack US shipping. As a result, American public opinion swung in favour of war. One later American work praised "Belgium's endurance" and "Britain's ready navy" that saved "civilisation which was the product of twenty centuries of human effort".[25] In 1919, President Woodrow Wilson was the toast of the Allies and also appeared to be the coming saviour of subject peoples in view of his talk of universal liberty with his Fourteen Points.[26] Then, abruptly, the United States retreated into isolationism, except in the western hemisphere and the Philippines, where it continued to pursue its own quasi-imperialist interests. Wilson, who had designed the League of Nations, failed to persuade his own nation to join the organisation. All the same, the war transformed America's position in the world in several ways which were critical for the future of the century.[27] Economically, the country initially benefited from the stimulus of war production, though prices doubled, as they did over much of the rest of the world. The United States rapidly pulled out of its pre-war recession and expanded into markets abandoned by the belligerent powers. It also became the world's greatest creditor as Britain, France and Germany struggled with massive debts accumulated during the conflict. Despite the government's retreat from international politics, Americans had moved across the world in great numbers during the war and its immediate aftermath, as technicians, soldiers, journalists and missionaries, and the nation's moral and intellectual, if not its political, isolation was breached for ever.

America's internal politics was also transformed by the war and the following slump. Women, who, as in Britain, played a prominent part in war production, began a campaign for a full adult franchise reminiscent of the British suffragettes. Finally receiving support from Wilson, the 19th Amendment, which gave women the vote, was passed in 1920.[28] Broadly, however, wartime patriotism hardened into a range of reactionary movements as the fighting came to an end. White Americanism reasserted itself. Immigrant labour was curtailed, while a rash of strikes in 1919 resulted in anti-Communist legislation, even though the American Communist movement was small in scale. When young white men had been consigned to Europe by the draft, black workers had been hired by northern factory-owners to fill their places. Racial tension arose as the soldiers returned from the war.

In the "white dominions" of South Africa and Canada, responses to the outbreak of war were idiosyncratic. In South Africa, memories of the Anglo-Boer War were still fresh, and this cautioned great circumspection with regard to the conquest of German South West Africa. The response in Canada was quite different. Canadians of British origin were keenly aware of the ambivalent attitude of their French-speaking population to Britain, despite France's own role on the Allied side. Equally, there had been a recent scare about annexation by the United States, however unlikely this eventuality actually was. Canada therefore poured men and supplies into the war on Britain's side: 458,000 troops were sent abroad, more than the 332,000 sent by Australia, and of these 57,000 became casualties. Per head of population and of the country's armed forces, Australia's sacrifice was greater, but the alacrity with which Canada's government and people responded to war was striking and, as in the United States, economic mobilisation gave a sharp, if temporary, boost to the economy.[29]

Perhaps Central and South America were the parts of the world most isolated from the direct effects of the war in Europe and the Middle East, though they served as a safe haven for both capital and labour during the conflict and its immediate aftermath. Nevertheless, these societies, and particularly Mexico, experienced locally generated conflict on an unprecedented scale. At the broadest level, some of the underlying social conflicts which brought Europe to the brink were seen here, too. In the late nineteenth century, South America had seen an export boom in raw materials to industrialising Europe and North America, much of it financed with British capital: Argentina and southern Brazil exported beef and grain; Guatemala, Colombia and central Brazil exported coffee and minerals. Across most of the southern continent, an oligarchy of commercialising landlords and newly wealthy urban interests dominated the state, speaking the language of paternalistic liberalism. Mexico's president, Porfirio Diaz, who held power from 1877 to 1911, was simply the longest lasting of these leaders.[30] But Brazil, more closely connected to Europe and influenced by North American ideas, became increasingly turbulent as rapid growth in both population and the economy created massive differences in wealth.

After 1900, Diaz became the target of more radical elements, including socialists and anarchists.[31] They could draw on a range of discontents which had grown up as landlords stripped peasants and tribal people of their common lands and a new and easily exploited urban working class emerged during the export boom. In 1906, the Mexican Liberal Party demanded "a completely secular education in all schools of the republic" and "that any extension of land that the owner leaves unproductive shall be confiscated by the state".[32] Demands for social reform spilled over into active resistance to Diaz in 1911 when the radical liberal Francisco Madero entered Mexico City. Meanwhile, Emiliano Zapata mobilised the peasantry of the central south of the country and the charismatic Francisco Villa's Division of the North brought together middle-class and urban radicals. Rapidly changing and increasingly militarised leaders came and went, culminating in a civil war between 1914 and 1915 which may have left a million dead overall, though one observer said of the Zapatistas that "beneath their terrifying exteriors [they] seemed more like harmless and valiant children than anything else".[33] As peace was restored in 1916 and 1917, the Mexican leadership inaugurated a new constitution with quite radical protection for labour and the peasantry as well as a tilt in the direction of state secularism on the French model. This move towards an interventionist state was paralleled in less radical forms in Argentina and Chile.

The Mexican Revolution has been overshadowed by the Bolshevik Revolution. But there were some significant similarities and differences which bear indirectly on the value of world history, given the physical and social distance between Mexico and Russia. Old landed oligarchs were challenged by urban radicals and peasant rebels in both Mexico and Russia. Mexico, which during these years collapsed into a congeries of revolutionary forces contending for power and promoting land reform, anticipated developments in Russia and Eastern Europe a few years later. Urban working-class organisations played a leading part in both uprisings, though urban workers were a relatively small part of both populations. Yet, there were also notable differences between the two cases. Most obviously, Mexico was not directly affected by the First World War.

Though soldiers were involved in overthrowing Diaz and his successors, there were not the millions of mutinous or discharged military personnel as there were on the Eastern Front in Europe.

Equally important, the various radical liberals, would-be military dictators and social reformers in the Mexican case were not bound by the fierce and hard-edged Communist belief of the Soviet vanguard, led by Lenin and Trotsky. Nor, finally, was Mexico subject to invasion by surrounding capitalist powers, as was the USSR, even if the United States meddled in its revolution on several occasions. Consequently, the social and political outcomes of revolution were less drastic in Mexico. The landlord elite and liberal bourgeoisie were temporarily weakened, though not destroyed, as was the case in the USSR. In fact, though to a lesser extent than in other parts of Latin America, politics in Mexico was to veer over the next century between populist regimes and military authoritarianism. The labour movement came to play a major role in politics despite the infant size of Mexico's industries. Peasant leaders acquired a voice in the state. But they were not subject to stringent control by a domineering party. Most striking was the socialist–aesthetic revolution which brought to prominence a whole range of radical artists, poets and novelists, of whom the most important were probably Frida Kahlo and Diego Rivera. Artistic freedom seemed to be moving in a similar direction in the USSR during its first ten years, but was later stamped out by Stalin.

CONVERGING GLOBAL CRISES 1911–1926: RETURNING TO EUROPE

The case of Mexico suggests some immediate reflections on the nature of the First World War and the "long world crisis" outside Europe. A straightforward narrative of how warfare spread beyond the Continent and led to clashes between European colonial powers in Asia and Africa is only part of the story. Taken as a whole, the world crisis had several different origins which converged between 1914 and 1918. The Middle East war could be seen as an autonomous development arising initially from the long struggle of the Ottoman Empire's Christian subjects for independence, which began as far back as the Greek revolt of 1821. It was also a consequence of the British Indian Empire's expansion into the Persian Gulf and southern Mesopotamia, which had accelerated during the viceroyalty of Lord Curzon (1898–1905).[34] Equally, the wartime and post-war conflicts in East Asia represented an extension of Japan's rise to prominence after the Meiji restoration of 1868. Regional tensions or conflicts, whether in India, South Africa, Canada or Mexico, contributed independently to the world crisis and did not simply follow from the assassination of the Archduke Franz Ferdinand in 1914. Many of the conflicts released by these crises, whether the Zionist–Palestinian struggle, the Chinese civil wars or ethnic conflicts in colonised Africa, continued long after the European continent itself achieved a degree of peaceful prosperity after 1945 in its western sector or in its eastern sector after 1990.

All the same, the 1914–1918 war and the Russian Revolution of 1917, which was a consequence of it, were indeed world-changing events, leading by stages to the Second World War, the destabilisation of the European empires, the rise of Communism across the world and, in time, the long American hegemony. So far, these first two chapters have attempted to decentralise the First World War from the great powers – Germany, France, Britain and Russia – and the Western Front. European historians, too, have been attempting to do this for some years. Michael Howard, Adam Tooze, Hew Strachan and Christopher Clark have emphasised the importance of the standoff between Austria–Hungary and the Serbians, who, supported by their Russian allies, wanted to constitute a new Slavic nation against the interests of the German-speaking powers. Strachan, in particular, brought the Ottoman Empire and Africa into the picture, and Tooze, China. By 1914, the Ottomans were no longer simply victims of the manipulation of their Christian populations by the great powers. With modernised armies, they actually took back ground in the Second Balkan War of 1913 and their revived military power was seen both in their stubborn resistance to British and French armies from 1914–1918 and later in the Turkish defeat of Greece and the stalemating of Britain between 1919 and 1923.

This geographical decentring of the origins of the war has been paralleled by reconsideration of the broader origins of the malign alliances that caused it. Despite the number of new studies forthcoming, however, the picture here has not greatly changed. For a century it has been rightly assumed that Germany's attempt to secure itself against the danger of encirclement by France and Russia, newly aligned after 1900, led it to build a powerful fleet. This in turn caused the British to ally with France and Russia after decades of hostility to these powers. Yet, despite these growing tensions and the pace of rearmament following the German Naval Laws of 1898, the passage to war was not predetermined. The failure of statesmen such as Theobald von Bethmann-Hollweg and Edward Grey to work resolutely for peace in July 1914 provides an equally compelling series of short-term causes.

What recent studies suggest, nevertheless, is a kind of hierarchy of causality. At the apex, the German fear of military encirclement and the British aversion to the domination of the Continent by any one power remain powerful causes of the scale of conflict. At the next level down, the fractious politics of Serbia and its neighbours and French determination to recover Alsace-Lorraine and avenge the humiliation of 1871 have perhaps achieved even greater significance. The intrusion into the war of those autonomous crises outlined here in the Middle East, in East Asia and even in Mexico seems significant at a yet lower level. Finally, as the first chapter suggests, the conditions for war had been created by the intertwining of capital and state power. The state and its local agents promoted economic rivalry across the world, which in turn fed back into political conflict between European powers.

Meanwhile, the consensus on the course of the war has hardly changed. Technical developments in machine-gunnery and the deployment of massed military power created a stalemate on the Western Front which neither the Allies or the Central Powers were able to break with the type of encircling attacks or rapid deployment of forces which had been successful in the wars of the nineteenth century. On the Eastern Front, it was the collapse of the Russian polity rather than the defeat of its armies which gave temporary victory to Germany. But in the west, again, the French and British were able to hold off German attacks until a new style of tank warfare and the arrival of American troops ensured their defeat.

The economic strains and distortions brought about by the War can now be put into a global context. In Europe, the mobilisation of capital and labour, including women's labour, for the production of armaments and munitions was quite unprecedented. An unequalled and rapid degree of urbanisation took place as rural labour was drafted into cities and soldiers mobilised from the countryside. This was especially true of Eastern Europe and Russia, which were still largely rural societies in 1914. The war also provoked an unprecedented level of state intervention in the economy, which set a precedent for later socialist experiments. Typical of this was the German Raw Materials Section (KRA), an organisation designed to control "war raw materials companies", which by the end of the war had spawned a bureaucracy of 20,000 people.[35] In France, meanwhile, as many as 287,000 workers for the munitions industry had been returned from the French army between the beginning of the war and June 1916.[36] Mechanisms for land and air war developed rapidly and one small bonus was the wristwatch, originally designed for the trenches.

European interests across the world were sold off to garner capital for the struggle. British operations in South America were pawned to the United States. Huge transfers of funds in 1916 and 1917 allowed the British to purchase materials from the Americans, stimulating an artificially large manufacturing boom there. Equally, though, German and Austrian wealth was drained off to Istanbul to support the Ottoman war effort. This massive mobilisation of resources had consequences, as we have seen, across the world. Whether it was the breeding of horses in Australia or Argentina, the drift of black labour from the South into the towns of the northern states of the United States or the rapid expansion and then collapse of Bombay mill production for the war effort, the results were profound. This was, without question, a connected history.

THE SOCIAL CONSEQUENCES OF CONFLICT: GOVERNMENTALITY AND REVOLT

One of the long-term social consequences of the war was a result of the unprecedented levels of social mixing: the mixing of classes, races and nationalities. Australian troops in Egypt mixed with Arabs and upper-class British officers. They appreciated neither, leading to the solidification of an Australian sense of selfhood centred on white "mate-ship" and a growing distrust of the supposed class-ridden stagnation of British society. Black workers from the French African and Caribbean colonies were recruited into French factories to replace men called to the front, and their relationship with white women caused deep unease.[37] Even more explosive was the use of black troops to police areas of the Rhineland seized by France from Germany after the war in recompense for the non-payment of reparations.[38] American troops in Europe astonished the embattled Europeans with their relative wealth and lack of concern for status. Equally, Indian, African and Chinese troops and labourers writing home and returning to their own countries after 1918 helped to destroy the myth of European racial superiority with their accounts of the destructive barbarism of their rulers.[39] Soon, garbled accounts of the Bolshevik Revolution spread across the world, apparently signalling the death knell of the old European and class-based order.

One under-appreciated aspect of this general crisis, seen in both the European and extra-European spheres, was the global popular revolt against militarised governmentality, which, temporarily at least, cracked the fabric of the old elite structures across the world, whether liberal or authoritarian.[40] This is a theme which brings together the collapse of German power in 1918 and the ensuing Spartacist revolt, the Bolshevik revolution of 1917, the rise of Gandhi in India, the May Fourth Movement of 1919 and numerous other events across Eurasia and Africa. I use the words militarised and Foucault's term governmentality deliberately, despite their ugliness. This was not just a matter of mutinies, riots and political objections to conscription, billeting soldiers on the civil population and the like – that is, direct reactions to the activity of armies. It also comprised objections to indirect applications of military organisation, discipline and extra-legal action and exclusion to processes which had formerly fallen within the realm of civil society.[41] Examples here were the transformation of civilian police into armed units. They also included the invasion of civilian areas by public health bodies using military methods and the imposition of military discipline on labourers and trades unions, practices that became common during the war and were perpetuated long after it had ended.

Even before the war, the threat of anarchism or terrorism had been adduced to justify such actions. During the war the authoritarian tendency of governments had grown exponentially and after the war, the spectre of the Bolshevik revolutions, agrarian movements in Eastern Europe and trade union militancy in Britain and France were invoked to extend indefinitely the period during which earlier civil liberties were suspended. This is where the word governmentality is useful. It was not simply the obvious dimension of government which had been militarised, but the whole area between formal government and the population, roughly Jürgen Habermas's civil society. The great expansion of press censorship, the interception of letters and telegrams was well known. Bodies such as the British Criminal Investigation Department or the US Bureau of Investigation[42] extended their purview deep into society, transforming the citizen into an agent of the newly diffused state.

Often, however, these moves were subtle and relatively unnoticed and had signal long-term effects. One example was the disarming of the civilian population during and after the war in Britain and France. Before 1914 many members of the ruling class and farmers had held weapons. Wartime surveillance and the fear of Bolshevism led to a stringent system of weapon registration after 1918. This, of course, did not happen to the same degree in the United States where the right of citizens to bear arms was loudly canvassed. These different outcomes had mixed results: in the United States it preserved liberty of a sort, but also led to an excess of numbers of gun murders there by comparison with Western Europe throughout the next century. Yet even in the United States, the "surveillance state" achieved greater prominence, in part because of the turbulence released by the world crisis. The Bureau of Investigation (BoI, forerunner of the FBI) had been established in 1909. Its remit expanded as what is now called people-trafficking became common and the pogroms in Russia and the conflicts in Eastern Europe before 1914 sent new waves of refugees in search of American shelter. During the war it targeted draft resisters and spies. One of the vaunted early successes of the BoI was the arrest of a large force of Mexican radicals on the US border in 1923.

At a yet more subtle level, militarised governmentality affected ideologies and practices throughout the world in the form of eugenic theory and social statistics. Eugenics had become fashionable by 1900 as social Darwinist theories were apparently validated by the rise and fall of nations and the fate of "races".[43] Physical and mental characteristics began to be introduced into debates about national fortunes in peace and war. Lord Curzon even bewailed the decline of the British race as the country suffered defeats in international sporting events, a situation that was to persist over the following century.[44] Robert Baden-Powell's Boy Scout movement with imitators across the world was avowedly eugenic and subtly militaristic. In his words, "You can only get discipline in the mass by discipline in the individual." Even liberals such as John Maynard Keynes were captivated by images of a better future and a stronger race.

The World War, therefore, gave a boost to those measuring social and mental facilities, as the failure of weak and enfeebled soldiers was linked to inbreeding and other forms of eugenic unfitness. Enlistment in armies provided opportunities for mapping and classifying men. After the war, military defeat could all too easily be attributed to the eugenic enemy within. The emergence of National Socialist ideology, targeting Jews, the mentally enfeebled and diseased, was only the most violent and obnoxious of these ideologies. The model of Soviet Man, particularly developed after Stalin took the reins in the USSR, had a military and eugenic as well as a class component. The important point was the manner in which these ideas inflected both government and civil society. Most countries had introduced controls on the sale and public drinking of alcohol during the war, for instance. This was ostensibly in order to prevent indiscipline and truancy affecting conscription and military discipline. But merged with local Protestant Puritanism this sensibility brought about Prohibition in the United States in the 1920s, once again with unintended consequences for public order and the control of crime.

If government had become more intrusive and had invaded civil society more deeply, popular revolt and resistance reached new levels after 1917. In time, groups of dissidents seized power themselves and created new types of states on both the left and the right of the political spectrum. As the Russian offensive of 1916 and 1917 was blunted and reversed by the German attack, thousands of

Russian soldiers mutinied and returned to their homes where they banded together with workers protesting against ever-harsher wartime labour conditions and the lack of essential commodities. In the countryside, a widespread peasant movement spurred on by sheer hunger had also emerged. This was the tipping point which removed first the tsarist government and then the moderate Provisional government which replaced it and provided the fundamental background for the Bolshevik Revolution of November 1917 which was effectively a coup organised by the ruthlessly centralising followers of Lenin.[45] It was the appearance of councils of soldiers' and workers' delegates across the country which undermined the moderates who had dismissed the tsarist government, negotiated for peace with Germany and established an elected Duma. Within a few months the Bolshevik leadership of Lenin and Trotsky, which had been a negligible political power at the beginning of 1916, was now in a pre-eminent position. On 16 April 1917, Lenin arrived in Petrograd, vowing "to place power in the hands of the proletarian and the poorest sections of the peasants". [46] By that autumn, the Bolsheviks had seized power in Moscow and Petrograd, so initiating the central phase of the European twentieth century.

The popular reaction against the wartime state was no less explosive in Germany. Despite its successes on the Eastern front, Germany's main ally, Austria–Hungary, was collapsing in a welter of strikes and mutinies and, from late 1917 into the summer of 1918, strikes in German cities among war supply workers were becoming more and more common. The Bolshevik revolution provided an ominous lesson in how unrest could become politicised by a resurgent left. It was this that caused Erich Ludendorff to approach President Wilson in October 1918 in search of a lenient peace. But this was not forthcoming. Germany's subsequent unconditional surrender followed by its humiliation at the peace conferences and the occupation of the Rhineland by France combined with unprecedented poverty and hunger in the country in late 1919 and 1920. Seizing their moment, German leftists launched the Spartacist revolt, a failed copy of the Bolshevik revolution, which was put down by the social democratic government in alliance with the anti-Communist militias of Freikorps.[47] The image of strikes, warfare in the streets and the ravages of bodies of ex-soldiers provided a powerful precedent for the forces of both Right and Left in the Weimar Republic. The failed leftist risings and murder of its leadership in 1919, notably Rosa Luxemburg and Karl Liebknecht, were followed by Hitler's failed putsch of 1923. Strikes, protests and minor movements of lesser violence also racked the cities of the victorious Allies over the next two years. In Britain, the Irish rebellion, suppressed violently in 1916, entered a new phase of civil war in 1921–1922. On the English mainland, striking workers in Liverpool, allegedly Communists, appeared so threatening to the British government that it despatched a battleship to the environs of the city in 1919.

Even in Spain, a country which had remained neutral during the war, powerful tremors shook the political scene.[48] Before and during the world conflict, Spain had been making an uneasy transition between an oligarchic form of representational government and a more directly democratic one, spurred by the rise of labour unions and urban liberalism. This transition was

Figure 5 A young Hitler with members of the 16th Bavarian Reserves Infantry Regiment during the First World War. Roger Viollet/Agence France-Presse/Getty Images.

interrupted by the abject failure of civilian politicians. They mishandled a movement among soldiers and urban workers in 1916–1917 protesting against low wages. Ironically, this had been caused by a burst of inflation, itself a gauge of the relative prosperity which Spain achieved by supplying France and the Allies during the war. Then, as across much of the rest of the world, a sudden slump occurred in late 1918 and early 1919 as wartime demand for goods and services collapsed and the labour unions organised a series of protests and strikes. In the case of Spain, this internal political crisis coincided with a "crisis of sub-imperialism" as the Spanish army initially faltered and fell apart in its war with the Moroccan rebel Abd el-Krim. Thus, Spain's late entry into the post-war political melee ended in humiliation and the scene was set for the dictatorship of General Miguel Primo de Rivera, a ruler who seemed to mimic the modernising bravura of Mussolini but presided over a much more archaic form of authoritarian government.

Internal revolt against militarised governmentality across the world in the eight years after the Armistice was paralleled by continuing armed conflict. As momentous as the Turkish War of Independence, the civil wars in China and the conflict in Afghanistan were the wars in Eastern Europe and Central Asia by which the emerging USSR sought to strengthen its borders and guard the revolution. Britain and France staged a failed military intervention in both these areas. But the Soviet armies rapidly gained the upper hand against them and the White Russian conservatives.[49] Despite their ideological differences, Muslim leaderships in the Caucasus and Russian central Asia also allied themselves with Lenin and the Bolsheviks because they, perhaps wrongly, believed that, organised into Soviet republics, the Muslim populations would have more autonomy than they did under the tsarist empire. Nevertheless, it took some years for the USSR to consolidate its hold in Vladivostok and the Far East, where White Russian armed resistance merged with Chinese warlordism and Japanese expansionist ambitions. Thus, in its peripheries, the consequences of the Bolshevik revolution completed the circle of decentralised conflict which was as much a significant feature of the world crisis as the bloody stalemate on the Eastern and Western fronts.

Not the least social and intellectual consequence of the long war was a further massive displacement of people it brought about. Russian conservatives and writers unsympathetic to the Leninist regime fled to Warsaw, Paris and the cities of the Chinese coast. Indian radicals fled the militancy of the colonial state whose callousness had been demonstrated by the Amritsar Massacre. Many Germans and Austrians dispossessed by the war tried to find their way to the United States, though the country was now closing its borders to foreigners, particularly to non-white migrants. Later, as fascist parties burgeoned across Europe, Jews and another wave of leftist radicals joined this stream of migrants. Not only did this forced migration lead to a new dispersed cosmopolitan sensibility, it also gave rise to a wave of reflection on war, conflict and the human condition, which imparted a feeling both of release and of deep sadness to the art and literature of what was to become the interwar period. The art of the futurists, vorticists and impressionists took on a new and radical form. War now represented a potential ontological rupture on a huge scale. The H. G. Wells film *Things to Come* (1936) pointed towards mass annihilation, something which was soon to be yet more feasible with the creation of atomic weapons. War had once been a continuation of politics by other means, but the unparalleled scale of death in the 1914–1918 conflicts undercut the validity of this aphorism. Since at least 1815, wars had seen the collapse of governments, but not, until 1917, the collapse of whole societies.

[3] AUTHORITARIANISM AND DICTATORSHIP WORLDWIDE, c. 1900–1950

> Nazism, Fascism and Communism: Distant Relatives?
> Authoritarian Rule in the Middle East
> Authoritarian Rule in East Asia
> Authoritarianism, Fascism and Nazism in the West
> Back to Communism
> A Typology of Early-Twentieth-Century Authoritarianism?

THE next four chapters extend the analytical narrative in Chapters 1 and 2, considering, in turn, authoritarian regimes, the fate of democracy and representative government, the Great Depression and the Second World War.[1] Democracy and authoritarianism were not, of course, wholly separate categories. Fascist regimes widely came to power through elections, while Communist regimes appeared to have mass support. In Latin America, politics moved from an endorsement of elite liberal democracies to military dictatorships and back again. The military leaders who came to power in the Middle East and East Asia over these years derived their legitimacy, in so far as it existed, from being modernisers while they maintained connections with ethnic and religious leaders. They relied as much on persuasion as on force. Indeed, the 1920s and 1930s were not simply an age of dictators, as they have sometimes been depicted. The Kaiser's Germany, for instance, already had a universal adult franchise in 1914, unlike Britain, while the Weimar Republic was a vibrant, if doomed, democracy. Outside Italy, much of Europe was still controlled by liberal or moderate socialist governments as late as 1930. Hitler's and Franco's rise to power, the fall of representative government in Eastern and Southern Europe and Stalin's lurch towards terror came after that date. All the same, the emerging conflict between two very different forms of authoritarianism in the USSR and Germany was profoundly to shape the remainder of the century.

NAZISM, FASCISM AND COMMUNISM: DISTANT RELATIVES?

As in the case of the world wars, the study of the authoritarian regimes of Europe in the first half of the twentieth century has been one of the most vibrant, lucrative and contentious areas of historical study over the last 50 years.[2] Numerous issues have been debated without a clear resolution. Were fascist and radical socialist regimes basically similar? Even Nehru, a democratic socialist, wrote in the 1930s, "Thus we have three types of dictatorship – the Communist type, the fascist and the military."[3] He implicitly added imperial dictatorship. Other historians on the left, or public intellectuals such as Slavoj Žižek, attempted to distinguish sharply between the regimes of Hitler, Mussolini and Franco, on the one hand, and Stalin, on the other, citing the former regimes' basic support for private property and private capital. By contrast, some liberal and right-wing scholars, among them the celebrated French sociologist and historian Francois Furet,[4] have emphasised their broad similarity in the destruction of opposition, individual rights and lives. This chapter takes the view that, though Communist and fascist regimes were all broadly authoritarian, and while they all arose from the violent conditions of the world crisis, there were fundamental differences between them in terms of their aims, structure and ideologies.[5] In addition, the term "authoritarian" is exceptionally broad and should be taken to include late colonial regimes, which also denied their subjects rights and often used extreme violence against them.

Even within the broad range of Nazi, fascist and anti-leftist authoritarian regimes in the Western world, there were significant differences in origin and form. This chapter aims to create a typology of such regimes. It also considers the origins of this worldwide shift in state forms. Were Nazism and fascism responses by an embattled bourgeoisie to popular movements after the war and during the Great Depression, or did they have deeper roots? The question of continuity between pre-1914 forms of governance and the later dictatorships has also been constantly debated, most pertinently around the question of Germany's *Sonderweg*, the teleology supposedly linking Otto von Bismarck through Kaiser Wilhelm II to Adolf Hitler. Another school of thought approaches the issue mainly from the perspective of international relations and stresses the importance of competing nationalisms, frustrated by the unequal treaties signed after 1918, and the retreat into semi-isolation of the United States, which might have provided a balancing element between the Allies and defeated Central Powers. Certainly, the contingent events of 1919 appear to have been more significant than any long-term trend towards authoritarianism in either Germany or Italy.

Some of these themes are discussed later in the chapter, but its main aim is once again to set the history of European dictatorships in a global context by bringing it into closer dialogue with events in the Middle East, Asia, Latin America and parts of Africa. Of course, there are dangers inherent in such a broad set of comparisons. European authoritarian regimes emerged in most cases out of periods of constitutional government, albeit sometimes on limited franchises, as in Weimar Germany, liberal Italy and Spain, or even the abortive dumas and the Russian provisional government. But in other parts of the world, forms of representative government were hardly in view before these central-ising dictatorships emerged. The Persian constitutional revolution of 1911, Sun Yat-sen's republicanism or caudillo-liberal regimes south of Mexico, for instance, had much shorter lifespans than their European or even Russian equivalents. The existence of relatively large working-class populations also differentiated most European from Asian, African and Latin American socie-ties, where industrialisation had only recently begun and urbanisation had been much slower. Asian and African despotic states generally emerged almost directly from governments previously dominated by large landlords, tribal elders and archaic civil or religious bureaucracies. Yet, most of the authoritarian regimes of the wider world were affected to some degree by European or American imperialism, even if this was only indirectly, as in China, Japan, Iran or Ethiopia.

On the other side, there is a danger of slipping into an easy Orientalism in which historians agonise over how apparently healthy Western representative systems succumbed to dictatorial coups, while the underdevelopment of other world societies is taken for granted and authoritarian regimes are naturalised. As in so much world historical writing, some kind of balance needs to be maintained between generalisation and sensitivity to specifics, between global arguments and regional or national conditions.

It is useful to distinguish different features which are sometimes lumped together in discussions of dictatorship and authoritarianism. As far as ideology is concerned there were fundamental differences in the understanding of the meaning of "the people", though most of these regimes purported to be modernising and populist in some respect. Populist racial mythology, for instance, was a formative feature of German, Italian and Spanish fascist ideology, though much more so in the case of Germany. In the southern Catholic countries, religious authority, represented by popes Pius XI and XII, compromised with fascist authoritarianism. As a leading Spanish fascist argued, "The regeneration of the race has to be backed up by the regeneration of the family institution . . . constituted in accordance with traditional principles of Christian morality."[6] In Germany, by contrast, tradition was progressively overwhelmed by a mythical sense of the people, a rejection of history and the imperative of race war. In the case of Japan, historicist themes were also invoked to tackle the challenge of modernity. These centred less on an idea of the mobilised people as on the royal dynasty, the Shinto religion and the *bushido* cult of the samurai warrior as embodiments of patriotic spiritual essence. Again, "the people" were invoked in the new Soviet regimes, but in these cases the concept arose from the ideology of the historical stages of class struggle rather than from an idea of racial essence. Despite these differences, the transnational ideological move against liberalism should not be underestimated. The leading intellectual to support Nazism, Carl Schmitt, challenged the legitimacy of parliamentary government, arguing for the dominance of executive power over all legal and political structures. For him, enmity not inclusion was the basis of politics.[7] Friedrich Nietzsche was adored by the Nazis, and Hitler particularly admired the American racialist Madison Grant, historicist of the "Nordic races". The Hindutva ideologue M. S. Golwalkar idolised Hitler, while Hitler praised Chiang Kai-shek for instituting "a strong state". Communist theorists excoriated "bourgeois authoritarianism", while much of the strength of authoritarianism arose from hostility to Communism.

The performative element in authoritarian politics also varied significantly between regimes. Many authoritarian rulers presented themselves through the media as great leaders, bridging the gap between the divine kings of the past and "the people". But while Mussolini invoked the Caesars, medieval populist leaders such as Rienzi and heroes of the cinema, Stalin and later Communist leaders, such as Ho Chi Minh, generally eschewed flowery rhetoric and grandiose public appearances as this might detract from their role as mouthpieces and reflections of the will of the proletariat. Personality cults later blossomed around them, but not to the same extent as around the fascist leaders. Yet, one theme common to almost all these regimes was an emphasis on youth: the Hitler Youth, the Soviet Young Pioneers, Chiang Kai-shek's New Life Movement[8] or his shadowy Blue Shirts and even the young zealots of the Rashtriya Swayamsevak Sangh (RSS) who promoted the politics of violence in opposition to Gandhi.[9] Here the themes of comradeship and sacrifice during the First World War and its "peripheral" equivalents blended with a sense that young men should create a fundamental break with the past to invigorate the nation.

The structure of authoritarian regimes varied greatly, too. Far from being a coherent and universally intrusive force, many of them were fragmented and internally contested between different groups of strongmen and their followers. This was as true of Franco's and Mussolini's governments as it was of Emperor Hirohito's or Chiang Kai-shek's. Nazi Germany was a more coherent political structure than any of these. But, even here, industrialists and the army with its Prussian roots retained some degree of autonomy and, similarly, the bureaucracy preserved its influence despite Hitler's periodic "charismatic interventions" and the fanaticism of the SA and SS.[10] In the Soviet regime of the 1920s and 1930s, by contrast, the universal reach of the Party and later Stalin's police and bureaucratic mechanisms was very clear. Rigidly centralised Communist Party leadership came to dominate the soviets, and from the outset Lenin had rejected the need for checks and balances, plurality and inclusiveness. There was to be "no distribution of power", he ruled.[11] Even in the central Asian republics, where tribal leaders barely disguised as party bosses initially held sway, Stalin's forced population movements and anti-kulak (rich peasant) policies created a rigid autocracy, later reinforced by purges of even mildly dissident voices. Yet, bringing extra-European forms of authoritarian rule into the picture from the beginning will help to provide a context for the developments of the period and avoid the danger of constantly seeing European forms diffused to the supposed peripheries.

AUTHORITARIAN RULE IN THE MIDDLE EAST

Most significantly, these authoritarian regimes emerged out of different conditions: war and frustrated nationalism in Europe and Latin America and colonial domination throughout much of the rest of the world. In the Middle East and North Africa, centralising regimes with many authoritarian characteristics came into being: in Turkey by 1923, Egypt by 1926, Iran in the 1920s and Iraq in the 1930s. A particular feature here was the British and French colonialists' desire to deal with effective local regimes for economic and strategic reasons in places where they could no longer afford to maintain direct rule.[12] These quasi-independent governments usually reflected a pact between modernising military figures which emerged out of the reforms of the late Ottoman Empire or the Iranian Qajar regime with ethnic leaderships which had been favoured during colonial or semi-colonial rule. Broadly speaking, their support bases were the landowners, the small middle class and merchant communities who wished to maintain their own privileges but had been disadvantaged by direct Western economic and political power.

Such regimes also relied quite heavily on the acquiescence of peasant farmers who often provided the bases of their military power. The army officers themselves were usually drawn from middle-level landholding communities but had moved through military academies set up in the latter stages of the old regimes. Their power evidently rested on their capacity to use new forms of military transport and weaponry to control the peripheries of their new, fragile states which had emerged when the earlier multi-ethnic polities were racked by war and European powers reduced their direct control. The attempts to foster an exclusive nationalism provided the ideological rationale for the dictators, both military and dynastic. So Atatürk gloried in Turkish history and the Turkish language, while the Sharifian rulers of Iraq and their military strongmen who became dominant in the 1930s projected a political ideology of Arabism which had supposedly prompted the first revolts of 1916–1918 against the Ottoman Empire. At the same time, these regimes further developed the rhetoric of modernisation: limited national school systems were established; scientific and military colleges proliferated; and language was purged and updated and, in the case of Turkey, rendered into the Roman script.

A more detailed consideration of some of these Middle Eastern societies will illustrate both the common features and the local differences which threw up these authoritarian regimes. The rulers of Egypt, Iran and even Turkey grappled with ethnic and religious plurality throughout the 1920s and 1930s. But these societies were all relatively homogeneous compared with Iraq, a composite of three old Ottoman provinces, divided by religion (between Sunnis, Shias, Christians and Jews) and by ethnicity (between Arab, "Marsh Arab" and Kurd).[13] In addition, the British had imposed an external Arab monarchy, the Sharifian dynasty of the Hijaz, on this disparate mix. In 1918, the British received the League of Nations mandate of the territory. They launched vigorous land and air assaults on Kurds and Shias, who revolted against them in the years 1919–1923. But, as in other parts of the bloated empire, they gradually withdrew as treaties were concluded with local powerholders in 1926 and 1932, leaving their vital interests in oil and communications safeguarded.

The regime the British left in Iraq was Sunni Arab and landlord dominated, and it soon came into contention with other suppressed ethnic and religious communities. King Faisal I had worked for the incorporation of minorities. But after his death in 1933 brutal war was fought against the Shias of the south in 1936. Conflict with the Kurdish leadership in the north continued throughout this period. The result was that the regime took on a more and more pronounced military character. Between 1932 and 1941, the Iraqi military, a predominantly Sunni force, expanded from 12,000 to 43,000 men and military officers became more and more dominant in the bureaucracy, a condition that was to persist until 2003 with the overthrow of Saddam Hussein. When Nazi Germany expanded its influence in the region, as the Kaiser's Germany had done before the First World War, the officer corps became yet more assertive, more authoritarian and hostile to residual British interests. This culminated in the coup of 1941 by officers of the so-called Golden Square, which allied formally with Germany. They were only dislodged later in that year by a British invasion mounted to secure the Persian and adjoining Iranian oilfields for the Allies. In 1958, the military and an elite Sunni organisation overthrew the monarchy and the new Baathist regime emerged. Military force and the careful distribution of oil revenues barely held the fragmented state together over the following two generations.

This style of authoritarian regime supported by military officers, a strong modernist party organisation and the support of small landowners was represented in a much stronger form by Kemal Atatürk's regime. Yet here, state ideology dispensed with all remnants of the Ottoman monarchy and divided itself sharply from religious institutions. Atatürk had based resistance to the Greek invasion and Allied intrusion in eastern Anatolia during 1919 and 1920. By 1922, Turks had regained control of Anatolia and Rumelia and had been recognised by the great powers. Atatürk then moved to disband the Sultanate and, in due course, the religious authority of the Khilafat and the madrasas (Muslim teaching institutions). By 1928, Muslim law was marginalised and the Swiss civil code became the model for a new Turkish legal system.[14] In 1925, a brief revolt by members of the old religious orders and their supporters was ruthlessly suppressed. Ankara became the capital of the new secular state, so distancing it from the memories of the old imperial capital and its great religious institutions. Atatürk inaugurated a nationalist party which owed responsibility to him as president through a national assembly.

The Depression, bringing about decline in the export prices of Turkish agricultural products, combined with continued resentment over the country's commitment to paying off Ottoman-era debt. The result was the introduction, as over much of the world, of a new economic policy, sometimes called etatism, which was an indigenous form of socialist five-year planning devoted to the establishment of industries and the diversification of the economy away from agriculture.[15] In this way, state intervention, though in support of private property rather than to its detriment, came to mirror the authoritative form of Turkish nationalist politics, a pairing which did not really come apart until the 1950s. Whether it was in Nazi Germany, contemporary Argentina or in Turkey, the use of state economic power to allay the period's economic problems reinforced popular support for authoritarian regimes.

Despite its resolute republican secularism, therefore, the interwar Turkish state had much in common with similar regimes across the world: a populist nationalist ideology, the existence of a ruling party with an authoritative president or newly coined king as leader, a strong and partly modernised military and broad middle-class and peasant support. Reza Shah Pahlavi, who seized power in Tehran in 1921, assumed the monarchy in 1925, deposing the last of the Qajar rulers.[16] Yet, he was a typical modernising military autocrat, building roads and discouraging the hijab, in this case trained by the Russians in the Persian Cossack Brigade. Benefiting from a share in oil revenues and holding the line between the Western powers and the Soviet Union, Reza Shah built a military–bureaucratic regime in the cities, but generally maintained good relations with rural tribal leaders.

A further variation on this theme in the Middle East was found in Egypt, which gradually released itself from indirect British control between the revolt of 1919 and the Anglo-Egyptian Treaty of 1936. Here the Wafd party, which had spearheaded the popular movement against Britain, inherited power.[17] Broadly an alliance of landowners and the urban middle classes of Cairo and Alexandria, it maintained better relations with the great religious institutions, especially the al-Azhar mosque and university, than Atatürk did in Turkey. Yet, religious groups, such as the Muslim Brotherhood, made little headway during the 1920s and 1930s and conflicts between Muslims and Christian Copts were relatively limited. The geographical term "Middle East" is of course a mere construct. If Africa had not still been controlled by European colonial powers, one might have seen the emergence of similar military–bureaucratic regimes there too. Certainly, in the one independent African state, Haile Selassie's regime combined some of the features which we have seen in Iran, Trans-Jordan and Iraq.[18] A refounded dynasty used religious observance, in this case Christianity, and military dominance over the major towns to create a kind of nationalist core within an agrarian rent-paying periphery.

AUTHORITARIAN RULE IN EAST ASIA

In East Asia, again, some aspects of this pattern were played out over the same period. For instance, the Thai monarchy, which had promoted a limited modernisation of society and economy since the mid-nineteenth century, outlived most of the Middle Eastern dynasties, poised between British, French and Japanese interests, but accepting military aid from all of them. The clearest comparison with the modernising military leaders of Iran, Turkey or Iraq was, however, Chiang Kai-shek's regime in China established in Shanghai after the civil wars of 1924–1925. The main difference with the Middle East lay in the fact that China was almost permanently at war between 1920 and 1950 after the brief "liberal moment" of Sun Yat-sen's revolution. Chiang was able to draw on nationalist resentment against the Allied presence in the coastal settlements.[19]

The British had ceded control of the city of Hankou, but they were still dug-in in Shanghai, controlling much of China's shipping and export industries. Chinese opinion was equally hostile to Japanese incursions in the north, which led ultimately to their occupation of Manchuria in 1931. Educated Chinese also realised that the persistence of regionalism and the continuing power of warlords meant that the nation was always under threat of "divide and rule" by its enemies. But informal Western, if not Japanese, imperialism had some advantages for Chiang's party, the Guomindang (GMD). The Chinese Maritime Customs Service, a British-dominated bureaucracy established in the 1860s, continued to control external taxation and the repayment of China's indemnities to European powers. It was able to provide a regular income to the government even during the wars of the 1920s and 1930s.[20]

Chiang consequently built up support among the urban middle classes of the southern coastal areas with their nascent industries and some local landholding communities. He reorganised the military and created a party system, not unlike Atatürk's, which owed loyalty to him as president. Lacking any single ideological basis, the party melded together features of a weak socialism with a reinvented version of neo-Confucianism which insisted on loyalty to the leader as "father of the national family". Chiang declared that China "needed a period of authoritarian rule". The promise of a strong central government was constantly undermined, though, by the persistence of local factions within the GMD leadership and its tendency to clientelism. In 1927–1928, Chiang broke with and expelled his erstwhile Communist allies from Shanghai. Yet, the GMD's purchase on the countryside remained weak. From the mid-nineteenth century Chinese regimes had ceded power and revenue to the provinces, often under external threat. As Mao Zedong put it in 1937, "China has been in the grip of two basic contradictions, the contradiction between China and imperialism and the contradiction between the mass of the people and feudalism."[21] Now, facing the Japanese on one side and a Communist Party garnering significant support in the northeast of the country following Mao Zedong's Long March (1934–1935) on the other, Chiang's position became vulnerable.

Japan itself was widely represented as a fascist state after the Second World War because of its support for the Axis powers. Japanese atrocities in China and against Allied soldiers and civilians allowed historians to make an easy comparison between the Nazis and the Hirohito regime. More recent scholarship has qualified this analysis.[22] The transition from the late Meiji form of government and Hirohito's more aggressive stance both in domestic affairs and also foreign policy was not brought about by any mass populist movement from below, like the fascist *squadristi* or the Brown Shirts; nor was there any sudden swing to the right by the electorate. Instead, a range of new political leaders and their clients, young military and naval officers, some from better-off rural families, with big business interests lined up behind the new emperor. Drawing on ideologies of cultural authenticity to challenge Western modernity,[23] they pushed for a more aggressive set of policies, believing that Japan had been humiliated by the Western powers.

Having reached the top diplomatic table after its pre-war victory over Russia, Japan seemed to be excluded again by the 1922 US–UK naval treaties and the

British "swing to the east", which entailed building up its naval bases in Hong Kong and Singapore in the 1920s. By the 1930s, young officers, such as Ishiwara Kanji, were calling for a "final war" with a resurgent Russia and the army and navy were vying for pre-eminence in a forward policy in Asia.[24] Rogue elements within the Japanese military assassinated moderate politicians. The lack of cabinet control over policy and the headstrong nature of Hirohito himself, deprived of the caution of the older Meiji leadership, added to this perfervid atmosphere. Religion was militarised and popularised through the *bushido* samurai cult. In parallel with this, Shinto was transformed from a royal cult into a state religion, while Buddhist organisations were disciplined into national training schools and members were forced to abandon their personal commitment to non-violence.[25]

The Japanese feeling of exclusion was compounded in 1931 when Japanese goods were locked out of European colonial markets and the currency had to be devalued. China's unsteady rise after Chiang's coup against the Communists was also viewed with alarm in Japan because the country had significant economic interests in northern China.[26] The internal and external pressures towards a more intrusive policy on the mainland were brought together by Japan's policy of trying to relieve rural hardship by removing peasant farmers from poor regions of central Japan to Korea and later northern China. The result was Japan's invasion of Manchuria in 1931 and its move to create the client state of Manchukuo. So began the long war with China which reinforced the militarised form of the Japanese state and ultimately brought it into conflict with the United States and Western colonial powers. Japanese farmers and shopkeepers generally supported a forward policy and internal dissent was more vigorously suppressed after Hirohito's accession. Yet, the basic social structures of Japan's unfinished modernisation stayed in place and there was no "rightist revolution" in the country. Military authoritarianism and expansionism characterised interwar Japan. But the similarities to European fascism, as opposed to Chiang's own regime or even contemporary Middle Eastern despots, were relatively less pronounced.

What all these regimes did have in common was, however, first, access to the new forms of warfare, communication and military control which had emerged during the First World War. This gave them a decided advantage, though not supremacy, over regional over-mighty subjects and religious and ethnic leaderships which had remained very powerful before 1914. Secondly, they drew on a growing hostility to the continued presence of the imperial powers in their lands directly or indirectly, but also a strong sense that those empires were waning and that subject nations were asserting themselves. Finally, there was no doubt a global exchange of information and aspiration which allowed military bureaucratic elites in Asia and the Middle East to believe that state-sponsored development and military bureaucratic authoritarianism provided a way forward through the political and economic dangers of the post-war and Depression years. To this extent, Mussolini and Hitler did indeed provide object lessons for would-be leaders, not only in Asia and Africa but even in Western democracies.

AUTHORITARIANISM, FASCISM AND NAZISM IN THE WEST

Some of these same conditions were reproduced in Latin America, though the continent was the scene of a wide range of political movements, from oligarchic parties backed by landlords and big urban capitalists with US connections through quasi-parliamentarian liberal constitutionalists to periodic democratic workers' movements. Nevertheless, there was a perceptible tilt towards more authoritarian government as these social, economic and ideological conflicts became more fraught. Many regimes, as in Chile, Peru and Cuba, sought to solve national problems "by executive action, combining economic developmentalism, outright repression and sometimes a veneer of populism".[27] In distinction to the situation in much of Europe, where the depths of the Depression helped propel the rise of fascist rulers, in Latin America the lesser economic shock registered in the region actually undermined several of the dictators of the 1920s and, at least initially, brought in nationalist social reform movements distantly comparable with those of Britain and France. But these regimes, notably that of Fulgencio Batista in Cuba, became more corrupt and authoritarian in the course of the 1930s. The period ended with the establishment of the government of Juan Perón in Argentina during the 1940s. In many respects, Perón's rule, which melded a tightly controlled labour movement with military nationalism, seemed an out-of-time echo of Mussolini's recently fallen regime in Italy. But more generally, the end of the Second World War in Europe discredited fascism and propelled Latin America back towards superficial forms of democratic politics, at least until the military dictators began to re-emerge, often with American support, in the 1950s and 1960s.

In Europe itself, as in the rest of the world, the First World War and the perceived failure of the old elites, military and liberal alike, to preserve the interests of the nation during the peace settlements and the Depression provided the background for the rise of authoritarian regimes. Even before the war, radical, even violent, political movements had been in evidence. Themes of military solidarity, sacrifice on behalf of the nation and a sense of betrayal by the power elites, whether political or commercial, pervaded Central and Southern Europe. The first Italian leagues for revolutionary action (*fasci*) had come into being in the autumn of 1914 to press for the country's entry into the war with the aim of liberating Italian-speaking areas still under control of Austria–Hungary.[28] The *fasci* were later joined by Mazzinians and socialist radicals, including Benito Mussolini himself. At the same time, the veneration of the ordinary soldier, comradeship in battle and military technology that came to the fore during the conflict acted against liberal and constitutional politicians. The war, wrote Alfredo Rocco, for example, had brought about the "revitalisation of national energies, of consciousness and national spirit".[29]

Then came disillusion with the failure of the peace to deliver on its promise. The radical Mazzinian and poet Gabriele D'Annunzio occupied the Italian town of Fiume, which had been designated a free port in the settlement, but was driven out of the city in 1919 while many Italian-speaking areas of the Alto

Adige remained controlled by the rump of Austria. The mobilisation of wartime nationalist organisations (the *squadristi*), which were fiercely anti-socialist and anti-liberal, culminated in the March on Rome in October 1922.[30] These bodies were quite socially diverse and included professional people, shop-keepers, former soldiers and peasants hit by the slump after 1919. Taking a dominant position in the weak coalition government that survived from 1919–1923, fascists, as they began to be called, gradually closed down the opposition press, outlawed labour movements and other socialist organisations on the grounds that they fractured national unity and renewal while promoting decadence and decline. The socialist leader Giacomo Matteotti was assassi-nated in June 1924.[31] Italy was to stand high in international life alongside the plutocratic societies of Britain and France and would be an essential element in the fight against Communism. In this, the last age of empire, Italy's self-respect, according to the fascists, demanded the maintenance of its colonial rule in North Africa and, ultimately, its extension to Ethiopia, which had humiliated Italy in the 1890s.

The importance of Italian fascism was that it provided a superficial model for similar forms of government, not just in Germany and later Spain but also in Eastern Europe and distantly in Latin America or China. What made it attractive was the sense of inclusiveness and devotion to social and artistic modernity it supposedly conveyed. Old elites, such as the frustrated upper-class men in Britain who supported Oswald Mosley or the conservative Catholics who joined Action Française in France, felt they could live with right-wing radicalism because of its anti-socialism and supposed anti-materialism. Shop-keepers and industrialists believed they would benefit from enhanced spending, particularly on the military. Even working-class people could continue to function within the tightly controlled fascist syndics which replaced the labour unions. Less obviously, the Italian regime conveyed a sense of thrusting modernity, rebuilding Italy's ancient cities, promoting a determined but effective art which fractured the classical tradition, but did not give rise to modernist anarchy. Ideologically, it supplemented and slowly displaced con-ventional static religion with patriotic fervour promoted by marching songs and secular hymns. Fascists glorified the male body, sport and youthful bonhomie for a generation haunted by the war but energised by the equality which it apparently created.

The First World War cast a similar corrosive cloud over Germany. The massive war reparations demanded by Britain and France, the French occupa-tion of the Rhineland and the seizure by the Allies and Japan of German colonies in Africa and Asia created a deep sense of humiliation. In 1919, the Marxist Spartacist rebellion traumatised the battered middle classes, most of whom had lost relatives or friends on the war fronts. The Weimar government that emerged from the defeat of Communism and the disastrous peace terms was plagued by a dysfunctional political system in which the president had excessive power and the constitution veered towards deadlock on a number of occasions. Yet, unlike the case in Italy, German democracy survived the war, reparations, the economic shock of 1923, which wiped out the savings of most citizens, and even the first few years of the Depression. The next chapter elaborates on this theme. Regardless of Germany's supposed responsibility for the outbreak of war in 1914, representative government had made considerable strides in the country before that date and the Social Democrats, albeit espousing a tame version of socialism, had established themselves as a major political force. Despite the Kaiser's erratic use of power, Germany had remained quite decentralised and democratic at the local level. Whatever the prestige the army had garnered on the Eastern Front during the war, a popularly based representative system emerged from it and the leftist uprisings which followed. The key to this lay in the strength of local democracy amongst small farmers, Bavarian Catholics and northern Protestant workers. These stood in contrast to the large *latifundia* of southern Italy and Sicily or Spain. Despite the charges of "*Junkerism*" levelled against the army, particularly in Prussia, military men had only indirectly influenced politics. Germany's total defeat in the war meant that the contrast with effete civilian politicians was not as sharp as it was in Italy.

Even though the war did not have the immediate effect on radicalising politics in Germany that it did in Italy, it let loose a whole range of organisations and political movements which destabilised the Weimar Republic and contributed ultimately to the triumph of Nazism. Numerous militant ideologies emerged in the 1920s from Catholic and Protestant opponents of "materialism" to old soldiers' organisations, anti-Communist youth movements and sports clubs, where violent nationalism found a home. Hostility to the French occupiers of the Palatinate was matched by an increased loathing of Anglo-American capitalism and its supposed local representative, the Jew. The ideological importance of anti-Semitism as a common factor in all these movements is difficult to overestimate and had been stoked up by publicists such as Theodor Fritsch since before the war. Fritsch urged the rediscovery of "a strong, healthy German national entity" free of "the clinkers of its own weaknesses and the cinders of alien perversion".[32] This sort of ranting, given academic respectability in Spengler's vision of a "German–Nordic race" surviving the "Decline of the West", was later elaborated on by Joseph Goebbels in his constant references to the "Jewish problem". Actually, the Jewish population was becoming increasingly assimilated into German society over the whole period since unification in the 1870s. But the myth of German racial purity, the canard that the Jews had contributed to defeat in 1918 and hatred of small capitalists generated by the disastrous inflation of 1923 and later the Great Depression brought together a whole range of social pathologies. Some historians continue to write of the "Nazi seizure of power" of 1933. But the Nazis actually garnered a whole range of support through what was initially a democratic process, even if President von Hindenburg chose Hitler to form a government because he felt he would be a useful tool against the socialists and was even considering reviving the monarchy.[33] Schmitt, consequently, argued that the weak and self-defeating nature of the Weimar legal system conferred legitimacy on this move: a rightful "seizure of power".

Whereas the Communist "vanguard" was a concentration of Marxist intellectuals and enlightened labour leaders, the Nazi elite were vitalist heroes, imbued with the spirit of Aryan Germanic history and devoted to the

Führerprinzip. Here the figure of Horst Wessel, martyr to the Nazi cause and creator of the Nazi anthem, *Die Fahne hoch* ("The Flag on High", otherwise known as the "Horst Wessel Song"), is instructive of the political fluidity of the period. Wessel remained a devout Lutheran throughout his life in a way that would have been impossible for a Communist hero. He moved from the far right of the monarchist party which survived after 1918 to become a leader of the SA, orchestrating its music and ceremonies as well as street battles with the Communists. He was killed in 1930, apparently in a banal conflict over rent with a landlady connected with local Communists. His grave, decorated by the Nazis with symbols of German history and its resurgence, became a place of pilgrimage after 1933 and his life became the subject of early Nazi films. Here again the theatrical and performative aspect of both Nazism and fascism was on display.[34]

Once Hitler became chancellor he benefited from a rapid expansion of state spending, especially on rearmament, and the tentative re-emergence of growth in the world economy.[35] Equally, suppression of the Communists, the *Freikorps* and other left-fascist groups and their organs of propaganda reassured a whole range of business and middle-class interests. It is important to remember that, however pernicious its ideology and practices, Nazism achieved great popular success, equivalent to Roosevelt's New Deal programme or the broad conservative consensus in Britain behind Stanley Baldwin. Hitler's popularity was greatly reinforced by his forceful position in foreign affairs, notably his reoccupation of the Rhineland, union with Austria and seizure of Upper Silesia from Czechoslovakia in 1938.[36] Socialist states and leftist Western academics constantly argued that Nazism and fascism were fronts for capitalism, as noted in the introduction, but they appealed to people at every level of society and not merely to the bourgeoisie.

Following the political revolutions which brought Mussolini and Hitler to power, the coup by the Spanish army against the Republic in 1936 and the civil war which followed clearly presaged the coming of the Second World War. While both Italy and Germany saw severe internal conflict generated by fascist gangs and their Communist opponents, these countries did not see open warfare in which their armies were involved. Why did this happen only in Spain, at least among European countries? One answer is that regional and social differences were deeper than even in Italy, with its north–south divide, and Germany, with Catholic Bavaria in its south.[37] Northern and central Spain, a land of small farmers, was relatively prosperous and remained profoundly Catholic and conservative. Southern Spain, dominated by great *latifundia*, serviced by numerous impoverished rural workers, had already seen the development of a kind of millenarian anarchism, deeply antithetical to the Church, which was castigated as a prop of the status quo. Another discrete form of society was found in Barcelona and the Catalan area, the only fully industrialised part of the country, with a large clothing industry, which suffered badly from the slump at the end of the First World War and later from the Depression. A more organised form of trade union syndicalism developed here, and this later came into uneasy alliance with the rural anarchistic strain. A second reason why political conflict spiralled into a major war was Spain's continuing colonial investment in North Africa where much of the army was based. For conservative elements within Spain this mini-empire was of great symbolic significance after the United States had seized Spain's overseas colonies in 1898. The role of the colonial army here was distantly comparable with the role of the French army in Indochina and Algeria a generation later.

Spain's first experience of dictatorship came immediately after the war, when a sudden collapse of demand sent labour unions onto the streets of the Barcelona industrial belt. The army intervened to "restore order" and the dictatorship of Primo de Rivera began. De Rivera managed to incorporate some of the labour movements into his conservative pact, in a manner reminiscent of Mussolini. But anarcho-syndicalist labour organisations proliferated and the onset of the Depression gave a further spur to leftist politics in town and country. In June 1931, following a collapse of the value of the peseta, the dictatorship ended and a left-wing republican government came to power.[38] But in a way quite different from the case of Russia after 1917, the old order remained very strong: landlords, the army and the Church bided their time. The civil war of 1936–1940 was in effect a resolution of the social tensions which persisted through the early 1930s. That resolution was ultimately brought about with ruthlessness by General Francisco Franco, who exploited the rivalries between different elements of the Left and drew in support from Italy and Germany.[39] Casting "reds", secularists, Jews and foreigners as the internal enemy, he was able to establish a more coherent right-wing consensus than de Rivera. Despite continuing local conflict during the Second World War, Franco's regime emerged relatively unscathed in 1945, having avoided direct involvement in the international conflict.

Eastern Europe and the Balkans, still largely rural, whose elites were fearful of the USSR to the East and still in thrall to the Roman Catholic or Orthodox churches, had more in common with Spain, Portugal and the south of Italy than with Germany. Their forms of interwar authoritarian rule, broadened and deepened by German occupation after 1939, were also similar. Despite ethnic conflict, the newly created state of Czechoslovakia remained a democratic outlier in the area until the Nazi invasion of 1938. Poland, however, succumbed to the rule of General Józef Piłsudski's dictatorship in 1926. Piłsudski had moved, rather like Mussolini, from left to right. Like Mussolini, he was able to find support among both moderate trades unions and also landowners who feared Communist interference. In Yugoslavia, a newly formed part democracy created in 1919, ethnic tension and pressure from Italy caused King Alexander I to suspend the constitution and imprison political opponents in 1929: the so-called January 6th Dictatorship. In 1936, a fully formed Croatian fascist movement, inspired by the Italian example, managed to create a semi-independent state within this patchwork of nationalities. During the Second World War, a partisan nationalism, led by Josip Broz Tito, positioned itself to take power and build a Communist state, though one that was less dependent on the goodwill of the USSR than its contemporaries in Poland, East Germany and Czechoslovakia.

BACK TO COMMUNISM

Finally, this chapter turns back to the issue of Communist authoritarianism and Stalin's dictatorship, which became more despotic and prone to resort to terror during the late 1920s and early 1930s as fascist leaderships were taking root in other parts of the world. Lenin and the Communist Party had come to power through what was effectively a coup in 1917 and the new USSR was gripped by what was known as "war Communism" for the first five years of its existence.[40] Having already dominated the urban working class, the Party not only seized large estates but also moved against well-to-do peasants, who often supported its opponents in the Social Revolutionary Party, by setting up gerrymandered committees of poor peasants to manage land redistribution. Emergency measures included the expropriation of food supplies to feed the towns and state organisation of industry and banks. After 1920, however, Lenin drew back from Party domination of the economy in his New Economic Policy. In 1922, a "Fundamental Law on Land Use" revived some inducements for the peasantry.[41]

Lenin's death in 1923 was followed by five years of factional struggle between Stalin and his competitors, notably Leon Trotsky and Nikolai Bukharin, but by 1928 Stalin had won out decisively and was determined to build "socialism in one country" through a massive refashioning of the USSR's economic and political structures.[42] The Politburo, which he now dominated, seized grain from the peasantry and initiated a dash for rapid industrialisation. Gross industrial output did increase by as much as 137% between 1927 and 1933. In 1930, Stalin vowed to eliminate the upper peasantry, the kulaks, whom he regarded as class enemies, and push forward a radical scheme of the collectivisation of agriculture. Over the next eight years, political opponents were sent to labour camps or executed after show trials; millions of rural people were displaced and many died as famine hit the Ukraine, southern Russia and Kazakhstan. Stalin's autocracy was indeed the most complete in modern history until Mao began his Great Leap Forward a generation later. Even before the Second World War, the human cost was enormous.

It is important, though, to note again some of the main differences between Communist and fascist regimes.[43] As a political order, and despite the mayhem in its upper leadership, the Communist Party of the USSR was always more coherent and politically omnipresent than the European or Latin American fascist parties, which were variously hemmed in by cliques of landowners, royalists, clerics or semi-autonomous military forces. Equally, the Italian fascists and German Nazis came to a kind of accommodation with big business, first to steer their countries out of the Depression and later through large state expenditure on rearmament. Conversely, in the USSR, the few concessions to private peasant entrepreneurship made through Lenin's New Economic Policy of the early 1920s were abrogated as Stalin became fearful of an independent landowning kulak class, especially after agrarian tensions, partly generated by the Depression, became visible in 1927–1928. The collectivisation of agricultural holdings and rapid drive for industrialisation did, in fact, represent a social revolution on a scale unknown in fascist societies. A virtual cultural revolution took place presaging the later movement in China.[44] Again, while Stalin dealt harshly with signs of dissent in the Ukraine and among other non-Russian nationalities, it is difficult to detect a strong anti-Semitic or anti-alien sentiment in Stalinism at this stage. This was despite Stalin's suspicion of socialist internationalists with experience in Germany and Western Europe, many of them Jewish. Stalin's policy was one of hectic modernisation by terror because, in his words, "We have fallen behind the advanced countries by fifty to a hundred years."[45]

Finally, an important aspect of Lenin's and Stalin's internal social revolution was the emphasis on expanding education at all levels.[46] In 1914, less than 40% of the Russian population was literate. The percentage rapidly increased during the 1920s and 1930s. Even if the 1939 percentage (95% of men and 79% of women) was exaggerated, the change was palpable and the next generation of Soviet leaders, such as Nikita Khrushchev and Leonid Brezhnev, came from poor working-class and rural backgrounds.[47] This was unmatched in fascist societies, let alone by the feeble educational attainments of the European colonies. But it was with the Five Year Plans that the policy of remaking the Soviet man or woman became most evident. The pressure on the individual to succeed for the community and state began in school and was transmitted to the workplace. In 1935, Alexey Stakhanov was proclaimed to have mined fourteen times his daily quota of coal in one day. Stakhanovite movements to emulate his success spread across industries throughout the Soviet Union, supposedly instilling discipline and selfless commitment to the collective.[48]

Conversely, there were several features of Stalin's despotism which were at least distantly reminiscent of Hitler's or Mussolini's. All these leaders dealt brutally with internal opposition both from the right and the left of their parties. In Stalin's case the years 1934–1935 saw an expansion of terror tactics against the old party leadership, people such as Grigory Zinoviev and Bukharin and other former allies of Leon Trotsky, at the same time as the liquidation of kulak farmers continued. Before his assassination, Leon Trotsky, himself formerly a ferocious centraliser, wrote that Stalin had replaced the French Sun King's dictum "*l'état, c'est moi*" with "*la societé, c'est moi*".[49] Persecution of "left deviationism" in the USSR was paralleled by Hitler's crackdown on the SA Brown Shirts. Stalin vigorously suppressed dissidence among industrial workers as Hitler and Stalin defeated and imprisoned or killed syndicalists and trades union leaders. While Stalin rarely resorted to the theatrical histrionics of either the Italian or the German leaders, the 1930s in the USSR saw a definite resurgence of a specifically Russian nationalism rooted in history and manifested in school textbooks, public utterances and Sergei Eisenstein's films, notably his *Alexander Nevsky* (1938). Peter the Great and Ivan the Terrible, once excoriated as feudals, now became champions of the Russian nation against external and internal enemies. By eliminating not only his perceived political enemies but also their whole families, Stalin saw himself as an inheritor of the strength of Ivan the Terrible.[50] In this sense, it would be appropriate to regard late colonial regimes and Stalin's dictatorship as outliers in an age of authoritarianism, which was fundamentally defined by Nazism and fascism.

A TYPOLOGY OF EARLY-TWENTIETH-CENTURY AUTHORITARIANISM?

This chapter stresses the individual trajectories of different societies which came under the control of anti-liberal, authoritarian states whose leaders valued national strength above individual rights and multiparty politics. Each case differed in detail from the next, but there were some broad preconditions which were common to all. Neo-Marxist arguments "from below", notably enunci-ated by Eric Hobsbawm, retain considerable force.[51] Across the spectrum, authoritarian government represented both a response to, and an attempt to contain, conflicts of economic interest between peasants and landowners, a growing urban working class, the middle class and big capitalists. These conflicts had been uneasily contained in the last decades of liberal government before 1914, though a degree of state intervention had already become common in Britain, France and Germany. The war itself and the Depression greatly exacerbated class conflict. But the relative weight of different social strata resulted in different outcomes. In Germany, the new Nazi regime built on a powerful business class and an entrenched working class. In Mexico, by comparison, landlordism remained more powerful and the resulting author-itarian regimes required strong rural support, often drawing on military families from the landed classes.

At this point, a purely class-based analysis becomes inadequate and it is important to consider the organisation of states, the degree of centralisation and the role of vested interests beyond simple class interest. Despite their origins as princely or *daimyo* "federations", Germany and Japan had been more unified states in the late nineteenth century than, for instance, southern Italy or the countries of Eastern Europe, South America or China. They had also built more powerful and mechanised armies. To this extent, the rulers of Germany and Japan in the 1920s and 1930s could build on and co-opt unified infra-structure networks, civil services, public sphere organisations, national trade unions and research universities. In the former states, vested interests – such as the Catholic Church, local bosses reflecting regional linguistic and cultural difference, criminal organisations and transnational diasporic subjects – acted as breaks on centralisation, producing forms of localised authoritarianism. A good example of this was the case of Yugoslavia, mentioned above, where a relatively weak type of monarchical absolutism was frustrated by a more vigorous Croatian fascism.

Broader ideological issues also retained a degree of autonomy in this contingent melee of structures, practices and ideas. Forms of Protestant and Catholic Christianity, secularised Islam, Shinto and "muscular Buddhism" all inflected these different state ideologies. In the semi-independent territories of the Middle East during the 1920s and 1930s, the military bosses and monarchs were constrained to limit their anticolonial ruling ideologies by pressure from the former colonisers. They also needed to temper their secular militarism through fear of Islamist resistance, especially in the rural areas. Nationalist ideology was a universal redoubt for authoritarian rulers, though it remained a difficult call in the multi-ethnic societies which were still the norm outside Western Europe and the Americas. For this reason, to one degree or another, anti-Semitism was a valued tool of dictatorships or authoritarian political parties, because this allegedly internal enemy was easier to persecute. In a relatively homogeneous Germany, assimilated Jews could be held responsible for wartime defeat. In Argentina in 1919, during the so-called Tragic Week, Jews could be attacked on the grounds that they had engineered damaging economic turbulence. Anti-Semitism also grew from small beginnings in the Arab world as a part of the armoury of dictatorship and this was greatly extended after the Arab–Israeli war of 1948 as the afterlife of authoritarianism produced the regimes of the Assads, Gaddafi and Saddam Hussein. Elsewhere, internal enemies such as Hakka Chinese merchants, Hindu moneylenders or Lebanese interlopers could justify repression. Soviet Communism was different. This was partly because the Party had completely dominated internal centres of power, and the commercial middle class, landowner and rich peasant had been largely eliminated. In part, though, it was because state ideology indicted both internal and external class, rather than ethnic, enemies. In terms of practice, nevertheless, Communist and nationalist authoritarianism had much in common.

Overall, the issue of broadly understanding interwar dictatorship, fascism and Communist authoritarianism at once reflects both the strengths and weaknesses of global history writing. In every case, class structure, state organisation and ideology interacted in different ways over different periods of time. To amalgamate all these national and local forms into a single phenomenon would produce a superficial form of history. Yet, against this, there were haunting similarities and even connections between them, not least because the different regimes and political parties involved constantly referred to each other and eyed each other's successes and defeats.

[4] DEMOCRACIES AND THEIR DISCONTENTS, C. 1900–1950

> The Impact of War and the Progress of Democracy: Britain and the United States
> War and Depression: The British Dominions
> Representation and Rights Among "Subject Peoples"
> Democracy on the Rack in Continental Europe: The 1930s
> Conclusion: Democracy and Its Travails

THE shadow of fascism and the turn of the Soviet Union towards Stalin's totalitarianism have caused many historians to take a gloomy view of the fate of democracy and popular representation during the age of the world wars and the Depression. Even in Western liberal states, authoritarian forces mobilised: Action Française and Mosley's British Union of Fascists were cases in point. In traditionally egalitarian northern European societies, such as the Netherlands and Sweden, fascist and Nazi parties made progress during the 1920s and 1930s. In some respects, it is argued correctly, the widening of the franchise and the operation of democratic party politics facilitated the rise of aggressive forms of populism. Equally, in mature democracies, such as the United States and Australia, racial exclusion persisted, or was even strengthened during this era. In their colonies, supposedly democratic states continued to maintain or even enhance authoritarian rule, with only small concessions to limited indigenous elites throughout the period.

Yet, there is a danger of making too negative an assessment of these several "dark continents".[1] For this was a period when both democratic politics and democratic ideology came into their own in many societies, even if in others they were submerged beneath authoritarianism and racism until the middle of

Remaking the Modern World 1900–2015: Global Connections and Comparisons, First Edition. C. A. Bayly.
© 2018 John Wiley & Sons Ltd. Published 2018 by John Wiley & Sons Ltd.

the century and beyond. To take the position of contemporary Marxists, capital itself was diffused and democratised between 1918 and 1950 so that liberal and left-leaning governments were constrained to buy the support of their electorates. Economic inequality was widely diminished, even if this was partly a consequence of the Depression.[2] At the same time, the moral value of the ordinary citizen was greatly enhanced by the experience of war and the expansion of education.

Even if democracy and authoritarianism ran together neck-and-neck during the interwar years, there were other positive developments. These included the slow enfranchisement of women during and after the First World War as a result of vigorous activism by women's organisations. In Britain, full female franchise was established in 1928. In Denmark, neutral during the war, this came as early as 1915. In France, the breakthrough came later, after the Second World War. Remaining barriers to full male suffrage were widely removed. Even in Germany, as the last chapter argues, it is easy to write off the democratic successes of the Weimar period in view of the rise of Nazism. The public memory of democracy certainly aided the establishment of West Germany's democratic institutions after 1945. Poland remained a democracy until 1926; Yugoslavia until 1929; and Czechoslovakia, despite its ethnic conflicts, right up to the Nazi invasion of 1938. The USSR was ever a "one-party state". Yet, even here, some degree of intellectual and artistic freedom, expressed through civil society organisations and Lenin's local committee structure, existed during the 1920s until it was suppressed by Stalin's turn to autocracy.[3]

While European colonial governments only gave their subjects very limited representation in their own territories, as in the British Gold Coast or India, or a few places in the Paris Assembly, the push for popular representation was now widespread. Historians who cling to the belief that the colonial powers implanted democracy in autocratic non-European societies point to these limited advances. Colonial elections, designed to secure the support of Indian or Malay landowners and African chieftains, certainly spread the notion of voting to subject peoples. Yet, it was nationalist mobilisation that laid the foundations for democracy in these societies, even if this was later subverted by dictators or ethnic conflict in many postcolonial states. Most nationalist parties in the colonies opted at least for adult male suffrage between 1918 and 1945. The Indian National Congress promised universal suffrage in 1931.

These pragmatically based demands for voting rights and influence were legitimated by a wide range of political theorists, inside the West and beyond, whose influence was now generalised through books, journals, the new medium of radio and the burgeoning popular press. In Britain, Harold Laski, prophet of "guild socialism", G. D. H. Cole, democratic socialist, and Bertrand Russell, maverick philosophical libertarian, or John Dewey, the "pragmatic liberal" in the United States, were examples of a new type of public figure who spoke to a wider audience of men and women and educated working-class people as well as to the elites. Dewey, in particular, stressed the role of education in "the development of mental and moral disposition" for a democratic society.[4] Gandhi, Muhammad Iqbal and Liang Qichao clearly, if idiosyncratically, preached democratic ideals to their countrymen. In this chapter, then, the word democracy has two meanings. In a broad descriptive sense, it refers to those societies which had not lurched towards authoritarianism but maintained a plural political system in the interwar years. At a deeper level, it means societies where civil society organisations continued to expand and incorporate new groups of people and political practices, even where this was a conflicted and uneven process and hardly affected their colonies at all.

THE IMPACT OF WAR AND THE PROGRESS OF DEMOCRACY: BRITAIN AND THE UNITED STATES

In Britain, as in other parts of Europe and the United States, the First World War provided a considerable impetus to the expansion of political participation. Returning heroes could not be denied the vote. In 1916, it was proposed to register all soldiers and people moving to do war work. Then women's representatives demanded full voting rights. The Representation of the People Act of 1918 conceded full manhood suffrage and created new constituencies of around 70,000 people, which inevitably caused political parties to scramble to attract votes.[5] Women over 30 with a modest amount of property in their or their husbands' names were also allowed to vote. The Labour government later abolished the property requirement.

Initially, the British general election of 1918 strengthened the Conservatives at the expense of both the Liberals and the Labour Party, though Labour's share of the vote increased considerably. Thereafter, one of the main forces driving the expansion of democratic politics was the rise of socialism, or, as many saw it, the danger of socialism. The expanded power of the trades unions, demonstrated powerfully during the general strike of 1926, caused other parties to redouble their efforts to "pull in the vote". Moderates within the labour movement were galvanised by the appearance of the British Communist Party and also by the spectre of the Soviet Union. The fruits of "the victorious struggle for political democracy" should be used to end "capitalist dictatorship", stated the Labour Party manifesto of 1928.[6] Just as significant was the moral and ideological change released by the war. Even if the mass death of young men in the conflict perpetuated the role of the pre-war elite in Parliament and business, the equalising effect of conscription and the trauma of the trenches spread the idea of rights and eroded the sense of social hierarchy. If the interwar years were overshadowed with anxiety, they were also hailed as a new beginning.[7]

Later, the Depression and mass unemployment further generalised the concept of rights, the minimum wage and the need for social security. Political philosophers became political advocates. R. H. Tawney published *The Acquisitive Society* in 1920, and its critique of the inequalities of capitalism, even if it sidestepped the issue of gender, came to be seen as doubly justified during the 1930s.[8] The crisis of the Wall Street Crash and the onset of the Depression emboldened Ramsay MacDonald's government to introduce ameliorative social measures. Even when constitutional crisis brought in the National government of 1931 and then Stanley Baldwin's Conservative government, the trend towards socially equalising politics could not be reversed.[9] Baldwin's own neo-Keynesian house-building project spread property ownership to the upper working class, so consolidating the idea of democratic rights and laying some of the popular foundations of the post-1945 welfare state. This was particularly significant because, since its foundation, the Conservative Party had broadly opposed state intervention in the economy. Mass politics required it to soften its stance between the 1930s and the 1970s. But the role of upper-class paternalism should not be discounted. Even conservatives were appalled by the poverty brought about by the Depression.

Yet, as in other parts of the world, the expansion of voting rights and democratic activity also stimulated conflict. In the British Isles, the emergence of the Irish Free State in 1922, the Irish Civil War and the separation of Northern Ireland bore a striking resemblance to the spread of nationalist majoritarianism in Eastern and Southern Europe. By 1920, the British government had realised that it could not contain the radical democratic nationalist forces which had been released in Ireland after the 1916 rebellion and strengthened by the "Wilsonian moment" across the world.[10] The notorious Black and Tans, who were reminiscent of the fascist *squadristi* in Italy, merely exacerbated confessional conflicts between Catholics and Protestants. Ultimately, though, Michael Collins's broadly independent government within the British Commonwealth suppressed the more radical nationalist rebellion in Dublin and compromised on the issue of the creation of Ulster as a continuing part of the United Kingdom.[11] Ireland badly needed peace and retrenchment, and Sinn Fein split on the issue. These events were a stark reminder that the spread of popular democracy did not necessarily bring peace between nations, or even within them.

Another outcome of popular democracy in the British Isles was the emergence in the 1930s of Oswald Mosley's British Union of Fascists, which, as in other parts of Europe, reflected an alliance between members of the militarised upper classes and dissident socialist followers from large cities.[12] British popular historical imagination represents an easy transition from the general male franchise created in 1918, through the Second World War to the welfare state and a stable mass democracy in the 1950s. Yet, the fascist marches and violent labour unrest of the 1930s might have augured a very different fate for British politics than the national unity which consolidated itself against the menace of Hitler and Nazi invasion.

The uneven pace of the expansion of democratic forms was equally in evidence in the United States, where issues of race and gender were even more stridently argued, while different definitions of liberty were often violently opposed to each other. During the First World War, for instance, President Wilson, who was regarded as a classical liberal in much of Western Europe, introduced conscription and also effectively nationalised the railways. These moves were opposed by libertarians on both the right and left of politics (in so far as those labels applied at all in the United States). In addition, German Americans objected to the US intervention in the war, though they were quickly silenced, while Irish Americans argued that American troops would be used to suppress revolts in Ireland at the behest of the British.

The effects of the peace were also ambivalent for American democracy. As in Britain, most women did not yet have the vote, except in a few states, such as California. But in the era of wartime women's labour and "Wilsonian democracy", they began to demand it more vociferously and pushed for an amendment to the constitution, staging protests along the lines of Britain's suffragettes. The jailing of middle-class women for "obstruction" in 1917 and 1918 sharpened the debate and put pressure on the White House.[13] After a long battle in Congress, women's suffrage was finally conceded in 1920, though equal rights for women were not enacted until later. Wilson's hesitancy and Congress's obduracy about women's rights were played out at an international level in the case of the United States' membership of the League of Nations. The president, of course, faced opposition from his former allies in Britain and France over his attempts to extend the principle of political autonomy to colonial or mandated territories. But no less vigorous were the attempts of domestic conservatives to obstruct America from joining an international body which was very much his own creation. The French, in particular, also objected to Wilson's attempt to water down the reparations imposed on Germany in order to aid its own nascent democracy. Critics in America constantly argued that, once in the League, the United States would inevitably be drawn into Europe's nationalistic wars and revolutionary upsurges, which they rightly observed showed no sign of ending after the defeat of Germany.

In domestic US politics, the partial victory of the women's movement was not followed in the early 1920s with other moves towards emancipation. In part, the 1917 revolution and its consequences had given rise to a reactionary frame of mind across the country. Strikes in major industries were put down vigorously, especially when the workers were recent foreign immigrants, supposedly infected with Communism. The so-called Red Scare of 1919–1920, when anarchists planned to blow up prominent congressmen, led to repressive legislation, a move to control immigration from Europe, Latin America and Asia and the rapid expansion of the Bureau of Investigation. Civil society activism could itself lead to an erosion of liberty. The classic case here was the temperance movement, which was successful, first, in having the import of liquor banned and, ultimately, in closing down legal domestic production, bars and "speakeasies".[14] The legislation had a distinctly ethnic and religious bias because many of the producers of liquor and owners of bars were Catholic Irish, Spanish or Italians, while the proponents of Prohibition were Anglo-Saxon or northern European Protestants by descent and puritans by ideology. Many of them feared that liquor consumption would embolden the supposed anti-social characteristics of blacks and immigrants. As is well known, Prohibition itself led to an upsurge of libertarian law-breaking, but also of criminal activity by the Mafia and other organised criminal networks, of which Al Capone, of Sicilian origin, became iconic.

Race relations became no easier during the 1920s and 1930s, and the issue of race set the United States apart from most other growing democracies – and, indeed, continued to do so throughout the century. The previous 20 years had seen a large-scale migration of black workers and later families from the southern states to expanding northern cities, where paid work had become more plentiful during the war. Many black soldiers fought in the First World War but were universally treated as second class to the extent that they had generally to serve under French, not American, officers.[15] But though black people in the north were less of an underclass than they were in the rural south, they were often discriminated against and their living quarters were of a very low standard. There was a serious race riot in Chicago in 1919 and minor outbreaks of violence through to the Second World War in this and other northern cities.

Meanwhile, the southern states themselves saw the expansion of the Ku Klux Klan movement, again an outgrowth of white Protestantism, often also connected with the Prohibition movement.[16] The white small-town population was alarmed by left-wing political activism, movements for emancipation, such as female suffrage, and the growth of urban cosmopolitanism. Widening democracy, even the appearance of the black icons of the jazz age, created its own populist backlash. All these contradictory trends were promoted and generalised by the movies which became central to American life during the 1920s and the Depression years. By 1928, there were 28,000 movie theatres in the United States with 65 million ticket sales each year.[17] Hollywood was often seen as a liberal redoubt, but a film such as D. W. Griffith's The *Birth of a Nation* (1915) also carried a subtle message of racial discrimination, depicting black men as subnormal creatures hankering after white women. Griffith's subsequent film *Intolerance* (1916) ended with a picture of class conflict in US cities. Democracy could easily meld into populism and racism.

The Great Depression took these social and political conflicts to a new level, as the next chapter shows. If conservative and small-town America was worried by the movements of the 1920s, the 1929 crash and its consequences brought the world crisis to every doorstep. The mass marches of the unemployed, the violent military action against unemployed former soldiers in 1932 masterminded by two future military heroes, Douglas MacArthur and George Patton, and growing poverty across the country spurred the state and federal governments to a new round of democratisation, but equally to measures of a quasi-socialist sort which were more characteristic of Western European states or the "White Dominions" of the British Empire. When the worst of the Depression propelled Franklin Roosevelt into the White House, he began to enact ameliorative economic measures which were aimed at shoring up democracy by extending economic rights. This was the New Deal. The Banking Act made it possible for ordinary people to access credit again; measures to create employment such as the Tennessee Valley Scheme, or the Works Progress Administration, gave the population jobs; the Social Security Act of 1935, modelled on European equivalents, created a limited system of public benefits.

In a way, though, Roosevelt's greatest act of democratic empowerment was to be his tortuous moves to enlist the United States in the war against the Axis and Japan. This was truly a device to help protect democracy abroad. But in the longer term it also consolidated the United States' unequalled strength as a domestic democracy. Enlistment and the war economy undid the ravages of the

Depression and signalled a new boom in national wealth. Women were finally and fully absorbed into the labour force. Above all, the enlistment of black soldiers during the war and their rise to leadership ranks had the effect of paving the way for black enfranchisement in the 1960s and 1970s.

WAR AND DEPRESSION: THE BRITISH DOMINIONS

Canada had suffered a greater loss of manpower during the First World War relative to the United States, while the collapse of its GDP was worse and its level of unemployment higher than in the United States during the Great Depression. In many ways, Canada's most obvious form of democratic empowerment during the interwar years was its decoupling from any form of control by the British government, the end to even informal imperialism.[18] A constitutional crisis, which set Canadian prime ministers against the British Governor General in 1927, was followed by almost complete independence under the Statute of Westminster of 1931, though Canada followed Britain into the war in 1939 after a decent gap of a week. As in the United States, immigration was restricted after 1918 and Native Americans made only limited gains in their demand for strengthened land rights during the interwar years. Women secured the right to vote in Dominion elections in 1918, though this was complicated by different rates of empowerment at the provincial level and exclusion until 1929 from the Dominion Senate. In this respect, Canada lagged behind Australia. In terms of social provision, it also trailed behind the United States, where measures such as the National Housing Act of 1937 and other significant relief acts came months if not years after Roosevelt's equivalents.

The other great democracies of European colonial settlement – Australia, New Zealand and South Africa – faced similar challenges, and here the paradox of the democratic empowerment of majoritarian exclusionism was yet more starkly in evidence. In South Africa, Gandhi had honed his political skills and the tactic of civil disobedience between 1904 and 1914 as the white authorities attempted to clamp down on Indian immigration by treating Indians as resident aliens.[19] The minority white settler population, British and Afrikaner, extended rights to women relatively rapidly following the establishment of the constitution of the new Union of South Africa in 1910. The small number of "coloureds" and Indians who had received the vote before this date retained it, but only "whites" were actually allowed to sit in the Parliament of the Union. Thereafter, and even before 1945, the government of General Jan Smuts was moving towards even greater restriction of the derisory electoral rights of the black population.[20]

The case of Australia is particularly instructive, however. Australia, like New Zealand, was far ahead of Britain, Canada and Western Europe, let alone the United States, during the late nineteenth century on the issue of popular representation. The adult male population and a large part of the female population already had the vote in both countries. A system of state benefits, again far ahead of anything in Britain, already existed. Yet, even before the First World War, this very democratic empowerment had resulted in hostile moves against Chinese and Indian immigrants and a slow disenfranchisement of the native Aboriginal population. Tensions of this sort increased as the effects of the First World War ate into the earlier prosperity of Australian society. During the war, the premier, Billy Hughes, clamped down ferociously on anti-war protests amongst Irish Catholics and others. In the aftermath of peace, anti-immigration legislation was tightened and Hughes seized German colonies in the Pacific and joined France in its desire to crush Germany. In 1924, the rise of a small Australian Communist movement led to a "red menace" scare, comparable to the one in the United States.[21] Even after 1929, when the Labor Party took power, fiscal austerity worked to demolish some of those very democratic safeguards which an earlier generation had sought to institute. Unemployed male workers were summarily despatched to work camps, for instance.

In New Zealand, as in Australia, the huge relative loss of men on the Western Front and, in particular, the ANZAC myth of Gallipoli had fostered the idea of national difference. New Zealanders began to imagine themselves as "kiwis" rather than loyal British subjects overseas; this identity emerged parallel to, but distinct from, the idea of the muscular Australian male. Here too, democratic governments turned against foreign immigrants, particularly the Chinese, who lost most of their rights. But this racist legislation was balanced to some extent by the creation of schemes to aid Maori groups in regaining title to land which had been denied them since the Treaty of Waitangi of 1840 during the wars of colonial settlement. Here the Maori were in a stronger position than the Australian Aboriginal people because they were more numerous, had a tradition of land cultivation and social organisation and, above all, many had fought in the war.[22]

This same paradox was seen in New Zealand gender relations. Women had voted since the 1880s, but they were still excluded, for instance, from the Upper House of the legislature. Women's war work and sacrifice gave a strong voice to women's movements, on the one hand. Wartime deaths, on the other hand, created a popular demand for women to return to the family and produce more children; and this idea was powered by a strong eugenic turn amongst the leadership, who, oddly, worried about the "physical and moral degeneration" of the country's youth.[23] An emphasis on the family was characteristic of other conservative white societies, notably in Eire with its Catholic state ideology. Yet, as in Australia and Canada, the Depression revived the pre-war push for health and retirement benefits which had been stalled by conservative governments in the 1920s. So, in the United States, Britain and Australia, full democratic empowerment at both the political and the social level awaited the end of the Second World War. The capacity of democracies, even as they evolved from established representative systems, in the West serves as a reminder that the path taken by Germany and Italy in the 1920s and 1930s cannot really be seen as a *Sonderweg* or special path. It is more appropriate to see their fate as representative of one end of the spectrum of populist upheavals created by the 1919 settlement, the economic turmoil of the 1920s and the Great Depression.

REPRESENTATION AND RIGHTS AMONG "SUBJECT PEOPLES"

European colonial empires saw, in many ways, the absolute opposite of the push for rights and representation which was taking place fitfully in the democracies of Western Europe and the Americas. Wartime and immediate post-war nationalist movements actually caused colonial authorities to crack down even more violently on political opposition of all sorts. In a sense this represented a further extension of the new imperialism of the 1880s and 1990s. The British and French mandates in the Middle East, supposedly "Wilsonian" creations to foster eventual self-government, saw the destruction of incipient nationalist assemblies in Damascus, the frustration of Palestinian hopes in Jerusalem and the imposition of a British-backed royal autocracy in Iraq. In French Indochina, the Depression years ushered in even greater French repression where moderate leaders were guillotined, paving the way for radical nationalists and Communists, such as Nguyen Ai Quoc, later known as Ho Chi Minh. Meanwhile, colonial governments were largely unaffected by the efforts of domestic states to ameliorate economic hardship by government intervention such as the schemes promoted by the leaders of the Popular Front in France and even Baldwin's Conservatives in the United Kingdom. Imperialism, in fact, took on a new, more militarised and hypernationalist form.

As noted above, some colonial governments did, however, introduce limited representation in local bodies and legislative councils in their colonies. The British did so through the Government of India Acts of 1919 and 1935 and similar policies in the Gold Coast, Nigeria and Malaya, for instance.[24] But these were broadly concessions to special interests: Indian and Malay princes, West African chiefs, groups of landowners and European residents everywhere. The National Congress of British West Africa was created in 1920 and it demanded the establishment of properly representative electorates. In 1925, a set of provincial councils was indeed set up in the Gold Coast, but these were once more selected from "paramount chiefs", had no more than advisory functions and were dominated by British civil servants and white settlers.[25] This tended to divorce the chiefly elite from the local populace. Non-official African members from the new educated classes were given a small role as late as 1943, when wartime pressures and military recruitment forced the British to make some further concessions to rising nationalist opinion.

An important comparative issue here was the density of European settlement in the African colonies, for the political rights of white settlers and business interests were often sharply opposed to the granting of even limited forms of representation to African populations. Liberal imperialists, such as Lord Lugard in West Africa, had aimed, through a system of "indirect rule", to empower African enterprise, particularly in agricultural development. The immediate beneficiaries were, again, tribal chiefs. But at least the existence of a degree of local responsibility in the Gold Coast and Nigeria prevented the emergence of the kind of white-dominated plantation system which had long existed in the Caribbean. Matters were different in East and Central

Africa. White settler populations had spread north into the Rhodesias at the end of the nineteenth century while, after 1918, the government had encouraged military officers to settle in Kenya and Uganda. Even though the British Colonial Office reaffirmed its desire to extend African education and local responsibility, it was the 33,000 European settlers who effectively took power in Southern Rhodesia after 1923. In the same way, by the later 1930s white settlers dominated local society and labour in Kenya, as the "Happy Valley" phenomenon of the expatriate search for wealth and status became stronger in the face of domestic economic hardship.[26]

Something similar occurred in French North Africa, where an even larger body of *colons* from France, the Iberian countries and Malta strengthened their hold on Algerian society during the 1920s and 1930s. Between 1900 and 1936, the French settler community there had doubled from 500,000 to about one million.[27] As full voting citizens of France, these *pieds noirs* were able to exert their power against the government in Paris and local governors to thwart attempts to expand the voting rights of indigenous people. Educated Muslims were, indeed, allowed to vote, but only if they abandoned Muslim for Christian law. In all these cases, therefore, a kind of white popular democratic empowerment blocked off African representation and economic growth. Even where the white settler population was smaller, Africans made little headway, even when a leftist democratic coalition came to power in France itself. In the French colonial world, the revolutionary past had enfranchised small groups of settlers and indigenous people in West Africa, North Africa and Indochina, for instance. These small electorates sent representatives to the Assembly in Paris. But they were hardly expanded between 1918 and 1939, and the authorities' insistence that such *évolués* give up native rights, customs and even land before being made French citizens was rigidly enforced. Outside Senegal, where there was an old electorate of French African citizens, only 2,000 out of 14 million French West African subjects had received French citizenship and could vote for the Assembly in 1930.[28] At best, the very limited voting rights which existed in the colonies acted as a spur and stimulant to local nationalists.

Even where colonial powers conceded limited forms of local representation, this could often exacerbate local tensions rather than help build democratic capacity. In Africa, there was a general hardening of "tribal" distinctions where colonial governments co-opted chiefly representatives into political decisions. In Kenya, the divide between the Luo and Kikuyu deepened; in the southern Sudan, distinctions between the Dinka and Nuer grew greater. In India, the British government moved in 1935 towards a federal system with an expanded electorate. But this system had the not entirely unintended consequence of dividing landowners from tenants, Muslims from Hindus and Brahmins from non-Brahmins. In Southeast Asia, limited patterns of community representation through chiefly representatives created a pattern of rivalry between Chinese and Malay, Karen, Shan and ethnic Burmese.

Under the surface of these repressive measures and painfully limited concessions, however, nationalist leaderships were emerging which were, at least initially, committed to political and social democracy. Bodies such as the Indian National Congress, the Nigerian Youth Movement and the Gold Coast's

National Congress of British West Africa staged long political campaigns to demand popular representation and dominion status within the British Empire. Gandhi's idiosyncratic political philosophy was relatively unconcerned with issues of representation as such, opposed positive discrimination in favour of Dalits, or untouchables, and lauded instead the archaic village community.[29] Yet, Gandhi did institute a huge popular movement which began to unite India's diverse peoples. More significant as an augury of its future democracy was the fact that as early as 1931, reiterated in 1938, Congress had voted decisively for universal suffrage, despite the worries of some political leaders about enfranchising the uneducated.[30] These aims were confirmed during the Constituent Assembly debates of 1946–1948 as the British left India. Equally, the Congress from 1938 embarked on a form of centralised planning which was designed to redistribute land and income in order to create a properly democratic nation. Even if many of these aspirations were not fulfilled after 1947, the leap to endorse universal suffrage cannot be underestimated as a foundational moment for the emergence of the world's largest democracy and its most elaborate system of positive discrimination.

Wartime and the distant prospect of independence had similar results in West Africa, leading to the beginnings of proper political representation in the Gold Coast in 1946 and Nigeria in 1947. The activities of political parties, often modelled on the Indian National Congress, were important here. But equally significant was the movement of young men from village to town and from country to country which in turn bred aspirations for personal empowerment and dignity. A whole range of civil society movements, cooperative societies and women's leagues had sprung up in West Africa after 1930, often representing attempts to lessen the effects of the Depression which had severely damaged the export sector of these economies.[31] Here the impact of wartime recruitment and the movement overseas of soldiers and commercial people made it clear to a new generation that white colonial rule and European society itself were morally and politically bankrupt.

A similar situation developed in the British and French Caribbean.[32] Returning soldiers and public figures, such as Marcus Garvey and later George Padmore, demanded popular representation and dominion status, fiercely denouncing colonial racism. The British Colonial Office introduced into legislative councils members chosen on a limited franchise in 1924. Middle-class activism and rural and urban strikes became common, especially in Jamaica, during the 1930s. But it was only towards the end of the Second World War and after, beginning with Jamaica in 1944, that new constitutions and adult franchises were instituted, mainly as a result of American pressure during the Roosevelt and Truman eras. France took a different path here, as across the rest of the colonial world. Small groups of French citizens voted representatives to the French assembly from Guadeloupe and Martinique as early as 1848. The franchise was gradually extended, though not to Indians until the 1920s. In 1946, both territories became overseas *départements* of France and, ultimately, some of the most distant parts of the European Union.

Elsewhere in the non-white British Empire, outside India, West Africa and latterly the Caribbean, representative government trod an even more difficult path. In Egypt, for instance, the British had conceded internal self-government in 1922, extended in 1936, subject to their continuing control over external affairs and the Suez Canal. A long battle ensued between the nationalist Wafd party, representing small Arab landowners, and the royal establishment in Cairo. The electorate remained small, representing the propertied and later military modernisers galvanised during the Second World War – a pattern repeated in Iraq. But purist Islamic ideology remained important here, by comparison with India, for instance. Neither right- or left-wing Indian politicians nor their more recent followers were hostile to democracy, political parties and the idea of the sovereign electorate. But this was the case with Sayyid Qutb, founder of Egypt's Muslim Brotherhood, who feared that they "might derogate from God's commands".[33]

Conflicts of this sort, between ideology, aspirations to popular empowerment, the sense of entitlement of old leaderships and vested economic interests, were played out across the British, French and Dutch empires and became more vigorous during the Second World War, when the colonial powers often hurriedly conceded more powers to their subjects who were now needed as soldiers and war workers in the global conflict. In 1943, Ceylon was promised self-government, and its leaders began to draw up a constitution, but in an atmosphere already bedevilled by suspicion between Sinhala Buddhists and Tamil Hindus. Though Jamaica was granted a full adult franchise in 1944, the issue of white landholding remained. The Gold Coast was finally given an African majority on its legislative council, but most members were picked by the chiefs. The scene was set for conflict with young radicals such as Kwame Nkrumah, like Jawaharlal Nehru, a Britain-returned socialist. Nehru remained deeply committed to popular government. Nkrumah ultimately established a form of personal rule, which many called a dictatorship. This divergence was a complex phenomenon. But one contribution to democracy's staying power in India was its plethora of liberal civil society organisations and vibrant journalistic tradition, both of which had developed rapidly in the interwar years. Not only did the Indian press circumvent British control to become more radical, but a large independent education sector, such as, for instance, the nationalist Jamia Millia Islamia university came into being and an Indian film industry emerged promoting romantic indigenous themes and Indian historical drama.

DEMOCRACY ON THE RACK IN CONTINENTAL EUROPE: THE 1930S

One link between the frustration of demands for popular government among colonised peoples and the political situation in Europe was that right-wing, Nazi and fascist interests were often complicit with hard-line colonial authorities. This helps explain the rise of a German-backed Nazi party in the Netherlands, where an intransigent position against self-government in the East Indies, which it reinforced, persisted through to the 1940s. Similarly, in the United Kingdom, Mosley's anti-Jewish racism merged easily with his post-war demands for a ban on mixed marriages and forced repatriation of Caribbean immigrants. Closely allied with imperial ruling families, his first wife was Lord Curzon's younger daughter.

In the European colonies, it was the desire of the powers to retain economic control and the special status of white settlers which hamstrung any but the smallest moves towards popular representation. In Europe, the 1930s often saw the rolling back of responsible democracy as the full implications of the 1919 settlement and the effects of the Depression took their toll. The German Weimar Republic, which formally existed between 1919 and 1945 but effectively came to an end between 1930 and 1933, has always been taken as the epitome of democratic failure in the twentieth century.[34] But even though it ultimately succumbed to the Nazis and their unthinking backers in the army and among conservatives, it represented one of the deepest and most surprisingly successful attempts to construct both social and political democracy in its time. The creation of a new constitution and the institution of universal suffrage, even in Prussia, the heart of the old military landowning class, was a remarkable achievement, especially as it came before female voting rights across much of Europe.[35] Equally, Prussia, like other former German states, preserved its internal autonomy, though now under moderate Social Democratic control. The federal constitution was maintained so that over-centralisation never became a problem for German democracy. Even before the Weimar constitution was established, the Council of People's Commissioners had extended the eight-hour working day and given legal force to wage agreements, so extending some of Bismarck's social legislation. Thereafter, the Weimar governments extended basic working rights farther and faster than in Britain before the institution of the welfare state in the 1940s, or the French Republic during the rule of the Popular Front after 1936, let alone the United States. All this occurred in a context of foreign demands for reparations and the open hostility of powerful factions on both the right and the left.

The Social Democratic Party had made continual gains even before 1914 and its social policies and commitment to local democracy should not be ignored, even though it functioned in the context of Wilhelmine autocracy and military imperialism. As Germany was scarified by the brutal ending of the war, numerous leftist coups occurred across the country, often led by soldiers and sailors. The Spartacist German Republic, graced by Rosa Luxemburg and Karl Liebknecht, took control of Berlin; a Red Army of the Ruhr emerged. Even after the Weimar government began to assume control, Hitler staged his failed Beer Hall Putsch in Munich in 1923. In 1922, the moderate Jewish foreign minister Walther Rathenau, who had signed the Treaty of Rapallo in 1922 with Russia in order to strengthen Germany's position against France, was assassinated by extreme nationalist and anti-Semitic former soldiers who regarded him as a traitor. The devastation of war was swiftly followed by French occupation of the Rhineland and its continuous demands for reparations and the hyperinflation of 1922–1923, which wiped out middle-class savings and a whole swathe of German business.

Yet, despite the pressure of left and right insurgency, the persistence of reaction in the army, the judiciary and the civil service, 89% of the enlarged electorate voted for social democratic parties in 1919. Again, despite the weakness of many of the succeeding coalition governments, the Nazi party (the NSDAP) secured only 19% of the popular vote and the Communists 13% as late as 1930, after the Great Depression had already set in. In other words, democracy was very well entrenched in the German Republic and this impression is strengthened by the vibrancy of civil society life. Germany retained the best universities and scientific tradition in the world; its intellectuals, the inheritors of Max Weber, along with Leo Strauss, Carl Schmitt and Martin Heidegger, despite the flirtation of the latter two with authoritarianism, ensured the highest level of political debate; Germany's filmmakers, playwrights and authors, debating societies and public religious figures were unequalled.

In addition, the Republic seemed to have emerged from the shadows as inflation eased in 1923–1924. The Americans, initially determined to avoid intervention in dangerous European affairs, devised the Dawes and later Young financial plans to ease German's load of debt. The British and other European powers finally ceased to abandon Germany to French rage in the treaties of Locarno of 1925, when its borders were legitimated and the French withdrew from the Rhineland. In this year, too, Germany joined the League of Nations, no longer a "pariah state". Between 1924 and 1929, the German economy recovered strongly, buttressed by the low value of the mark. The groundwork for a good deal of the growth, later attributed to Hitler and his rearmament drive, was already laid in this period, only interrupted by five years of deep depression. A series of cautious but skilled statesmen, notably Friedrich Ebert and Gustav Stresemann, steered the country's difficult external relations with France and the USSR.

Before 1929, then, it would have been difficult to predict the demise of democratic government in Germany. External pressures had been enormous. Hyperinflation had wreaked havoc and the weak, coalition-style of government with a powerful president looming over it threw up difficulties for the continuity of policies. These were slowly managed. But there were two interlinked weaknesses which ultimately came together in the atmosphere of social and economic crisis between 1929 and 1934. The first was the persistence of an older and angry cohort of former military commanders, many of whom had links back to the landed classes of Prussia. The Social Democratic leadership compromised with the military in the so-called Ebert–Groener pact of 1918, designed to secure social peace in Germany. But in time, the military were unable to secure a conservative government through the ballot box and entertained deep fears of the rise of Bolshevism, which they located in the Communist trade unions. They saw their salvation in the continued existence of semi-militarised bands of young middle- and lower-class men, who were equally nationalistic and hostile to Communism but now scarred by unemployment and depression. This was the second weakness in the Weimar state, which had some degree of responsibility itself for the persistence of armed gangs of this sort. For the immediate post-war leaders had also encouraged the *Freikorps*. It was from the residues of these militarised political factions that Hitler's mass support emerged. These same groups, which assisted his rise to power, were then disarmed by the putsch against the Brown Shirts. Capitalising on the crumbling of democratic power at the centre, the Nazis passed an Enabling Act which allowed the president to pass acts circumventing the Reichstag, or popular assembly.[36]

However unique the combination of intra-European imperialism and genocide which Hitler ultimately unleashed, the conditions of his rise to power did not necessarily reflect failings unique to Weimar democracy or any particularly German tendency to authoritarian rule. Similar conditions existed in Japan, Italy, Spain and Latin America, for instance, as the last chapter shows. Even in France, another advanced democratic state after 1936, there remained an old imperialist, Catholic and landed elite which hated social democracy and saw a disdained ally in right-wing nationalist youth activists descended from the anti-Dreyfusards and Action Française zealots of the immediate pre-war years. Yet, they could not grasp power until France's defeat by Germany in 1940.

As elsewhere in Europe, the example of the Russian Revolution resulted in a split in 1920 between avowed Communists and the rump of the French Socialists led by André Léon Blum. Weak left-wing coalitions gave way to centre-right governments and vice versa over the following 29 years with the left increasingly favoured by the electorate after 1929. But powerful far-right forces complicated the political scene, supported by Catholics, monarchists and colonial conservatives organised in movements such as Action Française and Croix-de-Feu. Political infighting reached its peak after the so-called Stavisky Affair of 1934, when a Jewish businessman who had sold huge quantities of false bonds was found dead. The right used this as an excuse to organise mass demonstrations against the socialist government, fired up by the anti-Semitism which was spreading across Europe. In 1935, the Communist International took fright at the spread of fascism and ordered its national parties to cooperate with moderates and socialists.

The main consequence was that the powerful Communist Party, which had so far refused to support the Socialists, formed the Popular Front with them, modelled on a similar leftist pact in Spain.[37] The Front won the 1936 elections and, following a general strike by Communist unions, conceded a far-reaching extension of social democratic rights, including collective bargaining, minimum annual leave for workers and a rise in the minimum wage. Concessions were made to leftist and national parties in Algeria and Senegal, where French citizenship was intended to be extended to a small number of indigenous people, though the Front government fell before this was enacted. In Indochina, where Communist and nationalist activists had been imprisoned and executed following a revolt in 1930, the leaders of the Indochinese Communist Party and nationalist Viet Nam Quoc Den Dang (VNQDD) were released from prison and allowed to function legally until war broke out again. Yet, the Front government only lasted eighteen months, and the deep fissures it created in French politics were later revealed after the German occupation of the country in 1940.

In the case of Spain, the deep conflicts within emerging democracies were redoubled. Here, as noted in the previous chapter, the power of the Catholic Church, large landowners and regional interests was pitted against an emerging workers socialist movement and a small middle class. In the relatively prosperous 1920s, Spain, which had not entered the First World War, was subject to a weak form of dictatorship represented by Primo de Rivera and legitimated by the king. The economic problems of the Depression undermined both de Rivera and the monarchy and led to the creation of the Second Republic, which survived from 1931 to 1939, when Francisco Franco triumphed in the civil war and inaugurated a further 40 years of dictatorship. But in 1931–1933, the auguries had still seemed favourable. Women achieved the vote, labour laws were put in place and farmers in the poorer south achieved some protection. But further economic tension served to bring to power a new conservative–Catholic–business coalition in 1933. In response to the new government's repeal of labour laws, workers in Catalonia rose in rebellion in 1934, with Falangist, fascist and anarchist groups taking up arms. By late 1935, a full-scale civil war was in view.[38] In many ways, Spain's lurch from dictatorship to multi-party democracy and back was more typical of South America, particularly Mexico and Argentina, than it was of Western Europe. Nevertheless, the closeness of the fascist regime in Italy and the image of Hitler's Germany created a very different international context for Spain, whereas the influence of the United States in Central and South America was more varied, promoting democracy by example, but periodically undermining it to frustrate "Communism".

CONCLUSION: DEMOCRACY AND ITS TRAVAILS

The previous chapter examines the shift to authoritarianism across the early-twentieth-century world. Here, however, some reasons for democracy's contemporary successes and failures over these same years have been advanced. Evidently, one important factor was experience itself. Those democracies which survived, at least to 1939, generally built on a long popular memory of forms of representative government, whether revolutionary and republican in the case of France, or parliamentary and representative in the case of Britain, the Netherlands and Nordic countries. Critical here was the degree to which the old ruling class and the newer, more democratised commercial interests had found ways to adjust to an expanded electorate and working-class demands. To some extent this outcome rested on the structure of an economy: where "gentlemanly capitalists" and upwardly mobile artisans and rural land-owners were predominant, serious class conflict could be avoided even when avowedly socialist governments came to power.

The constitutional and legal context was also critical, however. If the army remained under civilian control, the judiciary was relatively independent and civil society organisations were inclusive enough, the emerging democratic system was able to weather substantial economic and political storms. In the United States, the powerfully entrenched forms of local representation and democratic balance were always in place to hold back unacceptable initiatives from federal government. By contrast, where a monarch or president retained considerable discretionary power – and this was the case in Spain, Germany and Japan – powerful, military, landowning and old commercial interests were in a much better position to undermine elected regimes of which they disapproved. In this respect, it was notable that a political consensus in Denmark finally removed the monarch's power to dismiss the ministry in 1920. This paved the way for the dominance of the Danish Social Democrats during the 1930s and again after 1945.

Elsewhere, ideology intervened to empower political forces of the old order. Historically, the Roman Catholic Church and, to a lesser extent, the Orthodox Church in Eastern Europe or the Shinto cult in Japan had been powers wedded to, and mutually dependent on, central governments and the old elites for patronage and protection. By contrast, non-conformist and Protestant churches, or even neo-Hindu movements in India, such as the Arya Samaj and Theosophy, had historically been outside, or even hostile to, the ortho-doxies of established powerholders. They tended therefore to empower civil society organisations which kept a weather eye on any drift towards authoritar-ianism. They were also often founding agents of newspapers, educational institutions and forms of communication, which spread the idea of rights, racial and religious tolerance and citizenship.

Having said this, it is clear that these were only some of the preconditions for the emergence, or survival, of representative government and democracy. Political, military and economic shocks easily upset any or all of these condi-tions, as they did in the Weimar Republic. In the case of colonised societies, the memory in question was of mobilisation through civil society organisations or mass action against the colonial power itself. A few colonial authorities and missionary bodies attempted to empower their subjects through education and even limited political representation, but even here indigenous agency held the key to change. To one extent or another, however, all regimes – democratic, authoritarian or colonial – were impacted on by the Great Depression, which is considered in more detail in the next chapter.

[5] THE DEPRESSION: STATE INTERVENTION AND POPULAR RESISTANCE

> The Origin and Spread of the Depression
> India, Australia and Africa: The Pains of Colonial
>   Dependence and the Advantages of Autonomy
> Germany, Latin America and Japan: Economic Crisis and
>   the Drift to Authoritarianism
> The United States and the World: A Paradigm Shift?
> The Interwar Years: Historians, Economists and Their
>   Differences

THE Great Depression of 1929–1938 creates a conceptual bridge between the two world wars. The mismanagement of wartime debts and reparations and the febrile boom after 1922 helped create the conditions for the Depression and here human error was the key component.[1] In turn, the collapse of democratic government in Germany and Austria and the exclusion of Japanese goods from colonial markets in East and Southeast Asia spurred the conflicts that led to the Second World War. Once again, the miscalculations of politicians and capitalists concerning the gold standard intertwined with their global ambitions and created a new era of conflict. Yet, long-term economic and political changes, notably the slow development of industrial production beyond Europe and the United States, also accelerated during the Depression.

In many ways, the collapse in agricultural prices during this era, following on from the volatility of the First World War, constituted the biggest blow of the twentieth century against the rural population, especially smallholders and rent-paying peasants.[2] The gradual disempowerment of the peasantry across

Remaking the Modern World 1900–2015: Global Connections and Comparisons, First Edition. C. A. Bayly.
© 2018 John Wiley & Sons Ltd. Published 2018 by John Wiley & Sons Ltd.

the world has continued unabated into the twenty-first century, land reform in former colonial territories and Communist revolutions in East Asia notwithstanding. During the Depression, the collapse of food-grain and other agricultural prices drove poor people into the towns, initiating a long-term drift which reduced the rural population from about 85% of the world's population in 1930 to about 46% in 2014.[3]

Outside the European colonies, the Depression also drove forward government intervention as politicians sought to placate an angry workforce. Some of this spending went into the countryside, as in the case of the Tennessee Valley Project in the United States. But much of it went into big industrial towns, further increasing their attraction to the unemployed smallholder or rural labourer. Finally, the very considerable political, intellectual and even artistic changes that were spurred on by the Depression were of significance. In the field of economic theory, at least until the 1970s, most governments were persuaded by the theories of Keynes and his supporters, who pointed to the self-defeating nature of government cuts and "austerity" while the economy itself was in dire trouble.[4] When the Great Recession of 2008 unfolded, these debates were reignited.

THE ORIGIN AND SPREAD OF THE DEPRESSION

A number of circumstances, pondered over in great detail by economic historians, came together to provide the background for the collapse of the New York stock market in August 1929.[5] The United States was unsparing in its demands for the repayment of war loans to European and other governments after the mid-1920s. France, too, pressed Germany for war reparations. Both these conditions brought about significant deflation just at the point when the world economy remained highly volatile. This coincided with conditions beyond Europe and America, which contributed to yet greater instability. For instance, landlords and peasants, attempting to recoup wartime and immediate post-war losses, over-produced agricultural crops, something that was made easier by contemporary developments in technology. Equally important was the wrong move taken by financial authorities in London and New York in reinstituting the gold standard, which had supposedly provided stability to the international financial system before 1914. This proved a disaster because it locked the currencies of Western countries and their colonies into an unsustainable fixed global exchange rate which ultimately collapsed, leading to a renewed crisis of confidence.[6] The result was that for up to five years after the world's stock markets collapsed in 1929, triggering an international panic, countries resorted to "beggar-thy-neighbour" policies which helped drive prices down further. Many governments across the world, particularly European colonial authorities, initially refused to contemplate any kind of intervention to ameliorate the decline of prices. Consequently, rural producers were further squeezed between demands for taxes and rents and falling prices for their goods. Urban working people suffered across the world as overall demand in the economy fell and many were laid off. The oldest generation in the United

Kingdom remember the proliferation of billboards declaring, "No hands needed!"

As in other global conjunctures discussed in this book, the Depression was both transmitted across the world by forces of connection and took on particular forms in different contexts as a consequence of prevailing local economic problems and political crises. It was transmitted from the United States to Europe by two factors: first, the sudden withdrawal of American capital from the world market as a result of America's own recession and the diversion of funds into the New York bull market, which predated the stock market crash. The United States had replaced Britain as the world's largest lender after the war and this withdrawal of capital precipitated a collapse in prices, particularly in raw materials and food grains in Canada, Australia, central Europe and beyond. Secondly, the United States embarked early on its own policy of "beggar-thy-neighbour", that is a great increase in tariff protection through the Hawley–Smoot Act of 1930, which raised duties against foreign imports by nearly 50% and precipitated responses from most other developed countries.[7] The consequence was that countries which had taken loans from the United States during the 1910s and 1920s were unable to pay them off by exporting to it, thus fragmenting the world economy still further. In turn, the problems faced by European governments led them to impose similar preferential tariffs, such as Britain's Import Duties Act of 1932. This, along with the country's earlier abandonment of the gold standard, set off a further wave of deflation.[8]

Few countries were able to put together a coherent policy in response to these financial challenges. Even though the First World War had imparted the idea of a degree of central state planning, most national governments were not large or coherent enough to drive through ameliorative policies. The federal government in the United States was still much smaller in relation to GDP than it was to become after the Second World War. Britain, ruled by a Labour government as the crisis broke, was polarised between the interests of capital and powerful labour unions. Many governments, including those of the United States, France and Japan, were hamstrung by dependence on farmers' votes and farmers were determined to protect the value of their commodities by imposing tariffs. Germany, in turn, horrified by the consequences of the great inflation of 1922, was unwilling to consider fiscal easing. Two of the few democratic governments to avoid the worst of the Depression were Denmark and Sweden, which had both begun to plan industrial change and institute forms of welfare state in the 1920s. It is not surprising therefore that some of the governments which were most successful and active in countering the effects of the Depression were authoritarian ones, especially Mussolini's and Franco's governments in southern Europe, the increasingly militarised Japanese regime and, of course, Hitler's government in Germany after 1933, which provided large loans to business and began a massive process of military–industrial expansion. In the USSR, the attempt to mix socialism with individual enterprise that had informed Lenin's New Economic Policy of 1921 was abandoned when the first Five Year Plan was inaugurated in 1928.

Not least the most damaging effect of governments' tardy responses to the Depression was the attempt to expand areas of production through imperial expansion. Faced with being shut out of European colonial markets in Asia by protectionism, Japan redoubled its intervention in China which it had initiated for strategic and political reasons. Economic stresses contributed to the Italian decision to invade Ethiopia, while Hitler began to conceive his *Drang nach Osten* (Drive to the East), spurred on, in part, by the fantasy of creating a dependent agrarian empire in Central and Eastern Europe. This chapter now moves on to consider the causes and consequences of the Great Depression in a number of specific cases which illuminate the broader argument.

INDIA, AUSTRALIA AND AFRICA: THE PAINS OF COLONIAL DEPENDENCE AND THE ADVANTAGES OF AUTONOMY

The problems of Australia, India and colonial Africa during the interwar years vividly illustrate the difference between the fate of a self-governing dominion and disempowered colonies. Certainly, the Australian economy had a bumpy ride during the 1920s and suffered very badly from the onset of the Depression in 1929. Wool and wheat prices collapsed during the global crisis and this meant that Australia was unable to pay the interest on its very large loans, predominantly secured from British investors. In a move towards austerity, federal and state expenditure was cut along with wages. By 1931, a massive 28% of the population was unemployed, among them a large number of disabled war veterans. Differential living standards had widened rapidly by 1933 and shanty towns of the unemployed sprang up on the edge of cities, something inconceivable in the 1890s, when Australians had enjoyed probably the highest living standards in the world.[9]

Indian raw material exports of cotton, jute and tea suffered equally badly, but with its vast population of impoverished farmers and huge subsistence market, the financial shock was relatively milder initially, though even a small drop in living standards had a huge effect. In some respects, India even benefited slightly from the Depression. Because wages were so low, Indian manufactures became more attractive since their prices were also low. Even earlier in the 1920s, and partly in response to the financial crisis at the end of the war, the colonial government had slapped higher tariffs on British cotton imports. This, of course, was a move to help the government of India's finance and not a socially progressive economic development. But the result was a steady expansion of cotton manufacturing in Bombay and Gujarat, which continued into the 1930s.

Yet, after 1930, the different political status of India and Australia magnified the difference, making it extremely difficult for India to even begin to counteract the effects of the deepening Depression.[10] When Britain left the gold standard in September 1931, Sir George Schuster, Finance Member of the government of India, who had been forced by London over some years to implement a policy of deflation, tried to de-link the Indian rupee from sterling because the artificially high valuation of the rupee damaged Indian exports. London again refused to allow this, so deflation and the Depression created a vicious circle. By contrast, Australia was able to devalue its currency against sterling by about 25%. The UK Treasury attempted to stop this, but here the relative autonomy of the dominion and the Australian states proved its worth, allowing the Australians to benefit from Britain's abandonment of the gold standard. Ironically, this compounded India's problems because cheap wheat from Australia and other basic commodities now entered the subcontinent in volume. The Indian authorities were once again unable to take remedial action since they could not apply a protective tariff. The income of Indian peasants fell sharply, and this led to an outflow of gold from the rural economy and, indeed, out of the country altogether. Gold, of course, had increased massively in price since the United Kingdom left the gold standard. Ironically again, this meant that the British government of India, not its people, was the great gainer because the outflow of gold allowed it to continue to remit interest and salaries from India to the United Kingdom – the notorious "home charges". The Indian farmer was necessarily the greatest loser.

One should not underestimate the distress suffered by Australia in these years. Labour unrest was endemic, particularly in the coal and steel sectors. But the fact that the country could control its currency and tariffs limited the damage. Exports recovered rapidly after 1932 and capital began to flow into local industrial activity which had been stagnant for five years. Australia's relative political weight in the Empire's councils also allowed it to negotiate a preferential tariff for British imports and greater access to the British market for its farmers. Consequently, Australia's external debt eased. India's, meanwhile, increased until the approach of the Second World War forced the British to finance the re-equipment of the Indian army.[11] When the Second World War ended, Britain was net debtor to India for the first time in 200 years, a factor which was by no means unrelated to the relative speed with which London was forced to give the subcontinent its independence in 1947.

Both India and Australia were faced with political dissidence among the rural and urban working classes. Both sets of governments clamped down hard on Communist activity, working hard to coerce labour unions back to work. In India, this continued even when Congress governments took limited power in the provinces after 1937. Both countries also did little to alleviate discontent by active state intervention. Australians were generally better off because governments before 1914 had introduced a degree of health insurance. But laissez-faire economics remained politically dominant, even when it was beginning to be abandoned in 1930s Britain. India, with no state provision to speak of, once again fared worse. Indian nationalists, such as Nehru's confidant G. B. Pant, were well aware of this. He was in vigorous dispute in 1936 with the Finance Member of the Indian government Sir James Grigg. Pant argued that if Great Britain had already moved away from laissez-faire and was inspired in its programmes of housebuilding by major economists and politicians, such as Lloyd George, Roosevelt, Keynes and Harold Laski, "How was it that the Indian government still adhered to rigid ideas of small government?"[12] Only planning during the 1939–1945 war – and independence itself – ultimately shifted the Indian government towards state intervention. Much the same can be said of Australia, where conservative hostility to higher taxation stymied social legislation until the troops returned from the war in 1945.

As an exporter of primary produce, Africa suffered as badly as India during the Depression. Tea and coffee exports from East Africa declined dramatically, as did rubber exports from West Africa and wool and mining products from South Africa. Wages fell in all these areas and rural poverty increased as migrant labour lost its position in many towns. There was perhaps some degree of equivalence with the Australian situation in South Africa, where the prime minister, Jan Smuts, was able to let the pound float in 1933 and take the country off the gold standard. The country also benefited from the rising value of gold itself, a major export by the end of the 1930s. Yet, even here rural poverty increased significantly.

Elsewhere in Africa, the situation was dire. In northern Nigeria, for instance, colonial officials worked at cross purposes.[13] On the one hand, they tried to rebalance the rural economies towards growth. On the other hand, pressure from London and the local governments forced them, like their Indian equivalents, to increase taxes on valuable export cash crops. This resulted in a decrease in the cultivation of these crops as producers were unable to afford extra taxation and there was a consequent decline in tax revenues. This vicious circle, compounded by years of bad harvests and delay to the development of the colonies' very poor infrastructure, continued until 1939, when both the East and West African economies were artificially stimulated by recruitment and demand for commodities as the Second World War began. In northern Nigeria, however, there was a small glimmer of hope.[14] Since few could now afford imported textiles, local female handloom weavers in areas such as Sokoto found their business booming as people turned to local goods. This again paralleled developments in India, where a stimulus had been given to the country's long-embattled handloom industry, but also to local machine manufacture in cities such as Ahmadabad. In some respects, indeed, low labour costs and economic crisis in the West saw the beginnings of a "return of the global south",[15] especially in cotton manufacture. India and China, later Africa, began to see a ramping-up of industrial production as Japan had seen a generation earlier.

Nevertheless, East African British colonies, such as the Rhodesias and Kenya, suffered a similar medium-term fall in exports and increase in rural poverty, but the situation was influenced by another factor: the extent of white settlement, which found parallels in French Algeria and, to a lesser extent, the Belgian Congo. European immigration to these territories had been substantial during the volatile 1920s, falling off somewhat in the 1930s.[16] But Europeans were still able to maintain a much better lifestyle there than they could in Europe. A notable case in point was the luxurious and somewhat decadent lifestyle of the second-tier British aristocrats and business people who located to Kenya's so-called Happy Valley. The consequence of the Depression here and elsewhere, however, was that the white settlers used local political power and influence to deny Africans access to land, effectively "proletarianising" them and retaining them as an even cheaper labour force. This situation paralleled that of French Algeria, where during the 1920s and 1930s the powerful body of French *colons* was able to frustrate attempts by local governors to alleviate the exploitation of Arab labour and provide a minimum form of representation for the local population. Settler political movements here were closely associated with right-wing organisations in France, such as the Croix-de-Feu.[17] But, as elsewhere, mounting unrest associated with forced labour and raised taxes during the Depression resulted in the creation of anticolonial movements such as the National Liberation Front and the National Algerian Movement.

Broadly, the effect of colonial policies during the Depression could be seen as the third great blow to Africa's prosperity, following the slave trade and the imposition of taxation on commerce during the earlier depression of the 1870s and 1880s. Africa's living standards were not to revive against the world mean until the beginning of the twenty-first century. Meanwhile, the foundations of the insurgent movements of the late colonial era were laid. Men looking for work spread out of their home villages, relaying dissident political messages. Local Kikuyu resistance to what was effectively forced labour built up in the 1930s; in West Africa, local political associations began to take up issues of economic deprivation. In the Belgian Congo, where colonial companies such as Union Minière had dominated a lucrative export trade in copper, iron ore and palm oil, the collapse of prices resulted in a 70% decline in the mining population. Sporadic insurgencies against heavy taxation and impoverishment broke out, such as the Pende Revolt of 1931. This rocked the colony and a degree of stability was only regained when the Congo became the main source of copper and iron for the Allies after the fall of Malaya to the Japanese in 1942.[18]

In South Africa, a different political conjuncture was reached, and it was white settler labour that moved to the offensive. Economic hardship, particularly the replacement of poor white labour with even cheaper African labour, gave a fillip to the newly unified National Party and the move towards racial exclusion, which culminated in the creation of the apartheid state in the 1960s, had begun. Political racism was emboldened by the Depression in South Africa as it was in Europe and the United States.

GERMANY, LATIN AMERICA AND JAPAN: ECONOMIC CRISIS AND THE DRIFT TO AUTHORITARIANISM

Germany's inflation of 1922–1923 had caused great social unrest and long-term political consequences. It had wiped out much internal debt, but, critically, Germany's war reparations to France and Britain continued to stand. The former Allies refused to countenance any reduction in their level, because these countries were equally bound to repay their wartime loans to the United States. The result, throughout the mid- and late 1920s, was that Germany was locked into a conservative fiscal policy and protectionism that did little to stimulate its economy and created a crisis of unemployment, which had already reached nearly 23% by 1926. Germany's problems accelerated when cheap American credit dried up in 1928 and the Wall Street Crash hit in 1929, damaging what financial confidence remained. Unemployment increased further and the political system was weakened. Heinrich Brüning, the chancellor between 1930 and 1932, was unable to find ways of freeing the economy for growth. He pursued a deflationary policy and worked hard to keep Germany on the gold standard through vigorous import controls even after Britain itself had left it. This was because the 1923 inflation was still a vivid memory for Germans and gold appeared to offer some kind of financial stability. In 1932, Germany defaulted on the reparations it owed and a few months later Britain and France defaulted on their war debts to the United States. But by this point the crisis was so deep that there was little economic gain from these events.

The constitution of the Weimar Republic gave considerable power to the president, who could override the legislature and create a government in times of political deadlock. Now, as Chapter 3 demonstrates, Hitler and the National Socialists began to build a loose and internally contradictory coalition of groups that had been damaged by the financial crisis and Brüning's austerity measures, including land expropriation. These included industrialists who wanted lower taxes, the military which wanted further expenditure, farmers who were suffering from the collapse of prices and overproduction and even some conservative elements of the working class. Hitler's success at the polls in 1932 and again in 1933 stymied Franz von Papen, Brüning's successor. President Hindenburg, who was supported by industrialists and farming interests, judged that Hitler might prove a useful tool against any further lurch to the left provoked by more militant trade unions and asked Hitler to form a government. During the 1920s, German governments had introduced a number of measures, such as rigid exchange controls and mercantilist arrangements for foreign trade, which gave the state considerable power over the economy. Hitler's regime, guided by his finance minister, Hjalmar Schacht, made considerable use of these economic measures, while at the same time slowly reflating the economy.[19]

The Nazis, therefore, created a hybrid socioeconomic regime of a type which later came to be called "state capitalism". This had the great advantage of pleasing industrialists and mercantile interests, which, in contrast to the situation in the USSR, continued to retain autonomy. At the same time, a slow reduction in unemployment from the end of 1934 helped pacify the more privileged members of the working class just at the moment Hitler was crushing his erstwhile Communist enemies and the trades unions.[20] As across much of the world, the onset of rearmament in 1935–1936 also consolidated this process, so that by the outbreak of the Second World War, the German economy was expanding rapidly and full employment had virtually been secured once again. Yet, as rearmament gathered pace after 1936, inflation began to spike upwards once again and Germany's external debt increased. By then it became clear that Hitler had in mind the long-term political goal of European domination, rather than economic growth, and Schacht and the board of the Reichsbank, who urged caution on economic grounds, were dismissed.

Another context in which the Depression contributed to a shift of some governments towards authoritarian government mentioned in Chapter 3 was Latin America.[21] As in several of the European colonial societies, economies here were vulnerable to external shocks because they were heavily dependent on the export of raw materials and cash crops. Again, the impact of the crisis fell very heavily on poor peasant communities and landless labourers. Governments in the region were, however, in a better position than dependent colonial ones because, like Australia, they had a greater degree of autonomy and could move in the direction of rapid import substitution, devalue their currencies or leave the gold standard in a way that India, for instance, could not. In this respect it is instructive that Argentina, a country heavily dependent on trade with the United Kingdom in wheat and beef products and on British capital imports, was in a relatively weaker position. An agreement of 1933 imposed preferential tariffs for British goods on Argentina. The consequent further decline of the standard of living undermined representative government and paved the way for Juan Perón's autocracy after 1946.

Brazil offered a counter-example of greater economic stability, but also fell under autocratic rule. The country was able to control its coffee production and also to begin a programme of local industrial development, especially in textiles. At the same time, the Brazilian currency was allowed to depreciate, giving its exports a further stimulus. The move to a degree of economic autarchy was pushed forward under the rule of the dictator Getúlio Vargas. Vargas was supported by military officers and local smallholders with different interests from the major coffee producers, who supported the older liberal elite. He pioneered a new form of state intervention in the economy, left the gold standard in 1930 and adopted a new policy of import substitution, while at the same time summoning up a tide of Brazilian nationalism.

The situation in Japan, which also lurched further towards authoritarianism in these years, displays some similarities with both Germany and Brazil in terms of the economic impact of the Depression.[22] The massive Tokyo earthquake of 1923 destabilised Japan's finances just as the inflation of the same year had done in Germany. The difference was that, in order to finance rebuilding, Japan was forced to devalue its currency and was unable to rejoin the gold standard as Britain had done in 1925. As a result, Japanese exports, especially exports to the United States, increased dramatically and the country entered a new phase of industrialisation and urbanisation, marred only by inflation and the failure of some of its banks in 1927. This prompted a return to a more orthodox fiscal policy in 1929 and a badly mistimed return to the gold standard in 1930. Determined not to devalue or leave the gold standard, the Inouye government oversaw a massive outflow of Japanese gold and a decline in rice prices, which had reverberations across Asia,

Finally, the government fell and, by 1931, the yen had collapsed by as much as 60% and the country was forced off the gold standard once again. A serious conflict emerged between the interests of the now impoverished peasantry and big business, with the army supporting the peasantry and gradually assuming power within the country's fragmented political system by appealing to the new emperor, Hirohito. Most significantly, the army and peasant colonists found a common interest in aggressive expansionism within Manchuria and later, after 1936, in China proper. The finance ministry, under Takahashi Korekiyo, gradually reflated the economy through reductions of military expenditure. But he was assassinated in 1936 by extreme nationalists. By then, the pre-conditions for the long Second World War in Asia were in place.

The Great Depression is sometimes seen as a crisis of the capitalist world and its colonial dependencies, but the effects on the USSR were significant, if indirect. Lenin's New Economic Policy of 1921 had sought to revive the Soviet Union's economy, making concessions to revived rural entrepreneurship by allowing farmers to sell some of their goods on the market at fixed prices. That system came to an abrupt end in 1929 when the collapse of world wheat prices ruled out the possibility of financing local industrialisation through exports, which had been the aim of the New Economic Policy. As a result, in early 1930, Stalin decided on the wholesale nationalisation of peasant land and its incorporation into huge collectives.[23] The result was the death by murder or starvation of millions of peasant farmers and a collapse of Soviet national income by as much as 20% under the first Five Year Plan, 1928–1932. As much a policy of eradicating potential political rivals as a rational economic device, aspects of the Plan were nevertheless adapted by other socialist and newly independent "third world" governments over the next generation.

THE UNITED STATES AND THE WORLD: A PARADIGM SHIFT?

By empowering four aggressive authoritarian regimes – Germany, the USSR, Japan and Italy – the Depression provided the preconditions for a resurgence of the world crisis. At the same time, the reach of government both in the dictatorships and in the democracies was greatly extended to ward off its worst effects. Whether in the United States with the New Deal or the Soviet Union with the Five Year Plan, or the measures to stimulate housebuilding in Britain, Canada and Australia, a new world of economic planning was fitfully introduced. In 1932–1933, unemployment in the United States was as high as 24% of the total labour force, a figure which was never reached before or afterwards. Franklin Roosevelt's New Deal resulted in a string of interventionist measures by the federal government which would have been unthinkable without the imminent danger of political collapse of the sort that overtook governments in Europe.[24]

Striking at the heart of the problem, Roosevelt instituted measures to bail out banks and to close down those which were impossible to rescue. A three-day bank holiday was announced early in 1933. The Federal Reserve was authorised to issue additional notes should there be a run on the banks when they reopened. Later in the year the Glass–Steagall Act set up a system of federal insurance for bank deposits to try to restore confidence in savers and the market. The Democratic administration introduced bills to support industrial enterprises, get the young off the dole and provide aid to farmers whose prices had collapsed. A notable development was the move in 1935 by the Works Progress Administration to sign up five million people to help in construction projects and local improvement schemes rather than pay out unemployment benefit.[25] Massive developmental projects were instituted, notably by the Tennessee Valley Authority and the building of the Coulee Dam on the Columbia River. Most significant for the future was the Rural Electrification Scheme, which in the longer run allowed families to install refrigerators, vacuum cleaners and water pumps in their homes. Throughout, Roosevelt's "fireside chats" on the radio raised morale and generated a sense of unity.

Economic historians note that Roosevelt was quite committed to fiscal orthodoxy despite these dramatic measures. It is also clear that the effects of 1929 were not really eradicated until the middle of the Second World War. GNP had tumbled from $104 billion in 1929 to $56 billion in 1933, and though Roosevelt's measures provided relief to individuals, it did not reach the pre-Depression level until 1941, even slipping again in a second recession in 1937–1938. Unemployment similarly struggled back to its earlier peak only in 1942. Yet, the size of the federal administration grew markedly and measures reminiscent of European welfare states were put in place, such as the 1935 Social Security Act. Institutions such as the Reconstruction Finance Corporation and the Agricultural Adjustment Administration were active across the country in a form which had never been seen before in a decentralised form of government. This second phase of the modernisation of the United States which had begun after the Civil War was to have a transformative effect on world economics and politics. The New Deal prepared the country for the Second World War and for the consumer boom which occurred after 1945. These were to lay the foundations of American hegemony in the second half of the century.

THE INTERWAR YEARS: HISTORIANS, ECONOMISTS AND THEIR DIFFERENCES

The interwar years, considered in the last three chapters, have received great attention from historians even if not as overwhelming as the range of studies of the First and Second World Wars. Their interpretations have conventionally moved through stages reflecting the political and economic problems of later periods. During the Depression itself and for the generation after 1945, the emphasis lay on the failure of statesmen to guarantee peace after 1919, to avoid the rise of Nazism or to properly understand the nature of the economic slump. This led to a dangerous obsession with the gold standard: "irrational choice theory", as we might call it. Keynes's views on the need to stimulate the world economy during the downturn became standard after the Second World War. In the 1960s and 1970s, neo-Marxist arguments were also in vogue, indicting capital for the crash and the advent of Nazism, though Hobsbawm at least recognised that this was a multi-class phenomenon rather than a plot by business. Ideological arguments between monetarist economists, such as

Milton Friedman, and those who indicted political structures, such as Charles Kindleberger,[26] followed during the 1970s and 1980s as the success of state intervention appeared to be waning. At the beginning of the twenty-first century, the failures of statesmen and finance ministers were once more brought into a renewed debate about Keynesianism and the perfection of the market, a reflection of the world crisis of the 2000s. Economists such as Paul Krugman assailed the views of the now-embattled monetarists, pointing again to the Depression.

These last three chapters try to achieve two things. First, they argue that democracy and representative government were making considerable strides across the world for much of the period, *squadristi*, Brown Shirts and racial discrimination notwithstanding. Even in impoverished colonial territories, anticolonial movements took on an inclusive, proto-democratic form. Secondly, though, there is no doubt that misjudgement by Western leaders exacerbated deep economic inequalities and imbalances across the world, whether these were in the form of a lack of economic protection for local produce, currency manipulation or imbalances in import–export ratios. The damage was particularly severe in dependent colonial territories.

In addition, however, these chapters allude to what might be called the Third Age of Imperialism, following the "imperial meridian" of the period of the French and Napoleonic Wars and the new imperialism of the late nineteenth century. This was an extension of the imperial expansion during and after the First World War. It was reflected in the Japanese assault on China, Italian ambitions in East Africa and the German Reich's determination to build its own "empire" in Eastern Europe. New waves of white settlements in North and East Africa and even the East Indies compounded this further shift. These moves were matched by the desperate attempts of the existing European imperial powers to maintain their empires by force and coercion and by the burgeoning and development of the Soviet empire in its southern and eastern territories during Stalin's consolidation of power. In this sense, small wars such as the confrontation between Italy and Ethiopia, or between the USSR and Japan, or Japan's incursion into Manchuria, announced the coming of the next stage of the world crisis.

[6] THE SECOND WORLD WAR AND ITS CONSEQUENCES

Decentralising the World Crisis Again: Part I

The War in Europe and Asia, 1939–1942: Part II

The Climax of the World Crisis, 1942–1948: Part III

The Small Wars Beneath

The Broader Consequences of the War, Part I: The Political

The Broader Consequences of the War, Part II: The
  Economic

The Broader Consequences of the War, Part III: Social and
  Moral

IN THE light of its centenary, much historical writing was produced in the 2010s dealing with the causes and progress of the First World War, devoted particularly to the slaughter on the Western Front. As Chapter 1 suggests, a major issue was the debate about the culpability of Germany, which continued to be broadly accepted by historians such as Margaret Macmillan, while Christopher Clark and Sean McMeekin[1] presented a polycentric version of the origin of the war which also indicted the Serbs, Russians and the Allied powers for fomenting, or in Clark's case for "sleepwalking" into, the conflict. In a way, this debate replayed some of the issues raised much earlier in the 1960s, when the Oxford historian A. J. P. Taylor had engaged in the more hazardous enterprise of partially exonerating Hitler and Nazi Germany from starting the Second World War.[2] Here the polycentric version has had less purchase. While Germany undoubtedly continued to feel surrounded and hemmed in on both fronts, Hitler's ambition of creating a new empire in Eastern Europe cannot be ignored.[3] In general then, the more recent debate about the Second World

Remaking the Modern World 1900–2015: Global Connections and Comparisons, First Edition. C. A. Bayly.
© 2018 John Wiley & Sons Ltd. Published 2018 by John Wiley & Sons Ltd.

War has focussed on other issues than its origin, particularly the degree to which Roosevelt really wanted the United States to enter the war, Richard Overy's contention that the British began the bombing of civilian targets as early as 1940,[4] the military conduct of the war[5] or a discussion of how far the later mass destruction of German cities was a credible military tactic rather than a simple act of revenge.

This chapter accepts the contention that the German and Japanese governments were largely responsible for the coming of war, whatever the underlying fears and ambitions which provoked them. It seeks, however, once again to reconceptualise the war temporally, geographically and in terms of its effects on social and ideological forms across the world. In the case of time and geography, one cannot dissent from the view that the climax of the struggle was the epochal conflict between 1942 and 1945 on the Eastern Front between Germany, the USSR and their proxies. This was certainly one of the three most destructive and bloody encounters in history, killing perhaps 25 million soldiers and civilians. It dwarfed even the mortality of the Taiping Rebellion in nineteenth-century China, while exceeding fatalities in the First World War itself. In fact, as a global event, the Second World War touched more regions directly than the First World War and created a consciousness of fear and ideological conflict which was even more pervasive.[6] Above all, the war was coexistent with the Holocaust, the mass murder of European Jews by the Nazis, an event of such enormity that it forms the central act of Chapter 14. The scale of devastation and loss of life was one condition which made conceivable the use of atomic weapons against Japan in 1945.

Still, it is helpful to consider a decentralised view of the Second World War, seeing it in Churchill's terms again as the climax of a second, and yet broader, world crisis which stretched from about 1935 to 1948 and continued to incite small wars well after that date. The conflict between heavily armed and increasingly nationalistic powers began with the Italian invasion of Ethiopia (Abyssinia) in 1935, the expansion of Japan's war against China from the Manchurian borderlands to mainland China in 1936 and the Spanish Civil War. The next phase of this second world crisis saw the war between Germany, France and Britain with the occupation of France in 1940. The third phase, beginning in late 1941 and 1942, was dominated by the German invasion of the USSR, the central event of the period, Japanese attacks in the Pacific and Southeast Asia and the entry of the United States into the war. The final phase saw the dropping of the atomic bomb, the American conquest of Japan and the Anglo-American reconquest of Southeast Asia. It also encompassed the Soviet expansion into Eastern Europe, the Greek civil war, the standoff over Berlin and the outbreak of small wars throughout Asia and the Middle East.

Examining the consequences of the world crisis, this chapter emphasises the significance of the technical developments of the period: the harnessing of atomic power; the birth of the computer, the jet aircraft and the missile; and medical discoveries. It also stresses the importance of the moral changes that occurred, such as the final expansion of the mass electorate and the empowerment of women, the completion of the welfare state and government intervention in Europe. Other major consequences included the defeat, or at least temporary discrediting, of the fascist right by Communism and socialism and the emergence of internationalism in the form of the United Nations. Finally, the chapter stresses the profound moral questioning and interrogation of the human psyche which accompanied the vision of atrocity, mass murder and the potential for the very destruction of the human race itself.

DECENTRALISING THE WORLD CRISIS AGAIN: PART I

The events of 1935–1936 which inaugurated the period may now seem to be a premonition of novel forms of atrocity marked by the large-scale killing by the Japanese army in Nanjing (Nanking) and the bombing of Ethiopian civilians by Italian aircraft. Yet, in some respects these events also represented unfinished business of the First World War or even of the "new imperialism" of the late nineteenth century: a third imperialist surge, in effect. Italy before the fascist takeover was a frustrated great power which had been unable to benefit from its entry into the war in the Adriatic and felt at a disadvantage in North Africa, surrounded in its Libyan colony by British and French influence. Its attack on Ethiopia was an attempt to flex its muscles as an imperial power, to put into action the ideology of martial masculinity promoted by D'Annunzio and then taken to new heights by Mussolini himself.[7] The Nazi ascent in Germany seemed to indicate to Italians that the old democracies were on the wane and it was only a matter of time before their empires would dissolve under the pressure of nationalism and economic sclerosis.

Ethiopia, considered only half-civilised, was a soft target for this final stage of imperialism, but it was also an old target because in 1895 the Italians had failed in their attempt to conquer the Ethiopian kingdom of Menelik, suffering huge losses, which had brought down the Italian government of the time. Yet, by 1935, Italian technical superiority was overwhelming, and this involved the use of modern bombers and even mustard gas. A British officer wrote in a somewhat complacent manner, "Italy has the unique advantage of having first hand experience of the use in war of modern weapons and up-to-date equipment."[8] Pietro Badoglio, a close adviser of Mussolini, completed his "march of the will", Emperor Haile Selassie fled into British protection and, by the end of 1936, Mussolini could claim, "At last Italy has her empire!" amidst triumphant celebrations in Rome. World opinion was divided, with the United States and the League of Nations condemning the war. But Britain and France, working to shore up their respective imperial holdings through the 1935 Hoare–Laval Pact, were ambivalent and silent.[9] Nevertheless, fear of a future war began to grow. The British journalist Collin Brooks wrote, "Behind the Italian trouble there looms trouble with Germany and trouble in the Near East."[10]

One power which definitely approved of the Italian invasion of Ethiopia was the Japanese leadership, which was forwarding its own imperial ambitions to the concern of the League and the United States. The Japanese emperor congratulated Mussolini on his victory. Within a year, Japan's own forces had invaded and occupied the Chinese seaboard from their base in the client state of

Manchukuo (Manchuria) and were pushing up the Yangtze River in pursuit of the fleeing armies of Chiang Kai-shek.[11] Japan's empire in Asia had expanded since the beginning of the century following its occupation of Korea and Taiwan. Yet, Japan's increasingly militarised leadership believed that the country, like Italy, had not received sufficient credit for joining the Allied side in 1916. As noted in the last chapter, the Depression had made matters worse as Western countries had imposed trade restrictions which damaged Japan's nascent industries. A stronger hold on China would allow it to use its reserves of raw materials and minerals as well as support further colonists from the poorer areas of central Japan as Manchukuo had done. Yet, these broad aims were empowered by a particular type of localised imperial expansion. The Kwantung Army had become a law unto itself in China because of the weakness of the Japanese cabinet system. So, too, expatriate Japanese commercial interests played their part in pushing for an aggressive expansionist policy in China. Particularly significant here was the South Manchuria Railway Company, which linked together numerous small Japanese enterprises in the region. These Japanese colonial ambitions were given new urgency by the rise of Chiang Kai-shek's Guomindang, which had begun to corral local Chinese warlords into a nascent state system along the Manchurian border. Chiang was attempting not only to shield himself against Japanese aggression but also to reinforce the north against the increasingly powerful Communist forces which had regrouped after the Long March of 1933–1935.[12] Yet, the Japanese, too, feared Communism. Seeking to bend China to their will, one diplomat demanded, "China and Japan must jointly devise effective measures to prevent the spread of Communism."[13]

Though Japan had been the historic beneficiary of Chinese culture, the post-Meiji generation considered China a "backward nation" and had promoted an indigenous concept of racial hierarchy which applauded their own modernity and military prowess. The Japanese leadership was also bound together by service of Emperor Hirohito, who was much more enamoured of military adventures than had been his more cautious predecessors. As in the case of Mussolini's Ethiopian conquest and the later Nazi surge into the USSR, the Japanese invasion between 1936 and 1940 was openly described as an "annihilation campaign". Enemy soldiers and civilians were summarily executed and mustard gas and other chemical weapons were deployed. The last stage of the new imperialism of the nineteenth century was again reinforced by the racist militarism of the twentieth.

Japanese leaders had been distantly influenced by the European doctrines of rapid military deployment, or blitzkrieg, which had been developed to avoid a repeat of the murderous stasis of the First World War. Their thrust into southern China and the Yangtze valley was also counselled by fear of the Soviet Union, which had long been seen as a menace in the borderlands of northeast Asia.[14] Indeed, Japan and the Soviet Union were to be involved in a sharp and inconclusive war in 1940, as the world crisis deepened. The Japanese, however, were unable finally to defeat Chiang, whose forces retreated towards the southeast inland city of Chongqing (Chungking), where they entrenched themselves for the next eight years. The shape of the wider conflict was influenced by the decision of the British and the Americans to help to re-equip Chinese forces in order to deny total victory to the Japanese.

The first stage of the resurgent world crisis, then, centred on North Africa and East Asia, but there were other contemporary wars and revolts which were also to prove of long-term significance. The revolt of the Islamist tribal leader the Faqir of Ipi in 1935–1936 in Afghanistan and on the Northwest frontier of British India was long represented by historians as an antiquated anomaly pointing back to the colonial adventures in the region of 1839, 1879 and 1919. After the Soviet invasion of Afghanistan in 1980 and the rise of the Taliban, however, this militant alliance between ethnic patriarchy and Islamist ideology seemed like a premonition of a wholly modern style of ideological conflict which was to shake the world after 2001.[15] Yet, even in the context of the 1930s and early 1940s, the diversion of thousands of British and British Indian troops to the Northwest Frontier, as Japanese ambitions were unfolding on the borders of British Southeast Asia, was to be of great strategic importance.

A further minor colonial war of long-term significance took place in Palestine and spilled over into French Syria and beyond. This was the Arab revolt of 1936, directed not only against rigid British land-revenue management in Palestine but also against the influx of Jewish settlers, as Nazi anti-Semitism became more virulent in Germany and Austria. Between 1926 and 1932, the Jewish percentage of the population of Palestine grew from 18% to nearly 30% and in 1935 alone 62,000 Jewish refugees arrived.[16] The Arab revolt against this influx transformed Palestine. Up to 10% of the Arab population was killed, wounded or exiled as national strikes and the demand for independence turned to violence.[17] The resistance hardened Arab anticolonialism across the region and prepared the way for Egyptian, Syrian and Iraqi leaders to make links with Germany. Among them the Mufti of Jerusalem, Haj Amin al-Husseini, was a much more central figure than the Faqir of Ipi. Ironically, it was the British who had created the office of mufti with an oversight of all Palestine and a role in the Sharia Council. But the failure of the revolt and the mufti's flight, first to Syria and then to Berlin, underscored the transnational significance of the conflict. The need to protect their families and their settlements against Arab insurgents also gave an ideological advantage to radical Zionists and determined their quiet decision to arm both against the British authorities and against the Palestinian Arabs. Finally, the British deployed nearly 70,000 troops and armed police in Palestine alone to confront the rebellion. As in Afghanistan, events in Palestine distracted the British government from the Nazi menace in Europe, but they also inaugurated a form of terminal colonial repression which was later seen in Malaya and Kenya.

A final element in the "gathering storm" – Churchill's words again – and one which has received great attention because of the manner in which it reflected the ideological polarisation of Europe, was the Spanish Civil War 1936–1940.[18] Francisco Franco had managed to draw in military support from Italy and Germany in his attempt to overthrow the socialist government in Madrid, which had come to power in 1930 at the height of the Depression. The left, fragmented between democratic socialists, anarchists and Stalinists, received brave if amateur aid from the International Brigade of Socialists, including figures such as the British writer George Orwell. One aspect of the civil war which reinforces the arguments of this section was the fact that the triumphant fascist military forces were drawn in large numbers from Spanish colonial territories in North Africa, the so-called Army of Africa.[19] It was led by many officers with experience of the barbarity of the suppression of the Rif Revolt of 1921–1926. The mechanised warfare so vividly memorialised by Pablo Picasso in his painting *Guernica* merged once again with the last stages of imperialism in Africa. The conflicts of the supposed "periphery" once again invaded the centre. Hannah Arendt noted the link between colonial violence and the new barbarism of war and extermination in the "Dark Continent" of Europe.[20] Yet, the war, as Orwell later said, "was settled in London, Paris, Rome, Berlin – at any rate not in Spain."

THE WAR IN EUROPE AND ASIA, 1939–1942: PART II

The next stage of the second world crisis which has preoccupied most historians was much more like the long litany of European wars over the "balance of power" stretching from the late eighteenth into the nineteenth and twentieth centuries.[21] The main difference was not in its origins but in the level of violence and killing it entailed. In this phase, the enmities between France and Germany, reinforced by the peace treaties of 1919, were the underlying cause. Hitler's reoccupation of the previously neutralised Rhineland in 1936 signalled the collapse of international agreements. Britain and France attempted to work through the League of Nations and failed to achieve any concessions, so further damaging these international accords. Then Germany and Austria began to reassert their domination over Eastern and Central Europe, always a periphery of raw materials and peasant production for them. The German invasion of Austria and the subsequent union of 1938 represented an attempt by the Nazis to delineate the outer frontiers of the German national state, or indeed national empire, just as the persecution of the Jews represented the internal dimension of ethnic cleansing.[22]

Later in 1938, Hitler demanded that Czechoslovakia hand over to Germany the ethnic German populations of the so-called Sudetenland. Neither Britain nor France, terrified of the onset of a new world war, was able to prevent this violent destruction of the 1919 settlement. Neville Chamberlain, the British prime minister, was central in pressuring the Czechs to grant all Hitler's demands under the Munich Agreement of late 1938. It should be remembered, however, that at this time British opinion itself was divided between a left wing naively enamoured of Stalin and a right wing exemplified by Oswald Mosley's Black Shirts which saw in Hitler a powerful statesman, enemy of Communism and supporter of European empires. Arguments about fear of war and political miscalculation in Britain should not be allowed to blind historians to the widespread admiration of the Nazis among the upper classes as well as anti-

Semitic lower middle classes which was even reflected in major newspapers of the day, such as the *Daily Mail.* [23]

Hitler's attack on Poland in the summer of 1939, the event which precipitated the next phase of the world crisis, was, however, of a different order from these earlier and successful attempts to build a new *völkische Reich*. In the first place, the German–Soviet Pact of August 1939 had given Hitler an even freer hand. Stalin was aware how unprepared were his troops. Germany had poured huge sums of money into modernising its forces, building a powerful navy and air force since 1933. Indeed, this expenditure, which ended Germany's depression even more effectively than Roosevelt's New Deal for the United States or Stanley Baldwin's housebuilding programme for Great Britain, was a guarantor of Hitler's popularity in his own country. The ostensible reason for Nazi hostility to Poland was, once again, its control over German populations on the frontiers, which had been ceded to it by the treaties of 1919. But here, one also begins to glimpse a wider aim. Shut out of African empire after 1918, the Nazis intended to build a German empire in Central and Eastern Europe, one that was ultimately intended to stretch into the Soviet Union itself. Nazi policymakers saw the Poles and other "non-Aryans" as slave peoples, comparable to the indigenous inhabitants of the British, French and Dutch empires. They were sources of labour for farms, providing food for the greater German nation or raw materials for its industries. Only in this way could Germany match the growing power of the United States and overawe the declining power of the colonial empires of Western Europe.

This final blow to the balance of power in Europe forced the British and French governments to go to war against Germany with consequences that are only too well known. The German occupation of France and the Low Countries in 1940 led to the emergence of a conservative Catholic regime under Marshal Philippe Pétain in its southern regions, a further reminder that conservative neo-fascism had much support across Europe, as in Britain, in the later 1930s. The British were pushed back into their own islands, which were ferociously defended by the Royal Air Force. The British were also successful in fighting off Mussolini's attempts, as an ally of Hitler, to dominate the whole of North Africa. Here British power in the colonial periphery, in this case in Egypt, the Sudan and Iraq, was first manifested. Yet, for the first four years of the war, Britain remained consistently on the back foot. Attempts to aid the Scandinavian countries suffering Nazi invasion had failed. General Erwin Rommel then drove British forces back to the borders of Egypt in a manner that had eluded Mussolini's troops. American aid to Britain was invaluable but spasmodic and German submarines constantly threatened food and supplies moving across the Atlantic. What remained of the Allied alliance was no more successful in the Far East, which was soon to become the scene of a fateful move by Japanese military leaders. The Japanese had occupied French Indochina in support of the German invasion of France. They now attempted to finish the war with Chiang Kai-shek in Chongqing, whose forces were now supplied by the United States and Britain across the border from Lashio in British Burma.

It was at this point, in June 1941, that Germany invaded the Soviet Union and dramatically changed the whole nature of the war and the century's history.

Hitler appears to have been unconvinced of Stalin's fragile neutrality in the case of a long war with Britain, supported by US lend-lease. He believed he needed direct access to the industrial wealth of Russia and the oil of the Caucasus. This fitted well with the Nazi desire to create a huge empire in Eastern Europe. The evident unpreparedness of Soviet armed forces, demonstrated by its long failure against Finnish resistance, and the collapse of the apparently modern French army, encouraged Hitler's sense of vainglory. The war on the Eastern Front became, however, the bloodiest struggle in history, marked by massacres of civilians on both sides and the annihilation of much of the continent's Jewish population. During the German siege of Leningrad alone, a third of its population died of starvation.[24]

A similarly disastrous throw of the dice was made just six months later when the Japanese invaded the Southeast Asian empires of Britain, France and the Netherlands and attempted to pre-empt an American intervention by attacking the US fleet at Pearl Harbor. The immediate rationale seems to have been the perception that a more dangerous enemy, the USSR, was now wholly consumed with the war in the West. France and Holland were occupied by German forces and Britain was fighting for survival. Defeat of the British and the deflection of the American threat would also speed the final destruction of Chiang Kai-shek.

This massive miscalculation, which caused the United States to declare war on Japan, perhaps inevitably drew Germany in on Japan's side. Up to this point, the full participation of the United States in a war against the Axis powers was by no means inevitable.[25] In fact, even Roosevelt's lend-lease programme of 1940 was inaugurated in the face of considerable hostility across America. Isolationism amongst the middle class and business establishment was partly fuelled by the sense that Nazi Germany represented a strong bulwark against the even more dangerous force of Soviet Communism. The large German community, particularly strong in Chicago and the Midwest generally, opposed another war, as did the anti-British Irish Catholics of the East Coast. Well-placed Americans declared in 1939 that the coming war would be another "sordid imperialist adventure". Anti-Semitism was not negligible in the United States either. Indeed, Henry Ford himself had published a diatribe against Jews. Finally, German business interests retained considerable clout amongst major US firms because the United States was a large market for German goods and US expertise was important for German industry. To this extent, the Japanese made a critical contribution to the outcome of the war, though not the one they desired.

There is, however, a broader point to be made here. Japan was not simply absurdly optimistic about its capacity to fight the United States. It also rightly judged that it retained considerable support across Asia, even following its assault on China. After Japan's defeat in 1945, most historians dismissed Japan's "Pan-Asianism" as a fanatical self-delusion, merely blinding them to the hostility that their militarism stirred up in the minds of other Asians. While this is certainly true of the majority of Chinese outside Taiwan, the Japanese actually had good reason to feel that they would be well received by many Asian peoples. Aung San, the Burmese nationalist leader, had made early contact with

Japanese agents based in this British colony.[26] Radical Indonesian leaders had also forged secret liaisons with the Japanese. In India, the Japanese had long been admired as the first Asian nation to defeat a European power (Russia) and Indian radicals had found a base in Tokyo.

Just as historians have tended to underplay the very widespread fascist sympathy within European nations beyond Germany and Italy and also in the United States, so the post-war attempts to normalise Japan's history had the effect of marginalising the importance of Pan-Asian ideology. Japan's widespread support was, in fact, to be critical in the formation of Japanese client regimes in Burma, Malaya, the Philippines and Indonesia, and these worked well for Japan's empire until the Allies reinvaded their territories. Subhas Chandra Bose's Indian National Army, which fought alongside the Japanese, is another reminder of the fact that many Asians saw Japan as a less oppressive power than the Europeans – at least until the last year of the war.

Initially, then, the Japanese might have applauded their own courageous decisions. The British fleet in Asian waters was sunk; Singapore followed by Rangoon fell to the invaders. The majority of US forces had evacuated the Philippines, moving back towards Australia and leaving the remainder to be captured and subjected to the notorious Bataan "death march". By the middle of 1942, Japanese armies were poised on the borders of India, now engulfed by Gandhi's Quit India movement, which showed open sympathy with them. In the south, they had conquered most of the Dutch empire in Indonesia and seemed to be a growing threat to Australia itself. In the Pacific, they had apparently pushed the Americans back to Hawaii. As is well known, this was in the main an illusion. Japan's ally, Germany, had already been put on the defensive by a Soviet counter-attack shortly after Pearl Harbor. The United States had quickly regained the initiative at sea, though its forces had been driven from the Philippines. Soon the British had stalled the Japanese army in the Assam hills and fought back against Rommel at El Alamein on the borders of Egypt.

There was also a more fundamental reason for the beginnings of the defeat of Germany, Italy and Japan. As in the First World War, all the Allied nations had deep resource bases. The Americans dominated half the globe and both the Atlantic and Pacific oceans. With a large population and huge oil, mineral and industrial resources, they could never have been defeated. The perception of their political weakness was an illusion fostered by the apparent power of neutralism in the country. Equally, the Soviet Union had a deep hinterland of population and resources. Even when the Germans dominated and decimated much of western Russia, Stalin could move resources back towards Siberia and draw on his eastern populations for manpower. Britain, of course, was a small island, but its empire provided an equivalent type of deep resource base. The British dominions supported the "mother country" out of loyalty, but also shrewd self-interest. A pre-war Australian publication observed, "Besides involvement in the politics of the Old World, another danger threatens: the awakening of the Pacific in the struggle for new markets and the last of the empty lands."[27]

Nearly two million Indian soldiers fought in the British armies, not only against the Japanese but in North Africa and Europe. By the end of the war, well-trained African troops from the Gold Coast and Kenya under British command had joined the fighting in Burma. As the German submarine threat decreased by the middle of 1943, American and British ships could support the British homeland population. Supplies from Australasia continued to feed the embattled population. Even though it was defeated in Europe, the French government in exile could draw on resources from Indochina and West Africa. Germany, of course, dominated much of Europe in the early stages of the war, but later, as the USSR moved to the offensive and as Italy was reconquered by the Allies, its resources were gradually cut back and then systematically destroyed. One of the problematic features of historical teaching and research was its long-sustained division between "European", "imperial" and "American" history. It is not possible to understand the outcome of the First World War without taking account of empire and the wider world. That is even truer of the Second World War.

THE CLIMAX OF THE WORLD CRISIS, 1942–1948: PART III

The narrative of the last stages of the Second World War is well known beyond academia, not least because of the plethora of dramatic Hollywood movies and constantly recycled television programmes.[28] As a result of the caution of Churchill's government about the invasion of Europe from the north, the Allies first landed in Sicily and fought their way with great difficulty up the Italian peninsula, delayed with large casualties at Monte Cassino south of Rome. In June 1944, after the Americans had built up their forces in England, a huge amphibious landing took place in Normandy, deceiving the Germans, who had believed that the assault would be further east. Slowly, the Allies reconquered France supported by Charles de Gaulle, leader of French troops from the colonies that had avoided occupation and the few who had joined him in Britain in 1940. The Allies finally entered Paris in September, signalling the last stage of the war. Over the autumn and winter of 1944, British, American, Polish and French troops pushed northeast against the German defences, held up once again by fierce German resistance in the Ardennes. By the beginning of 1945, with many German cities reduced to rubble by continuous Allied bombing, culminating in the destruction of Dresden and tens of thousands of its citizens, the Allies stood on the threshold of Germany itself.[29]

Meanwhile in Eastern Europe, the Armageddon of Soviet–Nazi conflict had taken place. As early as December 1941 – ironically, only two days after the Japanese attack on Pearl Harbor – the Soviet army launched a massive counter-attack against the hitherto victorious Germans near Leningrad. Over the next year, they pushed back against their enemies and gradually destroyed them after the unparalleled standoff at Stalingrad.[30] In the following year, the reinvigorated Soviet Army smashed the German tank divisions at the Battle of Kursk in the Ukraine in July 1943, finally depriving the Nazis of access to the region's oil and food resources. Thereafter, a fight to the death occurred with the Soviet army pushing into Poland and eastern Germany, ruthlessly killing its enemies, raping German women and taking revenge for the terrible atrocities its own citizens had suffered over the previous three years. Finally, as US and Allied troops moved into western Germany and the Russians approached Berlin from the east, Hitler and his lieutenants committed suicide or fled. The world war in Europe was over, though small wars were to flourish.

As the victorious Soviet armies pushed into Eastern Europe and Germany, they rapidly destroyed all non-Communist opposition parties and military forces across Poland, Czechoslovakia, Hungary and eastern Germany.[31] But under the Yalta and later Potsdam agreements of February and July 1945 between the Allies, not only was Germany to be divided into four occupation zones but Britain, France, the United States and the USSR were all assigned sectors of Berlin.[32] Stalin, however, was determined to drive the Western allies from the city and initiated what was effectively a siege of Berlin in June 1948. Harry Truman, the then US president, stood firm and supplied the city with supplies through the so-called Berlin Airlift for nearly a year. This standoff, combined with fear of the expanding technology of nuclear armaments, gave rise to what became known as the Cold War, which is discussed in the following two chapters. While the Soviet bloc and America and its European allies came perilously close to war in 1962 during the Cuban Missile Crisis, historians agree that fear of nuclear war and the relative political homogeneity imposed on both the Western democracies and the Soviet bloc prevented both major and many minor wars in Europe until the Soviet Union was dissolved in 1991.

The end of the war in Asia has received almost as much attention in books and on screen as the end of the war in Europe.[33] The American fleet's recovery after Pearl Harbor, the seaborne campaign against the Japanese culminating in the Battle of Leyte Gulf of October 1944, with General MacArthur's return to the Philippines and the epic struggle at Guadalcanal have all been replayed again and again. Less well remembered is the long struggle in Southeast Asia with General Stilwell's support for Chiang Kai-shek, but also the reinvigoration of British military ambition in Assam and Burma as a British Indian army and many British and African troops fought a long and arduous war through mountain and jungle under the command of General William Slim.[34] In southern China, the final conflict between Japanese troops and those of Chiang Kai-shek at Changsha in Hunan during May 1944 opened the way for Mao and the Communists. But the depleted Japanese armies showed every sign of fighting to the end. They massacred perhaps 100,000 people in Manila in February 1945 and held out stubbornly against Allied forces in Burma.

By mid-1945, however, the Allies had reconquered Burma and were pushing into Malaya when the war was dramatically ended by the dropping of the atomic bombs on Hiroshima and Nagasaki. Emperor Hirohito announced his surrender: "Should we continue to fight it would not only result in the ultimate collapse and total obliteration of the Japanese nation, but also it would lead to the total extinction of human civilisation."[35] The Americans occupied a defeated Japan while the last stage of the war between resurgent Communist forces and the Guomindang raged between 1945 and 1948 as Mao's troops took over territories formerly dominated by the Japanese. An uneasy peace descended on East Asia as it had over Europe. The Korean War of 1950–1953 and the Indochina wars of 1950–1975 make it clear that there was another and different "cold war" in Asia. This was the consequence of the merging of a global ideological struggle with the problems of decolonisation and nation-building.[36] The conflict indeed "turned hot" on several occasions and left a legacy up to the time of confrontation between North and South Korea in 2013. Yet none of these conflicts, either in Europe or Asia, escalated in the way that the crises of 1914 and 1938–1939 had done.

THE SMALL WARS BENEATH

At a level beneath these world-changing events, other small wars, political conflicts and accommodations were taking place from 1942 to 1948. These also profoundly shaped the emerging postcolonial world and the coming Cold War and reflected the emergence of new forms of nationality and cultural cohesion. The analysis of these events is taken forward in the next chapter, but here we need to trace these conflicts from their origins during the war itself. In Europe, the Allied intervention in southern France, Italy and Greece suppressed local conflict and marginalised insurgent Communist parties. But three further examples make the case well. In Yugoslavia, a stronger Communist resistance to the Nazi invasion emerged in the small towns and countryside. It benefited from limited quantities of Allied supplies moving across the Mediterranean and the insurgents' ability to retire into the mountains when under attack. Tito, an able guerrilla fighter, emerged as its leader.[37] He received relatively little aid from the USSR and was distant from Stalin's forces that were pushing into Poland and eastern Germany. Tito had shown an early propensity to pursue his own course independent of Stalin's ambitions. In 1944, William Deakin, later Warden of St Antony's College, Oxford, was parachuted into Yugoslavia to meet Tito on Churchill's orders. British and American support and later their special forces followed this contact. After the end of the war, Yugoslavia's Communist regime remained more independent of the newly formed Communist bloc than most of its other states, maintaining diplomatic links with the West across the "Iron Curtain". Yugoslavia held together for another generation, but even before 1945 tensions had emerged between different linguistic and ethnic groups on the former southeast frontier of the Austro-Hungarian Empire.

In what had been British Burma, a distantly comparable situation developed. Aung San, a young leader of Burmese resistance to British colonial rule, had contacted the Japanese as early as 1939 and fought alongside the Japanese. But by 1944, the increasingly harsh nature of Japanese rule turned the Burmese liberation forces against the Japanese and they staged a revolt in early 1945 just as British forces under Slim were pushing into northern Burma from Assam.[38] When the British governor tried to return to the old form of colonial rule in 1946, Aung San's forces were in control of most of the country and the overall

British commander, Lord Louis Mountbatten, prudently decided to grant greater autonomy to the Burmese. By 1948, the British Labour government had given Burma full independence. But, as in the case of Yugoslavia and other states drawn into the war, ethnic and linguistic tensions rapidly fragmented into a series of small wars between the central government and the Karen, Kachin and Shan ethnic groups. These conflicts continued into the following century and were paralleled by Buddhist–Muslim and Burmese–Indian confrontations.

A further example, also from Southeast Asia, concerns Indochina, and this also had great significance for the future. The Indochinese Communist movement had emerged in the 1930s to fight French colonial rule. Its leader, Ho Chi Minh, returning from France, the USSR and China, moved to the remote countryside in 1941 to oppose the Japanese invaders, renaming his movement the Viet Minh and distancing it from association with both the Soviet and Chinese Communist parties.[39] The situation differed from the other cases mentioned because the French Vichy regime in the region became an ally of the Japanese. So, late in the war, Ho received aid from the United States and the British. As the Japanese regime collapsed in August 1945, Ho, sensing "the acceleration of history", proclaimed Vietnamese independence in the great square in front of the French opera house in Hanoi with a speech which was reminiscent of the American Declaration of Independence, electrifying his people and later generations of revolutionaries across the world.

Neither the Chinese nationalists, who occupied part of North Vietnam (as it was to become) nor the British, who, under General Douglas Gracey, occupied the south, nor, above all, the returning French under Admiral Thierry d'Argenlieu recognised this independence. After complex political machinations, in 1946, the French bombed Communist positions in Haiphong and drove the Viet Minh back into the rural northwest. It was from here in the early 1950s that Ho was to fight back, win the Battle of Dien Bien Phu and ultimately defeat the Western client state in the south and its US supporters. Significantly, and in parallel with Yugoslavia's alienation from Moscow, the Viet Minh remained suspicious of both the Chinese nationalists and also the Chinese Communists. This stance reflected historic fears of domination by their northern neighbour.

A similar pattern of armed national groupings or ideological movements, emerging in the latter stages of the war to challenge Japanese and German forces and then carrying the fight to the weakened colonial powers and central governments, was seen across much of Eurasia and North Africa. The Maoist challenge to Chiang Kai-shek's government was a case in point; the Indo-Pakistan war of 1948 over Kashmir saw armed groupings of Pakhtuns (Pathans), a traditional source of British military labour, taking a major part. Vietnam's Communist movement and Philippine and Indonesian radicals also took the war to the Japanese and then mobilised against the colonial powers as they tried to reassert their control. War spread weapons and aspirations, working at different levels of social power to fundamentally change the world order over these years. Quite apart from mass destruction by bombing, the global conflict had also demonstrated that guerrilla tactics supported by powerful ethnic or political ideologies could defeat and fragment major states, a lesson for revolutionaries over the next 70 years.

THE BROADER CONSEQUENCES OF THE WAR, PART I: THE POLITICAL

The following sections consider the effects of the Second World War on the politics, economies, societies and particularly the mentalities of the world's peoples. Perhaps the most obvious change was the worldwide defeat of far-right politics and the abeyance, or at least muffling and dispersion, of extremist nationalism for a generation or more. Only in Spain, Portugal and parts of Latin America did fascist parties survive the war, because these regions had played only a limited role in the conflict. While it is true that the zealots of Action Française were to play a part in the fall of the French Fourth Republic, liberal, democratic and socialist forms of government generally dominated the non-Communist bloc. These governments were, however, forced to intervene directly in their economies, extending a policy inaugurated during the Depression.[40] In Britain and much of Western Europe, wartime mobilisation, control of resources and movement of population were necessarily extended into the post-war period as governments attempted to feed their people, rebuild devastated cities and provide healthcare. The British Labour government of 1945–1951, for instance, built up the National Health Service, which was a continuation of various forms of wartime health provision and national insurance. In Germany, even conservative politicians, such as Konrad Adenauer, or his Christian Democracy coevals in Italy, were constrained to implement various forms of state interventionism simply to repair the massive devastation of war and re-educate their traumatised populations.[41]

Similar conditions obtained over much of the English-speaking world even when conservative governments were in power. In Australia, the post-war government of Sir Robert Menzies continued state provision which had been initiated during the Depression and the war, as the country struggled to resettle its very high proportion of returned military personnel. The need for state intervention was even clearer in newly independent governments. As India moved towards freedom from 1945 to 1948, the state preserved and extended the considerably greater range which it had achieved during the war when the mobilisation of men and resources reached new levels. Nehru's government from 1947 to 1964 is often regarded as socialist. India's new government certainly adapted aspects of the Soviet development model, but its form reflected wartime exigencies and was constrained by a democratic constitution and a free press. In Japan itself, the occupying US authorities under General MacArthur pursued a policy of strong state interventionism out of necessity, whatever their private political beliefs. A new democratic constitution was imposed. The emperor was turned into a constitutional monarch and agreed to foreswear his supposed divinity in order to foster stability.[42]

Perhaps the only deviation from this pattern of the victory of the liberal left was in the United States itself. Here, Roosevelt's New Deal policies had continued during the years of war and the Truman government worked hard to resettle, educate and provide for the families of returning soldiers. But two developments held back what in other circumstances might have been regarded as a form of American socialism. The first was the hectic growth of the non-state, capitalist economy which had occurred during the war as the country pulled out of the Depression and became the world's manufacturing hub. Swords became ploughshares, as tank and armament production was transformed into the manufacture of cars, radios and refrigerators. Private money, not government support, funded most of this massive development and it was the recovering Republican Party of capitalism, anti-statism and conservatism which ultimately benefited politically.

The second development was the growing fear of Communism, which infected the United States as the war ended and Stalin's USSR, now armed with atomic weapons, came to dominate Eastern Europe.[43] At the end of the war, radical "New Dealers", some with socialist leanings, seemed well positioned in Washington. But spy scandals such as the Alger Hiss case, when American atomic know-how was leaked to Moscow, and, later, the Korean War and the apparent triumph of Communism in Asia radically changed the political tone. Soon Senator Joseph McCarthy's pogrom against leftists and President Dwight Eisenhower's withdrawal from some aspects of state interventionism consolidated the return of the right. Even in Europe, the gradual recovery from wartime economic destruction and new technical developments saw a slow revival of the right, but state provision for health and pensions remained in place to the extent that US Republicans continued to regard Europe as "socialist". It was only well into the 1990s that radical nationalist and racialist parties re-emerged across the European continent. This was at least one long-term effect of the Second World War.

In areas only indirectly involved in the war, as in Latin America or Iberia, the left made less headway despite this broad triumph of democratic socialism. The Middle East also presents another more complex picture over these years. The wartime mobilisation of resources and associated urbanisation had weakened the old upper-class circles of moderate nationalists represented, for instance, by the Wafd in Egypt. A new younger generation of more radical nationalists emerged in the form of Gamal Abdel Nasser's supporters in Egypt and the Ba'ath parties in Iraq and Syria. The weakness of Britain and France and the collapse of Italy during the war resulted in a hard-edged, anticolonial drive which had begun even before 1945. But these young authoritarians were constrained to tread an uneasy path between socialist developmental planning with distant admiration of the USSR and their own conservative Muslim societies. In Egypt, the Muslim Brotherhood and elsewhere other Islamising parties had emerged in the 1920s as foes of colonialism and Westernisation. The military authoritarians and one-party leaders of the Middle East during the immediate post-war era were forced to take them into account, sometimes parleying with them, sometimes imprisoning them, as the British and French had done earlier. Between 1948 and 1952, British influence in Egypt and Syria greatly weakened. French control in Syria–Lebanon had been destroyed during the war, but the continuing grip of Paris on Algeria, with its three million French colonists, was a persistent source of both secular and religious radicalism in northwest Africa.

The widespread collapse of the right across the world, or at least its temporary restriction, was accompanied, as has been suggested, by the rapid decline of European colonialism. This was a product of the defeat of the colonial powers themselves across the whole of East and Southeast Asia and the Middle East, despite their late resurgence in these areas. Indian junior officers in India and Burma told their British officers that they would help them drive out the Japanese, but then the European colonialists must leave. French Gaullist soldiers and administrators who returned to Indochina and Indonesia found that even their domestic servants and café waiters had turned against them and that, however self-serving it was, the Japanese cry of "Asia for the Asians" had created new mentalities. For this was a moral as much as a political change. My landlady in the city of Allahabad in the 1960s remarked that the day Empire ended was when newly arrived American troops were seen rolling drunk in the city's streets in 1943. Even more than the First World War, the Second had finally destroyed the myth of white pre-eminence.

American influence was not simply negative, of course. Asians and Africans demanded that the Atlantic Charter become a universal and not simply a Euro-American announcement of freedom. Close contact with the relative wealth and openness of American soldiers and technical personnel, American films, cars and aircraft contributed to a large-scale change of perspective among subject peoples. Both the physical presence of colonial powers and the long-term consequences of colonial rule persisted over the next three generations, as I show in later chapters. But the death-knell of colonialism had clearly sounded between 1942 and 1947.

The third moral and political consequence of the war, examined further in Chapter 15, was the redoubling of efforts to bring nations together and create institutions which would avoid further global conflicts – an attempt to forward "internationalism in an age of nationalism" as it has been termed.[44] The failure of the League of Nations to avert conflict in Europe led to the creation of the United Nations even before the end of the war. This was soon accompanied by the growth of American-led voluntary international humanitarian organisa-tions, such as the Rockefeller Foundation. Nationalist leaders in newly inde-pendent African and Asian countries argued for colonial freedom at the United Nations and its subordinate organisations and brought into being the Non-Aligned Movement and the Bandung Conference of 1955, which sought to moderate the conflicts of the Cold War.

Even when these moves failed, they did create a moral alternative to the nation state in an era of nation-building and widening international communi-cation. So before 1947, plans were developed in Europe to bring into being a "European family of nations", first through economic and later through political cooperation. The American Marshall Plan, bringing aid to millions of victims of war, worked across the Continent. The end of the war also saw a great proliferation of non-governmental aid organisations (NGOs), working in different colonies, former colonies and countries ravaged by war. Organisations such as the Red Cross had existed since the nineteenth century. But mass observation by American and European soldiers and officials of the plight of large parts of the world's population gave urgency to the idea of economic aid and education. In a sense, the moral power which had previously been largely invested in Christian missionary activity took on a more secular form with numbers of US aid workers returning to the countries to which they had been posted during the war.

Balancing the expansion of democratic socialism, anticolonialism and internationalism was the rise of Communism across Eastern Europe, China and Southeast Asia during the war. Once again, the sheer force of Soviet military occupation in Europe and of Mao's ability to fill the vacuum left by the simultaneous collapse of the Japanese and Chiang Kai-shek's nationalists in China was critical here. But deeper moral and political forces were also at work. However brutal Stalinist oppression of his enemies and Mao's later purges were, the USSR and the CCP did build upon a sense of hope that Communism would bring equality, liberate the labour force and help rebuild the devastated wartime economies. Even a convinced democrat such as Sarvepalli Radhakrishnan, later second president of India, observed as an envoy in Moscow, in Eastern Europe and at the UNO that many ordinary people were still optimistic about their future under Communism in the later 1940s and early 1950s.[45] At least this new state seemed active in its attempt to spread the benefits of industrialisation in previously agrarian Eastern European societies.

Similarly, in areas occupied by the Chinese Communists during the later stages of the war, the authorities had initially sought to harness the power of the so-called middle peasant. Only later were large parts of the rural and urban labour force corralled into cooperatives and deprived of any sense of personal ownership and personal worth. In Indochina/Vietnam, the small businessman was not vilified as a class enemy but stood alongside the peasant and the worker. In Malaya, the Communists offered promise to the plantation workers who saw themselves as mere slaves. In many areas, Communists were able to meld their views with a socialistic and modernising form of nationalism which appealed in an age when the brutal force of fascism still dominated the collective memory. Much Western, particularly American, historiography, which is still influenced by the ideologies of Cold War, concentrates only on the oppressive aspect of Communist rule. But a system which controlled half of the world's population for several generations, even in a hollowed-out and often corrupt form, and still has its supporters today, cannot simply be written off as a history of violence and intimidation.

THE BROADER CONSEQUENCES OF THE WAR, PART II: THE ECONOMIC

The economic and technological consequences of the war were as dramatic as the political changes it brought, and these were clearly in evidence by the middle of 1944. Mass bombing, invasion, death and starvation had reduced the GDP of Germany, Japan, Russia and Italy by between 20% and 40%. Occupied countries, such as coastal China, Poland and even the Netherlands, suffered as badly. Even Britain saw the destruction of major parts of its cities and industries. By contrast, the effort of mobilisation for war finally propelled the United States out of the consequences of the Depression. By 1948, it was estimated to command 40% of world GDP, making it the greatest economic as well as political hegemon in history. In addition, the United States and its companies and manufacturing dominated Canada and much of Central and South America. Economically, indeed, the United States was half the world.

The case of the USSR was more complex. The country had lost perhaps 20 million of its own citizens, and cities such as Leningrad and Stalingrad had been devastated. Yet, it unquestionably emerged as the second great power. War had spread its manufacturing power to Siberia and the east in a kind of second industrial revolution. However relatively poor its citizens, even by comparison with those of war-torn Western Europe, it had developed significant technical knowledge during the conflict. The days of the Soviet H-bomb and the sputnik satellite were in sight. Meanwhile, the defeated states went through a phase of economic rearmament, partly as a result of American occupation and aid from the Marshall Plan, both designed to hold the line against Communism.[46] By the late 1950s, both Germany and Japan had reached their respective 1939 level of GDP once again. But the massive lead of the United States and the consequent dwindling of the economic power of Europe were never completely reversed.

Elsewhere in the world, in parts of Africa and Asia, colonial war economies were transformed into the centralised governments of new nation states determined to shield themselves against a recurrence of imperialist economic penetration. In India, business leaders and the Indian National Congress had already sketched the Bombay Plan for economic centralisation and development in 1944. By the early 1950s, "five year plans" modelled on the apparent success of the USSR were in place. As the war ended, Britain, France and Holland repatriated economic powers to colonies and semi-colonies such as Indonesia, Indochina and Egypt, even as they attempted to retain political leverage in them. As in the political realm, not all movements of the period were towards economic autarchy and closed economies. American "lend-lease" aid to the United Kingdom, the genesis of the Marshall Plan and bilateral agreements in Japan and Germany after the US occupations resulted in the sharing and diffusion of resources. Equally, the new cooperation between democratic governments in Europe in the years immediately after 1945 led slowly to collective pacts such as the European Coal, Iron and Steel Agreements of 1951–1952 and, ultimately, to the creation of the European Union itself. Statesmen and leading economists were determined to avoid a new Great Depression, which they rightly saw as the main cause of the Second World War.

Yet, once again these epochal changes in the macroeconomic world were accompanied by local technical developments of the greatest significance. The bright side of the war, though often put to malign use, was the development of atomic power, jet propulsion, radar, the computer, major medical advances in the treatment, for instance, of malaria and, ultimately, space travel. At a more mundane level, the mass production of food for troops produced new forms of preservation such as canning and freezing, which were soon adapted to civilian use, as Lizzie Collingham demonstrated.[47] The wartime need of governments to nourish their populations enhanced the fast delivery and mechanisation of supply lines, and this fed into the expansion of supermarkets and the mass manufacturing of food after 1945. Here again the American presence was vital. Certainly, the ebb and flow of war across Eurasia and North Africa had disrupted peasant farming and killed millions of rural dwellers. Yet, at the same time, war had encouraged intensive farming of food and resulted in whole new areas being turned over to farming both on a large and on a small scale. Wartime developments of intensive farming, for instance, fed into India's "Green Revolution" of the 1960s and 1970s.

THE BROADER CONSEQUENCES OF THE WAR, PART III: SOCIAL AND MORAL

The political and economic dimension of war accelerated enormous social changes across the world. To an even greater extent than in the First World War, the Second World War began to break down social hierarchies which had persisted and expanded since the beginnings of industrialisation. Throughout Western Europe, wartime hardship and the movement of population brought people of different classes together in an unprecedented manner. In Britain, for instance, poor children from urban slums in London and other major cities were sent for safety to small towns and the countryside. Middle-class women were thrown together in the "grow more food" campaigns, while the Territorial Army mixed urban and rural, upper- and lower-class males, creating a melting-pot later memorialised in the television series *Dad's Army*. The mass influx of US troops and airmen first into the United Kingdom and later into Western Europe and European empires had similar consequences. Europeans, Africans and Indians marvelled at the easy social manners and apparent mixing of the Americans, qualities that made many of their class and racial distinctions seem antiquated and pointless.

Americans themselves also began to experience the dissolution of hierarchies as black soldiers mingled with whites in campaigns and increasingly in military bases. Black soldiers took back the memory of this limited move to equality to the rural South and also to the cities of central and northern America and this became one of the most important influences on their push for civil rights in the following decades. Similarly, Algerian and African troops from south of the Sahara fighting in General de Gaulle's armies witnessed the moral and material failures of metropolitan France, consorted with, and occasionally married, white French women and also began to chip holes in the racial hierarchy, which both colonial officials and domestic conservatives had rigorously protected. Even the Pétainiste regimes in France and its empire had attempted to create social solidarity amongst its own citizens and outlaw demeaning racial language in colonies such as Indochina.

The partial dissolution of social divisions was not something which affected European and American societies alone. In India, caste and ethnic hierarchies already under pressure at the height of Gandhi's nationalist movement were further called into question by the events of the war. Military recruitment spread far beyond India's traditional "martial races" in the Punjab and the Northwest to people, such as Bengalis and Madrasis, long considered "non-martial" or even effeminate – and not only by the British. The mobilisation of Dalits, or untouchables, for war work served to raise their self-esteem and also made them more visible in the public sphere. B. R. Ambedkar, a leading Dalit, became Minister of Labour and, in 1946, began to draft the new Indian Constitution. Indian women, who had already played a greater part in the Congress movement, also achieved greater influence during the Second World War. Congress had voted for a universal franchise in 1939. Bose's Indian National Army had its own "Rani of Jhansi" women's battalion, named after the famous female freedom fighter of 1857. Woman's work in factories and on farms expanded over these years.[48]

In fact, the war had a partially liberating effect on the status of women generally. Male-only franchises disappeared from Western Europe. In Japan, the Americans imposed female suffrage and discouraged the public and private demeaning of women. Even in the Muslim world, women were recruited into hospitals and doctors' surgeries during wartime and some at least continued in these careers after 1945. In Western Europe, Australasia and North America, women flooded into professional and scientific jobs as their menfolk were called up to military service. Unlike the situation after 1918, they tended to stay in employment after 1945, since the urgency of social rebuilding had eroded common ideas of the sexual division of labour between the public and the domestic spheres. In Communist societies, too, the ideology of sexual equality was part of the revolutionary mentality since the disempowering of women was seen, at least theoretically, as a bourgeois ideology. Women's military forma-tions, labour corps and industrial work bands spread to newly Marxist Eastern Europe and the "liberated zones" of China and Vietnam. The presence of radical urban intellectuals in the villages promoted the liberation of women here, even if their lot remained no better than that of the average peasant or worker.

Perhaps the most dramatic effect of war on social hierarchy lay in the deeper invasion of the lands of those regarded as tribal peoples, whether in the uplands of South and Southeast Asia or in the Central Asian steppe or the Pacific Islands. Such communities had long been subject to penetration and exploi-tation by the colonial powers, missionaries, merchants and settlers from the plains. Conversely, colonial powers had sometimes tried to protect and wall them off from modernity as a counterweight to rising nationalism. From 1936 to 1948, however, successive intrusions by Japanese, British, Soviet and US troops largely remodelled these societies and their moral bases. Maoris and North American Indians drawn into the conflict began further to rebuild political self-respect. Tribal groups in north-eastern India, such as the Nagas, and the Shan and Kachin of Burma, or the Hmong of Indochina, were radicalised and armed, sometimes against the emerging postcolonial states. Pacific Islanders responded to the trauma of invasion with new religious movements, sometimes melding Christianity with ancestor cults. The forceful incorporation of these "tribes" into settled populations, which had begun in the early modern period, was now greatly accelerated

Figure 6 Japanese suffragists carrying 20,000 petitions to the Imperial Diet requesting a women's suffrage bill, 1920s. George Rinhart/Bettmann/Corbis/Getty Images.

As well as an assault on hierarchy, the war and its consequences brought about a revolution in the human physical environment. Before 1948, the urban social context was already being drastically remodelled as the first attempts were made to repair the physical destruction of the cities. Signalling the same ideological rupture with earlier forms of the representation of social hierarchy, new ultra-modernist and so-called brutalist forms of architecture began to appear in European cities. The neo-gothic and neo-classical were at a discount. The desire to rebuild working-class areas devastated by wartime bombing led planners and architects to implement styles of building derived from the Bauhaus tradition of the 1920s and 1930s, but usually supported by limited funds and consequently vulgarised. The desire to announce socialist modernity led the Communist German Democratic Republic (GDR), for instance, to create Stalinstadt, a new model working-class city (though it had become desolate and populated by the old before 2013).[49] This was not always the case. Despite now being under Communist control, the city of Warsaw, which had been almost completely destroyed in the last phase of the war, was rebuilt in the same neo-classical style, basically in order to commemorate the survival of the nation itself. By contrast, in India, Nehru experimented with the ultra-modernism of 1930s French architecture in building the new city of Chandigarh, breaking with both the Mughal and the British colonial past.

Art, cinema and literature reflected the deep impact of war across the world. One reaction was a further attempt to distance the artist and the viewer from history, which led to a greater emphasis on the abstract than had been seen even in the 1920s and 1930s. Picasso took this turn in his later years and it was seen particularly in the American tradition of Jackson Pollock. But the social mixing and collapse of the urban–rural divide was seen in much of Asia, where radical nationalists and Communists were influenced by village designs, lacquer paintings and bronzes. The discovery of "the people" during wartime was also reflected in the work of British painters. The conflicting priorities of wartime were seen in the work of authors such as Ernest Hemingway, who appears to have gloried in its destruction of status and polite language forms, or in the anti-hierarchical literature of Jean-Paul Sartre, Norman Mailer and Primo Levi. By comparison, the British writer George Orwell was scarified by the nature of tyranny and mind control. This, he believed, was the hallmark of the fascist and Communist regimes which created and survived the conflict. Revealingly, Orwell's *Animal Farm*, written in the last stages of the war, was rejected by numerous British publishers on the grounds that it was anti-Stalinist and might damage relations with an essential ally. By then, however, that ally was in the process of becoming the new enemy.

Yet, that enmity had been fundamentally transformed in August 1945 by the atomic bomb, bringing into question the very nature of what it was to be human with even greater force than the moral apocalypse of the First World War. From this point on, war could no longer be seen as "politics by other means", but as a means by which the human race might utterly destroy itself. The next chapter takes this broad narrative forward to the early 1950s and the following one considers world politics during the period of American dominance of the West and the climax of the Cold War during the 1960s and 1970s.

[7] PERIPHERAL CONFLICTS AND THE END OF OLD REGIMES, C.1945–1955

The Small Wars Beneath Continued, Part I: Israel and the
Arab World
The Small Wars Beneath Continued, Part II: Asia and
Independence
The Small Wars Beneath Continued, Part III: Africa and
Beyond
The Fate of the Major Combatants, Part I: Europe,
c.1945–1955
The Fate of the Major Combatants, Part II: The Americas
The Fate of the Major Combatants, Part III: Japan
Conclusion: An Age of Forced Compromise

THE final years of the first half of the twentieth century were consumed by two massive wars: the great Asian war of 1937–1945, terminated by the atomic bombing of Japan, and the European and Atlantic war of 1939–1945, which ended with the partition of the continent by the Allies and Soviet Union. Yet, as the last chapter shows, these great conflicts were entangled at their fringes with other wars, ethnic conflicts and political settlements, some of which had discrete origins before 1939 and all of which resulted in the overthrow of old-style regimes across the world. These included the Chinese Civil War, which had its origins in Mao Zedong's Long March, and the Arab–Israeli War of 1948, which settled the fate of the majority of old notable-dominated governments in the Arab world and laid the final foundation of the Zionist state. Equally, the two major wars had loosened the grip of European colonial powers, leading to the independence of India, Burma and the Gold Coast, with

Remaking the Modern World 1900–2015: Global Connections and Comparisons, First Edition. C. A. Bayly.
© 2018 John Wiley & Sons Ltd. Published 2018 by John Wiley & Sons Ltd.

ensuing conflicts between India and Pakistan in Kashmir, between local minorities and the Burmese centre, and between Indochina and the French colonial power.

A striking consequence of the two world wars, especially the Second World War, was the way in which the world became an ideological as much as a geographical space. Thereafter, the movement of ideas, practices and techniques became ever more dense and far-reaching, even if they were wholly reshaped in different national and social contexts. Not everything was connected, of course. Ideological conflict and decolonisation also led to the fragmentation of old entities, a hardening of the nation state and the localisation of ideologies, as this chapter demonstrates. Yet, a comprehensive global mentality and a global awareness had been formed and this would never be dispelled.

THE SMALL WARS BENEATH CONTINUED, PART I: ISRAEL AND THE ARAB WORLD

Of all these later small wars and settlements, the Arab–Israeli War of 1948–1949 had some of the most profound effects. It sparked a series of further conflicts and created one of the most serious diplomatic impasses of the century. It became a global event and source of debate.[1] The connection between the Second World War and events in Palestine was clear. The Holocaust of European Jewry was accompanied by a further outflow of Jewish refugees and the growth of extreme militancy among Jewish organisations outside and within the territory. The Irgun, the Stern Gang and armed underground movements linked up with local commanders in Palestine to give the cause a purpose and steeliness not matched by any of the disorganised Arab powers which opposed the emerging settler state. Indirectly, too, the Second World War had created the conditions for a successful Jewish coup by at least temporarily aligning British, American and even Soviet support for the Jewish people. A weakened and nearly bankrupt British government, already losing its grip on India, Burma, Malaya and now Palestine itself, was more prepared to cooperate with the settlers than with Jordan, Egypt or Syria.[2] Since the days of the Balfour Declaration of 1917, the British had seen the Jewish settlers as modernisers and better allies for the protection of the Suez Canal, which they still perceived as a vital interest for their dissolving empire.

The roots of the failure of the apparently superior Arab forces to impede the creation of a Jewish state led back to the conflicts of the 1920s and 1930s. The Zionist settlers were well organised in rural cooperatives and had achieved a dominant position in Palestinian commerce and agriculture before 1930. They had pushed forward electrification and water management in the Dead Sea.[3] During the Arab uprising of 1936, they had aided the British Mandate authorities and had received large quantities of weaponry and logistical aid from them. In addition, if the uprising cost a massive outpouring of money and men by the British, it also smashed the Palestinian leadership and destroyed the economic vitality of Arab society. The key ideological leader, the Mufti of Jerusalem, had fled Palestine for Beirut. In 1948–1949, he again ineffectively tried to direct the anti-Zionist alliance from outside Palestine. Meanwhile, the Arab forces of Egypt, Syria and Jordan fought for their own particular interests rather than working together for a united Arab cause. Christians and Druze remained neutral or even cooperated with the Zionists. Sunnis were suspicious of Shias and older Arab notables were suspicious of the younger radicals. Based on a strongly fortified area which they controlled between the Mediterranean coast and the city of Jerusalem, the Zionist regime surprised, divided and routed the half-hearted forces of the Arab states.

The consequences of the defeat of Arab armies by a relatively small, but much more effective, Jewish defence force were immediate. Large numbers of Palestinians fled their homes and lands in the new Israel. Initially, at least, this appears to have been the result of random attacks by Zionist militias. But there is later evidence of a deliberate Zionist policy of population transfer. This had, of course, been a radical technique adopted by different national interests since the break-up of the Ottoman Empire in 1918 and the emergence of the Irish Free State a few years later. It had been seen most recently in a particularly violent form in India. In the Middle East, population transfer resulted in the appearance in Syria, Lebanon and several of the conservative Arab states of bodies of younger, more militant Palestinian refugees demanding revenge against Israel.

Equally significant was the deep disillusionment of the Arab population with their feeble and ineffective rulers. Most of the existing Arab regimes of 1948–1949 were to collapse within a few years. Particularly significant was the fall of the Egyptian regime to a military coup which finally ended Britain's semi-colonial status in the country and again raised fears for the security of the Suez Canal. This led directly to the 1956 Anglo-French and Israeli attacks on the Egypt of Gamal Abdul Nasser and his new nationalistic and militarised Egyptian regime, with long-term implications for European and American diplomacy.[4] The old-style rulers of Jordan, Syria, Lebanon and Iraq were also dismissed, in the main because of their perceived failure to advance Arab nationalism, but also because of their inability to reduce Western influence or to foster local development. Syria suffered a series of coups and counter-coups after 1949. Meanwhile, Iraqis still smarted under a sense that they were occupied by British forces, even though they had achieved formal independence in 1930. They had sent a large contingent to fight the Zionists, but its failure to take the offensive left the regime open to the charge that it was merely helping King Abdullah of Jordan annex Arab Palestine rather than attacking the Israeli forces. Despite harsh repression over the next decade by the government of Nuri al-Said, popular anger grew until, in 1958, it exploded in a military coup of young officers determined to overthrow the monarchy and the central land-owning clique which was popularly regarded as totally corrupt.

These older regimes, whether in Egypt and Syria or ultimately in Iraq, were replaced by a younger generation of militarised and technocratic leaders supported by the commercial middle class that, in general, further distanced itself from the old Arab dynasties. The new military rulers edged towards, but did not fully promote, an Islamic style of politics which, at this time, was associated with the poor of the cities and half-educated mullahs. Yet, these new forms of urban-based authoritarianism had little more success than the old dynasts or the Mufti of Jerusalem in challenging the state of Israel, a formidable developmental polity, which benefited particularly from the devotion of American Jews and philanthropists and became a major force in US politics and international relations.

THE SMALL WARS BENEATH CONTINUED, PART II: ASIA AND INDEPENDENCE

The long-term forces of political and diplomatic chaos unleashed by the Second World War were equally in evidence in South, Southeast and East Asia. The end of British colonialism in India and Burma is often contrasted with the violent wars of independence which convulsed French Algeria and Indochina or the Dutch East Indies after the war. But even if British colonial power was more clearly aware of the forces of nationalism which opposed it and was weakened by financial and military over-extension, independence was far from painless even for the British – and for Indians it was tumultuous and murderous. Upward of half a million people were killed in religious pogroms between Hindus and Sikhs and Muslims, mainly in the Punjab and Bengal. Disbanded forces from the Indian princely states played a significant part in the slaughter and in the ensuing conflicts. Weapons from the Burma front also poured into Bengal in 1945–1946. Hundreds of thousands of people were displaced.[5]

As in the Middle East, the end of international war and decolonisation were followed by a series of small wars between local states. As the princely regime of Hyderabad tried to negotiate independence from India through the United Nations in 1948, the new Indian government invaded the state and defeated its small army. Concurrently, a tribal peasant Communist-led insurgency, the Telangana movement, broke out and the forces of independent India spent three years suppressing it.[6] In 1948 again, India and Pakistan took up arms about Kashmir whose ruler had acceded to India when most of the state's population was Muslim. Tribesmen from the Northwest Frontier province of Pakistan surged into Kashmir and established control in the west of the province as Indian and Pakistani commanders established a fragile peace. Thereafter, in 1950–1952, Afghanistan attempted to take advantage of a local ethnic movement among Pakhtuns (Pathans) on the frontier, demanding a separate state of Pakhtunistan. This led to low-level skirmishing between tribal leaders and the government of Pakistan, which was determined to maintain control over the frontier. The prevailing sense of danger persuaded Nehru, rather against his inclination, to remain in the Commonwealth, the postcolonial institution with which Britain hoped to maintain its declining world role.[7]

Initially at least, Pakistan under Jinnah retained a form of democracy. But a series of further wars with India and the difficulty of holding together a regional and fissiparous state, including East Pakistan, distanced from central government by thousands of miles, caused the army to intervene increasingly in the country's politics. The military leaders began to use the ideological shield of Sunni Islamic orthodoxy to legitimate themselves in a manner similar to contemporary regimes in the Middle East. Meanwhile, in northeast India and Assam, which had been close to the Burma front during the war, members of the Naga ethnic group were arrayed against the Indian authorities, also demanding a separate state. This insurrection was speedily put down, but sporadic revolts occurred in the area through to the beginning of the twenty-first century.

Burma and Southeast Asia, which had been directly occupied by the Japanese and reconquered by the Allies in 1944–1945, witnessed an even more continuous set of conflicts.[8] Initially, it seemed that British Burma might avoid protracted postcolonial warfare. As the last chapter notes, Aung San, as leader of the Burma Independence Army, had revolted against the Japanese occupiers in early 1945. He was angered by the oppression practised on the civilian population but had also begun to realise that the British under General Slim were on their way back. Louis Mountbatten, as Supreme Allied Commander, Southeast Asia, avoided the type of conflict with armed nationalists in which the French became embroiled shortly afterwards in Indochina. He and his successors, directed now by Clement Attlee's Labour government, moved Burma rapidly towards independence, keen to avoid further military commitments in the area.

Despite his earlier authoritarian proclivities, Aung San made reasonable compromises with local ethnic leaderships, notably the Karen in the south and the Shan and Kachin on the northern border. In August 1948, however, he was assassinated. Under Burma's constitution of 1948, U Nu, a modernist Buddhist, attempted to unify the newly independent country.[9] Yet, throughout the late 1940s and 1950s, a series of insurgencies sapped the authority of the civilian government: Communist factions, rebellions by the Karen and Shan and opposition from Guomindang forces which had fled China and established themselves in northern Burma. These insurgencies were contained by the early 1950s, but flickered on in the peripheries, ensuring that the military achieved more and more influence in Rangoon. Consequently, General Ne Win slowly built up his power, became prime minister in 1958 and ousted U Nu in a coup in 1962. Here, again, events in Burma echoed the rise of military autocrats over much of the former colonial world, notably in the Middle East and Africa.

Further south in British Southeast Asia, a series of equally violent insurrections, this time Communist in form, took place in Malaya.[10] Unlike Burma, or latterly India, the British had important economic interests in the colony. Its rubber and tin provided a valuable resource for the weakened British economy, and therefore, as in the case of East Africa, a continuation of empire in some form seemed desirable to London. Not only this, but the fact that Communism appeared to be making advances in China convinced the government to try to retain the colony and the vital naval base of Singapore. In 1948, the British declared a state of emergency in response to Communist guerrilla attacks, and war against the insurgency flared on until 1954.[11] The British were able to gain the upper hand, in contrast to the French in Vietnam, because, in general, they retained the support of the more conservative Malayan Muslim population, which feared Chinese domination if the British left abruptly. But this conflict was one of the "terminal wars of colonialism", which included the suppression of the pre-war Arab revolt and later events in Kenya, Cyprus and Aden which continued to sully the memory of the British governments of the period.

In terms of the scale of violence and their long-term political impact, events in French Indochina were to prove even more significant than the Malayan story. By 1946, Vietnamese nationalists in the south had been driven underground as the French and Allied forces which had occupied the country at the end of the war with Japan had refused to accept their independence. In the north, the French had also tried to stage a comeback. But controlling inland and northern parts of the country, the Viet Minh had established a form of self-government in what became known as the "inter-zones". They received support from Chinese Communist forces as they themselves reconquered southern China from Chiang Kai-shek in the course of 1948–1949. More distantly, the USSR aided the Vietnamese both practically and through international diplomacy. The scene was therefore set for the First Indochina War, or, as the Vietnamese put it, the "Anti-French War", which was to slowly transform itself during the 1950s into the "Anti-American War". Inevitably, it was the more highly motivated Vietnamese Communists under Ho Chi Minh, survivors of French repression in the 1930s, who came to lead the nationalist coalition.[12]

As one of the most successful revolutionary movements of the twentieth century, the Viet Minh started its long war with the French with some key advantages.[13] Despite the claims of the French, and later the Americans, that it was little more than a conspiracy directed by China and the USSR, it gained a great deal of support not just from the working class of port towns such as Haiphong and rural plantation labour but also from the French-educated middle class: doctors, lawyers and minor administrators, including many women. It became a national liberation party under the relatively inclusive leadership of Ho Chi Minh. Unlike the Chinese Communist Party, it was not hostile to small traders and merchants, an essential element of the local economy and a source of supplies. Resistance to the French during the 1930s and the Japanese after 1942 had given Viet Minh supporters a deep knowledge of the countryside, which allowed them to transform the inter-zones into effective bases for guerrilla war. This later became a more conventional conflict as the Viet Minh had managed to secure some of the weapons that had flooded into Southeast Asia during and after the Second World War. While Chinese and Russian help was vital in the final victory of the Vietnamese over the French at Dien Bien Phu in 1954, their clever deployment of mobile forces and knowledge of the country were even more important.

The Vietnamese insurgents also benefited from the international situation to an extent. Even though American anti-Communist rhetoric became more and more violent following the rise of Mao, the early 1950s saw an attempt by the newly independent nations of Southeast Asia to limit conflict in their region and avert intervention by the great powers. This culminated in the Bandung Conference of 1955. As the scale of the French defeat became clear, India and Indonesia were able to step in and arrange a truce between the French and their allies around Saigon and the Viet Minh power in the north of the country. The result was a stalemate which allowed Communist North Vietnam to rebuild and prepare itself for the next major conflict: war with the United States and the reconquest of the South.

In many respects, the Dutch East Indies, later Indonesia, took a similar path to Indochina/Vietnam. But, by the 1960s, the outcomes were radically different.[14] Whereas North Vietnam had become Communist and was fighting to free the South from an American alliance, the Indonesian government was on the point of massacring nearly a million of its Communist opponents, a substantial number of whom were of Chinese origin. The cause of these differences lay once again in the period immediately after the war. Japanese invasion had led to the fragmentation of an Indonesian nationalist movement which was already divided between left-leaning and Islamist components, as also between those who advocated violent revolution and a more moderate faction. In the 1930s, several peasant insurgencies had broken out in Java and been put down by the colonial power. Figures such as the leftist and Muslim revolutionary Tan Malaka fostered an anti-Dutch underground across Asia. During the Japanese occupation, a faction led by Mohammad Hatta had cooperated with the invaders, while another, led by the future leader Sukarno, had gone underground, to emerge in 1945 after the Japanese surrender and declare independence even before Ho Chi Minh.

Like the French in Indochina, the Dutch were initially determined to hold on to their former colony. This was partly to assuage the humiliation of Nazi occupation, but mainly because since the beginning of the century Indonesia had seemed to be an essential part of the Dutch economy. The high-technology and highly educated Holland of the 1960s and 1970s had not yet emerged and the country was still significantly dependent on agricultural and mineral exports from its eastern colony. The Dutch government, itself fractured and facing a domestic economic crisis, acquiesced in two "police actions" against the Indonesian nationalists, first in 1946 and later in 1949, which were similar to French attempts to reimpose their hold in Indochina. They met fierce and organised resistance from guerrilla forces with a strong base in the villages of Java and Sumatra.

Ultimately, though, the Dutch gave up the effort in 1949, following their second invasion, and Indonesia was recognised as independent by the United Nations. Holland was bankrupt and, perhaps more critically, the United States was not prepared to countenance a reimposition of "imperialism" in Indonesia. In Vietnam, by contrast, they gave tacit support (and later direct military support) to the French, in view of the rise of the spectre of Communism there. Whereas the radical nature of the regime in North Vietnam was fairly clear by 1950, this was not the case in Indonesia. Here conservative Islamists, the secularised version of modernised Islamic nationalism promoted by Sukarno and a more radical leftist movement, supported by many Chinese in the archipelago, were still in contention.[15] Tan Malaka, "the Muslim socialist", had been killed in 1946 and a Communist-led revolt in East Java in 1948 was suppressed by the new nationalist government. Leftist elements were gradually

Figure 7 President Sukarno and Marilyn Monroe at a party at the Beverly Hills Hotel, 1956. Bettmann/Getty Images.

marginalised over the next two decades, quite opposite to the situation in Vietnam.

In many ways the most momentous of this melee of post-war conflicts scattered around the fringes of the great battlegrounds of Europe and the Soviet Union was the Chinese Civil War of 1946–1949. Not only did this extend the range of the Cold War to Asia, but it also indirectly precipitated the Korean War of 1950–1953, which came perilously close to being an international conflict. As with so many of the other wars discussed in this chapter, its origins can be traced back to the early 1930s, when Mao Zedong's Communist fighters began to establish themselves in liberated zones in northern China (Shensi and Shansi provinces).[16] Chiang Kai-shek tried to crush the Communists before he faced the Japanese who had occupied Manchuria in 1931, but following a mutiny among his own troops, he was unable to do so. After 1937 he found himself fighting on two fronts as the Japanese invaded coastal China from the north and also, after 1942, from Burma. Chiang was forced to move his capital to Chonquing in the far south, where he was supplied by Allied forces under General Stilwell. This effectively laid northern China open to Mao and his Soviet allies when the Japanese surrendered in 1945, allowing Communist armies to race into Manchuria and the vital northern coastal cities in the late 1940s.

It is often stated that Mao's army became a peasant force and his appeal was essentially to the rural under-privileged. But this is a reading back of his later policies. In fact, Communist land-reform schemes in northern China also at first attracted the support of ordinary traders and urban people, who were tired of endless fighting between warlords and Chiang's government and suspicious of its links to big landlords and the Americans. As Communist armies entered the coastal cities when the civil war broke out, many supporters of the Guomindang regime also changed sides, having been offered an amnesty and in some cases posts as representatives of the new government in factories and businesses which they had once owned. Inflation was rampant; Chiang Kai-shek's old cronies seemed intent on re-establishing their corrupt forms of control, while at least the Communists seemed to offer a unified national government intent on restoring China's pride both against the warlord armies and China's former imperialist enemies. Nevertheless, a more balanced reading of the fall of the Guomindang emphasises the massive destruction that the war with Japan had visited on China and Chiang's armies.[17] In 1948–1949, these armies collapsed and he and his inner circle retreated to Taiwan, where they had secured a firm base after viciously suppressing a local rising there in February 1947.

In October 1949, Mao Zedong inaugurated the People's Republic of China.[18] During its first year, the Communist government reinforced its hold across the whole country, often using the officials of the former nationalist regime once they were "re-educated". Generous quantities of Soviet aid poured in, while the government used wealth seized from landowners and business-men, now including small traders, to set up cooperative credit societies and improve infrastructure. In the meantime, however, the international situation had changed. The American president, Truman, faced with a Communist China and Soviet occupation of Eastern Europe, was inclined to sense a worldwide Communist conspiracy.[19] While Communist North Vietnam escaped intervention, this was not the case with Korea. Following the defeat of Japan, the former colonial power, the country had been divided between an American-occupied South and a Chinese-occupied North. But in June 1950, North Korean forces invaded the South, triggering, first, a full-scale invasion by American and other Allied forces under General MacArthur and then, in 1951, a Chinese counter-intervention to support the embattled Communists. Mao had begun to fear encirclement by US forces when Japan and Malaya recovered as bastions of Western capitalism. The Korean War was one of the most dangerous spark points of the whole period of the Cold War and the uneasy ceasefire of 1953 left both parts of Korea shackled by different styles of authoritarian regime.

THE SMALL WARS BENEATH CONTINUED, PART III: AFRICA AND BEYOND

Africa south of the Sahara had not been directly affected by fighting during the Second World War as it had been between 1914 and 1918, but its effects were felt during the following decade and precipitated violence in several regions.[20]

Substantial numbers of soldiers from British East and West Africa had fought in Burma and Malaya and returned to their countries with radical ideas and new skills. One such was Idi Amin, future dictator of Uganda, who fought in Southeast Asia. Large numbers of black troops from French West Africa had also taken part in campaigns from Western Europe to Indochina. The first and most violent explosion in post-war Africa was the Malagasy revolt in Madagascar in 1947–1948. Madagascar nationalists, stirred by the Atlantic Charter, demanded independence as it became clear that France was intent on recategorising its colonial empire as the "French Overseas Territories". Malagasies crying "Let's abolish forced labour!" rebelled and occupied a substantial part of the island, but were suppressed by French North African troops, leading to the death of an estimated 20–30,000 people.

War had also spurred notions of colonial development or, rather, exploitation. Prices rose and collapsed as they had done during and after the First World War. But after 1945, the British, under severe economic pressure, attempted to spur agricultural exports from the continent and thus brought the pressure of the colonial state directly to bear on its farming populations. In general, these beginnings were not successful, as witness the abortive Tanganyika Groundnut Scheme, and the benefit to the British Treasury was much smaller than in Malaya, where tin and rubber exports increased despite the Communist insurgency. More seriously, they resulted in the transfer of land from African communities both to white farmers and to a small class of black rural entrepreneurs. In Kenya, this led quite directly to the Mau Mau insurrection among Kikuyu farmers from 1952–1960, a revolt which was put down violently by the British government and local white settlers.[21]

West Africa also saw strikes and demonstrations in the Gold Coast in 1948–1949, resulting in a limited expansion of local self-government by the British Labour government, but outright fighting remained limited in scope. In South Africa, Afrikaner sympathy with Germany during the war, the spectre of decolonisation in Asia and fear of the British Labour government saw a surge in support for the white National Party in the 1948 elections. The new government began introducing restrictive laws which ultimately underpinned the apartheid system and led to a 40-year struggle for dignity on the part of black South Africans.

This chapter began by shifting the focus from the outcome of the Second World War in its major theatres, Europe and the Soviet Union, to the east and the south, where its long-term consequences have continued to reverberate even after Europe and the USSR achieved a degree of stability after 1948. Yet, under the surface of these small, peripheral conflicts and accommodations, a number of broader social, economic and ideological changes can be seen. First, the ending of formal colonial rule over much of this area was accompanied by a shift from old authority figures – dynasts, princes and tribal elders – to new men who were technocrats and soldiers, or often both. They were influenced by modern ideologies, socialism, egalitarian Christianity or neo-Buddhism, for instance. This occurred in the Middle East, where European empires had been rolled back somewhat earlier, in the 1930s, and in parts of South and Southeast Asia and Africa after 1948. The command of machines, particularly machines of war, had given these new men much greater control over the countryside and the fringes of their realms.

Along with this, the idea of the will of the nation, seen at this time mainly in ethnic rather than religious terms, had supplanted charismatic and tribal authority. Finally, both within and outside what became the "socialist ecumene", the notion of development became the dominant ideology of the new states. War itself had spurred this change by mobilising men, machines and money on a grand scale. The irony was that this advance of the nation and the developmentalist state itself tended to harden, rather than weaken, local identities, which became "ethnicised" and, in the course of time, inflected with universalist religious ideas. "Hindu-ness" (Hindutva), Kurdish Sunni identity, Malayan Islamic identity and Kikuyu identity, for instance, began to emerge in more radical forms in the two generations after 1945. So, while the state became stronger everywhere, the wars, coups and political conflicts over its control also became more violent. Independence gave enormous advantages to colonised people, notably a new sense of self-respect. But the rolling collapse of European colonialism did not spell the end of international influences on their politics. Almost immediately, the ideological conflicts of the Cold War emerged and melded with local struggles, creating profound consequences for all world societies.

THE FATE OF THE MAJOR COMBATANTS, PART I: EUROPE, c. 1945–1955

The 1930s, the height of the Stalinist terror, had decimated the intelligentsia, purged the kulaks and had seen the mass displacement of smaller ethnic groups within the USSR. But these shocks were small compared with the impact of the Second World War. The crisis had uprooted whole communities as factories were shifted from the warzone to the east, out of the reach of the Nazi invasion. Labour, especially female labour, was drafted into the war economy on a massive scale. The destruction and death in the west of the country had been astonishing. At least 14 million Russians had been killed in the fighting itself or had died of starvation. As the Germans retreated after the epochal defeat at Stalingrad, thousands more communities had been disrupted and the Nazis had destroyed not only military buildings but also schools and hospitals.

The impact on the Soviet political system was equally great. Stalin, already in an unassailable position after his annihilation of political opponents, had become a national icon in view of his albeit tardy role in driving his armies and peoples to success. He vaunted his position not only as leader of the USSR but also more specifically of the Russian people, and the remaining leaders of the Supreme Soviet, such as Nikita Khrushchev, Vyacheslav Molotov and Lavrentiy Beria, quaked in fear of his lethal displeasure. Meanwhile, state security services pursued a relentless policy of repression within the borders of the USSR. Nearly three million Red Army soldiers were subject to interrogation on repatriation and many of these were sent to labour camps.[22] Stalin was also able greatly to extend his rule outside the realm of the Communist Party itself. The war had achieved what even the purges and deportations of the 1930s could not do. It had brought the Soviet state closer to every city, village and individual through conscription, war propaganda and the expropriation and redistribution of resources. Most of the old German-speaking cosmopolitan intelligentsia had been eliminated during the purges of the 1930s. The presence of Anglo-Americans in the USSR during the war had reopened a limited passage to the West. But, after 1945, a new "anti-cosmopolitan" campaign was instigated, and this was not confined to Jewish intellectuals.[23]

Stalin's dictatorial brutality persisted until his death in March 1953. Yet, significant changes were already underway in the Soviet economy and society which reflected the new technological and developmental pressures of the post-war era. In 1953 and after, the collective leadership attempted to increase the production of collective farms and to begin to put more land under agriculture in areas such as Kazakhstan. Attempts were made to boost light industry throughout the country. Further urgency was given to the nuclear programme. All this was set in the context of an attempt to scale down the Cold War and reach some degree of agreement with the United States. As Khrushchev and his acolytes achieved supreme power, they did little to loosen the bonds of the state security mechanism. But a new generation, too young to fight in the war, was coming to maturity. Fascinated at a distance by the West, these young people contributed to "the thaw" both inside the USSR and with its Cold War foes which began in the mid-1950s.[24]

In the meantime, east and southeast Europe suffered peripheral conflicts not dissimilar to those in the Middle East and Asia as Soviet control was imposed on them or partisan war in defence of nationhood and religion broke out. This was particularly intense in areas on the margins of the pre-war USSR, such as Estonia, Latvia, Lithuania, western Belarus and western Ukraine. Over much of Eastern Europe, in Poland, Hungary and Czechoslovakia, Communist leaderships which had been suppressed before the war and during Nazi occupation realised that they were dependent on the Red Army to defeat their liberal and socialist foes. Once they were in power, Stalin forced out and often killed any of them who showed the slightest interest in resisting his policy of turning them into little more than imperial provinces of the Soviet Union. First, the Soviets forced Communists into key positions in the cabinets of the coalition governments which emerged after the end of fighting. These then began to harass their liberal and socialist rivals and fix elections in their own favour. Finally, Stalin dispensed with Communists who got in his way, creating regimes of brutal sycophants in his own image. In Hungary, where the elections in November 1945 had returned a large anti-Communist majority led by the Smallholders Party, Communists nevertheless gained control of the security apparatus with the help of the Red Army and whittled down their opponents over the next two years. It is not surprising that Hungary was the scene of the first great rising against Soviet control little more than a decade later in 1956.[25]

It would be wrong to see this as a picture of simple Soviet conquest, however. In Poland, East-Central Europe and the Balkans, coalitions of powerful landlords and reactionary military cliques, often supported by Catholic or Orthodox hierarchies, had retained power during the 1930s and had become collaborators with the Nazi regime during the war. Among working people and even the lower middle classes scarred by war, the order and relative stability of Communist government had at least some appeal. In Czechoslovakia, for instance, home to a fairly large working class and a population still terrified of a reviving Germany, the Communists gained 38% of the vote in 1946 and became the largest single party, apparently without undue fraud. People hoped for a better future. Edvard Beneš, the president, stated, "We are not merely changing institutions . . . but we must create also a new man."[26] Communism also had a basic appeal in East Germany, where the military–*Junker* alliance had persisted into the Nazi and wartime era. Even in Berlin, once revenge atrocities perpetrated by the Red Army had ceased, there was a considerable amount of support among working people for Communism.[27] Nazism and the authoritarian socialist state which replaced it were different in ideology, in their attitude to international affairs and in their vision of the future. While anti-Semitic discourse and incidents continued to flare up in East Germany – the German Democratic Republic – the pathological fear of "Jewish conspiracy" and "barbarous" Czechs and Poles, born of ignorance, which had gripped the Third Reich, had dissipated. Yet, what many people felt they had in common was a strong commitment to the ordinary man, rather than to the upper-middle-class elite. In East Germany, particularly, and despite the constant petty spying and intervention by the Stasi secret police, large sections of the population in the 1950s and 1960s still had some faith in the system.[28] The awareness of the West culminating in John F. Kennedy's "Ich bin ein Berliner!" speech only developed when the effects of Marshall Plan money became visible and West Germany's economic revival gained in strength after the mid-1950s. This was much less true of Poland, Hungary and Czechoslovakia, where nationalism remained powerful and the USSR was widely seen as an occupying power.

One state which successfully resisted Soviet power was Yugoslavia, as noted in the previous chapter. Here Tito's partisans had staged a continuous and successful war of resistance against the Nazi invaders and had managed to regain control of the country by 1945, with little help from the Red Army. The Yugoslav Communists won the ensuing civil war with more moderate parties but showed little intention of adhering closely to Moscow's line. Preoccupied with their domestic problems and the devastation in West Germany, Britain and France had little leverage in Soviet-dominated Eastern Europe. Before late 1947, the Americans continued to give Stalin the benefit of the doubt. Only with Yugoslavia, where wartime alliances persisted, did the West maintain cordial relations. And only in Greece, which Churchill had long regarded as a critical strategic point, did the former Allies intervene to support non-Communist parties in the civil war which broke out in 1946.

France and Italy, both countries occupied by the Nazis and then invaded by the victorious Allied armies, had much in common as they tried to rid themselves of the taint of fascism and collaboration.[29] But France had one great moral advantage in the person of General Charles de Gaulle. Despite the relatively small scale of the Free French Army, de Gaulle made it his business to pose alongside the Allied victors and demand the respect of Churchill and

Roosevelt. Though the Italian resistance had put up a significant guerrilla struggle in the upland areas and had finished off Mussolini, it could not command the same international prestige as de Gaulle. In some respects, though, the Italian political system regained a degree of clientelist normality more rapidly than the French. In part, this was because the Italian Communist Party was more a communitarian grouping among lower-middle-class urban-ites and was less of a threat to conservative reformers than the French party, which had a larger proletariat base encouraged by the success of the Soviet Union. In part, too, it was because Italian conservatives and liberals could band together under the capacious flag of Christian Democracy.[30] Moderate Cathol-icism, indeed, proved a successful banner under which to exorcise fascism, dispense with the monarchy, which had compromised with Mussolini, and keep Marxism at bay.

A new constitution was established in 1946 and the Christian Democrats under Alcide de Gasperi maintained an easy, if somewhat corrupt, dominance over Italian politics for much of the next generation. Finally, and unlike the situation in France, they were helped by the absence of a "colonial question", now that Libya and Ethiopia were free under their own shaky monarchies. Two other factors aided this transition: first, the introduction of a limited welfare state which helped underpin Italy's small, productive family business sector. Italy by 1955 was beginning to experience "*il miracolo economico*".[31] Secondly, Italy benefited from the existence of a second ideological renovation in addition to Christian Democracy in the form of the push towards a united Europe, in which Italian statesmen were fully engaged. Rome was to be the location of the first and most important treaty on the way to European unification. Very rapidly, too, the imperial fascist persona of the city was displaced by the much more active presence of the Church and also by tourism, spurred on by wealthy holidaymaking Americans and the prestige of post-war Italian cinema.

France remained a struggling great power, as witnessed by its share in the spoils of Berlin and also its desperate attempt to hold on to an imperial role in Indochina and later Algeria. Indeed, the Free French Army had been very much an imperial army, recruited from Africa, Asia, the Caribbean and the Pacific, which had not fallen under German domination. But France's colonialist ideology, uninflected by the realism of the British, who had seen at close hand the Quit India movement and the Indian National Army, was one of the forces which injected instability into the Fourth French Republic founded in 1946. The almost excessive prestige of de Gaulle paralleled the exuberance of the French Communist Party and kept various liberal and socialist politicians in an almost constant state of paralysis in weak coalitions right up to 1958, when de Gaulle re-entered the scene via a constitutional *coup d'état*. It was this weakness which allowed governors and militarists in Indochina and Algeria to push forward their attacks on local nationalists, so deepening the domestic ideological divide and draining off French manpower into the army. All the same, this was not an era of total failure, since government intervention in infrastructure, its extension of social services and well-judged support for middle-sized rural industry pushed forward France's economy and living standards, which were already rising to the same level as Britain's by 1955, and there was further improvement with the introduction of the European free-trade movement.[32]

Germany's transition from a Nazi-ruled state fighting almost to the last moment against encircling enemies to a peaceable federal democracy was indeed remarkable.[33] A key factor here was, of course, the economic stimulus given by the $15 billion of Marshall Plan aid, much of which was directed at Germany by an America increasingly fearful of the rise of Communism in its European markets. In 1953, Germany's external debt was written off. The presence of American troops and military bases also gave a fillip to growth in the austere late 1940s and early 1950s. Germany also remained a technically literate and well-educated society in which existing business enterprises were quickly able to rebuild capital and manpower. No less significant was the changed political environment. "De-Nazification" was pursued at the top level of the state, as in Japan and Italy, where the wartime regimes were dismantled by the occupying forces. But below this level, the state apparatus was left largely intact and the business classes quietly washed off the taint of Nazism. A federal democratic structure was created on the basis of existing regional units. This was enshrined in the Basic Law of the German Federal Republic in 1949.

The new constitution emphasised the local structures of Weimar Germany and also gave the president a balancing role as against an over-mighty chancellor. Symbolically, the capital was moved from Berlin, the Nazi imperial capital, now divided amongst the powers, to Bonn, a provincial centre with few claims to grandeur. As in Italy, the emergence of a Christian centrist party, with strong support both in Catholic Bavaria and the Protestant north, gave an unexciting stability to German politics over much of the next generation. The omnipresent threat of the Communist German Democratic Republic to the east helped the Christian Democrats to project themselves as upholders of a Western, Christian way of life and peaceable partners of the United States, Britain and France.

In regard to France, a determination to end more than a century of hostility and military conflict led the West German leadership to embark on economic and later political moves to create a European Union. Even though the two countries had different political styles, France being much more centralised even before de Gaulle re-entered the political scene, the two countries were brought together by the growth of their economies. France rapidly urbanised and its new consumers bought German goods in large quantities as the Federal Republic of Germany entered a period of spectacular GDP growth after 1950. Konrad Adenauer, the long-serving chancellor (1949–1963), represented the features of caution and lack of flamboyance which set the new Germany apart from its Nazi and Wilhelmine predecessors. A devout Catholic and committed democrat, he had served as Mayor of Cologne in the Weimar era but had avoided close contact with the Nazi state. As chancellor, he insisted on the full integration of Germany with the Western alliance and limited rearmament. Reunification of Germany, in his view, could only come about when West German democracy and its economy were undeniable strong and this message had been understood by the Communist East.

War had everywhere further extended the scope of the state. It was, indeed, Conservative ministers who first planned to build the welfare state in Britain, though it was later almost exclusively associated with Attlee's post-war Labour government.[34] Depression-era Keynesian expansion and wartime interventions in housing, brought about by bombing and the subsequent relocation of families, were continued in order to improve inner cities. Wartime disbursements of food and medicines continued after the war in the age of austerity, floods and harsh winters that followed. Some pre-war eugenicist interventions in the health of children, which had continued for fear of disease during the fighting, were also extended into the later 1940s and early 1950s. Indeed, the broad agreement between Tories and Labour Party spokesmen about the role of the state, later described as "Butskellism" (after Rab Butler and Hugh Gaitskell, two chancellors of the Exchequer from different political wings), found its origin much earlier in the aftermath of the war.

Despite his yearning for the Empire, even Churchill, who had once been a radical Liberal, did little to challenge this left-drifting political consensus when he returned to power in 1951. In fact, to some degree this progressivist sensibility united much of the democratic world after 1945 and even found some echoes in the United States. In Britain, the Cold War never excited the same degree of anxiety as it did in the United States, at least not until the Kennedy era. Socialism and Communism, dimensions of internal British politics and intellectual life since the anti-fascist movements of the 1930s, were known and understood. Stalin was a revered war hero until Khrushchev began to denounce his murderous regime in 1956. It was the fate of empire, rather than deep ideological divisions between left and right about state intervention or the Cold War, which split the consensus. The Suez debacle was to prove much more divisive even than the Soviet invasion of Hungary in 1956. But even empire quickly became a mere memory.

THE FATE OF THE MAJOR COMBATANTS, PART II: THE AMERICAS

In the ten years after the end of the war, the United States apparently passed from an era of Democratic government under Roosevelt and Truman to a conservative Republican phase under Dwight D. Eisenhower, Allied commander-in-chief during the latter stages of the war. Truman strengthened the rhetoric of anti-Communism, intervening in Greece and Iran against Stalin's expansionism as the British proved unable to maintain their global reach. The president also intervened with great determination against the Soviet attempts to starve the Western sectors of Berlin into submission in 1948–1949. Then the Korean War broke out with Douglas MacArthur urging the use of the atomic bomb against the Communists. Violent anti-leftist rhetoric targeting domestic politicians and media figures poured from the mouth of Joseph McCarthy in the Senate. The U-2 incident saw the great powers on the edge of another war, when an armed American plane flew over the territory of the USSR. American schoolchildren were regularly sent into underground shelters for fear of atomic warfare. Lacking a strong tradition of leftist thought and politicised trades unionism, Soviet Communism provoked an almost existential fear in the United States, despite its wealth and the power of its military. This immediate post-war period of tension ended with the overthrow in 1956 by British and American forces of the moderate Iranian president Mohammad Mossadegh, in a blatantly imperialist move to pre-empt the country regaining control of its own oil assets.

Yet, these changes in US domestic and foreign policies, even after the Republicans surged back to power in 1952–1953, were in no way a premonition of the age of neo-liberalism and "humanitarian intervention" which was to transpire at the beginning of the end of the century. Instead, and particularly in its domestic policy, the state pursued surprisingly interventionist policies under both Truman and Eisenhower and this helped to perpetuate the wartime boom in construction and development.[35] Here, at least, the United States remained closer to other liberal democracies across the world that were initiating, or developing, more clearly and ideologically "socialistic" forms of the welfare state. Indeed, in its emphasis on medium-size industrial development and exploitation of its huge resources of potential agricultural land, the United States even had something in common with the contemporary USSR, a parallel the leaders on both sides would have vigorously rejected.

This was a period of low energy prices when the United States faced very little competition from the exhausted countries of Western Europe or their impoverished colonial territories. But active state intervention, even when accompanied by the rhetoric of free markets, also provided a powerful stimulus. The so-called GI Bill of Rights gave returning soldiers considerable cash benefits which they could invest in consumer products and also low-cost mortgages, sparking a renewed housing boom. During the Depression and wartime, few houses had been built. Now, with federal and state support, a new expansion began, using wartime methods of mass production. Government agencies insured the bulk of the cost of housing, making it easy for companies to borrow money for the construction of cheap dwellings. The reality of quite large-scale state intervention was disguised by the prevailing emphasis on the free individual: "No man who owns his own house and lot can be a Communist. He has too much to do," said one of the foremost proponents of affordable housing.[36] Mass production techniques emerging out of the war were also turned to automobile construction since politicians and economic planners believed that mobility would also diminish poverty and consolidate the national market. By the mid-1950s, three-quarters of American families owned a car, and added production could be diverted towards Europe, consolidating the Western style of life there too.

Babies, as well as houses and cars, "boomed", further stimulating consumer demand. The poverty level which had been high in the Depression years declined dramatically and American GDP shot upwards, accounting for something like 45% of total world income by the early 1950s. The supposedly conservative Eisenhower revealed himself as a covert disciple of Keynes. "Ike" presided over the expansion of social security. He released funds for the expansion of the interstate highway network and large-scale irrigation works. The idea of building up the domestic economy once again came together with the rhetoric and fear engendered by the Cold War. The highways were also intended to make it easier for the population to escape in the event of a nuclear attack. But equally, Eisenhower pressed for the racial integration of the army and the state school system. Even in foreign policy, he brought about the end of the Korean War and recalled MacArthur, attempting to damp down the conflict with China and the USSR. Moreover, he did all this while engineering a balanced budget and compromising with his political opponents in Congress, unlike his Republican successors 60 years later. To this extent the gulf between Western European or Canadian "socialistic" economies and the United States can be greatly exaggerated for this period.[37]

Yet, despite the boom, this was by no means a period without social tension. The return of black soldiers and their experience of relative desegregation in the army forced the issue of racial discrimination in the Southern states of the Union to the forefront of politics. Similarly, a further migration of millions of black people to better-paying jobs in the less segregated northern industrial cities raised the temperature of black politics, but also impelled Southern politicians to work hard against black emancipation, which might diminish their rural labour supply. In 1954, the Supreme Court ruled against racial discrimination in schools, but its judgment proved impossible to enforce given states' autonomy. Here again, the United States was a signal, but not entirely exceptional, society. The post-war liberation movements in European colonial empires along with the movement of Asian, African and Caribbean workers to Western countries as their economies improved had raised issues of racial equality across the world, a clear example of global "connection". As the South African National Party introduced apartheid, its opponents sought solidarity with the United States' restive black population and the leftist leadership of the post-colonies.

During the war and the decade after it ended, the Latin American economy, outside Argentina, which lost its former pre-eminence, also boomed as older trades in agricultural products and beef were supplemented by a surge in the production of consumer goods for its rapidly growing cities. One stimulant here was the direct investment of North American capital itself, which could evade the still-high tariff barriers maintained by these states. This provides another example of the huge boost given to the world economy by the United States. Yet, Latin American politics, by contrast, continued in many respects to follow the varied path set during the Depression and the war.[38] Old landowning and liberal elites vied for power with conservative militarists. Democratic and socialist elements were marginalised across much of the continent and even Mexico, home of an indigenous revolution, moved to the right. It is true that the end of the war tended to bring disrepute to those regimes which had proclaimed their support for Germany or had vaunted their fascist credentials very openly. But even initially democratic movements or military coups engineered by younger and more modern military men usually established autocratic, patronage-based regimes. The most striking example here was Argentina, where Juan Perón (president 1946–1956) established a state which bore a great deal of resemblance to Franco's Spain, though embellished with a certain degree of romance by his wife, Eva.

One main reason why Latin American regimes often lapsed back into authoritarianism during this period was, as in so many other parts of the world, the atmosphere of the Cold War. This was not entirely the result of American suspicion of leftist movements. Though there was no real evidence for direct control by Moscow, let alone Beijing, Communist support in the region did spring from rather similar sources as it had done across Asia: poor farmers oppressed by elite landowners exporting cash-crops; "tribal" peoples losing their land, particularly in the Andes; and urban workers. Bosses tried hard to keep the earnings of working people low, or even depress them. This was the only way to keep competitive with the flood of US products even after the impact of tariffs was taken into account. Supposedly democratic regimes often used anti-Communist rhetoric to justify their continuing hold on power through corrupt clientelism. In Chile and Costa Rica, Communist parties were banned and their leaders purged and driven into exile. When, after 1944, Guatemala's politics moved to the left and land redistribution began to threaten, among other interests, that of the United States' United Fruit Conglomerate, the CIA quietly orchestrated a coup which pushed the government back to the right.

Yet, the most notorious example of this alliance between US political and commercial interests and right-wing dictatorships was provided by Cuba. Here, Fulgencio Batista, an army sergeant and mild reformist before the war, took power again in the 1950s and through corruption and violence assiduously laid the ground for the later emergence of the one successful Communist movement in the region, that of Fidel Castro. In the 1950s and early 1960s, Che Guevara and Fidel Castro returned to the issue of the relationship between the state and the individual in speeches and writings.[39] Guevara sought to resolve the difference and refute the "capitalist" view that Communism destroyed individuality, by stressing the idea that the members of the socialist vanguard were enlightened individuals who sacrificed themselves for a better society. Once Communist government was established, the people would remake themselves through "self-education". Work and struggle were now commitments to society.

THE FATE OF THE MAJOR COMBATANTS, PART III: JAPAN

Japan was even more totally crushed than Germany at the end of 1945. The whole colonial empire which it had occupied a mere five years before in Manchuria, Korea, Formosa and the China coast had been occupied by enemy powers. Mainland Japan had been devastated by bombing which had culminated in the destruction of Hiroshima and Nagasaki and as many as fifteen million of its population had been killed. In order to preserve even a small element of continuity at the highest level of government, the American occupiers under Douglas MacArthur had preserved the imperial house in a de-mystified form, whereas most monarchies in the Arab world and Eastern Europe had disappeared. In other respects, the United States moved to eradicate the wartime order more completely than the Allies did in France, Germany or Italy.[40] Some major war leaders were tried and hanged. As many as 200,000 military, civil and educational personnel were purged and replaced with younger men less beholden to the defeated imperial order. But at a local level the governmental structure was maintained, as in Germany. The constitution was rewritten. Women were given new rights to vote and inherit, and, perhaps most significantly, land was redistributed to farmers who had previously been mere tenants.

The Japanese, traumatised by war, cooperated with the Americans, and their economy began to recover with remarkable speed, reaching pre-war levels of production by 1953–1954.[41] This was partly because of the adaptability and acumen of the business groups which had survived the war and a considerable development of local infrastructure by the occupying forces. But it was also partly a result of external circumstances. Referring to "Japan's amazing recovery", a contemporary noted that the country "enjoyed a substantial measure of prosperity in recent years, due in part to the United States military expenditures and a boom in trade following the outbreak of the Korean War".[42] Japan also benefited from the fact that its defence needs were entirely met by the United States until 1953 and remained at a very low level thereafter. This contrasted sharply with the situation in the late 1930s, when something like 60% of the country's income had been spent on the military. Despite its fear of Chinese Communism, the Japanese post-war governments developed bilateral trade arrangements with China, while also benefiting from the slow economic recovery in South Korea and Malaya.

The Japanese Liberal Democratic Party emerged as a stabilising force in the country's politics as the United States ended its occupation and gave its blessing to the so-called 1955 System. This liberal–conservative grouping concentrated on building an export-led economy, encouraging savings and a low interest rate for loans and building medium and light industry, a policy that was later followed by several developing economies, latterly by China itself. To an even greater extent than in Western Europe under the social democrats, political conflict was kept to a minimum. The Liberal Democratic Party was opposed in national politics by the Socialist Party, but this had a very similar middle-class support base and was highly averse to sparking strikes and industrial conflicts. In cinema, art, music and youth culture, the Japanese appropriated many aspects of Western life, a path they had erratically taken since the 1860s.

CONCLUSION: AN AGE OF FORCED COMPROMISE

Above and beyond the continuation of "small wars beneath" across the world, this chapter traces the emergence of the United States as the dominant world power following the decline of all other contenders, bar the Soviet Union. This was not simply a matter of overwhelming military superiority. People in Western Europe, Japan and Southeast Asia yearned for peace and order after decades of warfare and economic depression. The proliferation and local successes of Communist movements in China, Vietnam, Southeast Asia and

Eastern Europe reinforced this craving for security. It was in this context that the emergence of transnational organisations, such as the United Nations and the International Monetary Fund, came to embody a desire for diplomatic and economic order. The United States rapidly came to dominate both, so consolidating its world hegemony. As early as 1941, economists and policymakers in Britain and America were drawing up plans for a new range of economic treaties and institutions which were intended to avoid the recurrence of a depression, itself a significant cause of the rise of Nazism and fascism. The key figure here was the British economist Keynes, who had pointedly argued in his book *The Economic Consequences of the Peace* that the turmoil of the previous decades was due to bad policymaking in 1919.

Yet, it was the Americans who ultimately determined the form of economic governance which emerged in the Bretton Woods Conference of July 1944.[43] Britain was heavily indebted to the United States as a result of the lend-lease agreement which financially underpinned the United Kingdom after 1941. The country had agreed to open its markets to American goods, demolishing the system of Imperial preference and effectively making the British Empire redundant as an economic force. The aim of the subsequent meetings was to stabilise exchange rates and avoid the kind of "beggar-my-neighbour" devaluations which had occurred after 1929. There was no intention of going back to the discredited gold standard and the British and even many Americans believed that state intervention, rather than the economic austerity lauded by theorists such as Friedrich Hayek, was the only way to raise living standards and in the process limit the apparent attraction of Communist central planning.

Though Keynes tried to limit American economic dominance at Bretton Woods, in the year before his death it was assured by the fact that the dollar was the only widely available and stable currency across the whole world. The dollar effectively became the intermediate measure between gold and other currencies, and consequently the world's reserve currency. There is no doubt that the stability this helped bring about lasted at least until the late 1970s and helped to spur significant economic growth across the Western world. This was so even when the Soviets and China refused to participate and a country such as India felt disadvantaged by the Bretton Woods system and the policies of the IMF. Chapter 8 takes forward the story of the flawed hegemony of the United States and the re-emergence of prosperity across Europe and Japan. But these first ten years after the Second World War should be seen as an age of forced compromise. This was a compromise empowered by American domination of Europe and Japan and general fear of nuclear war. But under the nuclear standoff, numerous small wars continued, from Vietnam to Palestine. These were to shape the rest of the century.

[8] AMERICA'S HEGEMONY AND COLONIALISM'S FINALE, MID-1950s TO 1970s

America Regnant
The Struggle with "World Communism"
The Fate of "Democratic Socialism" in the New States: South Asia
Africa: The End of Colonialism and the Trials of Nation States
The Travails and Resurgence of Europe
Latin America and the Caribbean: Revolution and Reaction
Conclusion

NEVER before in world history was a new age announced with such ferocity than when the atom bombs fell on Hiroshima and Nagasaki in the summer of 1945, finally bringing the Second World War to an end. Yet, once the secret of atomic reaction was out, these weapons were soon in place in the USSR (1948) and Britain (1950). By the time the hydrogen bomb was tested in 1952 the level of possible destruction in an atomic war was clear. The military budgets of major states were increasingly spent on the development of atomic weapons and the missiles which would carry them. International tensions reached new heights and were paralleled by regimes of secrecy, surveillance and denunciation epitomised by Senator McCarthy's anti-Communist inquisitions in the United States and the monitoring by MI5 of prominent left-wing intellectuals and even historians, notably Christopher Hill and Eric Hobsbawm, in the United Kingdom.[1]

"The Bomb" stood as the dark antithesis to the ideology of high modernism which had already been announced before the war in art, architecture and

Remaking the Modern World 1900–2015: Global Connections and Comparisons, First Edition. C. A. Bayly.
© 2018 John Wiley & Sons Ltd. Published 2018 by John Wiley & Sons Ltd.

literature. Yet, the atomic age also saw a great explosion of peaceful scientific advances: the creation of nuclear power reactors, aircraft which could break the sound barrier and advances in medicine following the sequencing of DNA in the early 1950s. Indirectly, the Cold War and the fear of nuclear catastrophe powered a huge improvement in education across the world, while it focussed the minds of European statesmen on Europe itself, contributing to the final liberation of most colonial peoples by the mid-1960s. Advances in communication, notably television, expanded the range of youth culture and empowered a new form of democracy. Wartime advances in contraception and the later dissemination of "the pill" helped bring about the feminist revolution of the 1960s and 1970s. This chapter, then, examines the political paradoxes of the years from the mid-1950s to the late 1970s: the period of high scientific modernism and worldwide ideological conflict, which was also an unequalled period of popular liberation.

AMERICA REGNANT

In 1953, the American post-war boom was in full swing and the Korean War had ended, though in military deadlock. The Stalinist era was drawing to a close, Japan had been returned to diplomatic normality and Europe was beginning to emerge from the devastation of the Second World War. By 1979, European imperial rule had finally come to an end in Africa and the Iranian revolution was underway, signalling the beginnings of an Islamic revival across the world. This was soon to be followed by the Soviet invasion of Afghanistan and the death throes of the Communist system itself. China was by then emerging from the travails of Maoism, while the Western democracies were moving towards the free-market right wing. In retrospect, then, these intervening two and a half decades marked the peak of American economic hegemony across the world, even though its people were successively alarmed by the Cold War, the assassination of President Kennedy, the clash over black civil rights, the country's defeat in Vietnam and the sense of loss of direction under presidents Gerald Ford and Jimmy Carter.[2] A country at the peak of its power in real terms was haunted by a sense of decline. Even when Richard Nixon initiated a period of detente and withdrew from Vietnam in the early 1970s, the United States was soon racked by the Watergate scandal, which seemed to speak of the corruption of democracy. Despite the sense of American decline, Khrushchev's Soviet "leap forward" was a chimera while the debacles in Cuba and Vietnam stirred domestic conflict, but scarcely damaged US global power. By contrast, the years of Ronald Reagan and his successors from 1979 up to 11th September 2001 certainly saw a continuation of American global pre-eminence, underscored by the collapse of Communism in the USSR and Eastern Europe. Yet, by then, US economic dominance had been curtailed by the rise of Western Europe and Japan.

Even at its height in the mid-nineteenth century, Britain had never dominated the world in this manner. American hegemony between the 1950s and 1970s was largely maintained without direct military intervention, Cuba and

Vietnam being significant exceptions, though leftists continued to castigate "American imperialism". The great economic expansion which had begun with the return of the GIs at the end of the war rolled on and American technical dominance was revealed anew by space travel, the development of computing and the TV entertainment industry. The roots of this superpower status clearly lay in the technical developments of wartime and the release of savings which families had piled up between 1940 and 1945. But it was maintained by deeper demographic, cultural and social processes. The so-called baby boom which gathered pace after 1945 provided a surge in the numbers of working-age young people, who filled first America's expanding colleges and universities and then professional jobs in the 1950s and 1960s. Black workers, discriminated against in their own states in the South, and foreign workers from poorer countries, particularly Mexico, filled the factory and skilled technical positions. The baby boom was self-perpetuating, increasing demand for domestic goods, larger houses, automobiles and televisions. American optimism, badly dented by the Depression and military failures early in the war, was reignited. Unemployment in the late 1960s remained remarkably low, the crime rate and divorce rate dropped and the American version of liberalism, which produced Kennedy and Lyndon B. Johnson's social legislation along with moves against Southern racism, held the day.

In turn, the mass production of top-quality consumer goods spurred on American penetration of overseas markets in Europe, Southeast Asia and Japan. The United States was never dependent on exports to the same extent as smaller European countries were, because of the great size of its own internal market. Yet, the success of American companies abroad expanded the global market in financial services and consumer goods. Televisions and cars replaced the tobacco exports of the Southern states. This created a new form of "soft power", based on the accumulation of capital, but propagated by the communication of desired lifestyles. By 1969, for instance, IBM accounted for three-quarters of mainframe production across the world. Within ten years, Steve Wozniak and Steve Jobs had created Apple, and Bill Gates, Microsoft, which brought computing to the world's masses.[3] This revolution in communications was as profound as any political revolution in history. In Gates's words, the personal computer "has become the most empowering tool we've ever created".

The American lifestyle and envy of its prosperity spread globally, powered by youth culture and high levels of spending on leisure products.[4] Hollywood produced massive blockbusters that inspired imitation across the world. In India, for instance, "Bollywood", Bombay's Hollywood, produced its own hybrid of the American dream and Indian musical slapstick. The two influences of African American music and country music enthused a new generation of global musical celebrities: the Beach Boys, the Rolling Stones, the Beatles and Michael Jackson. Though political historians tend to emphasise the nuclear standoff and the Soviet invasion of Afghanistan, the rise of free-market conservatism and the retreat of socialism in the Western world owed much to the influence of American popular culture and technical expertise. In the longer run, it was a critical background to the fall of Communism in Russia and

Eastern Europe and even its reform in China. Young people saw no reason to sacrifice a more pleasant lifestyle for the sake of socialist perfection, and party bosses eventually got the message.

Yet contemporary observers, while acknowledging America's pre-eminence, still pointed to the profound internal racial and social tensions which the country exhibited[5] and the two disastrous ventures into liberal imperialism which it undertook in Cuba and Southeast Asia. The Civil Rights Movement was part of a much more general pattern of liberation movements across the world. Several sub-Saharan African nations had achieved independence in the late 1950s and early 1960s. The French had been fought to a standstill in Algeria, and America itself had loosened its hold on the Philippines after the war. Black leaders in the American South, in particular Martin Luther King, constantly pointed to the paradox that the United States apparently championed freedom abroad while its own black population was still denied basic rights in the South and remained second-class citizens in the northern cities to which many of them had migrated.[6] King summoned up the example of Gandhi and the fate of the Indian "untouchables", who in an earlier era had themselves been uplifted by the example of American reformers such as Wilson, Dewey and Roosevelt.

The massacre of black protesters at Sharpeville in South Africa in 1960 seemed to point to an international struggle against racial discrimination. This might easily have turned violent, as the examples of the African National Congress and the US Black Panthers were to show. Non-violent protest spread rapidly across the Southern states in the early 1960s. John F. Kennedy made little progress in dismantling racial legislation because of the relative autonomy of state governments. But Lyndon Johnson, himself a Southerner and a skilled backroom politician, made large strides in demolishing it. The 1964 Civil Rights Act which outlawed discrimination in public schools and the workplace was cleverly pushed through Southern Democratic and Republican opposition by Johnson, aided by a widespread mobilisation of public sphere organisations.[7] The 1965 Voting Rights Act gave black people in the South equality and a huge effort was made to get them onto the electoral register.

Johnson also embarked upon a wider, state-led programme of social reform, called "the Great Society", which dwarfed the advances of the 1930s. He proclaimed, "I'm a Roosevelt New Dealer . . . I'm no budget slasher."[8] His aim was to create a more equal society and head off the radical liberation movements which had begun to emerge within both the black and white populations. The provision of Medicare and Medicaid for the poor was greatly increased, though this continued to be a source of political tension for the next 50 years. Federal funds were put into education in poor areas. The direction of these changes was epitomised by the Economic Opportunity Act of 1964. In so far as these reforms succeeded, it was because they commanded the support of a large body of young and middle-aged citizens who had been mobilised by radio and television. The Democrats won a landslide victory in the 1964 elections. Youth culture, the feminist movement and black consciousness all contributed to the sense of change. Radical theologians, both Protestant and Catholic, steered their congregations towards more liberal positions.

Yet, this was no easy transition. Crime and racial politics became entangled. Riots in Detroit in 1967 led to a massive fire and hundreds of deaths, mostly of black people. The assassination of the black leader Martin Luther King in 1968 sparked a further set of disturbances. In the early 1970s, the Black Panther organisation was succeeded by the Black Liberation Army, both prepared to use force against pervasive racism.[9] This ferment also divided the liberals and created a conservative backlash, especially in the South. Many saw the excesses of youth culture – "free love", alcohol, drugs and bacchanalian music festivals – as a threat to social stability. Above all, society was deeply divided by the draft and Johnson's determination to prosecute the war in Vietnam. Here the consensus was dangerously split. Radical libertarians and anti-war protestors excoriated Johnson, while many liberals and conservatives viewed the war as a righteous struggle against coercive and godless Communism.

The Struggle with "World Communism"

The year between the spring of 1953 and the spring of 1954 provided the background for this fateful US military intervention in Asia and the launching of the last phase of Soviet Communism. In March 1953, Stalin died. Ironically, one reason for his sudden demise seems to have been the fact that all the best doctors in Moscow had been jailed as dissidents.[10] In July, the Korean War ended with a stalemate guaranteeing the existence of the Communist North and American-protected South Korea. During the spring of 1954, the French were defeated at Dien Bien Phu, signalling the emergence of a Communist state in North Vietnam. International Communism was advancing, but in the USSR itself the political temperature was changing. Nikita Khrushchev, once a member of Stalin's circle who had gradually assumed overall power, signalled a number of developments towards a more open society. It was hardly liberation but there was, at least, a loosening of coercion. This was important because all the indications were that, immediately before his death, Stalin was planning a further round of purges and repression.

Khrushchev was acutely aware that internal criticism of the Party was growing. Quite apart from the exile to the gulags, disappearance and death of numerous ordinary citizens, living conditions had hardly improved since the end of the war and many former soldiers had seen how much better off Germans and even Poles had been a few years earlier. Khrushchev gradually lifted controls on consumer products, but more importantly invested in a massive new housing programme.[11] Hundreds of thousands of families were moved from the communal housing of the Stalinist period to individual units in new blocks which sprung up around the major cities. This was not simply a physical relocation, because the new privacy made it possible for people to discuss and even criticise government measures without fear of surveillance. Beyond the Communist Party, civil society institutions were still largely absent and news from outside the country very limited, but a constrained internal dialogue had begun.

Khrushchev played out a long power struggle with more hard-line follow-ers of Stalin in 1953–1954, in part by expanding the Party's Central Com-mittee and using it against the Politburo. Again, this was hardly a move towards democracy and popular representation, but it did open the state to new influences, particularly those of scientists and technicians. Those who lost out in the power struggle were not executed or imprisoned as they would have been under Stalin. A limited degree of freedom was also given to novelists and artists. Yet, most important was Khrushchev's brave decision to criticise Stalin for tyranny and murder at the 1956 Party Congress in a "secret" speech, where he noted that, "three-quarters of the Central Com-mittee that had been put in place at the Seventeenth Party Congress in 1934 had been shot before the end of the decade".[12] This revelation had interna-tional repercussions. Communists and socialists in the Western world, who had naively believed that Stalin was a progressive statesman, were horrified. In Eastern Europe, only recently conquered by the USSR, significant resist-ance began. But Khrushchev quickly demonstrated the limitations of his reformism when he invaded Hungary in November 1956 as anti-Communist forces gained power there.

Over the next decade, the USSR still seemed secure in its great power status. Living standards improved marginally. Eastern Europe was stable and Com-munism seemed to be making headway in other parts of the world. In the GDR, a degree of economic success was recorded with the release of the Trabant motorcar in 1957. Sold across the Communist bloc, this dwarf-like vehicle seemed to be at least a runner-up to the spectacular success of West Germany's Volkswagens. With the launch of the space satellite, sputnik, in 1957, Soviet science seemed to be on a par with the United States. Even after Khrushchev's dismissal from power in 1964, a degree of political stability was preserved across the bloc. The ageing leadership maintained control throughout the 1970s. Communist state surveillance probably reached its height in East Germany in the 1950s and 1960s. The GDR was suspect in the eyes of the USSR because of its previous history of Nazism and the proximity of American and other Allied forces. Unlike Mao's China or even parts of the USSR, the country had rapidly built up its communications network and there is clear evidence of intrusive spying within families, schools and the workplace with dissidents being jailed or denied employment.[13]

Yet, it is important to remember that the aims of "the state" in the GDR were carried forward by ordinary people.[14] One picturesque case concerns the exploits of Hector the Bear, a kind of socialist Winnie the Pooh. Children were expected to watch this programme on a regular basis, applauding Hector's exploits, as the red scarf-wearing animal made contact with his fellow com-radely bears in the Ukraine or Azerbaijan. Children would be quizzed at school by the teachers the next day to make sure their parents had made them watch the programme, rather than the illegal, "Americanised" West German TV pro-grammes. Those in default would be sanctioned. Only very late in the decade, with the USSR's decision to invade Afghanistan, internal economic stagnation and the gradual filtering in of news through the West's new media, did the true fragility of these Communist regimes begin to be revealed.[15]

The USSR's external policy was also reshaped in the mid-1950s. Indeed, the background to the external traumas of the United States was the new direction of Soviet policy across the world after Stalin's death. Stalin's aim had always been to consolidate Communist power in Europe. Khrushchev shrewdly realised that the longer-term consequences of Marshall Aid and the revival of the European economies under the nuclear protection of the United States meant that little further movement could be made on that continent. The Soviet leadership was, of course, prepared to intervene militarily if any of their gains in Eastern Europe came under serious threat: this is what happened in Hungary in 1956. But Khrushchev had decided that world revolution, or rather Soviet hegemony, could be better served by the vaguely leftist anticolonial and anti-elite movements which had emerged in what was by then called the Third World. This is what lay behind American-based rightists' attempts to overthrow Castro's Communist mini-state in Cuba in 1962 and the subsequent Soviet intervention, only abandoned at the last minute when the world seemed close to nuclear war. The Communist state survived but was crushed by US sanctions for the next 50 years. The vicissitudes of Patrice Lumumba's rule in the Congo in 1960–1961 were part of the same international struggle. The United States even staged a partial rapprochement with India during Nehru's 1962 war with China.[16] But it was the Southeast Asian situation which had the greatest impact on both American foreign policy and its internal politics.

The defeat of the French by the Viet Minh in 1954 resulted in a tense peace in the region, comparable perhaps with the stalemate in Korea.[17] But the situation changed with the Sino-Soviet split of the later 1950s and the USSR's attempt to draw closer to the North Vietnamese, part of Khrushchev's Third World policy. As tension between the North and the non-Communist South increased during the 1960s, the United States, fearing a "domino effect", increased first technical assistance and then direct military support to the South.[18] In 1963, they even moved to overthrow President Ngo Dinh Diem, whom they regarded as an unreliable proxy ruler. In due course, Lyndon Johnson poured US troops into the country. This appeared to bring success until a major North Vietnamese counterattack, the so-called Tet Offensive of 1968, sounded a warning that an American defeat was approaching. This was despite huge Vietnamese losses, perhaps three million dead, compared with about 60,000 US troops.[19] Indeed, Ho Chi Minh himself had correctly prophesied, "You will kill ten of our men and we will kill one of yours and in the end it will be you who will tire of it."[20]

Basically, American politicians and the US high command had overestimated the effectiveness of their technological dominance against guerrilla warfare. They had also underestimated the hatred and opposition which the influx of foreign troops created among the local Vietnamese population, both North and South. Ho Chi Minh's revolution was always more a nationalist than an international Communist movement. This was later exemplified in the country's resistance to control by China and even the USSR. Compared with China, for instance, Vietnamese Communists always protected the indigenous small business class along with the peasant and worker. Even during the purges of Ho's rigid accomplice and later successor, Le Duan, Secretary General of the

Party in the 1960s, Vietnamese land policies were never as repressive as Mao's. Vietnamese Communists also gave a degree of protection to the country's more compliant Buddhist institutions, in stark contrast with the treatment of comparable bodies in China. Under the Cold War rhetoric of Communism and anti-Communism, both combatants were influenced, in fact, by deeper ideological commitments: national independence and Christian liberalism, respectively. Yet, in the case of the United States, a full-scale revolt against conscription and a pointless war began to undermine the national consensus at the same time as the struggle in Vietnam reached crisis point. Opposition within the US was dramatically demonstrated by the National Guard's shooting of demonstrators against Richard Nixon's war in Cambodia at Kent State University in 1970.

American failure in Vietnam, finally dramatised by the flight of its officials in helicopters from Saigon in 1975 and Richard Nixon's earlier visit to appease China, had significant internal consequences for the United States. While American youth, already stirred by pop culture and anti-establishment sentiment, "dodged the draft" and derided politicians, other Americans turned towards the right, and various forms of Christian revivalism. This shift, decisively signalled by Ronald Reagan's election to the presidency in 1981, was only temporarily interrupted by the White House tenures of Gerald Ford and Jimmy Carter. These two leaders made successful attempts to defuse international conflicts, such as the crisis between Israel and Egypt, but ultimately seemed weak in domestic politics.

If Khrushchev hoped vainly that the USSR had constructed a socialist state combining equality with the high technical modernism of the United States, Mao Zedong embarked during the late 1950s on one of the most disastrous social experiments in human history: the so-called Great Leap Forward.[21] After the end of the Korean War, China had been successful in repairing much of the damage of the earlier civil war and laying the foundation for modern industries. The urban population grew quite rapidly, though the population remained 75% rural in 1950. A brief attempt to institute collectivisation of peasant land in 1956–1957 was called off when production figures began to decline because of the chaos created. But Mao and his Central Committee were determined to transform China into a worker's society as quickly as possible. The aim was to overtake Britain in industrial production before the beginning of the 1960s and the policy required a great increase in food production in order to feed the burgeoning urban working class. This had increased by as much as 70 million people between 1957 and 1960. In the view of the leadership, this leap forward in food production could only be achieved by utterly transforming the mentality of the peasantry in the way they believed the Stalinist Five Year Plans had done in the USSR. The state would have to intervene on a huge scale, sequestering grain and forcing the rural labourers into communes with collective dining halls and labour distribution. Party officials believed that peasants were wedded to the family and consequently hid much of the grain they produced. If the state could extract this assumed surplus and sell it abroad as an agricultural producer, the resulting funds could be invested in industrial development.

The result of these policies was large-scale famine across some of the most isolated parts of central China. Officials vastly overrated the size of the harvests of 1958 and 1959, seized up to 40% of the crop, leaving local communes without food. The estimate of deaths varied greatly between 17 and 45 million, though early on one Chinese official admitted there had been "casualties . . . this is the price we have to pay".[22] Many of those who died were denied rations because they did not fall in line with the local cadres and were regarded as "bad elements". People survived by theft, criminal attacks on their fellows or by running away from the communes to the cities against the government's rules. Mao failed to heed the warnings of a few of his officials and believed in his own omnipotence as a seer of China's future. Despite his rural origins, he distrusted the peasantry and believed that they were hiding grain. He lived in an "echo chamber", as one historian has put it. The disaster was only brought to an end in 1960 when the cities themselves began to run short of food because of the disruption in the countryside. Finally, the Central Committee summoned up the courage to acknowledge the situation and Zhou Enlai began to ship food to the starving provinces.

China's population was given a breathing space for a few years before another violent attempt was made to drag them into socialist modernity in the form of the Cultural Revolution.[23] On this occasion, however, it was intellectuals and urban-dwellers rather than the peasantry who were the prime targets of the CCP's cadres. Ironically, the emergence, or re-emergence, of this "bourgeois" class – for many were members of the old elites who had survived civil war and revolution – was itself a result of the breakneck urbanisation which the Party had brought about. The failure of the Great Leap Forward – the impossibility of turning peasants into steel-producers overnight – diminished Mao's influence for some years. But in 1966, he and his clique regained power and began to denounce "revisionists and bourgeois elements" which had allegedly infiltrated the Party.

A corps of Red Guards was formed which sparked off power struggles in local Party units, factories, educational institutions and the People's Liberation Army. The mass imprisonment of "deviationists" followed. Many sceptics of the regime were murdered in local conflicts, though deaths were on a small scale compared with the famine of the Great Leap Forward. Educated people and intellectuals were forced out of the towns in the "Back to the Countryside" movement. Mass action persisted until 1971 when the scale of disruption and economic weakness again forced a slackening of Red Guard pogroms. Thereafter, the CCP was afflicted by a typical contest between right and left elements which only came to an end on the death of Mao himself in September 1976. With the help of the military leadership, which feared for the integrity of the country under leftist ideological domination, Deng Xiaoping and his supporters engineered a coup against the so-called Gang of Four. By 1978, Deng was urging "liberty of thought" at the Party Congress. This did not come to pass. Yet, China's own movement, over the following generation, towards a kind of state capitalism began to take form.

In part, the Cultural Revolution and its aftermath have to be seen against the background of international developments. Mao had long been concerned by what he saw as Khrushchev's revisionism and the lurch away from Stalinist forced planning. But Khrushchev's own deposition in 1964 seemed to him even more dangerous evidence of how a socialist state could begin to fragment in the context of popular discontent and American commercial success. Equally, China's lurch towards pragmatism under Deng Xiaoping can be seen in the context of the fears generated by the foreign policy of the USSR as it unfolded in Afghanistan and Southeast Asia, where Vietnam, victorious against both the French and the Americans, was seen as the USSR's, rather than a Chinese proxy. Vietnam's invasion of Cambodia in 1978 sparked a war between China and Vietnam. The latter's sound defeat of the much larger People's Liberation Army confirmed the post-Mao leadership in its fears that the Cultural Revolution had sapped China's vitality and so encouraged economic and political pragmatism.

A series of ideologically disparate and indeed antagonistic "cultural revolutions" were to mark the following half-century. The followers of the ayatollahs in Iran were quite soon destroying the Shah's art works and libraries, while pouring his first-growth clarets down the drain. Later, the Afghan Taliban smashed the Buddhas of Bamiyan, just as the Red Guards had destroyed their Chinese equivalents. The neo-Christian regime in post-Communist Hungary burned the archival records of its predecessors. A more recent manifestation of this phenomenon is ISIS's destruction of priceless Assyrian monuments. All these cases saw a use of new media – whether the radio, the press or cinema – and the harnessing of angry youth. This had been one aspect of revolutions as far back as 1789, 1773 or even 1642. Mass popular communication and the ideological lurch away from Marxist–Leninist sub-structuralism made it even more evident. Yet, Communist violence had one final outing before political insurgency took on this new, religious tinge. The seizure of power by the Khmer Rouge in Cambodia in 1975, in the wake of the reunification of Vietnam, led to localised mass murder on a proportionate scale not seen even in Mao's China. In this small country perhaps two million people were slaughtered.[24] Pol Pot, the Khmer Rouge dictator, apparently believed that Mao's Cultural Revolution had not gone far enough and that socialism could finally be achieved if the intelligentsia and covert capitalists of the towns were totally annihilated. Only a Vietnamese invasion of Cambodia in 1978 averted further killing.[25]

Another of these bloody eruptions had taken place in Indonesia in 1965–1966 when as many as a million Communist supporters, trade unionists and intellectuals were massacred by the Indonesia army following a failed coup against the government of President Sukarno. But as a non-Communist coup, tinged with ethnicity and religion, this was a clearer anticipation of events after 1979 in Iran. Ever since the Indonesian revolution against the Dutch, the country's leaders had sought an unstable balance between Communism and Islam, between Malay and Chinese. The increasing radicalism of the PKI (Indonesian Communist Party), spurred on by the example of Mao, brought Sukarno's balancing act to an end. The assassination of army officers during an attempted Communist coup resulted in a savage reaction by the army, which became an anti-Chinese pogrom.[26] In the following so-called New Order of the following president, Suharto, the use of the Chinese language and Chinese

Figure 8 Yogyakarta, Indonesia, 1948. © Charles Breijer/Nederlands Fotomuseum.

names was banned. As in other cases in Asia and Africa during the Cold War, ideological conflicts became forms of ethnic cleansing. The United States and Britain failed to register any protest over these events, the one already fighting Communists in Vietnam; the other concerned by the *Konfrontasi* ("confrontation") between West-leaning and now independent Malaysia and a volatile Indonesia.[27]

THE FATE OF "DEMOCRATIC SOCIALISM" IN THE NEW STATES: SOUTH ASIA

This chapter is concerned with the high modernist period of centralised planning, popular mobilisation and movements of liberation which dominated much of the world between the end of the Korean War and the beginning of the Iranian Revolution of 1979. These aspects of the period were seen at their most stark in Mao's China. But even the world hegemon, the United States, exceptional in its hostility to "socialism", saw a degree of state intervention both internally with the GI bills and Johnson's social legislation and externally through foreign aid. These features again were all evident in softer and modified form in independent India. From as early as 1938, the Indian National Congress had begun to consider a new constitution for the country as it became independent, but also created a Planning Commission which used Soviet centralised planning, though not its centralised pseudo-democracy, as a model. By the early 1950s, the country had embarked on the First Five Year Plan, which envisioned the establishment of heavy industries, massive dam and road construction and state intervention in financial provision. The Zamindari (landlord) Abolition Acts of 1949–1951 also superficially resembled the forced land redistributions which had taken place in the wake of the Russian and Chinese revolutions. P. C. Mahalanobis, one of Nehru's closest advisers, a top-down planner and statistician, wanted to remould the "village habits and psychology" and to force an engagement with "the industrial outlook with interests in tools, gadgetry and new innovations".[28]

The intention was to break down the bonds of caste and religion and, in one sense, it seemed to mirror Mao's Great Leap Forward. But there was one fundamental difference: the Congress Party was an all-India party, but it was not an organ of state control in anything like the manner of the Soviet or Chinese Communist parties. Nehru himself declared that he would like to introduce more socialistic policies but complained that most Indians were not socialists and so he could not implement them. This was a backhanded compliment to the strengths of India's form of representative democracy which had been instituted through a universal franchise immediately after independence, despite the concerns of many of the country's politicians. An attachment to popular rights which had been forged during the movement against colonial rule, alongside widespread respect for the practice of voting which had been unwillingly introduced by the British rulers, meant that ordinary people in India, however poor, genuinely believed in the democratic process. India's inheritance of numerous and complex civil society organisations further reinforced its democracy. Yet, politicians also had a shrewd understanding that, while a strong central government was required, the enormous linguistic, religious and social variety of the country meant that any attempt at autocratic rule from such a centre would rapidly be counter-productive, as Indira Gandhi was soon to discover.[29]

Indian society, however, remained poor and unequal, and this prompted the emergence of leftist movements and attempts to counter inequality. The recovery from the Depression and Second World War, combined with the state intervention which the British authorities had foresworn, resulted in a slow emergence of a bigger middle class and a relatively better-off rural population in many parts of the country in the 1950s. Famine was replaced with "scarcity", such as the one that occurred in northern India in the mid-1960s. But growth was held back by bureaucracy and the government's unwillingness, for historic reasons, to embrace foreign investment. Phrases like "permit Raj" and "the Hindu rate of growth" became common by the 1970s. The sluggishness of economic improvement and regional difference led to the success of Communist parties, particularly in Kerala and Bengal. These, however, still remained broadly democratic and did not move against other political parties. The failure of the institution of caste reservations in government jobs to give much help to Dalits ("untouchables") led their leader B. R. Ambedkar to draw many of them off into a neo-Buddhist movement, organised against the Hindu majority. Indian development remained slow by comparison with the rapid growth of Latin America and parts of Southeast Asia.

Nehru's daughter, Indira Gandhi, pressed the modernist and socialist policies of her father much further. Coming to power in 1966, she inaugurated the "Green Revolution", which was designed to increase food crop production through more scientific agricultural development.[30] This was a modest success and India became less dependent on foreign imports with the welfare of the urban poor improving considerably. It was, however, a centralising project, complemented by the nationalisation of the banks in 1969 and a revivification of economic and political relations with the USSR. After the electoral boost which Mrs Gandhi received following the country's defeat of Pakistan during the Bangladesh war of secession in 1971, her policies became more stridently centralising. She worked not only to destroy Congress's enemies in the states but also Congress chief ministers who appeared too powerful in her eyes. This was a significant break with her father's policies. The war on poverty of the early 1970s ("Garibi Hatao!") also spread centrally controlled welfare programmes across the country. India's desire to place itself as a modern, scientific power was also realised by its nuclear policy, which began in 1967 and resulted in the successful test of an atomic bomb in 1974. This, combined with India's hostility to American policy in Indochina, led to a further deterioration of relations with the United States and stronger ties with the USSR.

While her social policies had alienated sections of the business class and richer farmers, Indira Gandhi's lurch towards authoritarian government during the Emergency of 1975–1977 was brought about by a series of local judgments by Indian courts which convicted her of electoral malpractice and effectively removed her from office.[31] Using the constitutional provision for president's rule during a national "emergency", she imprisoned political opponents who had coordinated protests against her, gagged the press and allowed her son, Sanjay, a wide range of powers. Sanjay pressed ahead with social programmes which included the seizure and demolition of slum property and what was effectively forced sterilisation, an attempt to diminish India's soaring birth rate.

Commentators still disagree about the reason why Mrs Gandhi called off the Emergency in 1977, so suffering a massive defeat in the following general election at the hands of a centre and right-wing coalition, led by the Janata Party. She may have believed that she was more popular among ordinary people than she actually was. A lingering democratic sensibility may have urged her to seek popular legitimacy for her actions. What is clear is that ordinary people were, in fact, more wedded to a multiparty democratic system than her advisers believed. Though Mrs Gandhi returned to power in 1980, these events and the reaction to them began the slow demise of the Indian National Congress in its socialistic guise. Over the next ten years more and more economists and public figures began to call for a move towards a free-market economy in common with opinion across much of the rest of the world and, ultimately, in the USSR and China. One significant result of the Emergency was the new vigour it gave to the Hindu right and also to Sikh activists in the Punjab, so echoing the slow resurgence of religious politics which was a global phenomenon, gathering pace over the following half-century.

AFRICA: THE END OF COLONIALISM AND THE TRIALS OF NATION STATES

Modernism, centralisation and democracy remained dominant themes of the years between 1955 and 1979. While the balance between them varied greatly across the world, aspects of them appeared in all societies. Africa experienced them all in striking succession. The early 1950s saw a sharp increase in popular movements demanding independence from European colonial rule.[32] The combination of the image of independence in India, the defeat of France in Indochina and the encouragement of the USSR and, more ambivalently, the United States galvanised nationalist leaderships across the continent. After the war, Britain, France and Holland had attempted to reimpose colonial control in Africa and parts of Asia. Lacking US support, the Dutch were effectively removed from the East Indies by 1950. To American administrations a weak Islamic–socialist mix of regional leadership under Sukarno was preferable to Communism, which was growing in strength among the local Chinese population. By contrast, American foreign policy was generally uninterested in Africa, where the Communist threat was deemed less pressing.

French governments, already on the brink of failure in Indochina, were in no mood to compromise with insurgent Algerian nationalists, particularly in view of the support they received from the French settler population (*colons* or *pieds noirs*) who insisted that Algeria was an indivisible part of France itself.[33] There followed one of the most brutal anticolonial wars of the period as French troops, hardened by the Second World War and the Indochinese conflict, combated armed guerrilla bands, which received the support of the USSR and independent Arab states, such as the Egypt of Gamal Abdul Nasser, who had emerged triumphantly from a contest with the British, French and Israelis in 1956. Several elements combined to embitter the conflict, which lasted to 1958, when Charles de Gaulle returned to power and ultimately sought a political compromise, as only a military nationalist could have done.[34]

Why was the Algerian conflict so violent? First, the *colon* population, part French, but also part Maltese, Jewish, Italian and Spanish, was one million strong, but saw no place for itself in an independent Algeria. Secondly, French intransigence was strengthened by the feeling that the country was rapidly losing international influence at a period when the process of European integration, from which it was later to benefit so much, was only just beginning. Violence was further increased by the fact that this was a civil war as well as an anticolonial struggle to a much greater extent than it had been in Vietnam. Two hundred thousand Algerian fighters and civilians were killed and thousands of others tortured by French forces. But as many as 150,000 so-called *harkis*, who supported the French, were also massacred during and after, while most of the *colons* eventually fled back to France.

Not all the final stages of French imperialism were equally violent, however. In West Africa, French influence persisted through to the beginning of the twenty-first century and this contrasted sharply with the violence of the end of Belgian rule in the Congo. The factors which contributed to this relatively peaceful outcome were almost the opposite of those in Algeria. French colonists were in much smaller numbers in West Africa, being mainly teachers, technical experts and shopkeepers. They did not dominate the major towns like the Algerian *colons*. From an early period, small groups of West Africans, mainly French-speaking Christians, had voted for deputies to the French Assembly, maintaining an albeit limited sense of political participation. Equally important, West Africa was much less affected by the anticolonialism of the Arab world epitomised by Nasser's support of the Algerian revolutionaries with the tacit backing of the USSR.

In East Africa, meanwhile, the British were faced with a major uprising in Kenya, the Mau Mau rebellion of 1952–1960. In the aftermath of the end of its Indian empire in 1947, the British had concentrated on trying to make empire in Malaysia and Africa pay for the costs of the Second World War and domestic welfare state. In Malaya, they had been relatively successful in putting down a Communist movement, which was predominantly Chinese, with the support of Malay Muslim landowners and business groups. This preserved British investment in the country's lucrative rubber industry. Britain's persistence here encouraged them to violently suppress a nationalist movement in Kenya which emerged from the smallholding farmers of the predominant Kikuyu ethnic group.[35]

Here again, British administrators desired to protect lucrative white farms and the new agricultural areas which had been developed since 1940, though with much less success than their equivalents in Malaya. The British declared a state of emergency, which lasted from 1952 to 1959, during which many fighters were killed and hundreds of thousands of poor Kikuyu were displaced and in some cases brutalised by colonial soldiers and police. The murder of a small number of white settlers sparked hysteria both in Kenya and in Britain. But many times more Africans than whites were killed on both sides. Estimates suggest that 40 settlers were killed and perhaps as many as 100,000 Africans. More than a thousand of these were hanged by the authorities in dubious judicial circumstances. Yet, Mau Mau was not simply a movement of poor farmers. It also represented a new type of contested popular morality. It arose not simply out of hostility to the white farmers and colonial authorities but out of hostility to wealthy and corrupt Kikuyu who were selling the people's land. Its youthful, underground and violent character echoed many similar movements throughout the century from the Russian anarchists, through Ghadar to the al-Qaeda movement of the 1990s in the sense that it was not straightforwardly nationalist, nor could it easily be classified either as modernist or as "nativist". Ultimately, as across much of Africa, the British declined to spend more blood and treasure and moved to a compromise with moderate nationalists, in this case Jomo Kenyatta, a Kikuyu leader who himself had ambivalent relations with the Mau Mau insurgents.

Over much of East and West Africa, similar tussles with the colonial powers occurred, though, apart from the Algerian war, these were not as violent as the Mau Mau insurrection and its suppression. The classic case in the west was Ghana, which was arguably the most sophisticated of the African colonies with a substantial and educated urban population. Post-war intrusion by the colonial state had seen peaceful mass protests and strikes by unions in 1949, which had forced the Labour government to extend a degree of political representation to the population. Further concessions were forthcoming and following the general election of 1954 nationalist parties began to split on ethnic, regional and ideological lines. Kwame Nkrumah, a young British-educated socialist moderniser, typical of the era across the world, ultimately consolidated power and became president when the colony became one of the first to gain complete independence in 1957.[36]

Most other British African colonies achieved independence between 1960 and 1964. At the same time, Charles de Gaulle, returning to power, pushed through a French withdrawal from Algeria. The debilitating war was causing serious fractures within French society at exactly the time its leadership began to see the potentialities of European unification. Colonial warfare also seemed to be a distraction from the imminence of the Cold War conflict. In Algeria, the French were able to leave an intermittently stable, if socialist and hostile FLN nationalist, regime. In the Belgian Congo, the situation was, however, more chaotic, distantly reminiscent of events in Indonesia. A large increase in demand for minerals and rubber during the war was squandered as the country rapidly fell to kleptocratic military governments for the following five decades.[37] Nationalist bands, each loosely based on tribal groups, staged riots against the Belgian occupiers, which culminated in 1959, around the same time that other parts of Africa, including even French West Africa, were achieving a form of independence.

The Belgian government, fearing further loss of life amongst its white citizens and soldiers and financially straitened, rushed rapidly towards granting Congolese independence in 1960. The only viable national leader was the leftist Patrice Lumumba, but as he pushed forward nationalisation he encountered fierce resistance from tribal opponents, a secessionist movement in Katanga and Western mineral interests there. When Lumumba, despairing of United Nations support, called in Soviet troops, he was quickly overthrown and later murdered in a military coup with US and British backing, setting a precedent for the failed attempt to do the same in Cuba the following year. Thereafter, the Congo tipped regularly between military rule and tribally based democratic movements. An equally devastating postcolonial standoff faced Nigeria between 1967 and 1970, when the ethnically distinct Igbos of the southern provinces declared the independent state of Biafra. Estimates suggest that between one and three million people were killed or died of starvation in the consequent conflict. Only the Portuguese, a power which achieved significance at a world level because of its colonies, held on in Mozambique and Angola into the 1970s.

The main reason for the acceleration of European decolonisation – and the wars of consolidation and fragmentation which often followed – was the cost of colonial repression of insurgents and even peaceful nationalists at a time when the standoff with the USSR was consuming national budgets. Another was the disapproval of the United States and the non-aligned bloc at the United Nations. It seemed better to compromise with moderate socialists than to risk pushing nationalist movements towards Communist insurrection, as had taken place in Indochina. The cost–benefit analysis was also influenced by the gradual decline in the economic surplus of colonies as the value of their produce declined. After the boom which accompanied the world's emergence from wartime austerity and the Korean War, the price of commodities such as palm oil, coffee and minerals fell away. By the late 1950s, colonies were generally costing much more than they contributed to European economies. Western Europe could still benefit from indirect economic control through offshore companies, as the case of India had shown. Finally, there was a subtle ideological shift represented, for instance, by the British Prime Minister Harold Macmillan's speech in South Africa in 1960. He said, "The wind of change blowing through this continent . . . this growth of national consciousness is a political fact." Colonialism seemed old-fashioned and pointless, as the United States and the USSR pioneered space research and the European Union, ASEAN and the Union of American States replaced imperial coercion. In Africa itself, however, the small wars of consolidation and fragmentation, which derived from the anticolonial struggle, persisted and often became entangled with global conflicts. A case in point was the 1976 Entebbe raid in Uganda by the Israel Defense Forces on Palestinian militants who had hijacked a French airliner and threatened to kill its crew and Jewish passengers.

Yet, one area of the Western world where the dominant pattern of liberation and the concession of rights went into reverse was South Africa. The extension of the "global colour line" had seen indigenous people removed from electoral registers in several parts of the world, such as Australia, New Zealand and even Canada between the 1880s and 1930s. But in general the influence of the League of Nations and its successor the UN, together with fear of Communism, were curtailing this process by the 1940s. The participation of people as soldiers during the Second World War also brought about a reconsideration of objectives among colonial rulers and white minorities in the British dominions, a process that echoed the fitful extension of civil rights in the United States.

This was not the case in South Africa.[38] Here full white universal suffrage and even women's enfranchisement were conceded relatively early, by 1930. But this in itself was an aspect of reinforcing the "laager", an area of exclusive white domination. Smuts, interwar premier of South Africa, and one of the founders of the United Nations, believed only in differential rights. Blacks could remain in South Africa's towns as labourers and even secure health and welfare benefits, but they were not political equals. The Afrikaner nationalist government that came to power in 1948 was yet more rigid, determined to guarantee whites exclusive areas by shipping Africans and Asians into special areas, "Bantustans" and residual African kingdoms. Despite their racist radicalism, supported by a rigid Calvinism and Afrikaner historicism, the idea of physical segregation of ethnicities was not, of course, limited to southern Africa. It bore a distinct relationship to Zionist ideology, the attitudes of Southern American whites and even more distantly to the idea of what has been called by Faisal Devji "Muslim Zion", namely Pakistan.

Yet, the South African government came up against the liberationist fire of the African National Congress which had expanded to become a national alliance during the 1930s, bringing together white liberals, Indians, mixed-race people and nationalist and Communist Africans. The African National Congress certainly drew on specifically African themes similar to those common in Ghana and Kenya. But, like African leaderships in these areas, they had been galvanised by news of the Atlantic Charter, the UN, contacts with Gandhian Indians and the US Civil Rights Movement. Labour movements, strikes and public meetings became more raucous in the later 1950s as the apartheid policy became more intrusive. In 1960, however, the mass killings of political activists and striking labourers at Sharpeville radicalised large sections of the African National Congress, turning them towards Communism and revolutionary violence.[39] Rather than a demand for common South African citizenship, African leaders increasingly demanded a total end to white rule and property. Mass arrests, deportations and executions became commonplace in the 1970s. South Africa came under pressure as international libertarian movements, Communist and non-Communist, became stronger. But even as the Cold War drew towards its end, conservative governments such as those of Ronald Reagan in the United States and Margaret Thatcher in Britain abstained from further attempts to change the direction of the South African government. Only the impossibility of maintaining both a modern global commercial society and the continuation of apartheid led to its ultimate demise in the early 1990s.

THE TRAVAILS AND RESURGENCE OF EUROPE

Western Europe was dominated by fear of the Cold War for many years after 1945. This began to abate slightly with the Berlin Airlift of 1948–1949 but was revived by the building of the Berlin Wall in 1961 and the Cuban missile crisis of 1962. International ideological conflict found local echoes in many countries. In Italy the Red Brigades, more an anarchist than a Communist movement, terrified the state in the 1970s. In West Germany, similar violent anarchist groups undermined the sense of ease which the new Federal Republic sought to propagate after Allied control was removed in the early 1950s. Several European nations were simultaneously scarified by the conflicts of decolonisation mentioned earlier. France's bloody war in Algeria continued until 1960. Britain encountered the Mau Mau insurgency and the intractable problem of South Africa. Even Holland only finally gave up on its ambitions in Indonesia in 1949. Authoritarian regimes in Spain and Portugal persisted in linking internal dissent with continuing colonial power through to the late 1970s. In this case, again, these colonial problems had an impact on internal stability.

The return of displaced Algerian *pieds noirs* and the radical Algérie Française movement destabilised the French Republic and, on one occasion in 1962, they came close to assassinating de Gaulle himself. The Iberian authoritarian regimes of Franco and António de Oliveira Salazar were buttressed by the fury of displaced colonists and the continuing influence of the Catholic Church. Britain, however, generally avoided internal problems arising from decolonisation. This was because its dominions' populations had dominated and even exterminated native peoples, or, as in the case of India, because it had never promoted colonies of settlement. Yet, there were some domestic political

Figure 9 People strolling near the Berlin Wall, Bernauer Strasse, Berlin, 1969. Ullsteinbild/TopFoto.

frissons during the late 1950s and early 1960s. The Suez debacle saw the United States withdraw its support from Britain's and France's attempts, along with Israel, to unseat Nasser in Egypt, signalling the end of the old global imperialism. Later, security services and right-wing spokesmen for Empire deplored the British disengagement from "white rule" in Southern Rhodesia (later Zimbabwe) in the 1960s, and hatched some amateurish plots against the prime minister, Harold Wilson, who was regarded by them as a Communist lackey. Yet, Britain was continually rocked by the nationalist crisis and "the Troubles" in Ireland, which at the very least represented a quasi-colonial problem.

Nevertheless, Europe from the late 1950s through to the 1970s managed to regroup and, at least in the medium term, recover its position of one of the world's dominant three political and economic entities alongside the United States and what still seemed to be a stable Communist bloc.[40] The clearest reason for this was the military and financial shield that the United States held above Europe, because of ethnic affinity, support for democracy and fear of the USSR. The Marshall Plan to rebalance and flood capital into the European economies had begun to have a significant effect by the mid-1950s. US military support gave confidence to the newly formed Federal Republic of Germany, post-fascist Italy and, despite their constant kicking against the pricks of US dominance, even to the French republics as they first recovered from the European war and then the Algerian conflict. The stationing of American troops and aircraft in Britain, Germany and Italy also gave an indirect boost to these recovering economies which had begun to catch up with the United States in terms of GDP per head by the early 1960s. Harold Macmillan, for instance, claimed that "most of our people have never had it so good."

In turn, this external economic boost was consolidated by internal economic and social change. Determined to avoid the disaster of further wars, a group of predominantly Catholic politicians in France, Germany and Italy pushed for a new alignment of European states, both politically and economically.[41] The creation of the European Economic Community, the European Court of Justice and numerous other Continent-wide relationships signalled an attempt by European nations to join together to balance the predominant power of the United States and the USSR. From the beginning, however, profound differences emerged about the nature of the EEC. First, France, in particular, viewed the institution as a way of enhancing its national political significance by drawing a chastened, but already economically powerful, Germany into its slipstream. This was why de Gaulle vetoed British membership of the EEC on two occasions in the 1960s. But, secondly, there was wide disparity between the interests of those countries, particularly Britain, which regarded European integration as a means of creating a free-trading economic bloc, and those who demanded political integration centred on Brussels. These conflicts were to persist for two generations.

Yet, this was not simply a question of international politics. The war and its aftermath had promoted a new sense of possibility which began to manifest itself in the late 1950s and dominated the 1960s.[42] As class, gender and even racial hierarchies began to melt under the impact of the emergence of a new consumer economy and the international media, Europe began to experience the same sense of social liberation that had emerged earlier in America. As in America, this was not necessarily a comfortable process. Following the disturbances in California in 1969, an outcome of hostility to the Vietnam draft, youth disturbances spread around the world. The impact of the US disturbances in France during *les évènements* (the riots and disturbances in Paris and other cities) of May 1968 was particularly significant. Trades union agitation combined with massive demonstrations by students and their peers nearly brought down de Gaulle's government. Even in Britain, which remained generally more stable, the notorious Cambridge Garden House riot of 1970 against the Greek Colonels, whose seizure of power in 1968 seemed to reverse the general trend towards liberation, led to the unjust jailing of a number of young students.

It was not only popular movements but also the actions of governments which gave this sense of opportunity amidst rapid change to the later members of the baby boomer generation. Throughout Europe, further education expanded at a rapid rate. In 1950, barely 11% of the British population had attended university. By 1969, this had climbed to nearly 40% and numerous new universities had been founded. The Federal Republic of Germany produced an even greater number of graduates from an educational system which was deliberately structured to avoid any kind of state interventions in knowledge like those that had blighted both the Nazi past and the progress of its former compatriots in East Germany. Nor was it simply a question of institutional change. European and American intellect was challenged by a whole range of brilliant and purportedly libertarian thinkers on politics, philosophy and the social sciences: these ranged from Jean-Paul Sartre in the 1950s, through Jürgen Habermas, Michel Foucault and Jacques Derrida in the 1970s and 1980s. These figures became icons for educated, left-wing youth who wanted to challenge what they saw as the coercive structures of politics which had emerged during the Cold War.

Latin America and the Caribbean: Revolution and Reaction

Latin America also acutely felt the long-distance impact of the Cold War between the 1950s and 1970s, but its response was governed by aspects of its internal evolution which had been apparent since the turn of the twentieth century. Since the Mexican revolution, which itself has preceded other world revolutions, there had always been a strong radical tradition throughout the continent which had developed a fluctuating relationship with the USSR and later Chinese Communism, while itself veering between party–state socialism and anarchism. Rural workers, often indigenous people by origin, had, in common with urban intellectuals and some small commercial people, a desire to strip privileged landholding and commercial elites of their power and extend basic workers' rights. For their part, the elites looked to the United States for support and often had business and family interests there. Politics consequently shifted between periods when autocrats with middle-class and military support dominated and periods of leftist reformism. During the Perón period in Argentina, both aspects were brought together in a populist dictatorship.

In several other Latin American countries, there were similar standoffs between socialist and right-wing military elements which were hardly resolved until the so-called Pink Wave of democratic reforms began at the end of the century. A military regime dominated Brazil between 1964 and 1985 and a similar regime took power in Uruguay at this time. Chile provided a particularly potent example of the fragility of any kind of left reformism when, in 1970, Salvador Allende became president of the country, instituting nationalisation and land reform, policies which were instituted with covert Soviet backing. Allende was also alleged to have received Soviet financial support for his election.[43] In 1973, Augusto Pinochet overthrew Allende and imposed his personal rule on Chile, remaining in power until 1990. There is no doubt that the American government and the CIA under Richard Nixon and Henry Kissinger supported the coup financially and diplomatically. The United States had nearly a billion dollars of corporate holdings in the country and feared for their safety. But it was the mobilisation of local conservative forces in the army, business, the judiciary and Parliament which finally precipitated Allende's fall, as was the case elsewhere in Latin America.[44] In Argentina, in 1966, a military coup had inaugurated the hypocritically named "Argentine revolution". Rather than giving way to a civilian regime, as had the leaders of earlier coups, Argentine's rulers tried to establish a functioning military bureaucracy, curtailing the right to strike and suppressing left-wing groups within the universities. With the exception of a brief period when the ageing Perón returned to power, right-wing militarists held power until Argentina's defeat by the United Kingdom in the Falklands War of 1982.

Yet, there was another aspect to the Latin American political struggles which explains the obdurate American support for dictatorships, and this was a strain of left-wing armed revolution which also had its origins in the Mexican revolution. Here the key event was the Cuban revolution of Fidel Castro and Che Guevara which took place between 1956 and 1959 and was both inspired by and inspired armed revolutions across the world.[45] "A revolution," Castro stated in 1962, "is a struggle to the death between the future and the past." Castro had taken part in revolutionary movements in the Dominican Republic and Colombia before he and a group of revolutionaries established themselves in the Sierra Maestra area of his homeland in 1957. Unseating the American-backed dictator, Fulgencio Batista, Castro became prime minister and later president (1976–2008) of Cuba. He nationalised the banks, expropriated large American companies, such as Coca-Cola, and instituted a rigorous land redistribution programme. His victory against American-supported invaders during the Bay of Pigs incident in 1961 and the standoff over the Cuban Missile Crisis of 1962, as well as his support for leftist insurrectionists in Palestine and Angola, ensured his fame across the world. But the economic blockade established by the United States drove the country towards evergreater political dependence on the USSR, an error which was only revealed with the fall of the USSR in 1991.[46]

Throughout the years from the 1950s to the 1970s, liberal, socialist and even Christian movements sought to return South American societies to a semblance of democracy. Armed insurrectionists on the Cuban model fought military rulers in several states. Yet, broadly, this was a period of autocratic reaction across the continent which continued into the 1990s. Evidence later emerged that dictatorships in Argentina, Paraguay, Uruguay and Chile collaborated to detain and murder dissidents who crossed their borders. The governments of Brazil and Bolivia were aware of the policy and the US Central Intelligence Agency also knew of it. The influence of American policy and the Cold War was undoubtedly one reason why a Western European style of popular democracy did not emerge for three decades or more in Latin America. But it was also the case that conservative landed and business groups, along with the Catholic Church, provided a relatively powerful counterforce to the region's working class and urban intelligentsia. Faced with the alternative of constant strikes and economic dislocation, people acquiesced in the constant "return of the soldiers".

CONCLUSION

The world of the later 1950s, 1960s and 1970s presented a series of sharp contrasts even if there was a continuing widespread belief in the need for state intervention in the market. Western Europe and North America finally shook off the economic and political effects of the double world crisis between 1914 and 1945. Europe moved slowly towards economic and political union as industry recovered and the consumer society burgeoned. Capital turned from financing war and heavy industry to satisfying popular material needs. For the first time in 200 years, Western Europe, at least, was not consumed by armed conflict. Meanwhile, despite the trauma of Vietnam and the crisis over Cuba, the United States attained unchallenged economic and political dominance as "leader of the free world" and its politicians began to address the great internal problem of black subordination. Scientific advances came fast and furious with the personal computer, however big and unwieldy, coming onto the market by 1970. Elsewhere, the former British dominions of Canada, Australia and New Zealand further developed their generous welfare state provisions and relaxed immigration restrictions on Asians and Africans. In sharp contrast was the situation in the Communist world. Despite the loosening of political control in the USSR after the death of Stalin, these states vigorously suppressed opposition, notably in Hungary in 1956, and also continued to undertake internal purges and schemes of levelling on a grand scale, as in Mao's China, Cambodia and North Korea.

In the former colonial world – in Asia and Africa and in Latin America – regimes oscillated between democratic reform and varied types of authoritarian and military rule. One reason for this was the superior organisation and discipline of the army in many of these societies. The Second World War and the small wars of liberation were not far behind them and civilian political parties were fractured, dominated by particular interests and unable to agree on the scope and aims of the state. Yet, very widely this fragmentation was exacerbated by the longer-term effects of colonial ethnic, religious and linguistic differentiation which had become more pronounced as limited forms of local representation were introduced during the first half of the century. Different groups had certainly come together in larger anticolonial alliances, but when it was a question of assigning the social and economic fruits of independence, these divisions re-emerged with a vengeance, whether it was the conflict between Chinese and Muslim in Malaya and Indonesia or between the various ethnic groups in the Congo and Katanga. In India, the largest postcolonial democracy, these conflicts of ideology and interest were barely managed by transforming ethnic, caste and religious conflict into an agonistic form of representative politics. But this was at the expense of the subjugation of Kashmir and the Northeast and continuing conflict with Pakistan. Latin America, of course, had not seen any formal colonialism since the early nineteenth century. But here again, the superior organisation of the army allowed military rulers to intervene to quash the class, regional and ethnic divisions in its society.

One circumstance which pointed towards a very different future, even by the end of the 1970s, was a further expansion of communication. The continuing growth of mass printing and radio broadcasts, along with the expansion of television, pushed forward the process of globalisation. People in East Germany could see the growing wealth of the West; in China, the success of the Japanese economy was filtering back into the public mind. It was not only the vision of material ease which found a response across the world. Muslim, Hindu and Christian religious organisations were able to capitalise on the expansion of movement and communication and present themselves as servants of the people, soon to replace Communist movements as leaders of just insurgency against privilege and corruption. The world was approaching a "tipping point" when the Communist half of the globe dramatically changed direction, while elsewhere conservative religious and free-market politics reasserted themselves in what had once been hailed as an age of secularism and state-led development.

[9]   THE "TIPPING POINT": WORLD POLITICS AND THE SHOCK OF THE "LONG 1980S"

The Fall of the Soviet Union and Communist Eastern
    Europe
Islamic Revival and Sectarian Conflict
China and East Asia: A Revolution Contained
India: The Decline of a Centralised Economy
The Americas, Europe and South Africa: Liberation or the
    Legitimation of Social Inequality?
Conclusion

THE first half of the twentieth century, through to the dropping of the atomic bomb, the Chinese revolution and the onset of the Korean War, saw an almost perpetual political, economic and cultural crisis. By contrast, the second half of the century and the years through to 2008 seemed a period of relative stability despite major eruptions such as the US–Vietnam War and the Cultural Revolution in China. Ironically, one reason for this was the relative stasis of international politics created by the perils of the Cold War and fear of nuclear destruction. Equally, the apparently endless rise of living standards in Western Europe and the Americas, patchily extended to the middle class of the non-European world after 1960, seemed to have largely banished the fears of the Great Depression and its concomitant crisis of democracy, at least until 2007.

Over these years, however, there was one decade during which significant political and economic change took place in many parts of the world and which had signal repercussions into the twenty-first century. During the years 1978–1992, there occurred a series of sharp political changes which interacted with each other, though often in what standard international studies would

Remaking the Modern World 1900–2015: Global Connections and Comparisons, First Edition. C. A. Bayly.
© 2018 John Wiley & Sons Ltd. Published 2018 by John Wiley & Sons Ltd.

regard as the peripheries. The "Fall of Communism" and the Iron Curtain was evidently the most striking event of the decade which had repercussions across the globe. But equally significant was the Iranian revolution of 1979 against the Shah, which in retrospect was the first of a series of Islamic insurgences against semi-Westernised autocrats which stretched on to the beginning of the following century. Likewise, the collapse of socialism in Russia and Eastern Europe was matched by the freeing of markets in the world's two most populous societies, India and China, though in China what really happened in this decade was that the Communist Party itself became an entrepreneurial player. In Europe and America, the triumph of neo-liberal economics also widely marked a sharp break from the residue of earlier forms of state economic intervention. Finally, the last phase of decolonisation was reached in 1990, when the South African government was finally forced to abandon apartheid. I have called these years "the tipping point", a less pessimistic version of Hobsbawm's "the landslide", which is roughly contemporaneous with it.

These changes of the "long 1980s" partly reflected, and later encouraged, the movement of capital, production and forms of consumption across the world, which was entirely in keeping with the ideologies of free-market politicians, such as Margaret Thatcher in Britain and Ronald Reagan in the United States. Meanwhile, in "continental" Europe, this was an era when significant developments occurred towards the creation of a single market and, later, a single currency. Even if these moves sometimes resulted in no more than a Continent-wide form of protectionism and services remained heavily controlled, trade in goods did become freer. These political and economic realignments were legitimated by a group of free-market economists and political thinkers led by Milton Friedman, who worked in the tradition of F. A. Hayek and rejected Keynesian economics and the idea of systematic state intervention in the economy. The contemporaneous rise of Islamism and the advance of the free market were, in fact, linked phenomena, since the decline and fall of socialism across the world left room both for the resurgence of a new form of possessive individualism and also for various quasi-religious ideologies of liberation: Muslim, Hindu nationalist, Christian and even neo-Buddhist.

In part as a consequence of the developments of these years, there were few societies in which economic differences between the rich, middle and poor did not widen.[1] The growth of inequality derived partly from the creation of new wealth, whether through the explosion of financial services in the West or opportunities for entrepreneurship in formerly socialist societies. It also derived from the beginning of the freeing of markets as the post-war boom of the years after 1950 slackened. Yet, economic freedom, as this chapter shows, was by no means a stable bridge to political freedom.

What was most important, however, was the convergence of the consequences of these broader transformations of the 1980s in supposedly peripheral societies to create areas of tension and conflict in the years thereafter. The Iranian revolution of 1979, for instance, led to an eight-year-long war with Iraq, which undermined both regimes, but also pointed forward to the emergence of what came to be called the "Shia Crescent" and intensified conflict between the two main branches of Islam. In the meantime, the Iraqi dictator, Saddam

Hussein, had embarked upon another attempt to strengthen his friable borders by invading the recalcitrant kingdom of Kuwait to the south. In order to protect oil supplies and access to the Persian Gulf, the United States, supported by Britain, France and various Gulf Arab states, invaded Kuwait, expelled Iraqi forces but stopped short of toppling Saddam in what became known as the First Gulf War of 1991.

The moral, economic and diplomatic consequences of these conflicts were far reaching, raising tensions across the Arab and Muslim world which were to persist into the twenty-first century. Even the fall of the Soviet Union was in part caused by the failure of the USSR's military intervention to succeed against the Islamist insurgents in Afghanistan after 1979. But this, in turn, led to the rise of the Taliban Islamic radicals who had been armed by the United States against the Afghan leftists and their Soviet supporters. The breakaway of Caucasus and Central Asian republics from the USSR allowed the rise of Islamist parties in these areas as well. Across Europe and the Americas, the installation of governments devoted to the freeing of the market led ultimately to a further unsustainable boom during the late 1990s and early 2000s, which was in time once again to converge with the collapse of governments and the rise of Islamism across the world.

THE FALL OF THE SOVIET UNION AND COMMUNIST EASTERN EUROPE

By far the most resonant of the developments in this decade of change was evidently the collapse of the Soviet Union and the path away from Communism in Russia, the former Soviet republics and Eastern Europe.[2] Here the pivot of the tipping point was the year 1989 when Solidarity won the general election in Poland, protests in Hungary spelled the end of Communism there, the "Velvet Revolution" destroyed Communism in Czechoslovakia and Nicolae Ceau-şescu's regime collapsed in Romania. Meanwhile, the Berlin Wall fell and the Soviet regime began to fragment in the USSR itself.[3] Eastern European currencies hastily abandoned their peg to the rouble. This maelstrom had repercussions in every part of the world.

As in so many major crises, the specific calculations and miscalculations of leaders came together with underlying structural problems to create a critical rupture. In this case, the determination of the Soviet leader, Mikhail Gorbachev, to loosen, though not to destroy, the control of the Communist Party over Soviet society between 1987 and 1991 and the reaction of conservative Communist generals against this move in August 1991 created a seismic shift. This crisis had been put in train by several developments over the previous ten years: in particular US President Ronald Reagan's decision to capitalise on America's now huge technological advantage over the USSR in missile defences, which had helped to bankrupt the Soviets, who were also suffering from falling oil prices. The late imperialist designs of the elderly Soviet leadership to impose Communism on a recalcitrant, and increasingly Islamic, Afghanistan resulted in one of the many defeats of foreign forces there. Finally, there was the growing power of communications, radio, television and smuggled German newspapers, for instance, which showed to Russians and East Germans in particular that the West was increasingly prosperous. By contrast, the standard of living in Communist societies was at best stagnant and, in the case of the Russians, alcoholism and pessimism were shaving off more than ten years from their life expectancy compared with Western countries. With Saudi oil reaching the market in growing quantities in the 1980s, one of the USSR's key exports was also losing value.

Yet, viewed in the longer history of the twentieth century, the collapse of Communism was less surprising.[4] Centralised Soviet government and, above all, Stalinism had been consolidated during international war and depression. It had been perpetuated by the tensions of the Cold War, which meant that ordinary people in the "Second World" still clung to the state as ultimate protector and even provider of food and housing. This was as true in China, North Korea and Vietnam as it was in the USSR and Eastern Europe. But the practical and theoretical disadvantages of Communism had merely been concealed by the Second World War and Cold War. As Europe and the United States embarked upon a great post-war boom, the theory of a unified proletariat and the practice of governmental centralisation and bureaucratic assignment of economic tasks became increasingly redundant. The provision of services and consumption needs, high-calibre decentralised industrial production and civic socialism seemed more attractive in Europe; low taxation and individual enterprise flourished in the United States. Both now clearly outclassed Communist centralisation. The needs of capital and personal fulfilment appeared to merge.

Several Communist parties in urban north Italy, Hungary and Poland quite soon took the point and consequently survived longer than their more rigid cousins in the USSR and Eastern Europe.[5] By the 1980s, even the triumphant Communist parties of China and Vietnam had also begun to take note. Late-Maoist policies had not increased China's prosperity; rather, they had continued to cause millions of deaths from famine. By comparison, the liberal economic policies and quiet authoritarianism of Singapore, Hong Kong and South Korea had showed how capitalist development could apparently be combined with directive government. This was an important lesson for political leaders.

The consensus among historians is that Mikhail Gorbachev, considerably younger than most of the other Politburo members, was convinced of the need for economic and political reform, clinging to the idea of perestroika.[6] He was no enemy of the Soviet system and saw his role as instituting something like Lenin's New Economic Policy of the 1920s or Khrushchev's move away from Stalinism in the 1950s. The conflict was summed up in his statement that "more socialism means more democracy, openness and collectivism in everyday life". From 1988, he began to introduce reforms, allowing multiparty elections, standing down heavy state censorship and changing Stalin-era laws. His aim was to galvanise the Communist Party, which he still believed held out the best political future for the USSR. But, as often happened, the tide of political change could not be controlled by the leadership. Elections in March 1989 brought various non-Communist members and representatives of non-Russian nationalities to power from the Caucasus and the Baltic. Then Boris Yeltsin, a more radical politician, began to demand a wider political pluralism.[7] This apparently liberal revolution sparked, in turn, a political response from conservative military leaders which finally settled the fate of the old regime. One nationalist stated, "Gorbachev did not have the historic right to put an end to the activity of the Warsaw Pact, and he should have exterminated Yeltsin for the breakup of the Soviet Union."[8]

Even a few years after Gorbachev's intervention, it became clear that a new democratic state could not easily be created out of the USSR. The old elites and bureaucratic business interests clung to power in many parts of the country. Past Communist bosses retained their political control, particularly outside Moscow and St Petersburg. The economy was sustained mainly by the production of crude oil, which helped to underpin the European boom of the 1990s. The most important consequence of the victory of perestroika, however, was on the fringes and, indeed, outside the old Soviet Union itself. The collapse of the Soviet Union apparently handed a victory to the neo-liberal political politicians of the United States and Western Europe. This caused major political theorists, considering these events alongside the end of autocratic regimes in Latin America, to proclaim in Francis Fukuyama's phrase "the end of history", the final victory of democracy and economic liberalism.[9]

Nevertheless, the longer-term consequences were most significant in the provinces and countries surrounding Russia itself. While Gorbachev called for a looser, federal USSR, the result was the effective breakaway of large parts of the old Soviet Union, which to some degree can be regarded as one of the last moments of European decolonisation. The republics of the Caucasus regained virtual independence and throughout the following two decades a contest between resurgent Islamism and strongmen loosely allied to Russia took place. The Ukraine, Uzbekistan and eastern Soviet republics also acquired a large degree of independence, though partly populated by Russian citizens, a curious parallel to developments in East and South Africa, for instance, where earlier settler colonial groups retained a precarious foothold. Ukraine's own vote for separation within a new loose Commonwealth-like federation was itself decisive in the collapse of the USSR.

Though a great blow to Russian pride, the collapse of the USSR had certain welcome features. Unlike many imperial systems, the central republic – Russia itself – was far from the richest part of the Union but had to bear a considerable part of its overall costs, especially the costs of defence. The fragmentation of the western parts of the old USSR therefore removed a considerable burden from the Russian taxpayer. Yet, by far the most important changes were in formerly Communist Eastern Europe. Gorbachev's and Yeltsin's policies were not designed to make possible the breakaway from the Russian bloc of East Germany, Poland, Hungary or Czechoslovakia, but this took place never-theless. In the case of Yugoslavia, a bloody breakup began in 1991, with Russia backing the Serbs and the West backing the Croats and Bosnians. Communist parties were gradually relegated to the margins in these societies and various forms of anti-Communist, Christian and ethnic nationalists took power.

Poland provided a good example of this transformation and emphasises the point that local ideologies and social forms provided the preconditions for the rupture; the fall of the USSR only the break point. Poland's cities and especially the shipyards of the coastal city of Gdansk supported a labour force which was both Catholic and aware of the rising living standards in other Catholic countries and West Germany. In August 1980, Lech Wałęsa and Tadeusz Mazowiecki helped form the Solidarity trade union, a body which was not directly controlled by the Communist Party and fostered discussion and analysis often critical of it.[10] Poverty among farmers as well as rising discontent among the urban clerical and commercial classes sapped the legitimacy of the Party. Fortuitously, a Polish bishop, Karol Wojtyła, became Pope John Paul II in 1978 as Communist power began to disintegrate in the USSR. Catholics in Eastern Europe took heart from this and it helped fuel a newfound separatist nationalism. As in the case of Gorbachev's Russia, this was not an inevitable leap to plural democracy and capitalism. Mazowiecki, in particular, was a Catholic philosopher who believed that socialism embodied elements of justice and equality and needed merely to be Christianized from within.[11] He became prime minister of the country after it negotiated its exit from the Eastern Bloc in 1989. Ultimately, though, no "third way" could be found between Communism and economic liberalism, either in Poland, Czechoslovakia or in Hungary. Within a few months, East Germany, too, was reunited with the West, despite the qualms of many European politicians, who feared the re-emergence of the German domination of the Continent which they had fought against for a century; the French President François Mitterrand supposedly said, "I like Germany so much I would prefer to have two of them."

ISLAMIC REVIVAL AND SECTARIAN CONFLICT

It was of epochal importance that these convulsions in the European Communist world were contemporary with the emergence of new forms of Islamic politics to challenge the earlier pseudosecular military aristocracies of the Muslim world and Western cultural and economic domination. Here, as in the case of the USSR and Eastern Europe, the revival of submerged religious identities, urbanisation, the frustration of youth and the worldwide communication of ideas of popular liberation came together. But the first tremor was to shake not the Sunni Arab world but Shia Iran. In origin, the Iranian revolution, which reached its peak in 1980, was a liberal movement designed to roll back the Shah's autocracy and curtail the influence of his Western backers. It inherited the vaguely socialist and anti-imperialist ideologies of Mohammad Mosaddegh, who had attempted, in 1950, to appropriate some of the assets of Western oil producers. In 1953, Mosaddegh had been unseated by an American intervention, supported by the British. Over the next generation rising oil prices made possible an unstable expansion of Iran's economy and a very rapid growth of urban populations, especially in Tehran and the north of the country.

The Shah's lavish lifestyle and growing inequality triggered a major civil disobedience movement in 1978–1979, distantly supported by the USSR.

It was not, however, the left but the Shia clerical leadership, led by Ayatollah Ruhollah Khomeini, who were the beneficiaries of the rapid disintegration of the Shah's rule.[12] The Shi'a leadership based in the holy city of Qom had long distanced itself from political power and had also helped stimulate anticolonial movements both in Iran and in neighbouring Iraq. Its legitimacy was strengthened by the role that the clerical class played both in the countryside and among underprivileged young people in the towns, where madrassas provided one of the few sources of basic education. When the Shah fled the country in mid-1979, Khomeini, who had returned from exile in France, skilfully pushed aside the secular leadership, proclaiming, "We will break the poison pens of all those who speak of nationalism, democracy and such things."[13] Iran became the first modern Islamic state, with clerical officials dominating most departments of government. The hostility of the United States, which culminated in the embassy siege of 1992 and Ronald Reagan's intervention, confirmed the ayatollahs' hold on power.

In Iraq, Saddam Hussain, until he faced defeat in the First Gulf War of 1991, remained a secular dictator, buying off Sunni, Shi'a and Kurdish leaderships and ruthlessly suppressing dissidence. Yet, sectarian tensions within Iraq increased, as his relations with Shi'a Islam deteriorated and ended in a prolonged and inconclusive war. As in other parts of the Muslim world, sectarian groups benefited from the dispersal of arms which resulted from conventional war. This was also the case in Pakistan by the early 1990s.[14] In 1979, and with a weather eye to the Iranian revolution, General Zia-ul-Haq, the country's president, began a deliberate Islamisation of law codes and education. If, under Jinnah and his successors, Pakistan had been "a country for Muslims" it now began to take on the appearance of an Islamic state. Zia believed that this move would help to cement the army's legitimacy in the eyes of the religious establishments and urban lower classes and head off opposition from the more secular upper classes and judiciary. But the longer-term result was the exacerbation of sectarian splits, with Sunnis beginning to mobilise against the minority Shias, though the initial targets tended to be Christians, descendants of lower caste converts during the colonial period, and Ahmadiyyas, who were pilloried as heretics. With a brief respite in the early 2000s, murderous sectarian attacks continued to 2015, intensified by warfare in Afghanistan and on the Northwest Frontier.

Even though Shias were a minority within Islam and the ensuing Iran–Iraq and Gulf Wars exacerbated conflict between the two sects, the underlying changes, which caused the Iranian revolution and turbulence in its Arab and South Asian neighbours, could be seen in many other parts of the Muslim world. The disillusioned young urban male population and Muslim political leadership found different forms of radical Islamism more congenial ideologies than the increasingly discredited Marxism, which many clerics denounced as godless. The absence of a strict division between "church and state" made it easier for movements such as the Taliban and Muslim Brotherhood to move into positions of political power. Finally, Islamism provided a powerful antidote to the sense of humiliation which Muslims found in the face of Western Christian wealth and disparagement along with periodic armed interventions by the United States, its allies and the state of Israel.

CHINA AND EAST ASIA: A REVOLUTION CONTAINED

Perhaps the most important development of the era in the longer term was the loosening of China's economic system achieved by Deng Xiaoping. This was an aspect of the general decline of state control of the economy over the world, but one not accompanied by any kind of concession to a new civil society model.[15] Deng had survived the end of the Maoist era and the reign of the Gang of Four. A supreme pragmatist and a politician unconcerned with ideological purity, he was well aware by 1979 that China's economy was only developing at a glacial pace. The key external events were not so much the move of the capitalist world to free-market economics and the slow deterioration and ultimate collapse of the Soviet Union but the obvious success of Southeast and East Asian economies, notably Japan, Singapore, Malaysia, Taiwan, South Korea and even Thailand. Booming Hong Kong, still under British control until 1997, when it was handed back to the Chinese Communist Party (CCP), provided an even closer example of Chinese economic success. The proximity of all these regions and the fact that overseas Chinese played such an important part in trade and investment made them object lessons for Beijing. But the evident failure of rural development within China itself played an even greater part.

Deng moved to remove state economic controls from a large number of medium-level businesses. The big state-owned companies survived because they were huge employers and he could not afford major labour unrest. But the promotion of more efficient business outside this charmed circle was a major feature of the beginnings of China's export boom, which was to some degree modelled on Japan's economic successes of the 1960s and 1970s. In China, the concentration on exports revivified but also unbalanced its economy over the following decades. The result was the rise of local bosses, part old CCP officials, part local capitalists, who emerged particularly in the coastal regions but also in big inland centres away from Beijing, such as Guangzhou.

The about-turn by the Central Committee and the knowledge that political rigidity was under threat in Gorbachev's USSR and in Eastern Europe encouraged students and members of the urban middle classes to challenge the regime. The Tiananmen Square incident of 1989 in which thousands of protestors demanded democratic change and occupied one of Beijing's squares was the most dramatic display of this new political force. But Deng, always mindful of the fragmentation of the country in the 1920s and 1930s and of turmoil in the USSR, ruthlessly deployed the army against the protestors. The soldiers killed thousands because they "knew nothing about the democracy movement [or] the conditions in the city".[16] China therefore moved, in the early 1990s, towards a form of state capitalism. Peasant land was appropriated or put up for sale, a new urban middle class benefited from the export economy and large income differentials opened up between segments of the population and the regions. This was not preordained. In both South Korea and Taiwan, decades of anti-Communist autocracy collapsed over the same period of years and new democratic systems emerged in both countries. But in China the elite still feared civil war and foreign intervention, though by this stage neither the United States, the Japanese nor the former USSR were, in any sense, external threats to China's integrity.

Elsewhere in East Asia, Vietnam was to take a similar path to China in the 1980s and did so for similar reasons. After the reunification of the country in 1975, the more prosperous and formerly "capitalist" South was brought under centralised state control and larger landholdings were broken up. But even under the rule of Ho Chi Minh's successor Le Duan, the country never moved towards a rigidly Maoist-type model. The Vietnamese Communist Party was relatively more open to debate and dissension, in part because of the survival of the French- and later Russian-speaking intelligentsia.[17] Yet, in the 1970s, the economy appeared stagnant, lagging behind neighbouring states. Beginning with a quiet relaxation of controls on capital and labour after 1979, the country moved towards a form of liberalisation under the control of the Communist Party, *Doi Moi* ("renovation"), formally announced in 1986. Private businesses were allowed to function and many thousands came into existence over the following decade. Consequently, living standards rose modestly. Later, in the Philippines, the long-standing dictatorship of Ferdinand Marcos also came to an end in 1986. The United States, now less fearful of Communism and the loss of its major naval base there, withdrew its support for him and a hesitant democracy emerged.

Japan itself had also provided a distant model of economic growth for these Asian societies. Rapid investment directed to supplying American forces during both the Korean and the Vietnamese wars was followed by strong growth in export markets in Southeast Asia and the West. Japan moved from undercutting prices in basic consumer goods, such as textiles and toys, to a strong investment in high-technology production in the 1980s. The country benefited from continuing US protection, which absolved it from military spending, while internally the Liberal Democratic Party maintained its hold on power, creating stability, if also a degree of corruption. The political elite had encouraged the Japanese people to save during the days of poverty at the end of the war and this filled its banks with large capital reserves. This in turn led to the so-called credit bubble of the 1980s when huge sums of money were invested in property in the major cities. The yen appreciated and living standards apparently rose so fast that many commentators of the time were predicting that Japan would overtake the United States as the largest economy in the world. But the bubble burst in the early 1990s. This proved an early warning of what was to happen in 1997 to several East Asian economies, and more distantly the crash of the American and European economies after 2007. The economist Paul Krugman argued that Japan suffered this crisis because its population had saved too much and spent too little: "1990–2000 really was a lost decade: Japanese output per potential worker fell a lot relative to the US", though the results were nowhere near as bad as in the West during 2010–2012.[18]

INDIA: THE DECLINE OF A CENTRALISED ECONOMY

One historian wrote of the 1960s as India's "most dangerous decade", but the tipping point of 1979–1991 more obviously deserves this title.[19] During these years, the Indian National Congress (usually referred to as "Congress") declined in authority, identity politics became divisive and the economy moved towards crisis at the end of the decade. Here India reflected the worldwide revival of both free-market and religious ideologies. Yet, despite political and sectarian turmoil, India's electoral system and democracy survived. In some ways, this was one of the happier consequences of Indira Gandhi's "Emergency" of 1976–1977, which had resulted in her expulsion from power and the re-emergence of vibrant party politics. Even after she returned to power in 1979, Congress was faced with significant and organised opposition and its hegemony gradually crumbled. The Bharatiya Janata Party (BJP) represented a new strand of right-wing Hindu political sentiment which partly drew its inspiration from ideologues such as V. D. Savarkar and K. B. Hedgewar earlier in the century. During the later 1980s, L. K. Advani of the BJP staged a series of processions across India, promoting the idea that it was fundamentally a Hindu society. This posed a threat to Muslim identity locally, as was demonstrated by the demolition of a mosque in the town of Ayodhya and a series of savage anti-Muslim riots which took place across the country in 1992. But, in general, when Hindutva leaders achieved power they were forced to bargain and compromise with other political actors, as Congress had done earlier.

Other forms of identity politics grew in significance during the 1980s, with Dalit (or untouchable) leaders demanding further concessions in government jobs and educational establishments. This led so-called Other Backward Castes to demand similar preferment. The whole system of positive discrimination was given new form by the Mandal Commission, which pushed Indian democracy further towards caste-based mobilisation. It was Mrs Gandhi who had inaugurated the Mandal Commission in the hope of repairing Congress's fortunes by empowering well-off rural people, but during the 1980s no further action was taken on it. It was only when Congress dominance had further eroded that B. P. Singh's minority government made it into law. After 1990, 55% of all government jobs were subject to "reservation" for different groups and politics became increasingly caste-based.

Yet, the most dramatic example of identity politics was the Sikh movement which had emerged early in the 1980s and led to the assassination of Mrs Gandhi herself in 1984.[20] Since the 1920s, Sikhs had demanded a degree of local autonomy within the Punjab. As Mrs Gandhi had moved against over-mighty chief ministers, local politics became more volatile, especially amongst Sikh rural people who had not benefited from the so-called Green Revolution – the development of intensive farming in the state. Unrest came together under the leadership of Jarnail Singh Bhindranwale, who headed a loose network of groups which in 1984 occupied the Sikh holy place, the Golden Temple of Amritsar. Mrs Gandhi sent in the Indian army and Bhindranwale and many of his supporters were killed. In revenge, Mrs Gandhi was assassinated by her own Sikh guards, sparking the mass murder of Sikhs by Congress supporters in

Delhi and other cities. In this sense extreme violence and democracy continued to go hand in hand in India, a fact further exemplified by the Union government's use of armed force to suppress peripheral movements in predominantly Muslim Kashmir and in the "tribal" regions of the northeast of the country. Shruti Kapila argued that the events in the Punjab represented the end of "postcolonial India", the final termination of the consequences of the Partition of 1947.

Mirroring similar moves in the rest of the world, India also began to adopt neoliberal economics in 1991, a time when it faced a serious balance-of-payments problem and a collapse of its ability to raise money on the world market.[21] These moves, therefore, finally dismantled the centralised economic system of Nehru's period, which had become associated with bureaucracy and low growth. Economic change was pushed forward rapidly in the early 1990s by the Union finance minister Manmohan Singh against considerable opposition both from Congress and other parties. This pointed forward to a new India of Hindu nationalism and market reform which was to triumph in 2014.

THE AMERICAS, EUROPE AND SOUTH AFRICA: LIBERATION OR THE LEGITIMATION OF SOCIAL INEQUALITY?

The most powerful force driving the world towards free-market economics and neo-conservatism was, of course, the United States itself. Elected president in 1980, Ronald Reagan inherited a political system which seemed to be exhausted, even though Nixon and his successors had largely extricated the country from foreign wars and the economy was growing fast again after a brief downturn in the mid-1970s. This election signalled a shift in the very base of US politics and society.[22] Local conservatism, defined at the time as "neo-liberalism" because of its concern with liberty of the market, was beginning to merge with a slow Christian revival which was broadly fundamentalist. This affected both Protestants and Catholics, the latter once of poor Irish and Italian origin, increasingly moving to the right after generations of support for the Democrats as they became better off. Distancing himself from the near-socialism, as he saw it, of the Johnson era, Reagan stated: "Government's first duty is to protect people, not run their lives."

This combination of anti-Communism, economic liberalism and religion proved a powerful force that continued to drive American politics into the twenty-first century under President George Bush and his son George W. Bush. Reagan finally revealed what had long been the case: America's technological dominance, particularly military technology, which the Soviets could not match. As suggested earlier, their economic decrepitude soon encouraged a fundamental reworking of the Soviet system itself under Mikhail Gorbachev. Similarly, Reagan stymied the USSR in Afghanistan by arming Islamic radicals, the Taliban, with unintended longer-term consequences. His foreign policy was by no means always successful, as the so-called Iran–Contra Affair suggests.

But midway through Reagan's term of office it was already clear that the United States was the only remaining superpower.

In domestic affairs, Reagan reduced the tax rates on the wealthy in a move designed to encourage entrepreneurship and match the economic success of the European Union. Reagan was also concerned by the combination of inflation and relatively low rates of growth which had set in during the later 1970s, so-called stagflation. Reagan supported Paul Volcker, Chairman of the Federal Reserve, who pushed up interest rates as a necessary move to defeat rapid price inflation. When he entered the White House in 1981, Reagan also moved rapidly to cut income tax on the top rate from 70% to 50%. He slashed some of the welfare bills which had been introduced in the days of Johnson and Carter. This inaugurated a long political contention about the extent to which the state should aid its poorer citizens that was to persist for a generation. While the incomes of the middle class and poorer people had scarcely improved in relative terms by 2010, the rich had prospered mightily, as Piketty later argued.[23] Despite the cuts in state provisions, defence spending increased by 10% a year. Indeed, the so-called Reagan revolution seemed almost the antithesis of the New Deal and when he moved to cut support for the retirees and the disabled, he was resisted by both Democrats and Republicans, who depended on their votes. The economy, however, continued to flourish because of structural changes and latterly the rise of IT industries. Firms such as Microsoft effectively inaugurated a new economic era which saw laptop machines and mobile phones rapidly spread across the world.

Yet, it can be argued that, as in Asia and Latin America, so even in the United States, economic liberty was not necessarily matched by social democracy. Despite the elaborate system of primaries, the division of power between the two houses of Congress and other checks and balances, the growing disparities of wealth in the country began to produce a more ferocious battle over taxation. Business lobby groups and other special interests became increasingly active in promoting candidates in state and presidential elections. A highly conservative body, the National Rifle Association, directly championed Reagan's election in 1981, for instance. Similarly, "liberal" California and New England were increasingly pitted against more conservative and religious populations in the central and southern parts of the country.[24] Meanwhile, the long shadow of racial discrimination was seen in incidents such as the Alabama schools dispute of 1989 when black people alleged a new form of discrimination had emerged through the measurement of pupils' ability.

There also came into being by the later 1980s a tacit alliance between conservative groups which is best called "anti-statist". Religious conservatives abhorred the Supreme Court's ban on prayer in schools and its refusal to curtail abortion. Business groups and the wealthy were suspicious of the Internal Revenue Service and demanded a further lowering of taxation. Reagan himself and his foreign affairs advisers opposed "godless Communism" in Central America and in the USSR itself where freedom of religion became an issue as the country slipped towards dissolution. Reagan never managed to do a lot for either the economic libertarians or the Christian crusaders. Yet, he was better, in their eyes, than the alternative which emerged in the guise of Bill Clinton. In foreign policy Reagan first raised the stakes almost to the point of armed conflict in 1980–1983. He then relented and began to work with Gorbachev after his election as General Secretary of the Communist Party in 1985. Both moves had the partly unintended consequence of weakening the Soviet Union.

In Europe, the closest approximation to Reagan's version of economics were the policies followed by Britain's prime minister, Margaret Thatcher, between 1979 and 1990.[25] Their contexts were, however, rather different. Since the 1950s, the United Kingdom had had a powerful and entrenched labour movement and a very costly, though at this stage still generally effective, welfare system, both on a quite different scale from traditionally libertarian America. While Reagan diminished the role of the state to some degree, Thatcher actually expanded the central state and diminished local government, even while claiming to be doing the opposite. Both the US and the UK government during this period were, however, bent on "supply side" reforms, following the teaching of economists such as Friedman and, earlier, Hayek. Thatcher put great emphasis on controlling inflation, so creating a severe depression which increased unemployment to a peak of about 3.5 million in 1984. She also moved against what she and her economics minister, Keith Joseph, believed were the "over-mighty" unions, crushing the miners' strike of 1984–1985 and effectively destroying the mining industry, which had been a driver of economic growth in Britain, particularly in Wales, northern England and Scotland, since the Industrial Revolution. Privatisation of state-owned business was a major plank of this economic programme, with British Rail being the first target.

Reagan considered Thatcher his closest economic and political ally across the world, particularly in relation to the sclerotic politics and foreign policies of the USSR. Consequently, he unwillingly supported Britain in its costly and risky war with Argentina which had occupied the Falkland Islands in 1982. British forces reconquered the islands within a few months in an apparent reassertion of the country's world power. Yet, Margaret Thatcher was a divisive figure. Her policies found echoes in the governments of other English-speaking countries, such as Australia and New Zealand, which also struggled with powerful labour unions and spiralling social spending. She approved of the vision of the European Union as a free-trade area but objected to the statist policies of governments in France, Germany and Italy. She showed marked reluctance to move against the apartheid government of South Africa, even as racial division became increasingly obnoxious and unsustainable in the eyes of much of the world and, ultimately, even of many white South Africans. Thatcher's government pursued policies which widened income differentials and increased child poverty – policies which were tolerated even by her Labour successors.

This heightened the difference between the prosperous south of the country and the declining industrial north, while doing little to end the explosive campaign of the Provisional IRA. Yet, Thatcher decisively banished the sense of the inevitability of Britain's total decline which had been widespread in the late 1970s. The tipping point in the English-speaking countries, therefore, represented the collapse of the consensus about the necessary role of the state in social provision which had persisted since 1945, though the change was much greater in Britain, Australia and Canada than in the United States, which had long supported versions of economic neo-liberalism.

On the face of it, the economies of France and Germany pointed in different directions over this period.[26] François Mitterrand came to power in a landslide victory of the Socialist Party in 1981 and even brought the Communists into his coalition as junior partners. He pushed through various measures of nationalisation and raised tax in moves that contrasted sharply with events in Britain and the United States and even with the policies of Helmut Schmidt in West Germany, whose government also introduced anti-Keynesian measures, cut social welfare and moved to de-nationalisation. But faced with an economic crisis and loss of confidence by world markets, Mitterrand reversed his policies in 1983–1984 and returned France to something like the emerging Western norm of the period in economic policy. The main reason why these various political crises and changes of direction were less politically unsettling than they might have been was that the economy of the European continent continued broadly to prosper as the freeing of trade under the rules of the European Economic Community expanded the size of its market. The Italian leadership, for example, was clear that a closer link with Germany, now reunited, and France, now growing strongly, would banish its own political and economic crises.[27] With a still-large rural population slowly moving into the Continent's towns, wages remained relatively low, while medium-sized specialist enterprises in Italy, for instance, helped satisfy burgeoning consumer demand. Building on this success, the major European countries moved towards closer economic and political union in the Maastricht Treaty of 1992, preparing the way for the creation of the single currency a decade later.[28]

By far the most dramatic form of unification which took place over these years, however, was the unification of East and West Germany (FRG and GDR) in 1990. Tensions between the two Germanys had lessened with the Ostpolitik, or East–West bridge-building, of Willy Brandt in the 1970s. As Reagan and Gorbachev also began to work together in the mid-1980s, the position of the Communist government of East Germany became untenable. When Communism collapsed in Eastern Europe in 1987–1988, Hungary opened its borders and thousands of East Germans flooded into the West, attracted by the lure of a better life which was increasingly apparent to them from television, radio and smuggled newspapers. Following peaceful protests in 1989, which were supported by both Protestant and Catholic churches, among the few civil society organisations allowed to exist in the East, the GDR collapsed and new measures were introduced to amalgamate the government of the two states. The GDR government was faced with a choice between repression on a grand scale or compromise. It seems likely that the ideological bankruptcy of Party rule and the vision of a better life trumped their desire to hold on to power, in contrast to the situation in China. Meanwhile, the Berlin Wall was demolished with huge celebrations across the country.[29]

Again, it would be difficult to argue that the shift towards free-market economies which spread over much of the world in the late 1970s and early 1980s was always closely associated with the strengthening of the institutions of democracy. There were some spectacular examples of democratic resurgence as with the fall of the dictatorship of General Pinochet in Chile which was followed by a referendum to re-establish representative government. Similarly, the defeat of Argentina in the Falklands War in 1982 resulted in a turn back to multiparty democracy in the country. But in many parts of Latin America authoritarian regimes continued to rule until the economic growth of the 1990s and declining fear of Communism brought about a more general move towards democratic accountability.

Elsewhere, events such as Tiananmen Square or the growing influence of business lobbies and the rich in electoral politics across the Western world seemed to contradict this idea. In Russia and Eastern Europe, there was truly a sense of liberation and movement towards representative institutions over these years. Yet, in the former colonies liberated in the previous generation, profound social conflicts, ethnic differences and income inequalities served to frustrate these democratic movements in many countries. The picture in Africa south of the Sahara, for instance, was very mixed during the 1980s.[30] This was clearly the tipping point for the apartheid regime in South Africa, but elsewhere authoritarian command economies continued to exist. White rule collapsed in Rhodesia, but the style of centralised authoritarian government that Robert Mugabe instituted did little to improve living standards. In Nigeria, the 1980s saw a succession of highly corrupt military regimes which only came to an end with a return to democracy in 1998.[31] It is true that civil society organisations continued to exist and even expand in reaction to state oppression: Muslim organisations, especially in the federated north, charismatic Christian churches in the south and underground labour movements throughout the country. But this often served largely to increase ethnic and religious tension. A wide range of different regimes, from military dictatorships to ethnically based democratic governments, held power across the rest of the continent. Mismanagement and corruption afflicted many of these regimes. But, as basically primary produce exporters, they also found it difficult to establish effective import substitution programmes as they were affected by the peaks and troughs of economic growth across the world during the 1970s and 1980s.

Nevertheless, the liberation of black South Africa from apartheid was of great iconic significance, and the political dynamics here had some features in common with the transformation of Eastern Europe and the USSR. In a sense, it also helped mark the final end of white colonialism across the world. Since its electoral victory of 1948, the National Party had rigorously and often violently imposed its form of segregation, not only on the black but also on the Indian and other "coloured people" of South Africa. Control over army and police, surging income from mining during the European and American boom, the reluctance of Western governments to promote the African National Congress during the Cold War when it, too, seemed "Communist': all these factors played a part in maintaining a regime which violated every norm of the humanitarian internationalism which had struggled to life after 1945. Black spokesmen such as Oliver Tambo and Nelson Mandela were imprisoned for "seditious activities" in the 1960s and periodic outbreaks of rioting among impoverished and unemployed people in segregated townships such as Soweto were met with tear gas and live rounds. In 1966, President Hendrik Verwoerd, who had pulled the country out of the Commonwealth and banned the ANC, was assassinated. There followed further arrests, imprisonment and torture of suspected black activists. If anything, the small political advances made by black South Africans in the 1940s and 1950s had been systematically erased and the white dictatorship reached its peak during the rule of President P. W. Botha in the 1980s.

The preconditions for the sudden change in 1990, when Mandela and his colleagues were released from prison and President F. W. de Klerk announced a new regime of equal rights, were not dissimilar to those obtaining in the European Communist states.[32] The ANC continued to operate clandestinely in the towns and even in the Bantustan of Transkei after 1987.[33] The South African economy was in decline, in part because of the end of the mineral boom as Western economies cooled. Economic, political and sporting boycotts of the country had begun to undermine white income and morale. The slow drip-feed of information from the outside world, reaching even the segregated townships, presaged an even more violent upsurge by the young black population. Economic interests briefly came together with a popular desire for social liberalism. But, as in the case of Gorbachev, Mazowiecki or even Deng, the stance of politicians was critical. Mandela himself famously renounced the violence that he had advocated before his 27-year imprisonment and urged a new racial harmony, becoming in 1994 South Africa's first black president. De Klerk also played an important part by marginalising more obdurate elements within the white population and forcing a deal with what he called the "fundamentally socialistic" ANC. It is true that the Truth and Reconciliation Commission did little to identify and prosecute those who had persecuted and murdered black activists during the apartheid era. The ANC, like the Indian National Congress and the CCP, once leaders in decolonisation, quickly became victim to clientelism. Yet, South Africa avoided racial civil war and a new, albeit small, black middle class emerged during the 1990s.

CONCLUSION

Why did so many major social and political changes come about largely within this one decade? Clearly, the globalisation of capital following the Second World War played an important part. It enhanced the differences in income and life satisfaction between an affluent West and the rest of the world. Combined with an exponential growth in communications, regimes could no longer hive themselves off from developments elsewhere. South Africa could not both sustain economic relations with the rest of Africa, Europe and America and, at the same time, retain a system abhorrent to peoples and governments there. The Shah of Iran could not maintain his rule, quaffing Château Lafite Rothschild, when his people remained desperately poor, and Muslims across the world were beginning to see salvation in the politics of piety. Even European liberal and socialist parties could not remain immune to the collapse of Communism or the slow relative decline of personal incomes as the postwar boom ended in the 1970s.

Underlying all this was the diffusion of ideologies of popular liberation, whether Christian, Muslim or secular libertarian, which blended with indigenous concepts of the good life and personal self-respect. It is impossible either to deny the significance of the global spread of ideas, economic and political forms or, equally, to ignore the varied ways in which these developments were appropriated and "cannibalised" in different societies. In none of the examples treated in this chapter, though, did the outcome of movements for change see an easy or happy accomplishment of these aspirations to the good life. Ethnic conflict, religious and secular tyranny, widening disparities of wealth within regions and localised forms of state repression persisted. International capital had been globalised and had not only undermined socialism in the USSR but also, by the early 1990s, seen off trade union power over much of Europe and non-Communist Asia. Individualist consumerism had apparently trumped social radicalism. Yet, history, again in Gibbon's words, continued to be "philosophy teaching by example" and some at least of its lessons were progressive as democracy resumed its patchy growth. For this reason, it would be wrong to see the end of the century simply as a succession of political economic crises even though the next two decades did indeed spawn the terror of 9/11 and the recession of 2008.

[10] THE EXPANSION OF HUMAN KNOWLEDGE: THE TWENTIETH-CENTURY PERSON AND SOCIETY

The Sciences and the Reconsideration of the Universe
History, Archaeology and the Human Imagination
Knowledge and the Person: Anthropology
Economics and Sociology

THE NEXT six chapters move away from the earlier analytical narrative approach and consist of an examination of the concepts that have fundamentally formed the century: the human, demography and religion, in particular. This chapter and the next concern the manner in which "the human" was conceived and acted out in a period when knowledge and imagination expanded exponentially alongside astonishing levels of violence. Many general histories hive off their discussion of scientific and humanistic knowledge into a category separate from social and political change. Such works often give priority to demography or economics. Yet, major discoveries, artistic experimentation and even academic debates had a remarkable impact on the way people lived in the twentieth and twenty-first centuries. They deserve to be treated as powerful and productive forces in their own right. These breakthroughs in knowledge recast and redirected the entangled worlds of capital, state and communication which have been the focus of earlier sections. Human imagination experienced a second "cognitive revolution", a development of expectation and communication integrating experience and the learning process at a worldwide, indeed cosmic, level.[1]

This chapter, for instance, briefly touches on the work of Einstein, Fermi and other physicists and its ultimate products: the hydrogen bomb and the nuclear power station. Equally, the mapping of DNA in the 1950s took time to produce social results. Yet, the genetic classification of populations and their profiling by institutions ranging from police forces to palaeontologists was the longer-term consequence. Advances in chemistry led, via medical discoveries, to a powerful assault on diseases such as smallpox, malaria and polio. Meanwhile, a combination of new medicines, better understanding of nutrition and the X-ray helped to extend average human life expectancy by as much as 25% over the course of the century.

The chapter, however, also concerns the impact of the social sciences and humanities on the understanding and development of "the human" and begins with the great breakthroughs in the course of the century in dating and charting the evolution of the race itself. Such discoveries did not have the same social consequences as the splitting of the atom or the mapping of DNA. But they caused human beings to think about themselves differently and often to act differently. These advances did not specifically throw religion – the subject of Chapter 13 – into doubt. Yet, they did provide the basis for a broad "demystification" of knowledge in Max Weber's sense and had major consequences for political and ethical debate. Underlying these epochal changes was the diffusion of knowledge across the world by newspapers and, later, radio, television and the Internet. Publishing houses and broadcasters worked with scientists and humanist scholars to greatly increase human knowledge and create a global awareness of possible futures – but also dangers.

THE SCIENCES AND THE RECONSIDERATION OF THE UNIVERSE

Genetics, basically the study of inherited characteristics, developed rapidly in the first three decades of the century and profoundly shaped views of the person and their position in society. T. H. Morgan of Columbia University showed that the characteristics of life forms were determined by genes at particular points on the human chromosome. In the 1930s, scientists in the United States and Britain were able to make a considerable advance on the Darwinist theory of natural selection: "the recognition that while natural selection affects the survival of individuals, what changes in the course of evolution is the genetic make-up of the population to which the individual belongs."[2] This idea was deeply distrusted by the Communist Party of the USSR since it tended to question the key tenet of Marxist science, the idea that class struggle was the route to the perfection of the human. Attempts by Soviet scientists, beginning with T. D. Lysenko, to posit an environmental, rather than genetic, theory of evolution more consonant with Marxism failed to gain credibility. In the longer term, this was one factor in the decline of the intellectual and moral base of Communism itself. Purely genetic understandings of the person and society were, by contrast, cast in a deeply problematic light by Nazi experiments and racist categorisation before the Second World War. But as scientific knowledge advanced after 1945, the degree to which genetic inheritance determined the intelligence and aptitude of individuals became a topic of political conversation once again. The left still tended to argue that social conditions determined a child's ability and opposed any form of intelligence testing to determine admission to different forms of education. Conservatives tended to take an opposite view, some arguing that genetic make-up was all-important. Liberals argued for a middle position, attributing variable weight to both upbringing and inherited intelligence.

Genetic testing and the analysis of DNA made possible long-term advances in the profiling of family inheritance, the analysis of crime scenes and the determination of the sex of unborn children. In the last case, this led inexorably to the termination of unborn female children in richer Asian countries, which was to have dramatic social implications in the twenty-first century. Along with new reproductive technologies discussed later, these discoveries indeed began to change the nature of the family itself. A further consequence was the genetic profiling of disease, leading to early prevention and contributing to a rapid increase in longevity. The future was laid out by 2013, when Saudi Arabia announced that it would sequence the genomes of 100,000 of its citizens in an attempt to save money on medical treatment, as did England a little later.[3] It also became possible to match the genetic profile of unknown dead bodies with those of living relatives. Some campaigners, however, were concerned that, as in the case of the surveillance of electronic media, this might put the individual at risk from a malign government.

A further key scientific change from the 1890s onward was the application of electricity to the generation of power in both the public and domestic spheres.[4] Albert Einstein's formulation of the origin of electricity in 1905 led to the development of radio receivers in the early 1930s and the transistor by 1947. Yet, the social and political benefits and also dangers from new scientific knowledge were particularly evident in the related case of the emergence of atomic physics.[5] Early pioneers such as Paul Dirac and Patrick Blackett in the United Kingdom and Max Born, Enrico Fermi and Werner Heisenberg in Continental Europe and the United States were able to map and predict the movement of atomic particles. During the Second World War, this knowledge was applied to the development of weapons which could release chain reactions of hundreds of millions of volts of energy in the Manhattan Project.[6] A hidden race between Allied and Nazi scientists led to the development of the first atomic bomb by the team led by Robert Oppenheimer. The subsequent destruction of Hiroshima and Nagasaki in August 1945 ended the Pacific War, but also raised profound questions about the future of humanity itself. The Cold War generation grew up in an atmosphere of orderly fear. I remember my father waking me up on the morning when the Cuban Missile Crisis of 1962 peaked to announce that we were unlikely to survive the day. Yet, the promise of the peaceful use of nuclear power offered hope that millions could be lifted out of poverty. Scientific exhibitions held across the USSR and Nehru's India, or the 1951 Festival of Britain, countered this atmosphere of fear with a sense of great human potential.

Developments in air transport, as in electronic communication, impacted on the understanding of the twentieth-century person. From Guglielmo Marconi's invention of the electric telegraph, through the first flights by Louis Blériot to the launch of the USSR's sputnik satellite in 1957, there opened up almost unlimited vistas of progress, and further foreboding about future conflict. The vision of the earth from a man-made platform far in space as a small and distant sphere implanted a sense of awe and hope in human beings. But the inexorable development of land-based and terrestrial technology further enhanced the military competition of states in this "age of anxiety". To this extent, the expansion of knowledge, physics, chemistry and biology had fundamentally reshaped the notion of the person, and hence of world society, by 2015.

Yet, perhaps the most significant, but also the most mundane, development took place in the sphere of land transport, which revolutionised economies across the world but also initiated a period when the individual or family traveller was released from the disciplines of the railway.[7] Wartime developments in petrol-driven vehicles played a part, as did the desire to produce fast cars for the rich in the years after 1918. The need to reduce public health risks resulting from the deposit of horse dung and urine in the streets of rapidly expanding cities after 1900 was not insignificant either. But in the 1920s and 1930s, firms such as Chrysler, Ford, Volkswagen and Leyland began to produce cars for ordinary families.[8] Demand was increased by the need to move people, goods and government agencies rapidly across the land during the Depression and Second World War. It was further expanded by the great economic boom between 1945 and the 1970s. The motorcar produced a new sense of familial, personal and spatial freedom, which was critical for the triumph of Western individualistic and commercial society. Poor developing societies were introduced to the idea of the motor idyll by film. Communist societies hurried to catch up. Only after 2000 did traffic chaos and pollution counsel a return to the railway.

Figure 10 Fiat cars at Singapore Harbour. Singapore Press Holdings Ltd.

Towards the end of the century, another fundamental breakthrough in science and technology also began to remake the human person. This was the expansion of the Internet, mobile phone and other electronic media. The effect on economic productivity was much less than that of the great expansion of communication and infrastructure after 1945, except in the United States for a relatively brief period in the 1990s.[9] But the consequences for human sociality and the sense of opportunity, economic, political and even sexual, were very great, as the next chapter suggests.

HISTORY, ARCHAEOLOGY AND THE HUMAN IMAGINATION

A subtler and less direct re-envisioning of the human resulted from the development of the social sciences over the century, especially when they were entangled with these scientific developments. The academic debates about human origins, civilisation and the nature of society were not simply hypotheses floating above politics, but influenced them at a deep level. First, a combination of archaeological discovery, chemical and biological anthropology pushed back the age of the human race itself by nearly three million years from the estimates at the end of the nineteenth century, establishing a fundamentally different picture of the relationship of human evolution to that of other species. Critical here were the discoveries of the Leakey family, Louis, Mary and Richard, of ancient human skulls in the Zambezi basin in East Africa between the 1940s and 1970s.[10] Much later, DNA analysis of early human remains gave mankind a more complex picture of the varieties of hominid life and ignited a controversy about the connection between Neanderthal man and other humans, still unresolved in 2015. Meanwhile, marine archaeologists postulated that all animal brains were "descended" from marine creatures which lived as much as 600 million years earlier.[11]

Debates about the physical evolution of the human were paralleled by fundamental questions about the development of the human mind. The discovery of stone-age cave paintings at Lascaux in southern France in the 1930s initiated speculation about the beginnings of art and imagination. These debates continued into the 2010s, when some scholars proposed that the paintings were the work of women when their men had gone off hunting, an argument in tune with the period's emphasis on gender equality. In time, DNA sampling both of human remains and of current world populations also strengthened specialists' assertions that the human race originated in Africa and then spread out to the other continents.[12] Again, this train of thought marked a sharp difference from the biological racism of the later-nineteenth century which often wrote off Africa as a backward area.

Other archaeological and historical discoveries had subtle effects both on national and ethnic politics and the way in which humans saw their past and their present. The discovery and protection of "heritage" at home and abroad became a key resource for emerging nationalisms.[13] From the nineteenth century, Germany's political links and cultural reputation in the Middle East had been empowered by the country's linguistic and archaeological prowess in the study of Assyrian and proto-Greek civilisation. National reputation and the Bible drove German excavation in the Holy Land, both facilitating and made possible by the Kaiser's political links to the Ottoman government.[14] The excavation of ancient sites in China from the 1920s, as the GMD sought international recognition, consolidated the view that the Chinese had created the first advanced civilisation. With the re-emergence of China as a global power after 1980, numerous showings around the world of the famous ancient Terracotta Warriors revived this idea. Likewise, the discovery in 1922 of the ancient city of Mohenjo-daro in northwest Pakistan led to intense discussion of whether it was an import by "Aryans" from central Asia or an aspect of a long established, "non-Aryan" Indian civilisation, influencing the debate about Dravidianism and Aryanism in India. In this way the ethnic and racial conflicts of the nineteenth century were reignited by scientific discoveries of the twentieth century and were used as ammunition by Hindu right-wingers and their left-wing critics.

Earlier, the discoveries of Sir Arthur Evans at Knossos in Crete fundamentally revised the picture of classical Greek civilisation which had underpinned Europe's sense of cultural and racial superiority since the Enlightenment. The fact that this early Hellenic civilisation used the Greek language, as Cambridge scholars discovered in the early 1950s, but appeared to have cultural connections with Egypt and North Africa threw the study of ancient civilisations into a comparative mode at the very time when European empires were in rapid decline. This shift in perception culminated in Martin Bernal's *Black Athena* (1987), a book which sought to establish the African origins of Western civilisation.[15] By then, the longstanding effort, which had reached its height in Nazi Germany, to prove that Europeans, and particularly so-called Aryans, were biologically and culturally superior throughout history had largely collapsed. Yet, while "heritage" continued to empower nationalism, religion or cultural relativism, its destruction did the same in some striking cases, for instance the ravaging of temples during China's Cultural Revolution or "un-Islamic" monuments during fundamentalist rampages in Afghanistan, Syria and Iraq after 1980.

Medieval and modern history might not seem to have had much social impact but they were probably one of the most politicised, and politically influential, of all disciplines. Rigorous "Germanism"; supposed Gallic uniqueness in combining Celtic, Roman and Germanic cultures; the search for "democracy" in Saxon England or in ancient India; all these historians' debates both reflected and empowered significant political conflicts, especially during the 1920s and 1930s. The general tendency throughout the century was the move from a diffusionist understanding of cultural change to one which emphasised the inherent creative capacity of different societies, a shift which again contributed to the global rise of nationalist and ethnic self-assertion. The so-called Sapir–Whorf thesis of the 1930s, for instance, suggested that language determined consciousness rather than vice versa. This tended to undermine the view that peoples, such as the Hopi of North

America, were "backward" or "primitive", whereas, in fact, they simply saw the world differently.[16]

In West Africa, again, scholars fought hard against "Euro-centrism" to prove that the Benin bronzes were African cultural artefacts and not copies of European originals. Indian Muslim scholars asserted the "Indian-ness" of Islam in the subcontinent, especially those who worked with the Indian National Congress. Soviet historical writing and social sciences were heavily constrained by political censorship. But oriental scholarship maintained a degree of vitality in the interwar period. Wilhelm (Vasily) Barthold wrote on medieval Arabic and Persian society, implying that they enshrined some degree of communitarian consensus, so anticipating the development of Communist central Asia.[17] In the English-speaking world Arnold Toynbee's massive *A Study of History* brought together late-nineteenth-century idealism with an emphasis on the evolution of world civilisations which relativised Europe, Christian civilisation and the nation state.[18]

European empire, however, proved to be a constant source of controversy throughout the century, encapsulating issues of development and race. The attempt to unify the British Empire against regional nationalism and European rivals in the 1920s gave rise to an extensive popular and children's literature, for example *The Wonder Book of Empire for Boys and Girls* which announced "a new interest and feeling of pride in what has been so aptly described as 'Our Glorious Heritage'".[19] In India, Sir Jadunath Sarkar, writing in the 1920s, presented a liberal view of the Mughal Empire,[20] mirroring and supporting Nehru's more vigorously nationalist one. By the 1960s, both had been replaced by a resolutely Marxist position, reflecting the intellectual dominance of the left in India. This in turn faded under the influence of postmodern and postcolonial critiques. In the 1960s and 1970s, nationalist and Marxist critiques of imperial rule had become predominant even in Europe, though the older generation often vigorously defended the memory of imperial rule. The French case was, perhaps, different. The savagery of the Algerian war of independence tended to marginalise French imperial history in the Academy as also in popular perception. French academic history was dominated by studies of revolutionary France and the structuralism of Fernand Braudel, which avoided both Marxist and nationalist tropes by analysing agricultural and trade patterns.[21]

Towards the end of the century, the debate had shifted again as some neoliberal historians reasserted the uniqueness of European civilisation and the way that the British Empire, in particular, had supposedly fostered free trade and the freedom of the individual. In common with the public view that "America never had an empire", most US historians painted a picture of the country's hostility both to the European empires and to Soviet Communism, though Michael Mann, for instance, dissented from this view. It might be thought that historical writing and teaching had few social consequences and the turn back to instrumental scientific and economic knowledge in the early years of the twenty-first century seemed to prove this. Yet, historical themes persistently seeped into national and personal self-consciousness. In an important sense, the constant iteration in books, films and television programmes of the morality and humanity of the Allies' struggle with Nazi Germany, for instance, profoundly shaped politicians' attempts to raise support for various types of humanitarian intervention which changed world politics from Britain's and France's Suez adventure of 1956, through the American war in Vietnam to later military interventions in Serbia, Iraq and Afghanistan.

KNOWLEDGE AND THE PERSON: ANTHROPOLOGY

The emerging discipline of anthropology also played a significant part in providing a new way of understanding non-European peoples as colonialism frayed and declined.[22] By the 1920s, British and American anthropology had taken different trajectories, though both were in dialogue with the work of the French and German sociologists Émile Durkheim and Max Weber. The Americans, influenced by the German-Jewish expatriate cultural theorist Franz Boas, had moved away from a classification of higher and lower social groups.[23] Boas rejected an evolutionist notion of culture and race and emphasised instead the way in which the organisation of society served individual needs, so laying the foundations of American cultural anthropology. He denounced nationalism and racism in the United States and, later, Nazi race theory.

Meanwhile, the British were also rejecting evolutionary racism to create the new field of social anthropology which stressed social structure and function in a manner that distantly echoed developments in biology and engineering. The need of colonial governments for information was one imperative here. But these scholars also increasingly rejected the earlier idea of a hierarchy of advanced and backward societies and indirectly influenced the following generation of colonial nationalists. As early as the 1880s, James Frazer had begun to examine mythologies in their own right. A later turning point was A. C. Haddon's Torres Strait expedition of 1898, which collected precise data on social organisation and ideologies of the region's people.[24] W. H. R. Rivers published a detailed and dispassionate study of the Toda people of southern India in 1906. In the 1920s, Bronisław Malinowski's studies of the Trobriand Islanders of the Pacific also rejected racial evolutionism, influenced by linguistic and psychological studies. Malinowski again argued that supposedly primitive peoples had the same mental abilities as other humans, but simply used them in a different way.[25] His aim was always partly "to influence the makers of policy", as he put it. Malinowski's pupils A. A. Radcliffe-Brown, Raymond Firth and E. E. Evans-Pritchard went on to analyse kinship as the core human universal.

Malinowski's and his colleague G. C. Seligman's days at the London School of Economics in the 1930s proved highly productive in the development of social anthropology which influenced global intellectual elites at the critical phase when new national states were emerging. The Chinese former LSE scholar Fei Xiaotong, for instance, became an expert on the country's minority ethnic groups, later a director for its Centre of Nationalities and finally, after a period of forced labour during the Cultural Revolution, an elder statesman of the anthropological profession. Similarly, Jomo Kenyatta transformed the ideas of Malinowski and the London-based black activist George Padmore into a Kenyan ideology of statehood in his *Facing Mount Kenya* (1938) which was based on his LSE thesis. Kenyatta's knowledge of kinship and social networks of the Kikuyu later provided the background for his ethnic policies as first president of independent Kenya. Raymond Firth, based in London and then Sydney, provided an intellectual basis for the revaluation of Maori culture and the movement for self-respect among Solomon Islanders.

Meanwhile, American anthropologists in Chicago had combined some of Boas' and Malinowski's thought with the theoretical ideas laid down by Durkheim. The result was a great generation of American anthropologists, notably Ruth Benedict and Margaret Mead, whose worldwide fieldwork paralleled, but also contributed to, the rise of American world power.[26] This kind of psychological and moral anthropology aimed to understand and rectify the behaviour of nations. Benedict, for instance, helped justify the decision to retain Hirohito as Emperor of Japan after 1945, on the ground that "intense tribal feeling" around the imperial house "has functioned to maintain loyalty and cohesiveness" in the country.[27] At the same time they argued strongly against racial discrimination in the United States itself and provided intellectual support to the Civil Rights Movement in the 1950s and 1960s. After the invasion of Iraq in 2003, calls were heard in the United States to find "new Ruth Benedicts" to understand the culture of that country.

Taking the century as a whole, however, a most significant influence was the appropriation of Marxism and later reaction against it by social anthropologists across the world. Marx himself had moved in his later years away from a strict emphasis on a materialist understanding of the development of class society to a sense of the importance of culture. By the 1870s, he had come to a new valuation of the supposedly democratic form of the village community.[28] Early Soviet anthropologists and their Marxist colleagues in Western Europe, India and Latin America created a debate about the "structure" of social organisations, and this influenced later anthropologists, who disavowed strictly Marxist interpretations of the discipline. So, in particular, Claude Lévi-Strauss's examination of Amerindian societies in Brazil proposed a structuralist model of social organisation which proved influential through to the 1990s. Lévi-Strauss's "structure" was not one of class and historical materialism, however, but a logical dialectical framework which was itself influenced by contemporary developments in mathematics and linguistics.[29] Yet, more forcefully, Lévi-Strauss argued that the "savage mind" had the same logical structure as the "advanced mind" and that human societies were constructed out of the mental categorisation by the person of a whole web of relationships in both cases. The fundamental difference between Marxist and mental-linguistic structuralism was played out in a heated exchange in the 1950s between Jean-Paul Sartre, who remained a Marxist in politics despite his avowal of existentialism, and Lévi-Strauss, who argued that these two positions were totally incompatible.

The subtle relationship between anthropological experience or theory and global social and political developments was clearly indicated during the Second World War and the phase of non-governmental organisation (NGO) activity that followed it. Anthropologists serving in the main war zones seized new opportunities for research. Lévi-Strauss fled from Europe to escape Nazi persecution and made close contact with American anthropologists. So, too, the British anthropologist Edmund Leach began to develop his theories of the relationship between kinship, symbol and local power structures on the Burma front and the road through Lashio to southern China during the British army's war with Japan. In the age of NGOs, the anthropologist Bernard Cohn worked in northern India with the Peace Corps and began to reconceptualise the Indian village community. Clifford Geertz, who was regarded as the key exponent of symbolic anthropology in the second half of the century, had served in the US navy during the war and later went to Java with the Ford Foundation. His famous study of the Javanese cockfight showed how the close examination of the form and mentalities of social interaction during a ritual could help anthropologists to reconceptualise a whole society. Jack Goody, Ernest Gellner and James C. Scott began to create a partial reconciliation between history and anthropology as the age of strict functionalism and structuralism in their discipline came to an end in the 1980s.[30] In the broadest sense, these intellectual developments tended further to assert the vitality and difference of human societies and their various creative potentialities precisely at a time when transnational bodies such as the United Nations and UNESCO were emerging on the world stage.

There is no question that anthropology was initially a predominantly European and North American discipline. It was profoundly influenced by and, indeed, influenced the experience of colonialism and the worldwide reach of the West during the wars and the era of decolonisation. But Africans, Asians and Latin Americans, many trained in Europe and America, began to turn to anthropology as a discipline quite early in the twentieth century, in part to add their voices to the debate about their own societies. Indians, for instance, reconceptualised the village, but in particular developed a new view of the caste system, noting its mutability and fluidity, whereas many British officials, missionaries and anthropologists stressed its rigid structure, often in order to laud the consequences of colonial rule.[31] This trend came to its climax in the work of M. N. Srinivas, a pupil of Evans-Pritchard, who used the term Sanskritisation to describe how middle and lower castes elevated their ritual status. Srinivas's studies stood in contrast with those of Louis Dumont, the French anthropologist, who produced a sophisticated late-structuralist account of the caste system. Yet, both authors provided powerful intellectual resources for those politicians who urged decisive state action to humanise the untouchables and lower castes in the Indian mind.

Over the same period, Lévi-Strauss's stimulus to anthropology in Brazil and other parts of Latin America initiated a creative tradition of the discipline there which repatriated the study, particularly of Amazonian tribal societies, from the hands of European and American scholars. While these developments were not a direct consequence of decolonisation and the rise of nationalism, they reflected a broad mental change and a new construction of the human which was visible in many aspects of life. In common with the postcolonial and "subaltern studies" move in other human and social sciences, anthropology also became more politicised towards the end of the twentieth century. Edward Said's assault on "Orientalism" in the European and American social sciences generally was mirrored by scholars such as Talal Asad and Achille Mbembe, who assailed the manner in which his predecessors had stereotyped Arab and African societies generally.[32]

At a theoretical level, the postmodernist critique of the humanities and its tendency to relativise and fracture grand theory had its proponents in anthropology. Counter-intuitively, postmodernism emerged out of a sense of ease with political and social processes and also a sense of global movement and fluidity. This might seem a contrarian idea, since postmodernism and post-colonialism announced themselves as radical systems of thought. Yet, it was easier to emphasise the unauthored nature of discourse or the challenge of the subaltern to power structures in wealthy Western universities, far from areas of economic and social disaster during the period of relative peace and growth which stretched from the 1960s to 2008. At this time, the study of economies was in decline, along with economic history, while economics itself had retreated into a mathematical and predictive phase, often dwelling on the "perfection of the market". Yet, as in the 1920s, the eruption of a serious economic and social crisis after 2008 destroyed the certitudes of specialists and brought social knowledge, including anthropology, back into the domain of public debate.

ECONOMICS AND SOCIOLOGY

Of all the social science and humanities disciplines, economics, economic history and sociology had the clearest effects on the political and social life of the twentieth century and the understanding of individual motivation. As one of the most celebrated economists of the century, J. M. Keynes stated that the policies of present are often derived from the views of an "academic scribbler" of the some years earlier. Equally, though, the views of the scribblers were themselves formed in the context of massive events: the world wars, the impact of Communism, the Great Depression, the consequences of colonialism and the world dominance of the US economy. The major developments in economic thought during the century were consequently the creation of mathematical models to predict human economic behaviour and avoid risk. This added rigour to the analyses of the market and social organisation which had preoccupied theorists from Adam Smith, through John Stuart Mill and David Ricardo, to William Stanley Jevons before 1900.[33]

Secondly, and of even greater practical importance, was the debate among economists and policymakers about the role of the growing state in the regulation and control of the market. At one extreme of this contest were Marxist economists in interwar Germany and the USSR and later China and Eastern Europe who advocated state ownership of the means and modes of production. Notable here was Rudolf Hilferding, who argued that a turn to socialist economic planning was actually made easier by the "socialising of capital" as businessmen came to dominate politics. At the other extreme were advocates of the free market, such as the Austrian-born economist F. A. Hayek and later US economists, notably Milton Friedman, who leaned to the view that the market itself was a rational form which assigned value effectively and that interference in its workings was likely to be counterproductive.

Keynes himself and his pupils stood midway between these sharply different positions, advocating strong state intervention to allay the commercial crises which arose from warfare and wrongheaded policymaking. In order to protect the citizen, the state needed at times to depart from the laissez-faire ideology which had dominated the previous century and act to change exchange rates, provide monetary or practical stimuli, such as building new houses, or even to take control of financial institutions. Though marginalised in most histories of economics, Indian, African and Chinese economists consistently argued for protection for their nascent industries even while laissez-faire remained dominant among colonial officials. From the late nineteenth century in India, for instance, figures such as K. T. Telang, Dadabhai Naoroji and, later, D. R. Gaddiel, whom I call statistical liberals, were using colonial ethnologies, censuses and statistics against colonial stereotypes of the lazy and unproductive peasantry.[34] Rather than being conduits through which Western ideas were diffused, they anticipated and pre-empted many European and American critics of laissez-faire economics. By 1938, the Indian National Congress had established a National Economic Planning Committee, bringing together economists, politicians and business people. Similarly, in the early nationalist period in China, Liang Qichao had urged the government to promote industrial development well before Marxist economics became dominant in the country.[35]

The economic thought of the century, whether liberal, left-wing or conservative, therefore, derived from a concern with the improvement of people's living conditions as popular government became dominant. Alfred Marshall (1842–1924), the leading British economist who developed the concepts of supply and demand, marginal utility and diminishing returns with mathematical models, was himself of a non-conformist background and determined to find a way of limiting working-class poverty.[36] Keynes, who inherited and developed many of Marshall's ideas, showed how the economic conditions imposed on defeated powers in 1919 had distorted the world economy and how rigid adherence to the gold standard by Britain and other Western countries had impoverished not only the domestic economy but more particularly their colonial territories.

Keynes's advocacy of state intervention to stimulate growth, regardless of rising inflation, was widely influential, but stimulated vigorous criticism. One former supporter wrote that he had "thrown on the scrap-heap a large part of the orthodox economic theory in which I still believe".[37] The philosopher Bertrand Russell, hardly a self-effacing intellectual, remarked that "annihilating arguments darted out of him with the sharpness of an adder's tongue".[38] But Keynes's arguments had no purchase in European colonial territories where governments adhered to laissez-faire policies through to the Second World War. But after 1945, as we have seen, Keynes and other leading economists attempted in the Bretton Woods agreements to stabilise international currency transactions and avoid large rises and falls in currency values. The creation of the International Monetary Fund and the World Bank and the various

European economic agreements which preceded the European Union were also products of this post-war period of regulation. High taxation and government investment across the industrial world along with states' determination to expand educational opportunities meant that the post-war period was one era in which income inequality was reduced. In the newly independent states of Asia and Africa, governments widely turned to centralised planning and policies of import substitution. These policies were legitimised by left-wing economists who had trained at Cambridge or at the London School of Economics, such as Joan Robinson, a pupil of Keynes.[39] Their five-year plans mirrored those of the Communist countries, though the appropriation of property and capital in the systems they advocated was generally less severe.

During the 1970s and 1980s, the balance of economic thinking changed once again, reflecting developments in the real economy. This in turn influenced policies and social outcomes. Even in the 1930s and 1940s, F. A. Hayek, who proclaimed himself a classic liberal, argued that state control over the economy led to tyranny, notably in his 1944 work *The Road to Serfdom*.[40] As the post-Second World War boom ended and inflation with low growth ("stagflation") became a problem in many countries, economists working in the broad tradition of F. A. Hayek began to urge the freeing of the market and limitations on government intervention. The collapse of the Soviet Union seemed to underline the point that centralised economic planning led to disaster. One problem analysed by F. A. Hayek and his followers was that if governments "printed money" or over-invested, the individual businessman or shopkeeper would anticipate this by raising prices and thus negate the purpose of the stimulus. Milton Friedman, his pupil and an economic adviser to President Nixon, in turn argued against "naive Keynesianism", emphasising the need for strict monetary policy and minimal state intervention in the economy.[41]

This new academic orthodoxy was highly attractive to government leaders trying to reduce spending and helped legitimise the policies of Margaret Thatcher, George Bush and George W. Bush. The result was the beginning of the scaling back of government expenditure in most Western democracies and, in time, a further period of rising inequality.[42] The collapse of the Soviet Union, meanwhile, led to a dramatic loosening of central government control in Russia and Eastern Europe. Observing this, China followed suit in opening the economy, as did Vietnam in the so-called *Doi Moi* ("renovation"/liberalisation) period. India, suffering a dramatic balance of payments crisis, saw a neo-Keynesian finance minister and economist, Manmohan Singh, reducing state control over industry and beginning to allow certain types of foreign capital investment in the country, so reversing the policy which went back to Nehru's period. This position was later strongly supported by Jagdish Bhagwati, an Indian economist close to the neoliberal right and Indian business, who stressed the importance of free trade. By contrast, India's leading twentieth-century economist, Amartya Sen, remained a late neo-Keynesian, committed to the alleviation of the country's persisting income inequalities through state intervention.[43]

The retreat of the state in the former Communist societies often led not to the emergence of a free market but to a situation where former state managers and party officials became "oligarchs" dominating particular trades and industries. But in Western countries, too, the implementation of the new orthodoxy brought dramatic problems. The insistence that "the market knows best" and was a rational actor built on the rational calculation of millions of individuals was not universally accepted. The leading businessman and economic thinker George Soros believed, on the contrary, that markets were periodically fundamentally irrational. The sceptics were proved right as property prices ballooned and banks made excessive and unsustainable loans. By 2008, with the collapse of the American firm Lehman Brothers, the whole edifice of the neoliberal world economy collapsed into what was called the Great Recession.

The globalisation of capital and production meant that this American crisis spilled rapidly across the world, bankrupting governments, undermining the policies of the European Union and depressing living standards in poorer countries. A self-styled "new Keynesian" and advocate of the welfare state, the economist Paul Krugman, vigorously revived the argument for state intervention during periods of economic crisis.[44] A further battle ensued between neo-Keynesians, who urged government investment and money printing to restore prosperity, and proponents of government austerity, who believed that only by "balancing the books" would prosperity return. In the eurozone, there was a similar intellectual contest between German proponents of austerity, still living in the shadow of the inflation of the 1920s, and those who demanded state intervention to avert deflation and further unemployment. A later development cast doubt on the very nature of economics itself, arguing that the notion of risk could only be approached through a study of "emotion": economics was a pointless discipline unless it was paired with psychology and anthropology. Throughout the century, indeed, the economic scribblers had created major change at a global level and had not simply reacted to it.

The discipline of sociology had a less clear impact on social and political action during the twentieth century than economics. This was because it traversed a particularly broad range of disciplines between history and economics, influencing them all. The work of Emile Durkheim, who emphasised the way modern societies maintained coherence through collective dispositions in law and religion, informed all the human sciences. Equally, Max Weber's linking of the market and Protestant religion, and his idea of the disenchantment of the world, dominated historical writing throughout the century. Later functionalist arguments promoted by writers such as the American sociologist Talcott Parsons took centre stage.[45] Societies, according to this model, were holistic entities in which social processes and forms all had a function which helped determine and construct the whole. This was a concept that had salience in anthropology and economics over the same period. Perhaps the key intervention of sociologists was not in theory, however, but in the empirical investigation and statistical assessment of the life chances of ordinary people, especially in the 1950s and 1960s, when many studies prompted politicians to improve educational facilities and help break down social hierarchies. After the 1970s, sociology moved away from functionalism to an emphasis on conflict and, later, to postmodern studies of fractured ideologies and unauthored discourses, as did historians, anthropologists and economists.

At a deeper moral level, beneath these continuing disputes about the nature of the market or social organisation, one can observe the emergence of a view of the human across the social sciences which inflected political processes and moulded society. Broadly speaking, the ideologies of the nineteenth century had stressed racial and cultural evolution, even if thinkers from Marx to Mills had made room for the market. By the second half of the twentieth century, the notion of the human as an economic animal, either working cooperatively or pursuing an individualistic path of profit maximisation, was widely in the ascendant and even triumphed in the USSR after 1990. The survival of the biologically or socially fittest had now become the survival of the economically fittest.[46] Power and knowledge had become economic power and knowledge. Even religious belief was invaded by economic instrumentalism. So, in the United States, the Christian activists who came on the political scene at the beginning of the new century were both individualist devotees and neoliberal opponents of big government. Yet, these positions were constantly challenged, not only by Marxists and late democratic socialist thinkers but also by liberals, idealists and philosophers who attempted to rescue and understand the human beyond the limits of economic individualism. This latter strain of thought is considered in the next chapter.

[11]   THE SELF AND HUMAN SOCIETY

Sources of the Self Worldwide
Twentieth-Century Sciences of the Mind
Moulding the Person for Society: Gender and Sexuality
Educating and Disciplining the Person for Society
Sport: A Window on the Twentieth Century?
Sociality, Communication and the Craze for Possession
Conclusion: The Twentieth-Century Person

ALL THE emerging knowledge systems mentioned so far had a profound, but indirect, impact not only on how the human being was understood and represented but also on how she understood herself and her life. The psychological sciences and philosophical approaches to the self which emerged during the century, however, directly addressed these issues and moulded the self-perception of millions of individuals, particularly in the United States and Western Europe. These are the subject of the present chapter.

SOURCES OF THE SELF WORLDWIDE

Here it will be useful to consider a major philosophical attempt to describe the making of modern identity, Charles Taylor's *Sources of the Self*.[1] Discussing Euro-American modernity in the twentieth century, Taylor acknowledged the importance of technical change, war and communications in forging the modern self, but emphasised the moral changes, the search for different forms of the good life which have both empowered these perspectives and reflected on

Remaking the Modern World 1900–2015: Global Connections and Comparisons, First Edition. C. A. Bayly.
© 2018 John Wiley & Sons Ltd. Published 2018 by John Wiley & Sons Ltd.

them. He showed how Enlightenment rationalism, Victorian romanticism and the search for nature created a new sense of the human person, which sought for meaning not in a given divinely sanctioned ordering of being but in an inward discovery of subjective rights "relating to the natural sentiments within us".[2] This had resulted in the emergence of a "fractured moral horizon" along with, at least in the West, the rise of unbelief and utilitarianism roughly described as "secularism". This position had features in common with the writings of earlier British and American conservative writers such as Michael Oakeshott and Leo Strauss who deplored the loss of civil traditions, morality and respect for authority.[3]

Like them, Taylor rejected a nihilistic or instrumental version of the modern self of the sort that supposedly emerged from the thought of Nietzsche and, later, Foucault, arguing that people in the late twentieth century still sought the good in forms such as personal autonomy, companionate marriage, the family and political and economic liberty. As a believer himself, he put relatively less emphasis on the way that the sense of the divine, even in this disaggregated sense, has been appropriated constantly by exclusive, aggressive and murderous forms of religion, particularly Christian, for many centuries. He also over-hopefully referred to the "big arc of Sufi-dominated Islam", just when this was widely being demolished by Sunni extremism.[4] Yet, Taylor, along with other philosophers, certainly broadened the notion of human flourishing beyond simple economic liberty, which was a dominant theme of the age.

Taylor's overall picture is plausible for much of Europe, America and other European and formerly Christian societies across the world. How did it relate to other world civilisations? There is no doubt that an appeal to reason, as opposed to embodied religious faith, has been a feature of all societies and religions as they have sought to come to terms with science and technology and proclaim their own modernity. The attack on "polytheism" within Hinduism (the Brahmo Samaj and Arya Samaj) was a case in point, as was the distancing from Sufi spirituality within Islam, taken to extremes by Wahhabism. The modernised Buddhism, shorn of millenarianism, which has acted to reinforce the state in post-Communist societies in Asia, also promoted rational spirituality. All these not only glorified reason but also sought to empower the individual, rather than a priestly hierarchy in order to create the good society.

These ideas moved and were refashioned across the world. So, Muhammad Iqbal modified British communitarian liberalism and German idealism to argue for a more robust Muslim self.[5] Conversely, Gandhian non-violence and self-sacrifice were adapted to conditions in the United States and ultimately returned to South Africa. Again, if belief in God had declined in Western Christian countries from about 90% in 1900 to less than 50% in the more secular European societies, such as Britain, France and Eastern Germany,[6] by 2010, a smaller, but significant, fall was also registered amongst the professional and scientific elites of Asia, the Middle East and Africa. Here also a search for inner, natural meaning, and an emphasis on companionate marriage and social achievement, especially, of course, commercial achievement, were also in evidence as the goal of the good life.

The impact of socialist and Communist conceptions of the person and society should not be underestimated. At one extreme, socialist man represented an attempt to eliminate possessive individualism in the interests of a progressive community. This was the aim of Stalin's Terror, Mao's Cultural Revolution and even Pol Pot's murderous attempt to recreate the primitive equality of the village. This last idea had its roots in the late Marx's turn away from the evolutionary historical materialism which ordained a capitalist phase of society, mentioned in the previous chapter. More moderate versions of socialism, even Lenin's own position during the New Economic Policy, made room for individual action and the role of the socialist vanguard, a validation of the idea of the millenarian agency of the self. Yet, socialism ultimately failed to marry this purposive self with the construction of an equal and productive society.[7] By the end of the century, there was evidence that even in the remaining socialist societies in Asia a version of individualism – the search for personal fulfilment in areas such as marriage and the family – rather than communal sharing was beginning to replace the existing amalgam of communitarian ideologies, supporting Taylor's position.

The re-emergence of radical religious movements by 2000, paralleling the US "moral majority", anti-Darwinian Christians of the United States or the anti-gay fundamental Christians of East and West Africa, is considered in Chapter 13. Extreme forms, such as the Taliban or the Hindu RSS, seemed to reflect a broader movement back to communally sanctioned notions of the good. Yet, even these forms remained distinct from the sensibilities created by the earlier deistic ontological hierarchies and were themselves reflections of what might still be seen as secular modernity.[8] The self in these moral movements was also individuated yet bound by social norms which reflected fear of the other and the dangerous tendencies of that very inner self. So, democracy, as understood by Hasan al-Banna of Egypt; or women driving cars in Saudi Arabia; or girls being educated in north-western Pakistan were seen as evils to be avoided because they threatened an individualist male elite, even if these arguments were archaised with reference to God and the Prophet. Liberal critics understandably denounced these movements as a return to the "dark ages". But they were, in fact, counter-modernist movements, created by modernity itself, with only indirect connections to the theology or understandings of a divine spiritual order of the past. The fundamentalist self was no less a creation of the modern than the capitalist entrepreneurial self or the consuming self.

TWENTIETH-CENTURY SCIENCES OF THE MIND

Alongside this changing philosophical and neo-religious understanding of the self, the century also created more specifically scientific and medical appraisals of the human, pointing to secular forms of treatment which it was hoped could lessen the anxiety of people as they faced unprecedented social and political change. These interacted in complex ways with philosophies of the self.[9]

Here the career of Sigmund Freud is obviously of fundamental importance. Freud, working in Vienna and later, following the rise of anti-Semitism, in London, believed that he could account for human behaviour by distinguishing between different levels of consciousness, the Id and the Ego, as is well known. He argued that there was a level of impulsive human behaviour beneath the rational which derived from unacknowledged desires, particularly sexual desire and the related traumas of early childhood. Psychoanalysis, a procedure for discovering these desires, could mitigate their influence on behaviour. Another Austrian, Carl Jung, followed a more Nietzschean argument, stressing the human's will to power. Yet, Jung, who was particularly influential in India and China, reinserted the notion of communion with God into these new sciences of the mind. Later in the century, Jacques Lacan asserted, in distinction to Freud, that the unconscious was not a primitive level of being but a complex form of language. Foucault also argued that, far from being repressed, discussion and analysis of sexuality was fundamental to the creation of the modern person.[10] These "scientists of the mind" all established schools of psychiatric practice which appealed to wealthy Westerners and were very influential in the era of moral turmoil after 1945. In a sense, they replaced confinement, exorcism and confession as ways of remaking the person for social action. Equally, they all influenced the arts and literature. In their rejection of the idea of madness, they represented a break with the evolutionary rationalism which had dominated the social sciences and humanities in the nineteenth century.

By the 1960s, some commentators even claimed that it was society rather than the individual which was "mad". Yet, there was, alongside these forms of therapy, another strand of psychological science which tended to medicalise mental disturbance, whose practitioners prescribed different forms of drugs and tranquillisers and concentrated on finding its causes in the body's chemistry.[11] In the second half of the century, its proponents became dominant and were often dismissive of psychotherapy, particularly psychoanalysis. Some observers argued that it was the pressure of major drug companies to sell their products which resulted in this change of focus. This was partly true, but the shift also reflected a wider technicalisation of attitudes to the person towards the end of the century, evidenced equally in areas such as cosmetic surgery and the proliferation of recreational drugs. Advocates of a balanced interpretation of mental health argued that personality disorders had both existential and physical origins. These interacted with each other, so that the Cartesian mind–body split was a chimera.

These movements in American and European thought have also often been relegated into a separate, scientific category. But one could add that the reimagining of the human in these circles should be put in context with modernised versions of world religions which were also philosophies. These included Tolstoy's and Gandhi's notions of soul force, neo-Buddhist conceptions of deep spiritual nurture and even various forms of late Christian self-knowledge associated with thinkers such as Martin Heidegger and Edmund Husserl. Heidegger, in particular, was also influenced by the idea of "finding ourselves" behind the surface of rational enquiry, as he stated in *Being and Time*.[12] He was influenced both by early Christian writers such as St Augustine of Hippo and by eastern religion. African political and religious leaders merged indigenous ideas of the beneficent patriarch with notions of spiritual liberty drawn from Christianity and Western politics. An Indian idealist nationalist, such as Bhagwan Das, declared himself a Hindu theosophist, but also a socialist.[13]

This entangling of medical, philosophical and religious ideas of the person at a global level was typical of the way that communication in the twentieth century broke down cultural boundaries. At the same time, the search for the perfect human could itself empower new ideologies of power and exclusion. Heidegger briefly toyed with a philosophical version of Nazism. Carl Schmitt lauded the search for power and sovereignty. The coercive force of Mao's Cultural Revolution embodied a search for a flawless socialist person as much as it was a form of political domination. Idealist Zionism, the search for a new land and rural community, the kibbutz, as well as a new person, became exclusive of Arab Palestinians because of its own idea of perfection.

There is little doubt, however, that the eclectic range of ideas of the person formulated in the twentieth century had a profound effect not simply on individual self-understanding and social politics but also on the world of science, art and self-expression.[14] Just as the psychological sciences broke away from rationalism, so painting and sculpture broke away from the humanist formalism of the early era, as the next chapter suggests. The century was regarded as both the best and the worst in human history and the fate of formal philosophy seemed to embody this paradox. Anglo-American philosophy at the beginning of the century, represented, for instance, by Bertrand Russell and John Dewey,[15] could best be described as pragmatic idealism, a position more ambivalent than contemporary German idealism. By the 1920s and 1930s, linguistic philosophy, represented above all by Ludwig Wittgenstein, had given philosophy a scientific edge, appropriate for the period, which it maintained into the post-war years of university expansion and was set against the neo-Marxist idealism of Sartre and his European coevals.

Yet, the return to the English-speaking world of philosophy as liberal hypermorality was reflected in the work of Robert Nozick, Richard Rorty and John Rawls,[16] and even Taylor himself.[17] Their emphasis on the search for human goodness seemed to echo and also promote the hopes for a better world order embodied in the UN, UNESCO and the European Union. Yet, the ancient antagonism between realism and idealism – often represented as the difference between Hobbes and Rousseau – could not be banished. Drawing on Lenin and Nietzsche, a philosopher such as Robert Nozick, and later Raymond Geuss, had reinstated "real politics" by the beginning of the twenty-first century.[18] Human beings could wish for goodness and high ideals, but the practice of politics, and hence philosophical reflection on it, represented a blending of unstable elements of ideology in contingent historical time. The cover of Geuss's 2008 book made the point visually. It showed an armed man, presumably a partisan, standing over the dead body of another. The French political philosopher Pierre Rosanvallon made a related point, noting that growing popular distrust with democratic representatives across the world was not a sign of generalised political apathy.[19] Countless popular protests, from "green" environmentalist activism and riots against the killing by police of black people in the United States to demonstrations against sexual violence against women in Delhi, signalled a new form of democratic action in an "age of distrust" and fragmented sovereignty when the person had constantly to be wary of malign politics. This turn was matched by the growth of both popular and state surveillance of these fragmented aspirations. Their ideologies and practices were spread by the new electronic media.

MOULDING THE PERSON FOR SOCIETY: GENDER AND SEXUALITY

A common theme during the so-called sexual revolution of the 1960s and 1970s was a comparison between the nineteenth and early twentieth century's focus on religion and nationalism with the late twentieth century's concern with sex and enjoyment. This caricature of different generations did at least point to some profound changes in Western societies and among some non-Western elites. The number of women in the workplace greatly increased. Marriage declined in popularity after 1960 and homosexuality became socially acceptable in large parts of the West, so that by the beginning of the twenty-first century several American states and European democracies had legislated for same-sex marriage. None of these changes was universal. Radicals were often puritanical. Che Guevara, for instance, wanted to send all homosexuals to labour camps. Severe constraints on all forms of sexuality continued to exist in Muslim and, to a lesser extent, Hindu societies, as well as in the remaining socialist countries. In the West, parents worried about "sexting", the sending of sexually explicit text messages and pictures with mobile phones. Nevertheless, changes in the mundane forms of human sexual expression were widely visible and had even begun to penetrate patriarchal and authoritarian societies, often creating a moralising backlash.

In the case of gender equality, the situation in 1900 had hardly changed since the early modern period. Women were occasionally rulers, as in the case of Queen Victoria and Queen Wilhelmina of the Netherlands. They were teachers, secretaries and occasionally well-regarded literary figures or scientists. Yet, they were excluded from the national franchise, except in Australia and New Zealand. In local affairs some propertied women were allowed to vote. In Latin America *mestizo* women had acquired the right to vote for town councils after the revolutions of the early nineteenth century. Even in Bombay, women in purdah had secured the right to vote as early as the Portuguese period. Ironically, though, the British authorities insisted in the 1880s that women should actually appear personally at the ballot box to avoid fraud, and this deterred many from voting. Women also often suffered discrimination in law, as in the case of inheritance, and were largely unprotected against domestic violence. Children of unmarried mothers were treated as outcastes and denied a normal upbringing often because they might inherit the "moral flabbiness" of their errant parents.[20]

By the beginning of the century, radical women's groups, such as the British Suffragettes, had campaigned vociferously for the vote, but it was the First World War which initiated a major intellectual as well as social rupture in the patriarchal consensus.[21] As we have seen, women became indispensable in the workplace, owing to the dearth of men. The end of the war saw a conservative reaction, but women over 30 received the right to vote both in the United States and most European countries by 1925. In 1924, the Weimar Republic actually enfranchised women over 25 years of age. Progress continued to be made until after 1945, when adult women in virtually all Western democracies had been enfranchised. In the USSR, women also played an important role in the highly structured Party committees. This was trumpeted in Bolshevik pamphlets and newspapers, though it is unclear how much had changed in the countryside. In British colonial territories, where even the male franchise for local and provincial elections was tiny, progress was glacially slow. In Africa, Christian churches hoping to influence the family put women into positions of authority on church councils. But much more important were the examples of women, European and non-European, who played a part in nationalist movements against the colonial power. In India, Annie Besant, the Irish radical and theosophist, inaugurated the change and even before 1914 women in the Nehru family were taking part in political demonstrations.

The great expansion of public communication and the press throughout the first half of the century pushed these changes forward. Powerful leaders needed increasingly to entice the new women voters. Even if this served as a new form of patriarchy it nevertheless focussed attention on female ability. Madame Chiang Kai-shek and later Indira Gandhi and Golda Meir stood alongside Eleanor Roosevelt and Eva Perón as political icons. Women writers such as Hannah Arendt tied the issue of sexual equality to questions of race and self-expression which became the subject of debate on radio and television during and after the Second World War. Meanwhile, figures such as the "flappers" of the pre-war party scene in the United States or the Land Army women of wartime Britain acted as icons for women both as transgressors and as "pillars of society". Open discussion of sex and sexuality by post-war psychologists and sociologists and women writers and poets, such as Sylvia Plath and Anne Sexton, advanced the notion that sexual desire should be openly expressed and not hidden or denied, so that the rights of women to approach and attract men were gradually conceded, if only in richer Western societies. The changes of the 1960s and 1970s across the world consolidated the position of the educated or "celebrity" woman in society. The US feminist movement of the period embodied the idea of the woman as a new and liberating political force. Distantly, in Vietnam, "the heroine mother" and women military volunteers became a symbol of national resistance against American imperialism. The two strands came together when the American actress Jane Fonda flew to Hanoi to strengthen Vietnamese resolve against her own compatriots, while thousands of women joined the anti-war protests of that period in the United States.

A critical turning point here, reinforcing the notion of equal gender rights, was the variety of new forms of contraception and other reproductive technologies that became widely available, especially in the West, in the 1960s and

Figure 11 Eva Perón handing out election badges from her campaign train, February 1946. Juan Perón is in the background. Thomas D. McAvoy/The LIFE Picture Collection/Getty Images.

1970s. This began to create a radical divide between intimacy and sexual pleasure, on the one hand, and childbirth, on the other. Authors in the early part of the century, from Freud through Wilhelm Reich to Herbert Marcuse, had emphasised the forms of discipline and control which built up around sexuality and even Foucault seemed to assent to some of these ideas. But after "the sixties", not only young people themselves but also social commentators began to experience and write of the "democratisation of intimacy", "plastic sexuality" and female choice.[22] *In vitro* fertilisation and surrogate motherhood further modified the nature of sexuality and the form of the nuclear family. By the 1970s, this had even penetrated into Communist Eastern Europe and prepared the way for a loosening of party discipline.[23]

By the turn of the century, theorists were arguing that, at least among educated Western women, the old patriarchal family and its attitudes were being swept away. More women were unmarried and childless; those with children could now work at home, as did increasing numbers of men. Sheryl Sandberg, chief operating officer of Facebook, probably the most successful company in the world at that period, argued along these lines in 2012.[24] Yet, women were still relatively poorly represented among chief executives of major businesses and in the top level of national political institutions. Other indicators also suggested that this picture was too rosy. In fact, economic downturns, the increase of marital breakdowns and pornography on the Internet after 1980 may actually have increased rape and sexual abuse. A UN report noted that in Italy 37% of women between the ages of 16 and 75 had suffered abuse in the previous 20 years, according to a 2006 survey, and death and domestic violence at the hands of men were on the increase.[25] The movement of women in public had widely led to an increase in "stalking", while differing notions of sexual dignity between immigrant and local ethnicities had led to numbers of cases of grooming and abuse in Britain. By 2013, both the British and Italian governments were moving to legally penalise these abuses more severely.[26] The financial crisis after 2008 also diminished women's access to the labour market.

Middle-class women in the newly emerging consumer societies of China and India followed many of these trends after 1980, both favourable and unfavourable, but in the poorer parts of these societies, and over much of the Muslim world and in Africa, the situation was very different. In many legal systems, from male primogeniture to South Asian customary law, women were penalised throughout the century and beyond. Ironically, in the 1930s, the secularist Muhammad Ali Jinnah attempted to invoke Sharia law to empower women in cases of inheritance, but failed to bypass the bias against female inheritance in local legal systems. Systems akin to "bride price" persisted across many of these societies as a disincentive to having female children. In general, blatant female infanticide had been suppressed by the British Indian government and its independent successors, but, by the 1990s, new forms of ultrasound scanning made the abortion of female foetuses possible. The ratio of new-born boys to girls dramatically increased after this, presaging a longer-term social problem even more serious than the one caused by China's "One-Child Policy", which persisted from the 1970s to the 2000s.

Taken in combination with the increase of violence against women in many societies, the persistence of abuse and genital mutilation of women and girls, particularly in Africa, many concluded that the improvement of gender equality since 1900 had been partial at best. Indeed, in some Muslim societies there had actually been a reversal of the improvement in women's education. Access to public places in areas such as Northwest Pakistan, Afghanistan, Chechnya, parts of Egypt, Saudi Arabia and the Sudan had been set back by rising fundamentalist movements or conservative regimes. When Jacqueline Kennedy visited Pakistan in the 1960s, photographs show large numbers of unveiled women greeting her on the streets. By the 2000s, the full veil (burqa) was gaining in popularity as military rulers attempted to garner favour with conservative clerics and Saudi influence spread. Web services were established to stop young men and women conversing online.[27] Radical movements such as the Taliban in Pakistan, ISIS in Iraq and Boko Haram in Africa went further, destroying women's schools, kidnapping female pupils or in the case of Malala Yousafzai in Pakistan, actually attempting to murder this young spokeswoman for education. Still, the level of support for the full-faced veil was by no means universal. A 2014 survey of Muslim societies found that, while 74% of respondents favoured the niqab or burqa in Saudi Arabia and 35% in Pakistan, 44% of all respondents thought that a tight-fitting scarf was adequate and that the face should be uncovered. In Lebanon, a near majority favoured no head covering.[28]

Figure 12 Pakistan President Mohammad Ayub Khan with Jackie Kennedy. Tour of Pakistan, 1962. Art Rickerby/The LIFE Picture Collection/Getty Images.

As suggested, the semi-emancipation of women in the West had resulted from a combination of material change in the form of the birth control pill and the condom and the notion of democratic rights, which was universalised after the Second World War. In the case of sexual diversity – homosexuality, the transgendered and metrosexuality – the notion of human rights was also increasingly invoked. But the retreat of Christianity and its concept of natural law, along with travel and better communications, also played their part. The result was the widespread decriminalisation of homosexuality in the West between the 1950s and 1980s and the later licence given to same-sex marriage. The century began with the trial of Oscar Wilde for homosexuality in Britain and ended with mass gay marriages in California. Midway between these dates, writers such as William Burroughs began publicly to advocate homosexuality and the black singer Sylvester transformed the "soul" themes of the Pentecostalist church (from which he had been expelled) into gay lyrics.

Of course, the legal bars to homosexuality in most socioreligious systems in the early part of the century by no means implied that people were entirely inhibited from these relationships. Among elite groups of young males in schools, colleges and military units in Western Europe and America, this had occurred throughout history. Ronald Hyam has shown how same-sex relationships were common among young colonial officials.[29] They had been thrown into societies which had different attitudes to sexuality despite the fierce condemnation of homosexuality inherent in certain forms of Islam, purist Hinduism and Buddhism as well as in the traditions of some patriarchal African societies. But in many regions a form of covert sexual diversity existed in which particular groups or even castes were known to form such relationships, sometimes for companionship, sometimes in festivities, when controls on behaviour were relaxed, and sometimes for money. In Hindu society a quasi-caste group of transgendered males who adopted female sexual roles, called the Hijras, continued to exist. The anthropologist Tom Boellstorff's

The Gay Archipelago [30] discussed the situation in Indonesia, where, until the end of the century, the discourse of homosexuality and lesbianism merged acceptance of old cultural forms with ideas of national tolerance. In China, again, homosexuality attracted discussion, not only from Western observers but also from Confucian scholars and later Chinese nationalists. All these forms of covert and hierarchical diversity distantly paralleled liaisons contracted in English public schools, French North African *qasba*s and American summer camps.

The great difference between the 1930s and the 1980s, however, lay in the permeation of the discourse of rights into sexual relations and the decline of the idea that some forms of behaviour were unnatural. The partial empowerment of women in Europe and America, along with the notion of black civil rights after 1945, also encouraged urban male homosexuals and later lesbian women to create civil society organisations and argue against discrimination. Medical and philosophical opinion abandoned the idea that homosexuality was abnormal and could be "cured". Even the churches began to take notice of these rights claims, uneasily aware that significant numbers in the clergy were themselves sexually ambivalent. Only sexual acts with children were excluded from this new moral relativism. Opting for diversity was the rational act of adults; paedophilia was a form of criminal coercion. In fact, the change in the law and public attitudes to adult homosexuality towards the end of the century appeared actually to have increased the incidence of moral panic about paedophilia. Significantly, this affected two of the most conservative bodies in the world: the Roman Catholic Church and the British "establishment".

Perhaps the only constraint on the wider acceptance of homosexuality and freer heterosexual relations was the spread of the virulent HIV/AIDS disease across the world in the 1980s which was particularly prevalent amongst male homosexuals. The disease was first discovered in Uganda in 1981 and appeared to have been transmitted from monkeys or other primates. [31] It moved rapidly to major centres of population including South Asia, Europe, the Caribbean and the United States. It was evidently disseminated along major routes of migration and commercial exchange, especially where large communities of prostitutes existed in poverty-stricken surroundings. Between 1981 and 2010, more than 30 million deaths had been recorded. Newly liberated homosexual communities in cities such as London, Paris, New York and San Francisco were decimated as the disease was fatal in about 80% of cases in its early years. Prostitution and casual sexual activity had transmitted it to the heterosexual world and continued to do so. This was not surprising. It was estimated, for instance, that there were 45,000 sex workers in Nairobi alone in 2013. [32]

This existential threat to the person was as severe, if not as universal, as the fear of nuclear war at the height of the Cold War. In some African societies, it further promoted a new, chaste Puritanism and religious conversion which emphasised the good of the community and the need for community help. In the United States, where there were 1.2 million people with the disease at the end of the century, the emphasis was mainly focussed on the individual human rights of the sufferers. Elsewhere, particularly in conservative Catholic and Muslim countries, it led to attacks on gays and the end of the relative toleration which they had enjoyed for two decades. The discovery of retroviral drugs that alleviated the disease largely halted mortality by the 1990s. Many gay rights activists also began to work to promote awareness of and medical support for those afflicted by the disease. But AIDS, although not generally lethal, remained widespread in parts of southern Africa, among prostitutes and among gay people across the world. In some areas it was still spreading in the 2000s and babies continued to be born with it.

The wider revaluation of sexuality persisted and was pervasive, then, but it was by no means universal. African societies influenced by the notion of the virtuous paterfamilias and Christian Puritanism continued to outlaw homosexuality and punish it harshly. Even in areas of earlier tolerance such as Indonesia, Islamic disapproval combined with a growing sense that variant sexuality was a challenge to the "manliness" of the nation.[33] In Russia after 1990, gay rights were regarded with hostility, both in deference to the revived Orthodox Church and because they were seen as an aspect of the ultra-democracy which the Kremlin was by then fighting. US conservatives cut back gay rights, invoking religious "conscience".

EDUCATING AND DISCIPLINING THE PERSON FOR SOCIETY

One of the great changes of the century was the expansion of literacy, from perhaps less than 20% in 1900 to about 70% in 2000. The new person had to be an educated person. In Russia, the great increase occurred after the 1917 revolution so that literacy was more or less universal by the 1940s. In India, by contrast, progress was exceptionally slow under British rule, reaching perhaps 25% by 1940 and by 2000 perhaps 60%, with the rate lagging significantly among women. There was, of course, no area of personal or social life, from health through religious belief to politics, on which rates of literacy did not impinge. But it is equally obvious that education was deeply bound up with with ideology. It was about making the ideal person as much as it was about the imparting of skills in mathematics, technical subjects or broader national cultures. It also empowered a wide range of political forms, and not necessarily liberal politics.

In very general terms, the main conflicts of educational ideology throughout the century were between religion and secularism, with a particularly militant form of secularism entering the field after 1917. The struggle between the Catholic Church and proponents of secular education extended to all parts of the world from Latin America through southern Europe to the Philippines. But it was particularly fierce in France and its colonies. Here revolutionary secularism re-emerged in the late nineteenth century as the Third Republic attempted to repair the damage done by the Franco-Prussian War. Many French republicans believed that inadequate and faith-driven Catholic schools were responsible for their defeat by the technically superior Germans and that schools run by the Catholic orders inculcated anti-republican sentiment. After the Jules Ferry laws of 1881, education became free, then mandatory, then secular. By 1920, secular education had been complemented with civil marriage, legal divorce and the expulsion of chaplains from military regiments, all measures opposed by the Catholic right.[34] Religious education effectively became domestic and private. This pattern was only slowly followed in other Catholic countries, though the Spanish republic did attempt to develop secular education during its brief period of power before Franco's victory in 1938. Franco, seeking the support of the Catholic hierarchy, moved back towards schools run by religious orders.

In countries with a substantial proportion of Protestant Christians, the picture was mixed. In Britain, a large majority of schools and other institutions were formally designated Church of England schools.[35] But religious education was a feeble thing and non-Protestants were given leave not to attend morning services. By 2013, the supposed failure of state schools and the precedent of Anglican schools had prompted the government to allow the creation of "academies", some with clear religious and even fundamentalist aims. In Ireland and in some parts of the United States, by contrast, sectarian conflicts were sharp. After 1922, Ireland introduced compulsory Catholic education, while in Boston the issue of church schools played an important role in local politics.[36] In areas where the battle between secularism and religion was particularly fierce, the issue was not simply about the necessity of Bible study. History, politics and even literature were inflected with ideological force. With the persistence of Christian fundamentalism in the United States, the teaching of evolution was a source of violent conflict from the "Monkey Trials" of the 1930s to the 2000s, especially in the Southern states. The issue was the very nature, past and future of the human person. Regular worship, scriptural study and an understanding of social duty would produce a Christian society. By contrast, an understanding of progress, of the emergence of democratic forms to challenge the superstitions of the past would create a rational, modern society, according to secularist ideologues.

These wars about schooling reached a crescendo in the USSR after 1917 and in Eastern Europe, China and Vietnam after 1945. As early as 1919, Lenin proclaimed the need for the "liquidation of illiteracy" and established a Commissariat of Education. Schooling became compulsory and Young Communist Pioneers travelled to remote areas to educate the illiterate. In part, this constituted an effort to develop technical, scientific and military skills. But Party propaganda was an essential element of education. Children were indoctrinated with Leninist ideology through discussions of history and politics. Religion was expelled from the classroom, while genetics, which was regarded as heresy contrary to the notion of materialist progress, was banned from school and university and only began to be taught again after 1970. In China, the attempt to enforce Communist ideology and expel Confucianism, Buddhism and Christianity was even fiercer during the Great Leap Forward and the Cultural Revolution. Here, the attempt to remake the person was enacted in struggle and criticism sessions and by actively encouraging young people to destroy temples and churches. As remarked in a later chapter, it is notable that, as China and Vietnam moved towards market socialism, formal Confucianism and Buddhism were reconstituted as embodiments of good morals and nation-hood, if only to stop the population resorting to magical and divinatory practices. In theory, though not always in practice, they were to be comfortably distanced from flourishing revivals of geomantic, astrological and divinatory knowledge.

Across the European colonial empires, wholly secular education was only imposed with great circumspection. This was particularly true of the French territories, where policy differed sharply from the domestic emphasis on secularism.[37] Catholic schools were the norm across much of French Africa south of the Sahara as also in the Belgian Congo. Here, the notion of the French and Christian "civilising mission" held sway. In Syria and Lebanon, which were mandates under the League of Nations, the authorities allowed schools run by Catholic orders to flourish. The orders were particularly valuable to French governance, supplying information to the French authorities, some of whom were Catholic and even royalist supporters themselves. French involvement in the region since the time of the Crusades was sometimes adduced to legitimate these policies. Whether it was Jesuit schools or schools of the Mission laïque, the important point is that the teachers should be French patriots and, as far as possible, teach in the French language. As in the British Mandate of Palestine, Muslim and Jewish institutions were also given a good deal of independence in Syria and Lebanon. Much the same obtained in Algeria, except that the large French and Mediterranean settler population there and the fact that the territory was technically annexed to mainland France meant that French and French culture were promoted even more vigorously.[38] The situation was similar in Indochina, where a substantial Christian population had existed since the seventeenth century. Some secularist *lycées* did come into existence, though segregated between French settler children and Indochinese. The Viet Minh and Khmer revolutionaries were educated in both *lycées* and Catholic schools. The notorious Khmer Rouge leader, Pol Pot, started life as Paul Pot in a Jesuit school, for instance.

In India, the British had been hostile to missionary activity before 1857. Thereafter numbers of southern European Catholic societies set up schools, while American, British and German Protestants became increasingly active in the twentieth century. The British Indian authorities put little effort into promoting secular primary and secondary education, though the universities of Bombay, Calcutta and Madras developed solid reputations in the humanities and sciences in the course of the century. This lack of official concern and financial support led Indian leaders to establish educational colleges themselves. Notable here was the Mohammadan Anglo-Oriental College, later Aligarh Muslim University,[39] which sought to blend European learning with a modernised version of Islamic learning. This was paralleled by the Benares Hindu University founded in 1910. Both these institutions were "broad church" in their approach. But powerful neo-conservative madrassa-type institutions, such as the Dar al-Ulum at Deoband[40] also flourished and the rationalist Arya Samaj established schools in the Punjab. During the height of the Gandhian movement, Indian leaders also tried to distance themselves from the colonial government, establishing national schools and colleges which played an important educational role after independence. Education since 1947 in India, Pakistan and Bangladesh continued to be marked by controversies about the teaching of Hinduism, Islam and Sikhism, about the proper script to use in schools and also about the caste status of children. Decades after independence, private Catholic schools continue to excel, while higher education remained uneasily poised between the British and American models, between an emphasis on the humanities and social sciences and the insistence that only technological training was worthwhile in a developing society.

During the century, the moulding of the young person was not limited to formal education in religious or secular schools or to the classroom. In the English-speaking world, sports clubs and school sport were seen as vital arenas in which a healthy body could help foster a healthy mind. In English public (i.e. elite private) schools, sport achieved an almost religious status, charged with the unlikely task of improving personal morality. This ideology also pervaded the Boy Scout and Girl Guide associations, which developed in the early part of the century. Elites in Britain and its colonies believed that training bands of young people in the skills of self-help in the country or social service would keep immorality at bay and promote the service of society. This concealed social project was paralleled by openly political youth movements in fascist Italy and Nazi Germany. Young Japanese were inducted into Shinto cults devoted to the service of the emperor. In the USSR and China, Young Pioneers and Red Guards indoctrinated youth into radical Communism. Even in the democratic United States, the iconic summer camp and various youth leagues were believed to breed public morality among the young.

All these educational forms and training institutions persisted into the second half of the century, but the social and ideological context in which they operated changed significantly. The onset of the Cold War and the fear of a nuclear holocaust certainly allowed states to continue to inculcate the person with their ideologies. Yet, the era of peace across much of the world after 1945 appeared to render obsolete many of the pedagogical forms of "discipline and punish". For instance, the whipping or caning of children was widely abandoned and in many societies made illegal, even within the family. The advent of all-day television and radio changed the educational context, detracting from book learning and publication. In some Western countries, the decline of religion and its associated sociality tended to fragment social life and diminish the real, as opposed to virtual, public sphere. The youth revolution of the 1960s and 1970s created a culture of parody and disrespect, as many elders saw it, or a culture of freedom, as many young people believed. The sexual permissiveness and wide availability of contraception, mentioned in the last section, changed gender awareness and pushed the age of physical maturity back into the early school days. Drug and alcohol consumption expanded greatly among the young, while sports declined in many schools for both economic and cultural reasons. These changes in the demeanour of the person had wide political significance. The *événements* of 1968 in Paris and demonstrations against the conflict in Vietnam in the United States were cases in point.

Again, these changes were widespread but by no means universal. As already noted, in many societies, they were opposed by powerful religious and conservative forces that tried to limit sexual licence among the young and, in some Muslim nations, even prohibit female education. Dissent and the expression of individual political and artistic freedom were severely curtailed in China following the Tiananmen Square massacre of 1981. War was far from eliminated and the persistence of ethnic and class conflict or local revolt meant that the phenomenon of "child soldiers" was observed in conflict zones such as the Central African Republic and Bolivia, where both government and rebel forces appeared to be implicated in forcing children as young as ten into armed gangs. The growing wealth of the middle class in societies such as China, India and Russia undoubtedly spread the Western taste for partying, drinking, dancing and texting across the world. And this went far beyond Western taste, as witness the Korean "K-pop" style of dance. In parallel with this loosening of social discipline, the practice of child trafficking over large distances for sex, or to procure household labour, became a feature of organised crime.

Punishment is in part a negative form of education and social disciplining. Michel Foucault famously argued that the modern state, attempting to discipline the person, moved from condign and very public executions and other punishments to incarceration in the "panopticon" prison. Prison populations undoubtedly greatly increased over the century as family, community and religious sanctions became less effective and people became more mobile. Strikingly, the United States had one of the largest prison populations in the world throughout the century.[41] A high proportion of prisoners were young black men from underprivileged urban backgrounds who had fallen into a life of crime, drugs and gun culture. In many Western societies, it was also immigrants, people of minority religious or ethnic status and again mainly young black, and latterly Muslim, men who felt the disciplinary power of the state. Yet, political difference was also a powerful reason for disciplining the person. The gulag system prevalent in the Soviet Union from 1919 saw hundreds of thousands deported to Siberia and other outlying parts of the country. In Communist China "re-education" labour camps were established in 1957. The Party's political enemies or bourgeois dissidents were detained in them for years without charge or trial and in a different manner this practice persisted into the following century. Similar institutions were found in other Communist states, such as Vietnam, East Germany and, most notoriously, North Korea. Colonial states resorted to similar practices of mass arrest, deportation and detention. While emerging democracies generally punished individuals, colonial regimes had often resorted to placing sanctions on whole communities.

SPORT: A WINDOW ON THE TWENTIETH CENTURY?

The chapter now moves on to the role of sport in modern society which emerged simultaneously as a form of education or disciplining, but also as a field of personal fulfilment. Many world histories omit such a discussion or even a reference to sport. *The Birth of the Modern World*, for instance, did so and was criticised for this. To some extent, these omissions reflect a sense that sport is not serious in the way that economics and politics are. But this is definitely false, since sport has represented a huge international business since the end of the century. At the same time it is highly political in its influence while glorifying the individual human within society.[42] One need only remember Hitler's storming out of the Olympic Games in Berlin in 1936 when a black athlete won a medal or the exclusion of apartheid South Africa from sporting events until 1990. Yet, sport also reflected more subtle changes in ideas about the person and society throughout the century.

The emergence of organised sport in the nineteenth century was heavily impregnated with issues of class, privilege and entitlement. Hunting with horses had evidently been a sport of the rich, especially landholding elites, not only in Europe but also across much of Asia and Africa. Rising urban elites intruded into rural race meetings as "gentlemanly capitalists" became dominant in European societies. Colonial officials, often drawn from middle-class backgrounds, broke into the ranks of princely and elite families in India and Africa as the century wore on. Photographs, which now inspire a shudder of horror, show Lord Curzon, Viceroy of India, and governors of the Cape Colony surrounded by slaughtered tigers and other animals. A generally non-lethal aspect of this elite horseplay was the game of polo which developed from Mughal or Manchu games in which the horse continued to stand as the ultimate symbol of aristocracy.[43]

Elite sports also developed in private schools across Europe and America and in colonial outposts on other continents. The notion of youth "strong in mind and body" took hold as eugenic ideas and fear of sexual "perversion" became common in late Christian Western society. Youthful energy had to be siphoned off into safe activities and this led to the formalisation of games such as rugby, cricket, tennis and competitive swimming. Yet, it is also striking that the mass expansion of sport between the 1880s and 1940s took place in the shadow of the world wars. Fitness was seen as essential for the maintenance of conscript armies and play on the rugby pitch was paralleled by the transformation of marksmanship with rifles into a sport for schoolboys in Europe and America. The refusal of colonial authorities to allow young Indian men similar opportunities sparked nationalist rage.

Yet, the expansion of formalised sporting activity also reflected the democratisation of politics and even the increasingly strident demands for independence which were a hallmark of the age. In the nineteenth century, non-elite games had developed at informal gatherings of working people outside factories or trade union meetings. Mass mobilisation for war also impacted on the development of popular games, and football and American football in particular. Off-duty soldiers had to be distracted and given some form of enjoyment. Yet, by the 1950s, football and other popular sports had become a democratic form, an equivalent in a sense to the mass electorates. Money was pumped into them and, since they were not dependent on elite background or elite education, they became avenues for rapid social mobility for individuals from disadvantaged groups and, rather latterly, for women. The social visibility of black people in the United States was reinforced, for instance by televised epics of boxing between Muhammad Ali, Joe Frazier and George Foreman in the 1970s.[44]

In the United States, major universities also poured resources into sports in order to attract donations and register their pre-eminence. Black players were greatly over-represented in football and basketball at all levels. When Donald Sterling, a sports magnate, made disrespectful remarks about black players there in 2014, a firestorm of agonising about racial attitudes was unleashed. In Europe, Latin America, Asia and Africa players from the working class became celebrities and their appearance on radio, television and film further promoted sport as the critical popular activity. Women increasingly participated in what had once been regarded as male sports, such as football and rugby. A census of tweets carried out in the United Kingdom in 2013 found that a majority of regular electronic messages concerned football matches and celebrities. Sport had become a form of sociality, gratifying the person and now largely divorced from issues of eugenic body- and mind-building, since most of the participants took part as "armchair" sportspersons. Indeed, in many Western countries, the omnipresence of sports in the media was paradoxically linked to the actual decline of physical participation in them.

Elsewhere, sports became even more profoundly democratised. In Australia, New Zealand and South Africa cricket became first a game of the outback and then a national preoccupation.[45] In India, cricket threw off its English image as a game "for warm beer and lazy summer afternoons".[46] The "all-rounder" Sachin Tendulkar became a national icon whom some compared to Mahatma Gandhi.[47] Yet, at the same time, the creation of international sporting organisations, leagues and rankings also served to keep alive the sense of national competition which had influenced sport since the 1890s. During the 2010s, Brazil agreed to host the World Cup for reasons of political prestige, but large-scale riots broke out as protestors pointed to the cost to a country with huge inequalities of wealth. Russia agreed to hold the Winter Olympics, but gay rights groups agitated against it. The German chancellor stated she would boycott the games because of the homophobia of the Russian government, but also because of the tug-of-war between the European Union and Russia over the future of the Ukraine. The entangling of international sport, human rights and national pride which was apparent as early as the 1920s reached a new peak a century later. All the same, we should not lose sight of the fact that, these political, moral and eugenic issues aside, for millions across the world sport remained a form of individual self-realisation distant from these communitarian dimensions. Even when it was internationalised, this was sometimes in a spirit of friendship across national borders as well as a field in which nations could assert their superiority.

SOCIALITY, COMMUNICATION AND THE CRAZE FOR POSSESSION

The last two chapters have considered how social and scientific knowledge, perceptions of philosophy, the mind, sexuality and proper education formed the person in the twentieth century and impacted on society, politics and the economy. After the 1980s, however, new forms of virtual human communication, notably the World Wide Web, the mobile phone and associated social media, Facebook and Twitter, began to register a powerful influence on the way people related to each other, leading, according to some theorists, to a revolution in the nature of human sociality itself. Governments both promoted and attempted to control the enormous flows of information, economic and civil society activity that resulted from these technical developments.

The Internet, invented by Tim Berners-Lee in 1989, massively speeded up ordinary communication within and across national boundaries and languages. By 2015, there were half a billion registered websites, promoting everything from politics and Muslim radicalism through sport to commercial advertisements and dating services. Even more significant than the World Wide Web in empowering new forms of personhood and sociality was the mobile phone and its developments, the iPad and the Blackberry. From the mid-1990s, the number of mobiles worldwide grew exponentially while their price dropped dramatically so that quite poor people were able to access them.[48] In India alone, there were 800 million of them in use in 2012, in Africa 400 million and globally, perhaps, two billion. The most obvious effect of this was economic. Whole new industries sprang up in Scandinavia, Japan and the United States, while huge numbers of people in bazars and small towns worldwide began to make a livelihood selling or servicing these items. Small farmers and craftsmen were able to anticipate market demand and work more efficiently as a result.

The social and political effects were no less dramatic. In some obvious senses, the mobile enhanced liberty. People were able to make new personal connections with each other. Women in seclusion could phone relatives and friends. Children were further released from the control of their parents as they had been by the computer. The mobile became a symbol and an incentive. In India and Bangladesh, the attractive young female *maubile-wali* ("mobile chapess") became a symbol of liberation. New political movements were created and spread through mobile messages. So, for instance, the quasi-democratic movements against Vladimir Putin's hold on power in Russia or corruption in South Asia and China, or the explosion of the abortive so-called Arab Spring in 2012, were organised by activists using mobile phones and social media. In the United States, the Tea Party movement and other grassroots movements were given new life by the mobile. Across the world, this ultra-democratic form of communication was used to bypass state surveillance, but it also helped to create the sense that there existed a freely communicating individual of a new type.[49]

Yet, as so often with the social appropriation of new forms of technology, from the railway, to the radio and telephone, the effect was ambivalent and contested. Gandhi had denounced the evil of greedy commerce and corruption spread by the railways (even though he used them persistently). His successors in India feared that unrestricted access to the mobile would hasten the endtimes of the *Kaliyuga*, when women's sexuality would became uncontrollable, caste restrictions would break down and images of the gods could be downloaded onto iPads without the mediation of priests. In the Islamic world, new radical movements could form without the intervention of either religious scholars or the state. Al-Qaeda and ISIS, notoriously, were adept at spreading their message via the Internet and the mobile. At the extreme, criminal gangs and looters were able to organise mayhem through them. This was particularly notable in the case of the London riots of 2012 or those in the US township of Ferguson in 2014. While acting to empower individuals in some circumstances, the mobile could also be used to hunt and track down dissidents in China, errant women in the Muslim world and unauthorised journalists and children accessing pornography in Western countries. Above all, the question remained of whether these new forms of communication simply enhanced an existing sense of mobility and change – or of fear of these changes – or whether they brought into being a radically different form of human sensibility. Certainly, the volume of and access to new forms of communication changed relations within the family and group, broke down the distinction between work and leisure and public and private and also expanded the range of the political. Conversely, they also provided new resources for state surveillance, as the Wikileaks controversy showed.

Conventionally many sociologists make a distinction between mental and material life, between communication and possessions. Yet, over the century, objects and their possession became an ever-stronger badge of individuality and guarantee of status than in previous centuries and the new communications reinforced this.[50] The power of advertising impacted even on young children, latterly through Twitter and Facebook. The accumulation of the material took different forms in different societies. In Britain, for instance, house ownership was a *sine qua non* which ultimately distorted its economy, while in Germany renting was much more prevalent. Before 1939, the possession of a motor vehicle had become a badge of status for the rich, including African chiefs and Indian princes. After the Second World War, demand for Lambrettas and other motorbikes boosted the Italian economy, followed by the mass purchase of cars, radios and televisions as the Western economies became rapidly wealthier. Access to running water speeded the demand for refrigerators and washing machines.

Outside the West, conspicuous possession was often limited to party officials, rich businessmen, the military and surviving landowners before the 1980s. But better communication ensured that this economy of ownership continued to spread, playing a significant part in the fall of Communism in the USSR and Eastern Europe and the liberalisation of the Chinese economy when the populations of these states became aware of their personal deprivation. As the economies of the former peripheries boomed after 1990, elite forms of personal ownership spread across Asia, Africa and Latin America. In addition to the demand for a classical and charismatic material such as ivory, the new Chinese middle class demanded expensive clothes and personal accoutrements manufactured by Prada and Burberry. Dog ownership, once a privilege of the old European and American hunting classes, became widespread across Asia and Africa. In the United States, gun ownership, long widespread, became almost universal, with the country holding 60% of all weapons in the world. This reflected a mark of individual status as much as a sense of growing insecurity.

At the beginning of the century, dress – and undress – conventions were highly variable. Many rural and upland Africans, Naga peoples of India and inhabitants of Papua New Guinea, for instance, displayed status through bodily decoration and semi-nakedness. Others such as the Japanese Ainu or residents of the Canadian Arctic wore unmistakeable ethnic dress. By the end of the century, this variety had almost everywhere given way to the T-shirt and jeans, or in more formal circumstances jacket and tie. Ethnic dress survived only for religious ceremonies and days of festivity. In combination with the spread of mobile phones, iPads and other items of communication, these developments had come to mean that the person across large swathes of humanity was homogenised and socially networked in uniform ways. Yet, paradoxically, this also empowered the individual in a manner impossible in earlier hierarchical societies.

CONCLUSION: THE TWENTIETH-CENTURY PERSON

A wide range of ideologies – from the extreme libertarianism of the youth revolution and the Hindu guru cults of the 1970s to rigorous attempts to create socialist man, on the one hand, or promote the fearless business entrepreneur, on the other – have moulded, and been moulded by, the societies of the century. Ideologies emerging from the world wars tended to dissolve or at least recast the old hierarchies of class, race, tribe and caste. These included, for example, fascism, Bolshevism, Gandhianism and social developmentalism. Such strains of thought were generally modernist in that, unlike the historicist ideologies dominant in the nineteenth century, they urged a break with the past and the fostering of a new style of personhood, but within an empowered collective community. The post-1945 struggle between left and right provided the context for what came to be called postmodernism and postcolonialism. Emphasising the constraining power of language, the construction of the person through multiple discourses on sexual mores, and capitalism more broadly, the authors and publicists of that generation tried to alert the supposedly free peoples of Western societies and new nations to their continuing "epistemological subject status". People, nevertheless, continued to consume and regard themselves as possessive individualists.

These ideological moves were opposed by a body of theory which also stressed liberation, but in this case liberation from collectivism, so that the empowered citizen, freed from the constraints of the collective, could work and build families within a perfect global market. The small wars of fragmentation and widely advertised ecological crisis of the early twenty-first century, discussed in Chapter 18, created a further strain of thought, sometimes called "posthumanism" or "the anthropocene". This argued for a radical change to stress the relationship between the person and the wider environment of animals, plants and objects, based on empathy and drawing on non-Western and non-modernist "animism". It remained to be seen whether these ideas would gain traction in a globalised world where increasing disparities of wealth between individuals were justified on the grounds of expertise in communication, commercial and technical knowledge or political connection.

[12] ARTS, LITERATURE AND ENTERTAINMENT: CRISIS AND RECOVERY

> The Terror of War and the Creativity of Peace
> Making the "New Man" Through Art and Literature
> Post War in the West: Experimentation and the
>   Reconstitution of the Classical
> Popular Music and the Rise of Youth
> At the Turn of the Twenty-First Century

ART AND literature helped mould the twentieth-century person and society as powerfully, yet more subtly, than the formal ideologies and educational practices discussed in the previous two chapters. In no earlier period had such a wide range of styles been jostled together by the forces of political intervention, globalisation and communication. From the late nineteenth century, many artists and writers had begun to fashion a disruptive individualistic style, which was designed to assault "bourgeois norms". Yet, the arts were far from being a redoubt armed against the state and capitalism, the two key motors of change over the century. On the contrary, both the Communist and the fascist state tried to enforce new conformist orthodoxies on them, considering art and literature to be powerful moral forces endangered by "degeneration". More covertly, Western capitalist societies quietly disseminated political messages through forms of art and entertainment. The art market itself became a powerful engine for the growth of inherited wealth in the Western states and, after 1990, in India and China. The irony was perhaps that, as artists and writers attempted to become more "anti-bourgeois", anti-state and anti-representational, their work had less popular impact. It became a niche product, catering to the art market, occasional official performances and the specialist elite

Remaking the Modern World 1900–2015: Global Connections and Comparisons, First Edition. C. A. Bayly.
© 2018 John Wiley & Sons Ltd. Published 2018 by John Wiley & Sons Ltd.

consumer. Popular music, cinema, television and dance filled the space it had abandoned.

As Chapter 1 suggests, the long shadow of the First World War has tended to obscure major changes in politics, communication and sensibility which occurred immediately before it. The decade prior to 1914 would have stood out as an era of revolutionary change in many areas of human life but for the outbreak of the war. This was particularly true of the arts, literature and entertainment, where these years had witnessed significant breaks with the past, some of which amounted to a wholesale rejection of methods of representative forms which could be traced back to the Renaissance or to other classical traditions outside Europe. This artistic revolution both reflected and informed contemporary political changes and changes in communication. The avant-garde, represented in cubism and other forms of "geometric abstraction", began as an aesthetic mirror of the political vanguard determined to destroy the old order. Artists became, in a sense, aesthetic politicians.

In painting, Paul Cézanne's *Les Grandes Baigneuses* (*c*.1894–1905), which combined naturalistic idealism with a complete rejection of classical representation, announced the new age.[1] The early works of Picasso, Henri Gaudier-Brzeska's *Wrestlers* (1914), the images of Amedeo Modigliani and the general disruption of what was called a "dead world" by the Futurists signalled the sharpest change in the conventions of art for many generations. Picasso's *Les Demoiselles d'Avignon* (1907) initiated a more radical rupture with the past.[2] Artists were obsessed with the idea of breaking from the constraints of perspective, classical forms and the rigid frame of time itself, which they felt had dampened creativity in earlier eras. F. T. Marinetti's *Manifesto of Futurism* announced the death of time and its replacement by "eternal, omnipresent speed". Meanwhile, the world of music was also revolutionised by movements rejecting the classical forms of melody, such as Igor Stravinsky's *The Rite of Spring* (1913), which deliberately reached back to an imagined paganism and was suffused with aggressive rhythms and dissonances. In literature, Marcel Proust's *À la recherche du temps perdu* (1913), with its emphasis on the malleability of time and individual experience, also predated the war.

These artistic movements reflected a radical change in the way in which people understood the divine, the political and the nature of humanity itself. Several of the new generation of abstract artists, notably Wassily Kandinsky,[3] were influenced by theosophy, a neo-religion, which claimed to be universal and scientific, and placed the East rather than the West at the pinnacle of spirituality, so reversing nineteenth-century historicism. Artists, especially Paul Gauguin, were also influenced by African masks and statuary and themes associated with the Pacific. Kandinsky was linked to the modernist composer Arnold Schoenberg and, later, the Bauhaus artistic and architectural movement in Germany. The new secular age in France and the first Russian Revolution of 1905 provided a political context within which novelists, musicians and artists rejected the earlier classical and Christian virtues and their representation. There was no hint of the Christian musical tradition in Stravinsky and God played little part in the humanistic musings of Proust.

Beyond Europe and the United States, writers and artists similarly broke with the forms of the classical and European past which had widely been forced on them by colonialism. Yet, they did so not initially by moving into abstract or even modernist political art but through a rediscovery and recasting of indigenous idealism. Okakura Kakuzo, the Japanese artist and scholar, rejected the superiority of Western culture. In his *Ideals of the East* (1903)[4] he had lauded the Hindu–Buddhist tradition of spiritual arts which he found in the paintings in the ancient Ajanta Caves in India. His book produced a sensation because it was read at the very same time as the Japanese sank the Russian fleet at Tsushima. This move was eagerly taken up by Ananda Coomaraswamy, the Anglo-Ceylonese writer and artist who wanted to capture the essence of Indian culture (in which he included Ceylon). He aspired to record the stories of "every educated Indian, with whom I include all those illiterate but wise peasants and women whose knowledge of the Puranas has been gained by listening to recitations or reading, by visiting temples . . . or from folk songs or mystery-plays".[5]

In India itself the *Swadeshi* ideology of "our land" promoted a return to the native. The call was taken up by theosophists, such as Annie Besant, and Hindu reformers, such as Sister Nivedita. Rabindranath Tagore wrote powerfully of "the new century of blood", while Abanindranath Tagore founded the Calcutta School of Art which promoted the modern, if not modernism. In pre-World War One Indian art, Raja Ravi Varma subtly adjusted and expanded the forms of Indian miniature painting to present a heroic vision of India's present, but in a modern style. Almost immediately after the Chinese revolution of 1911, as the influence of the old elites collapsed, Western and Japanese styles of art and literature also spread beyond their redoubts in European-dominated port cities. But the most powerful call was again for the recreation of the native tradition as the so-called Shanghai School brought a new fluidity to classical painting.

This form of artistic modernity, the recapture of a vibrant indigenous subject, was not only an "Oriental" phenomenon. In Britain, the Arts and Crafts Movement, originating in the Victorian era, represented a response to urban modernity through a retreat to the simple and rural. It remained significant in the 1920s and 1930s. In Germany the *völkisch* artists and writers lauded the ancient spiritual past of Germany. In Russia, the *narodniki* ("motherland") radicals, associated with the first revolution of 1905, similarly reinvented a rural and cooperative past in their novels and stories. In Mexico, the artists associated with the 1913 revolution recalled the life of the pre-colonial and early colonial peasant, rejecting the "civility of the bourgeois".

The myriad of different movements and trends might seem contradictory. Futurism and Cubism pointed to a distant human future. Existentialism emphasised the significance of immediate human experience. The Austrian Jewish author Franz Kafka dwelt incessantly on alienation and misery, a theme which was common to Freud's burgeoning psychoanalysis, and took on many different forms amidst the extraordinary burst of artistic and intellectual creativity which occurred in his already endangered community.[6] *The Metamorphosis* (1912), which pictured an ordinary tradesman suddenly transformed into a vile, verminous insect, was iconic of this trope. Yet, even the prophets of indigeneity – the *völkisch*, the *Swadeshi* writers and the *narodniki* – imagined a radical break with the present often through a retreat to the distant past which would in time become their shining future.

The Terror of War and the Creativity of Peace

The First World War merged with the Bolshevik and Spartacist revolutions, the humiliation of China and the Ottoman Empire and a series of vicious smaller wars in Africa, to push all these tendencies towards more extreme forms in the 1920s and 1930s. The war's clearest artistic outcome was an explosion of writing in English, French, German, Russian, Turkish and Hindustani, which reflected the crisis of the individual and the human in the most extreme situations of peril, death and killing.[7] These poems, memoirs and novels spoke of horror, but also voiced a profound questioning of the institutions and ideologies which had brought about this mass murder. Among the English war poets, Wilfred Owen and Siegfried Sassoon were probably the best known after the war. Owen was killed a mere week before the Armistice in 1918. He wrote of needless loss and sacrifice and one line of poetry read significantly, "Germans he scarcely thought of", oblivious to their guilt as much as to their own suffering. One of Robert Graves' wartime poems began "When I'm killed", but it was his retrospective memoir *Goodbye to All That* (1929) which summed up his experiences and pointed to the manner in which patriotism was over-whelmed and replaced by atheism, socialism, pacifism and feminism. T. S. Eliot's poem *The Waste Land* (1922) seemed to reflect the fragmentation of European culture and the nihilism of war. Giuseppe Ungaretti, fighting on the Italian front, wrote moving poems of fear and fraternity in wartime. Similar themes emerged in the writing of the most celebrated of the German war veterans, Erich Maria Remarque's *All Quiet on the Western Front*, or *Im Westen nichts Neues* (1929), which also spoke of the profound rupture and alienation that war-returned soldiers felt in civilian society. This work provided a deep explanation of the emergence of ruthless radicalisms of both left and right in the following decades. In 1930, a film of the book was released and became a pinnacle of the realist, anti-establishment art forms that were typical of the late Weimar Republic. In parallel with this, the Austrian-born filmmaker Fritz Lang produced works of "expressionism" which merged violence, moral ambiguity and a sense of dread.

Also in Germany, the failed Communist revolts after 1919 produced a form of "workers' revolutionary art" typified by the paintings of Otto Griebel which paralleled early Bolshevik art in the USSR. These were deeply serious responses to the war. Yet, a different mood was reflected in the work of the so-called Dada movement, founded by French refugees in Switzerland in 1916.[8] These artists, or "non-artists" as they called themselves, rejected the horror of war by sneering at the bourgeois ideals, including traditional art, which had brought on the war. Typical productions were the "Mona Lisa with a moustache" and a urinal masquerading as a "Fountain". In the 1920s, this mood of comic revulsion was replaced with an emphasis on the unconscious, in an ironically conscious reference to Freud's now celebrated work. Writers such as Louis Aragon and André Breton created the Surrealist movement which became an artistic rallying cry for interwar French socialists and Communists. These forms of artistic anarchism posed a threat to the fascist and Nazi regimes as they consolidated. Here, state authority pushed back against Cubism and Surrealism and attempted to reinvigorate figurative styles, proclaiming the triumph of youth and the nation. The result was not always banal. Mussolini's government, for instance, emphasised design and founded the Mostra del Cinema (the Venice Film Festival).[9] The Nazis infamously staged a Degenerate Art Exhibition in 1937, featuring the works of Kandinsky, Picasso, Henri Matisse and Otto Dix, which attracted huge crowds.[10]

While the war and its memory scarified European society and its arts, another powerful factor influencing the world's self-perception throughout the 1920s and 1930s was American culture: novels, painting and, above all, cinema.[11] America emerged from the war with its reputation for optimism, progress and technical skill undamaged. Its popular and elite art, literature and drama seemed mutually compatible rather than hierarchical and class-ridden, as in Europe. Hollywood, thronged with creative artists of European origin, many of them Jewish, produced thoughtful films concerning social and political issues, such as Josef von Sternberg's *Underworld* (1927), as well as blockbuster popular entertainment such as Walt Disney's Micky Mouse (who first appeared in 1928), the *Jazz Singer* (1927) and numerous westerns. The introduction of effective Technicolor and "talkies" during the 1930s had a profound effect, not only on all art forms but also on the representation of politics and social criticism. Many Hollywood films gloried in robust individualism, reaching their apogee in a 1949 film version of Ayn Rand's *The Fountainhead* (1943). But films with a covert socialist message were few and far between and writers and artists who made them found themselves under threat during McCarthy's purges after 1945.

America was not alone in developing cinema as a form of both art and entertainment, with underlying political messages. German and French expressionist and realist films also marked a new chapter of post-war creativity. In the USSR, Eisenstein promoted a dramatisation of the victories of socialism and a reimagining of Russia's past, mirroring and promoting the contemporary shift from international socialism to "socialism in one country".[12] Arguably, the fast-paced populism of film also profoundly affected literature. The elite ruminations of novelists of the British Bloomsbury set, for instance, later gave way to the no-nonsense realism and radical stripping-down of the English language by authors such as Ernest Hemingway. Parallel to the fame of Charlie Chaplin, there was the worldwide discovery of the common man, though for different reasons in different places. In the United States, the writers Sinclair Lewis and John Steinbeck lauded rugged individualism.

The war and Depression was a world crisis and not just a European one. Indian soldiers in Mesopotamia and on the Western Front recorded their experiences in letters home which were intercepted by the British authorities and some of these contained pacifist literary themes. Rabindranath Tagore, in the United States in 1916–1917, wrote fierce attacks on the idea of nationalism which were quite clearly a reaction to the destruction of war.[13] He denounced the "fierce self idolatry of nation worship", "a terrible absurdity" which had "thriven long on mutilated humanity". Hindi writers such as Munshi Premchand created a new, modern Hindi shorn of "feudal elements" and Urdu words.[14] Meanwhile, the 1911 revolution in China, the country's humiliation by both the Western powers and Japan in 1919 and the ensuing May Fourth Movement coincided with and contributed to some fundamental changes in Chinese literature, poetry and drama. Most significant was the widespread abandonment of classical Chinese and its replacement with the vernacular language and modern styles of writing. Xu Zhimo, who had lived in England and met Bertrand Russell, Roger Fry and Katherine Mansfield, set up a society for new literature.[15] Significantly, Xu acted as translator for Tagore when he visited China in the 1920s.

These new literary figures argued that a dead language could not produce vibrant and contemporary art. Women writers greatly increased in numbers. There emerged later the League of the Left-Wing Writers, similar to movements in the USSR, and later the Progressive Writers' Movement in India. In the 1930s, Ba Jin wrote novels excoriating the Confucian family system as an anachronism which held back the nation. Again, the Peking Opera was a popular form which had roots in the later Qing period. But one significant change brought on by the 1911 revolution was the formal admission of women into its dance troupes. Significantly, the Guomindang nationalist party was founded in Peking Opera's main guildhall in the following year and modernist themes began to appear in performances well before the opera became a mouthpiece for the CCP after 1949.

Chinese art, meanwhile, had become open to Western and Japanese influences. Yet, in the late 1920s and 1930s, there was a renaissance of more traditional forms of landscape painting ("the Guohua revival"). This often featured craggy hills and luxuriant forests, reminiscent of the late Qing style, and was typified by the work of Fu Baoshi. Though the old elites had been displaced and art had become a popular pastime, the idolisation of the national heritage had become significant in the age of the Guomindang, as the art historian Michael Sullivan argues.[16] Japan in the 1920s and 1930s saw a similar movement, an attempt to protect the nation's artistic heritage. Called the Mokujiki Movement after a seventeenth-century monk devoted to carving, it sought to revive traditional ceramics, metalwork and textile-making. It provided a patriotic alternative to the modern Western forms being replicated in Japan.[17] This again had some parallels with the English Arts and Crafts Movement. But it also fed into the new Japanese nationalism of the 1930s.

In China, however, the coming of cinema had revolutionary effects, in both senses. The earliest film (in 1905) was "indigenous", projecting the career of an ancient emperor. But by the late 1920s and early 1930s, a genre of starkly realist films, often centring on women, was entrenched. While the West revelled in the "Orientalism" of Marlene Dietrich in *Shanghai Express*, Chinese filmmakers were producing *The Peach Girl* (1931) and *Street Angel* (1937). These films

Figure 13 *The Peach Girl*, 1931. Ryan Lingyu and Jin Yan. Liana Film Co/REX/ Shutterstock.

depicted the terrible life of marginal people in China's cities as the country was afflicted by the Depression and the Japanese invasion. Most of the producers were members of the fledgling CCP and their models were German realist films and early Soviet cinema before the chill of Stalinism set in.

MAKING THE "NEW MAN" THROUGH ART AND LITERATURE

One form which broke, apparently decisively, with late-nineteenth-century pictorial forms and narrative literature was the new art of the Soviet Union. Its aim was to mobilise through affect, by stirring the emotions of the ordinary worker or peasant to strive for a better society. In Leninist circles, art was an essential component of the life of the new human person, the new socialist state and the worldwide alliance of the proletariat. During the 1920s, there was a great upsurge of pictorial art, sculpture and literature heralding the dawn of the new age. Trotsky wrote in *Literature and Revolution* (1924), "The wall will fall not only between art and industry, but simultaneously between art and nature."[18] Painters such as Kazimir Malevich and El Lissitzky joined film-makers such as Eisenstein in depicting the power of popular emotion and attempting to create a socialist avant-garde.

Ten years later, this burst of creativity had been crushed by Stalinist uniformity. In April 1932, the Central Committee disbanded independent artistic groups and conscripted painters, writers and intellectuals into party-dominated unions. Innovative art faltered and then collapsed in the face of a return to the politicised figurative. Kazimir Malevich, for instance, turned back to figurative painting.[19] Many art historians saw this imposition of uniform and banal political images of worker heroism, often centred on Stalin himself, as a retreat to philistinism. An exception here was Boris Groys, a Russian writer who later taught in the United States. Groys lauded Stalinist art as a challenge to the supposedly bland and money-driven art of the West.[20] This position was endorsed by theorists such as Slavoj Žižek and Alain Badiou, who regarded modern European and American art as expressions of "capitalist animality", though they themselves were more ambivalent about the Stalinist period. Perhaps a lone area where art was not bent to the will of either Communist or fascist power was in the realm of music. Antony Copley argued that composers were able to express an underlying spirituality through musical composition. Indeed, Sergei Prokofiev was a Christian Scientist and Alexander Scriabin a theosophist. Several other composers were influenced by Indian spirituality.[21]

One socialist movement crushed neither by fascist nor Communist banality was the Mexican tradition epitomised by Diego Rivera and Frida Kahlo. Rivera moved from an early interest in Cubism around 1914 to figurative art, presenting Amerindian and Mexican populism. Kahlo, his wife, introduced similar themes, but is best known for her haunting self-portraits. Elsewhere, the struggle between the libertarian aspect of socialism and party orthodoxy took a parallel path to the USSR. In China, Maoist art took a similar turn to its Stalinist forebears, particularly after the Cultural Revolution. Posters showed happy peasants and workers greeting political leaders. One example was "By Premier Zhou's side", with Zhou Enlai wearing a Mao badge inscribed with the words "serve the people".[22] Portraits of Mao became omnipresent on badges and postage stamps during the Cultural Revolution. Mao "poetry" and revolutionary songs were promoted across the land. Meanwhile, a huge range of classical material was destroyed in the 1960s on the grounds that it was feudal, while the Western-influenced art of the 1930s and 1940s was disowned as bourgeois. Many artists were purged and sent to rural labour camps. Yet, after Deng's turn to state-controlled capitalism and the announcement of the "open door policy" to outside influences, Western-influenced styles began to reappear. Later, artists such as Qiu Zhijie emerged once again to put, alongside the depictions of heroic workers, images of mythological animals and cultural maps that quietly called to mind once again the delicate, naturalistic images of the former empire and nationalist period, previously targets of mass vandalism.[23] The art market in China, especially sales of items made before 1600, soared after 1990.

Much the same happened in Vietnam. The Chinese script had already been displaced. During the anti-French war, Parisian styles were abandoned and writers and artists on the war front were enjoined to respond to peasant craft works and rural stories of everyday life, eschewing radical anti-figurative forms.

Figure 14 Leon Trotsky and his wife with Frida Kahlo and others on arrival in Mexico, 1937. OFF/Agence France-Presse/Getty Images.

Later images of happy peasants and workers surrounding Bac Ho (Uncle Ho) were promoted in the war against the United States. After *Doi Moi* ("renovation"/liberalisation), however, aspects of French high art and a push for depictions of "modernity" became acceptable. Even while political posters continued to adorn the streets, the Vietnamese argued that words rather than images created national consciousness.[24] Here the successful mass literacy campaign, which raised the literate population from about 15% to 60% between 1960 and 2010, stirred the demand for popular literature. Across the still formally Communist world from China to late-Castro Cuba, intellectuals debated whether these forms of political exhortation had been mere design or true art.[25]

In Africa, indigenous art, originating from the production of religious and cult objects, flourished throughout the century. Here, perhaps, more than elsewhere, the persistence of rural artistic production was less affected by European styles. Increasingly, though, this work was destined for European purchasers either within or outside the Continent. In the 1950s, South African artists began to produce works melding indigenous themes with contemporary modernist ones.[26] By the 1990s, art galleries had opened in many of the capitals of independent African countries, and indigenous African artists began to produce similar hybrid productions to be displayed there. These often represented dancers in African costume, portraits based on indigenous masks or native animals. Makerere University in Uganda and Kenyatta University in Kenya developed flourishing art departments, and European and American collectors began to buy their productions. In this way, modern African art represented both a stylistic break with the past and an appropriation of its themes, as was the case across the world.

POST WAR IN THE WEST: EXPERIMENTATION AND THE RECONSTITUTION OF THE CLASSICAL

The great post-war boom in Europe and the Americas broadened the revolt against tradition which had begun at the beginning of the century. Picasso remained the icon of this movement, many of his later works becoming more abstract, at least until his final years. Figures such as Salvador Dalí had given this artistic turn a provocative, quirky form. In North America, Jackson Pollock and Andy Warhol and their followers captured the public imagination with works which completely erased naturalism, emphasising colour and geometry even more fiercely than Kandinsky and his generation. Mark Rothko and Barnett Newman produced an art of pure abstraction, a "counter art". The vibrant art market was enlivened by the demand of wealthy buyers, especially in New York and California, for works of ultra-modernity which matched the architectural innovation of the period. At the same time, these artists offered a political critique. Warhol's piled commercial boxes could be seen as a comment on capitalism; Robert Rauschenberg's image of a predatory American eagle perhaps anticipated his later activism against the US–Vietnam War.[27] This art was resonant but could hardly be seen as popular.

Many artists in Europe followed this pattern, but naturalism survived longer here even in a radically altered form. In Britain, for instance, Francis Bacon and Lucian Freud created a style which could best be described as counter-classical. Both painted portraits or pseudo-portraits, but disrupted them, the one with splashes of colour and ridicule (for example Bacon's *Seated Figure (Red Cardinal)*), the other with an obsessive focus on flesh, as if stressing both the beauty and ugliness of the human form. Though David Hockney spent time in California, his style was a similar reinvention of the classical, but one applied to the everyday life of the middle classes. L. S. Lowry's paintings of street scenes of dismal northern cities, their inhabitants reduced to matchstick-like shapes, seemed to deepen the ruminations on class that pervaded the post-war era in Britain. In sculpture, Henry Moore undertook a similar radical reinvention of the classical. Yet, his statuesque figures often seemed like outlandish carica-tures of the kind of works found in Renaissance gardens, decorated with the beaks of birds and sometimes moving towards a form of abstraction. This style persisted to the end of the century and beyond in the work of sculptors, notably Grayson Perry. Even in music, a composer such as Benjamin Britten was able to reproduce classical themes in a modernist idiom.

Some art critics have suggested that the difference between the vaulting abstractionism of American artists and the counter-classicism of British and European painters and sculptors can be attributed to the persistence of conservatism in its art schools, a reflection of the wider conservatism of a society only partially released from the bonds of class, status and empire. There is some truth in this, but at the same time, the heavyweights of English classical art, figures such as Anthony van Dyck or Joshua Reynolds, had a disciplining effect on younger artists. The same phenomenon can be seen in the work of mid-twentieth-century artists influenced by Spanish, Latin American or Italian masters. In Italy the so-called Transavantgarde movement of the 1970s and 1980s rejected conceptual art, reintroducing emotion, symbolism and figurative art. This was a transnational movement, a partial return to tradition after the political and aesthetic shocks of the early to mid-century. It was reflected even in China's quiet return to the artistic past, as noted above. In Spain and Portugal, the conservative instincts of the Franco and Salazar years, buttressed by the Catholic Church, similarly limited the scope of art which the earlier fascist regimes had regarded as degenerate.

France and Germany were somewhat different. In France, the artistic scene had already been revolutionised by Marc Chagall, Matisse and others in the early part of the century. The depiction of the ordinary, shorn of appearances of classical formality, was a dominant theme. In literature, the existentialism of Albert Camus and Jean-Paul Sartre, which represented a typical rejection of the past and a concentration on "the moment", held sway in the 1950s, representing a form of artistic melding with the rise of contemporary left politics. Sartre famously praised Stalin's USSR, even when evidence of its political atrocities had emerged. Yet, this was not the whole story. Authors such as Michel Déon continued to write social novels (in Déon's case, analysing the lives of interwar French people). This stood against the more abstract trend of the Existentialists, which tended to downgrade the agency of people in favour of ontological and metaphysical generalisations while still claiming "the People" as the agents of history. If Sartre in *Being and Nothingness* presupposed the general meaninglessness and absurdity of life, Déon and his coevals in a body called "Les Hussards" (the Hussars) wrote about the real lives of people struggling with everyday existence and conflict, with evident meaning for the 1950s and 1960s when France was embattled with conflict in Vietnam and Algeria.[28] This artistic realism was closely aligned with a commitment to the political right and anti-Communism. Several members of this grouping had shown sympathy with Action Française and monarchist and pro-colonial groups.

Yet, if in the first half of the century, both radicals and nationalists had discovered the common man, much literary effort in its second half was devoted to challenging the nature of the subject, paralleling the philosophical movement of Derrida and Foucault, which sought to decompose the idea of the individual with the message of post-structuralism. An important figure here was the Irish playwright Samuel Beckett, with his sparse, ruminative characters. The trend was clear, but by no means universal. By the 1960s there had been a revival of more classical forms of literature or variations on it. Jorge Luis Borges became a world-renowned novelist, combining allusion to the European and American literary canon with complex detective stories and science fiction. He was followed by other South American figures such as Mario Vargas Llosa and Gabriel García Márquez and later by the "magic realism" of the Indian-born writer Salman Rushdie.

On a different timescale and with different consequences, architecture followed a similar trajectory. The First World War finally displaced the historicist nostalgia of neo-gothic and neo-classical forms. New styles emerged in the 1920s and 1930s. But radical modernism was a product of the Second World War and a self-conscious search for a stylistic rupture. Buildings, for architects such as the French pioneer Le Corbusier, were "machines for living in".[29] The hard edges of these structures, their towering and sometimes intimidating piles of concrete, reflected the desire for a mathematical precision devoid of naturalism, which was seen in the painting of conceptual art and photography. This movement also spoke of a desire to have done with the past more dramatically even than in anti-classical art produced after 1918.

At the same time, the spread of what became known as Brutalist architecture reflected the worldwide influence of America and also the emergence of large construction firms which had a commercial interest in designing architecturally similar buildings. The earliest skyscrapers of Manhattan had been a response to a lack of urban space as the city of New York expanded after the 1890s. They were grand and geometrical, yet retained aspects of decoration and individuality. After 1945, however, uniformity set in and ultra-modernism, often in a second-rate form, was imposed on cities as widely separated as Chicago, Buenos Aires, Hong Kong and London. As in the realm of the visual arts, the reaction against ultra-modernism came late, after 1980. It was diffuse, varying between neo-traditionalism and attempts to humanise the modernist styles by reducing their scale or reintroducing colour and brickwork. A striking example of this was to be seen in Singapore. Here, many of the colonial buildings surrounding Raffles' Landing Site had been demolished in the 1960s and 1970s to mark the city's commercial modernism and also its liberation from colonial rule. But by the later 1990s, the authorities realised that tourists were flooding to more traditional venues. So, ersatz traditional Chinese-style shop-houses were built to recreate a sense of tradition. Architectural battles to save the past were recorded across the world from London's neo-Gothic St. Pancras Station, preserved following a campaign in the 1980s orchestrated by the poet John Betjeman, to Rangoon where Thant Myint-U and others launched a movement to save its classical buildings from destruction in the 2010s.

POPULAR MUSIC AND THE RISE OF YOUTH

By their very nature, the visual arts and literature remained elite forms of imagining even if they strove for modernity and gestured towards popular inclusion. If anything, "serious" music became less inclusive over the century. Anton Webern, Igor Stravinsky and Alban Berg moved sharply away from earlier harmonics. But classical music attracted a widening public as concerts and operas were popularised by great performers such as Maria Callas. This was even truer of popular music, now diffused by cinema, radio and television. Black American soul singing, distantly a product of the slave plantations, became a global phenomenon by the 1950s. Meanwhile, jazz, another product

Figure 15 The Beatles, 1967. "All you need is love". Getty Images.

of US black culture, preserved a form of harmonics which was specialist but still open to a wider public. The previously staid style of British music making was transformed by a plethora of new dance bands which domesticated themes from American music, even before jazz conquered the country during the Second World War. The dispersal of the US army across the world after 1942 and the explosion of record production and filmmaking helped to bring this about.[30] In a sense, pop groups such as the Beatles and Rolling Stones were "whited up" and less radical versions of these black groups. Rock music represented a further radicalisation of US musical styles. Popular music across the world absorbed these influences. This was the case with the French romantic ballads promoted by Edith Piaf, as also the Japanese popular music of the post-war years, represented, for instance, by the band Happy End which merged rock music with Japanese themes. Similarly, Indian Bollywood film scores were partly derived from older *qawwali* forms but modernised with American-style film themes.

There was a distinct social context for these waves of popular music. They often represented – and heightened – a revolt against the conservative values that still remained strong or had even reasserted themselves in the 1950s. Young people gathered in bars and nightclubs to express their moral and sometimes political independence of their elders. Psychedelic drugs, still legally banned, produced a new febrile style of music. Poetry and literature became radical, with figures such as Allen Ginsberg publicly announcing their homo-sexuality and women writers dismissing "family values".[31] The invention of the long-playing record also created a new narrative style of pop lyrics. Clothes and hairstyles reflected the rejection of earlier norms as with the British Teddy Boy craze of the later 1950s and its aping of fashionable Italian styles. In the United States, singers such as Bob Dylan and, most notably, Elvis Presley epitomised a musical and political reaction against the conservatism of the war years, the inequality of the black ghetto and, later, youth mobilisation against the conflict in Vietnam. This youth revolt reached its peak with the punk rock bands of the 1970s, which combined violent anti-establishment lyrics with short, aggressive musical forays, directed as much against what was now seen as establishment rock as against the sensibilities of the older generation. Some of the most startlingly aggressive of this music was associated with gay nightclubs and bars.

Popular youth music and dance continued to worry conservative forces, mothers and fathers throughout the century. This was particularly true of authoritarian governments. For instance, post-war South Korea remained a conservative neo-Confucian society, on edge because of the belligerence of its northern neighbour. The presence of American forces initiated a gradual change and, by the 1990s, Korean pop music had taken on a particular style, blending American themes with local romantic poetry and dancing. Within a decade K-pop had become a craze, not just in Korea but across Asia.[32] In 2012, a Korean singer called Psy released an "all-singing, all-dancing" video of himself performing in "Gangnam style", named after a suburb of Seoul. This clip went viral, as the contemporary phrase had it. It was seen worldwide and became the first video to be watched two billion times on YouTube. Meanwhile, schools were established across Korea to train youngsters in pop music, while fans from across Asia tuned in online. The teenage boy and girl bands sometimes seemed sexually ambiguous and this mass musical movement frightened parents in countries as far afield as Vietnam, who became concerned that it would distract their children from educational achievement or compromise them morally.

Indeed, pop music's disruptive, anarchistic persona induced fear in authority throughout the second half of the century. Rock music was banned from Russia until the 1970s and its final introduction was itself a sign of the weakening of the *ancien régime*. As conventional political resistance widely declined, cultural resistance became more pervasive. The irony here was that the great beneficiaries of the youth cultural movements had long been large music and communications commercial groups, HMV in the case of the Beatles and Bob Dylan, Hyundai in the case of K-pop. Psy himself was said to have made more than $27 billion for his own company.[33] It should not be thought, however, that the state and conservative elites entirely lost their power to control sentiment through art and entertainment even in Western societies. Second World War propaganda films were followed by films, books and TV promoting or explaining the Cold War[34] and the American war in Vietnam.[35] Even the hugely popular and generally mindless *Rambo* films ventured into politics with Sylvester Stallone supposedly defeating the Soviet invasion of the country in a film dedicated, ironically in view of later events, to "the brave people of Afghanistan".[36]

AT THE TURN OF THE TWENTY-FIRST CENTURY

Art continued, then, to alarm conservative governments throughout the century since it was able to convey subtle generalised political messages which were often difficult for them to interpret. Political insinuations at *mushairas*, or poetry contests, worried the British Indian authorities in the 1930s as the leftist Progressive Writers' Movement emerged.[37] Hitler's regime seized and destroyed "degenerate art" because it might influence the new German Man. Boris Pasternak's novel *Doctor Zhivago* was banned in the USSR because it depicted the Bolshevik revolution in an ambivalent light. Later in the century, the leading Indian painter M. F. Husain exiled himself from India when right-wing parties lambasted him for depicting a nude "Mother India" in the form of a stylised map. This was all the more ironic since classical Hindu sculpture venerated female nudity and this reaction seemed to represent a form of Islamisation of the Hindu right.

Yet, both the democratisation of artistic resistance and state repression were well represented at the Venice Biennale art festival in 2013. A Bangladeshi artist displayed an installation depicting a huge pile of strands of female hair, recalling the victims of the pogroms during the war of 1971 which severed the country from Pakistan. Later, one of the Islamist perpetrators of this violence was executed for these crimes, more than 40 years after the event. At the same festival, art acceptable to the Chinese state, depicting the earth from far in space, was displayed a few months before a Chinese spacecraft landed on the moon. Less than a mile away, though, the Chinese artist Ai Weiwei, exiled from the country because of his dissident style, had built an installation representing his incarceration and interrogation by the authorities. Representatives of societies ravaged by war could still sometimes express their regret and aspirations through art. The Biennale also featured an exhibition by the Iraqi artist Bassim al-Shaker of a series of humanistic depictions of the everyday life of the Marsh Arabs of southern Iraq. This was an area assaulted by the British during and after the First World War, decimated by Saddam Hussein and further ravaged by the Allied invasion after 2003.

In Western Europe, Japan and the Americas, artists and writers believed that they were engendering self-reflection among the public, though, as in the case of elite music and literature, their audience was tiny compared with that of popular music, crime novels, advertisements, posters and television, which all added up to a composite but contested visual culture. Even film, which had been a vehicle for social comment, particularly with the film noir of the 1950s, was now dominated by fantasy and science fiction extravaganzas, though both Bollywood and the Nigerian film studios' "Nollywood" continued to produce vibrant and musical social dramas. Boris Groys, of course, was convinced that, in so far as elite art and literature continued to exist in the West, it was wholly absorbed by the needs of capitalism. Yet, the installation art that made money and metropolitan celebrities of figures such as Marcel Duchamp, Yayoi Kusama, Tracey Emin and Damien Hirst forced the observer to consider the oddity of the everyday and the dominance of the machine. Emerging strongly after about 1980, installation art became a major form in museums and galleries by 2000. It was an existential statement, reflecting a desire to find something novel, once film and photography had seemed to render naturalistic art and portraiture redundant.

Throughout the century, the arts and literature remained poised between radical and existential critiques of society and politics and forms which tended to replicate them. Groys may well have been right in asserting that art in Western and even developing countries had widely been depoliticised, a trend which reflected a wider disengagement from formal politics across the world. New, fragmented forms of creativity powered by electronic media had seemed to disempower elite art, literature and politics by 2010, with the consequent decline of the book, the museum and the library mirroring the decline of voter turnout in elections. The state's attempt to control culture had widely failed in the West and, even if business dominated the form of the arts, at least this was now driven by individual taste. The classical forms of language, literature and painting had been demolished and the new aesthetic of the twenty-first century reflected immediacy, eclecticism and the evanescent. The classical lineage of art forms of earlier centuries had disappeared, and some specialists argued that the human brain itself, its visual and aural qualities, had evolved in new directions. Still, economic globalisation, democratisation and the speed of communication of ideas were the dominant features of the century and art and literature had signally contributed to the remaking of the human person.

[13] RELIGION: CONTESTATION AND REVIVAL

The Expansion of "World Religions"
Religion Contested: Burgeoning Cults and the Threat of
  Communism
The Trials of Christianity, *c.*1900 to 1970
"Leaps of Faith": The Late Twentieth and Twenty-First
  Centuries

MOST accounts of religion in the twentieth century begin with the changes in the great "world religions": Islam, Christianity, Hinduism and Buddhism and their often fractious, yet equally close, relations with the emerging state, domestic and colonial. Yet, throughout the century, a considerable (if diminishing) part of the human population had been only lightly touched by either "world religion" or the state. Indeed, the very notion of "religion" essentialises a whole range of everyday practices and assumptions which were not necessarily linked in the subjects' minds. Across the Pacific, over much of southern Africa and the plains of Siberia and Manchuria to the North Pole, there existed communities of pastoralists, populations of connected villages and mobile groups which lay mainly beyond both state and dominant religions. Some of these populations had suffered conflict, expulsion and oppression verging on mass murder earlier in the nineteenth century, particularly in Australia, New Zealand and the American West. Equally, even within the heartlands of the state and religion, there remained so-called tribal populations, loosely connected through familial leaders and served by local priests, shamans and soothsayers, which propagated forms of spiritual connection with the living and the dead. Often these specialists emphasised the overriding importance of

Remaking the Modern World 1900–2015: Global Connections and Comparisons, First Edition. C. A. Bayly.
© 2018 John Wiley & Sons Ltd. Published 2018 by John Wiley & Sons Ltd.

the spirit of the ancestors, in the broad context of celestial power, the importance of initiation into the group and the making of right life choices in relation to impersonal forces of the benign and the malign.

The ethical codes of these communities were products of right conduct in family and clan and communion with spirits.[1] Much of their personal and spiritual life is only known because missionaries of the world religions recorded them in the effort of conversion or because the discipline of anthropology burgeoned in the twentieth century.[2] It is important not to homogenise these peoples spread over vast areas of the globe or, worse, to see them as somehow primitive or archaic, as did the "civilising" missionaries of the period. As the French anthropologist Claude Lévi-Strauss pointed out in the books of his (admittedly brief) direct observations of the tribal groups of the Amazonian basin, their belief systems were complex, sophisticated and evolving.[3] As the case of the Maori of New Zealand showed, the role of rites, spirit-calling and the resort to seers had long been changing in form as a consequence of internal political and economic development. People such as the Dinka of the Sudan combined a sense of meeting personal spirits with a notion of a wider celestial sphere.[4] Again, the difference between the so-called world religions, themselves only slowly becoming more internally consistent, and these more dispersed forms of spiritual life should not be overdrawn. Hinduism, Buddhism and Christianity themselves often subsisted alongside, though they did not necessarily incorporate belief in spirits, the power of ancestors and the role of shamans. Yet, for many supposed converts, Jesus and the Prophet had merely been absorbed into these ecstatic and shamanistic forms of belief.

Nevertheless, these communities had not, at least since the sixteenth century, been entirely untouched by the state and world religions. In Latin America, particularly, European settlement and ecological change had provided the context in which tribal communities had been conquered, decimated and brought under the aegis of Iberian Christianity.[5] In North and West Africa and the Sudan, Muslim state-building on the fringes of the Ottoman Empire had created so-called jihad polities which survived into the twentieth century.[6] Here religious teachers, or sometimes Sufi mystics, had begun to spread the tenets of Islam. As settled agriculture had expanded across Asia, Hindu, Buddhist and later Christian religious establishments had merged with the local spiritual systems of the Nagas of north-eastern India, the Moi of northern Indochina and the tribal people of Manchuria.

THE EXPANSION OF "WORLD RELIGIONS"

Religion, then, is a term of convenience. But two developments after about 1880 made it a more consistent category. First, the public and academic understanding of religion developed rapidly. At one level, anthropologists and the more thoughtful missionaries had begun to analyse "tribal" beliefs in their own right rather than classify them as primitive. At another level, the nature of world religions themselves came under fresh scrutiny, particularly after the events of the World Parliament of Religions held in Chicago in 1893, attended among others by Swami Vivekananda on behalf of "Hinduism" and Anagarika Dharmapala for "Buddhism".[7] Late-nineteenth-century scholars and publicists had already begun to re-evaluate Buddhism and place it near to, but below, Christianity. A more balanced view of Hinduism understood it as a form of "polymorphous monotheism" rather than a backward and corrupt form of polytheism. This re-evaluation continued after 1900 with the work of Max Weber, in particular, which moved religious practice firmly into the realm of the social and economic.[8] While these intellectual changes did little to dislodge the claims of Europe to intellectual and cultural hegemony, they did at least reflect the slackening of the Christian civilising mission among Muslims, Hindus and Buddhists. Meanwhile, rational and scripture-based versions of these faiths emerged and began to match the charitable projects of the Christian missions and refute their purported moral superiority.[9]

Such developments promoted a more rapid appropriation by local populations of Christian beliefs and rituals. This occurred across much of sub-Saharan Africa powered by the new imperialism of the period. It was matched by an expansion of Muslim practice in North Africa, the Dutch East Indies and other parts of Southeast Asia. In southern and south-eastern Africa, the settler/colonial state encouraged its African accomplices to "become Christians", though the depth of this change was unclear in an area such as Buganda, where some existing rites continued even while local rulers attended newly built churches. The competitive expansion of mission activity – German Lutherans and British non-conformists in South Africa and Belgian Catholics in the Congo, for instance – was pushed forward as churches raised money, obtained the support of colonial governments and made use of the new communications and medical discoveries.[10] Yet, everywhere the key agents were indigenous people themselves, encouraged by new forms of sociality, economic links and forms of political practice extending beyond their localities. Consequently, the focus of the religious activity which evolved was often hybrid and in some respects diverged from West European and US Christianity. Generally speaking, for instance, African and Polynesian Christians placed less significance on themes of original sin or resurrection. The notion of God as a just lawgiver and Jesus as a charismatic leader played a greater role than in most European churches. This paralleled the form of Muslim expansion. Here it was street teachers, often referred to as "Sufi saints", who gave meaning to the faith rather than any general submission to the dictates of Sharia. Broadly, "conversion" to the world religions over this period was closely related to the emergence of new foci of power – military, administrative and especially communicative – which marked the dawning of the new century.

RELIGION CONTESTED: BURGEONING CULTS AND THE THREAT OF COMMUNISM

While the link between ethics and formal religious practice represented in scripture was common to the new Christianity, Buddhism, Vedantic Hinduism and "Sharia- minded" Islam, as Marshall Hodgson termed it,[11] this is not to say that religion everywhere took on a formal, text-based aspect. Outbreaks of spiritually informed animal slaughter persisted in parts of Africa. Dramatic announcements of the end of the world through messianic religion continued to occur in Buddhist–Confucian lands, though not on the scale of the mid-nineteenth-century Taiping rebellion. Most striking was the emergence of so-called cargo cults in Micronesia and Polynesia from the 1930s, where devotees prayed for material belongings from the gods, even in semi-Christian communities.[12] These varied from territory to territory, and anthropologists have disagreed widely over their meaning. Did they mark the advent of capitalism or an expression of notions of exchange, or were they unrelated expressions of popular messianism and belief in cosmic good unified only by the discourse of anthropology?

Expressions of unstructured spirituality were to persist throughout the mid- and late twentieth century, to the consternation of organised religions and the overweening state. Alongside these spiritualist upsurges, new religious sects continued to emerge. Theosophy, mixing Hindu and Buddhist belief with Western spiritualism, was followed by various versions of "New Age" religion. To existing forms of para-Christianity, such as Mormonism and Christian Science, the cult of Scientology was added in the 1960s, blending science, mysticism and messianism and built on donations from wealthy adherents like many such sects. Amongst Muslims, the Ahmadiyya movement challenged the finality of Muhammad's prophecy and was classed a heresy by the orthodox. The Cao Dai sect of Vietnam emerged as a complex of neo-Buddhism and veneration of great Francophone leaders such as Joan of Arc and Victor Hugo.[13] It was both patronised and repressed by the French authorities and later more

Figure 16 John Frum followers, Vanuatu. Thierry Falise/LightRocket/Getty Images.

or less tolerated by the incoming Communist governments in North and South Vietnam on the understanding that it gave up its French elements. By contrast, the Falun Gong cult in China, which emerged in the 1990s, was outlawed by the government even though it conveyed no obvious political message. Astonishingly, a wholly fictional "religion", so-called Jedi-ism, based on the *Star Wars* science fiction films, attracted 400,000 followers, according to the British census of 2001.[14]

These contestations and accommodations between cults, organised religion and state became more significant precisely because all three were extending their range over the century. The worldwide growth of the state, in its broadest sense, is well understood and frequently alluded to in previous pages. But partly in response to the state and partly in departure from it, religious authorities and organisations were venturing into areas previously untouched. In Spain and Latin America, for instance, the Catholic Church established growing numbers of savings banks (*cajas*) and self-help societies from the 1890s onwards, trying to tackle the economic problems of poor communities. Roman Catholic educational institutions exported their syllabi, competing with the laicising reformers of the state in France. In India, the radical neo-Hindu sect Arya Samaj similarly founded schools and colleges in competition with state organisations. Muslim madrassas, self-help societies and newspapers similarly expanded in numbers and range, stimulated both by the explosion of pilgrimage resulting from new steamship routes to the Hijaz and the Shi'a holy shrines in Mesopotamia.[15]

The world religions, however, faced more profound and direct challenges to their authority and even survival than they had in the nineteenth century. They surmounted those challenges with a degree of canniness and inner resilience which outshone that of the secular authorities, whom they sometimes

Figure 17 One of the symbols of Vietnam's Cao Dai religion of modernity. Xavier Rossi/StockPhoto/Getty Images.

challenged, but often co-opted as a source of strength. Even after the slow formalisation of belief and practice in the nineteenth century, religion remained a congeries of popular affects and sentiment only lightly touched in many cases by the moral codes and teachings of dedicated adepts: the ulama, priesthood or Brahman authorities. Here lay much of its strength: the manner in which it spoke to the aspirations and life crises of ordinary people. At the same time, though, religious leaders also found new strength as healers, counsellors in war and disaster and above all through new media: the expanded press, latterly radio, television and the Internet.

The greatest challenge to religion in the broad sense emerged from the Communist regimes of Eastern Europe, the USSR and East Asia, which initially explicitly rejected faith as a form of social oppression supported by feudal or capitalist ruling classes. Marx's position, often caricatured in view of his phrase about "the opium of the people", actually viewed religion not as an evil so much as a healing remedy for social alienation. Yet, he also thought that religion would naturally disappear when capitalist and feudal society had dissolved and the original village of gender equality and class-free living had itself been resurrected. Lenin and the Bolsheviks were more hostile towards Christianity, fearing priests such as Father Gapon of the 1905 revolution as potential rivals to the Party. Yet, it was only in the 1920 and 1930s under Stalin that religion of any form was denounced as a direct enemy of the Communist state.[16] The reason for this shift was the widespread alignment of Orthodox priests with the kulaks, or rich peasants, against the impending land reforms and the way in which ulama, Sufis and shamans rallied to tribal and minority revolts in the Caucasus, Kazakhstan and Mongolia. Consequently, over large areas of the USSR, priests and religious adepts were murdered and churches closed or demolished. The purge was accompanied by an intellectual assault on religious "superstition" which posited both a familial and political ethics totally independent of the divine.

A similar assault on religion occurred in China as Mao Zedong's rule became more oppressive. Chiang and other nationalist leaders and warlords had attempted to gain popular support by practising a form of Confucian Buddhist–Daoist nationalism, which conjured up Chinese tradition and piety, but also courted the better-off village leaders of the gentry class, who had remained powerful even as central government had declined in authority. Religion, piety and respect for ancestors were, additionally, a guarantee of social stability. Consequently, when the CPC initiated a full-scale assault on the village leadership during the land reform movements of the 1950s, the local religious establishments inevitably came under attack.[17] The Cultural Revolution consolidated the assault. Religion was driven underground and temples widely destroyed. One Party activist remembered, "At night we were ordered to go around to destroy the graveyards and turn them into farming land."[18] A secular religion of the socialist state was intended to replace popular piety.

For a time and in the most aggressive Communist states, the USSR, newly reunified China after 1949 and North Korea, people's committees were quite successful in scaling back public worship – Christian, Confucian and Buddhist – though families often quietly preserved private altars and forms of prayer. The position was more ambiguous in Eastern Europe, Indochina and Southeast Asia. In Poland, where the Communist Party had only achieved complete power in 1949, for instance, the powerful Catholic Church retained great influence and maintained public worship, not least because Polish Catholics could look outside the country to the Vatican and southern Europe for training, education and literature. Catholicism maintained its role, too, in the workers' unions, one of the few elements of the old civil society which survived. Over the long term, this situation encouraged the emergence of the Solidarity trade union, which played a key role in the eventual collapse of Communism in the country, as Chapter 9 notes.

One factor which kept Eastern European Christianity alive was its link with residual nationalism, which was subtly promoted by different varieties of East European Communists, particularly those with a peasant base. Warsaw, almost totally destroyed by the Germans, was rebuilt as an eighteenth- and nineteenth-century national symbol, not as a city of socialist modernity. It was natural therefore that church buildings and the local Catholic hierarchy played a part in this. An analogous situation developed in Vietnam following the Communist victory in the north in 1949. Ho Chi Minh rewrote Confucius's dicta to make them compatible with socialism. Hanoi's Confucian 'Temple of Literature' was not destroyed, as were so many Confucian and Buddhist sites during China's Cultural Revolution. Instead, it became a hallowed national shrine exalting 'love of learning' as a key virtue for educated socialist youth. Indeed throughout Southeast Asia, radical parties were strongly influenced by ethnic nationalism and hence very widely with a sense of "our religion".

Japan offered a rather different case. Here the Shinto patriarchal religion and nationalistic emperor worship in the form of the *bushido* cult of the military samurai, "Japan's traditional life force", as one devotee called it,[19] had proved serviceable to Japanese military expansionism, as also had a form of "muscular Buddhism". MacArthur moved to dismantle Shinto as a national religion in 1945, though it remained powerful in family settings. American occupation averted any potential Japanese march towards Communism here as had been envisaged by the British political scientist G. D. H. Cole during the war. After 1950, as a liberal democracy took shape in the country, more pacific forms of Shinto, *bushido*, Buddhist belief and Catholic Christianity proved serviceable to the new commercial and professional elite. A version of nationalistic Shinto even revived as the Japanese leadership became more self-confident after 1990. This was dramatised by their worship at the Yasukuni Shrine in Tokyo where Japan's war leaders, some of them executed by the Allies, were venerated, to the discomfiture of Chinese, Korean and Western commentators.

Across much of the late colonial world, religious organisation and ideology also faced significant challenges both from local Communist parties and from proponents of secularism determined that religion should not fragment the hard-won, anticolonial consensus. As elsewhere, establishments and ideologues responded by appropriating religion for the state and vice versa. In India the situation was particularly complex. Gandhi declared himself a devotee of the "eternal religion" (*sanatan dharma*) and introduced modified versions of traditional Hindu beliefs into his concept of soul force (*satyagraha*).[20] Yet, he had also linked the anti-British struggle to the Muslim campaign to protect the Khalifa and, even after 1924, when Atatürk abolished the office, professed to see Muslims and Muslim politicians as neighbours and brothers. Jawaharlal Nehru, a former theosophist and devotee of scientific modernity, argued for a secular constitution for a future independent India and insisted that any division between Hindus and Muslims was a recent development among the middle classes and was not reflected among the populace as a whole.

Nevertheless, the ambivalently secularist and inclusive state of the Indian National Congress did not persuade some Muslims, particularly leaders of Muslim majority areas in the northwest and east of the country, that religion should be excluded from politics. The British legal system had marginalised both Muslim law (Sharia) and the Hindu legal texts. The ideologue of the future Pakistan, Muhammad Iqbal, argued, however, for a place within India where Muslims could live by Sharia. Only later did his followers and other contemporaries begin to argue that what was needed instead was a separate state. By contrast, though radical Hinduism had not yet manifested itself and the Partition massacres were impelled by political and economic fear much more than by religious ideology, some Hindu leaders insisted that the future Greater India must be a Hindu state. Chief among them was V. D. Savarkar, proponent of Hindutva.[21] Savarkar's vision was as much ethnic and territorial as religious, but it provided a powerful rallying cry later in the century. India's constitution as it emerged from the Constituent Assembly debates of 1946–1948 was indeed broadly secular and inclusive, but sufficient room for manoeuvre was left in the provisions for Hindu and Muslim family legal codes or central and local government support of religious institutions for the politics of independent and secular India to be constantly scarified by issues of religious conflict. Moreover, political religion subsisted with a whole range of private religious beliefs and practices among Hindus, Muslims and Sikhs, which were being slowly modified by communication, as a later section suggests. One striking event was the way in which the leader of the nominally Hindu Dalits ("untouchables"), B. R. Ambedkar, despairing of secularism and seeking a remedy for the community's social oppression, initiated a move to Buddhism in the 1950s, which he regarded as a faith of equality.

The Middle East, part colonised, part independent, encountered challenges to Muslim and other belief systems both from political powers and from within faith communities. These were critical for the remaking of religion in the modern world. The clearest assault on the role of Islam within society came in Turkey, where the government of Kemal Atatürk abolished the office of Khalifa in 1924, established secular schools and pushed Sharia to the margins of the judicial realm even more thoroughly than had happened in British India.[22] These moves were not replicated to any considerable extent in the Arab world, a phenomenon that needs some explanation. Within the Ottoman Empire, religious institutions had always been state controlled to a considerable extent (unlike the situation in Shia Iran, for instance). The emperor's law (*kanun*), which some traced back to the Byzantine period, had always had a role particularly in view of the role in non-Muslim communities in the empire.

In the nineteenth century modernising reforms (*Tanzimât*) had created areas of legislative and public debate which were, once again, outside the purview of religious authorities.[23] Finally, religion became a difficult area as the new republic, fighting off European inroads and Arab insurgents themselves claiming the authority of the Prophet, sought to portray itself as an ethnically and linguistically Turkish entity, outside the Arab Middle East and devoted to modernisation.

The striking aspect of this distancing from Islam was that it occurred in an independent and formally Muslim polity. In Lebanon, Syria, Palestine, Iraq and more ambivalently in Egypt, by contrast, these secularising forces were greatly advanced by the colonial governments established after 1922 through the mandate system. British rule in Iraq and Palestine followed the pattern set in British India, where Sharia and Islamic judicial systems were preserved, but marginalised while new civil courts were established. In Lebanon and Syria, a modified version of French *laïcité* already operating for nearly a century in Algeria stood side by side with surviving Muslim courts and educational institutions.

Egypt, the most populous of the Arab countries, exhibited some of these tendencies. Mehmet Ali and his successors had instituted their own version of *Tanzimât*, giving the khedive (ruler) more control over religious courts and religious property. British occupation after 1882 had extended courts and other institutions from which the ulama were excluded. But there were two dimensions which tended to preserve the spirit and authority of Islamic ideology and practice. First, Egyptian nationalism from the 1870s, and particularly during the great risings against the British in 1919, was in part empowered by a specifically Islamic ideology: "Islam in danger" came together with the cry "Egypt for the Egyptians" in a way it had not in Turkey. The great prestige and power of the Muslim al-Azhar University in Cairo were critical. Secondly, Egyptian intellectuals, far from espousing secularism, constantly sought to merge modern forms with a reverence for Sharia and the finality of prophethood. Even modernisers such as Rashid Rida were prepared to accept Western scientific modernity only so far as it was compatible with the teachings of the Prophet.

In the 1920s and 1930s, a complaisant, landed ruling elite, conjoined in the Wafd Party, alternately fought and compromised with declining British power. But the period also saw a gradual strengthening of Islamic intellectual purism with the emergence of the Muslim Brotherhood.[24] Under the surface of Egyptian society the effects of "modernising" reform since the nineteenth century were apparent in the growth of a class of experts and later military officers whose significance was greatly increased between 1939 and 1948. These men finally achieved power in Nasser's revolution of 1954 and achieved fame during the 1957 Suez adventure by Britain and France. But, though they saw themselves as modernisers, they were not Atatürk. Nasser adapted "socialism" to Islamic ideology and the role of the ulama. The Muslim Brotherhood was persecuted, but it remained powerful and influential among the growing numbers of urban poor and in the countryside. It ultimately briefly returned to power at the beginning of the twenty-first century.

Through Italian-occupied Libya to the French colony of Algeria to the west and Ethiopia and Sudan to the south, similar conflicts between relatively secular modernisers and religious institutions buttressed by social conservatives in the countryside played out. In Libya, the Italians encouraged an urban middle class, planted Italian settlers and created neo-Islamic institutions, as the French did in Algeria. But rural revolts powered in part by varieties of Islamic ideology, both purist and Sufi, continued to erupt. The Second World War began to transform the situation. Whereas, as noted earlier, in Egypt the mobilisation for war tended to advantage modernising experts, at least for a time, the opposite happened elsewhere. In Libya after the occupation of the country in 1942, the British, suspicious of the urban population of Tripoli, advantaged the "tribes" of the east and south, mirroring their role in the Sudan. Equally, the Anglo-American occupiers of Algeria, wishing to diminish the power of the pro-Vichy elite, tended to support more conservative and rural forces after 1942.

This should not be seen as a policy applied only to Muslims. The US occupiers in Sicily and southern Italy similarly dismissed the semi-modernisers of the fascist establishment and gave a fillip to Catholic conservatism, a situation which applied to some extent in other parts of southern Europe, such as Greece and southern France. Here forces which supported collaboration with the Axis were regarded with as much hostility as the re-emerging Communists after the Allied conquest of Europe. As in the Muslim world, however, this was not simply a change determined by political instrumentality. When the formerly dominant fascist and modernising elites were pushed aside across Italy, people rallied again to religious symbols as a way of affirming their culture and autonomy.

One further major event in the central Islamic lands which was to resonate especially in the late half of the century was the re-emergence of a purist Wahhabi kingdom in central Arabia more than a century after the sect of Abdul Wahhab had been virtually destroyed by the armies of Mehmet Ali and Egyptian forces. After ibn Saud took Mecca and Medina in 1926, his followers destroyed many of the tombs and Ottoman structures, which the Wahhabis regarded as symbols of saint worship and polytheism, a process which continued for the following 90 years.[25] A modus vivendi of a sort was, nevertheless, established with less puritan Muslim populations and this allowed the continuance of pilgrimage by the large bodies of South and Southeast Asian, Sudanese and West African devotees. As Saudi Arabia benefited from the oil boom after 1960, it funded educational and military institutions in other Islamic societies, designed to propagate a rigorous version of the faith. This appealed to Muslim urban youth, disenchanted both with the old religious and landed establishments and also with the authoritarian modernisers who seized power across the Muslim world during the 1940s and 1950s.

THE TRIALS OF CHRISTIANITY, c. 1900 TO 1970

Before turning to the inner meaning of these changes in religious belief and practice, this chapter considers developments in the Christian, or post-Christian, West and its dependencies. Many of the same conditions observed in other religious systems also held true here: socialism and Communism initially appeared to offer an alternative to the "opium of the people"; the state, to one degree or another, promoted a division between itself and the church; urbanisation and new lifestyles undermined rites and dogmas associated with Catholic and Protestant Christianity, both of which had already been significantly modified by the spread of rationalism. At the ideological level, even non-socialist intellectuals ate away at the edges of religious belief. In fact, Darwinism and the development of a belief in science formed a more difficult menu to swallow for Christian churches than it did for Hindus, Buddhists or Muslims. Hindu thinkers had often proclaimed modern science perfectly compatible with the Vedas. For Muslims, since the Prophet was not himself a divine being, although the bearer of a divine message, evolution without the intervention of a deity was perfectly acceptable, even though some thinkers later came to reject this view.

For Christians, even in an advanced society such as the United States, largely unaffected by socialism, this balancing between science and religion was less easy to perform, as the famous American "Monkey Trials" of the 1920s showed. Paradoxically, in the United States, where the state and church had supposedly been divided by the founding fathers, local religious believers, both Protestant and Catholic, remained vigorous and politically powerful throughout the century. Churches offered a form of social mobility and social respectability. In the absence of strong socialist parties, black churches across the nation represented the yearning of the deeply disadvantaged populations for civil rights. American missionary activity, both Protestant and Catholic, expanded greatly between the wars. The United States, which had withdrawn from international diplomatic organisations after 1919, created a "spiritual empire" within the husk of European empires no less pervasive than the Catholic spiritual empire of the nineteenth century. American missionaries appeared as teachers and educators across the British Empire in the 1920s and 1930s. Protestant sects burgeoned with the development of communications. Preachers moved by motor car and there was an explosion of religious print. The Depression and the New Deal empowered some working-class groups and, in particular, brought American Irish Catholics into the mainstream of social life and overseas missions. American missions, both Protestant and Catholic, were active in China, where they educated important figures in the GMD and, later, Taiwanese elite and even a number of Communists. The delicate position of these missionaries was memorialised in the writing of Pearl S. Buck.[26] Secularism, indeed, made much less progress in the United States than in Europe. This meant that, with the coming of the neo-liberal age of Ronald Reagan in the 1980s, American Christian churches were in a position to play a strong political role, especially in the Midwest and the South.

In Western Europe, the impact of secularism, science and the process of distancing from religious rites proceeded at a very different pace between the Protestant nations and the mainly Catholic or Orthodox south of the Continent. In Britain, the very fact of the existence of a national church, however supposedly moderate, contributed to the growth of secular agnosticism in contrast to the United States. Children were less likely to remain believers when they were forced into religious services and religious instruction at school. The Christian socialism of the emerging Labour Party was a weak force. Some members of the elite constructed the Moral Re-Armament movement as a reaction against the murderous immorality of the First World War, the supposed indecency of urban areas and the chimera of Communism. Only in parts of radically Protestant Scotland and even more so in the Republic of Ireland and Ulster did religion remain a major political force. In Eire, it became a symbol of nationalist resistance to British oppression. The clerics of the Catholic Church and the Eire state became particularly close during the premiership of Éamon de Valera, whose anti-British stance even propelled him, perversely, towards the Axis powers during the Second World War.

The situation in Ireland bore some comparison with developments in Spain, Portugal and Italy. In all these cases, despite the onslaught of secular modernisers, a degree of accommodation was reached between the Catholic Church and an authoritarian state before 1939. In Italy, the Vatican had refused to recognise the legitimacy of the new unified state, leading to continuous legal conflict in the new Italy, particularly in matters of matrimony and church property.[27] Fearful of the rise of Communist trades unions, however, the church was enticed into a morally dubious compact with the fascist regime in the early 1930s. The irony is that, despite Catholic leaders' active collaboration with fascism and even Nazism during the Second World War, the Allied conquest of Italy saw a re-establishment of Catholic politicians and institutions after 1945, even though this took place in the name of Christian Democracy. The incoming Allies and returning moderate politicians had little choice, given the threat of anarchy and the great influence of both small-town and rural Communism in the country.

In Iberia, there was a similar, though far more violent, tussle between conservative Catholic and radical socialist thought and practice. The victory of radicals and socialists in the Spanish elections of the early 1930s was powered by the demands of urban workers, socialist ideologues and urban syndicalists in Catalonia, in particular. A major assault on the Catholic Church, implicated in conservative administrations since 1918, ensued, sparking a reaction which escalated into the Spanish Civil War of 1936–1939. General Francisco Franco brought together the Church, the colonial administration in Morocco, landowners and the commercial middle class to fight "socialism" with the aid of Nazi Germany and fascist Italy.[28] Franco is reported to have stated in 1945 that, "Hitler, son of the Catholic church, died while defending Christianity."

Similar compacts sustained conservative governments across Latin America. Only in Castro's Cuba, however, did radical anticlerical and Communist atheism win out when, in 1959, Castro suppressed the Church, a close ally of Batista's dictatorship. In Mexico, the secularist and socialist assault came earlier, even before the First World War, with the Mexican revolution, whose leaders moved rapidly to cut back the privileges of the Church during an era of reform which lasted from 1920 to 1934. As in Spain, conservative and Catholic forces fought back, sparking a near civil war there between 1926 and 1930. A precarious social peace prevailed after 1934, presided over by presidents who combined state-centred social welfare with some kind of rapprochement with the Church. Something similar happened in the southern cone (Chile and Peru) so that Latin American entered a period of autocratic military rule, less rigid than Franco's Spain, and combining some of the themes of Latin American socialism with religion and social conservatism. Revealingly, the Latin American autocracies began to crumble in the 1970s when Franco's did in Spain. Rapid democratisation, communications and the image of a democratic West: all these combined to make the older religious conservatives seem redundant. Importantly, however, the social policies of the Church itself began to change: Catholic radicals emerged, working amongst poor and disadvantaged groups. This shock to the old conservatives was not administered simply by the state or Catholic "liberation theologians",[29] but also by the appearance in Central and South America of evangelical Protestant missionaries from North America.

Finally, the struggle and accommodation between the state and religion impacted on northern and Eastern Europe. In France, the conflict between secularism and the religious establishment had been initiated early, before the First World War, as the radical government of 1905, composed of free thinkers, Protestants and even spiritualists, sought to "laicise society". The Dreyfus Affair had also highlighted a key element within right-wing thought: anti-Semitism. During the 1920s and early 1930s, the conflict waxed and waned in France only to be won decisively by the socialist left with the establishment of the Popular Front of 1936, a victory which had repercussions throughout the French Empire in Africa and Indochina. The progress of laicisation proceeded apace until it was abruptly interrupted by the Second World War. The defeat of France allowed the return of the social conservatism of the Vichy regime of Marshal Pétain, deeply Catholic and representative of *"La France aux Fran-çais"*. The political instability of early post-war France reflected the resurgence of the left, but also the fact that many of the supporters of Charles de Gaulle were relatively conservative Catholics, some of them with strong backgrounds in the French colonial armies.

An interesting parallel is to be found in the case of Miklós Horthy, Regent of Hungary between 1920 and 1944. Horthy invoked a notion of *"La Hongrie Profonde"*, siding with ideologues who viewed Hungary as separate from Pan-Slavic Europe and cognate with Asiatic powers and the Huns. Horthy was also, however, a devout Catholic and in this guise inaugurated one of the first anti-Semitic acts in post-First World War Europe, an echo of the Austro-Hungarian Empire before 1914. He established a census of Jewish students in Hungary's universities. The Stalinist conquest of Hungary in 1945 abruptly destroyed Pan-Turanism and the influence of the Church (though it retained an element of anti-Semitism). These themes were only revived after 1990 in the discourse of Hungary's right-wing, post-Communist governments.

In Germany and the Scandinavian states, hostility to religions and the reactions against it from Protestants and Catholics played a lesser part in politics after 1919. Some theologians, such as Karl Barth, fiercely opposed the advent of Nazism. But other Protestants and Catholics found it possible to tolerate Nazism's atavistic Aryanism because its leaders did little to alienate the church establishments. Under US tutelage, as Germany and Central Europe rebuilt after 1945, however, a revived democratic and largely Catholic Christianity re-emerged under Konrad Adenauer. This time it had the aim of national reconstruction, but also of building a new, pacific Europe, linking with similar policies and ideologies in France and Italy. In the 20 years after the Second World War, irenic political religion and secularisation went hand in hand. Over much of northern Europe religious attendance sharply declined while a hollowed-out official Christianity survived. The youth revolution of the 1960s and 1970s and women's sexual and social liberation played an important part here.[30] Combined with the impact of Communism across much of the rest of the world, the 1960s and 1970s seemed to be the nadir of religious belief. Yet, as the century ended, it became clear that Western Europe was an exception to wider global trends.

"LEAPS OF FAITH": THE LATE TWENTIETH AND TWENTY-FIRST CENTURIES

The resurgence of religion in politics between 1990 and 2015 is touched on in the final narrative chapters of this book, but some background is necessary. In the case of the Muslim world, it was marked by the clerical revolution in Shia Iran after 1979; the rise and then fall of the Muslim Brotherhood in Egypt; and the influence of Saudi Wahhabism and the expansion of radical Islam in the form of al-Qaeda, ISIS in Iraq, and Boko Haram, the latter a Nigerian terrorist group hostile to Western customs. In India, a muscular form of Hindutva, represented by the Bharatiya Janata Party (BJP) and supported by the Rashtriya Swayamsevak Sangh (RSS), waxed and waned in power between 1980 and 1990, but was once again on the upsurge after 2010. In China, Vietnam, Cambodia and Laos, Buddhism regained its status as these countries moved away from rigid Communism and this rational faith seemed both a national heritage and a protection against minority religions and local seers. Much the same happened to Christian institutions and advocates in Russia and Eastern Europe, while in the United States, right-wing politics was closely allied to various forms of Christian revivalism constituting what was called "the moral majority". When, in 2013, Pope Francis became leader of the Roman Catholic Church, it seemed that the forces of conservatism were on the decline here too and popular approval of the Church was gaining strength.

What were the wider changes underlying this resurgence of religion? On the negative side, the fall of Communism and the failure of the military and technocratic elites across the world left both an ideological gap and a sense of deep disenchantment among younger and poorer people. The movement of populations associated with globalisation also often created a moral void. The children of Muslim, Sikh and Hindu migrants to Western Europe, the United States, Canada and Australasia sought strength in religious institutions when the surrounding societies seemed uncaring, or even racist. Equally, the continued spread of modern education and mores into conservative local societies in Africa, the Middle East and southern Asia produced a reaction which favoured stricter forms of indigenous religion. "Western corruption" became a theme, especially when it was associated with scientific education, gay rights and the public drinking of alcohol. Political parties of all stripes, from American radical Republicans to Recep Erdoğan's Islamist supporters in Turkey, took advantage of these fears and magnified them.

Yet, there was also a positive side to this moral change. Religious groups had often taken the lead in providing education, social support and a sense of community in societies where the modernising state had failed. In Egypt, the Muslim Brotherhood had given poor rural and urban people financial support. In the Gaza Strip, the West Bank and Lebanon the radical Sunni group, Hamas, had done the same. In black American communities, across West Africa and even in South Korea, Pentecostalist Christian societies had imparted basic education and medical aid. In India, Hindu nationalism had managed to create a "Weberian compact" between Hindu religion and the rise of capitalism for lower-middle-class shopkeepers and business magnates alike. This was a major factor in Narendra Modi's and Erdogan's overwhelming electoral victories in 2014. Aspects of populism merged with modernising religion.[31] In Israel, too, immigrant Jews and a sense of solidarity against political danger strengthened forms of orthodox and nationalist Judaism after 1980. Even in Western Europe, where religious practice generally continued to decline, churches provided "food banks" for the poor during times of economic hardship, while many, especially women, continued to believe vaguely in God and the afterlife.

Yet, how had the inwardness of religious belief changed by the 2000s? Conversion to Christianity, Islam or other world religions of tribal peoples and inhabitants of "zomia" (areas beyond the reach of settled government) was a moral rupture, even when it involved the continued veneration of ancestors.[32] Communal worship, right comportment in dress and life rituals, perhaps a new notion of goodness and sin: all these were novel features of belief and practice. Almost as dramatic was the widespread decline of Sufi mysticism across the Sunni Islamic world and the growing power of text-based teaching and formal, disciplined practice instilled by the ulama. In a sense, religion became utilitarian. The leadership of local ulama, often radical reformists who based their teaching strictly on the Qur'an and hadith, was strengthened by the fall of the Khilafat and connection through the Hajj with Wahhabi puritanism. As the ayatollahs gained political power in Shia Islam a form of politicisation of religion occurred here, so that political and religious dissidence became two-headed forms of heresy. Equally, radical political activity, even terrorism, was validated in some of these contexts.

Christian spirituality had a perhaps more complex history. Some broad-church groups adjusted to secular knowledge, retaining the concept of an original creation and the ministry of Jesus yet leaving room for evolution. Even during the Communist onslaught, Christian groups, in Eastern Europe, for instance, were able to emphasise the levelling dimension of belief and match it with communitarian socialism. These adjustments were not necessarily the case with the Roman Catholic hierarchy or radical Protestant denominations. Quite apart from the issue of the Church's infallibility, the Catholic priesthood was in conflict throughout the century with secular authorities and even their own followers over issues such as contraception, abortion, paedophilia and homosexuality. These controversies were somewhat lessened in the 1960s and 1970s under Pope Paul VI and again after 2013 when Pope Francis seemed to announce a more forgiving attitude to homosexuals and a return to the Christian radicalism of the 1970s. Local Protestant churches, dominated by lay devotees, also made few compromises with modern science or secular ethics, whether in the southern United States or Africa. Millenarian themes about the end of the world had less purchase than earlier. Yet, these charismatic communities demanded immediate personal connection with God and still took the Bible as invariable truth. In all these contexts, though, God was domesticated and enlisted in the fight for human ends, as he had been throughout history.

Religious leaderships, whether Christian priests and Pentecostalist preachers, Buddhist monks or Muslim *alim*s, retained power and influence which was, if anything, strengthened by media and new forms of communication. But they could not monopolise them. In complex ways, these religious authorities fragmented and came to relate to their followers and congregations differently by the beginning of the new century. The devotee had become more independent, as much forming the community as being formed by it. Young people were indoctrinated over the Internet and travelled large distances of their own volition to proselytise, pray or engage in religious war. Religion had become a yet more populist and democratic form, just as it had invaded and reformed democracies and authoritarian states alike.

[14] A Century of Killing and a Century of Crime

"Ethnic Cleansing" Before the Holocaust
The Holocaust and its Memory
Killing, Ethnic Cleansing and the New States
The 1990s Generation and Humanitarian (Non)-
    Intervention
The "Downsizing" of Killing and the Small Wars of
    Fragmentation
A Century of Crime and Criminal Killing

IF the bright side of the twentieth century was the attempt to create an international order, the release of millions from colonialism and the subsequent lifting of parts of these populations from poverty, the dark side was the incidence of genocide and mass killing that occurred dramatically throughout the twentieth century and showed only limited signs of abating in the early twenty-first century. Crime, broadly understood, also took on new, diffuse and more malign forms over these decades.

Mass killing had been common throughout human history, associated with religion, imperialism and revolution. The European wars of religion, Francisco Goya's depiction of executions during the Spanish wars, Lord Wellesley's slaughter of wounded Indian troops on the battlefield, the horrors of 1848: all these are well documented. Yet, the scale, intensity and precipitating ideologies of the twentieth century's mass killing have convinced most historians that there was something new here. We can isolate several aspects of this novelty. First, and most prosaically, the weapons of killing became more sophisticated and devastating compared with the swords and muskets of earlier periods. Machine

Remaking the Modern World 1900–2015: Global Connections and Comparisons, First Edition. C. A. Bayly.
© 2018 John Wiley & Sons Ltd. Published 2018 by John Wiley & Sons Ltd.

guns and gas attacks killed more people more quickly. The "carpet bombing" of the Second World War in Europe killed hundreds of thousands of people. The industrially produced gas chambers of the Holocaust brought genocide to its scientific peak. Regardless of its justification, the atomic bombing of Hiroshima and Nagasaki also took the obliteration of whole populations to a new level.

Yet, the sheer capacity of civilian and military leaders to kill their assumed enemies is not in itself an adequate explanation. A change in mentality was also involved. In part, the hypernationalism, or genocidal democracy, of the late nineteenth century and early part of the twentieth century played a part.[1] In the words of Michael Mann, this was the "dark side of democracy" as well as an aspect of the hyperdefinition of the new and yet more powerful state. The sacred nation had to be purged of its internal enemies and resolutely sacrifice itself in order to crush its external adversaries. The central genocide of the century – the Shoah or Holocaust – was the supreme and also most obvious example of this. Yet, the attempt to create exclusive and unified polities, spurred on by readings of social Darwinism and notions of racial hierarchy, spread this mentality much more widely. The examples are numerous: the British versus the "degenerate" Kikuyu of Mau Mau, the Christian Serbs versus the "corrupted" Muslim Bosnians, Hindus versus Muslim "invaders". All of these speak to the policing and defining of the ethnic state, but also to the manner in which this was sustained by the feeding of popular prejudice spread through rumours and newspapers and later by radio, television, the Internet and the mobile phone.

A final dimension, alongside the instruments and ideologies of mass killing which distinguished the century, was, then, the communication of hatred. People moved in large numbers along shipping routes, through airports and by motor vehicles, and became perceived as a threat by sedentary populations. This was especially true if their whole lifestyle was one of movement, like the European Roma or gipsies, who were slaughtered alongside the Jews and persecuted throughout the century. The Jews themselves were perceived as a diasporic and rootless community even where they had settled and increasingly bonded with host societies for centuries before their mass annihilation. Supposed conspiracies by Armenians, Jews, Muslims, Sikhs, Tutsis and other internal enemies were broadcast to millions concerned about their livelihood or status. The result was pogroms much broader and more destructive than could ever have occurred in medieval or early modern societies. The "enemy" had always been on the doorstep, but now he was on the doorstep of compatriots, caste fellows or tribal members hundreds or even thousands of miles away. These conspiracies were now mobilised by the new media for self-protection or in order to purify their own societies.

Historians and, even more so, politicians have debated the nature of mass killing. Was the elimination of Armenians between 1916 and 1922 in the Ottoman Empire comparable with the genocide of the European Jews? Was the death of three million Indians in the Bengal famine of 1943 a deliberate act of genocide by Churchill, who denied them food, calling them the "next worst people" after the Germans? Were French campaigns against Algerian dissidents in the 1950s or the American bombing of Vietnamese cities in the 1960s a form of genocide? All these positions seem to be determined by politics and emotion. What is perhaps more important is how to contextualise them – how ideology, capacity and popular support came together to convert hatred into mass killing. The next sections try to provide a comparative background for some of these events.

"ETHNIC CLEANSING" BEFORE THE HOLOCAUST

The mass killing of the First World War on the Eastern, Western and Ottoman fronts were fully documented, almost excessively so, during the centenary celebrations of 2014. There were at least 40 million casualties, of which about 17 million were deaths, during the war, though the majority were military personnel, unlike the Second World War, when upwards of 60 million were killed. But during 1914–1918 and in the war's aftermath there began a series of annihilations of civilian populations which changed the nature of human society and reached a crescendo between 1935 and the 1970s. Before, during and after the First World War, for instance, there took place what has been called the Armenian genocide, that is the mass murder of up to 850,000 Armenian residents of the Ottoman Empire. Its description as genocide, which was further validated by Armenians in the United States, especially after the Holocaust, was echoed in 2012 by the French Assembly and later by Pope Francis, to the fury of the Turkish government. It was often argued that this extermination campaign was not carried out by the ruthless policy of a centralised administration, as in the case of the Holocaust, but that much of the impetus came from local militias, Muslim leaders and ordinary people. New evidence from Turkish and German sources suggests, however, that local governors and police chiefs did, in fact, deliberately initiate the killing.[2] Yet, questions of nomenclature aside, the key question is why did it happen, and what does it signify that these events took place on the fringes of the increasingly violent Western European nation states?

The three causative factors mentioned above certainly came into play.[3] The Ottoman army and militias were well armed, having been participants in the Balkan Wars of 1912–1913 and recently rearmed by Germany. The change in the nature of the state was also in evidence following the Young Turk revolution of 1908, which promoted a "Turkification" of the country and its language and had moved away from the more inclusive politics of the earlier sultans. In the context of two generations of war with Russia and the Balkan Christian powers, Armenian and Assyrian Christians, many of them intelligentsia, had themselves become potentially dangerous "others". Communication was also significant. The First World War had generalised the notion of the "danger within" and Russia, albeit an enemy of Turkey, had already embarked on a policy of denying civil rights to Jews, again many of them from the intelligentsia, in the generation before the war. The popular dimension of the killings was also reinforced by the cry "Islam in danger!" which had sustained the Khilafat movement and infected the contemporary nationalistic riots in Egypt and India in the aftermath of the war, when Coptic Christians were to come under attack and Hindu–Muslim riots resumed.

The interwar years continued to see mass killings in the context of the final stage of imperial expansion and coercion which the First World War had set in motion. Hundreds of thousands of Turks were expelled from the city of Salonika following the Greco-Turkish War of 1919–1922, and many did not survive. There was also heavy mortality among the Greeks in Turkey itself.[4] The Rif Revolt in Morocco ended with French and Spanish soldiers massacring rebels against colonial rule. Some of the officers in these atrocities later participated in violent repression during the Spanish Civil War. This "infection" of the domestic state by colonial atrocities is reminiscent of Hannah Arendt's belief that extermination campaigns carried out by German troops in German South-West Africa before and during the First World War created a civil and military mentality hospitable to mass killings by the state.

As the Second World War approached, three major events, mentioned in Chapter 6, pointed the way to the future expansion of mass murder. First, there was the brutality of the Italian campaign in Abyssinia. Secondly, among other Japanese atrocities in China there occurred the Nanjing (Nanking) massacre of 1937, when perhaps 300,000 Chinese citizens were killed by Japanese troops, which has envenomed relations between the two states ever since.[5] When Chiang's forces' defence of the city collapsed, Japanese soldiers ran amok, killing thousands of civilians whom they ostensibly suspected of being defecting Chinese soldiers. There were at least 20,000 rapes in the first month of the occupation alone. Clearly Japanese soldiers were enraged by the fact that Chinese resistance had been so fierce. Yet, there was also an issue of competitive nationalism here. A particular Japanese version of racial hierarchy had been fostered by Japan's military schools and this cast the Chinese as a backward and irrational people in need of Japanese tutelage.

The third great spate of pre-war mass killing was inaugurated by Stalin's Communist state, not only directed at internal dissidents but also against kulaks, supposedly intransigent rich peasants, and ethnic groups in Central and East Asia. Historians and public commentators are deeply divided about the ultimate cause of these atrocities. Michael Mann, for instance, saw Stalin's terror as a long-term consequence of the very Bolshevik emphasis on the Party as the unassailable voice of the people and vehicle of historical truth. If the revolution was to survive, "class enemies" had to be exterminated. But, as in many other examples of mass killing, state power unleashed many local vendettas, greatly increasing the death toll.[6] By contrast, Marxist historians saw the terror as Stalin's personal programme and were at pains to distance it from the subsequent Nazi genocide. Admittedly, Nazi and Communist ideology differed in fundamental respects, but both disdained and revolted against liberal humanism. Again, the imminence of world war provided the backdrop to this fear of the internal enemy. In Spain, one of Franco's collaborators wrote in 1936, "We have to terrorise, we have to show we are in control by rapidly and ruthlessly eliminating those who do not think as we do."[7]

THE HOLOCAUST AND ITS MEMORY

The Nazi genocide of the Jews, or the Shoah as the state of Israel came to describe it, was no doubt of a wholly different order of magnitude from these earlier events and horrific in its industrial form of killing.[8] The ideology of anti-Semitism had been transformed in the nation states of the late nineteenth century, particularly where these states were doubtful of their own multiple identities, as was the case in Austria-Hungary before 1914. Yet, the First World War and the defeat of the Central Powers transformed it. A "Jewish conspiracy", both internal and external to Germany and Austria, could be blamed for the collapse of their powerful war machine and the mobilisation of the United States on the Allied side, as Kaiser Wilhelm asserted. Former soldiers turned SA or SS recruits harboured deep resentment for the defeat and Hitler was able to build on this, casting the Jews as the hated "other" despite the fact that they had been increasingly absorbed into German society over the previous two generations and many had lived there for hundreds of years.[9] Equally, the role of Jews such as Rosa Luxemburg in the post-war Communist uprisings could be portrayed as a racist attack on the German nation. Between 1933 and 1939, the Nazis enacted a whole range of laws which gradually stripped Jews of their citizenship.

The immediate context of the genocide of six million Jews between 1942 and 1945 was, of course, the barbarism of the Second World War itself, a war where on the Eastern Front perhaps 20 million were slaughtered and whole cities razed to the ground by Allied bombing. The ideology of extermination seemed dominant and evil had become an everyday, banal matter, to paraphrase Arendt. As Heinrich Himmler blandly put it, "Thus the difficult decision had to be taken to make this people disappear from the face of the earth."[10] Along with the bombing of Hiroshima and Nagasaki, the Shoah is rightly seen as the culminating event of the twentieth century, dwarfing even the death of three million Bengalis in the 1943 famine or the Maoist terror of the 1960s. The mechanism of the Holocaust was not limited to the Germans. On the contrary, the Vichy authorities in France[11] and large elements of the Polish and other East European populations participated eagerly in the rounding up of Jews and their despatch to extermination camps. Nazi race theory had existed from the earliest days of the party. Hitler was determined to build an "empire" within Europe dominated by the Aryan Germans. Revealingly, he occasionally mentioned the British Indian Empire with respect. The Ukraine was to be his "new Indian Empire".[12] But it was the violence of the war itself, the desire to create a consolidated German heart of this empire and discipline a tame colonial labour force which created the impetus for targeted genocide. In a chilling "welcome speech" the deputy commandant of Auschwitz told his victims: "This is not a sanatorium, this is a German concentration camp and you can expect to live three months . . . there is only one way out of here and that's through the crematorium chimney."[13]

The end of the war saw massacres and counter-massacres by Communist and anti-Communist forces. Notorious here was the Katyn massacre of Polish anti-Communist prisoners of war by Stalin's forces in 1945. But across the whole range of collapsing fascist regimes and resurgent Communism, similar atrocities took place. Hundreds of thousands of German women were raped by the invading Soviet forces and men were killed out of hand. Slovenian Communists massacred defeated Italian fascist troops around Fiume. In

Greece, meanwhile, with the covert approval of the Anglo-Americans, anti-Communist forces eliminated and drove out Communists, forcing them back to the Albanian border. Even in the very last hours of warfare, the murder of Jews continued throughout Europe.

In some ways the consequences of the genocide of the Jews were almost as significant as the events themselves. Contrary to the "myth of silence" about the Holocaust, serious research and recording of the death toll began almost immediately after the war, first in Yiddish language circles and the Jewish state itself and shortly afterwards in Western Europe and the United States. As François Azouvi showed,[14] filmmakers, litterateurs and others took up the discussion almost immediately after 1945, though surviving Jewish communities in different parts of the world were divided about how far to memorialise the Holocaust. I vividly remember a BBC television programme in the early 1950s showing distressing pictures of corpses being piled into mass graves and the debate between my parents as to whether their young son should see such images. But Holocaust research was not Holocaust memory. As Tony Judt argued,[15] across Europe, even in the United Kingdom, the racial dimension of genocide was very often sidestepped by politicians and public figures. The Nuremberg war crimes trials and the later trial of Adolf Eichmann in 1962 raised public awareness. But most perpetrators had long escaped justice by fleeing to authoritarian countries in South America or they were simply too valuable to the victors to be tried. Similarly, in the Far Eastern theatre of war, both the GMD and the Communists were very uneven in their prosecution of Japanese war criminals, even those responsible for the Nanjing massacre. The idea of "Asia for the Asians" still held some resonance while the Communists were keen to promote themselves as a legitimate, but also superior, government of the people, seeking justice not revenge.[16]

For Judt, the analysis and discussion about the Holocaust and how to avoid its repetition was the most important accomplishment of European civilisation in the post-war age, even more significant than the formation of the European Union.[17] For the state of Israel and its supporters, by contrast, and particularly those in the United States, it became the fundamental guarantee of that state's survival. The atrocity filtered into modern human rights consciousness, though one important dimension of the post-war years was the failure of this consciousness to influence attitudes to violence and mass murder in colonial contexts. French liberals were often silent about examples of vicious oppression in Algeria in the 1950s, while many British liberals were silent about events in Malaya and Kenya during the Communist and Mau Mau insurgencies there. Hundreds of thousands were killed in these terminal wars of colonialism. There is good reason to think that British forces summarily executed large numbers of supposed Mau Mau fighters in acts of collective punishment while thousands of others were hanged or died in confinement.[18]

Leftists were equally silent about the mass murder and starvation enacted in China's Great Leap Forward and Cultural Revolution or the more limited purges enacted in Communist North Vietnam. Even the killings by the Pol Pot regime in Cambodia in the 1970s seemed to them dwarfed by the US assault on North Vietnam, though the bombing of civilian targets in Hanoi was indeed reminiscent of the saturation bombing of German cities in the Second World War. Two million Vietnamese died at the hands of the United States and its allies. While the Jews had acquired the status of world citizens by being the object of mass murder, non-white peoples waited much longer. Yet, the unyielding stance and occasionally ruthless actions of the democratic state of Israel against its Palestinian subjects and its neighbours often seemed to derive its legitimacy from the past suffering of the Jewish people. Indeed, across the dependent world, the discourse of the white "civilising mission" was persistent and unaffected by the horrors of European history.

Killing, Ethnic Cleansing and the New States

Mass killing was not, however, limited to the European theatre of the war or to the direct action of colonial powers with their backs against the wall. Perhaps a million and a half people were killed between 1946 and 1948 during the Partition of India. More were killed from 1948 to 1952 and again during the Bangladesh War of 1971. The mass killing of Sikhs in 1984 after the murder of Indira Gandhi may also be seen as the last act in this drama.[19] During the Partition itself, the preconditions listed above were once again clearly in evidence. The killings began in the aftermath of a major war. Weapons were plentiful and armed militias – in this case the troops of the princely states, Sikh and Muslim veterans and members of militant political groups – were spread across the subcontinent. The drift of weaponry into Bengal from the Eastern Front of the war with Japan seems to have been particularly significant in the killings in the summer and early autumn of 1946 in Calcutta and eastern India which inaugurated the tragedy. Historians such as Gyanendra Pandey showed how the rumours of atrocities sparked new atrocities as the railway brought trains from eastern Bengal or western Punjab into the Indian plains.[20]

Yet, while the failing colonial state was supine in the face of mass murder and Indian spokesmen continue to call for the trial in absentia of Mountbatten, there is no doubt that these events also represented the dark side of democracy. Nehru's failure to comprehend the power that had, if only latterly, become a form of Muslim nationalism; Jinnah's part in sparking off what became the Great Calcutta Killing of 1946 and, in desperation, calling for what he himself called a "moth-eaten Pakistan"; the malign influence of underground political forces such as the militant Hindu Rashtriya Swayamsevak Sangh (RSS): all these contributed to the scale of the violence. When the new government of India effectively invaded the former princely state of Hyderabad in 1948 to consolidate the Indian republic, bands of so-called Razakars killed Hindus and gangs, probably formed through the influence of the extreme nationalist RSS, responded, leaving at least 30,000 dead. Later, the leftist Telangana revolt resulted in thousands more casualties.[21]

The psychology of the conflict also bears consideration. Much of the political rhetoric of the previous generation had cast Hindus, Muslims and Sikhs as friends, neighbours and even brothers. Gandhi was in the forefront here. Shruti Kapila suggests that much of the later killing was "fraternal", as people who had lived together for generations took revenge on each other through intimate acts of murder, a distant echo of fraternal killing in the *Bhagavad Gita*.[22] Equally, though, the moral amnesia of movement could be invoked: people killed and moved on, wiping memory and guilt from their minds. The Urdu writer Saadat Hasan Manto, unsure of whether he was Indian or Pakistani, documented these killings in literary form. His 1950 story, *Thanda Gosht* ("Cold Meat"), was a tale of rape and murder between Sikhs and Muslims. His protagonist says, "The house I attacked . . . seven people lived in it . . . six I slaughtered . . . there was a girl very beautiful . . . I picked her up and carried her away."[23]

As with the Holocaust, the memory of Partition killing, long repressed, at least in public, had profound political and personal consequences. Hindus and Sikhs were driven out of Pakistan and later Bangladesh, though Muslims fared somewhat better in democratic India. All the same, continuous conflict over Kashmir, which in view of its Muslim majority should have become part of Pakistan, continued to distort the life of the subcontinent. As late as 2008, murderous attacks were launched against Mumbai (Bombay) by Kashmiri militants with the probable complicity of elements of Pakistani security services.

Nor was the security of the subcontinent improved by the escalation of conflict in Ceylon/Sri Lanka. Here, by comparison with India, a relatively peaceful decolonisation took place in 1948. However, rivalry over jobs, political authority and economic resources between an increasingly militant Tamil minority and the majority Sinhalese, with origins in the colonial period, became violent in the 1970s and 1980s. The "Tamil Tigers" (LTTE), seeking to maintain the Tamils' position as a better-educated and privileged group, attempted to carve out a state in the north of the island, promoting a violent rhetoric of separate identity.[24] Violence spilled into India when Rajiv Gandhi was assassinated by a Tamil suicide bomber, supposedly because of India's failure to come to the aid of their distant Tamil kinsfolk. The spectre of Chinese intervention on behalf of the Sri Lankan government explained Indian caution. The standoff was only ended in the 2010s when the Sri Lankan government smashed the Tamil Tigers, executing thousands of its fighters and violating the laws of war, according to many commentators. Perhaps at least 40,000 civilians were killed between 1983 and 2009 in this civil war. A feature of these events was the way in which a form of "ethnic demonisation" was again used to legitimate it. Tamils had always been "invaders" according to this populist rhetoric, though in fact the eighteenth-century kingdom of Kandy had been ruled by a Tamil dynasty and its culture was a Hindu–Buddhist hybrid.

If the massacre of perhaps two million "class enemies" by the Khmer Rouge in Cambodia in the late 1960s was one type of atrocity, led directly by a radical Communist state, the scene had been set in the opposite direction in Indonesia a few years before.[25] Here, an Islamising postcolonial government signalled to local leaders and militias that the elimination of up to a million "Communists", mostly Chinese civilians, was a national priority, as discussed in Chapter 8. This took place at the height of the Cold War and the beginnings of the conflict in Vietnam. The Middle East also remained a scene of violence after 1948 as Israel fought three major wars with its Arab enemies. Civilians suffered throughout. In 1982, for instance, as Israel went from the offensive to defensive war in Lebanon under Prime Minister Ariel Sharon, more than a thousand Palestinian refugees were murdered by Christian militias.

THE 1990S GENERATION AND HUMANITARIAN (NON)-INTERVENTION

Africa had also been a scene of mass killing since the First World War. Quite apart from the Mau Mau insurgency, perhaps half a million Ugandans died during Idi Amin's brutal rule from 1971 to 1979. But Central West Africa, in particular, had a miserable and turbulent history throughout much of the century. Belgian rule in the Congo was harsh, exploitative and long lasting. In the context of the Cold War, the Communist independence leader Patrice Lumumba was ousted in a violent coup in 1971. The Congo remained impoverished and prone to ethnic conflict until 2015. The Nigerian civil war of 1967–1970 may have killed more than a million through famine and direct killing.[26] Here, again, local rivalries were exacerbated by the international politics of the Cold War. During the struggle against apartheid, the area of Natal in South Africa was subject to significant violence.

Yet, it was in neighbouring Rwanda that one of the most notorious genocides of the postcolonial era took place.[27] Here too, the cause was ethnic competition between two main tribal groupings, the Tutsi and the Hutu, who competed for power and resources. In 1994, armed Hutu militias began the systematic killing of an estimated 800,000 Tutsis. Whole villages were wiped out while the "international community" stood by and looked on. Ultimately, the Tutsis armed themselves, regained the initiative and seized control of the country, driving many of the Hutu perpetrators over the border into the Congo and killing thousands more. This conflict continued to have local repercussions. Rwanda itself made considerable economic progress, not least because guilty Western powers poured in aid. By the 2010s, the lifespan of the average Rwandan had increased by 20 years. The country became a favoured spot for foreign investors. But the Hutu–Tutsi conflict continued under the surface of the regime of President Paul Kagame, a Tutsi, while the Rwandan army continued to intervene and foment conflict in the Congo, concerned that their erstwhile enemies might make a comeback.[28]

What had made the Rwandan conflict so violent was, to a significant degree, the colonial heritage. More obviously than even the British and French in Iraq and Syria, the Belgians had played the game of divide and rule to retain their own control of mineral and other resources. At the same time the fact that the two groups were of similar size and had access to arms across a troubled region also played its part. Finally, the inaction and incapacity of foreign powers was significant, as in the Armenian and Jewish genocides.

Another example of this set of preconditions for slaughter was the mass killing by rebels in Sierra Leone in the 1990s when Charles Taylor, the Liberian president, sent bands of irregulars across the border and more than 50,000 villagers were massacred. It is striking that, in 2012, Taylor himself was the first ever head of state to be prosecuted and imprisoned for crimes against humanity. However guilty Taylor had been, these events certainly suggest a degree of deliberate amnesia among Europeans, Americans and Asians. Yet, it was the Rwandan genocide and the near-contemporary killing of Bosnian Muslims by Serbs that convinced President George W. Bush and Prime Minister Tony Blair to intervene. This also had a profound impact on the decision to invade Afghanistan after the events of 2001 and then Iraq in 2003. Here, Saddam Hussein had unleashed mass killing against the Kurdish minority, following attacks on the "Marsh Arabs" and various Shia groups. Killing and counter-killing continued to 2015, when there emerged the murderous ISIS movement of Sunni militants.

The "Downsizing" of Killing and the Small Wars of Fragmentation

Horror at the continuation of mass killing at the end of the twentieth and into the twenty-first century, in Rwanda, Serbia, Syria and Iraq, for instance, should not be allowed to distract us from the very significant changes which have occurred since 1945 and even more so since the 1980s. The revival of anti-Semitism in France, Hungary and Ukraine since 2000 was indeed alarming, powered as it was by anti-Israel feeling amongst Muslims and a desperate search for new ideologies to bind nations perplexed by their decline as world powers or the collapse of Communism. But a general turn towards mass extermination seemed unlikely.

It was the concurrence of new communications, vigorous and often perverse state ideologies and their implementation by new methods of warfare that contributed to the mass genocide of the earlier eras. After the 1980s, however, the nature of killing changed. In terms of total numbers of deaths, it came nowhere near the toll of the two world wars, revolution and the genocide by authoritarian states between 1914 and 1970.[29] Interstate killing and ethnic cleansing certainly continued unabated, but it was fragmented into more limited conflicts between opposing rights and truth claims: local Christian versus Muslim conflicts based on ethnic distinction in the Middle East and Northwest Africa; intertribal wars, as between the hardened categories of Nuer and Dinka in the South Sudan after 2012; Buddhist versus Muslim pogroms, as in Myanmar/Burma; localised Sunni–Shia conflicts, as in Pakistan[30] and Iraq, and Tamil–Sinhala ones in Sri Lanka. The period ended with the violence unleashed by the failed "Arab Spring" across the whole Middle East.

In many respects, these events still reflected the dark side of democracy, but, equally, the morphology and fragmentation of the nation state had empowered numerous local militias, which often directed hatred and killing against other groups rather than drawing on the violence of the state itself. Here Achille Mbembe's notion of "necropolitics" is useful. Contrasted with Foucault's "biopolitics" (the social control of production, etc.), a politics defined morally and geographically by indiscriminate killing and sacrifice (drone strikes versus suicide bombers) seemed increasingly apparent.[31]

In Iraq after 2001, for instance, there was almost continuous conflict between Sunnis, various different groups of Shias and the Kurds. The victims of the killings were often people who happened to be in the market or the mosque at the wrong time, caught up in suicide bombings, rather than victims of the state, which was now fragmented and weakened. Even in major conflicts, such as the warfare from 2011 to 2015 in Syria or Iraq, much of the killing was carried out by local militias. Islamists fought with each other, as did Sunnis, Kurds and the remaining Christians. This sort of violence against a localised public had been foreshadowed in Northern Ireland and mainland Britain in the 1980s and 1990s, where bombs had been used by Irish nationalist radicals and their enemies to kill not the agents of the state but ordinary people in their everyday lives. Now violence itself fragmented further, as groups such as al-Qaeda, Boko Haram, ISIS and al-Shabab targeted civilians in revenge for state policies. To an extent, this was reminiscent of the anarchist killings of the 1890s and 1900s, but the target was more often ordinary civilians than the political leaders of the earlier era. Killing was democratised and internationalised as young religious zealots, recruited not by religious and political leadership but through the Internet, converged on warzones.

It is also important again to consider the underlying ideologies which informed these diffuse forms of killing. Evidently, revenge combined with an underlying demand for "our rights" played a part. At the same time, the suicide bomber gestured at a form of what we could call "reciprocal sacrifice" – "I can kill you because I am prepared to die myself" – and this was different from the socialised ethnic exterminations of the earlier period and reflected the new influence of neo-religion on mass murder. Religion, of course, had often legitimated exclusion and killing, despite its preachers' pious sermons about goodness and morality. But its rationale subtly changed with the fragmented religious passions of the late twentieth and early twenty-first centuries. At the same time, the deep moral misery of contemporary youth, sometimes denied income, but more so marriage, honour and a meaningful life, and put at the mercy of radical, Internet-based ideologues, played a part.

The state's ideologies and practices of killing also subtly changed. Mass bombings in the 1940s were legitimated by notions of uncontrolled warfare between states and "the will of the people". By the 2000s, guilt by association attended targeted killing by drones and other targeted assaults. The reasoning was something like: "If you are close to terrorists, even as a journalist or a guest at a marriage party, you deserve to die." This return to the communal punishments of the colonial period was made possible, once again, by technical advances in weaponry. Antimissile gunships and remotely controlled aircraft have been used in warfare since Hitler's V2 rockets in 1945. A new development were the plans, after 2000, to create robotic "drones" which would target supposed enemies electronically with no intervention by human agents, a move widely held to contravene the aims of the UN's conventions on weapons of mass destruction.

Feelings of despair, not necessarily based on indoctrination by any particular philosophy or religious leadership, but fuelled by rage, notions of difference and populist communication contribute equally to killing in supposedly modern settled societies. This was particularly true in the United States, where the murder rate remained at least three times the average of that in other developed societies and the gun murder rate in 2014 was ten times higher, indicating a kind of internal warfare based on gang identity and interracial contempt. This phenomenon provides a link to the following section on crime.

A Century of Crime and Criminal Killing

The chapter now moves on to the issue of criminal killing and then to the nature of crime itself over the century. Tens of millions were killed in family murders or conflicts between crime cartels. By the end of the century, the scale of criminal homicide itself reached the proportion of small wars in Mexico and Peru as the Latin American–United States drug trade ran riot. By comparison with the human cost of war, the cost of crime during the century was on a smaller scale. A study of the shape of crime does, however, raise important questions about law, accountability, the human mind and the exercise of power. The incidence and development of crime were influenced by several factors which have been fundamental to this study: urbanisation, population mobility, the storing of value, the traffic of empire and the incidence of warfare. The tendency of crime to globalise in the course of the century resulted in international efforts to counter it. The International Criminal Police Commission (1923) was expanded and renamed Interpol by 1956.[32]

The definition of crime itself was, however, highly contested not only by states, victims and perpetrators but also by anthropologists and sociologists. At the beginning of the century, with a relatively small urban population and a rural population still widely dispersed in relatively autonomous settlements, crime was largely defined by custom. Indeed, it is often better to see the cases that came before village elders, landlords or itinerant elite judicial agents as "transgressions" rather than crimes. The concept of crime can be seen to have spread only where the legal governmentality of the state coincided with, and swept into its purview, the range of customary transgressions which had been previously decided by local leaders.[33] There were also sharp conflicts of interpretation throughout the century between these different agencies. For instance, colonial government in Africa and Asia, alongside emerging nationalist legal systems in China and Japan, began to class infanticide as a crime, whereas much customary practice accepted or even endorsed it. The expansion of governmentality appears to have limited the practice by the 1950s, especially in regard to female infanticide and genital mutilation. But new conditions took hold thereafter. In China, the Maoist and post-Maoist "One-Child Policy" encouraged hidden infanticide.[34] Again, the emergence of clinical testing for the sex of unborn children after the 1980s led to a great increase in abortions, especially in India.[35] While custom stressed the need for male children, the state deplored sex-targeted abortion, even when it legalised other forms.

A rather similar situation prevailed in relation to sexual transgression across a wide range of Hindu, Muslim and even Buddhist societies. Tribal elders and local judges often ignored the killing of young people by family members when they were held to have sexually transgressed. Equally, assassinations or assaults in cases of so-called blasphemy often revealed a sharp difference between customary understandings of guilt and those of the expanding state. Towards the end of the century, what I have termed "counter-modernity" in supposedly traditional Muslim societies, in particular, led to the killing of women who had illicit sexual relations or had even taken advantage of local education in the case of Pakistan and Nigeria. At the same time, the roaming of poor unemployed males in growing urban centres also led to the rape and murder of vulnerable females in India and many other countries.

It should not, of course, be assumed that the modern state was a domain of rationality in this respect. Governments in colonial or semi-colonial societies often used violent group punishments to avenge attacks on their own officers. A particularly notorious example of this was the Murderous Outrages Act of 1867 employed by the British Indian government on its Northwest Frontier Province and later extended by the Pakistan government.[36] Government forces and police were legally empowered to avenge crime by mass arrests, executions or aerial bombardment of recalcitrant villages. Similar forms of retribution were used in Iraq and the Sudan. Even in cases of sexual activity, Western and non-Western states continued to make a crime of homosexual acts. Britain did not decriminalise homosexuality until the 1960s. Russia and India recriminalised it in the 2010s following the lead of many African countries. A similar problem arose in the case of legal discussions of prostitution and the trafficking of girls and women throughout the century. As Rachel Leow has shown, colonial authorities in British Malaya and imperial and later nationalist authorities in China refused to intervene in the practice of *mui tsai* by which young girls from parts of southern China were brought down into Malaya as polygamous wives, or often prostitutes. Was this crime or was it a cultural form accepted by custom?[37] Was female genital mutilation a crime? More broadly, how far was the state a moral agent and how far should it curtail individual sexual liberty on the grounds of morality? The problem was made more difficult by the fact that wealthy members of the establishment or, later, vulnerable ethnic communities were often involved in these acts. The debate about whether to criminalise prostitution – and the males who sought out prostitutes – continued throughout the century in several Western countries, even in France, where, since the days of Henri de Toulouse-Lautrec, brothels had been regarded as locations of culture, at least by some.

The drug trade provides a key case study of change over the century. As Carl Trocki has argued, drug trades were a fundamental aspect of empire and economic globalisation: opium, alcohol, tea and coffee built modern trade, and finance and colonial power were used to coerce and punish indigenous states that attempted to halt the death and misery heaped on their own citizens.[38] By the early twentieth century, however, the sale of opium and other drugs was criminalised in most Western countries as a result of humanitarian pressure and the rise of eugenic ideas. Colonial governments such as the British Indian government and the government of the Straits Settlements closed opium farms after 1909. All the same, the drug trade was bound to continue as demand could never be eliminated, and new drugs such as heroin and later chemical agents were seen as essential features of relaxation and pleasure, particularly among young people.

The state criminalised and withdrew from the trade, therefore, but elements of it surreptitiously connived in its continuation. For instance, the CIA supported anti-Communist "drug lords" in Korea and Vietnam and later anti-leftists in South America and Afghanistan. Middle-class professionals, some even associated with government, turned a blind eye to or participated in drug-taking. Equally, local drug-growing communities, whether in Bolivia or Afghanistan, viewed the cultivation of drugs as a natural right, guaranteeing their very survival. A large proportion of murders, theft and assaults across the world in the second half of the century were the result of drug trafficking. Sixty thousand people in Mexico alone were estimated to have been killed in drug wars between 2006 and 2012 and crime increased again in most European countries after the 2008 recession.

The difference between state or interstate notions of criminality and individual or local rights claims is also evident in the case of piracy. The consensus against piracy enshrined in treaties concerning "the law of the sea" was one of the earliest examples of the idea of universal jurisdiction. It evidently arose from the need of Western states and their empires to protect trade routes and commercial profits. But, as Simon Layton showed, from the eighteenth century the notion of piracy was increasingly used against small states which asserted their own sovereignty and rights to tax passing maritime traffic.[39] Areas such as the Strait of Malacca, the South China Sea, the Niger Delta and the environs of Aden were the scenes of sharp conflicts between imperial states that held "piracy" to be a crime and the small kingdoms which tried to impose maritime taxation, especially Wahhabi Arabia and the sultanates of Sumatra. These zones of conflict persisted into the twentieth century, when the takings from acts of piracy or, alternatively, legitimate taxation were swelled by oil revenues. Between 2008 and 2013, Somali pirates exacted £120 million per annum from passing shipping in the form of straightforward theft, hostage-taking and murder. Western governments and shipping firms hired private companies to protect their cargoes and personnel, while Somali gangs claimed that the seas belonged to them. Over the same period, the Russian government, determined to defend its claim to Arctic resources, chose to define Greenpeace environmental activists as pirates when they ventured into waters claimed by the government. The Japanese government likewise condemned antiwhaling activists as pirates when they tried to disrupt whaling ships.

Most commentators would agree that, however difficult the definition of crime and however contested between states, local agents and custom it was, straightforward murder and theft should be treated as crimes. And, to return to the point made at the beginning of this section, the form and location of such crimes changed considerably in the course of the century. The rise of the urban population was a clear factor here. Crime became more centralised in cities and better funded. In fact, it mimicked and was complicit with the evolution of capital, with the proceeds of crime often being invested in legitimate business, making it more difficult for police authorities to track.

At the same time, more archaic practices of ensuring loyalty by fear, patronage and family connection persisted. So, the almost feudal practices of fealty-giving and revenge, typical of the countryside, proved valuable not only in the case of the Mafia and other crime gangs drawn from Sicily and southern Italy but also for the Japanese Yakuza and the Chechen criminals, who rose to fame in post-Communist Russia. The Yakuza groups are a telling example of this nexus between money, group solidarity and capital-pooling.[40] They apparently emerged in the seventeenth or early eighteenth century as an association of peddlers who moved around from one Shinto festival to another and then combined with gambling fraternities in the cities. Once recognised by the Edo state before 1865, they were later regarded as an organised crime syndicate by the Japanese government and police but knew themselves as the Chivalrous Organisations. They spread abroad to Hawaii, the Philippines and Eastern Europe where they were involved in human trafficking for prostitution. Their ambivalent status, between organised criminality and the mimicking of civil society, was displayed when the Yakuza sent food and other aid into the areas devastated by the Tohoku earthquake of 2011.

The international migration of ethnic groups played a key part in the spread of criminality. The obvious example is, of course, the Mafia gang warfare in Chicago in the 1920s, forever associated with Al Capone and other Italian immigrants, and fuelled by America's idiosyncratic lurch towards temperance after 1918. War itself also played a part in the diffusion of criminality. As Allied troops invaded Sicily and southern Italy in 1944, they were sometimes forced to work with anti-state elements and their prosperous local backers, since Mussolini's fascists still had a degree of support across the land.[41] The Mafia and 'Ndrangheta received a new lease of life, having previously been embattled by the fascists in the 1930s. Again, after the fall of South Vietnam in 1974–1975, Thai pirates made a fortune from looting the escaping ships commandeered by members of the regime and ethnic Chinese who feared the revenge of Communist forces. Yet, the movement of criminals, including designated war criminals, was also aided by the relatively lax judicial systems of Latin American countries after 1945 and the rise of international tourism which allowed them to move outside the jurisdiction of local police systems. In response, the creation of Interpol and the European Court of Justice was an attempt to control such movements.

Perhaps the most important development in the latter part of the century in this aspect of society, as in so many others, was the transnational growth of electronic media and communication, especially banking "online". This allowed criminals to access and steal from bank accounts by "hacking" and also to move money electronically from site to site. Police authorities attempted to counter these often massive thefts of identities and value by enhancing surveillance. In time, this aggrandisement of state intelligence on criminal and terrorist acts itself raised questions about the legality of that surveillance: what if the state itself was acting in a criminal way?

Beyond these large-scale and even glamorous forms of crime, often guiltily celebrated in popular books, films and TV dramas, lay the whole quotidian range of murders, thefts and minor crimes which had a long genealogy throughout human history. It is difficult to be sure whether there was an aggregate increase of everyday crime through the century. Certainly, some major social changes made it both more obvious and arguably more prevalent. Policing and the spread of state power even to more distant rural communities and into families certainly increased knowledge of crime and hence heightened the sense of its prevalence. Sexual and physical abuse within families became a target of the moral power of the state and public opprobrium. Equally, the breakdown of joint-family systems and the loosening of sexual constraints, at least in Western societies, may also have given rise to an increase in "crimes of passion". Youth crime appeared to have grown in proportion to the total as parental control weakened and dysfunctional lifestyles were promulgated over the Web and by the media. Major differences between different areas and communities within mega-cities also probably raised the incidence of common theft.

Finally, the psychological and social sciences, combined with the greater visibility of crime statistics, brought about both an expansion and a narrowing of the definition of the criminal as a transgressive agent. The definition was widened so that criminality was no longer simply a matter of legality or a capitulation to evil but a product of sociality itself. The early Italian psychiatrist Cesare Lombroso wrote *L'uomo delinquente* (*The Criminal Man*) in 1876, postulating a hereditary tendency towards criminality. Though long scorned in favour of environmental interpretations of crime, the revival of reductionist genetics late in the twentieth century suggested that Lombroso's theory was by no means dead.[42] More common in the development of criminal psychology and criminal psychiatry were arguments that stressed childhood trauma and upbringing as a cause of criminal behaviour, echoing the main themes of the Freudian, Jungian and Lacanian psychic sciences. Judicial systems across the world took cognisance of these theories.

The plea of insanity was used to mitigate sentences or to distinguish between premeditated criminal acts and those driven by mental instability. The gradual retreat from the notion of evil and retribution also brought about an abandonment of capital punishment. This occurred in Britain and other European countries in the 1960s, and even in the United States, plagued by a very high murder rate by international standards, the number of executions rapidly diminished after 2000. It was perhaps some consolation to observers in the second decade of the twenty-first century, assailed by terrorism and drug-running, that killing whether by the state, by armed groups or even by criminals had probably declined as a percentage of the total population over the previous 50 years.

[15] INTERNATIONALISM AND TRANSNATIONALISM IN THEORY AND PRACTICE

Alternative Internationalisms
Internationalism and Individual Rights after 1945

THE devastating experience of mass killing spurred on the creation of a large number of international organisations purporting to promote cooperation between states and, only later, personal freedom. The earliest major example, the League of Nations itself, was an umbrella for numerous labour, police and developmental organisations, such as the International Labour Organization and the Permanent Court of International Justice. After 1945, the United Nations Organization (UNO) provided a rather more robust and inclusive version of internationalism. These liberal and socialist bodies were paralleled by, and in part a reaction to, the Moscow-based Comintern, which flourished in the same post-First World War context of transnational movement, publicity and ideological conflict.

Alongside the impact of war and the consequent need to establish borders for the new states which emerged from the century's conflicts, two other issues helped give rise to this internationalist sentiment. The first was anticolonialism itself. While the mandate system after the First World War did little but gesture towards freedom from colonial rule, the UNO and contemporary gatherings of new nations after 1945 forced the issue of the termination of colonialism onto the agenda of all states. The second stimulus arose indirectly from the gathering pace of migration and the question of the rights of migrants. The Jewish diaspora across the whole period, the later Palestinian forced migrations, the immigration of people from former colonial or semi-colonial regimes into rich Western countries, the constant flight of the victims of local wars: all these

Remaking the Modern World 1900–2015: Global Connections and Comparisons, First Edition. C. A. Bayly.
© 2018 John Wiley & Sons Ltd. Published 2018 by John Wiley & Sons Ltd.

developments demanded solutions at an international level. Finally, global disease and crime accelerated by these migrations foregrounded the need for international solutions.

Some of the impetus for these internationalist aspirations had developed before the First World War, as statesmen and public figures became alarmed at the menacing single-mindedness of the nation state. The Red Cross, indeed, dated from the wars of the mid-nineteenth century, and, before 1914, branches had been established in Japan and the organisation was mobilised during the Boer War. Pan-Islamism and the fate of the Khilafat brought into being a parallel Red Crescent Society, which worked in India and the Middle East during the Balkan Wars and the First World War. Most liberal and socialist parties had sections devoted to promoting a transnational sensibility, and a variety of civil society bodies of this sort had sprung up well beyond the boundaries of Europe and North America. The Inter-Parliamentary Union (1889–1914) was in many respects a precursor of the League. Equally, the Hague Peace Conferences of 1899 and 1907 were convened to address the issue of growing expenditure on armaments.[1]

While they were not the originators of internationalism and were in many ways "profoundly conservative",[2] President Woodrow Wilson and his right-hand man, Colonel Edward M. House, nevertheless gave a huge fillip to thinking transnationally with their Fourteen Points and world travels after 1918. Early hopes for international cooperation were, however, rapidly dashed by the United States' refusal to join the League, the blatant self-interest of the peace conferences and heightened racial tensions across the globe. International bodies, therefore, tended to remain dominated by European national interests. Glenda Sluga has analysed the "international turn" in detail, showing how national interests pervaded the new international organisations.[3] The League, formally responsible for the mandated territories of the colonies of the former Central Powers in Africa, Asia, the Middle East and the Pacific, became a kind of council of the surviving imperial powers. National liberation movements found it difficult to have their voices heard in its chambers or in its subordinate bodies. Though mandated countries were formally supposed to become independent and join the League when they had reached the appropriate "stage of development", the only one to do so was the Kingdom of Iraq in 1932. Even here, British power remained significant. Japan, which had often argued ambivalently for racial equality at a world level, withdrew from the League in 1933, though this was because Western powers objected to its expansionism in Manchuria. In Europe, too, the shadow of the pre-war period remained. German claims to the whole of Upper Silesia were ignored and the richer mining areas of the region were given to Poland in 1922, to the fury of German public opinion.

More influential, perhaps, in a world worried by Communist internationalism, the International Labour Organization remained dominated by the national, racial and gender attitudes of the pre-war period. The International Labour Charter, drawn up in 1919, specifically stated that "differences of climate, habit and customs, of economic opportunity and industrial traditions make strict uniformity in the conditions of labour difficult of immediate attainment".[4] That is to say, colonised and aboriginal peoples and black people in the United States could not expect to use the rhetoric of "justice and humanity" to improve their own wages and conditions of work to the level of white Europeans and Americans. Similarly, the demands of women's international organisations to make women's rights a subject of international debate were also ignored. Predictably, the Maharaja of Bikaner and the Japanese delegates at the 1919 peace conference supported Woodrow Wilson's view that women's rights should be a prerogative of national self-determination, meaning that the gender prejudices of different societies would remain unassailable.

Blocs of nations with assumed common interests also developed in the interwar years alongside these international bodies. The idea of the British Commonwealth supposedly moved colonial power towards a more representative form. A pan-European Union came into being in 1926 with the aim of preventing conflict and promoting growth in African colonies during the Depression. Yet, this French–German axis viewed Britain and the United States with distrust and harboured designs on future internal colonies in Eastern Europe and the USSR, foreshadowing the policies of the Third Reich. Meanwhile, Italy under Mussolini led the way in ignoring the League's calls for the negotiation of international conflicts. In 1923, Italy seized the Greek island of Corfu and thereafter the powers routinely violated League norms: Japan in Manchuria, Hitler in the Rhineland, Italy again in Abyssinia in 1935. The League's structure made it impossible to establish a consensus about what constituted aggression.[5]

Despite such manifest failures, the League and its subordinate organisations did exercise a powerful demonstration effect. Alternative versions of internationalism found new institutional form: W. E. B. Dubois' Pan-African Congress, convened in Paris in 1919, was one such institution, building on the thought of Edward Blyden.[6] League and International Labour Organization officials circulating across the world from Geneva kept alive a humanitarian discourse directed against war, racism and nationalist aggression. The large numbers of League societies in different countries and non-governmental organisations associated with it maintained surveillance over international telegraph and telephone infrastructure, shipping regulations and control over airspace, for instance. Dubois, the Haitian, Dantès Bellegarde and other public figures of Caribbean, African and Asian origin used League connections to highlight racial injustices across the world in the 1920s and 1930s.

ALTERNATIVE INTERNATIONALISMS

At first sight, the Third Communist International (Comintern), 1919–1943, seems a totally different type of transnational force and it has rarely been studied together with the League or the International Labour Organization. In fact, it had a number of features in common with its more liberal coevals. Devoted formally to the overthrow of capitalism and imperialism and the creation of a worldwide Soviet republic, it quickly became mired in conflicts between

Stalinist and Trotskyite factions in the USSR.[7] By 1924, its dominant element had effectively become a tool of the foreign policy of the USSR, just as a few powerful nations dominated the League and other liberal internationalist bodies. The Comintern gave only inconsistent and partial support to Asian Communist movements in French Indochina, Dutch Indonesia or British South and Southeast Asia. Domestic Soviet struggles caused the Comintern to advocate the Chinese Communists' near-disastrous break with the GMD in 1926. But, equally, ignorance of circumstances outside the West played as much a part in its flawed policies as simple self-interest. Most activists in Moscow were unable to see that Marx's stages of evolution through bourgeois capitalism to Communism could not work in Asia or Africa because the industrial proletariat in these countries was tiny.

The Comintern did, however, give intermittent moral support to radical colonial liberation movements and European and American leftists. Its publications, particularly the *International Press Correspondence* (*Inprecor*, in English and German), were widely disseminated. Along with the *League of Nations Official Journal*, its propaganda helped foster an international mentality. The Comintern's agents were a number of migrant political intellectuals who were sometimes in favour in Moscow but often not, particularly after the fall and flight of Leon Trotsky himself. One example was Henk Sneevliet, a Dutch Communist, who linked up with the Indonesian independence movement when he was resident in the Netherlands East Indies from 1913–1918. He later appeared in Moscow, disastrously urged the Chinese Communists to ally with the GMD and was eventually murdered in a concentration camp in 1942, having organised resistance to the Nazis.[8] M. N. Roy, the Bengali Marxist radical, was a similar migrant figure, who founded the Mexican Communist Party, advised the Comintern on relations with India but eventually found himself in a British jail on the subcontinent.[9] After the Second World War, Roy abandoned Marxism and became a "radical humanist". Again, Tan Malaka, the Indonesian radical mentioned in Chapter 7, tried to adapt rigid Marxist–Leninist principles to the situation in his homeland where an Islamised peasantry was the dominant force in opposition to colonialism. Malaka shifted between the Netherlands, Moscow, South China and Indonesia, where he was eventually killed during the revolt of 1946–1948.[10] Finally, Nguyen Ai Quoc, or Ho Chi Minh, was probably the most important of all the leftist intellectual cosmopolitans associated with the Comintern. He moved through London, Paris, Moscow and South China. He only came to rest in his native Vietnam to lead the revolution there in 1945, when he was 55 years of age.[11]

For many of these itinerant leftist intellectuals, the experience of prisons distant from their homelands proved to be another formative personal experience. It brought them face to face with the oppression of the authoritarian state, while encouraging some of them to reformulate their theories of revolution. In the European context, Antonio Gramsci's reflections in Mussolini's prisons became an iconic text for later Marxists globally. So too did Tan Malaka's *Prison Diaries* become a classic statement on an Indonesian form of revolution, as did Ho Chi Minh's similar writings on his imprisonment in British Hong Kong, where he narrowly avoided extradition and probable execution by the French. Nor were these experiences exclusive to the radical left. So, for instance, V. D. Savarkar's *Hindutva: Who is a Hindu?*, written in a British jail in the Andaman Islands, became the founding text for right-wing Hindu nationalism both inside and outside India. Probably the most telling result of imprisonment, however, was the way in which it enhanced the celebrity status of the intellectuals in question and spread word of their struggles well beyond their homelands through the hints and gossip of indigenous warders, doctors and the like. Prisons were always friable, as Peter Zinoman argued.[12]

Ho Chi Minh and Mao Zedong had much in common intellectually with these Comintern migrant intellectuals in that they also tried to inject a sense of the contingent and the local into Marxist–Leninism. But Mao was no traveller, while Ho worked in Paris and London and journeyed to Moscow and China, before seizing the leadership of the Viet Minh at a critical stage of the anticolonial struggle in 1945. The success or failure of all these radicals depended as much on the particular conditions in their homelands at the end of the Second World War as it did on the strength of their international support base and transnational ideologies. Chin Peng, the Malaysian Communist, was in a strong position amongst the Malayan Chinese guerrillas who had fought the Japanese between 1942 and 1945. He found little support among the Malay Muslim community, however, and was also persuaded to stand down his secret forces in the face of the returning British and Indian troops.[13]

Finally, this form of "localising internationalism" could be extended to religious internationalism which in some cases interacted both with their liberal imperialist and socialist coevals. Fear of further wars gave rise to movements such as Moral Re-Armament, which attempted to bind people across and beyond Christian societies.[14] American missionaries established large networks of Christian associations across Asia and Africa by 1930. Opus Dei and Catholic revivalist organisations attempted to bring the faithful together across the bounds of the nation state. The abolition of the Khilafat was a serious blow to the Muslim *umma* but populist and internationally minded organisation such as the Muslim Brotherhood or Tablighi Jamaat rapidly filled the void. As with the Geneva-based organisations, all these associations attempted to offer education and aid during the Great Depression and the local wars of the 1930s. Like them, too, they thrived on the expansion of print, publicity and international travel.

INTERNATIONALISM AND INDIVIDUAL RIGHTS AFTER 1945

The years from 1945 to 1955 are rightly regarded as the high point of international aspiration for the whole century. In spite of the intransigence of old white colonial interests, represented above all by Jan Smuts and the French and Dutch leaders who tried to cling to their colonies, it was the multiracial and inclusive form of international organisation which appeared to have won out in the UN Charter and the founding principles of UNESCO.[15]

An important aspect of the movement, by comparison with the League, was its emphasis on individual as well as state rights. The Charter of 1945 reaffirmed "faith in fundamental human rights . . . in the equal rights of men and women and of nations large and small".[16] True, some of the exclusions, which undermined the League's drive for equality, persisted into the 1950s. White Europeans and Americans continued to dominate the Security Council and UNESCO. Educational projects in East Africa and Haiti secured only limited results and were mired in waste and corruption. But, on the other side, figures such as the African-American activist Ralph Bunche, and representatives of newly independent India, including Nehru's sister, Vijaya Lakshmi Pandit, were able to push forward their anticolonial and antiracist agenda more effectively. This reached its climax in the Universal Declaration of Human Rights of 1948. The disapproval of the new "world community" played some role in hastening the end of colonial rule in Africa, though four decades of pressure on South Africa failed to end apartheid, which, ironically, was consolidated after the National Party's election triumph in the year 1948 itself. As in the 1920s and 1930s, the push for inclusive international cooperation was matched by transnational, but more localised, movements to realise rights. The Bandung Pact of 1955 was intended to bring together the neutral postcolonial societies of Africa and Asia. In 1963, the Organisation of African Unity was founded to eliminate colonialism and promote development, though it quickly became polarised between different visions of this unity. The year 1967 saw the foundation of the Association of Southeast Asian Nations. Meanwhile, the fragments of British and French colonial power became, respectively, "the Commonwealth" and Francophonie.

Thereafter, the optimism of the United Nations' early years faded, as had the promise of the League before it.[17] If the abandonment of the League by the fascist powers and Japan in the 1930s had crippled the League, the onset of the Cold War did much the same to the UN and its agencies. The USSR was suspicious of UNESCO from its inception and only joined the organisation in 1953 after Stalin's death. Yet, at the same time, the United States was infected with fear of Communism and harangued by McCarthy. There was a damaging "purge" of UNESCO by President Truman when the loyalty of US citizens working for the organisation was called into question. During the 1970s and 1980s, the auguries for international action were mixed. The UN recognised the activities of the non-governmental organisations for education, health development and equity. But as more former colonial states joined the organisation and made their voices heard in New York, Western countries began to distance themselves from it, especially during the years of conservative government associated with Reagan and Thatcher. In a sense, the "summit" or face-to-face meetings between Western and Communist leaders, as in Vienna in 1961 or Geneva in 1985, represented the residue of the aspiration to international accord which had suffused the UN.[18]

The collapse of Communist internationalism after 1989, the unification of Germany and the development of the European Union seemed to presage a new era towards the end of the century. Novel, regional forms of transnationalism in the Americas, Europe and Southeast Asia were still expected to develop lower-level transnational ties. The end of the Cold War was expected to free the UN's ability to deal with local conflicts across the world, which it did to some extent.[19] Yet, new shifts in international politics once again frustrated many of these hopes. First, Western powers, and the United States, Britain and France in particular, began to voice the notion of "humanitarian intervention" and the "war on terror" which sidestepped, bypassed or rendered redundant the activities of the UN Security Council in the Middle East conflicts after 1992. Secondly, the Council was hamstrung in several cases, notably in regard to conflict in Syria in 2012 or tensions in the South China Sea, by the resurgence of Russia and China, which vetoed UN involvement in a manner which recalled the problems of the League or the standoff during the Cold War. Equally, the United States' obdurate support of Israel's conservative government made it more difficult for negotiations between Israel and Palestinian groups.

An important ideological change also accompanied the small wars of fragmentation after 1980. Insurgent radical groups, now more often Islamist than leftist, refused to accept either the legitimacy of nation states or any universal notion of human rights. Again, the UN and UNESCO seemed to lose some of their importance as rapid economic development in the 1990s and 2000s began to reduce income differentials between the West and the developing world. In sub-Saharan Africa, UN educational and poverty-eradication programmes continued with moderate success, but it was the demand for oil and raw materials, especially from China, which began to lift populations out of poverty.

In the first decades of the twenty-first century, in fact, internationalism seemed to have taken a new form in which formal world-level organisations were less important. If the UN was paralysed by the stance of China and Russia and failed to act decisively in any of the conflicts or global epidemics which emerged after 9/11, the IMF and the World Bank continued to play a role in the alleviation of poverty in developing economies. Yet, they could do little but watch and advise as the world economic crisis unfolded after 2008. The World Health Organization was similarly impeded in its response to the Ebola epidemic of 2014–2015 in West Africa by differences within the world community. Meanwhile, the rapid regional movement of populations within the EU, the Organization of American States and Southeast Asia, were at one and the same time forming broader social relations and arousing resentment and nationalistic reactions. The diffusion of Indian populations to the United States was beginning to feed back into the development of technical industries in Bangalore. Christian churches and Islamic organisations were building new transnational links. Western universities were becoming global, establishing new campuses in Asia, Africa and Latin America. Satellite television and the Web had brought populations into contact and frustrated attempts to preserve the indigenous, whether languages, styles of dress or the deportment of the young. In a sense, globalisation had superseded internationalism, both as a promise and a threat to national governments and ethnic groups.

[16] THE SHADOW OF EMPIRE IN THE MODERN WORLD

> Empire, the European World and the Redefinition of Race
> The Residual Colonialism of Language
> Political Representation and the Consolidation of Religious
>   and Ethnic Difference
> Colonialism's Shadow in Economics and Social Control
> Economics and Empire

THIS chapter considers the inheritance of late-colonial rule for postcolonial societies across the world, a theme which has appeared in several earlier chapters but needs to be treated more coherently.[1] By far the most extensive and complete investigation of this topic has been carried out by economic historians, who discussed the "development of under-development" in the context of world-systems theory.[2] They argued that the drain of wealth from colonial societies to service domestic expenditure and debt, along with the frustration of early industrialisation by colonial laissez-faire ideologies and the over-taxation of the peasantry, contributed to the profound inequalities of wealth and opportunities in most parts of the non-Western world. These global distortions were only beginning to be lessened by the beginning of the twenty-first century.[3] Conversely, some historians have insisted that colonial empires did, in part at least, bring economic advantages by expanding world trade and providing a relatively strong state favourable to commerce and scientific knowledge.[4] A related theme which became more prevalent during the "globalisation turn" of the 1990s was the migration of Asians and Africans across the world as a consequence of imperial commerce. Parsis from western India

Remaking the Modern World 1900–2015: Global Connections and Comparisons, First Edition. C. A. Bayly.
© 2018 John Wiley & Sons Ltd. Published 2018 by John Wiley & Sons Ltd.

established themselves in Aden; Gujaratis, in East Africa and Europe; South Indians, in Malaya and Fiji; Chinese, in Malaya and also Indonesia.[5]

This chapter, however, is particularly concerned with the moral, social and political, rather than the purely economic, consequences of European empire for the extra-European world. The notion of empire is interpreted broadly here to include some areas of "informal empire", such as China, and also areas of older European settlement, North America, Australasia and Latin America, where European societies were still expanding into new lands during the nineteenth and early twentieth centuries, creating deep cultural as well as economic hierarchies. Non-European peoples, of course, also had highly developed notions of relative human virtue, whether reflected in the Indian caste system or the East Asian sense of higher and lower civilisations. These interacted with appropriations or impositions from Europe in complex ways to reinforce class, ethnic and religious subordination. Yet, colonial concepts of race, the dissemination of languages and understandings of religion proved particularly powerful consequences of the European empires long after they had largely dissolved in the 1960s. The chapter returns, in conclusion, to the issue of the economic and social consequences of empire, having examined these cultural themes.

EMPIRE, THE EUROPEAN WORLD AND THE REDEFINITION OF RACE

It is appropriate to start with the issue of the legacy of empire for racial attitudes. Empire spread white populations across the globe, heightening the ideologies of racial supremacy that were necessary to sustain the legitimacy of those empires. Equally, the end of empire, far from diminishing racial ideologies in world politics, served instead to reinvigorate them, as immigrants from former colonies or semi-colonies migrated to Western Europe and North America and Australasia when Western economies were booming after 1945. Though marginalised by many historians of empire and its aftermath, racialism was a critical aspect of both these phases.

Very broadly, we could distinguish three broad types of racial ideology which evolved through the nineteenth into the twenty-first centuries. First, there was the civilisational racial thought of the Enlightenment and early-nineteenth-century empire, which posited the superiority of the Hellenic or Aryan world and often focussed on language and religion as its definitional markers. Secondly, towards the end of the nineteenth century, this loose assemblage of ideologies was permeated by social Darwinism and so-called scientific racism, which used inherited bodily and supposed mental characteristics as its markers. During the early twentieth century, the idea of racial hierarchy coexisted with this pseudo-scientific thought, buttressing the power of fading colonial empires, but also empowering the continued dominance of European-descended populations over former slave or so-called tribal peoples in the Americas, Australasia and South Africa. Finally, after the age of decolonisation and global diaspora, there emerged in the West what could be called democratic racism, an emphasis on the right of "our people to inhabit our territory". Practices of exclusion in the West reinforced in turn the resentment of the non-Western world. These different forms of racialism, of course, intermingled and coexisted. They were linked through time. But they remained determined by context, as Francisco Bethencourt argued, and were never innate features of humanity.[6]

In themselves racial attitudes were not, of course, simply a product of territorial empire. They were already present in the so-called Age of Discovery, often tied to notions of religious supremacy.[7] They were evident in William Shakespeare's works and the southern European writers who belittled the "Moors", a discourse which was later transferred to the Americas. Atlantic slavery promoted a particularly malignant form of racism. Yet, what Nicholas Dirks called the colonial ethnographic state of the nineteenth century certainly deepened and universalised racial and ethnic discrimination, even if it did not originate it.[8] Colonial censuses, legal and prison systems categorised racial types and subordinated them to the dominant white population. Sexual fear and sexual desire also consolidated racial difference and indirectly repatriated it to Europe.[9] This often reached its peak towards the end of colonial rule, not at its beginning. Tellingly, it was also often particularly prevalent in societies which were the most liberal in relation to their own white populations.

The model and precursor here was the United States itself, where political freedom from British rule and the development of a mass democracy in the nineteenth century coexisted with severe racial subordination of black Americans, notably in the Southern states.[10] The ending of slavery after the Civil War allowed blacks to move more freely, and, after 1900, they migrated for work in numbers to Northern cities. The result was an early democratisation of racism leading to a spate of lynching in the South in the 1920s and 1930s and attacks on black people in Northern cities. As in Australia and New Zealand, racial discrimination here persisted into the twenty-first century. In South Africa, outright discrimination by the state was only formally lifted in 1994. And in these cases, white civil and democratic societies were as active as authoritarian states in perpetuating racial exclusion.

So, for instance, the condescension of the Australian colonies towards their Aboriginal peoples after 1880 led to the disenfranchisement of the few who had received the vote before that date.[11] Yet, Australia had been one of the first countries in the world to concede votes to women and establish an adult franchise. A figure such as H. B. Higgins, who opposed colonial wars and argued for Australian autonomy from Britain, was vehement in his denunciation of Chinese and Indian immigration, stating that "the inferior races drive out the superior".[12] Aboriginal children and children of mixed race were removed from their parents by government action. Even up to the 1970s, the Australian government did its best to exclude Chinese and Indian migrants. Immigration remained a toxic issue in Australian politics, as the 2013 election and intervention by the United Nations demonstrated.

Similarly, in South Africa it was the rise of white supremacists and "scientific racism" after 1900[13] and the victory of the National Party in 1948 which initiated intensified racial discrimination, with black people being shipped out of city suburbs to so-called Bantustans.[14] Here again, a mass electorate for whites had been established very early, largely as a bulwark against black representation. What ensued was a virtual race war in South Africa with black populations fighting back against discrimination and land seizures by whites. The issue continues to envenom relations not only in South Africa but also in other African colonial territories, such as Zimbabwe and Kenya, the latter still scarred by memories of the violent British campaign against Kikuyu rebels during the Mau Mau insurgency of the 1950s. The massacres of Algerians both during the independence war and in Paris in 1961 paralleled these events in the former French Empire. In all these cases, white settler racialism empowered local governments.

This high point of colonial racism, the results of which were still in evidence in 2015, was not simply a consequence of the land wars of late imperialism, however. It was also informed by the sense of difference generated by the racialist ideologies of the nineteenth and early twentieth centuries, the legacy of Joseph Arthur, Comte de Gobineau, of social Darwinism, scientific eugenics and the white supremacist ideologies of the Southern states of America. A key text here was Madison Grant's, *The Passing of the Great Race*,[15] which bemoaned the decline of the dominant "Nordic race" in the United States and across the world. Hitler referred to this book as "my bible". But it is important to remember that it was not only the right, buoyed by fascism, which promoted European racial eugenics. Self-styled socialists espoused eugenic intervention and even the liberal economist John Maynard Keynes was a member of the British Eugenics Society. Attempts to promote interracial understanding such as the Universal Races Congress of 1911 continued to relegate non-whites to the "waiting room of history".[16]

Nor was racial thinking confined to white Europeans and Americans. These ideas filtered into conceptions of the Indian caste system, as the untouchable leader B. R. Ambedkar vigorously argued. The historian Gyanendra Pandey has examined the connection between American black liberation movements and the Indian revolt against caste.[17] The Chinese, Vietnamese and Japanese also honed their own conception of civilisational difference in dialogue with European racial ideology. Africans, in particular, were often assigned to a lower status, which they still occupy in the popular mind in these countries. In twenty-first-century Thailand, for instance, Buddhist monks and politicians discriminated against Muslim Rohingyas, not simply because they were of a different religion but because they were considered racially inferior.

The appearance of black people, Indians and Chinese as colonial soldiers and labourers in Europe during the world wars began to generalise and democratise racism within Europe. Black French troops occupying the German Rhineland after 1919 were subjected to abuse and racist posters.[18] Mass immigration to European societies after the 1940s reignited racial fears and racial discrimination, which took the form of Islamophobia after 9/11. There were race riots in Britain as early as 1948 brought on by Caribbean immigration and these became violent during the recession years of the early 1980s. Since then, black communities in city suburbs in Britain, France and even Sweden have fought back against discrimination.

The ideological base of racial antagonism had, however, shifted. During the late colonial period, ideologies of racial supremacy were deployed against nationalist movements and in order to control the labour of colonised people. It was a hierarchical form. Later, the struggle was between parochial notions of rights, equity and entitlement, on the one hand, and transnational under-standings of the same entitlements, on the other: a lateral or democratic form of discrimination. Right-wing parties across the European world complained that immigrants were "taking our jobs" and the left often took up this call. But this was not confined to Europe. East African regimes moved against Indian immigrants after independence. In West Africa during the 1960s, residual French anti-Lebanese racism merged with fears among Africans about Leba-nese commercial "interlopers".[19] Later, European politicians baulked at using national resources to fund foreign aid. Yet, the dying hierarchical racism of empire sometimes merged with and empowered this exclusivist racialism of equity. In 2013, a British politician from a right-wing party, UKIP, attacked foreign aid on the grounds that money should go to England, not to "Bongo-Bongo Land". This was a racist jibe at African countries, coined at the height of imperialism. Debates on what was called "liberal interventionism", both for and against, were tinctured with elements from the old racial ideologies of empire.

In societies such as the United States and Latin America, countries where racial attitudes were formed and deployed internally rather than externally through empire, the workings of democracy brought benefits. The Civil Rights Movement in the United States during the 1960s and 1970s and expanded education created a stratum of successful non-white people who increasingly achieved status and office, culminating in Barack Obama's electoral victory in 2008. Yet, black people remained disproportionately represented among both the poor and the prison population. Public discourse was largely purged of racist language and institutional racism had diminished, but the long shadow of slavery still hung over the United States in 2014 with public agonising over riots caused by the police shooting of a black teenager in Missouri.[20] In the former colonial territories and the former colonial metropolitan societies, the rise of Asian and African states after 1990 went some way to reduce racial attitudes and racial suspicion among former subject peoples. But racialism merged with forms of political and religious chauvinism both in the West and outside.

THE RESIDUAL COLONIALISM OF LANGUAGE

A second critical feature of the cultural legacy of empire and European conquest for the globalised world of the twenty-first century lay in the area of language and communication. Of course, the earlier multi-ethnic empires broadened communication across their territories by spreading the use of Mandarin Chinese, Ottoman Turkish, Persian and Urdu, for instance.[21] But Western colonial empires created globalised languages on a much larger scale and these in turn influenced the earlier language forms and their social status. Spanish, English and French, and to a lesser extent Portuguese and

Dutch, were exported and imposed on whole new territories. About 700 million people worldwide spoke English in some form in 2010, while there were around 400 million Spanish and 200 million French speakers. These imperial languages hastened communication in commerce, legal forms and in scientific and technical knowledge. Yet, they also served to deepen class, "tribal" and caste divisions across the world and have remained a source of conflict about entitlement, identity and cultural authenticity. Gandhi, a polished English speaker, wrote as early as 1909, "To give millions a knowledge of English is to enslave them."[22] Postcolonial writers, notably Homi Bhabha, have adapted Derrida's ideas to postulate that the "epistemic violence" supposedly wrought by the imposition of these languages created "fragmented subjectivity" and "morally disempowered" subject peoples.[23] That is now probably too negative an assumption, as the imposition and appropriation of these languages also empowered subject peoples, who came to occupy knowledge-hubs such as Silicon Valley, Bangalore, Singapore and Hong Kong. But the imposition of colonial languages and conflict with indigenous languages certainly persisted throughout the century.

The English and French languages in the colonial and postcolonial worlds remain key examples. Clearly, in areas such as what became the United States, Canada, Australia, New Zealand and the Caribbean, the near total extirpation of indigenous peoples reduced their languages to philological antiquities in the face of English.[24] This was a development with a long history. Perhaps the earliest forms of English linguistic expansion were in the pre-modern colonies of Gaelic Scotland and Ireland, where Celtic languages were slowly marginalised. By 2011, for instance, only one parish in the ancient heartland of Scots Gaelic, the island of Skye, was predominantly Gaelic-speaking. These indigenous languages have often only been revived as democratic politics has allowed local leaders to build constituencies by calling on marginal and minority groups to assert language rights. After 1922, Eire attempted to revive the Irish language, with limited success. The same was true of the Welsh government's language revival campaigns after 1945.

Again, as New Zealand forces drew increasingly on the supposed "martial" characteristics of the Maori people in the two world wars, Vietnam and even Afghanistan, Maori language and supposed local forms of self-government have been allowed to flourish as a kind of payoff.[25] By 2000, some white New Zealanders called themselves by the Maori word *pakeha*; others deplore the use of the word. Ironically, this word *pakeha* apparently first appeared in a letter of 1831 written by North Island Maori to the British king asking for protection from the "French strangers". After 2010, parties based on Maori and Pakeha identities entered New Zealand politics. Less populous and more harshly victimised peoples, such as the Australian Aboriginal peoples and American or Canadian Indians, were only able to assert their language and cultural rights as the global communication of the concept of native peoples and Left angst over their fate infected world media.

The role of imperial languages in larger world societies was subject to constant interrogation before and after decolonisation. In India, English began to spread from the end of the eighteenth century as a language of trade, government and law. In Bengal, merchant intermediaries with the British were called *dubashe*s – literally, people of two languages, *do bhasha*. But it was T. B. Macaulay, Law Member of the Governor-General's council, who in 1835 penned a minute on the language of education in India which ignited controversies which long continued. Even though nationalists and postcolonial scholars have asserted otherwise, Macaulay neither wished uniformly to impose English nor completely marginalise Arabic, Persian and Sanskrit.[26] In fact, he seems to have thought that a class of Indians "English in taste and manners" would seed indigenous languages or "dialects" as he called them with modern knowledge. But Macaulay's rhetoric against Hindu culture and assertion that "a shelf of English books" was worth more than the whole of Oriental literature continued to enrage Indians.

In the later stage of Nehru's government in the 1960s, right-wing Hindu parties annexed an anti-English message to their policies. Riots occurred. I vividly remember the denunciations of English as a colonial import and attacks on merchants in the city of Allahabad on the River Ganges at this time. On one occasion, a shopkeeper, his English signs destroyed by a mob, asked what the time was of one of the leaders of the protest. When shown the time, the shopkeeper smashed the agitator's expensive watch with a hammer, shouting, "These numbers are in English as well, aren't they!" In 2013, the Taliban leader who wrote – in English – to the Pakistani schoolgirl Malala Yousafzai, whom they had attempted to murder because of her support for women's education, damned Macaulay by name. He added, "Why do they want to make all human beings English? Because Englishmen are the staunch supporters and slaves of the Jews!"[27] Religious hatred, misogyny and linguistic contempt merged here.

English survived and flourished, of course, in part because of its propagation among India elites through Roman Catholic schools and more recently worldwide computer companies. It remained an essential "link language" because, among other reasons, Hindi, though now the national language, was not acceptable in large parts of southern India which belonged to non-Sanskritic language groups. Meanwhile, at a quieter level, some of the grammatical forms of English percolated into Indian regional languages and into Hindi simply as a result of the growth of communication.[28] The return of a more resolutely Hindu populist government to power in 2014 gave new impetus to the project of promoting Hindi. Delhi elites, however, continued to disdain "HMTs" ("Hindi-Medium Types").

Meanwhile, in other British Asian colonies, English had a quieter life. Singapore and to a lesser extent Malaysia were the scene in recent years of controversies not about the use of English itself, as in India, but about the need to impose standard English on what had come to be called "Singlish", Singapore-English patois.[29] The authoritative former prime minister, Lee Kuan Yew, took on the role of proponent of English, demonstrating that liberal imperialism still had its uses. English, he argued, was a common language between Chinese, Malays, Indians and resident Euro-Americans, an essential tool of national integration. Meanwhile, in Hong Kong, local people resisted the Chinese central government's attempts to impose

Figure 18 A march past performed by Bukit Panjang Government School pupils during the coronation of Queen Elizabeth II, 1953. National Archives of Singapore.

Mandarin, not only because they spoke a local Chinese language but also as an assertion of political autonomy.

In Southeast Asia, French had less staying power. Many of the leaders of the Viet Minh were fluent French speakers and some of the oldest generation remained so.[30] But, as Vietnam sought the support of the USSR, political leaders moved away from the French inheritance and began to promote the use of Russian as their international language, especially in view of the large number of specialists who were travelling to the USSR and Eastern Europe. Later again, English made its reappearance in schools and colleges, not because of the United States, let alone Britain, but because of the importance of Singapore and Malaysian English speakers in the regional economy. French survived strongly, however, in West Africa and elsewhere as a link between local languages and ethnic communities.[31] In Algeria, the independent government after 1962 first attempted to discourage the use of French, which had been the official language of the colony, and replace it with Arabic and Berber. Teachers were brought in from Egypt and Syria. But the value of French as a language of commerce, media and international communication meant that it could never be banished. The expansion of satellite television in the 1990s gave it a new thrust, and by 2013, 33% of the Algerian population spoke French, while in the street, a mixture of French and Arabic was spoken. This media-informed type of Franco-Arabic was different from the older mixture of French, Hebrew, Maltese and Arabic spoken by the French *colons*, as studied by Joëlle Bahloul.[32]

There is no doubt that the imposition of imperial languages from the time of the Spanish and Portuguese New World in the sixteenth century onward has indeed tended to fragment consciousness and erect barriers of class and sensibility within colonised nations, as postcolonial writers argue. Many public intellectuals assert that the use of these former colonial languages has disempowered indigenous languages and perpetuated lateral social divisions. So, Sri Lankan Tamils denounced English as *kaduwa* – "the sword" – severing them from Sinhalese.[33] In India, radicals denounced the role of *kala angrez*, the "black English" elites, a cry that was heard in 2013 at celebrations for the centenary of the foundation of the Ghadar revolutionary movement. Yet, it is not clear either that the existence of a single indigenous national language, whether it is Japanese, or English in Britain, in any way averted the development of social hierarchies. Indeed, indigenous languages whether Hindi, Urdu, Javanese, Indonesian or Kikuyu were all remodelled in structure and grammar under colonial rule and their "proper use" continued to empower elites as against rural or local people.[34] An example was the way in which European empires in Africa extended the use of Swahili to large areas of the continent, such as the Congo, where numerous local languages existed. Swahili, like the European languages on a lesser scale, acted as a powerful resource and badge of privilege for elites mediating between the colonial power or later agents of the world economy and the locals.[35] Much the same can be said of Chinese, which became a new world language after 2000 as Australian schools, in particular, began to teach it.

POLITICAL REPRESENTATION AND THE CONSOLIDATION OF RELIGIOUS AND ETHNIC DIFFERENCE

Perhaps an equally potent legacy of colonialism in the modern, globalised world lies in the area of religious and ethnic identity. Chapter 13 is concerned with the fate of religions throughout the century generally. Here the colonial context is briefly examined again, as a precursor to a discussion of ethnic differentiation in the social and political realm. Not only did Western European empires and settler societies export and impose Christianity on other cultures but also non-Christian religions became more coherent in doctrine and practice as a result of these encounters. Common features included the strengthening of formal religious leadership by the colonial powers, for example the Sharia Council in British Palestine in the 1930s, the creation of Anglo-Muhammadan law or the formalisation of Anglo-Hindu law in South and Southeast Asia over the nineteenth and twentieth centuries in the British and Dutch realms. Consequently, more formal and written versions of spiritual texts and traditions were sought by the colonial powers for legal and political reasons. This tended to create in turn forms of "scripture" and also formal teaching institutions for Hinduism, Buddhism and Shinto which paralleled the Bible, the Quran and the various Muslim and Christian academies.

The drive of the colonial powers and their ambivalent missionary allies for information and consistency was empowered by the desire of indigenous religious teachers themselves to establish their authority and, later, civil society organisations claiming in the name of religion to speak for Buddhism, Hinduism or Islam against those very colonial authorities. In fact, much of the religious landscape of the former colonial world of the late twentieth century was formed by organisations resisting colonial power on the basis of faith because formal political mobilisation was widely suppressed. In South Africa, for instance, independent black Christian churches emerged in the 1920s, challenging the pre-eminence of white and particularly Afrikaner clerics in religious institutions. These churches played an important role in the later movement against apartheid in the 1960s and 1970s.[36] Again, in French North Africa, the bias of the local colonial governments towards Catholic organisations catering to the settler population created a fierce backlash from Tunisian and Algerian Muslims as early as the 1920s.[37] Alongside secular and leftist organisations, movements founded during these years played a large part in the anticolonial war of the 1950s and 1960s, though, in turn, these secular and religious leaderships came into conflict with each other in the 1980s and after.

If, therefore, the impact of colonialism resulted in a broadening, theorising and popularising of Christianity and Islam and in the making of other "world religions", in Weber's sense, it also fomented conflicts between them and promoted what might be called religious intransigence.[38] I am referring to the proliferation, particularly after the 1920s, of radical movements within several traditions: the RSS and various Hindutva organisations within Hinduism and Salafi revivalist groups, such as the Muslim Brotherhood and others powered by Saudi money.[39] In turn, vigorous Protestant evangelical churches, which recorded great success in the former East and West African colonies, stirred conflict with Catholic and Muslim organisations. There was, of course, no simple teleology directly linking radical late-twentieth-century religious movements to colonialism. The fall of Communism in the 1980s and the general development of religious organisations after independence, along with the role of youth unemployment and unrest, should all be taken into account. Yet, the imprint of colonial government and later the neo-colonialism of "humanitarian intervention" by the United States and its allies remind us that there were longer-term causative factors at work here.

The chapter now moves on to politics and the economy, areas in which the continued impact of colonial rule for the globalised world of 2015 remained equally clear. Here, the dimensions mentioned earlier – racial attitudes, communication and religion – were all intertwined with politics through colonial policies of representation. There is still a widespread belief among European nationalist historians and the general public, especially in Britain and Holland, that empires brought the benefits of political representation, and even democracy, to non-European peoples. The British and Dutch did, indeed, establish limited forms of local representation, as had the Portuguese before them. The French tended, by contrast, to create small electorates which could select indigenous representatives, properly Gallicised, to the French Assembly. These electorates survived, particularly in West Africa. Yet, the real break-through to democracy came when anticolonial resistance movements opted for mass electorates.

A particularly potent and long-standing consequence of colonial political ideologies for the contemporary world within these electoral systems was, however, the practice of ethnic categorisation which brought together lan-guage, religion and class as political units, in turn encouraging local leaders to mobilise along these lines. This phenomenon occurred not only in formal colonial territories in Asia and Africa but also in the informal realms of European (and American) domination, such as the Middle East, Central America, the Caribbean and the Pacific. In the Middle East, Ottoman forms of government had acknowledged religious difference, but as European influence expanded after 1914, ethnic categorisation of populations in regard to law and access to authority became yet more widespread. In Egypt, Syrian, Coptic and Mediterranean Christians and Jews could have their cases tried in different courts from the ordinary Muslim citizen. In the mandate system, such categories became the basis of politics. A particularly resonant example of this was the 1930 constitution of Syria–Lebanon, following various risings of Sunni populations against French rule and compromises forged with Druze, Alawites and other Shias. In Iraq, meanwhile, the British gave special privileges to the minority Sunni and Kurdish populations to buy their support in control of the Shia majority. Much of the political instability as late as the 2000s arose from attempts by these privileged minorities to protect their power from increasingly radicalised majority populations.

In South and Southeast Asia, colonial concessions and favours to elite minority groups similarly impacted on local politics throughout the century. The British gave Muslims and, in southern India, non-Brahmins a role in various quasi-representative systems from the 1880s onwards. Although some Congress Muslims supported its decision to retreat from special electorates in the interwar period, the Pakistan project of Muhammad Ali Jinnah and his successors was a direct consequence of this religious and ethnic categorisation. One does not need to regard Indian or Indonesian or Malay leaders as simple dupes of colonial government to recognise that the existence of such legal and political categories provided an easier route for political self-expression for leaders of minority groups than long-term engagement with majorities would have entailed.

One final element which brings together colonial political economy, ideology and social change was the development of civil society organisations, meaning a form of association-making, which, in Jürgen Habermas's sense, lay between state and society, but interrogated both. The public creation of associations was a relatively late development in Europe itself, associated with representative bodies, the coffee house and heterodox religious associations such as the Quakers. In the colonised world forms of association and debate which predated colonialism had also developed: discussions outside mosques and temples, poetic and political meetings or *mushairas*, even the literary meetings in the houses of courtesans.[40]

High colonial rule, however, greatly expanded the range of public associations in two distinct ways. First, associations developed on the fringes of the very limited representative institutions through which the authorities had tried to reduce the costs of direct government. So, for instance, rate payers' associations and "people's associations" began to develop in colonial societies. Alongside this, the type of ethnic and religious categorisation described earlier also had the effect of bringing people together to protect their beliefs or sectional interests. The Muslim Brotherhood in Egypt and the Hindu Mahasabha in India represent examples of this sort of activity, as did the Kikuyu Central Association in Kenya. Colonial pressure may have caused their formation, but thereafter, indigenous agency and local connections of marriage, education and military service, for instance, maintained and strengthened them. Associations of this sort penetrated society, particularly expanding urban societies, creating new relationships between belief, family, work and subsistence. Ultimately, too, political ambition, government oppression and new forms of communication brought representatives of these associations together in much broader groupings, which asserted that they represented the whole nation. The Indian National Congress, the Wafd in Egypt and the African National Congress are all examples of this form of amalgamation. All of them exerted powerful influence on postcolonial politics in their respective societies. Critically, they spread radical and anticolonial knowledge across the world, while at the same time appropriating many of the knowledge practices of the colonialists themselves. Even though the Indian National Congress instituted non-English-language subdivisions in 1916, it continued to operate in English to a large extent up to the present day.

COLONIALISM'S SHADOW IN ECONOMICS AND SOCIAL CONTROL

Finally, this chapter considers the policies of some of the immediate post-independence governments and the manner in which they sometimes inherited, but often radically reinterpreted, colonial ideologies and practices. When theorists speak of the postcolonial, they often apply little sense of time to it. Arguably, the postcolonial era lasted from about 1950 to the 1990s. Thereafter, the long-term effects of colonial rule were still apparent, especially in the areas already discussed, such as ideologies of race, religion, as also in economic differentials. But world societies had developed in new directions and moved beyond the postcolonial, except perhaps in its use as an academic tool.

First, it is striking how the experience of empire had changed understandings of the person, the family and community with consequences which were only beginning to play themselves out in the twenty-first century. For India, the historian Brian Hatcher coined the term "bourgeois Hinduism" for a this-worldly form of being, which stressed social activism and developed in the early nineteenth century, partly under the influence of Christian missionary activity.[41] Formal and informal empire spread a notion of the activist subject which partly dissolved earlier social hierarchies and ranged far beyond religious belief and practice. Secondly, colonial policies tended to diminish hierarchical status differences within non-European societies. Rich merchants came to stand on equal footing with Brahmins and mandarins, at least in civil society organisations. Tribal leaders, rajas and *raises* (magnates) were forced into the same social categories as ordinary people, both by colonial law and governance and also as a consequence of the mass mobilisation of anticolonial movements. Conversely, colonialism tended to strengthen "vertical" differences between people and these have often been extended, as postcolonial governments introduced majoritarian politics and consequently used resources to strengthen their own democratic resource base. So, for instance, economic interest groups loosely designated Kikuyu were set against Luo; Ibo against others; Berbers against Arabs; Malay Muslims against Chinese; and so on.

Yet, more significantly, the huge increase in the urban population, only beginning in the late colonial period, moved the percentage of those who lived in towns and cities from at most 20% in 1900 to more than 60% by 2015. The peasant, the key figure of the scholarship and political activism of the 1960s and 1970s in the colonial world, was revealed as the century's greatest loser. While heavy colonial revenue regimes in rural areas and forced labour service certainly disadvantaged the rural poor, the massive increase in urban industrialism and the sale of rural land for development pushed forward this process after the end of colonial rule. Colonialism therefore initiated, but did not complete, the slow "death of the peasantry", which was regarded as the key agent of political change as late as the 1970s. In towns, society changed dramatically. Some advocates of the rights of the underprivileged, such as the Indian low-caste leader B. R. Ambedkar, decried the village as a place of discrimination and a "sink of backwardness".[42] Caribbean nationalists agreed, believing that towns would emancipate rural workers and break down racial barriers. Certainly, the rise of the town has seen a disintegration of the joint family, a limited growth of cross-status marriages and a partial empowerment of women. Yet, urbanisation also brought into sharp relief massive differentials in living standards, health and mortality. Postcolonial governments continued to drive peasants and tribal people off the land.[43]

It is important not to overgeneralise. The inheritance of colonial thought and practice in post-independence societies was quite uneven, often reflecting wartime experience and the form of the anticolonial struggle. In Indochina and Indonesia, the impact of the Japanese invasion and nationalist wars against the French, Dutch and, later, Americans erased many of the structures and ideologies of colonial rule. Across much of the rest of Asia and particularly Africa, often not decolonised until the 1960s, the impact of colonial rule and colonial ideologies was more pervasive. During the independence era, the earlier themes of national and social idealism were absorbed into rather than displaced by ideas of democracy, developmentalism and science, as a whole generation of colonial leaders was brought into direct contact with European, American and Japanese radical academics. After all, Jawaharlal Nehru had once been a theosophist before he replaced this with an idolisation of science. But the shift was palpable. Gandhi was indeed a latter-day idealist: the village community and its councils were for him perfect societies. Yet, for Nehru and his co-workers, such as D. R. Gadgil, the panchayat, or local council, was at best a structured low-level organisation to push forward economic change in the context of the new five-year plans; the so-called Panchayati Raj. So, in the long term, the colonial knowledge of British philosophers such as James and John Stuart Mill and Henry Maine, which had cast these bodies as the "primitive societies" at the base of despotism, had been challenged. First, by the assertion that they were really original democratic institutions; then, that they were premonitions of an ideal society. Finally, in the twentieth century, they were to become agents of economic development and social engineering. In this sense, postcolonial ideologies and practice across much of the world can be seen as historically contingent amalgams of ideologies and practices created both by colonialism and by anticolonial appropriations of many of its forms.

There were similar developments in empires of knowledge elsewhere in the colonial world. The myth of the original Arabic *shura* or "consultation" was transformed into a claim for political representation. In East Africa, Julius Nyerere's village developmental system, called *Ujamaa*, or "familyhood", was to become the basis of the socialist state after 1962.[44] The ideological basis of *Ujamaa* was, not unlike Panchayati Raj in India, a blending of ideas of indigenous village-level self-reliance, intended to break down "tribalism", merged with elements of British Fabian guild socialism. But whereas Gadgil's or Nehru's programmes remained politically liberal in the manner of Harold

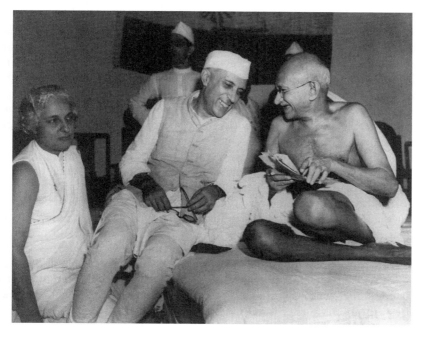

Figure 19 Gandhi and Nehru at a Congress meeting, 1946. Ruhe/Ullstein Bild via Getty Images.

Laski's original teaching, Nyerere's project soon became oppressive, forcibly moving rural people into new villages, in a small-scale version of Mao's Great Leap Forward, but one that also drew on precedents in colonial rule.

A general ideological move in late colonial and early postcolonial society was towards a contextualisation of developmentalism in economic history and theory. In part, this resulted from a radicalisation of colonial economic knowledge and practice. Even before the Depression, Frank Swettenham had written on the village and the plantation system in *British Malaya* (1906). J. S. Furnivall's *Netherlands India* (1939), dwelling on local credit systems, and Malcolm Darling's disquisition on *The Punjab Peasant in Prosperity and Debt* (1928) were more obviously products of gathering economic crisis. But despite this, the colonial powers adhered to rigid laissez-faire policies. Nationalist writers took up these themes and imbued them with a profound sense of local grievance and also knowledge of wider economic ideas. Nehru's *Discovery of India* (1946), written in a British jail, contained long sections on the destruction wrought by unbalanced capitalism in British India.

ECONOMICS AND EMPIRE

Aspects of these arguments are developed in earlier chapters, but it is now possible to suggest a basic typology of the economic consequences of empire which contributed to the persistence of great income inequality across the world. First, there were cases where colonial powers deliberately worked against the development of indigenous industry or agricultural development. The British opening of India to unlimited British imports of machine-made cloth goods before 1919, denounced by Indian economists from Dadabhai Naoroji to D. R. Gadgil, provides a good example of this.[45] Few former colonial territories had developed technically sophisticated industries with a well-paid labour force before 2000. In the agrarian sphere, the seizure of the best lands by European colonists in French North Africa or Anglo-Dutch East and South Africa illustrates the point equally strongly.[46] Large imbalances of wealth persisted even when new indigenous elites replaced European farmers.

Secondly, there were cases where the unintended consequences of colonial rule clearly held back indigenous development, for instance the failure of the colonial powers to foster basic literacy or technical education to any great extent or the small size of colonial civil services, limiting economic oversight. Finally, there were developments which cannot be attributed directly to the effects of colonial rule but enhanced these forms of underdevelopment and prolonged them well beyond the 1970s. An important contributory factor here was the very rapid growth of population during the twentieth century in Asian and African countries which were already relatively poor in 1850.[47] A balanced judgement might conclude, in the words of Rajnarayan Chandavarkar, that European empires did, in fact, foster development "up to a point, but only to a limited extent and largely in their own interests".[48] The construction of railways, initially more for reasons of control and troop movement, or later for the importation of European goods, than for local development, is a case in point.

The profits of railway expansion in the colonial world were almost everywhere remitted to the respective metropolis rather than being invested in the locality, as was the case with US railway building.

Yet, knowledge of wider economic thought did not necessarily lead all late-colonial and early independence nationalists to the same forms of state intervention. Like Nehru, Lee Kuan Yew of Singapore was influenced by Fabianism in Britain. But as leader of the independent country, now severed from Malaysia, he was more profoundly responsive to the American free-market model. Speaking in Delhi in November 2005, he lamented the bureaucratisation of Nehru's India.[49] He said he had abandoned Fabian-style welfareism in Singapore because it "sapped the people's self-reliance". Rather than pushing for industrialisation through import substitution and holding multinationals at arm's length, he invited them in and had achieved a much higher level of growth. All the same, the state did not wither away. On the contrary, Lee approved of state control of the media, punishments including the whipping of miscreants and intervention in family life characteristic of government in the colony, but now legitimated by the national concept. The themes of the politician as society's doctor curing the disease of backwardness through eugenic planning were widely found throughout Southeast Asia after the 1950s. The Malaysian leader Mahathir Mohamad, for instance, produced a eugenic version of the old colonial conception of the plural society. But these were not always simple adaptations of Western ideologies. Burhanuddin al-Helmy, president of the Pan-Malaysia Islamic Party, resorted to Sufi as well as homeopathic medical knowledge in his writing on the Malay race and social planning.

In trying to build a more cohesive and disciplined Chinese citizen in Southeast Asia, Lee Kuan Yew was reflecting and adapting some of the tropes of race and eugenics which were a significant feature of late colonialism and indigenous nationalism. Omnia El Shakry's *The Great Social Laboratory* [50] shows how contemporary Egyptian intellectuals sought to move on from British and French colonial stereotypes of oriental lassitude through a social engineering of the peasantry, using social psychology, geography and population studies. In India, deeply connected with British scientific thought and its racism, this turn was particularly associated with another of Jawaharlal Nehru's aides, P. C. Mahalanobis, mentioned in Chapter 8. For Mahalanobis, progress was dependent on knowledge: knowledge of irrigation statistics, of educational statistics and particularly of statistics about the size, shape and capabilities of people.[51]

In South Africa, the colonial legacy extended into the 1990s in two different, racially segregated forms. In a sense, the apartheid regime reflected an extreme version of eugenic and disciplinary control: supposedly inferior people were physically moved, corralled and denied rights. Conversely, the white population was given the advantages of free-market wealth creation. Elsewhere in Africa, there was great continuity between the economic and social conditions of the colonial period and those of the first decade of independence after 1960.[52] Despite the interventionist efforts of the new postcolonial leadership, urban and rural poverty persisted. Rural famines were rare, but rapid urbanisation created an impoverished class of unemployed city dwellers which suffered badly during the depression of the 1980s. Only with the boom in demand for food and raw materials, in particular from China after 2000, did poverty in some parts of Africa begin to diminish. Empire in the broadest sense, as a discourse and a set of social and economic residues, remained a dominant force throughout the twentieth and on into the twenty-first century.

[17] THE PRESSURE OF PEOPLE

The Stagnation of Population: Western Europe, Japan and
   Russia
Pressures on the Human Body
Human Population and the Elimination of Other Species
Alleviating the Pressure of People

THE revival and spread of religious politics and the persistence of the shadow of empire across much of the world in the years in the generation after 1980 elicited much public and academic comment. But the other critical subjects of discussion were population, environment and sustainability. The pressure of people in the title of this chapter refers both to highly uneven demographic pressure on the world's land, food supplies and animal and vegetable life and also to the pressure of politics on the environment as both authoritarian and democratic polities drove to expand and develop it. The concept of *Lebensraum* – living space – could be applied not only to the Nazi drive into agrarian Eastern Europe and Russia but also to the final waves of expansion of settler colonists in northern Canada, Australia and New Zealand and the Brazilian rain forests, for instance. The chapter also considers the pressure of the environment on the human body itself. It ends with a discussion of the ideologies and practices that humans developed to explain and control the unparalleled expansion of human population that occurred over the century. By the beginning of the twenty-first century, scientists and historians had come together to postulate the long development of "the anthropocene", an understanding of the world that brought together the life of humanity, animals, plants and even inanimate objects.[1] Humanity was increasingly indicted for fundamentally distorting

Remaking the Modern World 1900–2015: Global Connections and Comparisons, First Edition. C. A. Bayly.
© 2018 John Wiley & Sons Ltd. Published 2018 by John Wiley & Sons Ltd.

conditions of life on the planet, a process that dramatically speeded up during the twentieth century.

World population stood at about 1.63 billion in 1900. It had risen to 7.2 billion in 2013 and was projected to reach over 8 billion by 2025. Population density stood at about 25 per square mile on average in 1800 and 400 per square mile in 2000. Though Asia was often seen as the centre of rapid population growth, its proportion of the total remained relatively stable over the century, while it was Africa that recorded the greatest proportionate growth from about 138 million to 700 million over the period.[2] In the Congo alone there were 15 million people in 1960, 71 million in 2014 and were expected to be 150 million by 2050. In 1900, land was abundant across Africa, but labour was scarce; by 1980, labour had become abundant and land scarce.[3]

The reasons for the unparalleled surge of human population over the century were fairly clear. Medical improvements that began with the taming of malaria at the end of the nineteenth century continued into the mid-twentieth century, when further wartime discoveries and the determination of newly independent countries to institute public health schemes further reduced death rates from disease. Periodic outbreaks of disease, from the revival of bubonic plague between 1890 and 1920, the influenza epidemic of 1919, the outbreak of AIDS and SARS towards the end of the century and Ebola in 2014–2015, killed hundreds of thousands and spread panic, particularly in Africa. But the broader picture was more benign. The death rates of children under five years were pushed down rapidly after 1950 as better maternity care was applied and basic health education was given to young women.[4] Finally, there is evidence that agrarian settlement, raising the demand for labour and the propensity of families to have children, also promoted population growth in parts of Africa and Asia.

At the same time, better communications and development policies by governments that rejected the earlier complacency of the colonial and elite rulers drastically reduced the incidence of famine. In so far as famine persisted, it was the result of war and political error, as in the Bengal famine of 1943, Mao's Great Leap Forward, the central African famines of the 1980s or the starvation that accompanied the Syrian and Iraqi civil wars of 2011–2015. A better understanding of nutrition and the work of aid agencies and non-governmental organisations contributed to longevity. Also critical here was the so-called Green Revolution, a surge of worldwide increased food production that peaked in the 1960s and 1970s.[5] As late as 1961, India and parts of Africa remained endangered by scarcity, if not famine. The rapid introduction into Asia, Africa and Mexico of high-yielding seed varieties, especially food grains, may have saved up to a billion lives over the following generation. New crops were supported with expanded irrigation systems, new fertilisers and pesticides. Better management in many countries led to a new era of food security. India, for instance, achieved self-sufficiency in cereal production in 1974. World population continued to grow after the 1960s, though at a slower rate. Combined with better nutrition and food provision, this resulted in a period of growing prosperity across the developing world that played some role in promoting a degree of political stability.

The role of the other great feature of the century – urbanisation – in population growth is less certain.[6] The expansion of the urban population from under 20% to over 60%, alluded to in the last chapter, was an astonishing change which led to the emergence by 2000 of cities with populations of over 30 million, such as Delhi, Calcutta, Beijing or Buenos Aires. In itself, urban living may not have greatly increased the average birth rate. But access to medicines, even in the worst city slums, may have alleviated death rates to some extent. Experts predicted, however, that these conditions would not necessarily continue into the twenty-first century. Some old killer diseases, such as cholera, tuberculosis and polio, reappeared because of poor medical services alongside the new scourges like AIDS and later Ebola. Certain bacterial infections also began to show alarming signs of resistance to medical treatments as antibiotics were deployed too thoughtlessly by practitioners under pressure. Opinion remained divided between those who insisted that the planet could contain a continuing, if slower, rise of population in the twenty-first century and those who predicted, in a late-Malthusian style, a return of conflict and starvation as "demand for food outstripped supply".[7] A balanced judgement might insist that the earth could sustain a substantial increase in population, but only if resources were more evenly divided. For instance, population pressure had certainly brought about a decline in water tables and the appearance of "dust bowls" in parts of Asia and Africa, while, as will be seen, population had stagnated or declined in some parts of Europe and Japan. Yet, the structure of world politics and residual perceptions of racial difference made any significant movement of population to alleviate poverty extremely contentious, even in the case of refugees from war.

THE STAGNATION OF POPULATION: WESTERN EUROPE, JAPAN AND RUSSIA

The huge expansion of population across the world, in particular in the developing world, towards the end of the century was not in evidence everywhere. In Western European countries such as Italy and Germany, the indigenous population was hardly reproducing itself by the end of the twentieth century. Here the demand for labour was increasingly met by immigration from Africa, Asia and Eastern Europe. The causes for the fall in rates of reproduction were complex. But the desire to hold on to the new wealth, the decline in infant mortality, so reducing the need to "hedge" by having more children, and a sharp reaction against Roman Catholic and other religious prohibitions on birth control appeared to have been among them. In Japan, the cost of child rearing, late marriage and inherent caution resulted in a projected decline of population after 2020. In a very different situation, indigenous peoples in Arctic Canada, Alaska and parts of the Australian outback also dramatically declined in fertility, leaving many of these communities on the point of disappearance. The main reason here was often excessive alcoholism. But psychic depression among peoples whose earlier lifestyles, such as hunting and fishing, had disappeared and whose other employment opportunities hardly existed was also an underlying cause.

Both these conditions were apparent in a much larger context: the Soviet Union, or later Russia. Here the birth rate slowly declined from the First World War onwards and estimates suggested that by 2050 the population will have declined by 20%, even from its diminished number around 2000.[8] Villages were depopulated even in the heart of Russia. The reasons for this were, once again, varied. It seems clear that a critical contributing factor was the death of millions of young people, especially young men, first, in the state-induced famines, forced collectivisation and gulags of the Stalinist period. Secondly, the fatalities of the Second World War were on a massive scale in the USSR. Apparently reliable estimates suggest that nearly 40% of all men between the ages of 20 and 49 were killed as a result of Nazi outrages and battle deaths on the war fronts. Altogether 45 million Russians may have died between 1914 and 1945, as excess deaths from war, famine and political terror. Yet, population growth did not pick up again after 1945. In part this was because death rates remained particularly high in the USSR, and later Russia, because of unhealthy lifestyles and poor medical care. Home-brewed vodka is said to have been a common killer. Remarkably, death rates in China and later India were better than those in Russia by the end of the century. Finally, *perestroika* and the end of Communism did not seem to have alleviated the problem, as optimistic European and American commentators had suggested. On the contrary, the dislocation, unemployment and existential worry caused by the collapse of Communism seem to have had the opposite effect.

As in Western Europe and the southern United States, one answer to the decline of labour power and demographic density in Russia might have been immigration from former non-Russian republics, or even from other parts of Asia. But here demographic imbalances had already showed signs of increasing social tension. Anti-immigrant parties sprang up in Russia after 1990, as they had done in Western Europe and the United States after 1945. The pressure of people in some parts of the world and the decline of populations in others seem to point not to a peaceful rebalancing but to premonitions of further societal and international conflict.

One particular emerging problem for the developed economies of the Western world was the growth of the number of elderly people over 65 and the massive costs this implied for them, their families and, indeed, for the welfare states that had been created, particularly in Europe.[9] There were several reasons for the relative growth of the elderly population as a proportion of the population as a whole. On the one hand, from the 1950s onward, people began to have fewer children. In the nineteenth and early twentieth centuries, families were larger and this had a demonstration effect. Equally, high death rates for the young, the need to have many hands earning for the family and, indeed, a sense that people owed it to the nation and the community to reproduce were very much in evidence. This began to change after the 1940s. The mass deaths of war and famine were over. More importantly, the widespread dissemination of methods of birth control encouraged a more targeted and rational approach to conception and birth.

Some states also changed their attitudes to procreation. The fear of the CCP in China that high birth rates would overwhelm any advances made in general living standards resulted in the "One-Child Policy", which dramatically limited family sizes. It was estimated that the policy averted the birth of 400 million children between 1960 and 2013. But in a population which was more than 1 billion by the latter date, this resulted in a serious youth "demographic deficit". By the end of the century, the young population had significantly shrunk as a percentage of the whole and this made it increasingly difficult for older people, especially in the rural areas, to enjoy a comfortable old age. The policy was partially relaxed in 2013 and scrapped in late 2015. In India, by comparison, the cultural determination to have male children, a result of pervasive gender prejudice and patterns of male inheritance and bride price, resulted in a rapid decline in the number of females born, especially to the middle classes, which now had access to scientific ways of determining a child's gender in the womb. This presaged a major problem for the country's future generations.

The decline in the birth rate was particularly severe in some of the countries of Western Europe, and this was only partly compensated for by immigration from Asia and Africa. In the United States, the same phenomenon was apparent, but immigration from Mexico and other parts of Latin America largely made up for this deficit. Even in Germany, one of the richest and most successful countries of the late twentieth century, the problem was becoming acute by the early 2000s. Up to half a million elderly Germans were unable to finance their old age provision and this population was growing at 5% a year. In part, this was because the cost of health services was soaring in a wealthy country. Elderly Germans were increasingly being shipped off to Eastern European and even Asian countries, where the wage costs of health professionals were much lower.

Overall, the emerging problem was that better life survival rates conflicted with the cost of paying for the inevitable diseases and disabilities of old age. The result was an enormous drag on the wealth of the younger members of these societies and a huge burden on the budgets of states such as Italy and even France and Germany, where the average birth rate was less than 1.5 children for every two adults. To some degree this had the effect of once again expanding family size that had been contracting through much of the century even in more conservative Asian countries. Children stayed with their parents or moved back into the family home. By 2010, in Italy, for instance, more than half of young men aged between 25 and 34 were still living with their parents. These financial pressures coincided in due course with the need to bail out banks crippled by the 1996 and 2008 financial crises and by the costs of foreign interventions and military costs or the development of newer sources of energy provision.

PRESSURES ON THE HUMAN BODY

A substantial part of the world's population was lifted out of poverty over the century. Nutrition improved for many as a result of the development of intensive agriculture and husbandry and state provision of aid by the newly independent nations. Famines which had been endemic in the late nineteenth century as the result of poor communication or the state's lack of concern were, in the twentieth century, more likely to be the result of warfare and the total breakdown of communication and political will, as in the Bengal famine or the African scarcities of the 1920s–1980s, which reflected the decline of the colonial or settler capitalist economies there.[10] As a consequence, the human frame itself began to change in form and size. In many areas this took decades to register. Rural populations in Africa and Asia remained small and thin through to 2015. The long period of war and scarcity from the 1930s to the 1990s ensured this. Even in Western Europe, working-class populations remained poorly nourished and small in stature throughout the first half of the century. Towards the end of the Second World War, for instance, the population of the Netherlands suffered a severe scarcity. The early "baby-boomer" generation of the 1940s and 1950s in Europe and the United States remained relatively undersized, giving rise to eugenic worries and the regular measurement of children in school.

After 1970, more adequate nutrition and the pressure of democratic politics began to produce a larger and healthier generation, at least in Western cities. This was reinforced by the expansion of sports facilities and the promotion of ideal body images through television and magazines. Yet, by the beginning of the twenty-first century, a new threat to the human body and health had emerged in the form of obesity and its attendant diseases. Not only in Europe and America, but also among the wealthy in Asia and Africa, substantial parts of the population were now overweight. The total had reached 2.1 billion.[11] This was accompanied by the appearance of heart disease and diabetes among populations that were widely ageing. In 2013, there were 30% more obese people in the world than undernourished ones. In India, where the poor remained very poor, 27% of the population was obese nevertheless.

Experts remained divided about why this relatively sudden shift from emaciation to obesity had occurred in many societies, bar the obvious fact of the greater availability of food. Many specialists pointed to the sugar, salt and fat poured into mass-produced food by companies hoping to exploit the demand for easy and fast eating. The figures seemed to prove their point. Sedentary lifestyles and the decline of sports provision at schools after 2000, as national budgets came under pressure and working hours became longer, were also indicted. Globalisation and communication also played their part. Burger bars and restaurants spread from the United States to Europe, Asia and Africa, where previously less fattening and more nutritious food had been available, at least for the middle classes. Children, in particular, were seduced into eating rich food by television and later mobile phone adverts, peer pressure and revulsion against the healthy foods promoted by their parents. Diets of fish and vegetables, widespread and relatively cheap in the 1950s, had become expensive as a result of overfishing and the policies of supermarkets. It was by no means clear that the improvement in the size, shape and health of the human body that had begun in the 1950s would persist far into the twenty-first century. Twenty-five % of children were overweight by this date, an increase of 10% since 2004. Malaysia had the highest rate of type 2 diabetes in the world. Almost

25% of American adolescents had type 2 diabetes in 2012, up 10% from the 1990s.[12]

These physical problems were compounded by drug addiction and mental health issues which were widely believed to have been exacerbated by the decline of the family and the pressures of the age of the Internet and mobile phone. ADD (attention deficit disorder) was singled out as a new scourge of late modernity. Eleven % of US children under eighteen had been diagnosed and medicated on account of this disease by 2014 and it was closely correlated with obesity and a sedentary lifestyle. Even the incidence of anorexia was indirectly linked to the widespread consumption of fast food. Peer pressure exerted by the new media also appeared to have contributed to a large increase in the demand for cosmetic surgery and skin whitening to enhance sexual attraction, not just in the West but also in Asian countries.

Industrialisation and urbanisation also caused the growing problem of air pollution from the beginning of the twentieth century, another effect of growing populations. By the 1940s and 1950s, rapidly growing cities in developing societies were often afflicted by air pollution from wood burning during the winter months. This was notably the case in Delhi, Lahore and other Pakistani cities, where companies as well as the urban poor devastated woodlands to find fuel. Cities in developed countries suffered from excessive burning of coal. So-called smog was a common feature of winters in London and Paris during the 1940s and 1950s until it was reduced by "clean air acts" that limited domestic and industrial fires. The problem never diminished in the developing world and was particularly intense by the end of the century in China, where industrialisation and the urban population had expanded at a great pace since the 1980s and large numbers of cars had come onto the roads. By 2013, air pollution in Beijing had reached six times the maximum recommended by the World Health Organization. Deaths from lung cancer had surged five times since the 1980s and politicians began to worry that the mental and physical health of Chinese people had been severely affected. Xie Zhenhua, the vice-chairman of the powerful National Development and Reform Commission, blamed the "obsolete development model of China's companies for the social damage" and predicted "it would take decades to change".[13]

HUMAN POPULATION AND THE ELIMINATION OF OTHER SPECIES

The basic pattern of humanity's relationship with the animal and vegetable worlds over the twentieth and twenty-first centuries was one of ruthless exploitation, punctuated by sentimentality. The destruction of animal life in warfare, an ancient feature of human history, reached its apogee in 1916 and 1917 before the tank appeared on the battlefield. Several million horses were killed on the various war fronts. After the war, many surviving animals were butchered for their meat as the post-war hunger set in, their use in battle now diminished. Thousands of dogs were also used by the various armies in a watch-and-ward capacity and later abandoned. Love of dogs and horses was nevertheless an entry point into human concern for animal life and the environment. This paradoxical relationship between man and the animal world was revealed by the career of the American canine star of silent movies, Rin Tin Tin, who "like the British royal family was actually German".[14] An American soldier had rescued him as a puppy from the Western front. He was part of a litter of German shepherds that the Kaiser's army used to patrol their lines but was abandoned after the German surrender. In the 1920s, he was transformed into a symbol of American individualism and heroism and one of the most popular "actors" in the burgeoning celebrity caste of Hollywood. Animal celebrities stretched back to the time of the Roman Emperor Caligula's horse, but film and television gave them a new charisma and reach. Later in the century, dogs in Russian sputniks and "Uggie" the terrier in the cult film *The Artist* (2011) filled similar roles.

Meanwhile, the steady erosion of animal habitats led to a sharp decline in the number of extant species. By the end of the twentieth century, the fall of the water table and the destruction of forests across the globe was said to be destroying species at the rate of five every day. In part, this was simply a result of the human demand for *Lebensraum*. A dramatic example is the fate of the North American buffalo. In the early nineteenth century, there were estimated to have been 60 million buffalo in the plains. By 1906, there were a mere thousand.[15] In India during the colonial period, it was estimated that about 17,000 tigers were slaughtered each year, mainly to protect livestock, but also for sport. In 2010, the total population was barely 1,700. This extermination was mainly a consequence of the epochal spread of farmland and railways so that, by the mid-century, the majority of tigers languished in zoos. But also damaging was the burgeoning demand for the body parts of exotic creatures: the horns of the rhinoceros, the tusks of elephants and the skins of tigers, leopards and lions. The increasing wealth of East Asian societies, which prized animal parts for medical and necromantic reasons, spurred species erosion on to a new height. But equally in the West, cruelty to animals took on a new, industrialised form in the expansion of the factory farming of chickens, turkeys and other animals after the 1970s.

Human sentimentality and regret about the destruction of non-human life was only transformed into action to a small degree by the activities of organisations devoted to the limitation of cruelty to animals and the preservation of global life forms. Some protection was provided in the late colonial and early independence periods for the preservation of forest, animal habitats and "tribal" areas. In 1948, in India, for instance, the committed moderniser Nehru helped create a wetlands project to preserve water supplies and the environment in Central India. But population pressure and the demand for timber and other resources had widely dented this effort by the end of the century. As Mahesh Rangarajan pointed out, however, rather than total environmental destruction, a patchwork of protected areas and protected species survived across much of the developing world.[16] Some success was also registered in Alaska and other parts of North America. Native peoples' reservations were transformed in the 1970s into development areas where attempts were made to establish small-scale industries which helped preserve the lifestyle of the inhabitants, but also their natural environment and local species.

Parallel to this, the general discourse of rights, which became pervasive after the Second World War, was extended to animal rights. In Europe, in particular, groups campaigned, sometimes violently, against hunting, the treatment of animals in circuses and the battery farming of animals. In 2014, a chimpanzee (with some human assistance) sued his keepers in an American court. Again, if some religious sensibilities in Buddhism or Hinduism had promoted a kind of transcendent morality in relation to the life of animals, other counter ideologies, counselling humanity's exploitation of the natural world for both religious and practical reasons, had proved more powerful even before colonialism.[17] As with the maintenance of forests in parts of the world, such as Indonesia and Brazil, the imperatives of rapid development and commercial rapacity proved more powerful influences. Towards the end of the long twentieth century, the image of stranded polar bears, isolated among melting icebergs, became a symbol of wider human fears about global warming and the fate of mankind itself in "the age of the anthropocene".[18] But the global economic shock after 2008 and the pressure of business interests constrained those few intergovernmental agreements that had been put in place to limit damage to the environment.

ALLEVIATING THE PRESSURE OF PEOPLE

From early-twentieth-century debates in a neo-Malthusian frame to early-twenty-first-century arguments about environmental protection versus the exploitation of resources, the issue of population pressure and its consequences have been profoundly political. Concern about population growth did not suddenly come into focus after the Second World War as the Green Revolution began. In fact, discussion of population in the context of land, resources and reproduction emerged as a transnational debate in the generation before the First World War and flared up with added urgency after 1919 when it was entangled with issues of global governance and eugenics. As Raymond Pearl wrote in 1927, there were three primary variables in the study of population, "natality, mortality and migration" or, as Alison Bashford put it later, "birth, death and space".[19] In liberal and even socialist circles, the debate on population before the 1940s was often framed by the discourse of eugenics: how to create a better race and discourage excessive reproduction among the poor and backward. Intellectual luminaries such as John Maynard Keynes and the Indian anti-colonialist and advocate of regional development Radhakamal Mukerjee both voiced eugenic ideas and argued that the poor should be urged to limit their birth rate.

A more radical version of these ideas was found in the works of the British neo-Darwinist and eugenicist Karl Pearson, a pupil of Francis Galton, who openly approved of "race war".[20] This self-styled socialist and republican wrote that nations should be recruited from the "better stocks" and national efficiency should be maintained "chiefly by way of war with inferior races". Pearson opposed Jewish immigration to Britain in 1925 on the grounds that Jews were generally inferior to the native British. These themes drew on fears of racial degeneration and population decline in Europe, particularly in France. Anglo-American worries about the rapidly increasing non-white populations also became more pressing between 1890 and 1930. Alarm was sounded about the "Yellow peril", supposed lascivious "negro" attention to white women as the black population spread into northern US cities and the malign consequences of mass non-white immigration into Europe, North America and Australasia. Galton influenced the proponents of enumeration and finger-printing in South Africa,[21] while his protégé, Pearson, was mentor of Nehru's associate P. C. Mahalanobis and associated with proponents of apartheid in South Africa. The whole genre, of course, reached its climax in Nazi Germany with the murderous assault on Jews, gipsies and the so-called degenerates. While less dominated by specifically racist themes, Japanese expansionism in Korea and China was also justified by the need to relieve population pressure in the homeland.

After 1945, these earlier fears about population pressure and the destruction of earth's natural resources came together with the novel terror of atomic warfare. Mankind's capacity to destroy itself had been redoubled. The United Nations was to reduce the danger of war and nuclear cataclysm while UNESCO would press for population control, a position that seemed practical now that cheap methods of contraception had become available. Fear of the "population bomb" also impelled national and transnational "food for peace" programmes and provided a particular incentive for the scientific work that went into planning for the Green Revolution. Concern about population, resources and migration were certainly diminished during the period of growth and development which followed the Second World War, but they periodically resurfaced, especially in Asia. Some Southeast Asian countries continued to impose stealthy eugenic policies to "improve the national stock". At the beginning of the twenty-first century, however, fears about global warming created by human populations releasing CO_2 gas into the atmosphere became widespread and received much scientific support.

At the same time, several Western European societies expressed alarm about the number of Asian, African and even Eastern European migrants crossing their borders. Population pressure on social services was often used to justify the emergence of chauvinistic anti-immigration parties. Racialist eugenics, as such, was rarely invoked, but the discourse was replaced by moral panics about violent Islamism and other covertly racialist views. Global disease, "jihadism", immigration and the destruction of the environment had merged into a new fear of the apocalypse by 2015. As the IMF and even the US military came to present their fears about the earth's future, academic opinion and the environmental movement began to create a new metanarrative of the anthropocene and the earth's decline which brought together scientific studies of plant and animal life with economics, natural history and anthropology, creating a new "deep history" which ranged from the earliest humans to the present.[22] So-called perspectivism in the latter discipline urged humans to see the world from the vantage point of the hunter, the hunted animal or the devastated forest. An ethical element became predominant in this discourse.

Much of the environmental damage that became increasingly evident at the end of the century had been put in train during the late colonial period or by business and government interests in independent states concerned simply with profit. The overexploitation and destruction of the forests of Indonesia and Brazil, for instance, were particularly disastrous examples of this. Yet, the irony was that some of the major developments in agriculture initiated to protect populations against scarcity in the middle of the century had begun to have detrimental effects by its end. So, for instance, the expansion of corn production in drier parts of the American Midwest resulted in a significant fall in the water table over the next two generations. A similar fate overtook parts of Rajasthan in India as the less beneficial effects of the Green Revolution began to be felt. By contrast, the logging of the Himalayas to provide wood for families during the cold north Indian winters disrupted water courses across the subcontinent and led to increased flooding and the destruction of crops in Bangladesh. The debate in the second decade of the twenty-first century, therefore, remained polarised between neo-Malthusian, environmentalists' gloom and the urgent need to push forward development to feed the world's growing population. This was a truly vicious circle.

[18] BETWEEN TWO CENTURIES: ECONOMIC LIBERALISATION AND POLITICAL FRAGMENTATION, C. 1991 TO 2015

The Small Wars of Fragmentation Redoubled: The West, Africa and the Muslim World

The Spectre of Jihadism and Further Humanitarian Intervention

Why Conflicts Racked the Muslim World

Small Wars of Fragmentation Redoubled: Africa and Latin America

The Triumph and Crisis of Capitalism

Globalisation, Prosperity and Crisis

The Pains of Globalisation and the Return of the National

THE 25 years after the fall of European Communism were marked by the resurgence of Western intervention and localised conflict. Further small wars of fragmentation accompanied and followed these so-called humanitarian interventions, as different ethnic groups attempted to create independent states or, latterly, caliphates. Broadly, the Western democracies persisted with the neo-liberal policies which had taken hold in the 1980s, while the leaders of Russia, China, Vietnam and other former socialist states loosened their control over their economies. By 2015, China was steadily overtaking the United States as the world's largest economy, though the country's GDP per head remained low. Consequently, while differences of wealth between countries tended to lessen, inequalities within countries, including the rapidly developing countries of the East, tended to grow. If anything, the economic crisis of 2008 and the "Great Recession" which followed it actually intensified this inequality.

Remaking the Modern World 1900–2015: Global Connections and Comparisons, First Edition. C. A. Bayly.
© 2018 John Wiley & Sons Ltd. Published 2018 by John Wiley & Sons Ltd.

Commentators wrote of a new "age of uncertainty" or drew parallels with the decades before 1914.

THE SMALL WARS OF FRAGMENTATION REDOUBLED: THE WEST, AFRICA AND THE MUSLIM WORLD

The period was profoundly marked by the proliferation of local conflicts. One estimate was that between 1990 and 2010 there were 50 small wars in Asia, 37 in Africa, fifteen in the Middle East and five in Europe.[1] The numbers had significantly increased by 2015. These decades began with the crises in Iraq, Bosnia, Rwanda and Chechnya. They witnessed further US intervention in Iraq and Afghanistan and ended with the so-called Arab Spring and the disintegration of Syria and Libya, along with extreme turbulence in Afghanistan, Pakistan, Sudan, western China, Ukraine and some West and Central African countries.

An earlier period of small wars, from the 1840s to the 1870s, had reflected attempts by nation states to consolidate their power. Those between 1918 and 1960 were brought about by the collapse of empires following the world wars. But these later events were caused by the fragmentation of existing smaller, national polities on ethnic or religious lines. In Libya, between 2011 and 2015, for instance, the contest between radical Islamists, "moderates", including the Muslim Brotherhood, and the army further overlaid a conflict between people of Arab origin and Circassians, Berbers and Turks. This in turn concealed divisions between local populations, the Misuratis and Zintanis.[2] These disputes were deepened by modern communications, the press and media located in the Gulf States. In all these cases, again, postcolonial, post-imperial military states fought to hold these fragments together, or to limit tendencies to fission at the margins of their territories.[3]

Yet, these lines of fragmentation also recapitulated the elements of much earlier imperial formations. For instance, the problems of Iraq and later Syria had deep lineages stretching back to the tactics and political patterns of the late Ottoman Empire and the European mandated powers, those in Libya to Italian colonialism and the British wartime intervention. Similarly, long genealogies can be drawn for the events in Bosnia and Rwanda, which captured international attention because of the "ethnic cleansing" that took place there: the fragmentation of Yugoslavia harked back to the days of Austria-Hungary and the Ottoman Empire and, in Rwanda, to French and Belgian colonialism. Even in the case of Chechnya and the problems on the fringes of the collapsing Soviet Union after 1990, the lines of fragmentation recalled the earlier expansion of the tsarist empire. In several instances, notably in Bosnia, the combatants specifically recalled these deep histories in order to justify political murder. If the Jewish Holocaust of the 1940s arose from the expansion of the Nazi empire, the ethnic killings of the 1990s arose, by contrast, from the breakdown of smaller states in a context of fluid and uncertain international governance. The wide reach of pre-war anti-Semitism was replaced by what Arjun Appadurai called "the fear of small numbers".[4] In addition, the revolt of young people against established structures empowered both liberal and purist religious and political movements.[5]

The breakup of the former socialist state of Yugoslavia between 1991 and 1999 followed hard on the collapse of the USSR itself.[6] Slovenia and Croatia had achieved independence by 1995 after a series of short wars. But the situation in the south of the former Yugoslavia, the territory of Kosovo inhabited by Bosnian Serbs and also by Albanian-speaking Muslims, led to the rape and mass killings of Muslims by forces determined to build a Greater Serbia, acting under the loose control of politicians in Belgrade.[7] The resulting international outcry led to the bombing of Serbian Yugoslavia and, in 1999, an invasion by NATO forces and the establishment of an International War Crimes Tribunal for the former Yugoslavia, which brought some Serbian political leaders to account. The situation in the Central African state of Rwanda, discussed in Chapter 14, provided a distant comparison with events in the former Yugoslavia.[8] Ethnic manipulation by the earlier Belgian colonial government set Tutsis against Hutus. After 1991, a murderous civil war broke out. In turn, France, as the major postcolonial power in the region, sent a "peacekeeping force" into the country.

The most important general outcome of both the Bosnian and Rwandan crises, then, was to reinforce the notion of "humanitarian intervention" by NATO and other Western forces, whether under the auspices of the United Nations or, increasingly, not. This type of policy initiative also drew strength from the US-led invasion to support Kuwait against Iraqi occupation in 1991. All these moves were approved by the Western press and seemed, initially at least, to have had some effect in limiting mass killings by disempowering oppressive local regimes. In Iraq, however, it ultimately had the opposite effect, as Saddam Hussein attempted, soon after 1991, to immobilise Kurdish opposition by attacking its civilian population with chemical weapons. This in turn set the scene for the US invasion of Iraq in 2003, which was again justified in terms of humanitarian intervention and an attempt to stop the dictator from developing atomic and chemical weapons.[9]

A further comparable small war of fragmentation occurred in the northern Caucasus region of the former tsarist empire and Soviet Union which had been conquered from the Ottomans in the early nineteenth century. With the breakup of the Soviet Union, Chechnya declared independence in 1992.[10] A Muslim majority here, as in neighbouring Dagestan, was opposed by a long-standing Russian diaspora. The independent republic survived for some years, despite heavy fighting in the First Chechen War from 1994 to 1996. In 1999, alarmed by an invasion of neighbouring Dagestan by radical Islamic mujahidin, Russia's new prime minister, Putin, entered Chechen territory. The Russian Federation was ultimately able to reimpose control. But a low-level guerrilla war and terrorist attacks in Moscow, similar to those in London and New York, persisted through to the 2010s. Here then, political fragmentation, itself the long-term result of imperial domination and ethnic–religious conflict, was further intensified by the loose, global spread of militant jihadism. Meanwhile, an astonishing three million people of mainly Russian origin left Azerbaijan to the northeast, a number almost equivalent to émigrés from the partition of India, but without the same level of violence.

THE SPECTRE OF JIHADISM AND FURTHER HUMANITARIAN INTERVENTION

The attack by two commandeered aircraft on New York's World Trade Center on 11 September 2001 – "9/11" as it came to be known – marked the true beginning of the twenty-first century.[11] Planned by a dispersed group of Islamist exiles and conspirators with loose links to Saudi Arabia and Afghanistan, rather than by a nation state, it was a supreme example of violent "gesture politics" and not a move intended to be immediately politically productive. Muslims, according to Osama bin Laden, should "pool all their energy and resources to fight the Americans and the Zionists and those with them".[12] Al-Qaeda's policy resembled the high-profile assassinations and attacks of the late-nineteenth-century European anarchists, the Indian Ghadar conspirators of the First World War or the murder of Israeli sea and air passengers by Palestinian militants in the 1970s and 1980s. Yet, its targets were infinitely more iconic and the level of slaughter on a different scale altogether. It represented, in fact, a kind of democratisation of assassination. The attacks of 9/11 also marked a shift in the nature of Islamist resistance. Islamism – a modern rigorous version of Islam – had become transfixed on an attempt to revive customary practice in dress and gender relations, for instance. In the process it had lost much of its spiritual content. Similarly, jihad, or holy war, had abandoned its religious connotation as a struggle against evil (the "greater jihad") and had instead been reduced to an earthly fight against supposed infidels, which could entertain the murder of hundreds or thousands of men, women and children. Thus, the organiser of 9/11, bin Laden, was neither the leader of a state nor a cleric but a lone exile who moved to an Afghan tribal zone in order to attract followers, as nineteenth-century figures, such as Sayyid Ahmad of Rai Bareilly, had done before him.

The new millennium also witnessed several examples of lesser jihadist gesture politics of this sort with attacks in Somalia, Nigeria and Kenya, the London bombings of 2005 or the murder of hundreds of residents of the city of Mumbai in 2008 by the organisation Lashkar-e-Taiba, which had Pakistani and Kashmiri connections. Yet, even though the dispersed organisation which oversaw 9/11 had no defined political objective itself, the consequences of the attacks were profound and came to dominate the following generation. Most obviously, it brought together the US-led coalition which invaded Afghanistan in October of that year and expelled the Islamist Taliban government which had sheltered bin Laden. The ensuing war became one of the longest ever fought by the Western alliance, and had no clear outcome even by 2015. The warlike atmosphere so created, in particular the relationship between the US president George W. Bush and Britain's Tony Blair, led to a situation that made possible the invasion of Iraq in 2003. It also set the scene for a retreat

of individual rights in Western democracies of which the notorious US detention centre at Guantanamo Bay and the widespread use of torture by the CIA
were only the most blatant examples.

The perception that the Iraqi dictator, Saddam Hussein, was sheltering
Islamist conspirators, building up atomic weapons and slaughtering his own
people made possible the next of these humanitarian interventions. Tony Blair
apparently combined realpolitik with Christian moralising, allegedly insisting
that "the man [Hussein] is evil, isn't he?"[13] Yet, neither the war in Afghanistan
nor the one in Iraq was effectively managed and these conflicts significantly
increased the underlying tensions between the Western powers, the Muslim
world and Russia, which was still hankering after its former global importance.
Equally significant was the enormous strain that continuous military expenditure put on the budgets of the United States and Britain in particular. The
financial consequences played an important part in the crumbling of the global
financial system after 2008. Emerging economies in China, India and South
America, which played no part in this attempt to police the world, gradually
assumed greater importance in the international economy.

While the consequences of 9/11 for the West and world politics were
profound, the distorting effects of the consequent invasions, wars and political
fragmentation in the Middle East and West Asia were even more significant.
Ethnic and religious divisions were exacerbated, raising regional tensions
between states, not least because India, Pakistan and Israel were nuclear powers
and Iran was rapidly acquiring nuclear expertise. In Afghanistan itself, the
conflicts between the revivalist Taliban movement, which had harboured bin
Laden, and the Kabul-based government supported by the US and its allies
only lightly covered a complex set of ethnic divisions. The Taliban was
particularly strong among the large Pakhtun (Pathan) section of the population,
while in Kabul Turkic speakers from the north and east of the country were
more influential.

As the consequences of the Afghan War were felt in Pakistan, similar
divisions were heightened there. The Pakistani Taliban, which opposed the
presence of Western troops in the region, took strength from among Pakistan's
own Pakhtun ethnic groups in the northwest, while other revivalist movements
opposing Western "licence" grew stronger in the Punjabi heart of the country.
Members of the Pakistani intelligence service, the ISI, were covertly supporting
the insurgents in Afghanistan and local Islamists. It was discovered in 2011 that
bin Laden himself was being sheltered close to the Pakistani capital. Relations
between the United States and Pakistan further deteriorated when bin Laden
was assassinated by US special forces and attacks by airborne drones apparently
killed members of civilian populations on both sides of the Pakistan–Afghan
border.

These multiple conflicts were responsible for tremors elsewhere. Relations
between India and Pakistan, always uneasy because of India's police actions
against Muslim insurgents in Kashmir, worsened after the Mumbai attacks of
2008 and the perception that India was really the closest ally of the US in the
region. To the west, meanwhile, Iranian politicians watched with suspicion
Pakistan's shift to an anti-Shia form of Islamism and its neighbour's albeit

increasingly unwilling cooperation with the United States. This, along with fear and hatred of Israel, was a key reason for its rapid strides towards nuclear status and its support of Shia movements from Syria, through Palestine to Yemen. Whereas the conventional metaphor used to describe the conflicts of the Cold War was the falling of dominos, in these later conflicts the dominos themselves fragmented. Conflict moved from the peripheries to the centre of power politics, rather than vice versa.

In Iraq, foreign intervention caused a similar upsurge of ethnic and religious division. Since the country was created by the British as an amalgam of the former Ottoman provinces of Basra, Baghdad and Mosul in 1916–1926, only strong and often oppressive rule by Baghdad-based Sunni leadership had kept its Shia and Kurdish populations quiescent. The exploitation of oil reserves, even if unequally shared out across the country, had aided centralisation. But there had been constant local rebellions since the 1960s. It was this which accounted for the particular brutality of Saddam Hussein's moves against the "Marsh Arabs" in the south and the Kurds in the north. Fear of Iranian influence amongst the dominant Shia population also precipitated his long and disastrous war with Iran. Equally, Saddam's irritation with the local politics of the Arab princely rulers to the south caused his 1990 invasion of Kuwait which had sparked off the First Gulf War and US intervention. This war inaugurated a new period of conflict in international relations characterised by the humanitarian intervention of the type described above.

In turn, the 2003 invasion virtually destroyed Baghdad's hold on the country and led to an intensification of Kurdish, Shia and Islamist movements, leading to hundreds of thousands of deaths and the creation of a political quagmire from which the United States, Britain and other allies had only begun to extricate themselves by the time the financial crisis hit in 2008. What emerged from these conflicts was what came to be called the "Shia triangle" constituted by Iran, a now Shia-dominated Iraq and the Shia and Alawite populations of Palestine and Syria. Distantly, the Shia majority in Bahrain became more restive under the rule of its Sunni majority. In turn, radical Sunnis reacted against the Shia domination of Baghdad and attempted to create their own Sharia-dominated Khilafat. By 2015, an aggressive Sunni military movement, ISIS (the Islamic State of Iraq and Syria), dominated much of north-central Iraq. As Faisal Devji argued, this movement, even more than al-Qaeda, largely abandoned the millenarian element in earlier Islamist jihadism.[14] It was simply determined to impose a quotidian, democratic form of Sharia, fuelled by hatred of "Western values".

WHY CONFLICTS RACKED THE MUSLIM WORLD

Yet, it is difficult to understand these wars without taking account of Israeli policies which had likewise moved from millenarian idealism to an emphasis on state security and expansion. The consequence of the Gulf War encouraged a moderate Labour government to try to find common cause with the Palestinian leadership on the West Bank and this was encouraged by Bill Clinton's

Democrat government in the United States. But, later, the Sunni–Shia struggle and assertion by Kurds and other minorities across the region had been compounded by a lurch to the right in Israel. After Prime Minister Yitzhak Rabin was assassinated by a Jewish extremist in 1995, the new government formed by Benjamin Netanyahu restarted Jewish settlements in the Palestinian West Bank.[15] America's own move to the right under George W. Bush (2001–2009) ensured that Israel could adopt this more intransigent policy with few international repercussions. The build-up of Palestinian militancy on the West Bank, and particularly the Gaza Strip, spelled future conflict. This was especially true after the fall of Hosni Mubarak's regime in Egypt in 2011 and the accession of a Muslim Brotherhood government in Cairo which supported Hamas, a Palestinian militant group. In 2014, Netanyahu's determination to destroy this movement in the Gaza Strip led to an assault on the area which killed hundreds of its inhabitants and turned much of world opinion against Israel.

More broadly, events in Iraq, Libya, Afghanistan and even Pakistan counselled against Western intervention. As the linguist and expert on the Muslim world Rory Stewart came to realise, humanitarian intervention by foreigners of a different faith and without local knowledge could never achieve the state-building goals that Western optimists hoped for.[16] This lesson had been partially learned by the time of the Syrian civil war of 2011–2013. The destruction of indigenous regimes merely led to local conflict and social fragmentation and the emergence of yet more radical movements.

It remains difficult to comprehend such a multiplicity of divisions without returning once again to the earlier history of these regions. The Ottomans, despite their reputation for despotism, ruled their diverse empire by hiving off political power to ethnic–religious units (the *millets*) and to acculturated local leaderships. As the empire began to modernise, this decentralisation proved difficult to maintain with the result that Arab, Turkish, Kurdish and other patriotisms became more assertive. Western colonial powers used their military and economic superiority to suppress revolt, but nevertheless relied on the acquiescence of local rulers, whether it was the Pathan tribes of the Northwest Frontier or the Sunni rulers of Trans-Jordan and Iraq, or the Zionist settlers in Palestine.[17] When the European colonial powers withdrew, unwilling to bear the costs of empire, they found that the best way to maintain their vital interests in global strategy or oil extraction could be met by supporting, directly or indirectly, a range of authoritarian rulers who could hold together their disparate societies by political bribery and force. This accounts for the longevity of figures such as Hosni Mubarak, Muammar Gaddafi, the Assad family in Syria, Saddam Hussein in Iraq or even, to some extent, the military governments in Pakistan. All these regimes had crossed the Western powers in one way or another, notably in the case of the apparent Libyan destruction of a US passenger plane over Lockerbie in Scotland in 1984. Yet, the dangers of their removal were considered by Western governments potentially greater than any advantages, as indeed proved to be the case between 2003 and 2015.

After 1991, these despotic governments found it particularly hard to maintain control of the populations they ruled, and the small wars of fragmentation became more general.[18] At the local level, Muslim religious and cultural movements became increasingly powerful, affecting even the Uighur population of western China.[19] In many cases, these were the only organisations offering social services and a kind of civil society in authoritarian states. Equally, the massive growth of the young, particularly the young male, population made societies across Africa and Asia more volatile. It was quite evident that the great increase in oil revenues was only benefiting small elites and the Western powers. Improved communications and the penetration of Western lifestyles created envy, but also revulsion and hatred in equal measure. These complex problems were only worsened when, out of economic self-interest or humanitarian compulsions, Western powers actually sent armed forces into these societies.

SMALL WARS OF FRAGMENTATION REDOUBLED: AFRICA AND LATIN AMERICA

Regional and local conflicts of this sort were not confined to the Middle East or Afghanistan, though this region remained the centre of attention between 1991 and 2015. In Algeria, for instance, ferocious armed conflict broke out in 1991 ostensibly between Islamist militants and the inheritors of the more secular and increasingly corrupt FLN regime which had been in power since the French withdrew from the country.[20] Yet, this little-reported war came about because of complex disputes within the army and civil bureaucracy and between groups which classed themselves as Arab and Berber respectively. Ethiopia and later West Africa and Sudan saw similar insurgencies which were reported as contests between Islamists and secular or Christian elites. Very often, however, these could only be understood in terms of local ethnic and linguistic divisions, compounded by differences of wealth between areas which had benefited from oil and other exports to the West and impoverished and often dry interiors. When, in 2013, the Christian South Sudan became independent after a long conflict with the overwhelmingly Muslim North, a further civil war soon broke out in the South, in essence between the Nuer and Dinka tribal groups, whose rivalry had been formalised during British colonial rule.[21]

Historians of international relations have sometimes attempted to classify long historical periods on the basis of the types of conflicts and alliances which characterised them. The period after 1991 clearly differed from the new imperialism of the late nineteenth century, the European and East Asian struggles of the 1930s and the Cold War period itself. In this later era, the withdrawal of the former Soviet Union from its forward foreign policy stance meant that the world was not divided, as it had been earlier, between two strong and contending systems of power. Secondly, the years after 1991 were characterised, as argued here, by the acceleration of internal conflicts between ethnicities and submerged nationalities, which had been held in check by relatively strong imperial and post-imperial centralised states. Sometimes, these took the form of leftist insurrections or "little revolutions", as in Latin America or Indian "Maoism". But these movements had little in common with the earlier networks of the International. Instead, they were loose groupings of marginalised tribal and ethnic groups who used the language of Marxist–Leninism to signal their anti-statism.

In central India, for instance, the "Maoism" of the Chhattisgarh region represented a rebellion of "tribal" groups against the appropriation of their common lands by mining companies and incoming settlers from the lowlands. With the support of some radical urban intellectuals, this movement had succeeded in holding the police and army at bay. Even taking account of its massive population, it was striking that in 2014 "India witnessed 190 IED explosions, putting it just behind Pakistan and Iraq",[22] many planted by "Maoists". Similar events happened somewhat earlier in Latin America. In Chile, the state continued to oppress the Mapuche Indians.[23] In the southern Mexican hill region of Chiapas, the Zapatista revolutionary movement emerged in the 1980s and 1990s, besieging the town of San Cristóbal de las Casas in 1994.[24] They were recruited from indigenous tribal groups which were marginalised, losing their holdings to landowners and urban interests. Their title harked back to the Mexican revolution of 1911–1917 and they also displayed images of the Cuban Marxist revolutionary Che Guevara and invoked Mao.

The Zapatistas and other anti-state groups founded local collectives which provided healthcare and financial support to the destitute. In some cases, where these local revolutionary groups managed to link up with the grievances of mainstream cultivators and urban working classes, they created local or even state-level governments. One example of this was the rule of Hugo Chávez in Venezuela, from 1999 onwards.[25] This was one of the few cases of a late-century socialist government which had not adopted neo-liberal norms. Finally, the phenomenon of international connection and the transfer of money, goods and ideas, which was increasingly termed "globalisation", also served to spread loose networks of transnational insurgency. Islamist and other neo-religious networks received great attention. Yet, "democratic" versions, often tipping over to violence themselves, included the "Occupy" movements in the United States and Europe, protests against gross expenditure on football in Rio, against corruption in India and Bangladesh and pro-democracy movements in Hong Kong and the Middle East. Theorists began to write of political forms not orientated to power, with no firm leadership or objective, merely the desire to communicate anger within a fragmented system of representation. This marked a sharp break with the long-standing emphasis on state power in the work of intellectuals from the dominant school, notably Michel Foucault and Pierre Bourdieu.[26] In searching for any kind of parallel, the historian of international relations would probably have to reach back to late-nineteenth-century anarchism or the radical groups of the 1840s which fomented the revolutions of 1848.

THE TRIUMPH AND CRISIS OF CAPITALISM

Over the period from about 1991 to 2015, militant jihadism, these little revolutions and the small wars of fragmentation were characteristic, unsurprisingly, of poorer regions of the world which had not benefited from the resurgence of free-market capitalism and the decline of orthodox Communism from the later 1980s. Conflicts in "marginal" areas such as Iraq and Afghanistan, Somalia and dry northern Nigeria impacted on international politics to some extent during the long boom of the Western world, China, India and Brazil. Yet, initially, these conflicts did not impede the apparent growth of global wealth, which seemed to presage the worldwide triumph of so-called neo-liberalism both in societies formally democratic and also in those such as China and Vietnam which were still dominated by centralised Communist parties. Russia and India also moved towards the free-market model, though here democratic processes took on new and particular forms.

After 1985, Boris Yeltsin and Mikhail Gorbachev pushed through reforms which had privatised the USSR's state industries and introduced multiparty elections and free speech. The old industries had been structured to complement each other across large areas of the Soviet Union and often did not operate as coherent localised units. Their demise caused considerable economic distress and threw many former state employees into poverty. This, along with disillusion and nostalgia, was the background to the attempted pro-Communist coup in August 1991 against the Yeltsin government. Its failure confirmed the reformers in power, led to the disbanding of the Communist Party of the Soviet Union and hastened the end of the Cold War.[27] The pace of economic change then increased dramatically after 1992, but immediately created great disparities of power and wealth, particularly between newly rich business tycoons and former state employees. This led to a further conflict between Yeltsin and more conservative forces in 1993.[28] What maintained the momentum towards a semi-free market was the fact that many of those who benefited from the privatisation of state property and had bought shares in it in 1993 were themselves former Communist officials who were disinclined to part with their new riches. There emerged a class of industrialists and financiers who were sometimes called oligarchs. Of these, some became the new elite of the Putin era of the 2000s while others became Vladimir Putin's arch-enemies and were driven abroad or imprisoned.[29]

By 2003–2004, the territory of the former USSR and its eastern European Communist allies had apparently stabilised remarkably quickly. Yeltsin, Gorbachev and even, initially, Putin had refrained from intervention when neighbouring states, including Latvia and Lithuania, had refused to join any new, Russian-led union. Moscow had even remained quiet when the former East Germany joined NATO. Only in parts of the Caucasus, where Russian leaders feared the rise of Islamism, were Russian troops deployed. By the early years of the new century, the Russian economy, too, had begun to recover from the shock of fragmentation. This was a consequence of the country's vast and often newly discovered oil and energy reserves, which helped fuel the febrile economic boom of these years in Europe and also rising consumption in China. Agriculture also recovered as world food prices rose and the spread of the computer and new technologies played an important role, as it did in the West.

It was this that supported the centralising tendencies of Putin, who continued to dominate the country both as president and prime minister.[30] Richer urban Russians, particularly in Moscow, felt increasingly cheated of the democracy they thought had been instituted during the Gorbachev–Yeltsin years. But ordinary Russians, especially rural people, supported by the Orthodox Church, compliant oligarchs and improving living standards brought Putin back to power, despite his slow erosion of the liberties granted in 1991. State marketisation and constrained democracy therefore characterised the new Russia just as it was symptomatic of change across much of the world. Putin was often represented by domestic and Western critics as a dictator returning Russia not to murderously egalitarian Stalinism but to something more like interwar fascism.

Certainly, like those earlier dictators, Putin benefited initially from growing prosperity and the belief that he was reversing the humiliations of the past. He even seemed intent on reviving the old Soviet federation by using strong-arm tactics in Ukraine, a policy that, in 2014, led to the first significant war in Europe since the 1950s. Yet, Putin cleverly avoided over-centralisation by supporting local governance and placating the Orthodox Church. During his time, the feminist art collective Pussy Riot, which had staged a rave in a Moscow cathedral, was imprisoned for "undermining the spiritual foundations of the state".[31] Putin also improved relations with China. Paradoxically, perhaps, he had emerged as one of the most admired men in the world, according to an international survey in 2014.

In Eastern Europe, which had been firmly under the control of Communist parties as late as 1988, the collapse of the USSR did not lead to direct warfare outside the former Yugoslavia. The assimilation of East into West Germany was entirely peaceful, despite the fears of many Western leaders. Yet, tendencies to fragmentation still remained when the old quasi-imperial systems of rule collapsed. In 1993, for instance, Czechoslovakia broke into two states. Across the region, the tendency was for the re-emergence of small and sometimes aggressive nationalisms. After 2000, there was a resurgence of anti-Semitism in several of the states of the former Eastern bloc, regardless of the fact that the vast majority of the Jewish population had been massacred during the Holocaust. Roma gypsies were persecuted in Hungary which spawned a neo-fascist movement, the Jobbik Party, which harked back to the 1930s.[32] Hard-line Catholicism and Orthodox Christianity re-emerged and not only former Communist but socialist institutions came under attack. In Germany, a neo-Nazi Party reformed to the great embarrassment of Germany's liberal rulers. Chauvinist anti-immigration parties emerged in Western Europe as a response to the free movement of people between EU states as well as renewed immigration from the Middle East, Africa and Asia caused by conflict and globalisation.

These fissiparous tendencies, though largely non-violent, also occurred in countries which had not been under Communist rule. Now that the European Union and later the single currency were in operation, the power of the more established and larger nation states seemed to have diminished. At the same time, old and new social media could generate enlarged groups of activists who operated outside the bounds of the older institutions of civil society. Italy faced the separatism of the Lega Nord; France, Corsican nationalism; Britain the growing influence of the Scottish National Party and the UK Independence Party: all separatist parties, albeit with very different aims.[33] Two of the most striking examples of this were, first, the split between Walloons and French-speakers in Belgium, which virtually paralysed the country in the early years of the new century; secondly, the rise of Catalan nationalism, where the richest region of the country increasingly resented what was thought to be the predatory actions of the Madrid elite.[34] The decline of the Spanish economy after 2008 only strengthened this separatist movement. Broadly, therefore, the end of the Cold War and the rise of globalised market capitalism inaugurated a new, more fluid international order and one in which new and often more localised forms of ethnic and religious conflict replaced the old contests between states and blocs. Some were non-violent democratic movements; others, implicated in the small wars of fragmentation.

These forms of hyperreactive modernity and anti-globalisation saw the concurrence of movements of regional solidarity against the centre in many countries. But they sometimes coalesced with other protest groups, as when marches against the François Hollande government in France in 2013 saw Breton nationalists, "anti-gay marriage" Catholics and opponents of road taxes all marching together. Even in the United States, the religious right, reacting to Obama's pro-diversity liberalism, took on a similar form. Its proponents combined religious conservatism, hostility to taxation, state benefits and gun control. This ideology was sometimes infused with a covert racism, especially in the Southern states. In Japan, right-wing nationalists of the Nippon Kaigi group rejected notions of the country's war guilt, demanded the rewriting of school textbooks, generated suspicion of gender equality and campaigned for Japanese control of islands in the South China Sea.[35]

In China, surprisingly, the transition from Communism to a politically centralised free-market society was rather easier, even following the ravages of late Maoism. Despite the violent suppression of dissidence after Tiananmen, the new economy emerged earlier and apparently with less pain. This was in part because, even during the Cultural Revolution, a low level of farmer entrepreneurship was allowed to develop across much of the country. Farmers were not given direct title to their land, but having fulfilled their state quotas, they were allowed to sell on the open market. By the beginning of the new century a body of relatively wealthy farmers had emerged which sold agricul-tural products to the new wealthy of the towns. Equally, though Deng Xiaoping and his allies had been ruthless in suppressing political opposition at a wider level, local Communist cadres became somewhat more open to debate so that some level of inclusiveness re-emerged. The Chinese authorities were acutely aware of the danger of national fragmentation, apparent in the case of the USSR, but, equally, they appreciated the threat of internal sclerosis that had manifested in the days of Leonid Brezhnev and his peers. Hong Kong and Chinese societies in Southeast Asia also provided a model, expertise and ultimately capital for the development of a controlled, but economically aspiring, society.[36] At the beginning of the twenty-first century, Mao was still taught in schools and remained a party icon, especially for some powerful local bosses. But on the 120th anniversary of his birth in December 2013, he might, to use the phrase uttered by the Roman Emperor Vespasian on his deathbed, have felt himself "becoming a god". At his former residence rural people burnt incense, left gifts and called upon his spirit for his blessings. Other Communist founding fathers, including Ho and even Stalin, experienced a similar epiphany, their old ideas on political economy now masked by a semi-divine status.

As in the former USSR, state enterprises in China were privatised and allowed to build up capital for expansion. The People's Liberation Army was particularly adept at investing in modern armament production and benefiting from sales to countries which were suspect to the Western powers: Iran, Iraq, Pakistan and, notably, North Korea. Unconstrained by world markets, the authorities embarked upon a massive expansion of road and rail networks, which in turn realised the value of real estate across the country. The economic model was definitely export-orientated, imitating the earlier success of Japan, Hong Kong, Singapore and South Korea, and this worked well while Europe and America were going through their boom period between 1995 and 2007. Thereafter, the Beijing authorities began to redirect economic growth towards the domestic market. Broadly, this tactic seemed to be as successful as the earlier boom in Japan during the 1970s and 1980s. But its longer-term result remained in doubt.

Observers pointed to coming problems: demographic imbalances and the destruction of the environment, where, as in India, the water table fell precipitously. Many rural people were left behind in this dash for wealth, though control of the media meant that their dissidence was little known, compared with developments in South Asia or Latin America. Equally, the former Party and military bosses who had enriched themselves as Chinese versions of Russian oligarchs began to pose a threat to the Beijing rulers. This was particularly true if they were dominant in some region distant from the capital and could summon up a sense of nostalgia about the Maoist past while still pandering to the new rich. Intellectuals and exiles warned the Central Committee that political tensions were again building up dangerously. Still, China's wealthy new elite, which looked forward to overtaking the United States itself in gross GDP within a decade or so, seemed acquiescent enough and largely uninterested in the formal trappings of democracy, free speech and a multiparty electoral system.

The other huge Asian society, India, which was expected to overtake even China as the largest human population on the planet by 2020, still remained a formal democracy which, despite pervasive internal and external criticism, was a remarkable circumstance. The period began badly with a major balance of payments crisis in 1990–1991 when India almost went bankrupt, gold had to be remitted to London to appease creditors and the IMF had to bail the country out. The prime minister, P. V. Narasimha Rao, appointed the economist Manmohan Singh as finance minister and he immediately introduced policies of liberalisation. Tariffs were reduced, a certain amount of direct foreign investment was allowed, state enterprises were broken up and privatised while the rupee was devalued to promote exports. Continuing fear of "foreign capitalists", tinged with the historical memory of the English East India

Company, limited further liberalisation, especially of the retail trade. But, powered by wider global expansion, the Indian economy reached a reasonable level of 7% growth per annum by 2000. This was essential in view of the continuing rise in population.[37] As in other major economies, the value of real estate around the major cities moved rapidly upwards. Equally, differentials of wealth widened. By 2005, it was calculated that the well-off Indian middle class numbered about 300 million. But numerous suicides amongst poor farmers, trapped by falling demand for their products, provided evidence that wealth did not necessarily "trickle down".

Nevertheless, following the report of the Mandal Commission of 1990, India embarked upon a further massive round of positive discrimination which alleviated inequality for some significant sections of the population.[38] B. R. Ambedkar's role in the making of the constitution of independent India had secured quotas in government jobs for Dalits (or "untouchables"). Mandal ensured that so-called Other Backward Castes (OBCs) also received similar quotas and other forms of support. This led to what some have seen as the "casteisation" of democracy, with politicians pitching their policies to garner the support of these newly advantaged groups, which reached 40% of the total population in some areas. The vigour of representational politics, however, showed no sign of diminishing over the following 20 years, especially since the Bharatiya Janata Party (BJP) had emerged as a viable opposition for the Congress at a national as well as regional level. Parties representing Dalits and OBCs also took power in key northern states after 2000.

The rise of the "Hindutva" politics of the BJP and the later emergence of the Aam Aadmi Party (the "Common Man Party") did not restrain the liberalisation of the economy, since these parties were supported by the business community and the overseas Indian diaspora. Yet, the prevailing discrimination against Muslims, powered by hostility to Pakistan and the spectre of Islamism, had effects which alarmed Indian moderates. In 2002, a pogrom against Muslims was instituted in the western state of Gujarat, while in the city of Mumbai (Bombay) and its vicinity an anti-Muslim and anti-southerner party, the Shiv Sena, gained greater influence. No more than in China, Europe or the United States did economic liberalisation necessarily lead to the further diffusion of democratic norms. In India, as elsewhere, powerful vested interest came to dominate politics and the media. Yet, India's democratic forms, albeit increasingly casteised and *sui generis*, did maintain a degree of openness which was not in evidence across most of the rest of Asia, Africa and the Middle East and was by no means universal across Europe and the United States. That openness finally allowed the BJP to return triumphantly to power in 2014, led by Narendra Modi, apparently heralding a major change in India's economic and social policy with a tilt towards Hinduism and business interests alike. The very widespread support for Modi appeared to trump regionalism and casteism, at least in the medium term.

The most important event in Africa during these years, as noted in Chapter 9, was the final end of the apartheid regime in South Africa, a rare case of true political liberation, but one connected to other major themes of this era. Between 1990 and 1994, Prime Minister F. W. de Klerk repealed most of the legislation which had condemned the black majority to second-class, segregated status. The social effects of this political liberation were much slower to manifest themselves. The massive, impoverished black townships which had grown up in the apartheid era grew even further in size.[39] New black elites, led by Nelson Mandela, emerged from within the African National Congress which took power after elections in 1994 and held it thereafter, becoming viewed by many as corrupt, even by its own youth wing. Large sections of the former white ruling class also retained their hold on capital, resources and land. This was in marked contrast to the situation in Zimbabwe to the north, where whites were progressively stripped of their land and resources during the autocratic rule of Robert Mugabe, who held power from 1980 to 2015, despite the desire of Britain and other Western powers to see him gone.

Elsewhere, the majority governments which came to power after the end of colonial rule have varied greatly in effectiveness, finding themselves at the mercy of sharp changes in the value of commodities on the world market, the AIDS epidemic of the 1990s and, later, religious conflicts which set Islamists against Christian populations in Nigeria and the former French West Africa. Forms of democratic government emerged in Kenya and Tanzania, but over much of the continent small ruling groups hung on to power through their control of reserves of raw materials and connections with international business and tourism. In Kenya, free elections were held in 2002 and 2008 and former ethnic conflicts were allayed to some extent. In Nigeria, 34 years of military rule ended in 1999 and elections were held in that year, 2003 and 2011, though amidst widespread charges of vote rigging. Ethnic and religious violence remained pervasive. Nevertheless, by the 2010s, many observers were marking out Africa as the continent of the future. Here wealth was finally beginning to "trickle down", not least because China and other Asian countries had a heavy investment in African raw materials. Representative government had also emerged from the doldrums in which it had languished in the "long 1980s".

In Latin America, free-market capitalism also registered some gains between 1991 and 2013 and democracy was restored in parts of the continent.[40] The pressure from, and example of, the huge American economy to the north played an important role here, with residents in the United States drawn from these countries acting as a kind of commercial diaspora and remitting funds and expertise. The rising value of raw materials and oil during the great boom also helped countries such as Brazil and Venezuela to raise standards of living and develop a consumer society. These new middle classes were not prepared to maintain the old economic nationalism of tariffs and strict controls on foreign investment, even if the result was unemployment and the growth of inequality. Some of these moves towards economic liberalism had already begun under previous military rulers, as in Pinochet's courting of the neo-liberal "Chicago Boys" in Chile. But they were generally extended under the civilian governments which came to power in the later 1990s. The great exception was Cuba, but even here quiet moves to allow small farmers to own their land were under way as the rule of Fidel Castro drifted into history and the United States finally lifted its sanctions.

Latin America was largely spared the small wars of fragmentation which afflicted the former Soviet Union, the Middle East and parts of Africa. But forms of internal insurgency – perhaps small revolutions – flared up in Colombia, for instance. These left many thousands dead during the 1990s in battles between the authorities and an armed resistance movement, FARC (Revolutionary Armed Forces of Colombia). At the beginning of the decade, 52% of the land in the country was owned by less than 2% of the population and much of the elite's accumulated wealth was parked abroad as international capital flows intensified. Another kind of internal war of fragmentation, distinct from the Zapatista insurgency, broke out in Mexico, a state with a strong democratic tradition. The insatiable demand for drugs in the United States and migration across the Mexican–US border as the American economy expanded empowered huge criminal organisations. These gangsters indulged in competitive slaughter which brought about a situation where parts of the country were effectively out of control of Mexico City, which was forced to deploy the army in 2007–2008. The drug wars continued unabated up to 2014, when the murder of dozens of students nearly brought down the government.

As in other parts of the world, the relationship between neo-liberalism and democracy remained complex. In Brazil, Chile and Uruguay, stable constitutional governments and plural political systems maintained themselves for much of the period. In Brazil, for instance, the left-wing Workers' Party, which came to power in 2002, successfully balanced a programme to reduce poverty with an open market and downward pressure on inflation, so gaining credit on the world market. By the end of the 2000s, Brazil had supposedly overtaken Britain's economy in size, at least for a time. There was little sign during this period of new military coups, even if the army remained a force in several of these states. Authoritarian government had generally failed to raise living standards during the 1980s, and had tended to speed internal fragmentation. The "democratic dawn" of the 1990s had widely improved living standards. But this did not rule out moves to the left in some countries. Hugo Chávez's government in Venezuela embarked on a massive redistribution of wealth based on oil revenues.[41] The opposition of the formerly prosperous middle class was suppressed. Towards the end of the 2000s, the Cristina Kirchner government in Argentina also adapted a populist mien, nationalised foreign interests and reignited the nationalist quarrel with the United Kingdom over the Falklands (Malvinas). Even though the Cuban government relaxed its firm control over private land ownership and foreign investment in the last years of the Castro regime, the Communist Party retained its firm grip on power.

Overall, the media of the early 2000s took a dismal view of the world situation, reminiscent in some ways of the foreboding of the 1900s or 1930s. Small wars, terrorist attacks and the politics of inequality dominated newspapers, radio and television and were popularised through Facebook and Twitter. Yet, as the next section suggests, inequality, at a global level at least, was diminishing and there had been a sea change towards democratic, multiparty government in several major countries. In the meantime, though, the world economy suffered its greatest crisis since the 1930s.

GLOBALISATION, PROSPERITY AND CRISIS

Several public figures, economists and journalists attempted to explain the "boom to bust" period between the First Gulf War and the world recession which began in 2008 with the collapse of Lehman Brothers, the US investment bank.[42] Surviving Marxists, such as Eric Hobsbawm, argued that the globalised world of capitalism, which emerged in the second half of the twentieth century, was inherently unstable. Late-Keynesian economists asserted that the problem was the doctrine of "the perfection of the market", supposedly promoted by figures such as Milton Friedman, which encouraged political leaders to let credit get out of hand and allowed states to build up huge deficits which eventually had to be tackled by regimes of austerity. Others came forward with a political argument. They claimed, for instance, that George W. Bush's Republican administration had a series of ideological goals all of which massively expanded the deficit and encouraged an explosion of personal debt. The war against Islamist terrorism came together with the need to encourage the Republican Party's wealthy backers and business interests by reducing taxation. At the same time, the exigencies of American popular politics required lending institutions to pour cheap credit into the housing market to appease lower-middle-class and working-class people, especially black and Hispanic people. Certainly, the combination of mass democratic politics, globalised money flows and Islamist insurgency meant that this latest "crisis of capitalism" was significantly different from earlier ones. It is true, as economic historians have pointed out, that major economic crises seem to strike the world economy every two generations or so: in the 1820s, 1870s, 1930s, 1970s, and in 2008–2015. But the underlying causes of this had shifted dramatically over these 200 years.

Even though the early-twenty-first-century crash was a worldwide phenomenon, there were also more specific local cultural differences which contributed to it. Here the case of Japan was instructive. Japan's "lost decades" began in 1991, well before any similar phenomenon was detected in the rest of the Western world.[43] The crisis had in common with later Latin American, US and European experience a massive property boom. But the underlying causes were subtly different in each case. In Japan, the propensity of families to save, inherited from the dark days of post-war poverty, meant that banks had huge sums of money to lend. The Bank of Japan was, moreover, a much more Keynesian animal than its European and American partners. The idea had been to speed Japan to the top of the international league of wealth by pumping money into the economy. Here the bank found a useful ally in the Liberal Democratic government which had held power since the 1950s. Its dominance arose from its appeal both to the salaried and entrepreneurial middle class that enjoyed low taxation and easy credit and to the still-substantial farming community. The government invested heavily in infrastructure, atomic energy plants, roads and bridges which apparently benefited rural people wishing to get their goods to market. In fact, many of these bridges and roads were, as critics later argued, "routes to nowhere". But, as in the United States and the welfare states of Europe, democratic politics encouraged the government to spend heavily on favoured parts of the electorate. Only very high productivity could fund this indefinitely and, outside Germany, many governments were to learn this the hard way after 2008.

Japan, however, had already suffered this fate.[44] When the "bubble" burst in 1990–1991, it was because asset prices, particularly the price of property in Tokyo and other major cities, had reached such heights that foreign investors and, latterly, the local business community suddenly realised that they were unsustainable. As asset prices plummeted, the banks and ordinary people were crushed with bad loans; the stock market collapsed, while Japanese consumers, who had always been risk-averse, ceased to buy. Economic growth dropped to less than 1% per annum compared with the 5–7% before the crash. Although Japanese manufacturers, notably the specialist automobile producers and computer giants, continued to find a ready market overseas, a weak recovery in 1994–1995 was aborted by a parallel financial crash in Japan's eastern markets in Singapore, Malaysia, Indonesia and Thailand in 1997–1998.[45]

At the time, the Bank of Japan was criticised for failing to act fast enough to prevent the country from drifting into deflation and for continuing to direct credit to failed companies. Yet, it is not difficult to see why cautious policies were adopted in view of the historical context. Japanese memories of the social crisis of the Second World War and its aftermath were still fresh, while the idea of printing yen on an even greater scale and artificially creating inflation was deeply worrying in a country concerned with social stability and predictable foreign relations. A devaluation of the yen might have sparked competitive devaluations of other currencies, damaging exports which broadly remained the best hope for recovery. In fact, by comparison with the later credit crisis in Europe and the United States, Japan's crisis was relatively mild. Political and social stability was broadly maintained, even though the Liberal Democratic government was criticised as incompetent and corrupt. By 2015, Japan's decade of deflation seemed to ease, but growth remained low and national debt unsustainably high.

By contrast, then, with the financial crises of earlier decades, a major common feature of the events of the 1990s and 2000s across the world was that these were, at one level, democratic crises of capitalism. Governments, banks and even international bodies such as the IMF, the World Bank and the EU were all trying to benefit mass electorates. In the case of the United States and Europe, reducing income tax and fomenting credit provision for house purchases had the same effect. It is often assumed that the income tax reductions put in place by George W. Bush benefited only the rich. It is certainly true that wealthy Americans commanded a massive slice of the country's GDP by 2007.[46] Yet Reagan, and Bush, like Clinton, had also significantly reduced the tax burden on middle and lower income families which spurred property purchases and created conditions in which federal loan institutions collapsed after 2007. Similarly, in the United Kingdom, Tony

Blair's and Gordon Brown's lax monetary policy was designed to pull sections of the urban working class out of poverty and also, of course, to secure their own re-election. In mainland Europe and the "white Commonwealth", fiscal negligence resulted from continuing competition between moderate socialist parties and conservatives who believed in low taxation to spur entrepreneurship. There was, however, a further consideration which marked out the European and US crises from the earlier Japanese one and, indeed, from the Great Depression of the 1930s. In addition to the "bursting of the asset bubble", when property, stocks and shares collapsed in value, the globalisation of finance and labour along with the severity of the sovereign debt crises in most developed countries made it even more difficult for governments and banks to respond to the turmoil. The globalisation of finance resulted in an increased ability for big companies, particularly highly successful products of the new "high-tech" economy, such as Microsoft and Google, and the Japanese computer "giants", to move their earnings to tax havens and avoid contributing to the revenues of the United States and European nations, precisely when these earnings were particularly badly needed. The example of the European Economic and Monetary Union was a case in point. The euro had made it possible for relatively weaker economies in southern Europe to borrow from those in the northern states, particularly France and Germany, at low rates of interest. Property prices surged in Spain, Portugal and Greece after 2000. But government debt also grew very fast because of welfare provision and an ageing population. When, after 2007, governments were required to bail out banks in the EU and Britain government debt became so severe that they were forced to put into effect economic measures which pushed the whole continent into a severe recession. After the recession, officials of the US treasury argued that only by bailing out the banks, however negligent, could an even greater collapse have been avoided. Some economists argued that the state should have aided householders struggling with negative equity and so preserve their purchasing power and the wider economy.[47]

The recession had shown only moderate signs of abating by 2015, making it, indeed, the worst financial crisis since the Great Depression. This had serious political and social consequences. Poverty grew, especially as poorer people were hit concurrently by a significant rise in the cost of food and clothing as a consequence of world demographic growth and poor agricultural seasons. Radical parties, reminiscent of, or in some cases with a direct ideological lineage back to, the 1930s, grew in popularity, opposing immigration and sceptical of the moves to European unity which had taken place over the previous 50 years.

Despite its very different political system, some of the same problems emerged in the United States after 2007. The collapse of Lehman Brothers in that year, when the federal government refused to intervene to bail it out, marked the beginning of the high point of the world financial turmoil. The following crisis of confidence led to the collapse of real estate prices and the stock market alongside a sharp jump in the debt burden on ordinary families. But once again this was a crisis of democracy as well as a crisis of capitalism. A multitude of divisions over the role of government emerged, between

Republicans and Democrats, rich and poor, mid-Americans and the east and the west coasts, young Latinos and blacks against ageing whites. Democrats had long argued that democratic government required the extension of health insurance and pensions to the poor. They also backed liberal objections to intervention on issues such as prayer in schools and abortion. Republicans, by contrast, were far from the conservative centralisers of Europe. They believed that democracy required a small state, low taxation and minimal legislative intervention except on a moral issue such as abortion. On the radical right, the Tea Party movement, which merged Christian values with a call for low taxation and localised government, gained influence in Congress during the 2000s.[48] Some left-wing commentators have implied that this was an issue between rich capitalists and the middle and lower classes. Certainly, business and even bodies such as the National Rifle Association supported the Republican right in electoral contests. Yet, the key issue here remained the relationship between the individual and the state: in other words, the meaning of democracy itself.

There was also a wider issue which struck at the heart of democracy and affected all the major developed economies. In addition to the issues of state–citizen relations and wealth disparity, there was the question of age. The so-called baby boomer generation was hostile to taxation, even to corporate taxation, because its pension funds were significantly supported by big companies which evaded taxation by using overseas havens. Yet, they wanted health-care and social support provision for their old age. The question then arose: in a democracy, should the old, often in positions of power, be able to control public policy in their own interest?

That this crisis of capitalism was in fact a crisis for democracy became clearer as Western governments and Japan tried to deal with the aftermath of their financial crises. In Japan, the long years of Liberal Democrat Party (LDP) domination were abruptly ended when Prime Minister Shinzo Abe was ejected from office in 2009. But the incoming coalition government proved inept in many respects. It failed to tackle Japan's huge national debt which had grown ever larger since 1991. It failed to act decisively in the aftermath of the tsunami of 2011 which had threatened north central Japan with a major nuclear disaster. It did little in its short term of office to dismantle the vested interests which were perceived to be frustrating Japan's recovery from the long period of economic stagnation. As other countries began pumping money into their own withering economies, the yen rose in value, making Japanese exports yet more expensive at the very moment that an increasingly bitter territorial conflict with China stalled the country's exports to the mainland. The result was a further election in which the "old guard" of the LDP returned to power under Abe and began to pump money into the economy along the lines of the Federal Reserve and the Bank of England.

Japan's government at least remained an elected one. In the eurozone, democracy proved less resilient as governments grappled both with sovereign debt and the collapse of the credit bubble. The eurozone authorities, the IMF, the stronger European governments and the World Bank all responded to the crisis by attempting to impose austerity, that is cutting wages of state employees, raising taxes and curtailing expenditure in order to reduce deficits and government debt. This saw harsh terms being imposed on Greece by a "troika" of unelected European officials in return for monetary aid. In Italy, meanwhile, a "technocratic" government led by an unelected prime minister, Mario Monti, replaced the elected but discredited government of Silvio Berlusconi. Spain and Portugal saw similar policies imposed on them by governments reacting to indirect threats from the European authorities. Even Britain, which retained the luxury of its own currency and could therefore devalue, suffered severe spending cuts under the government of David Cameron. To remaining neo-Keynesians, such as the American economist Paul Krugman, these seemed precisely the wrong economic policies, since depressing growth would actually increase sovereign debt in the medium term. The globalisation of finance and financial prediction meant that governments which actually increased spending would be punished by international markets and downgraded by international credit rating agencies. This impasse was in some respects reminiscent of the 1930s. Yet, while America's New Deal was often invoked, economic historians were aware of the fact that Roosevelt's measures were only partly successful until massive wartime expenditure supervened to boost the US economy for the next two generations.

While Europe faced a restriction of democratic accountability, the United States, if anything, saw an excess of democracy. A new alliance of the young people, blacks and Hispanics had ensured a Democratic victory in the elections of 2008 and 2012. But President Barack Obama faced huge problems in implementing measures which could reduce the country's large deficit, brought about by Bush's tax reductions and the long wars in Iraq and Afghanistan. The Tea Party movement had pulled the Republican Party far to the right, to the extent that it came close to vetoing any tax rise whatsoever. Since it also refused any reduction in military spending, the consequence could only be cuts in welfare benefits, education and other federal spending. This the Democrat majority in the Senate refused and, given the complex division of powers which was still enshrined in the US constitution, well-targeted economic policies were difficult to formulate. The success of Obama's main policy initiative, the proposal to implement compulsory social security, was still in doubt in 2015, a year after mid-term elections had given Republicans control of both houses of Congress, though a reasonable rate of economic growth had been achieved again.

THE PAINS OF GLOBALISATION AND THE RETURN OF THE NATIONAL

At the beginning of 2015, international opinion and the media continued to exude a sense of unease. Economists noted that, though living standards were much higher worldwide than they had been in the 1930s and famine had been banished except in parts of East Africa, the economic downturn had lasted even longer than the Great Depression itself. Europe seemed destined for a long period of further stagnation and the recovery in the United States remained fragile. The rise of Brazil, India, China and Southeast Asia gave some hope of a new stimulus to the world economy and some prophesied the gradual demise of the West and the rise of the East in a manner which echoed the earlier prophecies of Oswald Spengler. Yet, closer observers noted the severe problems which were yet to reveal themselves in these societies. All of them suffered from huge regional differences of wealth between town and country, though these were less visible in China, where information was tightly policed. China and India suffered from demographic imbalances, as the previous chapter indicates. In Argentina, one of the richest countries in the world in 1900, the political crises of the 1940s and 1950s, followed by defaults in 2002 and 2014 which shut it out of global financial markets, had greatly reduced its relative standing and wealth.[49]

These economic, demographic and environmental problems overlapped and intersected with widespread political instabilities. One-issue radical political parties, organised to oppose immigration, austerity or political integration, emerged strongly in Europe, while American politics remained dangerously polarised. Russia seemed destined to a new form of authoritarian rule under Vladimir Putin, even though he had come to power through an election and enjoyed popular support. Various insurgencies afflicted other parts of the world. Leftist "Maoist" risings continued to occur in Latin America and India. Islamist movements divided ethnicities and religious groups in much of Africa, Pakistan and even Burma and Thailand. Most striking was the Arab world's "Spring" – or rather its "1848" – in which movements of young people pushing for democratic representation ultimately hatched new forms of authoritarian states, often with an Islamist tinge. In Turkey, hailed at least after the 1960s for being both secularist and increasingly democratic, the Recep Erdoğan government of the 2010s appeared to be swinging towards authoritarianism and Islamism, while at the same time it was denounced as corrupt even by its erstwhile Islamist supporters. In India, the BJP under Narendra Modi, regarded with suspicion by leftist and Muslim voters as a Hindutva ideologue, came to power in 2014. There were few years over the previous century in which pessimistic commentators had found such a confluence of challenges to prosperity and peace. Especially in the Western world, economic and political confidence appeared to have drained away more completely than at any time since 1945.

Yet, OECD and national statistics painted a more complex and in some respects a more encouraging picture. Inequality in Western societies had certainly grown rapidly after about 1990 and was actually increased by the Great Recession of 2008–2015. Capital continued to benefit from movement and globalisation, even during this period. But wages stagnated or declined as jobs moved to cheaper Asian or African locales and world demand pushed up fuel and commodity prices. Especially in the United States, corporate governance awarded executives large pay rises while ordinary workers languished.[50] President Obama himself noted that in the United States, "the top ten per cent no longer takes one third of our income – it now takes one half." Whereas, in the 1980s, "the average chief executive made about 20 to 30 times the income of the average worker, today's CEO makes 273 times more".[51] And that was a serious understatement in regard to major businesses. Blacks and Hispanics were overrepresented amongst those whose incomes had fallen between 2008 and 2013. Internationally, economies were staffed by easily replaceable service sector workers. Yet, surveys in 2014 revealed that Canada had overtaken the United States on the measure of median income. The middle classes and poor citizens in Western Europe were rapidly overtaking their American equivalents even though GDP per head in the United States remained unrivalled. Social mobility had stagnated relative to Europe and even Britain, despite the illusion of the "American Dream". The rush of governments to join the Chinese Development Bank in 2015 was both a response to persisting inequality and an augury of the end of the United States' financial dominance which had begun in 1918.

Piketty argued that this growing inequality had deep historic roots.[52] Those who had acquired capital had always been able to invest more, create more capital and hence pull away from the rest of society. The result was that inherited wealth, rather than ability, would dominate the "rich list" of the 2030s, as it had that of the 1890s. Equally, large international companies had established intrusive databases of citizens' wealth and consumer predilections which worked in parallel to, and were often complicit with, state surveillance organisations such as the FBI. Wealthy corporations consequently further maximised their profits and rewarded their shareholders and higher-level employees at the expense of ordinary citizens and fought against attempts to increase top-rate income tax. Meanwhile, neo-liberal economics converged with ethnic fragmentation to foster a significant rise in crime and disorder in many former colonies.[53]

This growing level of inequality was compounded in the West by inter-generational inequalities between the "baby boomers" of the post-war years and the generations born after 1970. Political parties seemed unlikely to benefit from this form of disenchantment in the short run even to the extent that the US Progressive movement at the turn of the twentieth century or the European socialists in the 1930s had done. Democratic politics had fragmented and middle-class people had turned to self-empowerment through media and sport. The poorest, often racial minorities, were too heavily policed or under-educated to protest except through local violence. Heavy state investment in education might have bucked the trend, but this was by no means in evidence in 2015.

Yet, the movement of jobs offshore, particularly in the industrial sector, had powered the rise of India, China and other parts of Asia and Latin America, creating an ambitious middle class. The international Gini index of global inequality, which measured income per capita regardless of residence, actually fell significantly between 2002 and 2008, probably for the first time since the "Great Divergence" of the early nineteenth century. Yet, this more optimistic picture concealed the fact that income of the bottom 5%, not only in Asia and sub-Saharan Africa but also in the West, had stagnated relative to the rest of world society. Even in China it was calculated that 1% of the population held 30% of its wealth.[54] The rich were becoming richer, while the poorest were becoming poorer everywhere.

The political and social picture was as mixed as the economic. Observers noted the decline of popular engagement with politics in the United States, even as the middle-class Tea Party movement took off. In Western Europe, some young people expressed a total lack of interest in politics and conventional social life, retreating instead to the virtual individualism of electronic media. Though *Discipline and Punish* was published in 1975, it seemed that Foucault's panopticon model had less relevance to the second half of the century, at least outside societies such as North Korea and Saudi Arabia. Across Western societies, self-surveillance and the demands of capital and debt rather than the "disciplining state" seemed to hold sway. Zygmunt Bauman posited the importance of sexuality in social control of the individual by directing desire, an evident feature of modern consumerism.[55] Others noted the importance of self-surveillance through a wide range of interventions by the media and peer pressure through electronic communication. Nevertheless, the Edward Snowden affair of 2012, when reams of intelligence material were released into the public domain, reaffirmed the continuing role of state surveillance.

Finally, although women were in a stronger position in most Western countries than in the Muslim world or even India, the financial crisis of 2008–2015 apparently pushed a higher percentage of women out of the labour market. Here they were already relatively poorly represented, especially in the higher ranks of business. These trends continued to play out well into the early decades of the twenty-first century. Left-wing writers, such as Jacques Rancière, Alain Badiou and Slavoj Žižek, predicted that this new age of capital, inequality and state surveillance would ultimately bring back the spectre of proletarian revolution,[56] contradicting optimists of a mere 20 years earlier such as Francis Fukuyama, who hoped for the end of history and glimpsed "a worldwide liberal revolution".[57] The picture was evidently more complex than either of these positions admitted.

Conclusion: Periods
and Prophecy

> The Person and the Self
> Society and Economy
> The Triumph of Human Imagination

It is a nearly impossible task to conclude a book about more than a century through which many of us lived, surrounded by memories, constant political conversation, radio or television programmes, along with more than a million academic studies and reminiscences of its history. Such studies are in constant danger of slipping between the obvious and the kind of usually erroneous prophecy with which some authors end their histories. A sage model, however, is represented by the two essays that ended the *Oxford History of the Twentieth Century* (1998), a short book, but one which has nevertheless been invaluable for the present study. The authors of the final essays in that volume, William Roger Louis and the late Ralf Dahrendorf, succinctly summarised issues which have remained central to this book.[1] Reflecting on the end of the twentieth century, Louis pointed to the continuing swathe cut through humanity by genocide, war and disease, particularly AIDS, in the latter case. Yet, he carefully balanced this picture with his assessment that the "record of the 1990s was emphatically positive", potentially a "golden age"[2] with rising living standards, declining death rates in warfare and better diet across much of the world. In his own essay, Dahrendorf, however, alluded to another "age of uncertainty": the decline of the ability during the 1990s of even the United States to control the force of globalisation, with its concomitant political conflicts, let alone the ecological problems which were already alarming experts and politicians. Dahrendorf also pointed to the "return to the tribe", a theme

Remaking the Modern World 1900–2015: Global Connections and Comparisons, First Edition. C. A. Bayly.
© 2018 John Wiley & Sons Ltd. Published 2018 by John Wiley & Sons Ltd.

popularised by Karl Popper, meaning the dangerous rise of local ethnic and religious absolutisms which he saw as a response to globalisation.[3]

How had the picture changed in the following two decades? Some of Dahrendorf's more negative predictions seemed entirely justified. What I have called the small wars of fragmentation moved more dangerously to the centre of world politics, spreading from Bosnia, Serbia and Rwanda in the 1990s, to the massive turmoil of the Arab Spring, the Syrian civil war, the breakup of Iraq and the fighting in Afghanistan and Pakistan in the 2010s. This turmoil threatened to spark major conflicts between Iran, Israel and Saudi Arabia, while the rise of Islamism seemed to spill over into Lebanon, Turkey and the Muslim communities of Western Europe and even the United States. Al-Qaeda and related dispersed insurgencies in the Caucasus spread political murder to New York, Boston, Madrid and London. In 2014, conflict in Ukraine even seemed to presage a return to a Cold War between Russia and the West. The apparent steady growth of prosperity during the 1990s and the early 2000s, cited by Louis, came to an abrupt halt in 2008 with the onset of the global financial crisis known as the Great Recession, and questions remained over the longer-term growth prospects of China, India and Brazil which had moved rapidly ahead as neo-liberal economics provided at least medium-term benefits. On the other side, the gradual diminution of the gap between rich and poor nations was accompanied by the stagnation of the living standards of those at the bottom in all world societies, a theme popularised by Thomas Piketty.

Did the two decades after Louis and Dahrendorf wrote represent a new era in global history or a continuation and acceleration of some of the trends they mentioned? The answer must be both, an answer which represents the historian's typical ambivalence. Still, the problem of dealing with periodisation remains critical for anyone attempting to write contemporary world history. For the century after 1900, this book has broadly followed the periods proposed by the *Oxford History* and by writers such as Michael Mann and Eric Hobsbawm, but with some significant modifications. The first period, the age of multinational rivalry and mass killing, 1914–1945, needs in my view to be prefaced by a discussion of the "Idealist Age" and the great acceleration of social and technological change between about 1890 and 1914, without which it is difficult to explain the later era.

The shift of dominant political thought and practice in the capitalist West from liberal individualism to democratic communitarianism, historicist national idealism and internationalist socialism was not eradicated by the First World War. This was the case even though a more muscular historicism and authoritarian socialism became a dominant form after 1918. Idealist thinkers such as the Italian poet Gabriele D'Annunzio fed into the fascist ideologies of the interwar era. In a more pacific and idiosyncratic manner, Gandhi himself remained more of an idealist of the pre-war period than a nationalist seeking a powerful state. Again, the rise before 1914 of working class and women's movements across Europe and America and in some colonised societies fundamentally influenced post-First World War politics, even if the working class was corralled into the nationalist disaster of 1914 and women were selectively excluded from political and economic life until the 1940s. In some respects, Marxist thinkers were correct to argue that the war, a muscle-flexing by older landed, military and commercial elites, can be seen as a way in which they suppressed emerging class and industrial antagonisms. Finally, a significant feature of the world before the war was the rise of Asian and Middle Eastern nationalisms which became a dominant theme over the following two generations. The Persian and Chinese revolutions, the Swadeshi movement in India and the rise of the Wafd in Egypt all pointed to a new era in which colonialism and the forces of anticolonialism would be engaged in a more violent confrontation.

The Eastern and Western Fronts and the war in Europe after 1939 have rightly engaged the attention of historians in view of the massive damage done to the world's most powerful nations and the eventual rise to dominance of the United States. But if we widen the lens to the world outside Europe and beyond 1914–1918 and 1939–1945, it is clear that there was no real interruption of this long world crisis, as Churchill termed it. A succession of regional conflicts, such as the Rif Revolt in Morocco of 1920–1926, the Third Anglo-Afghan War of 1919–1920 and the Russian civil war, harried the 1920s. The 1930s saw the Japanese invasion of Manchuria and, after 1936, of central and southern China. The Italian invasion of Ethiopia and the Spanish Civil War heightened international tension and fed back into Europe's arms race.

During the Second World War, the epochal struggle between Germany and the USSR and the mobilisation of the United States for the invasion of Europe once again dominate the historical writing. Yet, the Japanese invasion of Southeast Asia as well as the war in North Africa and the Pacific were critical in the collapse of European empires and the rise of Communist China, which, within two generations, had become the world's second largest economy and most populous nation. Even in areas relatively distant from open warfare, notably India and Africa south of the Sahara, wartime mobilisation brought forward a new generation of young leaders and set the scene for decolonisation.

Yet, more generally, this age of global warfare and economic turmoil resulted in a great increase in the competence and aims of the state, not only under Communism and fascism but also in the Western democracies. Mass mobilisation made inevitable a mass electorate, female enfranchisement and the expansion of mass media. The world was democratised, sometimes in dangerous ways. The demands of war, particularly after 1941, made the long-term political manipulation of prices, wages and investment unavoidable. In the new states of Asia and Africa and the turbulent societies of Latin America, deeper state intervention in the economy during wartime provided the model for the developmental state and technical explosion of the 1950s and 1960s. Even in the locally governed United States, the state made its entrance during the Depression and the Second World War and had hardly retreated before the 1980s.

After 1945, the world again entered a period of forced stability until the "tipping point" between 1979 and 1991 initiated a much sharper series of ruptures in the global political order. The first years after 1945 saw the full emergence of the postcolonial states, the erosion of authoritarian Communism in the USSR and Eastern Europe and the high point of US political and economic hegemony in the West and over much of what was then called the "Third World", the examples of Cuba and Vietnam notwithstanding. The sense of change before 1979 was powered by the recovery of Europe, the new wealth of the US middle classes and the escape of much of the colonial world from colonialism, famine and racial discrimination. The explosion of youth culture and counter-politics in the later 1960s echoed across the West. The sense of optimism was palpable. Yet, at the same time, the Cold War made possible the excesses of the Great Leap Forward and the Cultural Revolution, on the one hand, and the mass murder of "Communists" in Indonesia, on the other.

The "tipping point" after 1979 and its ambivalent legacy through to the Great Recession and small wars of fragmentation after 2008 remained a subject of popular and historical debate well into the twenty-first century. What is clear, however, is that the demand to "free the market", the fall of Western Communism, the lurch of China and other states towards state-controlled economic liberalism combined with the rise of political Islamism to rupture many social and political trends which had been dominant since the late nineteenth century. The decline of socialism and the limiting of state intervention in the economy, along with the check to secularism and semi-secular dictatorships, marked a major change in the world community which arose both from the force of globalisation and from local reactions to it. Global capital remained a powerful force: capital moved away from areas of high state taxation to safer havens of low taxation. Large multinational companies moved production to areas of cheap labour, outsourcing production to countries such as Bangladesh, the Philippines or the Congo. Huge mining companies invaded tribal lands with impunity, whether in central India, Mexico or Southeast Asia. People moved across borders on a large scale, threatening the English language's dominance in the United States, sparking chauvinist movements in Europe and murderous riots in South and Southeast Asia. Globalisation, indeed, engendered a revival of the parochial.

In a sense, capitalism, whether Western or Chinese, no longer needed the carapace of formal imperialism. Its highest stage could be reached by exploiting the fragmented and corrupt states and broken nationalisms of the post-1991 world, a position vigorously proposed by Hardt and Negri. At the level of producers and consumers, feudal landed dominances had been replaced by forms of local entrepreneurial capitalism which everywhere intertwined with big figures in national and regional politics. Lenin's "Capital" had been real enough, but by the early twenty-first century the superstructure and sub-structure had merged. In the case of Chinese business in Africa, or the influence Putin's Russia in the former USSR, capitalism had itself become "the highest stage of imperialism". Elsewhere, it roamed free, buying its way into and compromising local states, becoming the pioneer of globalisation.

The small wars of fragmentation often seemed to reflect the rise of ethnic and religious difference. These were also intertwined. In Malaysia, for instance, it was the revival of earlier contests between Chinese and Malay versions of nationalism which gave the appearance of the rise of a more rigid form of Islamism in the country, while many religious teachers remained quite inclusive. In France, the rise of anti-Semitism concealed a right-wing reaction against proposals for "gay marriage", the apparent failure of the socialist government and regional inequalities as well as hostility born in the poor African and Arab *banlieues*. It is too easy constantly to characterise all these splits as simple contests between Islamism and secularism. Even in countries such as Pakistan and Syria, where this was undoubtedly a powerful element, regional differences and sectarian or local ethnic issues were also part of the story. Global communication helped to transform local grievances and loyalties into broad alliances of the angry and those for whom individualistic consumption provided no moral compass.

"Globalisation" was a term which achieved great currency towards the end of the century and has often appeared in this book. In the academic world after 1990, some advanced it as a theory which posited the undermining of state- and regional-centred approaches to the human and social sciences. In popular debate, it was either a premonition of a new human age of global partnership or a source of fear as "the foreign" invaded home space. It is impossible to avoid the conclusion that movement, commerce, communication and, of course, warfare did indeed knit the world more closely together over the century. Yet, globalisation was not an inexorably expanding or straightforwardly cumulative process, as the "theory" of globalisation seemed to assert, so much as a series of conjunctures, periodically ruptured by a reassertion of the power of the local, regional and national. So, for example, the regional and the national reasserted their power after 1918 and did so again after 2000, but in both cases in a dialectical relationship with the forces of globalisation. The state, drawing on feelings of nationalism or chauvinism, showed little sign of relinquishing the role it had played for 200 years but needed, nevertheless, to come to terms with global interconnections. Historians have had a great time arguing for or against global connections, the existence of the anthropocene or the need for "deep", long-term history. But the intelligent reader would probably conclude that none of these positions need be exclusive.

THE PERSON AND THE SELF

Underlying and informing these broad global changes, the century witnessed major shifts in the concept of "the human being itself" and the manner in which people related to family, locality and society more broadly. Anthropologists distinguished between the inner concept of the self and the more abstract, social concept of the person. Powerful states and capital throughout the century attempted to make the self reflect their understanding of the person, whether it was "fascist man", "socialist man" or, most successful of all, "the person as consumer". The trend in social and political theory in the early part of the century pointed away from the ideal of the free rational individual of liberal theorists towards a belief in the need for individuals to work for community, represented in the ideology of figures such as T. H. Green, John Dewey and, in a very different way, Mohandas Gandhi or Muhammad Iqbal. Psychological theory had meanwhile eroded the notion of the rational individual from the inside.

Later in the century, existentialist and postmodernist thinkers came to see the person as an amalgam of different urges and predispositions dominated by the "un-authored discourses" of race, gender and capital. Language itself, as in the theories of Jacques Derrida, was seen as a fluid form of social action which did not necessarily represent a series of rational statements.[4] Derrida's assertion that "there is nothing outside the text" aligned his difficult linguistic philosophy of "deconstruction" with other so-called poststructuralists and postmodernists who broadly dissented from Cartesian rationalism which, they argued, had dominated the West for too long. Meanwhile, anthropologists posited that large parts of mankind, especially in Asia and Africa, had always understood the person as a fluid being, constructed of relations between the self, spirits, animals and place.[5] The irony here, though, was that, however philosophically challenged the idea of the rational individuated person became, the actual practice of the rights-bearing individual as perpetual consumer and accumulating owner of property became more and more powerful and widespread as the century progressed. By 2015, formerly Maoist China, for instance, was the greatest market in the world for luxury German vehicles, Italian handbags and Japanese mobile phones.

This was paralleled by observable changes which made large parts of human society more fluid and, at least initially, challenged earlier views of discipline, religious faith and social commitment. The wars and authoritarian states of the first half of the century gave way, after 1950, to youth and student dissent, the decline of marriage, sexual freedom and the erosion of parental, academic and legal authority over much of the West. The shift was particularly notable in the widespread contempt for anti-drug laws, with millions taking banned substances which seemed to change the very nature of consciousness. Liberal political and economic freedoms of the Western democracies in the earlier part of the century were replaced by notions of "free-loading" and the rightful pursuit of pleasure. Even outside the West, urbanisation and rising living standards created similar breaks with the past, with the decline of Communist activism in China and Vietnam and the erosion of the caste system, at least among the wealthy, in Indian cities. Admirable movements towards freedom of speech, freedom of social interaction and freedom of movement were paralleled by a rise in political and economic corruption and crime cartels which at times brought parts of countries such as Mexico into a state of near warfare. Nevertheless, these aspirations towards freedom and democracy persisted even as the economic crises and the small wars of fragmentation gathered force after the millennium. Large states such as Russia, China and India began to roll back freedom of expression while religious norms were re-imposed, though vigorously challenged.

SOCIETY AND ECONOMY

Just as the notion of the independent, rational individual was widely abraded over the century and replaced with the concept of a fluid or porous, but actively consuming, person, the idea of hierarchy within and between societies came under attack from theorists and activists, though with mixed results. The emergence of anthropology after 1890 in the United States, and later Europe and its colonies, saw experts rejecting the idea that some societies were primitive. From Boas to Lévi-Strauss, studies showed that so-called tribal and backward societies were, in fact, organised both socially and linguistically in complex and sophisticated ways. Guilt over the earlier slaughter and destruction of indigenous peoples and their continued marginalisation resulted, by the middle of the century, in "first nation" movements in countries such as Canada, Australia, New Zealand and some parts of Central and South America. By 2015, the Australian constitution was amended to make Aboriginal peoples the "first nation" and to erase the idea that the country had been *terra nullius* before the arrival of Europeans. Social conservationists and indigenous leaders worked, with mixed success, to preserve such societies from exploitation by logging and mining companies or settlers from the majority communities.

The struggle for national independence from colonialism, the creation of new states and the liberal academy had also led to a proscription of language which implied that Africans, Asians and Pacific peoples were more primitive than Europeans. The legacy of "scientific" and fascist racism, and the idea of war against inferior races at the beginning of the century, had apparently been nullified by the adoration of Gandhi, Martin Luther King or Nelson Mandela. Racial discrimination was banned in most legal codes, even if many social groups, and not only whites, continued to regard Africans and South Asians as inferiors. Certainly, a century of "counter-preaching" by individuals such as Lin Yutang, who elevated Chinese Confucianism, and Sarvepalli Radhakrishnan, who elevated Hindu "detachment", combined with the effects of the two world wars on European morale, had severely dented the self-confident superiority of Europeans and white Americans.

In general, the associated claim that Christianity was the only true religion, or at least the most caring and advanced one, had been formally abandoned by most religious leaderships. The move had become evident with the World Parliament of Religions in Chicago in 1893. It was pressed forward as all religions came under attack from Marxists and atheists and culminated at the end of the century with numerous forms of "interfaith dialogue". Of course, various forms of fundamentalist religion – Christian, Muslim and even Hindu – dissented from any compromise over truth or right conduct. It was notable, though, that intransigent faith communities came to resemble each other more and more and to promote standardised and widely promulgated norms. The variety within and between these faith communities in 1900 had been significantly reduced by 2000. The Universal Declaration of Human Rights and UN bodies had played some part in banishing discrimination on the grounds of both race and religion.

The widespread recruitment of women into wartime work and the expansion of women's education along with the patchy effects of feminist movements across the world had also begun to erode the notion of female inferiority, which had often underpinned both racial and religious discrimination. Women were still poorly represented in key government and business positions in many societies. In Saudi Arabia they were legally prevented from driving cars. But even in Islamic societies, women had made some gains in terms of mobility, marriage choice and inheritance by 2000, though strong counterforces prevailed after that date. The rapid increase in the numbers of women in higher education in the English-speaking world, outnumbering male students in Britain by 2014, for instance, was a pointer to future social equality, though this was still far off.

Yet, social hierarchies within societies apparently often remained quite resilient despite the effects of mass mobilisation during war and the widespread adoption of democratic forms of government. In these cases, what had happened was that, while class and other forms of hierarchical language and manners had persisted, the actual composition of these different groups had changed considerably. In many Western societies, the "white working class" continued to languish with low educational attainment and poor employment prospects, as did blacks in the United States. The economic crises of the 1970s and 2000s had impacted badly on them. But the decline of mining and industrial production, as it was offshored to Asia from places such as Sheffield and Detroit, meant that much of the old labour elite had disappeared by the end of the century. While the poorest in 1900 had been rural labourers, in 2015 it was jobless urban men or women, often unmarried with large families. The middle class had expanded very greatly in all Western societies and even in former Communist societies after 1990. By 2015, it appeared that the very wealthy, who were often financial entrepreneurs, were rapidly pulling away from the remainder of this large middle class in terms of disposable income. Increasingly, the wealthy transformed wealth into political power, transforming democracies into something more like oligarchies.

The emerging pattern, then, was one of a very poor surviving working class scattered with single-parent and large families surmounted by a substantial middle class whose income was stagnant compared with the top 5% of earners. The language and practice of hierarchy had also changed. Across much of the world, the old gentlemanly or intellectual elites had largely been displaced by the commercial middle class and entrepreneurs. The Indian caste system retained vitality, but it was the merchant classes and the middle rural entrepreneurs, rather than the Brahmins, who came to dominate the social, if not the ritual, hierarchy. In China and earlier in Japan, it was also successful urbanites who had come to the fore, replacing samurai and mandarin elites as they were wiped out by war and Maoism.

The century was pre-eminently a century of economics. The laissez-faire economy of late liberalism was ruptured by war and the resurgence of economic protectionism in both nationalist and Communist forms. Yet, after 1945, and even more after 1990, the great expansion of transnational economic linkages of capital, trade and migration meant that shocks or growth in one part of the world economy were instantaneously passed on to the rest, with significant political consequences. This was the most powerful aspect of globalisation. It was a century of economics in another sense, too: economics emerged as a separate and powerful discipline, closely allied with power-holders and dominating the debate about the future shape of society. The lines of battle were drawn up in the 1920s and 1930s, as a response to the shocks of war and the

Depression. On the one hand, disciples of John Maynard Keynes and economists in Asia and Africa, such as Amartya Sen, pushed for and often achieved state intervention to boost economies through public spending on housebuilding and infrastructure. On the other hand, devotees of free-market capitalism, such as the popular writer Ayn Rand and the scholar F. A. Hayek, opposed such intervention on the grounds that it stifled entrepreneurship and distorted economic growth in the long term. As both Western socialism and Communism waned in influence after 1980, the latter thinkers became popular once again. Finally, as the post-2008 Great Recession took hold, state intervention returned to the agenda in the form of "quantitative easing", that is, printing money. The statistically supported economic theorising which posited that the market was itself a perfect force for allocating value without any political intervention came under assault both from perceptive financiers, such as George Soros, and from socially minded economists.

Underlying these loudly broadcast debates, which rocked the IMF and the World Bank as well as national governments, international capital flows and links of supply and demand drove the world economy more tightly together, so that Chinese consumption became a major factor in the late growth of the African economy and Western companies offshored their production even more aggressively to East and South Asia and Eastern Europe. The speed of the rise and fall in incomes in both developed and developing markets baffled governments, so that NGOs and religious organisations often stepped in to provide basic resources and care. In a sense, the political, social, ethical and economic began to move back into the same frame, as they had once been in the era of John Stuart Mill. One important aspect of the debate about the economic future related to the exploitation of natural resources and the destruction of animal and plant habitat. Short-term political calculations by national governments were paralleled by the emergence of the "green" ecological movement and fears about climate change. Certainly, massive deforestation in countries such as Brazil, Nigeria, Democratic Republic of the Congo and Indonesia and fears about air pollution in China or falling water tables in India, along with over-fishing in the world's oceans, increasingly focussed the policies of international bodies as well as national governments. The melting of polar ice and the onset of extreme weather conditions in the 2010s initiated a ferocious debate between the majority of scientific opinion and "climate-change deniers". Along with global terrorism, ecological issues were poised to dominate political debate well into the mid-twenty-first century.

THE TRIUMPH OF HUMAN IMAGINATION

This conclusion has considered how politics, economics and the self might have changed in theory and in practice over the century. It ends with the issue of the human imagination, a force which has encompassed all the major "drivers" considered in this book: the state, capital and communication. One of the most striking developments of all was the burgeoning of the scientific, social and artistic imagination after 1900, powered forward by warfare, on the one hand,

and the professionalisation and global spread of education and research, on the other. Human curiosity, the envisioning of multiple alternatives – social, political and religious – expanded exponentially with the human population. Two images were iconic here. The first was the explosion of the hydrogen bomb over the Pacific in 1954 which was the cover image for the *Oxford History of the Twentieth Century*. The second was the view of the earth from the surface of the moon after the first landing there in 1971. The ability to imagine the absolute destruction of the human race and, simultaneously, humanity's insignificant place in the universe was the unequalled accomplishment of the century.

Yet, these images were themselves products of a range of creativity much wider than scientific investigation and imagination. Novelists such as H. G. Wells had imagined the "war of the worlds". Science fiction writers such as Isaac Asimov imagined space travel to distant planets and comets and the creation of sentient robots years before these became scientifically feasible. Asimov, indeed, was employed at one point in the 1950s to inform US scientists how to use imagination for the purposes of scientific discovery. The USSR and Communist China also produced a whole range of science fiction in stories and films which pointed to a perfect socialist society on those distant planets, while the American version tended to privilege the pioneering individual explorer. Artists such as Marc Chagall and playwrights such as Samuel Beckett had "deconstructed" the human in parallel with Freud's "discovery" of the unconscious and the sequencing of DNA. The century of unbridled imagina-tion slipped after 2000 into a new age when the urge to find other planets on which to settle – or on which to exploit a different range of natural resources – was accompanied by bloody struggles on earth itself to found new liberal democracies, new caliphates or new godly communities of the "faith of our fathers". People imagined, and began to create, a world in which all work and even much of its thinking would be done by robots, something which only science fiction writers had dreamed of earlier. The human imagination of scientists and artists alike reached a new vaulting high when some claimed that humanity would eventually discover the means to make life eternal, something which, for earlier generations, only God could have accomplished.

NOTES

INTRODUCTION

1 Some material in the introduction and conclusion replicates parts of my review C. A. Bayly, "Michael Mann and Modern World History", *Historical Journal* 58, 1 (2015), pp. 331–341; see also Lynn Hunt, *Writing History in the Global Era* (New York, 2014).

2 Semantic discussions about the meaning of "world" and "global" have produced little of value. Here "world history" is taken to mean a study of the interactions, or lack of them, of major events and trends across the world. "Global history" in turn suggests a method which is alert to the use and appropriation of ideas and practices which derive from outside the particular locality, nation or region. It could, for instance, be applied to a study of how such ideas were transformed in one particular society. But it does not necessarily engage geographically with the wider world.

3 Jürgen Osterhammel (tr. Patrick Camiller), *The Transformation of the World: A Global History of the Nineteenth Century* (Princeton, 2014); Emily S. Rosenberg (ed.), *A World Connecting, 1870–1945: A History of the World* (Cambridge, 2012); Michael Mann, *The Sources of Social Power*, 4 vols (Cambridge, 1986–2013); E. J. Hobsbawm, *The Age of Revolution*; *The Age of Capital*; *The Age of Empire*; *The Age of Extremes* (London, 1988–1998).

4 Michael Werner and Bénédicte Zimmermann, "Beyond Comparison: Histoire Croisée and the Challenge of Reflexivity", *History and Theory*, 45, 1 (2006), pp. 30–50; see also Mathias Albert (ed.), *Transnational Political Spaces: Agents, Structures, Encounters* (Frankfurt, 2009), and Kenneth Pomeranz, "Histories for a Less National Age", *American Historical Review*, 119, 1 (2014), pp. 1–22.

5 Francis Fukuyama, *The End of History and the Last Man* (New York, 1992).

6 Justin Rosenberg, "Globalization Theory: A Post Mortem", *International Politics*, 42, 1 (2005), pp. 3–74.

7 Thomas Piketty (tr. Arthur Goldhammer), *Capital in the Twenty-First Century*, (Cambridge, 2014).

8 A good example of a global approach to the issue of racial inequality is Francisco Bethencourt, *Racisms: From the Crusades to the Twentieth Century* (Princeton, 2013).

Remaking the Modern World 1900–2015: Global Connections and Comparisons, First Edition. C. A. Bayly.
© 2018 John Wiley & Sons Ltd. Published 2018 by John Wiley & Sons Ltd.

9   For a robust version of this argument, see Michael Hardt and Antonio Negri, *Empire* (Cambridge, 2000).

10 See Prasenjit Duara, *The Crisis of Global Modernity: Asian Traditions and a Sustainable Future* (Cambridge, 2015).

11 David Bell, "This is what happens when historians overuse the idea of network", *New Republic* (25 October 2013).

12 Samuel Moyn, "Book Review: The Transformation of the World by Jürgen Osterhammel", *Prospect Magazine*, July 2014.

13 Jo Guldi and David Armitage, *The History Manifesto* (Cambridge, 2014).

14 Deborah Cohen and Peter Mandler, "The History Manifesto: A Critique", *American Historical Review*, 120, 2 (2015), pp. 530–542.

15 Samuel Moyn, "Bonfire of the Humanities", *The Nation* (21 January 2015).

16 In fact, one of the earliest and most balanced discussions of the strengths and limitations of global history is Michael Geyer and Charles Bright, "World History in a Global Age", *The American Historical Review*, 100, 4 (1995), pp. 1034–1060.

17 P. K. O'Brien, "Global history for global citizenship", in Toyin Falola and Emily Brownell (eds), *Africa, Empire and Globalization: Essays in Honor of A.G. Hopkins* (Durham, 2011), pp. 447–458.

18 Ranajit Guha and Gayatri Spivak (eds), *Selected Subaltern Studies* (Delhi, 1988).

19 Kenneth Pomeranz, *The Great Divergence: Europe, China, and the Making of the Modern World Economy* (Princeton, 2000).

20 Jean-Laurent Rosenthal and Roy Bin Wong, *Before and Beyond Divergence: The Politics of Economic Change in China and Europe* (Cambridge, 2011).

21 Engseng Ho, *The Graves of Tarim: Genealogy and Mobility across the Indian Ocean* (Berkeley, 2006).

22 Notably, Michael Mann, *The Sources of Social Power*, vol. 3: *Global Empires and Revolution, 1890–1945*, and vol. 4: *Globalizations, 1945–2011* (Cambridge, 2012–2013); see C. A. Bayly, "Michael Mann and Modern World History".

23 A. G. Hopkins (ed.), *Globalization in World History* (London, 2002).

24 A. G. Hopkins (ed.), *Global History: Interactions between the Universal and the Local* (Basingstoke, 2006).

25 Marshall McLuhan, *Understanding Media: The Extensions of Man* (Cambridge, 1994).

26 Marshall G. S. Hodgson, *The Venture of Islam: Conscience and History in a World Civilization*, 3 vols (Chicago, 1974).

27 V. I. Lenin, *Imperialism: The Highest Stage of Capitalism* (1917; repr. Lenin Internet Archives, 2005). Accessed: www.marxists.org/archive/lenin/works/1916.

28 Colin Bird, *An Introduction to Political Philosophy* (Cambridge, 2006), p. 290.

29 Stuart Jeffries, "Why Marxism is on the rise again", *The Guardian* (4 July 2012).

30 Marshall McLuhan, *Understanding Media* (New York, 1962).

CHAPTER 1 THE WORLD CRISIS, C. 1900–1930: EUROPE AND THE "MIDDLE EAST"

1   Directly around the war's centenary: David Reynolds, *The Long Shadow: The Great War and the Twentieth Century* (London, 2013); Frank Furedi, *First World War: Still No End in Sight* (London, 2014); Adam Tooze, The Deluge: *The Great War and the Remaking of Global Order, 1916–1931* (London, 2014); the latter is a truly global history.

2 Particularly useful here for both world wars is Heike Liebau *et al.* (eds), *The World in World Wars: Experiences, Perceptions and Perspectives from Africa and Asia* (Leiden, 2010).

3 James Cowan, *The Maoris in the Great War: A History of the New Zealand Native Contingent and Pioneer Battalion* (1926; repr. Melbourne, 2006).

4 Aleksandr Etkind, *Internal Colonisation: Russia's Imperial Experience* (Cambridge, 2011).

5 Avner Offer, *The First World War: An Agrarian Interpretation* (Oxford, 1989).

6 V. I. Lenin, *Imperialism: The Highest Stage of Capitalism* (London, 1948).

7 A. G. Hopkins and P. J. Cain, *British Imperialism Innovation and Expansion, 1688–1914* (London, 1993); *idem, British Expansion: Crisis and Deconstruction, 1914–1990* (London, 1993).

8 See Michael Howard, "The Dawn of the Century", in Michael Howard and Wm. Roger Louis (eds), *The Oxford History of the Twentieth Century* (Oxford, 2000), pp. 3–9.

9 John A. Thompson, *Progressivism* (Durham, 1979).

10 David Motadel (ed.), *Islam and the European Empires* (Oxford, 2014).

11 Andrew Gordon, *A Modern History of Japan: From Tokugawa Times to the Present* (New York, 2003).

12 Archie Brown, *The Rise and Fall of Communism* (New York, 2009), pp. 35–37, 40–47.

13 Alfred J. Rieber, *The Struggle for the Eurasian Borderlands: From the Rise of Early Modern Empires to the End of the First World War* (Cambridge, 2014), pp. 424–531.

14 Christopher Clark, *The Sleepwalkers: How Europe Went to War in 1914* (London, 2012); Margaret Macmillan, *The War that Ended Peace: How Europe Abandoned Peace for the First World War* (London, 2012); Sean McMeekin, *July 1914: Countdown to War* (London, 2013).

15 Cited in Hew Strachan, *The First World War*, vol. I: *To Arms* (Oxford, 2001), pp. 63.

16 Fritz Fischer, *Germany's Aims in the First World War* (London, 1967).

17 Strachan, *The First World War*, I, and *idem, The First World War: A New Illustrated History* (London, 2003).

18 David Stevenson, *1914–1918: The History of the First World War* (London, 2004).

19 Tooze, *The Deluge*.

20 A very useful compendium of such approaches is Heike Liebau *et al.* (eds), *The World in World Wars*.

21 Stevenson, *1914–1918*, pp. 57–60, 73–74.

22 Offer, *The First World War*.

23 W. R. Scott and J. Cunnison, *The Industries of the Clyde Valley During the War* (Oxford, 1924), p. 185.

24 Tooze, *The Deluge*, pp. 88–106.

25 Geoffrey D. Schad, "Competing Forms of Globalisation in the Middle East: From the Ottoman Empire to the Nation State", in A. G. Hopkins ed. *Global History: Interactions Between the Universal and the Local* (Basingstoke, 2006), pp. 191–228.

26 Feroz Ahmed, *The Making of Modern Turkey* (London, 1993).

27 Rashid Khalidi *et al.* (eds), *The Origins of Arab Nationalism* (New York, 1991).

28 George Antonius, *The Arab Awakening: The Story of the Arab Nationalist Movement* (London, 1938).

29 Leila Tarwazi Fawaz, *A Land of Aching Hearts: The Middle East in the Great War* (Cambridge, 2014).

30 Toby Dodge, *Inventing Iraq: The Failure of Nation–Building and a History Denied* (London, 2003); Charles Tripp, *A History of Iraq* (Cambridge, 2000).

31 Eugene Rogan, *The Fall of the Ottomans: The Great War in the Middle East, 1914–1920* (London, 2015).

32 The most refreshing recent intervention on this heavily studied topic is Avi Shlaim, "The Balfour Declaration and its Consequences", in Wm. Roger Louis (ed.), *Yet more Adventures with Britannia: Personalities, Culture and Politics in Britain* (London, 2005), pp. 251–270.

33 James Gelvin, *The Modern Middle East: A History* (Oxford, 2005).

34 Elizabeth Monroe, *Britain's Moment in the Middle East, 1914–71* (London, 1981).

35 John Darwin, *Britain, Egypt and the Middle East: Imperial Policy in the Aftermath of War, 1918–22* (London, 1981).

36 Christopher Andrew and A. S. Kanya-Forstner, *France Overseas: The Great War and the Climax of French Imperial Expansion* (London, 1980).

37 Dodge, *Inventing Iraq*.

38 D. K. Fieldhouse, *Western Imperialism in the Middle East 1914–1958* (Oxford, 2006).

39 Gertrude Bell to her father, 10 April 1920, in Gertrude Bell, *Letters of Gertrude Bell*, vol. II (London, 1927), p. 47.

40 Nadine Méouchy and Peter Sluglett (eds), *The British and French Mandates in Comparative Perspective* (Leiden, 2004).

41 Andrew and Kanya-Forstner, *France Overseas*.

42 Albert Sarraut, *La mise en valeur des colonies françaises* (Paris, 1923); Martin Thomas, *The French Empire Between the Wars: Imperialism, Politics and Society* (Manchester, 2005).

43 Benjamin T. White, *The Emergence of Minorities in the Middle East: The Politics of Community in French Mandate Syria* (Edinburgh, 2011).

44 Avi Shlaim, *The Iron Wall: Israel and the Arab World* (London, 2014).

45 Zeina Ghandour, *A Discourse on Domination in Mandate Palestine: Imperialism, Property, Insurgency* (Abingdon, 2010).

46 M. E. Yapp, *The Making of the Modern Near East, 1792–1923* (London, 1987).

47 Andrew Mango, *Atatürk* (London, 2004).

48 Antonius, *The Arab Awakening*.

CHAPTER 2 THE WORLD CRISIS, C. 1900–1930: AFRICA, ASIA AND BEYOND

1 An honourable exception to this on television was BBC 2's *The World's War: Forgotten Soldiers of Empire* by David Olusoga.

2 James Roslington, "The Rif War (Morocco, 1921–26) and the Coming World Crisis", unpublished PhD dissertation (University of Cambridge, 2013; Sebastian Balfour, *Deadly Embrace: Morocco and the Road to the Spanish Civil War* (Oxford, 2002).

3 Strachan, *The First World War*, I, pp. 495–599.

4 John Iliffe, *Africans: The History of a Continent* (Cambridge, 1995).

5 Strachan, *The First World War*, I, pp. 544–557.

6 David van Reybrouck, *Congo: The Epic History of a People* (London, 2014).

7 Terence Ranger, "Africa", in Howard and Louis, *Oxford History*, pp. 264–276.

8 Paul Emil von Lettow-Vorbeck, *East African Campaigns* (New York, 1957), pp. 300.

9 Ervand Abrahamian, *A History of Modern Iran* (Cambridge, 2008).

10 Maia Ramnath, *Haj to Utopia: How the Ghadar Movement Charted Global Radicalism and Attempted to Overthrow the British Empire* (Berkeley, 2011); Shruti Kapila, *Violence and the Indian Political*, forthcoming.

11 Mohammad Gholi Majd, *Great Britain and Reza Shah: The Plunder of Iran 1921–1941* (Gainesville, 2001).

12 Francis Robinson, *Separatism Among Indian Muslims: The Politics of the United Provinces' Muslims, 1860–1923* (London, 1974).

13 Gail Minault, *The Khilafat Movement: Religious Symbolism and Political Mobilization in India* (New York, 1982).

14 B. R. Tomlinson, *The Economy of Modern India from 1860 to the Twenty-First Century* (Cambridge, 2013).

15 Jawaharlal Nehru, *An Autobiography* (London, 1940), pp. 56.

16 Shahid Amin, *Event, Memory, Metaphor: Chauri Chaura 1922–92* (Delhi, 1996).

17 Faisal Devji, *The Impossible Indian: Gandhi and the Temptation of Violence* (Cambridge, 2012).

18 John K. Fairbank (ed.), *The Cambridge History of China*, vol. 12: *Republican China, 1921–49, Part I* (Cambridge, 1983).

19 Hans van de Ven, "China and the First World War", unpublished conference paper University of Oxford, 2014.

20 Chow Tse-tsung, *The May Fourth Movement: Intellectual Revolution in Modern China* (Cambridge, 1960).

21 Mao Zedong, "A Single Spark Can Start a Prairie Fire", January 1930, in *Selected Works of Mao Tse-Tung*, vol. 1 (Peking, 1967), pp. 119.

22 Hans van de Ven, *Breaking with the Past: The Maritime Customs Service and the Global Origins of Modernity in China* (New York, 2014), pp. 172–216.

23 Andrew Gordon, *A Modern History of Japan: From Tokugawa Times to the Present* (New York, 2003).

24 Stuart Macintyre, *A Concise History of Australia* (Cambridge, 2009), pp. 156–174.

25 E. W. Young, *The Wilson Administration and the Great War* (Boston, 1922), p. 9.

26 Erez Manela, *The Wilsonian Moment: Self Determination and the International Origins of Anticolonial Nationalism* (Oxford, 2007).

27 David Reynolds, *America, Empire of Liberty: A New History* (London, 2009), pp. 302–336.

28 John A Thompson, *Woodrow Wilson* (London, 2002).

29 J. B. Brebner, *Canada: A Modern History* (Ann Arbor, 1960).

30 Peter Bakewell, *A History of Latin America: c.1450 to the Present* (Oxford, 2003).

31 Alan Knight, *The Mexican Revolution* (Cambridge, 1986).

32 "Programme of the Mexican Liberal Party, 1906", cited in James D. Cockcroft, *Intellectual Precursors of the Mexican Revolution, 1900–1913* (Austin, 1968), pp. 240–243.

33 Cited in Charles C. Cumberland, *Mexican Revolution: Genesis under Madero* (Austin, 1952), p. 174.

34 Guillemette Crouzet, "Genèse du 'Moyen Orient': Les Britanniques dans le Golfe Arabo-Persique, c.1800–c.1914", unpublished Thèse de Doctorat, Université de Paris-Sorbonne, 2014.

35 Strachan, *First World War*, I, p. 1023.

36 Ibid., p. 1054.

37 Tyler Stovall, "Love, Labor and Race: Colonial Men and White Women in France During the Great War", in Tyler Stovall and Georges van den Abbeele (eds), *French Civilisation and its Discontents: Nationalism, Colonialism, Race*, pp. 297–321.

38 Keith L. Nelson, "The 'Black Horror on the Rhine': Race as a Factor in Post-World War I Diplomacy", *Journal of Modern History*, 42, 4 (1970), pp. 606–627.
39 David Omissi, "Europe Through Indian Eyes: Indian Soldiers Encounter England and France, 1914–18", *English Historical Review*, 122, 496 (2007), pp. 371–396.
40 M. Dean, *Governmentality: Power and Rule in Modern Society* (London, 1999).
41 The work of Giorgio Agamben, notably *Homo Sacer: Sovereign Power and Bare Life* (Stanford, 1998), traces the theme of radical exclusion by the state through the century.
42 Reynolds, *America*, p. 324.
43 Alison Bashford and Philippa Levine (eds), *The Oxford Handbook of the History of Eugenics* (Oxford, 2010).
44 Richard Lynn, *Eugenics: A Reassessment* (London, 2001).
45 Brown, *The Rise and Fall*, pp. 61–62, 72.
46 V. I. Lenin, "The Tasks of the Proletariat in the Present Revolution", (1917; repr. Lenin Internet Archive, 2005). Accessed: www.marxists.org/archive/lenin/works/ 1917.
47 Brown, *The Rise and Fall*, pp. 79–80.
48 Raymond Carr, *Spain, 1808–1975* (Oxford, 1982), pp. 560–590.
49 Alexander Werth, *Russia at War, 1941–45* (New York, 1964).

CHAPTER 3 AUTHORITARIANISM AND DICTATORSHIP WORLDWIDE, C. 1900–1950

1 For a general view see Richard Overy, *The Inter-War Crisis, 1919–39* (Harlow, 1994).
2 For a useful compendium see Roger Griffin (ed.), *Fascism* (Oxford, 1995).
3 Jawaharlal Nehru (ed. Saul Padover), *Glimpses of World History* (New York, 1960), p. 265.
4 Francois Furet, *Le passé d'une illusion: Essai sur l'idée communiste au XXᵉ Siècle* (Paris, 1993); see also Daniel Steinmetz-Jenkins, "Revolutionary rights", *TLS*, 19 November 2014, p. 25.
5 Michael Geyer and Sheila Fitzpatrick (eds), *Beyond Totalitarianism: Stalinism and Nazism Compared* (Cambridge, 2009).
6 Antonia Vallejo-Nagera, 1937, cited in Griffin (ed.), *Fascism*, p. 191.
7 The best brief analysis of this complex, highly quoted and controversial thinker is "Carl Schmitt", *Stanford Encyclopaedia of Philosophy*. Accessed: plato.stanford.edu/ entries/schmitt.
8 Hans van de Ven, *War and Nationalism in China, 1925–45* (London, 2003), pp. 164–167.
9 Shruti Kapila, *Violence and the Indian Political*, forthcoming.
10 Ian Kershaw, *Hitler: A Profile in Power* (London, 1991); *idem, Hitler, 1936–1945* (London, 2008).
11 A. J. Polan, cited in Archie Brown, *The Rise and Fall*, p. 57.
12 D. K. Fieldhouse, *Western Imperialism in the Middle East, 1914–1958* (Oxford, 2006).
13 Dodge, *Inventing Iraq*.
14 Bernard Lewis, *The Emergence of Modern Turkey* (London, 1961), p. 267.
15 Ibid., pp. 280–283.
16 Cyrus Ghani, *Iran and the Rise of Reza Shah: From Qajar Collapse to Pahlavi Power* (London, 1998).

17 Janice J. Terry, *The Wafd, 1919–1952: Cornerstone of Egyptian Political Power* (London, 1982).

18 Harold G. Marcus, *A History of Ethiopia* (London, 1994).

19 Rana Mitter, *A Bitter Revolution: China's Struggle with the Modern World* (Oxford, 2004).

20 Hans van de Ven, *Breaking with the Past*, pp. 216–258.

21 Mao Zedong, "The tasks of the Chinese Communist Party in the period of resistance to Japan", 3 May 1937, in *Selected Works of Mao Tse–Tung*, I, p. 263.

22 W. G. Beasley, *Japanese Imperialism, 1894–1945* (Oxford, 1987).

23 Harry Harootunian, *Overcome by Modernity: History, Culture and Community in Inter-war Japan* (Princeton, 2002).

24 Mark R. Peattie, *Ishiwara Kanji and Japan's Confrontation with the West* (Princeton, 1975).

25 David C. Holtom, *Modern Japan and Shinto Nationalism* (1943; repr. New York, 1963).

26 Rana Mitter, *The Manchurian Myth: Nationalism, Resistance and Collaboration in Modern China* (London, 2000).

27 Alan Knight, "Latin America", in Howard and Louis, *Twentieth Century*, pp. 277–291.

28 The most detailed narrative remains Paolo Alatri, *Le Origini del Fascismo* (Rome, 1956); the most accessible general history of Italy is Simona Colarizi, *Storia del Novecento Italiano* (Milan, 2000).

29 Alfredo Rocco, "Dalla vecchia alla nuova Italia", tr. in Griffin (ed.), *Fascism*, p. 32.

30 Alatri, *Le Origini*, pp. 186–234.

31 Giuseppe Finaldi, *Mussolini and Italian Fascism* (London, 2008).

32 Theodor Fritsch, "Hammer-Ziele" ("The Goals of the Hammer"), cited in Griffin (ed.), *Fascism*, p. 103.

33 Richard J. Evans, *The Coming of the Third Reich* (London, 2003).

34 Evans, *Third Reich*; Michael Burleigh, *The Third Reich: A New History* (London, 2003).

35 Joachim Fest (tr. Richard and Clara Wilson), *Hitler* (London, 1974).

36 Richard J. Evans, *The Third Reich in Power, 1933–1939* (London, 2005).

37 Helen Graham, *The Spanish Republic at War, 1936–1939* (Cambridge, 2002).

38 The classic account is Gerald Brenan, *The Spanish Labyrinth: An Account of the Social and Political Background of the Civil War* (Cambridge, 1950).

39 Paul Preston, *Franco: A Biography* (London 1993).

40 Archie Brown, *The Rise and Fall*, pp. 56–78.

41 E. H. Carr, *The Bolshevik Revolution, 1917–1923*, vol. II (Oxford, 1963), p. 289.

42 The classic study is Robert Service, *Stalin: A Biography* (London, 2005).

43 Moshe Lewin and Ian Kershaw (eds), *Stalinism and Nazism: Dictatorships in Comparison* (Cambridge, 1997).

44 Sheila Fitzpatrick, *The Russian Revolution* (Oxford, 2008), pp. 130–148.

45 *Pravda*, 5 February 1931, cited in Service, *Stalin*, p. 273.

46 Sheila Fitzpatrick, *Education and Social Mobility in the Soviet Union, 1921–1934* (Cambridge, 1979).

47 Brown, *The Rise and Fall*, pp. 65–66.

48 Fitzpatrick, *Education and Social Mobility in the Soviet Union*, pp. 237, 252.

49 Leon Trotsky (tr. Charles Malamouth), *Stalin: An Appraisal of the Man and his Influence* (London, 1947), p. 421.

50 Service, *Stalin*, pp. 340–341.

51 Hobsbawm, *The Age of Extremes*.

CHAPTER 4 DEMOCRACIES AND THEIR DISCONTENTS, C. 1900–1950

1 Mark Mazower, *Dark Continent: Europe's Twentieth Century* (London, 1998), pp. 1–106.
2 Piketty, *Capital*.
3 R. Pethybridge, *The Social Prelude to Stalinism* (London, 1974); Neil Harding, "The Marxist–Leninist Detour," in John Dunn (ed.), *Democracy: The Unfinished Journey, 508 BC to AD 1993* (Oxford, 1992), pp. 155–186.
4 John Dewey, *Democracy and Education: An Introduction to the Philosophy of Education* (New York, 1916), p. 143.
5 Charles Loch Mowat, *Britain Between the Wars, 1918–40* (London, 1955), pp. 5, 343; still the most accessible study of inter-war Britain.
6 "Labour and the Nation", drawn up by R. H. Tawney, cited in Mowat, *Britain Between the Wars*, p. 350.
7 Eric Hobsbawm, "C (for Crisis)", review of Richard Overy, *The Morbid Age: Britain Between the Wars* (London, 2009), in *London Review of Books*, 31, 15 (August 2009), pp. 12–15.
8 Susan Pedersen "Only Men in Mind", review of Lawrence Goldman, *The Life of R. H. Tawney* (London, 2013), in *London Review of Books*, 36, 16 (August 2014), pp. 29–30.
9 Mowat, *Britain*, pp. 353–412.
10 Manela, *The Wilsonian Moment*.
11 Deirdre McMahon, "Ireland and the Commonwealth, 1900–1948", in Judith Brown and Wm. Roger Louis (eds), *The Oxford History of the British Empire*, vol. 4: *The Twentieth Century* (Oxford, 1999), pp. 138–162.
12 Colin Cross, *The Fascists in Britain* (London, 1961).
13 Reynolds, *America*, pp. 309–314.
14 Ibid., pp. 326–7.
15 David Olusoga, "The World's War", episode 2, BBC 2, 13 August 2014.
16 Reynolds, *America*, pp. 329–330.
17 Lary May, *Screening out the Past: The Birth of Mass Culture and the Motion Picture Industry* (New York, 1990), p. 26; Reynolds, *America*, pp. 327–328.
18 Arthur R. M. Lower, *Colony to Nation: A History of Canada* (Toronto, 1957).
19 Ramchandra Guha, *Gandhi Before India* (London, 2013).
20 Shula Marks and Stanley Trapido (eds), *The Politics of Race, Class and Nationalism in Twentieth Century South Africa* (London, 1987).
21 Stuart Macintyre, *Australia*, pp. 172–4.
22 Philippa Mein Smith, *A Concise History of New Zealand* (Cambridge, 2005), pp. 147–149.
23 Ibid., pp. 102–104, 136.
24 Brown and Louis, *Oxford History*.
25 F. M. Bourret, *Ghana: The Road to Independence 1919–57* (London, 1960).
26 Bruce Berman and John Lonsdale, *Unhappy Valley: Conflict in Kenya and Africa*, 2 vols (London, 1992).
27 Roland Oliver and Anthony Atmore, *Africa Since 1800* (Cambridge, 2004), p. 187.
28 Ibid., p. 177.
29 Anupama Rao, *The Caste Question: Dalits and the Politics of Modern India* (Berkeley, 2009).

30 Sunil Khilnani, "India's Democratic Career", in Dunn (ed.), *Democracy*, pp. 189–205; see also *idem*, *The Idea of India* (London, 2003).
31 Toyin Falola and Matthew M. Heaton, *A History of Nigeria* (Cambridge, 2008), pp. 141–146.
32 B. W. Higman, *A Concise History of the Caribbean* (Cambridge, 2011).
33 Derek Hopwood, "Introduction", in John Cooper, Ronald Nettler and Mohamed Mahmoud (eds), *Islam and Modernity: Muslim Intellectuals Respond* (London, 1998), p. 7.
34 Eberhard Kolb (tr. P. S. Falla), *The Weimar Republic* (London, 1988); John Hiden, *The Weimar Republic* (London, 1996).
35 Christopher Clark, *The Iron Kingdom: The Rise and Downfall of Prussia, 1600–1947* (London, 2006), pp. 619–654.
36 Evans, *The Coming of the Third Reich*.
37 Julian Jackson, *The Popular Front in France: Defending Democracy 1934–38* (Cambridge, 1988).
38 Graham, *The Spanish Republic at War*.

CHAPTER 5 THE DEPRESSION: STATE INTERVENTION AND POPULAR RESISTANCE

1 John Maynard Keynes, *The Economic Consequences of the Peace* (London, 1919).
2 Dietmar Rothermund, *The Global Impact of the Great Depression, 1929–1939* (London, 1996).
3 Anon, "Datawatch", *Financial Times*, 27 October 2014.
4 Michael Stewart, *Keynes and After* (London, 1986).
5 The classic account remains Charles P. Kindleberger, *The World in Depression, 1929–39* (London, 1973).
6 Michael Kitson, "Britain's Withdrawal from the Gold Standard: The End of an Epoch", in Randall Parker and Robert Whaples (eds), *Handbook of Major Events in Economic History* (London, 2013), pp. 127–137.
7 Reynolds, *America*, pp. 335–58; the classic analysis was J. K. Galbraith, *The Great Crash, 1929* (London, 1955).
8 Eric Rauchway, *The Great Depression and the New Deal: A Very Short Introduction* (Oxford, 2008).
9 Macintyre, *Australia*, pp. 178–183.
10 Rothermund, *The Great Depression*, pp. 87–97.
11 B. R. Tomlinson, *The Economy of Modern India from 1860 to the Twenty-First Century* (Cambridge, 2013).
12 M. Chalapathi Rau, *Govind Ballabh Pant: His Life and Times* (Delhi, 1981) pp. 140–141.
13 Falola and Heaton, *A History of Nigeria*, pp. 118–124.
14 Moses E. Ochonu, *Colonial Meltdown: Northern Nigeria in the Great Depression* (Athens, 2009).
15 Sven Beckert, *Empire of Cotton: A New History of Global Capitalism* (London, 2014), pp. 378–426.
16 I. D. Talbott, *Agricultural Innovation in Colonial Africa: Kenya and the Great Depression* (Lewiston, 1990).
17 Samuel Kalman, *French Colonial Fascism: The Extreme Right in Algeria, 1919–39* (New York, 2013).

18 Osumaka Likaka, *Naming Colonialism: History and Collective Memory in the Congo, 1870–1960* (Madison, 2009).

19 Harold James, *The German Slump: Politics and Economics, 1924–36* (Oxford, 1986).

20 Evans, *The Third Reich in Power*.

21 Bakewell, *Latin America*, pp. 441–443.

22 Rothermund, *Great Depression*, pp. 110–119.

23 Service, *Stalin*, pp. 269–272.

24 Hugh Brogan, "The United States, 1900–45", in Howard and Louis, *Oxford History of the Twentieth Century*, pp. 136–137.

25 Reynolds, *America*, p. 347.

26 Kindleberger, *The World in Depression, 1929–1939*.

CHAPTER 6 THE SECOND WORLD WAR AND ITS CONSEQUENCES

1 Christopher Clark, *The Sleepwalkers: How Europe Went to War in 1914* (London, 2012); Sean McMeekin, *July 1914: Countdown to War* (London, 2013).

2 A. J. P. Taylor, *The Origins of the Second World War* (London, 1961).

3 Wm. Roger Louis (ed.), *The Origins of the Second World War: A. J. P. Taylor and his Critics* (New York, 1972).

4 Richard Overy, *The Bombers and the Bombed: Allied Air War Over Europe, 1940–1945* (London, 2013).

5 Jeremy Black, *World War Two: A Military History* (London, 2003).

6 Alongside Black, the fullest analytical narrative is provided by Peter Calvocoressi and Guy Wint, *Total War: Causes and Courses of the Second World War* (London, 1979) which this chapter follows; cf. Gerhard Weinberg, *A World at Arms: A Global History of World War II* (Cambridge, 1994).

7 David Nicolle, *The Italian Invasion of Abyssinia, 1935–6* (London, 1997).

8 Major E. W. Polson Newman, *Italy's Conquest of Abyssinia* (London, 1937), p. 307.

9 Colarizi, *Novecento Italiano*, pp. 226–228.

10 Journal, 12 October 1935 in N. J. Crowson (ed.), *Fleet Street, Press Barons and Politics: The Journals of Collin Brooks 1932–1940* (Cambridge, 1998), p. 132.

11 Rana Mitter, *China's War with Japan, 1937–1945: The Struggle for Survival* (London, 2013).

12 Jay Taylor, *The Generalissimo: Chiang Kai-shek and the Struggle for Modern China* (London, 2008).

13 Hirota's "Fundamental Principles", cited in P. H. B. Kent, *The Twentieth Century in the Far East: A Perspective of Events, Cultural Influences and Policies* (London, 1937), p. 285.

14 Hans J. van de Ven, *War and Nationalism in China*, pp. 209–252.

15 Elisabeth Leake, "The Politics of the North-West Frontier of the Indian Sub-continent, *c.*1936–65", unpublished PhD dissertation University of Cambridge, 2013.

16 Rashid Khalidi, "The Palestinians and 1948: The Underlying Causes of Failure", in Eugene Rogan and Avi Shlaim (eds), *The War for Palestine: Rewriting the History of 1948* (Cambridge, 2001), p. 24.

17 Ibid., p. 26.

18 Graham, *The Spanish Republic at War*.

19 Ibid., pp. 105, 110.

20 Richard H. King and Dan Stone (eds), *Hannah Arendt and the Uses of History: Imperialism, Nation, Race and Genocide* (New York, 2007).
21 Calvocoressi and Wint, *Total War*.
22 Mazower, *Dark Continent*, pp. 141–184.
23 Richard Griffiths, *Fellow Travellers of the Right: British Enthusiasts for Nazi Germany, 1933–39* (London, 1980).
24 Richard Overy, *Russia's War* (London, 1997).
25 David Reynolds, *America*, pp. 358–372.
26 Timothy Harper and Christopher Bayly, *Forgotten Armies: The Fall of British Asia, 1941–1945* (Cambridge, Mass., 2005).
27 Ion. L. Idriess, *Must Australia Fight?* (Sydney, 1939), pp. 8–9.
28 Richard Overy, *Why the Allies Won* (London, 1995).
29 Richard Overy, "Dresden: When moral force was lost amid the brutality of war", *The Times*, 28 February 2015.
30 Antony Beevor, *Stalingrad* (London, 1998).
31 Wilfried Loth, *The Division of the World, 1941–1955* (London, 1988).
32 David Reynolds, *Summits: Six Meetings that Shaped the Twentieth Century* (London, 2007), pp. 96–151.
33 Harry A. Gailey, *The War in the Pacific: From Pearl Harbor to Tokyo Bay* (Novato, 1995).
34 Louis Allen, *Burma: The Longest War, 1941–1945* (London, 1984).
35 "Imperial Rescript", 14 August 1945, cited in H. T. Cook and T. F. Cook, *Japan at War: An Oral History* (New York, 1992) p. 401.
36 Heonik Kwon, *The Other Cold War* (New York, 2010).
37 Richard West, *Tito and the Rise and Fall of Yugoslavia* (London, 1994).
38 Timothy Harper and Christopher Bayly, *Forgotten Wars: The End of Britain's Asian Empire* (London, 2007).
39 William J. Duiker, *Ho Chi Minh* (New York, 2000).
40 Mark Mazower, Jessica Reinisch and David Feldman (eds), *Post-War Reconstruction in Europe: International Perspectives, 1945–1949* (Oxford, 2011)
41 Colarizi, *Novecento Italiano*, pp. 336–360.
42 Seymour Morris Jr., *Supreme Commander: MacArthur's Triumph in Japan* (New York, 2014).
43 Reynolds, *America*.
44 Glenda Sluga, *Internationalism in the Age of Nationalism* (Philadelphia, 2013).
45 Sarvepalli Gopal, *Radhakrishnan: A Biography* (Delhi, 1989).
46 Jeffrey M. Diefendorf, Axel Frohm and Hermann-Josef Rupieper (eds), *American Policy and the Reconstruction of West Germany, 1945–1955* (Cambridge, 1993).
47 Lizzie Collingham, *The Taste of War: World War Two and the Battle for Food* (London, 2011).
48 Geraldine Forbes, *Women in Modern India* (Cambridge, 1996), pp.189–222.
49 Melissa Eddy, "East German model city rusts, quarter-century after Berlin Wall's fall", *The New York Times*, 3 November 2013.

CHAPTER 7 PERIPHERAL CONFLICTS AND THE END OF OLD REGIMES, C.1945–1955

1 Shlaim and Rogan (eds), *The War for Palestine*.
2 Wm. Roger Louis, *Ends of British Imperialism, The Scramble for Empire, Suez and Decolonisation* (London, 2006), pp. 419–451.

3 Ronen Shamir, *Current Flow: The Electrification of Palestine* (Stanford, 2015).
4 Louis, *Ends of British Imperialism*, pp. 589–689.
5 Vazira Zamindar, *The Long Partition and the Making of Modern South Asia: Refugees Boundaries, Histories* (New York, 2007); Yasmin Khan, The Great Partition: *The Making of India and Pakistan* (London, 2007).
6 Sunil Purushotham, "Sovereignty, Violence, and the Making of the Postcolonial State in India, 1946–52", unpublished PhD dissertation University of Cambridge, 2013.
7 Harshan Kumarasingham, *A Political Legacy of the British Empire: Power and the Parliamentary System in Post-Colonial India and Sri Lanka* (London, 2013).
8 Bayly and Harper, *Forgotten Wars.*
9 Michael Charney, *A History of Modern Burma* (Cambridge, 2009).
10 Barbara Andaya and Leonard Andaya, *A History of Malaysia* (London, 1982).
11 Robert Jackson, *The Malayan Emergency: The Commonwealth's Wars, 1948–1966* (London, 1991).
12 Pierre Brocheux (tr. C. Duiker), *Ho Chi Minh: A Biography* (Cambridge, 2007).
13 W. J. Duiker, *The Communist Road to Power in Vietnam* (Boulder, Col., 1996).
14 Anthony Reid, *The Indonesian National Revolution, 1945–50* (Hawthorn, 1974).
15 Rex Mortimer, *Indonesian Communism under Sukarno: Ideology and Politics* (London, 1974).
16 Stuart R. Schram, *Mao Tse-tung* (London, 1966).
17 Van de Ven, *War and Nationalism*, pp. 293–296.
18 Jonathan Spence, *Mao Zedong* (New York, 1999).
19 Odd Arne Westad, *The Global Cold War: Third World Interventions and the Making of Our Times* (Cambridge, 2007).
20 Oliver and Atmore, *Africa*, pp. 265–266, 255–257.
21 Louis, *Ends of British Imperialism*, pp. 553–589.
22 Service, *Stalin*, p. 493.
23 Timothy Johnston, *Being Soviet: Identity, Rumour and Everyday Life Under Stalin* (Oxford, 2011).
24 Juliane Furst, *Stalin's Last Generation: Soviet Post-War Youth and the Emergence of Mature Socialism* (Oxford, 2010).
25 Brown, *The Rise and Fall*, pp. 267–278.
26 Cited by Holly Case, "Reconstruction in East–Central Europe: Clearing the Rubble of Cold War Politics", in Mazower, Reinisch and Feldman (eds), *Post-War Reconstruction in Europe*, p. 77.
27 Eric D. Weitz, *Creating German Communism, 1890–1990: From Popular Protests to Socialist State* (Princeton, 1997).
28 Neal Acherson, "Little People Made Big", review of Maxim Leo, *Red Love: The Story of an East German Family* (London, 2013) and Franz Fuhmann, *The Jew Car* (Chicago, 2013), in *London Review of Books*, 36, 1 (9 January 2014), pp. 23–24.
29 Alan S. Milward, *The Reconstruction of Western Europe, 1945–51* (London, 1984).
30 Colarizi, *Novecento Italiano*, pp. 325–343.
31 Michele Salvati, *Economia e politica in Italia dal dopoguerra a oggi* (Milan, 1984).
32 Tony Judt, *Postwar: A History of Europe since 1945* (London, 2010), pp 241–353.
33 Timothy Garton Ash, *In Europe's Name: Germany and the Divided Continent* (New York, 1993).

34 David Kynaston, *Austerity Britain, 1945–51* (London, 2007).

35 Reynolds, *America*, pp. 387–406.

36 Bill Levitt cited in ibid., p. 388.

37 Jean E. Smith, *Eisenhower in War and Peace* (New York, 2012).

38 Knight, "Latin America", in Howard and Louis (eds), *Twentieth Century*.

39 Che Guevara, "Socialist man in Cuba", and "From Algiers to Marcha, 12 March 1965", in David Deutschmann (ed.), *Che Guevara Reader* (Melbourne, 2003).

40 John Dower, *Embracing Defeat: Japan in the Aftermath of World War Two* (London, 1999).

41 Howard Schonberger, *Aftermath of War: Americans and the Remaking of Japan, 1945–1952* (London, 1989).

42 Jerome B. Cohen, *Japan's Postwar Economy*, (Bloomington, 1958), p. viii.

43 Jamie Martin, "Were We Bullied?", review of Benn Steill, *The Battle of Bretton Woods: John Maynard Keynes, Harry Dexter White and the Making of a New World Order* (Princeton, 2013), in *London Review of Books*, 35, 22 (21 November 2013), pp. 16–18.

CHAPTER 8 AMERICA'S HEGEMONY AND COLONIALISM'S FINALE, MID-1950S TO 1970S

1 Cahal Milmo, "Revealed: How MI5 watched the wrong Marxist Oxbridge academics – Christopher Hill and Eric Hobsbawn", *The Independent*, Friday 24 October 2014.

2 William Chafe, *The Unfinished Journey: America since World War II* (New York, 1991).

3 Reynolds, *America*, pp. 520–521.

4 James Baughman, *The Republic of Mass Culture: Journalism, Filmmaking and Broadcasting in America since 1941* (Baltimore, 1997).

5 Richard Polenberg, *One Nation Divisible: Class, Race and Ethnicity in the United States since 1938* (New York, 1980).

6 Peter B. Levy, *The Civil Rights Movement* (London, 1998).

7 Clay Risen, *The Bill of the Century: The Epic Battle for the Civil Rights Act* (New York, 2014).

8 David Runciman, "What if He'd Made It Earlier", review of Robert Caro, *The Years of Lyndon Johnson*, vol. 4 (London, 2014), in *London Review of Books*, 34, 13, (5 July 2012), pp. 18–22.

9 Tim Walker, "Assata Shakur: Black militant, fugitive cop killer, terrorist threat . . . or escaped slave?" *Independent*, 18 July 2014.

10 Brown, *The Rise and Fall*, p. 222.

11 William Taubman, *Khrushchev: The Man and his Era* (London, 2003).

12 Brown, *The Rise and Fall*, p. 243.

13 Peter Grieder, *The German Democratic Republic* (Basingstoke, 2012).

14 Neal Acherson, "Little People Made Big".

15 Brown, *The Rise and Fall*, pp. 398–414.

16 Benjamin Zachariah, *Nehru* (London, 2004), pp. 241–250.

17 James M. Carter, *Inventing Vietnam: The United States and State Building, 1954–1968* (Cambridge, 2008).

18 George Herring, *America's Longest War: The United States and Vietnam, 1950–1975* (Philadelphia, 1986).

19 James M. Carter, *Inventing Vietnam*, pp. 232–248.

20 Cited in Kim Megson, "Vietnam Dispatch: On the beach where US troops landed 50 years ago, a new Vietnam flourishes", *The Guardian*, 28th February 2015.

21 Yang Jisheng (tr. Stacy Mosher and Guo Jian), *Tombstone: The Untold Story of Mao's Great Famine* (London, 2012); Frank Dikötter, *Mao's Great Famine: The History of China's most Devastating Catastrophe* (London, 2011); see the review by James C. Scott, "Tyranny of the ladle", in *London Review of Books*, 34, 23 (6 December 2012), 21–28.

22 Chen Yi, Chinese Foreign Minister, quoted in Dikötter, *Great Famine*, p. 70.

23 Paul Clark, *The Chinese Cultural Revolution: A History* (Cambridge, 2008).

24 Brown, *The Rise and Fall*, pp. 347–349.

25 Grant Evans and Kelvin Rowley, *Red Brotherhood at War: Vietnam, Cambodia and Laos since 1975* (London, 1990).

26 Robert Elson, *Suharto: A Political Biography* (Cambridge, 2001).

27 Michael R. R. Vatikiotis, *Indonesian Politics under Suharto: The Rise and Fall of the New Order* (London, 1993).

28 Cited by Khilnani, *Idea of India*, p. 87; see also Ashok Rudra, *Prasanta Chandra Mahalanobis: A Biography* (Delhi, 1996).

29 Khilnani, *Idea of India*; Ramachandra Guha, *India after Gandhi: The History of the World's Largest Democracy* (London, 2008).

30 Paul Brass, *The Politics of India since Independence* (Cambridge, 1994).

31 Francine Frankel, *India's Political Economy 1947–77: The Gradual Revolution* (Princeton, 1978).

32 Oliver and Atmore (eds) *Africa*, pp. 226–302.

33 John Ruedy, *Modern Algeria: The Origins and Development of a Nation* (Bloomington, 1992); see also Charles Robert Ageron (tr. Michael Brett), *Modern Algeria: A History from 1830 to the Present* (London, 1991).

34 Julian Jackson, *Charles de Gaulle* (London, 2003).

35 Bruce Berman and John Lonsdale, *Unhappy Valley*, vol. 2, pp. 316–458.

36 David Birmingham, *Kwame Nkrumah: Father of African Nationalism* (Athens, 1998).

37 Van Reybrouck, *Congo*.

38 William Beinart, *Twentieth Century South Africa* (Oxford, 1994).

39 Tom Lodge, *Sharpeville: An Apartheid Massacre and its Consequences* (Oxford, 2011).

40 Mazower, *Dark Continent*, pp. 290–332.

41 Anne Deighton, "The Remaking of Europe: 1945–1989", in Howard and Louis (eds), *Twentieth Century*, pp. 190–203; Milward, *The Reconstruction of Western Europe*.

42 Judt, *Postwar*, pp. 390–421.

43 Nathaniel Davis, *The Last Two Years of Salvador Allende* (Ithaca, 1985).

44 Alain Rouqie, "The Military in Latin American Politics since 1930", in Leslie Bethell (ed.), *Latin America: Politics and Society since 1930* (Cambridge, 1998), pp. 145–219.

45 Jules R. Benjamin, *The United States and the Origins of the Cuban Revolution: An Empire of Liberty in an Age of National Revolution* (Princeton, 1990).

46 Leslie Bethell, *Cuba: A Short History* (Cambridge, 1993).

CHAPTER 9 THE "TIPPING POINT": WORLD POLITICS AND THE SHOCK OF THE "LONG 1980s"

1 Piketty, *Capital*.
2 Brown, *The Rise and Fall*, pp. 481–522.
3 Steve Crashaw, "Fall of the Berlin Wall: A people's uprising that grew until it remade Europe", *Independent*, 28 October 2014.
4 Judt, *Postwar*, especially pp. 585–633.
5 Brown, *The Rise and Fall*, pp. 522–548.
6 Archie Brown, *The Gorbachev Factor* (Oxford, 1996).
7 Roy Medvedev (tr. George Shriver), *Post-Soviet Russia: A Journey Through the Yeltsin Era* (New York, 2002).
8 Aleksandr Dugin, 2005, cited in Brown, *The Rise and Fall*, p. 563.
9 Fukuyama, *The End of History*.
10 Alain Touraine, *Solidarity: The Analysis of a Social Movement: Poland, 1980–1981* (Cambridge, 1983).
11 Piotr H. Kosicki, "After 1989: The life and death of the Catholic third way", *Times Literary Supplement*, 13 December 2013, pp. 13–15.
12 Baqer Moin, *Khomeini: The Life of the Ayatollah* (London, 2009).
13 Speech to students in Qom, 13 March 1979, cited in *Time*, 7 January 1980.
14 Ian Talbot, *Pakistan: A Modern History* (London, 1998).
15 David Shambaugh (ed.), *Deng Xiaoping: Portrait of a Chinese Statesman* (Oxford, 1995).
16 Interview with Timothy Brook, *Frontline*, 11 April 2006.
17 Susan Bayly, *Asian Voices in a Post-Colonial Age: Vietnam, India and Beyond* (Cambridge, 2007).
18 Paul Krugman, *The New York Times*, 9 January 2012; cf. Krugman, *The Return of Depression Economics and the Crisis of 2008* (New York, 2009).
19 Martha C. Nussbaum, *Democracy, Religious Violence and the Future of India* (Cambridge, 2007).
20 Kapila, *Violence and the Indian Political*.
21 Robert Stern, *Changing India: Bourgeois Revolution on the Subcontinent* (Cambridge, 2003).
22 Reynolds, *America*, pp. 507–537.
23 Piketty, *Capital*.
24 William Martin, *With God on Our Side: The Rise of the Religious Right in America* (New York, 1996).
25 Hugo Young, *One of Us: A Biography of Margaret Thatcher* (London, 1991).
26 Judt, *Postwar*.
27 Colarizi, *Novecento*, pp. 494–498.
28 Judt, *Postwar*, pp. 526–534.
29 Charles S. Maier, *Dissolution: The Crisis of Communism and the End of East Germany* (Princeton, 1997).
30 Frederick Cooper, *Africa since 1940: The Past of the Present* (Cambridge, 2002); Paul Nugent, *Africa since Independence: A Comparative History* (London, 2012).
31 Falola and Heaton, *A History of Nigeria*, pp. 209–242.
32 S. Terreblanche, *A History of Inequality in South Africa, 1652–2002* (Pietermaritzburg, 2002).
33 Timothy Gibbs, *Mandela's Kinsmen: Nationalist Elites and Apartheid's First Bantustan* (Woodbridge, 2014).

CHAPTER 10 THE EXPANSION OF HUMAN KNOWLEDGE: THE TWENTIETH-CENTURY PERSON AND SOCIETY

1 According to Don LePan, the first "cognitive revolution" occurred during the Renaissance, *The Cognitive Revolution in Western Culture*, vol. 1: *The Birth of Expectation* (Basingstoke, 1989). The work of Jean Piaget would expand this to a global level.

2 John Maddox, "The expansion of knowledge", in Howard and Louis (eds), *The Oxford History of the Twentieth Century* (Oxford, 1998), p. 36.

3 "NHS mission to map DNA of entire British population", *The i*, 1 August 2014.

4 T. P. Hughes, *Networks of Power: Electrification in Western Society, 1880–1930* (Baltimore, 1983).

5 Steven Weinberg, "The Great Reduction: Physics in the Twentieth Century", in Howard and Louis (eds.) *Oxford History*, pp. 22–34.

6 Richard Rhodes, *The Making of the Atomic Bomb* (London, 1988).

7 T. C. Barker, "The International History of Motor Transport", *Journal of Contemporary History*, 20, 1 (January 1985), pp. 3–19.

8 Michael L. Berger, *The Automobile in American History and Culture: A Reference Guide* (Westport, 2001).

9 Claire Guélaud, "Le manqué d'innovation menace la croissance", *Le Monde*, 2 September 2014.

10 Virginia Morell, *Ancestral Passions. The Leakey Family and the Quest for Humankind's Beginnings* (New York, 1995).

11 Jonathan Lake, "We're all intellectual shrimps", *The Sunday Times*, 8 March 2015.

12 Robin McKie and Chris Stringer, *African Exodus: The Origins of Modern Humanity* (London, 1997).

13 Paul Betts and Corey Ross (eds), *Heritage in the Modern World*: *Historical Preservation in International Perspective* (Oxford, 2015).

14 Neil A. Silberman, *Digging for God and Country: Exploration, Archaeology, and the Secret Struggle for the Holy Land, 1799–1917* (New York, 1982).

15 Martin Bernal, *Black Athena: The Afroasiatic Roots of Classical Civilisation*, vol. 1: *The Fabrication of Ancient Greece, 1785–1985* (London, 1987).

16 Cf. John H. McWhorter, *The Language Hoax: Why the World Looks the Same in Any Language* (Oxford, 2014).

17 See, e.g., V. V. Barthold (tr. Shahid Suhrawardy), *Mussulman Culture* (Calcutta, 1934).

18 Krishan Kumar, "Civilized Value: The Return of Arnold Toynbee", *TLS*, 24 October 2014, pp. 16–17.

19 Harry Golding (ed.), *The Wonder Book of Empire for Boys and Girls* (London, 1920), p. 8.

20 Dipesh Chakrabarty, *The Calling of History: Sir Jadunath Sarkar and His Empire of Truth* (Chicago, 2015).

21 Fernand Braudel (tr. Sian Reynolds), *Civilisation and Capitalism, 15th–18th Century*, 3 vols (London, 1979).

22 See Robert Layton, *An Introduction to Theory in Anthropology* (Cambridge, 1997).

23 Herbert S. Lewis, *In Defense of Anthropology: An Investigation of the Critique of Anthropology* (New Brunswick, 2014), pp. 123–185.

24 Keith Hart, "The Cambridge Torres Strait Expedition and British social anthropology", blog post, 6 November 2009. Accessed: memorybank.co.uk.

25 Raymond Firth (ed.), *Man and Nature: An Evaluation of the Work of Bronislaw Malinowski* (London, 1957).

26 Peter Mandler, *Return from the Natives: How Margaret Mead Won the Second World War but Lost the Cold War* (Newhaven, 2013).

27 Ruth Benedict, *The Chrysanthemum and the Sword: Patterns of Japanese Culture* (Boston, 1946); Elson Boles, "Ruth Benedict's Japan: The Benedictions of Imperialism", *Dialectical Anthropology*, 30, 1–2, (January 2006), pp. 27–70.

28 "Introduction", to Gareth Stedman Jones (ed.) *Karl Marx and Friedrich Engels: The Communist Manifesto* (London, 2002).

29 Marcel Henaff (tr. Mary Baker), *Claude Lévi-Strauss and the Making of Structural Anthropology* (Minneapolis, 1998).

30 Henrika Kuklick (ed.), *A New History of Anthropology* (Oxford, 2008).

31 C. A. Bayly, *Recovering Liberties: Indian Thought in the Age of Liberalism and Empire* (Cambridge, 2012).

32 Talal Asad (ed.), *Anthropology and the Colonial Encounter* (London, 1973); Achille Mbembe, *De la postcolonie: Essai sur l'imagination politique dans l'Afrique contemporaine* (Paris, 2000).

33 Mark Blaug, *Economic Theory in Retrospect* (Cambridge, 1985).

34 Bayly, *Recovering Liberties*.

35 Xiaobing Tang, *Global Space and the Nationalist Discourse of Modernity: The Historical Thought of Liang Qichao* (Stanford, 1996).

36 Stewart, *Keynes and After*.

37 Lecture 2 May 1936 in Henry Clay (ed.), *The Inter-War Years and Other Papers: A Selection from the Writings of Hubert Douglas Henderson* (Oxford, 1955), p. 160.

38 Richard Davenport-Hines, *Universal Man: The Seven Lives of John Maynard Keynes* (London, 2015).

39 Nahid Aslanbeigui and Guy Oakes, *The Provocative Joan Robinson: The Making of a Cambridge Economist* (Durham, 2009).

40 See Bruce Caldwell, "Introduction", in F. A. Hayek, *The Road to Serfdom: Text and Documents* (Chicago, 2007), pp. 1–22.

41 Milton Friedman, *Capitalism and Freedom* (Chicago, 1962); William Ruger, *Milton Friedman* (London, 2011).

42 Piketty, *Capital*.

43 Nupur Acharya, "The Friday Briefing: Battle of the Economists", *The Wall Street Journal India*, 25 July 2013.

44 Paul Krugman, *The Return of Depression Economics*.

45 Heinz Maus, *A Short History of Sociology* (London, 1962).

46 Craig Calhoun (ed.), *Sociology in America: A History* (Chicago, 2007).

CHAPTER 11 THE SELF AND HUMAN SOCIETY

1 Charles Taylor, *Sources of the Self: The Making of the Modern Identity* (Cambridge, 1989).

2 See also Georges Vigarello, *Le sentiment de soi: Histoire de la perception du corps, XVIe–XXe Siècle* (Paris, 2014).

3 Robert Devigne, *Recasting Conservatism: Oakeshott, Strauss, and the Response to Postmodernism* (New Haven, 1996).

4 Ben Rogers and Charles Taylor, "Charles Taylor interviewed", *Prospect Magazine*, February 2008.

5 Javed Majeed, *Muhammad Iqbal: Islam, Aesthetics and Postcolonialism* (London, 2007).

6 David Charter, "God and socialism still divide Germany", *The Times*, 4 November 2014.

7 John Dunn, *The Politics of Socialism: An Essay in Political Theory* (Cambridge, 1984).

8 Humeira Iqtidar, *Secularizing Islamists? Jama'at-e-Islami and Jama'at-ud-Da'wa in Urban Pakistan* (Chicago, 2011).

9 Thomas Hardy Leahey, *A History of Psychology: Main Currents in Psychological Thought* (London, 1985).

10 Michel Foucault (tr. Robert Hurley), *History of Sexuality*, 3 vols (London, 1979–1984).

11 Edward Shorter, *A History of Psychiatry: From the Era of the Asylum to the Age of Prozac* (New York, 1997).

12 Charles B. Guignon (ed.), *The Cambridge Companion to Heidegger* (Cambridge, 2006), introduction, pp. 1–42.

13 D. P. S. Khanna, *Dr Bhagwan Das as a Social Thinker* (Delhi 1983).

14 Darrin M. McMahon and Samuel Moyn, *Rethinking Modern European Intellectual History* (Oxford, 2014).

15 Alan Ryan, "Staunchly Modern, Non-Bourgeois Liberalism", in Avital Simhony and David Weinstein (eds), *The New Liberalism. Reconciling Liberty and Community* (Cambridge, 2001), pp. 184–204.

16 Chandran Kukathas and Philip Pettit, *Rawls: A Theory of Justice and its Critics* (Stanford, 1990).

17 Ellen Frankel Paul, Fred D. Miller Jnr and Jeffrey Paul (eds), *Liberalism: Old and New* (Cambridge, 2007).

18 Raymond Geuss, *Philosophy and Real Politics* (Princeton, 2008).

19 Pierre Rosanvallon (tr. Arthur Goldhammer), *Counter-Democracy: Politics in an Age of Distrust* (Cambridge, 2008).

20 Jane Robinson, *In the Family Way: Illegitimacy between the Great War and the Swinging Sixties* (London, 2015).

21 Jane Purvis (ed.), *Women's History: Britain 1850–1945* (London, 1995).

22 Anthony Giddens, *The Transformation of Intimacy: Sexuality, Love and Eroticism in Modern Societies* (Stanford, 1992).

23 Roger Boyes, "I had a snog – not enough for a Stasi file. That came later", *The Times*, 4 November 2014.

24 Paul Seabright, "Sexual distinctions", *TLS*, 28 June 2013, pp. 3–5.

25 "Femminicidio, pene piu severe", *Il Gazzettino*, 9 August 2013.

26 Elisabetta Povoledo, "Growing perils for women in Italy", *New York Herald Tribune*, 19 August 2013.

27 Faiza Zerouala, "Curriculum voilée", *Le Monde*, 10 September 2014.

28 Lizzie Dearden and Ian Johnstone, "Full face veils find little support across the Middle East, survey shows", *The i*, 10 January 2014.

29 Ronald Hyam, *Empire and Sexuality: The British Experience* (Manchester, 1990).

30 Tom Boellstorff, *The Gay Archipelago: Sexuality and Nation in Indonesia* (Princeton, 2005).

31 John Iliffe, *The African AIDS Epidemic: A History* (Athens, 2006).

32 Jeremy Laurance, "A journey to the heart of Africa's AIDS epidemic", *The i*, 18 November 2013.

33 Tom Boellstorff, "The Emergence of Political Homophobia in Indonesia: Masculinity and National Belonging", *Ethnos*, 69, 4, (2004), pp. 465–486.

34 W. D. Halls, *Education, Culture and Politics in Modern France* (Oxford, 1976).

35 William Boyd, *The History of Western Education* (London, 1954).

36 James Hennesey, *American Catholics: A History of the Roman Catholic Community in the United States* (New York, 1983).

37 Gail P. Kelly (ed. David Kelly), *French Colonial Education: Essays on Vietnam and West Africa* (New York, 1998).

38 Martin Thomas, *The French Empire Between the Wars: Imperialism, Politics and Society* (Manchester, 2005).

39 David Lelyveld, *Aligarh's First Generation: Muslim Solidarity and English Education in Northern India, 1875–1900* (Chicago, 1975).

40 Barbara Metcalf, *Islamic Revival in British India: Deoband, 1860–1900* (Princeton, 1982).

41 David Garland (ed.), *Mass Imprisonment: Social Causes and Consequences* (London, 2001).

42 Chris Nawrat, Steve Hutchings and Greg Struthers, *The Sunday Times Illustrated History of Twentieth Century Sport* (London, 1997).

43 Allen Guttmann, *Games and Empires: Modern Sports and Cultural Imperialism* (New York, 1994).

44 Richard Hoffer, *Bouts of Mania: Ali, Frazier, Foreman and an America on the Ropes* (London, 2014).

45 See Richie Benaud, *Anything but an Autobiography* (London, 1999).

46 James H. Mills (ed.), *Subaltern Sports: Politics and Sport in South Asia* (London, 2005).

47 Sachin Tendulkar, *Playing It My Way: My Autobiography* (London, 2014).

48 Jon Agar, *Constant Touch: A Global History of the Mobile Phone* (Cambridge, 2004).

49 Howard Gardner and Katie Davis, *The App Generation: How Today's Youth Navigate Identity, Intimacy and Imagination in a Digital World* (New Haven, 2014); Lynn Schofield Clark, *The Parent App: Understanding Families in the Digital Age* (Oxford, 2013).

50 John Brewer and Frank Trentmann (eds), *Consuming Cultures, Global Perspectives: Historical Trajectories, Transnational Exchanges* (Oxford, 2006).

CHAPTER 12 ARTS, LITERATURE AND ENTERTAINMENT: CRISIS AND RECOVERY

1 Paul Cézanne, *Les Grandes Baigneuses*, National Gallery, London.

2 Sue Roe, *In Montmartre: Picasso, Matisse and the Birth of Modernist Art* (London, 2014).

3 Hartwig Fischer and Sean Rainbird (eds), *Kandinsky: The Path to Abstraction* (London, 2006).

4 Okakura Kakuzo, *The Ideals of the East with Special Reference to the Art of Japan* (London, 1903) includes an introduction by Sister Nivedita.

5 A. Coomaraswamy and Sister Nivedita, *Myths of the Hindus and Buddhists* (London, 1913), p. vi.

6 Stanley Corngold, *Lambent Traces: Franz Kafka* (Princeton, 2004).

7 Vincent Sherry (ed.), *The Cambridge Companion to the Literature of the First World War* (Cambridge, 2005).

8 M. Biro, *The Dada Cyborg: Visions of the New Human in Weimar Berlin* (Minneapolis, 2009).

9 Colarizi, *Novecento Italiano*, pp.178–183.

10 Richard J. Evans, "Artists Under Hitler", review of Jonathan Petropoulos, *Artists under Hitler: Collaboration and Survival in Nazi Germany* (New Haven, 2014), in *The Sunday Times*, 1 February 2015.

11 Kristin Thompson and David Bordwell, *Film History: An Introduction* (London, 2003).

12 Ronald Bergan, *Eisenstein: A Life in Conflict* (London, 1999).

13 Rabindranath Tagore, *Nationalism* (London, 1918).

14 Munshi Premchand, *Premchand ki Sarwashrest Kahaniyan* (Allahabad, Uttar Pradesh, 1960).

15 Xu Zhimo, *Encyclopaedia Britannica*. Accessed: www.britannica.com/biography/Xu–Zhimo.

16 Michael Sullivan, *Art and Artists of Twentieth-century China* (Berkeley, 1996).

17 Alice Rawsthorn, "'Mokujiki Fever' Endures", *The New York Times*, 24–25 December 2013.

18 L. Trotsky (tr. Rose Strunsky), *Literature and Revolution* (Chicago, 2005), p. 13.

19 Tony Wood, "At Tate Modern", *London Review of Books* (21 August 2014), p. 13.

20 Boris Groys (tr. David Fernbach), *Introduction to Antiphilosophy* (London, 2012).

21 Antony Copley, *Music and the Spiritual: Composers and Politics in the 20th Century* (Delhi, 2013).

22 Helen Wang, *Chairman Mao Badges: Symbols and Slogans of the Cultural Revolution* (London, 2008), p. 82.

23 Qiu Zhijie, "The Unicorn and the Dragon", Fondazione Querini Stampalia, Venice, May–August 2013.

24 Susan Bayly, "Beyond 'propaganda': Images and the Moral Citizen in Late-Socialist Vietnam", forthcoming article.

25 Benjamin Kunkel, "Just Don't Think about it", review of Boris Groys, *Introduction to Antiphilosophy*" (London, 2012), *London Review of Books* (8 August 2013), pp. 33–37.

26 Monica Visona *et al.*, *A History of Art in Africa* (Upper Saddle River, 2001).

27 Both items were shown at the Pesaro Palace, Venice, in the summer of 2014.

28 Marc Dambre (ed.), *Les Hussards: Une génération litteraire* (Paris, 2000).

29 William J. R. Curtis, *Le Corbusier: Ideas and Forms* (London, 1986); for the link to modernism in photography, see Peter Galassi (ed.), *Henri Cartier Bresson: The Modern Century* (London, 2010).

30 Gary Giddins, *Visions of Jazz: The First Century* (New York, 1998).

31 "Great Poets in their Own Words", BBC Four, 20 August 2014.

32 Sun Jung, *Korean Masculinities and Transcultural Consumption: Yonsama, Rain, Oldboy, K-Pop Idols* (Hong Kong, 2011).

33 Choe Sang-Hun, "Cramming for stardom at Korea's K-Pop schools", *The New York Times*, 9 August 2013.

34 For example, *The Third Man*, the film of *Dr. Zhivago* or the spy thrillers of John le Carré.

35 For example, *Miss Saigon* or Oliver Stone's trilogy of films including *Heaven & Earth* (1993).

36 *Rambo III* (1988). Ironically, the real-life equivalents of these brave resisters were to become the United States' fiercest opponents, the Taliban.

37 Muhammad Amir Ahmad Khan, "Rhetorics and Spaces of Belonging among North Indian Muslims 1850–1950", unpublished PhD dissertation, University of Cambridge, 2015.

CHAPTER 13 RELIGION: CONTESTATION AND REVIVAL

1 Classic studies include Fredrik Barth, *Ritual and Knowledge among the Baktaman of New Guinea* (New Haven, 1975), and I. M. Lewis, *Ecstatic Religion: An Anthropological Study of Spirit Possession and Shamanism* (Harmondsworth, 1978).
2 Antonia Mills and Richard Slobodin (eds), *Amerindian Rebirth: Reincarnation and Belief among North American Indians and Inuit* (Toronto, 1994).
3 Edmund Leach, *Lévi-Strauss* (London, 1970).
4 The classic account is still Godfrey Lienhardt, *Divinity and Experience: The Religion of the Dinka* (Oxford, 1961).
5 For example, Gabriela Ramos, *Death and Conversion in the Andes. Lima and Cuzco, 1532–1670* (Notre Dame, 2010).
6 Amira K. Bennison, "Dynamics of Rule and Opposition in Nineteenth Century North Africa", *The Journal of North African Studies*, 1, 1 (1996), pp. 1–24.
7 Julius Lipner, "The rise of 'Hinduism,' or How to Invent a World Religion with Only Moderate Success", lecture delivered at Gandhi Center, James Madison University, 13 October 2005.
8 Frank Parkin, *Max Weber* (London, 2002).
9 John L. Esposito, Darrell J. Fasching and Todd Lewis, *World Religions Today* (Oxford, 2005).
10 Oliver and Atmore, *Africa*, pp. 164–167.
11 Marshall G. S. Hodgson, *Rethinking World History: Essays on Europe, Islam and World History* (Cambridge, 1993).
12 P. Worsley, *The Trumpet Shall Sound: A Study of "Cargo" Cults in Melanesia* (London, 1957); cf. Martha Kaplan, *Neither Cargo nor Cult: Ritual Politics and the Colonial Imagination in Fiji* (Durham, 1995).
13 Pierre Rondot, *Caodai Spiritism: A Study of Religion in Vietnamese Society* (Leiden, 1976).
14 Beth Singler, "Return of the New Gods: Jedis, Auras and Online Witch Schools", blog post, 24 Oct. 2014. Accessed: http://www.cam.ac.uk/research/features/return-of-the-new-gods-jedis-auras-and-online-witch-schools.
15 John Slight, *The British Empire and the Hajj, 1865–1956* (Cambridge, 2015).
16 Service, *Stalin*, pp. 267–268.
17 Frank Dikötter, *Mao's Great Famine: The History of China's Most Devastating Catastrophe* (London, 2010), pp. 167, 267, 268.
18 Ibid., p. 172.
19 Oleg Benesch, *Inventing the Way of the Samurai: Nationalism, Internationalism and Bushido in Modern Japan* (Oxford, 2014), p. 182.
20 Devji, *Impossible Indian*.
21 V. D. Savarkar, *Hindutva: Who is a Hindu?* (Delhi, 2003); Dhananjay Keer, *Savarkar and his Times* (Bombay, 1966).
22 Ahmed, *The Making of Modern Turkey*.
23 Murat Siviloglu, "The Emergence of Public Opinion in the Ottoman Empire, 1826–1876", unpublished PhD dissertation, University of Cambridge, 2015.
24 Richard P. Mitchell, *The Society of the Muslim Brothers* (London, 1969).
25 Madawi al-Rasheed, *A History of Saudi Arabia* (Cambridge, 2002).
26 Peter J. Conn, *Pearl S. Buck: A Cultural Biography* (Cambridge, 1996).

27 John Pollard, *Catholicism in Modern Italy: Religion, Politics and Society since 1861* (London, 2008).

28 Graham, *The Spanish Republic at War*, pp. 4–6, 27–31, 340–341, 386.

29 Phillip Berryman, *Liberation Theology: Essential Facts about the Revolutionary Movement in Latin America and Beyond* (New York, 1987).

30 For example, Callum G. Brown, "Gendering secularisation: locating women in the transformation of British Christianity in the 1960s", in Ira Katznelson and Gareth Steman Jones (eds), *Religion and the Political Imagination* (Cambridge, 2010), pp. 275–295.

31 Humeira Iqtidar, "Colonial secularism and the genesis of Islamism in North India", in Katznelson and Stedman-Jones, *Religion and the Political Imagination* (Cambridge, 2010), pp. 235–253.

32 James C. Scott, *The Art of Not Being Governed: An Anarchist History of Upland Southeast Asia* (New Haven, 2009).

CHAPTER *14* A CENTURY OF KILLING AND A CENTURY OF CRIME

1 The phrase is that of Michael Mann. His book *The Dark Side of Democracy: Explaining Ethnic Cleansing* (Cambridge, 2005) remains the key text on this issue.

2 Eugene Rogan, *The Fall of the Ottomans: The Great War in the Middle East, 1914–1920*.

3 Raymond H. Kévorkian, *The Armenian Genocide: A Complete History* (London, 2011).

4 Mark Mazower, *Salonica, City of Ghosts: Christians, Muslims and Jews, 1430–1950* (London, 2004).

5 Mitter, *China's War with Japan*, pp. 117–138.

6 Mann, *Dark Side of Democracy*, pp. 326–330.

7 General Emilio Mola, cited by Helen Graham, *The Spanish Republic at War*, p. 117.

8 Inga Clendinnen, *Reading the Holocaust* (Cambridge, 1999).

9 Mazower, *Dark Continent*, pp. 161–184.

10 Speech to Gauleiter, Poland, 6 November 1943, in Griffin, *Fascism*, p. 162.

11 Robert Gildea, *Marianne in Chains: In Search of the German Occupation, 1940–1945* (London, 2002), pp. 272–280.

12 Mazower, *Dark Continent*, p. 150.

13 Karl Fritzch, cited by Josef Paczynski, a survivor, Tony Paterson, "Auschwitz survivors remember the horror of the camp 70 years on", *The Independent*, 25 January 2015.

14 François Azouvi, *Le Mythe du Grand Silence: Auschwitz, les Français, le Mémoir* (Paris, 2012).

15 Judt, *Postwar*, pp. 803–822.

16 Barak Kushner, "Pawns of Empire: Postwar Taiwan, Japan and the Dilemma of War Crimes", in Adam Culow (ed.), *Statecraft and Spectacle in East Asia* (London, 2010), pp. 108–130.

17 Judt, *Postwar*, pp. 803–822.

18 David Anderson, *Histories of the Hanged: Britain's Dirty War in Kenya and the End of Empire* (London, 2005); Caroline Elkins, *Britain's Gulag: The Brutal End of Empire in Kenya* (London, 2005).

19 Shruti Kapila, "1984: Sacred violence and Militant Sikhism", unpublished work-shop paper, Cambridge, 2012.

20 Gyanendra Pandey, *Remembering Partition: Violence, Nationalism and History in India* (London, 2001).

21 Sunil Purushotham, "Destroying Hyderabad and making the nation", review of A. G. Noorani, *The Destruction of Hyderabad* (Delhi, 2013), in *Economic and Political Weekly*, XLIX, 22 (31 May 2014), pp. 28–33.

22 Shruti Kapila, "A History of Violence", *Modern Intellectual History*, 7, 2 (August 2010), 437–457.

23 Sayyid Hussein Manto (tr. Nasreen Rehman), *Thanda Gosht* (1950), p. 7; copy in translator's possession.

24 Jonathan Spencer (ed.), *Sri Lanka: History and the Roots of Conflict* (London, 1990).

25 Adrian Vickers, *A History of Modern Indonesia* (Cambridge, 2005).

26 Falola and Heaton, *A History of Nigeria*, pp. 175–180.

27 Mann, *Dark Side of Democracy*, pp. 428–473.

28 David Kampf, "How Rwanda Threatens its Future", *The International Herald Tribune*, 17 August 2013.

29 The argument about the long-term decline of killing is still in doubt; see Victor David Hanson, "The Aztec Road", review of Ian Morris' *War! What is it Good For? The Role of Conflict in Civilisation from Primates to Robots* (London, 2014), in *TLS*, 26 September 2014, pp. 9–10.

30 Ahmed Rashid, *Descent into Chaos: How the War against Islamic Extremism is being Lost in Pakistan, Afghanistan and Central Asia* (London, 2008).

31 Achille Mbembe, "Necropolitics", *Public Culture*, 15, 1 (Winter 2003), pp. 11–40.

32 Fenton S. Bresler, *Interpol* (London, 1993).

33 Michel Foucault's (tr. Alan Sheridan), *Discipline and Punish: The Birth of the Prison* (London, 1977) inevitably comes to mind.

34 Elisabeth Croll, Delia Davin and Penny Crane (eds), *China's One-Child Family Policy* (London, 1985).

35 L. S. Vishwanath, *Female Infanticide and Social Structure: A Socio-Historical Study in Western and Northern India* (Delhi, 2000).

36 Mark Condos, "License to Kill: The Murderous Outrages Act and the Rule of Law in Colonial India, 1867–1925", *Modern Asian Studies*, forthcoming.

37 Rachel Leow, "Do you Own Non-Chinese Mui Tsai? Re-Examining Race and Female Servitude in Malaya and Hong Kong", *Modern Asian Studies*, 46, 6, (November 2012), pp. 1736–1763.

38 Carl A. Trocki, *Opium, Empire and the Global Political Economy: A Study of the Asian Opium Trade, 1750–1950* (London, 1999).

39 Simon Layton, "Discourses of Piracy in the Age of Revolutions", *Itinerario*, 35, 2, (August 2011), pp. 81–97.

40 David E. Kaplan and Alec Dubro, *Yakuza: Japan's Criminal Underworld* (London, 2003).

41 William Balsamo and George Carpozi Jr., *The Mafia: The First Hundred Years* (London, 2009).

42 Mary Gibson, *Born to Crime: Cesare Lombroso and the Origins of Biological Criminology* (London, 2002).

CHAPTER 15 INTERNATIONALISM AND TRANSNATIONALISM IN THEORY AND PRACTICE

1 Adam Roberts, "Towards a World Community? The United Nations and International Law", in Howard and Louis (eds), *Twentieth Century*, pp. 305–318.
2 Tooze, *The Deluge*, p. 516.
3 Sluga, *Internationalism in the Age of Nationalism*.
4 Ibid., p. 50.
5 Roberts, "Towards a World Community", p. 308; F. S. Northedge, *The League of Nations: Its Life and Times, 1920–1946* (Leicester, 1986).
6 Joseph DeMarco, *The Social Thought of W. E. Dubois* (Lanham, 1983).
7 Kevin McDermott and Jeremy Agnew, *The Comintern: A History of International Communism from Lenin to Stalin* (Basingstoke, 1996).
8 Tony Saich, *The Origins of the First United Front in China: The Role of Sneevliet (alias Maring)* (Leiden, 1991).
9 Kris Manjapra, *M. N. Roy: Marxism and Colonial Cosmopolitanism* (Delhi, 2010).
10 Bayly and Harper, *Forgotten Wars*, pp. 166–7, 181; Tim Harper, *The Imperial Underground: World Revolution and the Rise of Asia*, forthcoming.
11 Brocheux, *Ho Chi Minh*.
12 Peter Zinoman, *The Colonial Bastille: A History of Imprisonment in Vietnam, 1862–1940* (Berkeley, 2001).
13 Bayly and Harper, *Forgotten Wars*.
14 Tom Driberg, *The Mystery of Moral Re-Armament: A Study of Frank Buchman and his Movement* (London, 1964).
15 Mark Mazower, *No Enchanted Palace: The End of Empire and the Ideological Origins of the United Nations* (Princeton, 2009).
16 Preamble, Charter of the United Nations (San Francisco, 1945).
17 Clive Archer, *International Organisations* (London, 1992).
18 Reynolds, *Summits*.
19 United Nations, *The Blue Helmets: A Review of United Nations Peace-Keeping* (New York, 1996).

CHAPTER 16 THE SHADOW OF EMPIRE IN THE MODERN WORLD

1 For a comprehensive survey of British imperialism, see Bernard Porter, *The Lion's Share: A Short History of British Imperialism, 1850 to the Present* (Harlow, 2012); for France, etc., see Marc Ferro, *Colonization: A Global History* (London, 1997); for a broad but incisive study of empires and identity, see Frederick Cooper, *Colonialism in Question: Theory, Knowledge, History* (Berkeley, 2005).
2 André Gunder Frank, *On Capitalist Underdevelopment* (Bombay, 1975); Immanuel Wallerstein, *The Capitalist World Economy* (Cambridge, 1979).
3 A good summary remains B. R. Tomlinson, "Imperialism and After: The Economy of the Empire on the Periphery", in Brown and Louis (eds), *The Oxford History of the British Empire*, vol. 4 (Oxford, 1999), pp. 357–378.

4 Notably, Niall Ferguson, *Empire: How Britain Made the Modern World* (London, 2003).

5 Sunil Amrith, *Migration and Diaspora in Modern Asia* (Cambridge, 2011).

6 Bethencourt, *Racisms*.

7 Ibid., pp. 137–158.

8 Nicholas Dirks, *Castes of Mind: Colonialism and the Making of Modern India* (Princeton, 2001), but see also Susan Bayly, *Caste, Society and Politics in India from the Eighteenth Century to the Modern Age* (Cambridge, 2001).

9 Ann Laura Stoler, *Race and the Education of Desire: Foucault's History of Sexuality and the Colonial Order of Things* (Durham, 1995).

10 Reynolds, *America*, pp. 232–236.

11 Macintyre, *Australia*, pp. 155–159.

12 H. B. Higgins, "Australian Ideals", in *The Austral Light*, 1 January 1902, pp. 9–10, 12–13.

13 Saul Dubow, *Scientific Racism in Modern South Africa* (Cambridge, 1995).

14 William Beinart, *Twentieth Century South Africa*.

15 Madison Grant, *The Passing of the Great Race* (New York, 1916).

16 Tracie Matysik, "Internationalist Activism and Global Civil Society at the High Point of Nationalism: The Paradox of the Universal Races Congress, 1911", in Hopkins, *Global History*, pp. 131–159.

17 Gyanendra Pandey, *A History of Prejudice: Race, Caste and Difference in India and the United States* (New York, 2013).

18 See posters in section on 1919–1925, Deutsches Historisches Museum, Berlin.

19 Andrew Arsan, *Interlopers of Empire: The Lebanese Diaspora in Colonial French West Africa* (London, 2014).

20 For example, Monica Davey, John Eligon and Alan Blinder, "Shift in tactics fail to calm Missouri town", *International New York Times*, 20 August 2014.

21 For the context, see John Darwin, *After Tamerlane: The Rise and Fall of Global Empires, 1400–2000* (London, 2008).

22 M. K. Gandhi, *Hind Swaraj and other Writings* (Cambridge, 1997), p. 103.

23 Homi K. Bhabha, *The Location of Culture* (London, 1994).

24 David Crystal, *English as a Global Language* (Cambridge, 1997).

25 Smith, *New Zealand*, pp. 19, 226–237.

26 Macaulay to Bentinck, February 1835, *The Correspondence of Lord William Cavendish Bentinck, Governor-General of India, 1828–1835*, vol. 2: *1832–5* (London, 1976), p. 1413.

27 Rob Crilly, "Senior Pakistan Taliban figure explains why they shot Malala", *The Daily Telegraph*, 22 July 2013.

28 R. K. Agnihotri and A. L. Khanna, *Problematizing English in India* (Delhi, 1997).

29 Hwee Hwee Tan, "A War of Words over 'Singlish'", *Time Magazine*, 22 July 2002.

30 Bayly, *Asian Voices in a Post-Colonial Age*.

31 Paul Zang, *Le Français en Afrique: Norme, tendances évalutives, dialectisation* (Munich, 1998).

32 Joëlle Bahloul (tr. Catherine Ménagé), *The Architecture of Memory: A Jewish–Muslim Household in Colonial Algeria, 1937–62* (Cambridge, 1996).

33 I thank Sujit Sivasundaram for this point.

34 Joseph Errington, *Linguistics in a Colonial World: A Story of Language, Meaning and Power* (Malden, 2008).

35 Johannes Fabian, *Language and Colonial Power: The Appropriation of Swahili in the Former Belgian Congo, 1880–1938* (Berkeley, 1986).

36 Nigel Worden, *The Making of Modern South Africa: Conquest, Segregation and Apartheid* (Oxford, 1994), pp. 54, 81, 106.
37 Julia Clancy-Smith, "Islam and the French Empire in North Africa", in David Motadel (ed.), *Islam and the European Empires*, pp. 90–111.
38 S. A. Nigosian, *World Religions: A Historical Approach* (Basingstoke, 2008).
39 Natana J. DeLong-Bas, *Wahhabi Islam: From Revival and Reform to Global Jihad* (Oxford, 2004).
40 Khan, "Rhetorics and Spaces of Belonging."
41 Brian Hatcher, *Bourgeois Hinduism, or the Faith of the Modern Vedantists: Rare Discourses from early Colonial Bengal* (New York, 2008).
42 D. R. Jatava, *The Political Philosophy of B. R. Ambedkar* (Agra, 1965), pp. 53–55.
43 For example, John Simpson, "Hunted by their own government: The fight to save the Kalahari Bushmen", *The Independent*, 26 October 2013.
44 William R. Duggan and John R. Civile, *Tanzania and Nyerere: A Study of Ujamaa and Nationhood* (Maryknoll, 1976).
45 Dharma Kumar and Meghnad Desai (eds), *The Cambridge Economic History of India*, vol. 2: *c.1757–c.1970* (Cambridge, 1983).
46 John Iliffe, *The African Poor: A History* (Cambridge, 1987), pp. 4–6, 143, 233–235.
47 William H. McNeill "Demography and Urbanization", in Howard and Louis (eds), *Twentieth Century*, pp. 10–21.
48 Communication to the author, *c.*2005; see also R. S. Chandavarkar, *The Origins of Industrial Capitalism in India: Business Strategies and the Working Class in Bombay, 1900–1940* (Cambridge, 1994).
49 Atanu Dey, "Lee Kuan Yew on India", blog post, 18 December 2005. Accessed: http://www.deeshaa.org/2005/12/18/lee-kuan-yew-on-india.
50 Omnia El Shakry, *The Great Social Laboratory: Subjects of Knowledge in Colonial and Postcolonial Egypt* (Stanford, 2007).
51 Ashok Rudra, *Prasanta Chandra Mahalanobis: A Biography* (Delhi, 1996); see also Sunil Khilnani, *The Idea of India*, pp. 82–93.
52 Iliffe, *The African Poor*, pp. 235–240.

CHAPTER 17 THE PRESSURE OF PEOPLE

1 See particularly Dipesh Chakrabarty, "The Climate of History: Four Theses", *Critical Enquiry*, 35, 2, (Winter 2009), pp. 197–222.
2 The most accessible brief summary remains William H. McNeill, "Demography and Urbanization", in Howard and Louis, *Twentieth Century*, pp. 10–21.
3 Iliffe, *The African Poor*, p. 277.
4 G. Robina Quale, *Families in Context: A World History of Population* (Westport, 1992).
5 John H. Perkins, *Geopolitics and the Green Revolution: Wheat, Genes and the Cold War* (Oxford, 1997).
6 Paul Bairoch (tr. Christopher Braider), *Cities and Economic Development: From the Dawn of History to the Present* (Chicago, 1988).
7 Suzanne Goldenberg, "Lester Brown: 'Vast dust bowls threaten tens of millions with hunger'", *The Guardian*, 24 February 2015.
8 A useful summary of recent work is Tony Woods, "Russia Vanishes", in *London Review of Books* (6 December 2012), pp. 39–41.
9 Richard Bernstein, "Aging Europe finds its pension is running out", *The New York Times*, 29 June 2003.

10 John Iliffe, *Famine in Zimbabwe 1890–1960* (Gweru, 1990).
11 *The Lancet*, May 2014, reported in *The Independent*, 29 May 2014.
12 Barbara J. King, "Beyond the Bliss Point", review of Robert Lustig, *Fat Chance: The Bitter Truth about Sugar* (New York, 2012); Michael Moss, *Salt, Sugar, Fat: How the Food Giants Hooked Us* (New York, 2013); Georges Vigarello (tr. C. Jon Delogu), *The Metamorphoses of Fat: A History of Obesity* (New York, 2013), in *TLS*, 16–23 August 2013.
13 Leo Lewis, "Chinese girl, 8, diagnosed with lung cancer", *The Times*, 6 November 2013; cf. Wu Wencong and Zheng Xin, "Beijing considers 'air corridors' to reduce pollution", *China Daily*, 3 August 2014.
14 Jennifer Schuessler, "Rin Tin Tin: American Hero", review of Susan Orlean, *Rin Tin Tin: The Life and Legend* (New York, 2011), in *The New York Times*, 20 October 2011.
15 John Sutherland, "How the Wild West was butchered", review of reprint of John Williams, *Butchers Crossing* (2013), in *The Times*, 23 December 2013.
16 Mahesh Rangarajan, *Fencing the Forest: Conservation and Ecological Change in India's Central Provinces, 1860–1914* (Oxford, 1996).
17 Prasenjit Duara, *The Crisis of Global Modernity: Asian Traditions and a Sustainable Future* (Cambridge, 2014).
18 Amidst this vast new literature, see, with for example, William F. Ruddiman, *Plows, Plagues and Petroleum: How Humans Took Control of Climate* (Princeton, 2005); Timothy Cooper, "Why we Still Need a Human History in the Anthropocene", blog post, 6 February 2014. Accessed: https://blogs.exeter.ac.uk/historyenvironmentfuture/2014/02/06/167.
19 Alison Bashford, *Global Population: History, Geopolitics, and Life on Earth* (New York, 2014), p. 19.
20 For example, Karl Pearson, *National Life from the Standpoint of Science* (London, 1901).
21 Keith Breckenridge, *Biometric State: The Geopolitics of Identification and Surveillance in South Africa, 1850 to the Present* (New York, 2014).
22 Jo Guldi and David Armitage, *The History Manifesto*, especially Chapter 2; Bruno Latour, "Facing Gaia," Gifford Lectures, Edinburgh University (February 2013). Accessed: www.ed.ac.uk/humanities-soc-sci/news-events/lectures/gifford-lectures.

CHAPTER 18 BETWEEN TWO CENTURIES: ECONOMIC LIBERALISATION AND POLITICAL FRAGMENTATION, C. 1991 TO 2015

1 Dan Smith, *The Penguin State of the World Atlas* (London, 2012).
2 David D. Kirkpatrick, "Strife in Libya Could Presage Long Civil War", *The New York Times*, 24 August 2014.
3 Mary Kaldor, *New and Old Wars: Organised Violence in a Global Era* (Cambridge, 2012).
4 Arjun Appadurai, *Fear of Small Numbers: An Essay on the Geography of Anger* (Durham, 2006).
5 For example, Juan Cole, *The New Arabs. How the Millennial Generation is Changing the Middle East* (New York, 2014).

6 Laura Silber and Allan Little, *Yugoslavia: Death of a Nation* (New York, 1996).

7 For example, the notorious Srebrenica massacre of 1995, see Kati Marton, "Bosnia, in Peril Once More", *The New York Times*, 28 November 2013.

8 Oliver and Atmore, *Africa*, pp. 343–349.

9 Toby Dodge, *Iraq: From War to a New Authoritarianism* (London, 2012).

10 Richard Sakwa, *Chechnya: The Pre-Politics of Partition* (London, 2001).

11 Anthony Summers and Robbyn Swan, *The Eleventh Day: The Full Story of 9/11 and Osama Bin Laden* (London, 2011).

12 Videotape of conversation, May 1998, cited in Faisal Devji, *Landscapes of the Jihad: Militancy, Morality, Modernity* (London, 2007), p. 82.

13 Cole Moreton, "Iraq invasion 2003: The bloody warnings six wise men gave to Tony Blair as he prepared to launch poorly planned campaign", *The Independent on Sunday*, 25 January 2015.

14 Faisal Devji, communication to the author, August 2014.

15 Avi Shlaim, *The Iron Wall: Israel and the Arab World* (London, 2001).

16 Decca Aitkenhead, "Rory Stewart: The secret of modern Britain is there is no power anywhere", *The Guardian*, 3 January 2014.

17 Yaroslav Trofimov, "The fractured legacy of the mapmakers", *The Wall Street Journal*, 11–12 April 2015.

18 Rashid, *Descent into Chaos*.

19 Andrew Jacobs, "In China, Myths of Social Cohesion", *The New York Times*, 18 August 2014.

20 Hugh Robert, *The Battlefield: Algeria, 1988–2002: Studies in a Broken Polity* (London, 2003).

21 Justin Willis, "Where division is not enough", review of James Copnall, *A Poisonous Thorn in Our Hearts: Sudan and South Sudan's Bitter and Incomplete Divorce* (London, 2014) in *TLS*, 22 and 29 August 2014, p. 13.

22 Deeptiman Tiwary, "Year of living dangerously: India more unsafe than Syria in 2014", *Times of India*, 12 February 2015, p. 11.

23 Ed Stocker, "Chile: The nation that's still waging war on Native Americans", *The Independent*, 11 December 2013.

24 George A. Collier *Basta!: Land and the Zapatista Rebellion in Chiapas* (Oakland, 2006); Neil Harvey, *The Chiapas Rebellion: The Struggle for Land and Democracy* (London, 1998).

25 Barry Cannon, *Hugo Chávez and the Bolivarian Revolution: Populism and Democracy in a Globalised Age* (Manchester, 2009).

26 Sandra Laugier and Albert Ogien, *Le Principe Démocratie: Enquête sur les Nouvelles Formes du Politique* (Paris, 2014); see also the interview by Julie Clarini, "Sandra Laugier: 'Une forme de politique qui n'est pas orientée par le pouvoir'", *Le Monde des Livres*, 3 September 2013.

27 Brown, *Rise and Fall*.

28 Roy Medvedev, *Post-Soviet Russia: A Journey Through the Yeltsin Era* (New York, 2000).

29 Richard Sakwa, *Russian Politics and Society* (Abingdon, 2008).

30 Allen C. Lynch, *Vladimir Putin and Russian Statecraft* (Washington DC, 2011).

31 Fernanda Eberstadt, "Pranksters into prophets", review of Masha Gessen, *Words Will Break Cement: The Passion of Pussy Riot* (New York, 2014), *TLS*, 18 July 2014, p. 7.

32 Owen Jones, "Anti-Jewish hatred is rising: We must see it for what it is", *The Guardian*, 11 August 2014.

33 Peter Walker and Paddy Allen, "Europe's 'nationalist populists' and the far right", *The Guardian*, 6 November 2011.

34 Sandrine Morel, "Nouvelle démonstration de force des indépendantistes Catalans", *Le Monde*, 12 September 2014.

35 Norihiro Kato, "Tea Party politics in Japan: Japan's Rising Nationalism", *The New York Times*, 12 September 2014.

36 Brantly Womack (ed.), *China's Rise in Historical Perspective* (Lanham, MD, 2010).

37 Nandini Gooptu (ed.), *Enterprise Culture in Neoliberal India: Studies in Youth, Class, Work and Media* (London, 2013).

38 Christophe Jaffrelot, *India's Silent Revolution: The Rise of the Lower Castes in North India* (London, 2003).

39 R. W. Johnson, *South Africa's Brave New World: The Beloved Country Since the End of Apartheid* (London, 2009).

40 Duncan Green, *Silent Revolution: The Rise and Crisis of Market Economics in Latin America* (London, 2003).

41 Nikolas Kozloff, *Hugo Chávez: Oil, Politics and the Challenge to the US* (New York, 2006)

42 Martin H. Wolfson and Gerald A. Epstein (eds), *The Handbook of the Political Economy of Financial Crises* (New York, 2013).

43 Jennifer Amyx, *Japan's Financial Crisis: Institutional Rigidity and Reluctant Change* (Princeton, 2004).

44 Tim Callen and Jonathan D. Ostry (eds), *Japan's Lost Decade: Policies for Economic Revival* (Washington DC, 2003).

45 Anon, "Lost Decades: The Japanese Tragedy", *Economist.com*, 3 August 2012. Accessed: http://www.economist.com/blogs/freeexchange/2012/08/lost-decades.

46 Joseph E. Stiglitz. *Freefall: America, Free Markets and the Sinking of the World Economy* (New York, 2010).

47 Atif Mian and Amir Sufi, *House of Debt* (Chicago, 2014); cf. Timothy Geithner, *Stress Test: Reflections on Financial Crises* (New York, 2014).

48 Anthony DiMaggio, *The Rise of the Tea Party: Political Discontent and Corporate Media in the Age of Obama* (New York, 2011).

49 Ambrose Evans-Pritchard, "Argentina accuses US of judicial malpractice for triggering needless default", *The Daily Telegraph*, 31 July 2014.

50 David Leonhardt and Kevin Quealy, "The American middle class no longer world's richest", *The New York Times*, 22 April 2014.

51 Cited in John Gapper, "Capitalism: In search of balance", *The Financial Times*, 23 December 2013.

52 Piketty, *Capital*.

53 John Comaroff and Jean Comaroff (eds), *Law and Disorder in the Postcolony* (Chicago, 2006).

54 Jonathan Kaiman, "China gets richer but more unequal", *The Guardian*, 28 July 2014.

55 Zygmunt Bauman, *Globalization: The Human Consequences* (New York, 1998).

56 Jeffries, "Why Marxism is on the rise again."

57 Fukuyama, *The End of History*, p. 339.

CONCLUSION: PERIODS AND PROPHECY

1 Wm. Roger Louis, "The Close of the Twentieth Century", Howard and Louis (eds), *Twentieth Century*, pp. 319–333; Ralf Dahrendorf, "Towards the Twenty-First Century", ibid., pp. 334–343.
2 Ibid., p. 333.
3 Ibid., p. 338.
4 Jacques Derrida and Geoffrey Bennington, *Jacques Derrida* (Chicago, 1993).
5 For example, Marilyn Strathern, *Property, Substance and Effect: Anthropological Essays on Persons and Things* (London, 1999).

BIBLIOGRAPHY

BOOKS

Abrahamian, Ervand, *A History of Modern Iran* (Cambridge, 2008).

Agamben, Giorgio, *Homo Sacer: Sovereign Power and Bare Life* (Stanford, 1998).

Agar, Jon, *Constant Touch: A Global History of the Mobile Phone* (Cambridge, 2004).

Ageron, Charles Robert (tr. Michael Brett), *Modern Algeria: A History from 1830 to the Present* (London, 1991).

Agnihotri, R. K. and A. L. Khanna, *Problematizing English in India* (Delhi, 1997).

Ahmed, Feroz, *The Making of Modern Turkey* (London, 1993).

al-Rasheed, Madawi, *A History of Saudi Arabia* (Cambridge, 2002).

Alatri, Paolo, *Le origini del fascismo* (Rome, 1956).

Albert, Mathias (ed.), *Transnational Political Spaces: Agents, Structures, Encounters* (Frankfurt, 2009).

Allen, Louis, *Burma: The Longest War, 1941–1945* (London, 1984).

Amin, Shahid, *Event, Memory, Metaphor: Chauri Chaura 1922–92* (Delhi, 1996).

Amrith, Sunil, *Migration and Diaspora in Modern Asia* (Cambridge, 2011).

Amyx, Jennifer, *Japan's Financial Crisis: Institutional Rigidity and Reluctant Change* (Princeton, 2004).

Andaya, Barbara and Leonard Andaya, *A History of Malaysia* (London, 1982).

Anderson, David, *Histories of the Hanged: Britain's Dirty War in Kenya and the End of Empire* (London, 2005).

Andrew, Christopher and A. S. Kanya-Forstner, *France Overseas: The Great War and the Climax of French Imperial Expansion* (London, 1980).

Antonius, George, *The Arab Awakening: The Story of the Arab Nationalist Movement* (London, 1938).

Appadurai, Arjun, *Fear of Small Numbers: An Essay on the Geography of Anger* (Durham, 2006).

Archer, Clive, *International Organisations* (London, 1992).

Arsan, Andrew, *Interlopers of Empire: The Lebanese Diaspora in Colonial French West Africa* (London, 2014).

Asad, Talal (ed.), *Anthropology and the Colonial Encounter* (London, 1973).

Aslanbeigui, Nahid and Guy Oakes, *The Provocative Joan Robinson: The Making of a Cambridge Economist* (Durham, 2009).

Azouvi, François, *Le mythe du grand silence: Auschwitz, les Français, le mémoir* (Paris, 2012).

Bahloul, Joëlle (tr. Catherine Ménagé), *The Architecture of Memory: A Jewish–Muslim Household in Colonial Algeria, 1937–62* (Cambridge, 1996).

Bairoch, Paul (tr. Christopher Braider), *Cities and Economic Development: From the Dawn of History to the Present* (Chicago, 1988).

Bakewell, Peter, *A History of Latin America: c. 1450 to the Present* (Oxford, 2003).

Balfour, Sebastian, *Deadly Embrace: Morocco and the Road to the Spanish Civil War* (Oxford, 2002).

Balsamo, William and George Carpozi Jr., *The Mafia: The First Hundred Years* (London, 2009).

Barth, Fredrik, *Ritual and Knowledge among the Baktaman of New Guinea* (New Haven, 1975).

Remaking the Modern World 1900–2015: Global Connections and Comparisons, First Edition. C. A. Bayly.
© 2018 John Wiley & Sons Ltd. Published 2018 by John Wiley & Sons Ltd.

Barthold, V. V. (tr. Shahid Suhrawardy), *Mussulman Culture* (Calcutta, 1934).

Bashford, Alison, *Global Population: History, Geopolitics, and Life on Earth* (New York, 2014).

Bashford, Alison and Philippa Levine (eds), *The Oxford Handbook of the History of Eugenics* (Oxford, 2010).

Baughman, James, *The Republic of Mass Culture: Journalism, Filmmaking and Broadcasting in America since 1941* (Baltimore, 1997).

Bauman, Zygmunt, *Globalization: The Human Consequences* (New York, 1998).

Bayly, C. A., *Recovering Liberties: Indian Thought in the Age of Liberalism and Empire* (Cambridge, 2012).

Bayly, Susan, *Asian Voices in a Post-Colonial Age: Vietnam, India and Beyond* (Cambridge, 2007).

Bayly, Susan, *Caste, Society and Politics in India from the Eighteenth Century to the Modern Age* (Cambridge, 2001).

Beasley, W. G., *Japanese Imperialism, 1894–1945* (Oxford, 1987).

Beckert, Sven, *Empire of Cotton: A New History of Global Capitalism* (London, 2014).

Beevor, Antony, *Stalingrad* (London, 1998).

Beinart, William, *Twentieth Century South Africa* (Oxford, 1994).

Bell, Gertrude, *Letters of Gertrude Bell*, vol. 2 (London, 1927).

Benaud, Richie, *Anything but an Autobiography* (London, 1999).

Benedict, Ruth, *The Chrysanthemum and the Sword: Patterns of Japanese Culture* (Boston, 1946).

Benesch, Oleg, *Inventing the Way of the Samurai: Nationalism, Internationalism and Bushido in Modern Japan* (Oxford, 2014).

Benjamin, Jules R., *The United States and the Origins of the Cuban Revolution: An Empire of Liberty in an Age of National Revolution* (Princeton, 1990).

Bentinck, William (ed. C. H. Philips), *The Correspondence of Lord William Cavendish Bentinck, Governor-General of India, 1828–1835, vol. 2: 1832–5* (London, 1976).

Bergan, Ronald, *Eisenstein: A Life in Conflict* (London, 1999).

Berger, Michael L., *The Automobile in American History and Culture: A Reference Guide* (Westport, 2001).

Berman, Bruce and John Lonsdale, *Unhappy Valley: Conflict in Kenya and Africa*, 2 vols. (London, 1992).

Bernal, Martin, *Black Athena: The Afroasiatic Roots of Classical Civilisation, vol. 1: The Fabrication of Ancient Greece, 1785–1985* (London, 1987).

Berryman, Phillip, *Liberation Theology: Essential Facts about the Revolutionary Movement in Latin America and Beyond* (New York, 1987).

Bethell, Leslie, *Cuba: A Short History* (Cambridge, 1993).

Bethencourt, Francisco, *Racisms: From the Crusades to the Twentieth Century* (Princeton, 2013).

Bhabha, Homi K., *The Location of Culture* (London, 1994).

Bird, Colin, *An Introduction to Political Philosophy* (Cambridge, 2006).

Birmingham, David, *Kwame Nkrumah: Father of African Nationalism* (Athens, 1998).

Biro, M., *The Dada Cyborg: Visions of the New Human in Weimar Berlin* (Minneapolis, 2009).

Black, Jeremy, *World War Two: A Military History* (London, 2003).

Blaug, Mark, *Economic Theory in Retrospect* (Cambridge, 1985).

Boellstorff, Tom, *The Gay Archipelago: Sexuality and Nation in Indonesia* (Princeton, 2005).

Bourret, F. M., *Ghana: The Road to Independence 1919–57* (London, 1960).

Boyd, William, *The History of Western Education* (London, 1954).

Brass, Paul, *The Politics of India since Independence* (Cambridge, 1994).

Braudel, Fernand (tr. Sian Reynolds), *Civilisation and Capitalism, 15th–18th Century*, 3 vols (London, 1979).

Brebner, J. B., *Canada: A Modern History* (Ann Arbor, MI, 1960).

Breckenridge, Keith, *Biometric State: The Geopolitics of Identification and Surveillance in South Africa, 1850 to the Present* (New York, 2014).

Brenan, Gerald, *The Spanish Labyrinth: An Account of the Social and Political Background of the Civil War* (Cambridge, 1950).

Brewer, John and Frank Trentmann (eds), *Consuming Cultures, Global Perspectives: Historical Trajectories, Transnational Exchanges* (Oxford, 2006).

Brocheux, Pierre (tr. C. Duiker), *Ho Chi Minh: A Biography* (Cambridge, 2007).

Brown, Archie, *The Gorbachev Factor* (Oxford, 1996).

Brown, Archie, *The Rise and Fall of Communism* (New York, 2009).

Burleigh, Michael, *The Third Reich: A New History* (London, 2003).

Calhoun, Craig (ed.), *Sociology in America: A History* (Chicago, 2007).

Callen, Tim and Jonathan D. Ostry (eds), *Japan's Lost Decade: Policies for Economic Revival* (Washington DC, 2003).

Calvocoressi, Peter and Guy Wint, *Total War: Causes and Courses of the Second World War* (London, 1979).

Cannon, Barry, *Hugo Chávez and the Bolivarian Revolution: Populism and Democracy in a Globalised Age* (Manchester, 2009).

Carr, E. H., *The Bolshevik Revolution, 1917–1923*, vol. 2 (Oxford, 1963).

Carr, Raymond, *Spain, 1808–1975* (Oxford, 1982).

Carter, James M., *Inventing Vietnam: The United States and State Building, 1954–1968* (Cambridge, 2008).

Chafe, William, *The Unfinished Journey: America since World War II* (New York, 1991).

Chakrabarty, Dipesh, *The Calling of History: Sir Jadunath Sarkar and His Empire of Truth* (Chicago, 2015).

Charney, Michael, *A History of Modern Burma* (Cambridge, 2009).

Clark, Christopher, *The Iron Kingdom: The Rise and Downfall of Prussia, 1600–1947* (London, 2006).

Clark, Christopher, *The Sleepwalkers: How Europe Went to War in 1914* (London, 2012).

Clark, Lynn Schofield, *The Parent App: Understanding Families in the Digital Age* (Oxford, 2013).

Clark, Paul, *The Chinese Cultural Revolution: A History* (Cambridge, 2008).

Clay, Henry (ed.), *The Inter-War Years and Other Papers: A Selection from the Writings of Hubert Douglas Henderson* (Oxford, 1955).

Clendinnen, Inga, *Reading the Holocaust* (Cambridge, 1999).

Cockcroft, James D., *Intellectual Precursors of the Mexican Revolution, 1900–1913* (Austin, 1968).

Cohen, Jerome B., *Japan's Postwar Economy* (Bloomington, Ind., 1958).

Colarizi, Simona, *Storia del novecento Italiano* (Milan, 2000).

Cole, Juan, *The New Arabs: How the Millennial Generation is Changing the Middle East* (New York, 2014).

Collier, George A., *Basta!: Land and the Zapatista Rebellion in Chiapas* (Oakland, Calif., 2006).

Collingham, Lizzie, *The Taste of War: World War Two and the Battle for Food* (London, 2011).

Conn, Peter J., *Pearl S. Buck: A Cultural Biography* (Cambridge, 1996).

Cook, H. T. and T. F. Cook, *Japan at War: An Oral History* (New York, 1992).

Coomaraswamy, A. and Sister Nivedita, *Myths of the Hindus and Buddhists* (London, 1913).

Cooper, Frederick, *Africa since 1940: The Past of the Present* (Cambridge, 2002).

Cooper, Frederick, *Colonialism in Question: Theory, Knowledge, History* (Berkeley, Calif., 2005).

Copley, Antony, *Music and the Spiritual: Composers and Politics in the 20th Century* (Delhi, 2013).

Corngold, Stanley, *Lambent Traces: Franz Kafka* (Princeton, 2004).

Cowan, James, *The Maoris in the Great War: A History of the New Zealand Native Contingent and Pioneer Battalion* (1926, repr. Melbourne, 2006).

Cross, Colin, *The Fascists in Britain* (London, 1961).

Crowson, N. J. (ed.), *Fleet Street, Press Barons and Politics: The Journals of Collin Brooks, 1932–1940* (Cambridge, 1998).

Crystal, David, *English as a Global Language* (Cambridge, 1997).

Cumberland, Charles C., *Mexican Revolution: Genesis under Madero* (Austin, 1952).

Curtis, William J. R., *Le Corbusier: Ideas and Forms* (London, 1986).

Dambre, Marc (ed.), *Les Hussards: Une génération litteraire* (Paris, 2000).

Darwin, John, *Britain, Egypt and the Middle East: Imperial Policy in the Aftermath of War, 1918–22* (London, 1981).

Darwin, John, *After Tamerlane: The Rise and Fall of Global Empires, 1400–2000* (London, 2008).

Davenport-Hines, Richard, *Universal Man: The Seven Lives of John Maynard Keynes* (London, 2015).

Davis, Nathaniel, *The Last Two Years of Salvador Allende* (Ithaca, 1985).

Dean, M., *Governmentality: Power and Rule in Modern Society* (London, 1999).

DeLong-Bas, Natana J., *Wahhabi Islam: From Revival and Reform to Global Jihad* (Oxford, 2004).

DeMarco, Joseph, *The Social Thought of W. E. Dubois* (Lanham, Md., 1983).

Derrida, Jacques and Geoffrey Bennington, *Jacques Derrida* (Chicago, 1993).

Deutschmann, David (ed.), *Che Guevara Reader* (Melbourne, 2003).

Devigne, Robert, *Recasting Conservatism: Oakeshott, Strauss, and the Response to Postmodernism* (New Haven, 1996).

Devji, Faisal, *Landscapes of the Jihad: Militancy, Morality, Modernity* (London, 2007).

Devji, Faisal *The Impossible India: Gandhi and the Temptation of Violence* (Cambridge, Mass., 2012).

Dewey, John, *Democracy and Education: An Introduction to the Philosophy of Education* (New York, 1916).

Diefendorf, Jeffrey M., Axel Frohm and Hermann-Josef Rupieper (eds), *American Policy and the Reconstruction of West Germany, 1945–1955* (Cambridge, 1993).

Dikötter, Frank, *Mao's Great Famine: The History of China's Most Devastating Catastrophe* (London, 2010), pp. 167, 267, 268.

Dikötter, Frank, *Mao's Great Famine: The History of China's Most Devastating Catastrophe* (London, 2011).

DiMaggio, Anthony, *The Rise of the Tea Party: Political Discontent and Corporate Media in the Age of Obama* (New York, 2011).

Dirks, Nicholas, *Castes of Mind: Colonialism and the Making of Modern India* (Princeton, 2001).

Dodge, Toby, *Inventing Iraq: The Failure of Nation-Building and a History Denied* (London, 2003).

Dodge, Toby, *Iraq: From War to a New Authoritarianism* (London, 2012).

Dower, John, *Embracing Defeat: Japan in the Aftermath of World War Two* (London, 1999).

Driberg, Tom, *The Mystery of Moral Re-Armament: A Study of Frank Buchman and his Movement* (London, 1964).

Duara, Prasenjit, *The Crisis of Global Modernity: Asian Traditions and a Sustainable Future* (Cambridge, 2014).

Duara, Prasenjit, *The Crisis of Global Modernity: Asian Traditions and a Sustainable Future* (Cambridge, 2015).

Dubow, Saul, *Scientific Racism in Modern South Africa* (Cambridge, 1995).

Duggan, William R. and John R. Civile, *Tanzania and Nyerere: A Study of Ujamaa and Nationhood* (Maryknoll, 1976).

Duiker, W. J., *The Communist Road to Power in Vietnam* (Boulder, Col., 1996).

Duiker, William J., *Ho Chi Minh* (New York, 2000).

Dunn, John, *The Politics of Socialism: An Essay in Political Theory* (Cambridge, 1984).

El Shakry, Omnia, *The Great Social Laboratory: Subjects of Knowledge in Colonial and Postcolonial Egypt* (Stanford, Calif., 2007).

Elkins, Caroline, *Britain's Gulag: The Brutal End of Empire in Kenya* (London, 2005).

Elson, Robert, *Suharto: A Political Biography* (Cambridge, 2001).

Errington, Joseph, *Linguistics in a Colonial World: A Story of Language, Meaning and Power* (Malden, Mass., 2008).

Esposito, John L., Darrell J. Fasching and Todd Lewis, *World Religions Today* (Oxford, 2005).

Etkind, Aleksandr, *Internal Colonisation: Russia's Imperial Experience* (Cambridge, 2011).

Evans, Grant and Kelvin Rowley, *Red Brotherhood at War: Vietnam, Cambodia and Laos since 1975* (London, 1990).

Evans, Richard J., *The Coming of the Third Reich* (London, 2003).

Evans, Richard J., *The Third Reich in Power, 1933–1939* (London, 2005).

Fairbank, John K. (ed.), *The Cambridge History of China: vol. 12: Republican China, 1921–49, Part I* (Cambridge, 1983).

Falola, Toyin and Matthew M. Heaton, *A History of Nigeria* (Cambridge, 2008).

Fawaz, Leila Tarwazi, *A Land of Aching Hearts: The Middle East in the Great War* (Cambridge, 2014).

Ferguson, Niall, *Empire: How Britain Made the Modern World* (London, 2003).

Ferro, Marc, *Colonization: A Global History* (London, 1997).

Fest, Joachim (tr. Richard and Clara Wilson), *Hitler* (London, 1974).

Fieldhouse, D. K., *Western Imperialism in the Middle East, 1914–1958* (Oxford, 2006).

Finaldi, Giuseppe, *Mussolini and Italian Fascism* (London, 2008).

Firth, Raymond (ed.), *Man and Nature: An Evaluation of the Work of Bronislaw Malinowski* (London, 1957).

Fischer, Fritz, *Germany's Aims in the First World War* (London, 1967).

Fischer, Hartwig, and Sean Rainbird (eds), *Kandinsky: The Path to Abstraction* (London, 2006).

Fitzpatrick, Sheila, *Education and Social Mobility in the Soviet Union, 1921–1934* (Cambridge, 1979).

Fitzpatrick, Sheila, *The Russian Revolution* (Oxford, 2008).

Forbes, Geraldine, *Women in Modern India* (Cambridge, 1996).

Foucault, Michel (tr. Robert Hurley), *History of Sexuality*, 3 vols (London, 1979– 1984).

Foucault, Michel (tr. Alan Sheridan), *Discipline and Punish: The Birth of the Prison* (London, 1977).

Frank, André Gunder, *On Capitalist Underdevelopment* (Bombay, 1975).

Frankel, Francine, *India's Political Economy 1947–77: The Gradual Revolution* (Princeton, 1978).

Friedman, Milton, *Capitalism and Freedom* (Chicago, 1962).

Fukuyama, Francis, *The End of History and the Last Man* (New York, 1992).

Furet, Francois, *Le passé d'une illusion: Essai sur l'idée communiste au XXe siècle* (Paris, 1993).

Furst, Juliane, *Stalin's Last Generation: Soviet Post-War Youth and the Emergence of Mature Socialism* (Oxford, 2010).

Gailey, Harry A., *The War in the Pacific: From Pearl Harbor to Tokyo Bay* (Novato, Calif., 1995).

Galassi, Peter (ed.), *Henri Cartier Bresson: The Modern Century* (London, 2010).

Galbraith, J. K., *The Great Crash, 1929* (London, 1955).

Gandhi, M. K., *Hind Swaraj and other Writings* (Cambridge, 1997), p. 103.

Gardner, Howard and Katie Davis, *The App Generation: How Today's Youth Navigate Identity, Intimacy and Imagination in a Digital World* (New Haven, 2014).

Garland, David (ed.), *Mass Imprisonment: Social Causes and Consequences* (London, 2001).

Garton Ash, Timothy, *In Europe's Name: Germany and the Divided Continent* (New York, 1993).

Gelvin, James, *The Modern Middle East: A History* (Oxford, 2005).

Geithner, Timothy, *Stress Test: Reflections on Financial Crises* (New York, 2014).

Geuss, Raymond, *Philosophy and Real Politics* (Princeton, 2008).

Geyer, Michael and Sheila Fitzpatrick (eds), *Beyond Totalitarianism: Stalinism and Nazism Compared* (Cambridge, 2009).

Ghandour, Zeina, A Discourse on Domination in Mandate Palestine: Imperialism, Property, Insurgency (2010).

Ghani, Cyrus, *Iran and the Rise of Reza Shah: From Qajar Collapse to Pahlavi Power* (London, 1998).

Gibbs, Timothy, *Mandela's Kinsmen: Nationalist Elites and Apartheid's First Bantustan* (Woodbridge, 2014).

Gibson, Mary, *Born to Crime: Cesare Lombroso and the Origins of Biological Criminology* (London, 2002).

Giddens, Anthony, *The Transformation of Intimacy: Sexuality, Love and Eroticism in Modern Societies* (Stanford, 1992).

Giddins, Gary, *Visions of Jazz: The First Century* (New York, 1998).

Gildea, Robert, *Marianne in Chains: In Search of the German Occupation, 1940–1945* (London, 2002).

Golding, Harry (ed.), *The Wonder Book of Empire for Boys and Girls* (London, 1920).

Gooptu, Nandini (ed.), *Enterprise Culture in Neoliberal India: Studies in Youth, Class, Work and Media* (London, 2013).

Gopal, Sarvepalli, *Radhakrishnan: A Biography* (Delhi, 1989).

Gordon, Andrew, *A Modern History of Japan: From Tokugawa Times to the Present* (New York, 2003).

Graham, Helen, *The Spanish Republic at War, 1936–1939* (Cambridge, 2002).

Grant, Madison, *The Passing of the Great Race* (New York, 1916).

Green, Duncan, *Silent Revolution: The Rise and Crisis of Market Economics in Latin America* (London, 2003).

Grieder, Peter, *The German Democratic Republic* (Basingstoke, 2012).

Griffin, Roger (ed.), *Fascism* (Oxford, 1995).

Griffiths, Richard, *Fellow Travellers of the Right: British Enthusiasts for Nazi Germany, 1933–39* (London, 1980).

Groys, Boris (tr. David Fernbach), *Introduction to Antiphilosophy* (London, 2012).

Guha, Ramachandra, *India after Gandhi: The History of the World's Largest Democracy* (London, 2008).

Guha, Ramchandra, *Gandhi Before India* (London, 2013).

Guha, Ranajit and Gayatri Spivak (eds), *Selected Subaltern Studies* (Delhi, 1988).

Guignon, Charles B. (ed.), *The Cambridge Companion to Heidegger* (Cambridge, 2006).

Guldi, Jo and David Armitage, *The History Manifesto* (Cambridge, 2014).

Guttmann, Allen, *Games and Empires: Modern Sports and Cultural Imperialism* (New York, 1994).

Halls, W. D., *Education, Culture and Politics in Modern France* (Oxford, 1976).

Hardt, Michael and Antonio Negri, *Empire* (Cambridge, Mass., 2000).

Harootunian, Harry, *Overcome by Modernity: History, Culture and Community in Inter-war Japan* (Princeton, 2002).

Harper, Tim, *The Imperial Underground: World Revolution and the Rise of Asia* (London, 2015).

Harper, Timothy and Christopher Bayly, *Forgotten Armies: The Fall of British Asia, 1941–1945* (Cambridge, Mass., 2005).

Harper, Timothy and Christopher Bayly, *Forgotten Wars: The End of Britain's Asian Empire* (London, 2007).

Harvey, Neil, *The Chiapas Rebellion: The Struggle for Land and Democracy* (London, 1998).

Hatcher, Brian, *Bourgeois Hinduism, or the Faith of the Modern Vedantists: Rare Discourses from early Colonial Bengal* (New York, 2008).

Henaff, Marcel (tr. Mary Baker), *Claude Lévi-Strauss and the Making of Structural Anthropology* (Minneapolis, 1998).

Hennesey, James, *American Catholics: A History of the Roman Catholic Community in the United States* (New York, 1983).

Herring George, *America's Longest War: The United States and Vietnam, 1950–1975* (Philadelphia, 1986).

Hiden, John, *The Weimar Republic* (London, 1996).

Higman, B. W., *A Concise History of the Caribbean* (Cambridge, 2011).

Ho, Engseng, *The Graves of Tarim: Genealogy and Mobility across the Indian Ocean* (Berkeley, 2006).

Hobsbawm, E. J., *The Age of Revolution; The Age of Capital; The Age of Empire; The Age of Extremes* (London, 1988– 1998).

Hodgson, Marshall G. S., *The Venture of Islam: Conscience and History in a World Civilization*, 3 vols (Chicago, 1974).

Hodgson, Marshall, *Rethinking World History: Essays on Europe, Islam and World History* (Cambridge, 1993).

Hoffer, Richard, *Bouts of Mania: Ali, Frazier, Foreman and an America on the Ropes* (London, 2014).

Holtom, David C., *Modern Japan and Shinto Nationalism* (1943, repr. New York, 1963).

Hopkins, A. G. (ed.), *Globalization in World History* (London, 2002).

Hopkins, A. G. (ed.), *Global History: Interactions between the Universal and the Local* (Basingstoke, 2006).

Hopkins, A. G. and P. J. Cain, *British Expansion: Crisis and Deconstruction, 1914–1990* (London, 1993).

Hopkins, A. G. and P. J. Cain, *British Imperialism Innovation and Expansion, 1688–1914* (London, 1993).

Howard, Michael and Louis Wm. Roger (eds), *The Oxford History of the Twentieth Century* (Oxford, 2000).

Hughes, T. P., *Networks of Power: Electrification in Western Society, 1880–1930* (Baltimore, 1983).

Hunt, Lynn, *Writing History in the Global Era* (New York, 2014).

Hyam, Ronald, *Empire and Sexuality: The British Experience* (Manchester, 1990).

Idriess, Ion. L., *Must Australia Fight?* (Sydney, 1939).

Iliffe, John, *The African Poor: A History* (Cambridge, 1987).

Iliffe, John, *Famine in Zimbabwe 1890–1960* (Gweru, 1990).

Iliffe, John, *Africans: The History of a Continent* (Cambridge, 1995).

Iliffe, John, *The African AIDS Epidemic: A History* (Athens, 2006).

Iqtidar, Humeira, *Secularizing Islamists? Jama'at-e-Islami and Jama'at-ud-Da'wa in Urban Pakistan* (Chicago, 2011).

Jackson, Julian, *The Popular Front in France: Defending Democracy, 1934–38* (Cambridge, 1988).

Jackson, Julian, *Charles de Gaulle* (London, 2003).

Jackson, Robert, *The Malayan Emergency: The Commonwealth's Wars, 1948–1966* (London, 1991).

Jaffrelot, Christophe, *India's Silent Revolution: The Rise of the Lower Castes in North India* (London, 2003).

James, Harold, *The German Slump: Politics and Economics, 1924–36* (Oxford, 1986).

Jatava, D. R., *The Political Philosophy of B. R. Ambedkar* (Agra, 1965).

Jisheng, Yang (tr. Stacy Mosher and Guo Jian), *Tombstone: The Untold Story of Mao's Great Famine* (London, 2012).

Johannes, Fabian, *Language and Colonial Power: The Appropriation of Swahili in the Former Belgian Congo, 1880–1938* (Berkeley, 1986).

Johnson, R. W., *South Africa's Brave New World: The Beloved Country since the End of Apartheid* (London, 2009).

Johnston, Timothy, *Being Soviet: Identity, Rumour and Everyday Life Under Stalin* (Oxford, 2011).

Judt, Tony, *Postwar: A History of Europe since 1945* (London, 2010).

Jung, Sun, *Korean Masculinities and Transcultural Consumption: Yonsama, Rain, Oldboy, K-Pop Idols* (Hong Kong, 2011).

Kakuzo, Okakura, *The Ideals of the East with Special Reference to the Art of Japan* (London, 1903).

Kaldor, Mary, *New and Old Wars: Organised Violence in a Global Era* (Cambridge, 2012).

Kalman, Samuel *French Colonial Fascism: The Extreme Right in Algeria, 1919–39* (New York, 2013).

Kapila, Shruti, *Violence and the Indian Political* (forthcoming).

Kaplan, David E. and Alec Dubro, *Yakuza: Japan's Criminal Underworld* (London, 2003).

Kaplan, Martha, *Neither Cargo nor Cult: Ritual Politics and the Colonial Imagination in Fiji* (Durham, 1995).

Katznelson, Ira and Gareth Steman Jones (eds), *Religion and the Political Imagination* (Cambridge, 2010).

Keer, Dhananjay, *Savarkar and his Times* (Bombay, 1966).

Kelly, Gail P. (ed. David Kelly), *French Colonial Education: Essays on Vietnam and West Africa* (New York, 1998).

Kent, P. H. B., *The Twentieth Century in the Far East: A Perspective of Events, Cultural Influences and Policies* (London, 1937).

Kershaw, Ian, *Hitler: A Profile in Power* (London, 1991).

Kershaw, Ian, *Hitler, 1936–1945* (London, 2008).

Kévorkian, Raymond H., *The Armenian Genocide: A Complete History* (London, 2011).

Keynes, John Maynard, *The Economic Consequences of the Peace* (London, 1919).

Khalidi, Rashid et al. (eds), *The Origins of Arab Nationalism* (New York, 1991).

Khan, Yasmin, *The Great Partition: The Making of India and Pakistan* (London, 2007).

Khanna, D. P. S., *Dr. Bhagwan Das as a Social Thinker* (Delhi, 1983).

Khilnani, Sunil, *The Idea of India* (London, 2003).

Kindleberger, Charles P., *The World in Depression, 1929–39* (London, 1973).

King, Richard H. and Dan Stone (eds), *Hannah Arendt and the Uses of History: Imperialism, Nation, Race and Genocide* (New York, 2007).

Knight, Alan, *The Mexican Revolution* (Cambridge, 1986).

Kolb, Eberhard (tr. P. S. Falla), *The Weimar Republic* (London, 1988).

Kozloff, Nikolas, *Hugo Chávez: Oil, Politics and the Challenge to the US* (New York, 2006).

Krugman, Paul, *The Return of Depression Economics and the Crisis of 2008* (New York, 2009).

Kukathas, Chandran and Philip Pettit, *Rawls: A Theory of Justice and its Critics* (Stanford, 1990).

Kuklick, Henrika (ed.), *A New History of Anthropology* (Oxford, 2008).

Kumar, Dharma and Meghnad Desai (eds), *The Cambridge Economic History of India, vol. 2: c.1757–c.1970* (Cambridge, 1983).

Kumarasingham, Harshan, *A Political Legacy of the British Empire: Power and the Parliamentary System in Post-Colonial India and Sri Lanka* (London, 2013).

Kwon, Heonik, *The Other Cold War* (New York, 2010).

Kynaston, David, *Austerity Britain, 1945–51* (London, 2007).

Laugier, Sandra and Albert Ogien, *Le Principe Démocratie: Enquête sur les Nouvelles Formes du Politique* (Paris, 2014).

Layton, Robert, *An Introduction to Theory in Anthropology* (Cambridge, 1997).

Leach, Edmund, *Lévi-Strauss* (London, 1970).

Leahey, Thomas Hardy, *A History of Psychology: Main Currents in Psychological Thought* (London, 1985).

Lelyveld, David, *Aligarh's First Generation: Muslim Solidarity and English Education in Northern India, 1875–1900* (Chicago, 1975).

Lenin, V. I., *Imperialism: The Highest Stage of Capitalism* (1917, Petrograd, repr. 2005). Accessed: www.marxists.org/archive/lenin/works/1916.

LePan, Don, *The Cognitive Revolution in Western Culture, vol. 1: The Birth of Expectation* (Basingstoke, 1989).

Lettow-Vorbeck, Paul Emil von, *East African Campaigns* (New York, 1957).

Levy, Peter B., *The Civil Rights Movement* (London, 1998).

Lewin, Moshe and Ian Kershaw (eds), *Stalinism and Nazism: Dictatorships in Comparison* (Cambridge, 1997).

Lewis, Bernard, *The Emergence of Modern Turkey* (London, 1961).

Lewis, Herbert S., *In Defense of Anthropology: An Investigation of the Critique of Anthropology* (New Brunswick, 2014).

Lewis, I. M., *Ecstatic Religion: An Anthropological Study of Spirit Possession and Shamanism* (Harmondsworth, 1978).

Liebau, Heike et al. (eds), *The World in World Wars: Experiences, Perceptions and Perspectives from Africa and Asia* (Leiden, 2010).

Lienhardt, Godfrey, *Divinity and Experience: The Religion of the Dinka* (Oxford, 1961).

Likaka, Osumaka, *Naming Colonialism: History and Collective Memory in the Congo, 1870–1960* (Madison, 2009).

Lodge, Tom, *Sharpeville: An Apartheid Massacre and its Consequences* (Oxford, 2011).

Loth, Wilfried, *The Division of the World, 1941–1955* (London, 1988).

Louis, Wm. Roger (ed.), *The Origins of the Second World War: A. J. P. Taylor and his Critics* (New York, 1972).

Louis, Wm. Roger, *Ends of British Imperialism: The Scramble for Empire, Suez and Decolonisation* (London, 2006).

Lower, Arthur R. M., *Colony to Nation: A History of Canada* (Toronto, 1957).

Lynch, Allen C., *Vladimir Putin and Russian Statecraft* (Washington DC, 2011).

Lynn, Richard, *Eugenics: A Reassessment* (London, 2001).

Macintyre, Stuart, *A Concise History of Australia* (Cambridge, 2009).

Macmillan, Margaret, *The War that Ended Peace: How Europe Abandoned Peace for the First World War* (London, 2012).

Maier, Charles S., *Dissolution: The Crisis of Communism and the End of East Germany* (Princeton, 1997).

Majd, Mohammad Gholi, *Great Britain and Reza Shah: The Plunder of Iran 1921–41* (Gainesville, 2001).

Majeed, Javed, *Muhammad Iqbal: Islam, Aesthetics and Postcolonialism* (London, 2007).

Mandler, Peter, *Return from the Natives: How Margaret Mead Won the Second World War but Lost the Cold War* (New Haven, 2013).

Manela, Ere, *The Wilsonian Moment: Self Determination and the International Origins of Anticolonial Nationalism* (Oxford, 2007).

Mango, Andrew, *Atatürk* (London, 2004).

Manjapra, Kris, *M. N. Roy: Marxism and Colonial Cosmopolitanism* (Delhi, 2010).

Mann, Michael, *The Sources of Social Power*, 4 vols (Cambridge, 1986– 2013).

Mann, Michael, *The Dark Side of Democracy: Explaining Ethnic Cleansing* (Cambridge, 2005).

Manto, Sayyid Hussein, *Thanda Gosht* (1950).

Marcus, Harold G., *A History of Ethiopia* (London, 1994).

Marks, Shula and Stanley Trapido (eds), *The Politics of Race, Class and Nationalism in Twentieth Century South Africa* (London, 1987).

Martin, William, *With God on Our Side: The Rise of the Religious Right in America* (New York, 1996).

Maus, Heinz, *A Short History of Sociology* (London, 1962).

May, Lary, *Screening out the Past: The Birth of Mass Culture and the Motion Picture Industry* (New York, 1990).

Mazower, Mark, *Dark Continent: Europe's Twentieth Century* (London, 1998).

Mazower, Mark, *Salonica, City of Ghosts: Christians, Muslims and Jews, 1430–1950* (London, 2004).

Mazower, Mark, *No Enchanted Palace: The End of Empire and the Ideological Origins of the United Nations* (Princeton, 2009).

Mazower, Mark, Jessica Reinisch and David Feldman (eds), "Post-War Reconstruction in Europe: International Perspectives, 1945–1949", *Past and Present* Supplement 6 (Oxford, 2011).

Mbembe, Achille, *De la postcolonie: Essai sur l'imagination politique dans l'Afrique contemporaine* (Paris, 2000).

McDermott, Kevin and Jeremy Agnew, *The Comintern: A History of International Communism from Lenin to Stalin* (Basingstoke, 1996).

McKie, Robin and Chris Stringer, *African Exodus: The Origins of Modern Humanity* (London, 1997).

McLuhan, Marshall *Understanding Media: The Extensions of Man* (Cambridge, 1994).

McMahon, Darrin M. and Samuel Moyn, *Rethinking Modern European Intellectual History* (Oxford, 2014).

McMeekin, Sean, *July 1914: Countdown to War* (London, 2011).

McWhorter, John H., *The Language Hoax: Why the World Looks the Same in Any Language* (Oxford, 2014).

Medvedev, Roy (tr. George Shriver), *Post-Soviet Russia: A Journey Through the Yeltsin Era* (New York, 2002).

Méouchy, Nadine and Peter Sluglett (eds), *The British and French Mandates in Comparative Perspective* (Leiden, 2004).

Metcalf, Barbara, *Islamic Revival in British India: Deoband, 1860–1900* (Princeton, 1982).

Mian, Atif and Amir Sufi, *House of Debt* (Chicago, 2014).

Mills, Antonia and Richard Slobodin (eds), *Amerindian Rebirth: Reincarnation and Belief among North American Indians and Inuit* (Toronto, 1994).

Mills, James H. (ed.), *Subaltern Sports: Politics and Sport in South Asia* (London, 2005).

Milward, Alan S., *The Reconstruction of Western Europe, 1945–51* (London, 1984).

Minault, Gail, *The Khilafat Movement: Religious Symbolism and Political Mobilization in India* (New York, 1982).

Mitchell, Richard P., *The Society of the Muslim Brothers* (London, 1969).

Mitter, Rana, *The Manchurian Myth: Nationalism, Resistance and Collaboration in Modern China* (London, 2000).

Mitter, Rana, *A Bitter Revolution: China's Struggle with the Modern World* (Oxford, 2004).

Mitter, Rana, *China's War with Japan, 1937–1945: The Struggle for Survival* (London, 2013).

Moin, Baqer, *Khomeini: The Life of the Ayatollah* (London, 2009).

Monroe, Elizabeth, *Britain's Moment in the Middle East, 1914–71* (London, 1981).

Morell, Virginia, *Ancestral Passions. The Leakey Family and the Quest for Humankind's Beginnings* (New York, 1995).

Morris Jr., Seymour, *Supreme Commander: MacArthur's Triumph in Japan* (New York, 2014).

Mortimer, Rex, *Indonesian Communism under Sukarno: Ideology and Politics* (London, 1974).

Moss, Michael, *Salt, Sugar, Fat: How the Food Giants Hooked Us* (New York, 2013).

Motadel, David (ed.), *Islam and the European Empires* (Oxford, 2014).

Mowat, Charles Loch, *Britain Between the Wars, 1918–40* (London, 1955).

Nawrat, Chris, Steve Hutchings and Greg Struthers, *The Sunday Times Illustrated History of Twentieth Century Sport* (London, 1997).

Nehru, Jawaharlal, *An Autobiography* (London, 1940).

Nehru, Jawaharlal (ed. Saul Padover), *Glimpses of World History* (New York, 1960).

Newman, Major E. W. Polson, *Italy's Conquest of Abyssinia* (London, 1937).

Nicolle, David, *The Italian Invasion of Abyssinia, 1935–6* (London, 1997).

Nigosian, S. A., *World Religions: A Historical Approach* (Basingstoke, 2008).

Northedge, F. S., *The League of Nations: Its Life and Times, 1920–1946* (Leicester, 1986).

Nugent, Paul, *Africa since Independence: A Comparative History* (London, 2012).

Nussbaum, Martha C., *Democracy, Religious Violence and the Future of India* (Cambridge, 2007).

Ochonu, Moses E., *Colonial Meltdown: Northern Nigeria in the Great Depression* (Athens, 2009).

Offer, Avner, *The First World War: An Agrarian Interpretation* (Oxford, 1989).

Oliver, Roland and Anthony Atmore, *Africa Since 1800* (Cambridge, 2004).

Osterhammel, Jürgen (tr. Patrick Camiller), *The Transformation of the World: A Global History of the Nineteenth Century* (Princeton, 2014).

Overy, Richard, *The Inter-War Crisis, 1919–39* (Harlow, 1994).

Overy, Richard, *Why the Allies Won* (London, 1995).

Overy, Richard, *Russia's War* (London, 1997).

Overy, Richard, *The Bombers and the Bombed: Allied Air War Over Europe, 1940–1945* (London, 2013).

Pandey, Gyanendra, *Remembering Partition: Violence, Nationalism and History in India* (London, 2001).

Pandey, Gyanendra, *A History of Prejudice: Race, Caste and Difference in India and the United States* (New York, 2013).

Parkin, Frank, *Max Weber* (London, 2002).

Paul, Ellen Frankel, Fred D. Miller Jr. and Jeffrey Paul (eds), *Liberalism: Old and New* (Cambridge, 2007).

Pearson, Karl, *National Life from the Standpoint of Science* (London, 1901).

Peattie, Mark R., *Ishiwara Kanji and Japan's Confrontation with the West* (Princeton, 1975).

Perkins, John H., *Geopolitics and the Green Revolution: Wheat, Genes and the Cold War* (Oxford, 1997).

Pethybridge, R., *The Social Prelude to Stalinism* (London, 1974).

Piketty, Thomas (tr. Arthur Goldhammer), *Capital in the Twenty-First Century* (Cambridge, 2014).

Polenberg, Richard, *One Nation Divisible: Class, Race and Ethnicity in the United States since 1938* (New York, 1980).

Pollard, John, *Catholicism in Modern Italy: Religion, Politics and Society since 1861* (London, 2008).

Pomeranz, Kenneth, *The Great Divergence: Europe, China, and the Making of the Modern World Economy* (Princeton, 2000).

Porter, Bernard, *The Lion's Share: A Short History of British Imperialism, 1850 to the Present* (Harlow, 2012).

Premchand, *Premchand ki Sarwashrest Kahaniyan* (Allahabad, 1960).

Preston, Paul, *Franco: A Biography* (London 1993).

Purvis, Jane (ed.), *Women's History: Britain 1850–1945* (London, 1995).

Quale, G. Robina, *Families in Context: A World History of Population* (Westport, 1992).

Ramnath, Maia, *Haj to Utopia: How the Ghadar Movement Charted Global Radicalism and Attempted to Overthrow the British Empire* (Berkeley, 2011).

Ramos, Gabriela, *Death and Conversion in the Andes. Lima and Cuzco, 1532–1670* (Notre Dame, 2010).

Rangarajan, Mahesh, *Fencing the Forest: Conservation and Ecological Change in India's Central Provinces, 1860–1914* (Oxford, 1996).

Rao, Anupama, *The Caste Question: Dalits and the Politics of Modern India* (Berkeley, 2009).

Rashid, Ahmed, *Descent into Chaos: How the War against Islamic Extremism is being Lost in Pakistan, Afghanistan and Central Asia* (London, 2008).

Rau, M. Chalapathi, *Govind Ballabh Pant: His Life and Times* (Delhi, 1981).

Rauchway, Eric, *The Great Depression and the New Deal: A Very Short Introduction* (Oxford, 2008).

Reid, Anthony, *The Indonesian National Revolution, 1945–50* (Hawthorn, 1974).

Reybrouck, David van, *Congo: The Epic History of a People* (London, 2014).

Reynolds, David, *Summits: Six Meetings that Shaped the Twentieth Century* (London, 2007).

Reynolds, David, *America, Empire of Liberty: A New History* (London, 2009).

Reynolds, David, *The Long Shadow: The Great War and the Twentieth Century* (London, 2013).

Rhodes, Richard, *The Making of the Atomic Bomb* (London, 1988).

Rieber, Alfred J., *The Struggle for the Eurasian Borderlands: From the Rise of Early Modern Empires to the End of the First World War* (Cambridge, 2014).

Risen, Clay, *The Bill of the Century: The Epic Battle for the Civil Rights Act* (New York, 2014).

Robert, Hugh, *The Battlefield Algeria, 1988–2002: Studies in a Broken Polity* (London, 2003).

Robinson, Francis, *Separatism Among Indian Muslims: The Politics of the United Provinces' Muslims, 1860–1923* (London, 1974).

Robinson, Jane, *In the Family Way: Illegitimacy between the Great War and the Swinging Sixties* (London, 2015).

Roe, Sue, *In Montmartre: Picasso, Matisse and the Birth of Modernist Art* (London, 2014).

Rogan, Eugene, *The Fall of the Ottomans: The Great War in the Middle East, 1914–1920* (London, 2015).

Rondot, Pierre, *Caodai Spiritism: A Study of Religion in Vietnamese Society* (Leiden, 1976).

Rosanvallon, Pierre (tr. Arthur Goldhammer), *Counter-Democracy: Politics in an Age of Distrust* (Cambridge, 2008).

Rosenberg, Emily S. (ed.), *A World Connecting, 1870–1945: A History of the World* (Cambridge, 2012).

Rosenthal, Jean-Laurent and Roy Bin Wong, *Before and Beyond Divergence: The Politics of Economic Change in China and Europe* (Cambridge, 2011).

Rothermund, Dietmar, *The Global Impact of the Great Depression, 1929–1939* (London, 1996).

Ruddiman, William F., *Plows, Plagues and Petroleum: How Humans Took Control of Climate* (Princeton, 2005).

Rudra, Ashok, *Prasanta Chandra Mahalanobis: A Biography* (Delhi, 1996).

Ruedy, John, *Modern Algeria: The Origins and Development of a Nation* (Bloomington, 1992).

Ruger, William, *Milton Friedman* (London, 2011).

Ryan, Alan, "Staunchly modern, non-bourgeois liberalism", in Avital Simhony and David Weinstein (eds), *The New Liberalism: Reconciling Liberty and Community* (Cambridge, 2001), pp. 184–204.

Saich, Tony, *The Origins of the First United Front in China: The Role of Sneevliet (alias Maring)* (Leiden, 1991).

Sakwa, Richard, *Chechnya: The Pre-Politics of Partition* (London, 2001).

Sakwa, Richard, *Russian Politics and Society* (Abingdon, 2008).

Salvati, Michele, *Economia e politica in Italia dal dopoguerra a oggi* (Milan, 1984).

Sarraut, Albert, *La mise en valeur des colonies françaises* (Paris, 1923).

Savarkar, V. D., *Hindutva: Who is a Hindu?* (Delhi, 2003).

Schonberger, Howard, *Aftermath of War: Americans and the Remaking of Japan, 1945–1952* (London, 1989).

Schram, Stuart R., *Mao Tse-tung* (London, 1966).

Scott, James C., *The Art of Not Being Governed: An Anarchist History of Upland Southeast Asia* (New Haven, 2009).

Scott, W. R. and Cunnison, J., *The Industries of the Clyde Valley During the War* (Oxford, 1924).

Service, Robert, *Stalin: A Biography* (London, 2005).

Shambaugh, David (ed.), *Deng Xiaoping: Portrait of a Chinese Statesman* (Oxford, 1995).

Shamir, Ronen, *Current Flow: The Electrification of Palestine* (Stanford, 2015).

Sherry, Vincent (ed.), *The Cambridge Companion to the Literature of the First World War* (Cambridge, 2005).

Shlaim, Avi, *The Iron Wall: Israel and the Arab World* (London, 2014).

Shorter, Edward, *A History of Psychiatry: From the Era of the Asylum to the Age of Prozac* (New York, 1997).

Silber, Laura and Allan Little, *Yugoslavia: Death of a Nation* (New York, 1996).

Silberman, Neil A., *Digging for God and Country: Exploration, Archaeology, and the Secret Struggle for the Holy Land, 1799–1917* (New York, 1982).

Slight, John, *The British Empire and the Hajj, 1865–1956* (Cambridge, 2015).

Sluga, Glenda, *Internationalism in the Age of Nationalism* (Philadelphia, 2013).

Smith, Dan, *The Penguin State of the World Atlas* (London, 2012).

Smith, Jean E., *Eisenhower in War and Peace* (New York, 2012).

Smith, Philippa Mein, *A Concise History of New Zealand* (Cambridge, 2005).

Spence, Jonathan, *Mao Zedong* (New York, 1999).

Spencer, Jonathan (ed.), *Sri Lanka: History and the Roots of Conflict* (London, 1990).

Stedman Jones, Gareth (ed.), *Karl Marx and Friedrich Engels: The Communist Manifesto* (London, 2002).

Stern, Robert, *Changing India: Bourgeois Revolution on the Subcontinent* (Cambridge, 2003).

Stevenson, David, *1914–1918: The History of the First World War* (London, 2004).

Stewart, Michael, *Keynes and After* (London, 1986).

Stiglitz, Joseph E., *Freefall: America, Free Markets and the Sinking of the World Economy* (New York, 2010).

Stoler, Ann Laura, *Race and the Education of Desire: Foucault's History of Sexuality and the Colonial Order of Things* (Durham, 1995).

Strachan, Hew, *The First World War, vol. 1: To Arms* (Oxford, 2001).

Strachan, Hew, *The First World War: A New Illustrated History* (London, 2003).

Strathern, Marilyn, *Property, Substance and Effect: Anthropological Essays on Persons and Things* (London, 1999).

Sullivan, Michael, *Art and Artists of Twentieth-century China* (Berkeley, 1996).

Summers, Anthony and Robbyn Swan, *The Eleventh Day: The Full Story of 9/11 and Osama bin Laden* (London, 2011).

Tagore, Rabindranath, *Nationalism* (London, 1918).

Talbot, Ian, *Pakistan: A Modern History* (London, 1998).

Talbott, I. D., *Agricultural Innovation in Colonial Africa: Kenya and the Great Depression* (Lewiston, 1990).

Tang, Xiaobing, *Global Space and the Nationalist Discourse of Modernity: The Historical Thought of Liang Qichao* (Stanford, 1996).

Taubman, William, *Khrushchev: The Man and his Era* (London, 2003).

Taylor, A. J. P., *The Origins of the Second World War* (London, 1961).

Taylor, Charles, *Sources of the Self: The Making of the Modern Identity* (Cambridge, 1989).

Taylor, Jay, *The Generalissimo: Chiang Kai-shek and the Struggle for Modern China* (London, 2008).

Tendulkar, Sachin, *Playing it My Way: My Autobiography* (London, 2014).

Terreblanche, S., *A History of Inequality in South Africa, 1652–2002* (Pietermaritzburg, 2002).

Terry, Janice J., *The Wafd, 1919–1952: Cornerstone of Egyptian Political Power* (London, 1982).

Thomas, Martin, *The French Empire Between the Wars: Imperialism, Politics and Society* (Manchester, 2005).

Thompson, John A., *Progressivism* (Durham, 1979).

Thompson, John A., *Woodrow Wilson* (London, 2002).

Thompson, Kristin and David Bordwell, *Film History: An Introduction* (London, 2003).

Tomlinson, B. R., *The Economy of Modern India from 1860 to the Twenty-First Century* (Cambridge, 2013).

Tooze, Adam, *The Deluge: The Great War and the Remaking of the Global Order, 1916–1931* (London, 2014).

Touraine, Alain, *Solidarity: The Analysis of a Social Movement: Poland, 1980–1981* (Cambridge, 1983).

Tripp, Charles, *A History of Iraq* (Cambridge, 2000).

Trocki, Carl A., *Opium, Empire and the Global Political Economy: A Study of the Asian Opium Trade, 1750–1950* (London, 1999).

Trotsky, Leon (tr. Charles Malamouth), *Stalin: An Appraisal of the Man and his Influence* (London, 1947).

Tse-tsung, Chow, *The May Fourth Movement: Intellectual Revolution in Modern China* (Cambridge, 1960).

United Nations, *The Blue Helmets: A Review of United Nations Peace-Keeping* (New York, 1996).

van de Ven, Hans, *War and Nationalism in China, 1925–45* (London, 2003).

van de Ven, Hans, *Breaking with the Past: The Maritime Customs Service and the Global Origins of Modernity in China* (New York, 2014).

Vatikiotis, Michael R. R., *Indonesian Politics under Suharto: The Rise and Fall of the New Order* (London, 1993).

Vickers, Adrian, *A History of Modern Indonesia* (Cambridge, 2005).

Vigarello, Georges, *Le sentiment de soi: Histoire de la perception du corps, XVIe–XXe siècle* (Paris, 2014).

Vishwanath, L. S., *Female Infanticide and Social Structure: A Socio-Historical Study in Western and Northern India* (Delhi, 2000).

Visona, Monica, et al., *A History of Art in Africa* (Upper Saddle River, 2001).

Wallerstein, Immanuel, *The Capitalist World Economy* (Cambridge, 1979).

Wang, Helen, *Chairman Mao Badges: Symbols and Slogans of the Cultural Revolution* (London, 2008).

Weinberg, Gerhard, *A World at Arms: A Global History of World War II* (Cambridge, 1994).

Weitz, Eric D., *Creating German Communism, 1890–1990: From Popular Protests to Socialist State* (Princeton, 1997).

Werth, Alexander, *Russia at War, 1941–45* (New York, 1964).

West, Richard, *Tito and the Rise and Fall of Yugoslavia* (London, 1994).

Westad, Odd Arne, *The Global Cold War: Third World Interventions and the Making of Our Times* (Cambridge, 2007).

White, Benjamin T., *The Emergence of Minorities in the Middle East: The Politics of Community in French Mandate Syria* (Edinburgh, 2011).

Wolfson, Martin H. and Gerald A. Epstein (eds), *The Handbook of the Political Economy of Financial Crises* (New York, 2013).

Womack, Brantly (ed.), *China's Rise in Historical Perspective* (Lanham, 2010).

Worden, Nigel, *The Making of Modern South Africa: Conquest, Segregation and Apartheid* (Oxford, 1994).

Worsley, P., *The Trumpet Shall Sound: A Study of "Cargo" Cults in Melanesia* (London, 1957).

Yapp, M. E., *The Making of the Modern Near East, 1792–1923* (London, 1987).

Young, E. W., *The Wilson Administration and the Great War* (Boston, 1922).

Young, Hugo, *One of Us: A Biography of Margaret Thatcher* (London, 1991).

Zachariah, Benjamin, *Nehru* (London, 2004).

Zamindar, Vazira, *The Long Partition and the Making of Modern South Asia: Refugees Boundaries, Histories* (New York, 2007).

Zang Zang, Paul, *Le Français en Afrique: Norme, tendances évalutives, dialectisation* (Munich, 1998).

Zedong, Mao, *Selected Works of Mao Tse-Tung, vol. 1* (Peking, 1967).

Zinoman, Peter, *The Colonial Bastille: A History of Imprisonment in Vietnam, 1862–1940* (Berkeley, 2001).

ARTICLES FROM JOURNALS AND NEWSPAPERS, BOOK CHAPTERS, BLOG POSTS, REVIEWS, DISSERTATIONS, LECTURES AND UNPUBLISHED PAPERS

Acharya, Nupur, "The Friday Briefing: Battle of the Economists", *The Wall Street Journal India*, 25 July 2013.

Acherson, Neal, "Little People Made Big", review of Maxim Leo, *Red Love: The Story of an East German Family* (London, 2013).

Aitkenhead, Decca, "Rory Stewart: The secret of modern Britain is there is no power anywhere", *The Guardian*, 3 January 2014.

Anon, "Lost Decades: The Japanese Tragedy", *Economist.com*, 3 August 2012. Accessed: http://www.economist.com/blogs/freeexchange/2012/08/lost-decades.

Anon, "Datawatch", *Financial Times*, 27 October 2014.

Barker, T. C., "The International History of Motor Transport", *Journal of Contemporary History*, 20, 1 (January 1985), pp. 3–19.

Bayly, C. A., "Michael Mann and Modern World History", *Historical Journal* 58, 1 (2015), pp. 331–341.

Bayly, Susan, "Beyond 'propaganda': Images and the Moral Citizen in Late-Socialist Vietnam", forthcoming.

Bell, David, "This is what happens when historians overuse the idea of network", Books, *New Republic*, 25 October 2013.

Bennison, Amira K., "Dynamics of Rule and Opposition in Nineteenth Century North Africa", *The Journal of North African Studies*, 1, 1 (1996), pp. 1–24.

Bernstein, Richard, "Aging Europe finds its pension is running out", *The New York Times*, 29 June 2003.

Betts, Paul and Corey Ross (eds), "Heritage in the Modern World: Historical Preservation in International Perspective", *Past and Present*, Supplement 10 (Oxford, 2015).

Boellstorff, Tom, "The Emergence of Political Homophobia in Indonesia: Masculinity and National Belonging", *Ethnos*, 69, 4 (2004), pp. 465–486.

Boles, Elson, "Ruth Benedict's Japan: The benedictions of imperialism", *Dialectical Anthropology*, 30, 1–2 (2006), pp. 27–70.

Boyes, Roger, "I had a snog – not enough for a Stasi file. That came later", *The Times*, 4 November 2014.

Bresler, Fenton S., *Interpol* (London, 1993).

Brook, Timothy, Interview, *Frontline*, 11 April 2006.

Caldwell, Bruce, "Introduction" to F. A. Hayek, *The Road to Serfdom: Text and Documents* (Chicago, 2007), pp. 1–22.

Chakrabarty, Dipesh, "The Climate of History: Four Theses", *Critical Enquiry*, 35, 2 (Winter 2009), pp. 197–222.

Chandavarkar, R. S., *The Origins of Industrial Capitalism in India: Business Strategies and the Working Class in Bombay, 1900–1940* (Cambridge, 1994).

Charter, David, "God and socialism still divide Germany", *The Times*, 4 November 2014.

Clarini, Julie, "Sandra Laugier: "Une forme de politique qui n'est pas orientée par le pouvoir", *Le Monde des Livres*, 3 September 2013.

Cohen, Deborah and Mandler, Peter, "The History Manifesto: A Critique", *American Historical Review*, 120, 2 (2015), pp. 530–542.

Comaroff, John and Jean Comaroff (eds), *Law and Disorder in the Postcolony* (Chicago, 2006).

Condos, Mark, "License to Kill: The Murderous Outrages Act and the Rule of Law in Colonial India, 1867–1925", *Modern Asian Studies*, 50, 2 (2016), pp. 479–517.

Connor, Steve, "NHS mission to map DNA of entire British population", *i*, 1 August 2014.

Cooper, Timothy, "Why We Still Need a Human History in the Anthropocene", blog post, 6 February 2014. Accessed: https://blogs.exeter.ac.uk/historyenvironmentfuture/2014/02/06/167.

Crashaw, Steve, "Fall of the Berlin Wall: A people's uprising that grew until it remade Europe", *The Independent*, 28 October 2014.

Crilly, Rob, "Senior Pakistan Taliban figure explains why they shot Malala", *The Daily Telegraph*, 22 July 2013.

Croll, Elisabeth, Delia Davin and Penny Crane (eds), *China's One-Child Family Policy* (London, 1985).

Crouzet, Guillemette, "Genèse du 'Moyen Orient': Les Britanniques dans le Golfe Arabo-Persique, c.1800–c.1914", unpublished Thèse de Doctorat, Université de Paris-Sorbonne, 2014.

Davey, Monica, John Eligon and Alan Blinder, "Shift in tactics fail to calm Missouri town", *International New York Times*, 20 August 2014.

Dearden, Lizzie and Ian Johnstone, "Full face veils find little support across the Middle East, survey shows", *i*, 10 January 2014.

Dey, Atanu, "Lee Kuan Yew on India", blog post, 18 December 2005. Accessed: http://www.deeshaa.org/2005/12/18/lee-kuan-yew-on-india.

Eberstadt, Fernanda, "Pranksters into prophets", review of Masha Gessen, *Words Will Break Cement: The Passion of Pussy Riot* (New York, 2014), *TLS* (18 July 2014), p. 7.

Eddy, Melissa, "East German Model City Rusts, Quarter-century After Berlin Wall's Fall", *The New York Times*, 3 November 2013.

Evans, Richard J., "Artists Under Hitler", review of Jonathan Petropoulos, *Artists under Hitler: Collaboration and Survival in Nazi Germany* (New Haven, Conn., 2014), in *The Sunday Times*, 1 February 2015.

Evans-Pritchard, Ambrose, "Argentina accuses US of judicial malpractice for triggering needless default", *The Daily Telegraph*, 31 July 2014.

Fuhmann, Franz, *The Jew Car* (Chicago, 2013), in *London Review of Books*, 36, 1 (9 January 2014), pp. 23–24.

Furedi, Frank, *First World War: Still No End in Sight* (London, 2014).

Gapper, John, "Capitalism: In search of balance", *The Financial Times*, 23 December 2013.

Geyer, Michael and Charles Bright, "World History in a Global Age", *The American Historical Review* 100, 4 (1995), pp. 1034–1060.

Goldenberg, Suzanne, "Lester Brown: 'Vast dust bowls threaten tens of millions with hunger,'" *The Guardian*, 24 February 2015.

Guélaud, Claire, "Le manqué d'innovation menace la croissance", *Le Monde*, 2 September 2014.

Hanson, Victor David, "The Aztec Road", review of Ian Morris, *War! What is it Good For? The Role of Conflict in Civilisation from Primates to Robots* (London, 2014), in *TLS* (26 September 2014), pp. 9–10.

Harding, Neil, "The Marxist–Leninist Detour", in John Dunn (ed.), *Democracy: The Unfinished Journey, 508 BC to AD 1993* (Oxford, 1992), pp. 155–186.

Hart, Keith, "The Cambridge Torres Strait Expedition and British social anthropology", blog post, 6 November 2009. Accessed: memorybank.co.uk.

Hobsbawm, Eric, "C (for Crisis)", review of Richard Overy, *The Morbid Age: Britain Between the Wars* (London, 2009), *London Review of Books*, 31, 15 (August 2009), pp. 12–15.

Hopwood, Derek, "Introduction", in John Cooper, Ronald Nettler and Mohamed Mahmoud (eds), *Islam and Modernity: Muslim Intellectuals Respond* (London, 1998).

Jacobs, Andrew, "In China, Myths of Social Cohesion", *The New York Times*, 18 August 2014.

Jeffries, Stuart, "Why Marxism Is on the Rise Again", *The Guardian*, 4 July 2012.

Jones, Owen, "Anti-Jewish hatred is rising: We must see it for what it is", *The Guardian*, 11 August 2014.

Kaiman, Jonathan, "China gets richer but more unequal", *The Guardian*, 28 July 2014.

Kampf, David, "How Rwanda Threatens its Future", *The International Herald Tribune*, 17 August 2013.

Kapila, Shruti, "A History of Violence", *Modern Intellectual History*, 7, 2 (August 2010), pp. 437–57.

Kapila, Shruti, "1984: Sacred violence and Militant Sikhism", unpublished workshop paper, Cambridge, 2012.

Kato, Norihiro, "Tea Party politics in Japan: Japan's Rising Nationalism", *The New York Times*, 12 September 2014.

Khalidi, Rashid, "The Palestinians and 1948: The Underlying Causes of Failure", in Eugene Rogan and Avi Shlaim (eds), *The War for Palestine: Rewriting the History of 1948* (Cambridge, 2001), pp. 12–36.

Khan, Muhammad Amir Ahmad, "Rhetorics and Spaces of Belonging among North Indian Muslims 1850–1950", unpublished PhD dissertation, University of Cambridge, 2015.

Khilnani, Sunil, "India's Democratic Career", in John Dunn (ed.), *Democracy: The Unfinished Journey: 508 BC to AD 1993* (Oxford, 1992), pp. 189–205.

King, Barbara J., "Beyond the Bliss Point", review of Robert Lustig, *Fat Chance: The Bitter Truth about Sugar* (New York, 2012).

Kirkpatrick, David D., "Strife in Libya Could Presage Long Civil War", *The New York Times*, 24 August 2014.

Kitson, Michael, "Britain's Withdrawal from the Gold Standard: The End of an Epoch", in Randall Parker and Robert Whaples (eds), *Handbook of Major Events in Economic History* (London, 2013), pp. 127–137.

Kosicki, Piotr H., "After 1989: The life and death of the Catholic third way", *TLS* (13 December 2013), pp. 13–15.

Kumar, Krishan, "Civilized Value: The Return of Arnold Toynbee", *TLS* (24 October 2014), pp. 16–17.

Kunkel, Benjamin, "Just Don't Think about it", review of Boris Groys, *Introduction to Antiphilosophy* (London, 2012), *London Review of Books* 35, 15 (8 August 2013), pp. 33–37.

Kushner, Barak, "Pawns of Empire: Postwar Taiwan, Japan and the Dilemma of War Crimes", in Adam Culow (ed.), *Statecraft and Spectacle in East Asia* (London, 2010), pp. 108–130.

Lake, Jonathan, "We're all intellectual shrimps", *The Sunday Times*, 8 March 2015.

Latour, Bruno, "Facing Gaia", Gifford Lectures, Edinburgh University (February 2013). Accessed: www.ed.ac.uk/humanities-soc-sci/news-events/lectures/gifford-lectures.

Laurance, Jeremy, "A journey to the heart of Africa's AIDS epidemic", *i*, 18 November 2013.

Layton, Simon, "Discourses of Piracy in the Age of Revolutions", *Itinerario*, 35, 2 (August 2011), pp. 81–97.

Leake, Elisabeth, "The Politics of the North-West Frontier of the Indian Subcontinent, *c.*1936–65", unpublished PhD dissertation, University of Cambridge, 2013.

Lenin, V. I., "The Tasks of the Proletariat in the Present Revolution", Lenin Internet Archive (2005). Accessed: www.marxists.org/archive/lenin/works/1917.

Leonhardt, David and Kevin Quealy, "The American middle class no longer world's richest", *The New York Times*, 22 April 2014.

Leow, Rachel, "Do you Own non-Chinese Mui Tsai? Re-Examining Race and Female Servitude in Malaya and Hong Kong", *Modern Asian Studies*, 46, 6 (November 2012), pp. 1736–1763.

Lewis, Leo, "Chinese girl, 8, diagnosed with lung cancer", *The Times*, 6 November 2013.

Lipner, Julius, "The rise of "Hinduism" or How to Invent a World Religion with Only Moderate Success", lecture delivered at James Madison University (13 October 2005). Accessed: www.jmu.edu/gandhicenter/wm_library/juliuslipnerlecture.pdf.

Martin, Jamie, "Were We Bullied?" review of Benn Steill, *The Battle of Bretton Woods: John Maynard Keynes, Harry Dexter White and the Making of a New World Order* (Princeton, 2013), in *London Review of Books*, 35, 22 (21 November 2013), pp. 16–18.

Marton, Kati, "Bosnia, in Peril Once More", *The New York Times*, 28 November 2013.

Mbembe, Achille, "Necropolitics", *Public Culture*, 15, 1 (Winter 2003), pp. 11–40.

McMahon, Deirdre, "Ireland and the Commonwealth, 1900–1948", in Judith Brown and Wm. Roger Louis (eds), *The Oxford History of the British Empire, vol. 4: The Twentieth Century* (Oxford, 1999), pp. 138–162.

Megson, Kim, "Vietnam Dispatch: On the beach where US troops landed 50 years ago, a new Vietnam flourishes", *The Guardian*, 28 February 2015.

Milmo, Cahal, "Revealed: How MI5 watched the wrong Marxist Oxbridge academics: Christopher Hill and Eric Hobsbawn", *The Independent*, 24 October 2014.

Morel, Sandrine, "Nouvelle démonstration de force des indépendantistes catalans", *Le Monde*, 12 September 2014.

Moreton, Cole, "Iraq invasion 2003: The bloody warnings six wise men gave to Tony Blair as he prepared to launch poorly planned campaign", *The Independent on Sunday*, 25 January 2015.

Moyn, Samuel, "Bonfire of the Humanities", *The Nation* (21 January 2015).

Moyn, Samuel, "Book Review: *The Transformation of the World* by Jürgen Osterhammel", *Prospect Magazine* (July 2014).

Nelson, Keith L., "The 'Black Horror on the Rhine': Race as a Factor in Post-World War I Diplomacy", *Journal of Modern History*, 42, 4 (1970), pp. 606–627.

O'Brien, P. K., "Global history for global citizenship", in Toyin Falola and Emily Brownell (ed.), *Africa, Empire and Globalization: Essays in Honor of A.G. Hopkins* (Durham, 2011), pp. 447–458.

Omissi, David, "Europe Through Indian Eyes: Indian Soldiers Encounter England and France, 1914–18", *English Historical Review*, 122, 496 (2007).

Overy, Richard, "Dresden: when moral force was lost amid the brutality of war", *The Times*, 28 February 2015.

Paterson, Tony, "Auschwitz survivors remember the horror of the camp 70 years on", *The Independent*, 25 January 2015.

Pedersen, Susan "Only Men in Mind", review of Lawrence Goldman, *The Life of R. H. Tawney* (London, 2013), in *London Review of Books*, 36, 16 (August 2014), pp. 29–30.

Pomeranz, Kenneth, "Histories for a Less National Age", *American Historical Review* 119, 1 (2014), pp. 1–22.

Povoledo, Elisabetta, "Growing perils for women in Italy", *New York Herald Tribune*, 19 August 2013.

Purushotham, Sunil, "Destroying Hyderabad and making the nation", review of A. G. Noorani, *The Destruction of Hyderabad* (Delhi, 2013), *Economic and Political Weekly*, XLIX, 22 (31 May 2014), pp. 28–33.

Purushotham, Sunil, "Sovereignty, Violence, and the Making of the Postcolonial State in India, 1946–52", unpublished PhD dissertation, University of Cambridge, 2013.

Rawsthorn, Alice, "'Mokujiki Fever' Endures", *The New York Times*, 24–25 December 2013.

Rogers, Ben and Charles Taylor, "Charles Taylor interviewed", *Prospect Magazine* (February 2008).

Rosenberg, Justin, "Globalization Theory: A Post Mortem", *International Politics*, 42, 1 (2005), pp. 3–74.

Roslington, James, "The Rif War (Morocco, 1921–26) and the Coming World Crisis", unpublished PhD dissertation, University of Cambridge, 2013.

Rouqie, Alain, "The Military in Latin American Politics since 1930", in Leslie Bethell (ed.) *Latin America: Politics and Society since 1930* (Cambridge, 1998), pp. 145–219.

Runciman, David, "What if He'd Made it Earlier", review of Robert Caro, *The Years of Lyndon Johnson*, vol. 4 (London, 2014), *London Review of Books*, 34, 13 (5 July 2012), pp. 18–22.

Sang-Hun, Choe, "Cramming for Stardom at Korea's K-Pop Schools", *The New York Times*, 9 August 2013.

Schuessler, Jennifer, "Rin Tin Tin: American Hero", review of Susan Orlean, *Rin Tin Tin: The Life and Legend* (New York, 2011), *The New York Times*, 20 October 2011.

Scott, James C., "Tyranny of the ladle", *London Review of Books*, 34, 23 (6 December 2012), pp. 21–28.

Seabright, Paul, "Sexual distinctions", *TLS* (28 June 2013), pp. 3–5.

Shlaim, Avi, "The Balfour Declaration and its Consequences", in Wm. Roger Louis (ed.), *Yet more Adventures with Britannia: Personalities, Culture and Politics in Britain* (London, 2005), pp. 251–270.

Simpson, John, "Hunted by their own government: The fight to save the Kalahari Bushmen", *The Independent*, 26 October 2013.

Singler, Beth, "Return of the New Gods: Jedis, Auras and Online Witch Schools", blog post, 24 October 2014. Accessed: www.cam.ac.uk/research/features/return-of-the-new-gods-jedis-auras-and-online-witch-schools.

Siviloglu, Murat, "The Emergence of Public Opinion in the Ottoman Empire, 1826–1876", unpublished PhD dissertation University of Cambridge, 2015.

Steinmetz-Jenkins, Daniel, "Revolutionary rights", *TLS*, 19 November 2014.

Stocker, Ed, "Chile: The nation that's still waging war on Native Americans", *The Independent*, 11 December 2013.

Stovall, Tyler, "Love, Labor and Race: Colonial Men and White Women in France During the Great War", in Tyler Stovall and Georges van den Abbeele (eds), *French Civilisation and its Discontents: Nationalism, Colonialism, Race* (Lanham, 2003), pp. 297–321.

Sutherland, John, "How the Wild West was butchered", review of John Williams, *Butchers Crossing* (2013), *The Times*, 23 December 2013.

Tan, Hwee Hwee, "A War of Words over 'Singlish'", *Time Magazine*, 22 July 2002.

Tiwary, Deeptiman, "Year of living dangerously: India more unsafe than Syria in 2014", *Times of India*, 12 February 2015.

Trofimov, Yaroslav, "The fractured legacy of the mapmakers", *The Wall Street Journal*, 11–12 April 2015.

van de Ven, Hans, "China and the First World War", unpublished conference paper (Oxford, 2014).

Vigarello, Georges (trans C. Jon Delogu), *The Metamorphoses of Fat: A History of Obesity* (New York, 2013), in *TLS*, 16–23 August 2013.

Walker, Peter and Paddy Allen, "Europe's 'nationalist populists' and the far right", *The Guardian*, 6 November 2011.

Walker, Tim, "Assata Shakur: Black militant, fugitive cop killer, terrorist threat . . . or escaped slave?" *The Independent*, 18 July 2014.

Wencong, Wu and Zheng Xin, "Beijing considers 'air corridors' to reduce pollution", *China Daily*, 3 August 2014.

Werner, Michael and Bénédicte Zimmermann, "Beyond Comparison: Histoire Croisée and the Challenge of Reflexivity", *History and Theory* 45, 1 (2006), pp. 30–50.

Willis, Justin, "Where division is not enough", review of James Copnall, *A Poisonous Thorn in Our Hearts: Sudan and South Sudan's Bitter and Incomplete Divorce* (London, 2014), *TLS* (22 and 29 August 2014), p.13.

Wood, Tony, "Russia Vanishes", *London Review of Books*, 34, 23 (23 December 2012), pp. 39–41.

Wood, Tony, "At Tate Modern", *London Review of Books* 36, 16 (21 August 2014), p. 13.

Zerouala, Faiza, "Curriculum voilée", *Le Monde*, 10 September 2014.

INDEX

'Ndrangheta, 261
1848 revolutions, 306
1955 System, 137
9/11, 178, 269, 273, 301, 302

Aam Aadmi Party, 311
Abdullah of Jordan, King, 120
Abe, Shinzo, 317
Aborigines, 38, 74, 265, 272, 275
Abyssinia, 97, 250, 265
Action Française, 59, 67, 81, 109, 225
Adenauer, Konrad, 109, 132, 244
Advani, L. K., 171
African National Congress, 142, 155, 156, 176, 281, 312
Afrikaners, 31, 73, 127, 155, 279
agricultural reforms, 54, 63, 75, 84, 85, 94, 119, 124, 127, 129, 134, 135, 146, 151, 153, 185, 232, 284, 291, 297, 307, 309, 316
Ahmadiyya, 168, 234
AIDS, 204, 205, 288, 289, 312, 323
Alawites, 22, 280
Alexander I of Yugoslavia, King, 62
Alger Hiss case, 110
Algerian War of Independence, 185
Algérie Française, 156
Ali, Mehmet, 239, 240
Ali, Muhammad, 210
Aligarh Muslim University, 207
Allahabad, 111, 276
Allende, Salvador, 159
Allied Powers (First World War), 13, 96

Ambedkar, B. R., 115, 150, 238, 273, 282, 311
American Civil War, 94
American Constitution, 109, 318
Amin al-Husseini, Haj, 100
Amin, Idi, 127, 255
Amritsar Massacre (1919), 30, 48
anarchism, 5, 10, 44, 61, 159, 219, 306
Andaman Islands, 267
Anglo-Boer War, 16, 31, 39
Anglo-Egyptian Treaty (1936), 55
Anglo-Hindu law, 278
Anglo-Iraq treaties; (1926), (1932)
Anglo-Muhammadan law, 278
Anglo-Russian Entente (1907), 22
animals in war, 210, 295
Antarctica, 15
Anthropocene, 214, 287, 295, 296
Anthropology, 8, 179, 183, 186–189, 192, 232, 234, 296
anti-fascist resistance, 133
Anti-French War, 123
anti-hunting protests, 210, 295
anti-Nazi resistance, 65
anti-Semitism, 16, 60, 66, 81, 100, 103, 197, 243, 251, 256, 299, 308
Anti-US War, 123
anti-Vietnam War protests, 143, 200
Antonius, George, 22, 28
Apartheid, 90, 127, 135, 156, 163, 174, 176, 210, 255, 268, 279, 285, 296, 311, 312
Appadurai, Arjun, 6, 299

Remaking the Modern World 1900–2015: Global Connections and Comparisons, First Edition. C. A. Bayly.
© 2018 John Wiley & Sons Ltd. Published 2018 by John Wiley & Sons Ltd.

Apple, 141
Arab revolt in Palestine (1936), 26, 100, 123
Arab separatism, 15
Arab Spring, 2, 27, 212, 256, 299
Arabia, 26, 181, 196, 202, 240, 260, 301, 321
Arabic, 22, 185, 276–278, 283
Arab–Israeli War (1948), 66, 118, 119
Aragon, Louis, 219
architecture, 116, 139, 226
Arctic, 214, 260, 289
Arendt, Hannah, 101, 200, 250
Argentina, 40, 43, 55, 58, 66, 82, 92, 135, 159, 160, 174, 176, 313, 319
Argentine revolution (1966), 159
Armenian genocide, 249
Armistice, 20, 47, 218
Armitage, David, 5
art, 10, 15, 48, 59, 116, 137, 139, 148, 183, 198, 203, 215, 217–226, 228–230, 308
art market, 215, 222
Arts and Crafts Movement, 217, 220
Arya Samaj, 83, 195, 207, 235
Asad, Talal, 188
ASEAN, 155
Asia, 5–9, 16, 20, 21, 23, 24, 29–48, 51, 55–57, 59, 71, 76, 84, 85, 87, 92, 93, 97, 99, 101–104, 107, 108, 110–113, 115, 117, 121–127, 129, 131, 136, 137, 141–143, 148–152, 161, 169–170, 178, 184, 185, 191, 195, 196, 204, 211–213, 228, 232, 233, 236, 237, 244, 250, 252, 264, 266, 268, 269, 277, 278, 280, 282, 285, 288–292, 296, 299, 302, 305, 308–311
Asian economic crash (1997–1998), 315
Asimov, Isaac
Assad family, 304
Atatürk, Mustafa Kemal, 23, 26
Atlantic Charter (1941), 111, 127, 156
Atlantic Ocean, 104
atomic weapons, 48, 97, 110, 139, 302
Attlee, Clement, 122
Auschwitz, 251
Austerity, 74, 85, 87, 91, 133, 138, 155, 192, 314, 317, 319
Australia, 13, 23, 38, 39, 43, 67, 73, 74, 87–89, 92, 104, 109, 155, 161, 174, 175, 199, 211, 231, 272, 275, 278, 287, 289
Austria, 8, 17, 42, 43, 46, 48, 58, 59, 61, 84, 100, 101, 189, 197, 217, 218, 251, 299
Austria–Hungary, 17, 42, 46, 58, 251, 299
Ayodhya, 171
Ayodhya mosque destruction (1992), 171
Azerbaijan, 144, 300
al-Azhar, 55, 252
Azouvi, François, 252

Baath Party (Iraq), 110
Baath Party (Syria), 110
baby boom, 141, 158, 292, 317, 320
Back to the Countryside Movement, 147
Bacon, Francis, 224
Baden-Powell, Robert, 45
Badiou, Alain, 10, 222, 321
Badoglio, Pietro, 98
Baghdad Province, 22
Bahloul, Joëlle, 278
Baldwin, Stanley, 61, 69, 70, 75, 102
Balfour Declaration (1917), 25, 119
Balfour, Arthur, 23
Balkan Wars (1911–1914), 26, 33, 249, 264
Balkans, 13, 20, 21, 62, 129
Bandung Conference, 111, 123
Bangladesh, 151, 208, 212, 229, 253, 254, 297, 306
Bangladesh War (1971), 151, 253
Bank of Japan, 314, 315
al-Banna, Hasan, 196
Baoshi, Fu, 220
Barth, Karl, 243
Barthold, Wilhelm (Vasily), 185
Bashford, Alison, 295
Basic Law of the German Federal Republic, 132
Bataan "death march", 104
Batista, Fulgencio, 58, 136, 160
Battle of the Marne, 19
Bauman, Zygmunt, 321
Bay of Pigs (1961), 160
BBC, 252
Beach Boys, 141
Beatles, 141, 227, 228
Beckett, Samuel, 225

Beijing, 36, 136, 169, 289, 293, 310
Belgian Congo, 31, 89, 90, 154, 207
Belgium, 19, 31, 38, 309
Bell, David A., 4, 265
Bell, Gertrude, 24
Bellegarde, Dantès, 265
Benares Hindu University, 207
Benedict, Ruth, 187
Benes, Edvard, 130
Bengal; -partition of, 16
Berber, 30, 277, 282, 299, 305
Berg, Alban, 226
Beria, Lavrentiy, 128
Berlin Airlift (1948), 106, 156
Berlin Olympic Games, 210
Berlin Wall, 156, 164, 174
Berlin–Baghdad railway, 9
Bernal, Martin, 184
Berners-Lee, Tim, 212
Besant, Annie, 200, 217
Bethencourt, Francisco, 272
Betjeman, John, 226
Bhabha, Homi, 275
Bhagwati, Jagdish, 191
Bharatiya Janata Party, 2, 171, 244, 311
Bhindranwale, Jarnail Singh, 171
Bismarck, Otto von, 50
Black and Tans, 70
Black Liberation Army, 143
Black Panthers, 142
Blackett, James, 181
Blair, Tony, 256, 301, 302, 316
Blériot, Louis, 15, 181
Blum, André Léon, 81
Blyden, Edward, 265
Boas, Franz, 186
Boellstorff, Tom, 203
Boko Haram, 8, 202, 244, 257
Bolivia, 160, 209, 260
Bolshevik Party, 8, 13, 15, 23, 30, 33, 40, 44, 46–48, 200, 218, 229, 236, 250
Bombay Plan, 113
Bonn, 132
Borges, Jorge Luis, 225
Bose, Subhas Chandra, 104
Bosnia, 21, 166, 248, 256, 299, 300
Bosnian Muslims, 21, 256
Bosnian War, 256
Botha, Louis, 31
Botha, P. W., 177
Bourdieu, Pierre, 306

bourgeois Hinduism, 281
Boxer Rebellion (1900), 15, 35, 37
Brahmo Samaj, 195
Brandt, Willi, 175
Braudel, Fernand, 7, 185
Brazil, 3, 16, 40, 92, 159, 160, 187, 188, 211, 287, 295, 297, 307, 312, 313, 319
Breton nationalism, 309
Breton, André, 219
Bretton Woods Conference (1944), 138
Brezhnev, Leonid, 64, 309
Britain, 4, 15–20, 22, 24, 31–33, 36, 38, 39, 42, 44, 46, 47, 49, 55, 58, 59, 61, 65, 68, 69, 71, 73, 74, 78, 79, 82, 86–88, 90–93, 97, 98, 101–106, 109, 110, 112–114, 120, 121, 130–133, 138–140, 146, 152, 153, 156–158, 163, 164, 174, 175, 180, 181, 186, 190, 195, 200, 202, 203, 206, 208, 213, 217, 224, 239, 241, 257, 259, 262, 265, 269, 272, 273, 277–279, 285, 296, 301–303, 308, 312, 313, 315, 316, 318, 320
British Colonial Office, 76, 77
British Communist Party, 69
British Empire, 13, 14, 72, 77, 138, 185, 241
British Gold Coast, 68
British Mandate, 119, 207
British Nyasaland, 31
British Union of Fascists, 67, 70
Britten, Benjamin, 224
Brooks, Collin, 98
Brüning, Heinrich, 251
Buchan, John, 32
Buck, Pearl, 241
Buddhas of Bamiyan, 148
Buddhism, 7, 65, 195, 203, 206, 207, 231–233, 237, 238, 244, 279, 295
Buddhist-Muslim relations, 108
Buenos Aires, 226, 289
Bukharin, Nikolai, 63
Bunche, Ralph, 268
Bureau of Investigation, 44, 45, 71
Burma, 102, 104–108, 111, 115, 118, 119, 121, 122, 125, 127, 188, 256, 319
burqa, 202
Burroughs, William, 203
Bush, George, 172, 191
Bush, George W., 172, 191, 256, 301, 304, 314, 315
bushido, 51, 57, 237

Butler, Rab, 133
Butskellism, 133

Cain, P. J., 13
Calcutta, 207, 217, 253, 289
Calcutta School of Art, 217
Caligula, Emperor, 294
Callas, Maria, 226
Cambodia; -Vietnamese invasion of, 148
Cambridge House Riot, 158
Cameron, David, 30, 318
Canada, 13, 16, 39, 41, 73, 74, 86, 93,
    113, 155, 161, 172, 244, 275, 287, 289,
    320
Canudos rebellion, 16
Cao Dai, 234, 235
Cape Colony, 210
capital, 3, 4, 6, 7, 9, 10, 13, 14, 17, 26,
    39–43, 50, 54, 58, 60, 61, 65, 68, 69,
    80, 82, 84, 86, 88, 91–94, 110, 125,
    126, 132, 135, 136, 141, 147, 148, 157,
    160, 161, 163–165, 167, 169, 170, 179,
    189, 191, 192, 260–262, 309, 310, 312,
    313, 319–321
Capone, Al, 71, 261
cargo cults, 234
Caribbean, 16, 43, 75, 77, 79, 131, 135,
    159–160, 204, 265, 273, 275, 280, 282
carpet bombing, 248
Carter, Jimmy, 140, 146
Castro, Fidel, 136, 159, 313
Catalan nationalism, 309
Catalonia rebellion (1934), 82
Catholic Church, 65, 81, 83, 156, 160,
    175, 204, 205, 225, 235, 237,
    242, 244
Ceauşescu, Nicolae, 164
Central African Republic, 209
Central Powers (First World War), 13,
    19, 23, 36, 42, 50, 251, 264
centralisation, 65, 79, 113, 152, 165,
    303, 304, 308
Ceylon, 78, 217, 254
Cézanne, Paul, 216
Chagall, Marc, 225
Chamberlain, Neville, 101
Chandavarkar, Rajnarayan, 284
Chaplain, Charlie, 219
Chauri Chaura, riots (1922), 34
Chávez, Hugo, 306, 313
Chechnya, 202, 299, 300

chemical weapons, 20, 99, 300
Chicago, 15, 72, 103, 187, 226, 232, 261,
    312
Chicago Boys, 312
Chicago race riot (1919), 72
child poverty, 174
child soldiers, 209
Chile, 40, 58, 136, 159, 160, 176, 243,
    306, 312, 313
China, 3, 5–7, 9, 13, 20, 21, 29, 30, 35–
    38, 42, 47, 51, 55–57, 59, 64, 65, 87,
    89, 93, 95, 97, 99, 103, 106, 108, 112,
    115, 122, 123, 125, 126, 135–138, 140,
    142, 144–148, 149, 151, 161–163, 165,
    169, 170, 175, 184, 188–191, 197, 202,
    204, 206, 208, 209, 212, 215, 218, 220–
    223, 225, 235, 236, 241, 244, 250, 252,
    258–260, 266, 269, 271, 286, 290, 291,
    293, 296, 298, 299, 302, 305, 307–312,
    317, 319, 320
Chinese Civil War (1924–1925), 41, 118,
    125
Chinese Communist Party, 123, 169
Chinese Development Bank, 320
Chinese Maritime Customs Service, 56
Chinese Revolution (1911), 150, 162,
    217
Chonquing, 125
Christian Democracy (Italy), 109, 131,
    242
Christian revival, 146, 172, 244
Christian Science, 234
Christianity, 7, 18, 55, 65, 115, 127, 198,
    203, 206, 231–234, 236, 237, 240, 242,
    244, 245, 278, 279, 308
Chrysler, 182
Church of England, 206
Churchill, Winston, 19, 23, 30, 97, 100,
    105, 107, 130, 133, 248
CIA, 136, 159, 260, 302
cinema, 52, 116, 131, 137, 148, 216,
    219–221, 226
Circassians, 299
civil disobedience, 73, 168
Civil Rights Act (1964), 142
Civil Rights Movement, 142, 156, 187,
    274
civil society, 44, 45, 68, 69, 71, 77, 78,
    80, 82, 83, 143, 150, 169, 175, 176,
    204, 212, 237, 261, 264, 279, 280, 282,
    305, 308

Clark, Christopher, 17, 42, 96
climate change, 3
Clinton, Bill, 173, 303
Cohen, Deborah, 5
Cohn, Bernard, 188
Cold War, 7, 9, 106, 107, 112, 117, 125, 126, 128, 129, 133, 135, 140, 146, 149, 154, 156, 158–160, 162, 165, 176, 181, 204, 208, 228, 254, 255, 268, 269, 303, 305, 309
Cole, G. D. H., 68
collaboration with Nazis, 242
collectivisation, 63, 146, 290
Collingham, Lizzie, 113
Collins, Michael, 70
Colombia, 40, 160, 313
Colonialism, 7, 9, 30, 37, 100, 110, 111, 121, 123, 128, 139–161, 176, 187–189, 217, 247, 252, 263, 266, 268, 274–285, 295, 299
colons, 76, 90, 152, 153, 278
Columbia University, 180
Comintern, 263, 265–267
Comintern International Press Correspondence, 266
Commonwealth, 24, 70, 121, 166, 177, 265, 268, 316
communications, modern, 299
Communism, 7, 10, 11, 42, 50–52, 59, 63–64, 71, 80, 82, 98, 99, 103, 110, 112, 122, 124, 130, 132–134, 136, 137, 140, 143–149, 152, 155, 156, 159, 163–165, 167, 170, 172, 173, 175–177, 180, 185, 189, 208, 213, 225, 233–239, 241, 242, 244, 251, 256, 266, 268, 279, 290, 298, 307, 309
Communist Party (Indochina), 81
Communist Party (Italy), 131
Communist Party (Mexico), 266
Communist war with Guomindang (1945–1948), 106–107
Comte de Gobineau, Joseph Arthur, 273
Confucianism, 56, 206
Congo, 31, 89, 90, 145, 152, 154, 161, 207, 233, 255, 278, 288
Conscription, 14, 30, 31, 38, 44, 45, 69, 70, 129, 146
Conservative Party (UK), 70
Constituent Assembly debates (1946–1948), 77, 238

Constitution of India, 115, 149, 238, 311
Consumerism, 178, 321
Coomaraswamy, Ananda, 217
Copley, Antony, 222
Copts, 22, 55
Corfu, 265
Corsica, 14, 308
Corsican nationalism, 308
Costa Rica, 136
cotton manufacturing, 89
Council of People's Commissioners, 79
Court of International Justice, 263
credit bubble, 170, 317
crime, 45, 141, 143, 181, 209, 229, 247–262, 264, 300, 320
Criminal Investigation Department, 44
Criminality, 260–262
Croatia, 62, 65, 300
Croix de Feu, 81, 90
Crusades, 25, 207
Cuba, 58, 106, 136, 140, 142, 145, 154, 156, 159, 160, 181, 223, 242, 306, 312, 313
Cuban Missile Crisis (1962), 106, 156, 160, 181
Cuban Revolution (1956–1959), 159
Cultural Revolution, 63, 147, 148, 162, 184, 186, 196, 198, 206, 222, 236, 237, 252, 309
Curzon, Lord (George), 41, 45, 79, 210
Czechoslovakia, 27, 61, 62, 68, 101, 106, 129, 130, 164, 166, 167, 308

D'Annunzio, Gabriele, 58, 98
d'Argenlieu, Admiral Georges Thierry, 108
Dada movement, 218
Dagestan, 300
Dahrendorf, Ralf, 323–324
Dalí, Salvador, 224
Dalits, 77, 115, 150, 238, 311
Danish Social Democrats, 83
Daoism, 236
Dar al-'Ulum, Deoband, 207
Darling, Malcolm, 284
Darwinism, 241, 248, 271, 278
Das, Bhagwan, 198
Dawes and Young Plans, 80
de Gasperi, Alcide, 131
de Gaulle, Charles, 105, 130, 152, 154, 243

de Klerk, F. W., 177, 312
de Rivera, Miguel Primo, 47, 62, 82
de Toulouse-Lautrec, Henri, 259
de Valera, Eamon, 242
Deakin, William, 107
debt, 39, 54, 80, 84, 88, 90, 132, 270, 284, 314–318, 321
deconstruction
deflation, 85, 86, 88, 91, 192, 315
deforestation, 294
Delhi, 172, 199, 276, 285, 289, 293
democracy, 2, 9, 10, 17, 30, 35, 49, 59, 60, 62, 67–72, 76–83, 95, 109, 121, 131, 132, 140, 144, 150, 152, 157, 160–162, 165–173, 176, 178, 184, 196, 237, 253, 256, 272, 274, 279, 280, 282, 306, 308, 310–313, 316–318
Democratic Party (US), 67
demographics, 141, 287, 290, 291, 310, 316, 319
De-Nazification, 132
Denmark, 68, 83, 86
Déon, Michel, 225
Derrida, Jacques, 158
Detroit, 143, 330
Detroit riots (1967), 143
Devji, Faisal, 155, 303
Dewey, John, 68, 198
Dharmapala, Anagarika, 233
diabetes, 292, 293
Diaz, Porfirio, 40
Diem, Ngo Dinh, 145
Dien Bien Phu, Battle of (1954), 108, 123, 143
Dietrich, Marlene, 220
Dinka, 76, 232, 256, 305
Dinka and Nuer relations, 76, 256, 305
Dirac, Paul, 181
Dirks, Nicholas, 272
Division of the North, 40
Dix, Otto, 219
Doi Moi, 170, 191
Dominican Republic, 160
Dominion Senate, 73
domino effect, 145
draft dodging, 146
Drang nach Osten, 87
Dresden, bombing of, 105
dress, 213, 214, 245, 269, 301
Dreyfus Affair, 243
drug cultivation, 260

drug trade, 258, 259
drug wars, 260, 313
Druze, 25, 120, 280
Dubois, W. E. B., 265
Duchamp, Marcel, 229
Dumont, Louis, 188
Durkheim, Emile, 186, 192
Dylan, Bob, 227, 228

East Germany. See GDR
East India Company, 310
East Java revolt (1948), 124
East Pakistan, 121
Ebert, Friedrich, 80
Ebert–Groener Pact (1918), 80
Ebola, 269, 288, 289
economic development, 6, 58, 87, 232, 269, 283
Economic Opportunity Act (1964), 142
Economics, 1, 3, 6, 7, 9, 10, 13, 14, 17, 20, 23, 24, 32, 34, 37–39, 42, 43, 53–55, 57–59, 63, 65, 66, 68, 72, 74–79, 82–95, 98, 110–114, 120, 122, 124, 127, 130–132, 134, 137–138, 140–142, 144, 147, 148, 150, 155, 157, 158, 160–167, 169, 170, 172–177, 179, 182, 183, 185, 186, 189–193, 195, 196, 201, 208, 209, 212, 228, 230, 232, 233, 235, 245, 254, 255, 259, 264, 269, 270, 281–286, 295, 296, 298–321
Edo state, 261
Egypt, 2, 15, 21–24, 26, 27, 37, 43, 53, 55, 78, 102, 104, 110, 113, 119, 120, 146, 152, 157, 184, 196, 202, 239, 240, 244, 245, 249, 277, 280, 281, 304
Egyptian uprisings (1919), 30
Eichmann, Adolf, 252
Einstein, Albert, 179, 181
Eisenhower, President Dwight, 110, 133, 134
Eisenstein, Sergei, 64
El Shakry, Omnia, 285
el-Alamein, battle of, 104
elections, 2, 49, 68, 69, 73, 81, 127, 129, 142, 146, 151, 154, 159, 164–166, 172–174, 180, 200, 201, 230, 242, 268, 272, 307, 312, 316–319
Eliot, T. S., 218
el-Krim, Abd, 30, 47
Emden, battleship, 18, 33

Emergency (1975–1977), 151
emigration, 89, 161, 263
Emin, Tracey, 229
Enabling Act, 81
Engels, Friedrich, 10
English, 4, 5, 38, 46, 109, 174, 185, 198,
    204, 208, 211, 218–220, 225, 266, 274–
    278, 281, 310
English Revolution, 2
Enlai, Zhou, 147
enlightenment, 184, 195, 271
Entebbe raid (1976), 155
environmentalism, 180, 260
epidemics, 269
Erdoğan, Recep, 245
Estonia, 129
Ethiopia, 51, 59, 87, 95, 97–99, 131,
    240, 305
ethnic cleansing, 27, 101, 149, 249, 253,
    256, 299
eugenics, 38, 45, 273, 285, 295, 296
Europe, 2, 3, 5–9, 12, 13, 15, 17–27, 29–
    31, 33, 36, 38–53, 55–59, 61–82, 84–
    87, 89, 91—116, 118–121, 125–145,
    152, 154–160, 162–178, 184–192,
    194–213, 216–219, 222–225, 229, 232,
    233, 236, 237, 239–251, 256, 260–264,
    266, 268–273, 277–284, 287, 289–292,
    295, 298–301, 304– 311, 314–321
European Coal, Iron and Steel
    Agreements (1951–1952), 113
European Court of Justice, 158, 261
European Economic Community, 158,
    175
European unification, 131, 154
European Union, 77
Euroscepticism, 2
eurozone, 5, 192, 317
Evans, Sir Arthur, 184
Evans-Pritchard, E. E., 186
évolués, 76

Fabianism, 285
Facebook, 201, 212, 213, 313
Faisal I, King, 54
Falangist, 82
Falklands War (1982), 159, 176
Famine, 22, 63, 147, 150, 165, 248, 251,
    255, 288, 290, 292, 318
FARC, 313
Farsi, 274

fasci, 58
fascism, 17, 27, 50, 57–62, 65–67, 81,
    102, 112, 130, 131, 138, 214, 242, 273,
    308
Federal Bureau of Investigation, 44
Federal Reserve, 93, 173, 317
female education, 209
female franchise, 68
female infanticide, 202, 258
feminism, 218
Ferdinand, Archduke Franz, 17
Ferguson riots (2014), 213
Ferguson, Niall, 17
Festival of Britain (1951), 181
fingerprinting, 296
Finland, 16
First Anglo-Afghan War
    (1838–1842), 33
First Chechen War (1994–1996), 300
First Five Year Plan (Russia) (1928), 86
First Gulf War (1990–1991), 164
First Indochina War (1946–1954)
First Italo-Ethiopian War
    (1895–1896), 98
First Sino-Japanese War
    (1894–1895), 37
First World War (1914–1918), 12, 15,
    17–19, 21, 23, 25, 29, 32, 34, 35,
    37, 40–42, 47, 52, 54, 57–59, 61, 68,
    69, 73, 74, 82, 84, 95–99, 105, 111,
    114, 117, 127, 200, 216, 218, 226,
    229, 242, 243, 249, 250, 255, 263,
    290, 295, 301
Firth, Raymond, 186, 187
Fischer, Fritz, 17
Fiume, 58, 251
Five Year Plan (India), 150
Five Year Plan (Russia), 86, 93
Flanders, 19, 30
FLN, 154, 305
Fonda, Jane, 200
forced migration, 48, 263
forced sterilisation, 151
Ford, 182
Ford Foundation, 9, 188
Ford, Gerald, 140
Ford, Henry, 103
Foreman, George, 210
Formosa, 136
Foucault, Michel, 158, 195, 197, 201,
    209, 225, 256, 306

France, 4, 6, 14, 16, 18–20, 22, 24, 25, 30, 33, 37, 39, 42–47, 58, 59, 65, 68, 71, 74–77, 79–82, 85, 86, 90, 91, 97, 98, 101–103, 105–108, 110, 113, 114, 127, 130–132, 137, 152, 157, 158, 164, 168, 174, 175, 183, 185, 195, 205, 207, 216, 225, 235, 239, 240, 243–244, 256, 259, 269, 273, 291, 296, 300, 308, 309, 316
Francis, Pope, 244
Franco, General Francisco, 62, 242
Franco-Prussian War, 205
Frazer, James, 186
Frazier, Joe, 210
Free French Army, 130
free trade, 174, 185, 191
free-market capitalism, 307, 312
free-market economics, 169, 172
free-trade movement, 132
Freikorps, 46, 61, 80
French (language), 207, 275
French Caribbean, 77
French Communist Party, 131
French Empire, 243
French Fourth Republic, 109
French Indochina, 13, 75, 102, 123, 266
French Overseas Territories, 127
French Revolution (1789), 3
French West Africa, 76, 312
Freud, Lucian, 224
Freud, Sigmund, 15, 197
Friedman, Milton, 95, 163, 174, 189, 191, 314
Fritsch, Theodor, 60
Front National, 4
Fry, Roger, 220
Fukuyama, Francis, 2, 166, 321
Furnivall, J. S., 284
further education, 158

Gaddafi, Muammar, 66, 304
Gadgil, D. R., 283, 284
Gaelic, 275
Gaitskell, Hugh, 133
Gallipoli, 13
Galton, Francis, 295
Gandhi, Indira; -assassination of, 150, 151, 171, 200, 253
Gandhi, Mohandas, 15, 34
Gandhi, Rajiv, 254
Gandhi, Sanjay, 151

Gang of Four, 147, 169
gang warfare, 261
Gapon, Father, 236
Gates, Bill, 141
Gaudier-Brzeska, Henri, 216
Gauguin, Paul, 216
gay rights, 205, 211, 245,
Gaza Strip, 245, 304
Geertz, Clifford, 188
Gellner, Ernest, 188
Genetics, 180, 206, 262
genome sequencing, 181
George, Lloyd, 26
German Democratic Republic (GDR), 116
German Empire, 102
German invasion of Poland (1939), 102
German invasion of the USSR (1941), 97
German Naval Laws (1898), 42
German occupation of France (1940), 97
German occupation of the Rhineland, 46
German orientalism, 188
German seizure of Upper Silesia (1938), 61
German South-West Africa, 250
German union with Austria (1938), 61
German–Soviet Pact (1939), 102
Germany, 8, 13, 15–25, 30, 31, 38, 39, 42–44, 46, 49–52, 54, 55, 59–62, 64, 65, 68, 71, 74, 79–83, 85, 90–93, 96–98, 100–109, 112, 113, 127, 130, 132, 135–137, 144, 156–158, 161, 166, 167, 174, 175, 184, 185, 189, 195, 208, 209, 213, 216–218, 225, 242, 243, 249, 251, 268, 289, 291, 296, 307, 308, 315, 316
Geuss, Raymond, 198
Ghadar Movement, 278
Ghana, 153, 156
GI Bill of Rights, 134
Glass–Steagall Act (1933), 93
global warming, 295, 296
globalisation, 2, 4, 5, 7, 11, 161, 177, 192, 215, 244, 259, 269, 270, 314–318
Goebbels, Joseph, 60
Gold Coast, 105
gold standard, 84
Golden Square coup (1941), 54
Golden Temple occupation (1984), 171
Golwalkar, M. S., 52
Gong, Falun, 235

Goody, Jack, 188
Gorbachev, Mikhail, 164
Gove, Michael, 4
Government of India Acts (1919 and 1935), 75
Goya, Francisco, 247
Gracey, General Douglas, 108
Gramsci, Antonio, 266
Grant, Madison, 273
Graves, Robert, 218
Great Calcutta Killing (1946), 253
Great Depression (1929–1938), 72, 73
Great Leap Forward, 63
Great Recession (2008–2015), 319
Great Society, 142
Greater Serbia, 300
Greece, 26, 42, 107, 130, 133, 240, 251, 316
Greek Civil War (1946–1949), 97
Greek Colonels, seizure of power (1968), 158
Greek War of Independence (1821–1832), 41
Green Revolution, 114, 151, 288, 295–297,
Green, T. H., 327
Greenmantle, 32
Greenpeace, 260
Grey, Edward (1st Viscount Grey of Fallodon), 42
Griebel, Otto, 218
Grigg, James, 88
Groys, Boris, 222
Guadeloupe, 77
Guantanamo Bay, 302
Guatemala, 40
Guevara, Che
Guldi, Jo, 5
Gulf statesm, 299
gun rights, 45
Guomindang (GMD), 56

Habermas, Jürgen, 280
Habsburgs, 16
Haddon, A. C., 186
Hague Peace Conferences (1899, 1907), 264
Haiti, 265, 268
Hamas, 304
Happy Valley, 76, 89
Hardt, Michael, 6

Hatcher, Brian, 281
Hatta, Mahomed, 124
Hawley–Smoot Act (1930), 86
Hayek, F. A., 138, 163, 189, 191
Hebrew, 278
Hector the Bear, 144
Hedgewar, K. B., 171
Heidegger, Martin, 80, 197, 198
al-Helmy, Burhanuddin, 285
Hemingway, Ernest, 117
Higgins, H. B., 272
Hijaz, 21, 22, 26, 53, 235
Hijaz Railway, 22
Hilferding, Rudolf, 6, 189
Hill, Christopher, 139
Himmler, Heinrich, 251
Hindenburg, Field-Marshal Paul von, 19
Hindi, 220, 276, 278
Hindu Mahasabha, 281
Hinduism, 195, 203, 208, 231–233, 238, 279, 281
Hindu–Muslim riots, 249
Hindutva, 7, 52, 128, 171, 238, 244, 267, 279, 311, 319
Hirohito, Emperor, 52
Hiroshima, 30, 106, 136, 139, 181, 248, 251
Hirst, Damien, 229
histoire croisée, 4
Hitler Youth, 47
Hitler, Adolf, 50
Hizbullah, 2
Ho Chi Minh, 52, 75, 108, 123, 124, 145, 170, 237, 266, 267
Ho, Engseng, 6
Hoare–Laval Pact (1935), 98
Hobsbawm, Eric, 139, 163, 314
Hockney, David, 224
Hodgson, Marshall G. S., 7, 234
Hollywood, 72, 105, 141, 219, 294
Holocaust, 97, 119, 208, 248–250, 252, 254, 299, 308
homeopathy, 285
homosexuality, 199, 203–205, 227, 246, 259
Hong Kong, 165, 169
Hongzhang, Li, 36
honour killing, 257
Hopi people, 184
Hopkins, A. G., 7, 13
Horthy, Miklos, 243

House, Edward M., 264
Howard, Michael, 42
Hughes, Billy, 74
Hugo, Victor, 234
human rights, 203, 204, 211, 252, 268, 269
humanitarian intervention, 134, 186, 269, 276, 298, 301–303
Hungarian anti-Soviet uprising (1956), 133, 134
Hungary, 42, 106, 129, 130, 133, 144, 145, 148, 161, 164–167, 175, 243, 256, 308
Husain, M. F., 229
Hussein, Saddam, 229, 256
Husserl, Edmund, 197
Hutu, 255, 300
Hyam, Ronald, 203
Hyderabad, 121, 253
hydrogen bomb, 139, 179
hyperinflation, 79, 80

IBM, 141
Immigration, 71, 73, 89, 161, 263, 272, 273, 289–291, 296, 308, 316, 319
Imperial preference system, 166
Imperialism, 5, 6, 9, 10, 13, 16, 21, 25, 30, 35–41, 56, 73, 75, 79, 95, 101, 124, 141, 152, 200, 233, 247, 265
Import Duties Act (1932), 86
India, 2, 5, 8, 13, 15, 16, 18, 23, 24, 26, 29, 30, 32–37, 41, 44, 48, 68, 73–78, 83, 87–89, 100, 104–106, 108, 109, 111–123, 131, 138, 141, 142, 145, 149–156, 161, 163, 171, 172, 176, 177, 181, 184–191, 197, 198, 200, 202, 205, 207–213, 215, 217, 219, 220, 222, 225, 227, 229, 232, 235, 237–239, 244, 245, 247–249, 251, 253, 254, 258, 259, 264, 266–285, 288, 290–297, 301, 302, 305–307, 310, 311, 319–321
India-China War (1962), 122
Indian Army, 23, 88, 106, 171
Indian National Army, 104, 115, 131
Indian National Congress, 16, 68, 76, 77, 113, 149, 151, 171, 177, 185, 190, 238, 281
Indian Ocean, 18
Indian Planning Commission, 149
India-Pakistan War (1948), 108

indigenous people, 13, 76, 81, 155, 159, 233, 275, 289
Indochina, 13, 25, 62, 75, 76, 81, 102, 105, 108, 111–115, 119, 121–124, 127, 131, 151, 152, 155, 207, 232, 237, 243, 266, 282
Indochina wars (1950–1975), 107, 123; See also US-Vietnam War (1962–1973)
Indonesia, 104, 108, 111, 113, 124, 148, 149, 154, 156, 161, 204, 205, 254, 266, 271, 278, 280, 282, 295, 297, 315
Indonesian Communist Party (PKI), 148
Indo-Pakistan war (1948), 108
Industrialisation, 51, 63, 92, 93, 112, 114, 270, 285, 293
Internal Revenue Service, 173
International Brigade of Socialists, 101
International Criminal Police Commission, 258
International Labour Charter, 264
International Labour Organization, 263–265
International Monetary Fund (IMF), 138
International War Crimes Tribunal, 300
Internet, 7, 180, 183, 201, 212, 213, 236, 248, 257, 293
Inter-Parliamentary Union, 264
Interpol, 258, 261
Ipi, Faqir of, 100
Iqbal, Muhammad, 195, 238
IRA, 174
Iran, 27, 30–33, 51, 53–55, 133, 134, 140, 148, 163, 167, 168, 172, 177, 238, 244, 302, 303, 310
Iran–Contra Affair, 172
Iranian revolution (1979), 140, 149, 163
Iran–Iraq War, 168
Iraq, 8–10, 21–27, 32, 37, 53–55, 75, 78, 100, 102, 110, 120, 163, 164, 168, 184, 186, 187, 202, 229, 239, 244, 255–259, 264, 280, 288, 299–304, 306, 307, 310, 318
Iraq revolt (1920), 24
Iraqi army, 54
Iraqi Kurds, 8, 27, 53, 257, 303, 304
Ireland, 16, 38, 70, 157, 206, 242, 257, 275
Irgun, 119
Irish, 16, 38, 46, 70, 71, 74, 103, 120, 172, 200, 225, 241, 257, 275

Irish Free State, 70, 120
Irish rebellion (1916), 46
Iriye, Akira, 1
Iron Curtain, 107, 163
ISI, 302
ISIS, 2, 8, 202, 212, 244, 256, 257, 303
Islam, 21, 26, 65, 148, 163, 168, 185, 195, 203, 208, 231–234, 238, 239, 244, 245, 249, 279, 301
Islamisation, 168, 229
Islamism, 7, 11, 18, 19, 26, 163, 164, 166, 168, 264, 296, 301, 302, 307, 311, 319
Israel, 21, 66, 119–121, 146, 152, 155, 157, 169, 245, 250, 252–256, 269, 301–304
Israel Defense Forces, 155
Israeli–Lebanese War (1982), 66
Italian Constitution, 131
Italian invasion of Abyssinia (1935), 97
Italian invasion of Libya (1911), 24
Italian–Ottoman War (1911), 26
Italy, 16, 37, 49–51, 58–62, 65, 70, 74, 81, 82, 93, 95, 98–100, 104, 105, 107, 109, 110, 112, 130–132, 137, 156, 157, 174, 202, 208, 225, 240, 242, 244, 261, 265, 289, 291, 308, 318
Ivan the Terrible, 64

Jackson, Michael, 141
Jamaica, 77, 78
Jamia Millia Islamia, 78
Janata Party, 151
Japan, 9, 11, 13, 16, 21, 29, 30, 35–38, 41, 48, 51, 55–57, 59, 65, 72, 81–84, 86, 87, 89, 90, 92, 93, 95, 97–99, 102–118, 122–126, 132, 136, 137, 140, 161, 169, 187, 188, 208, 212, 214, 217, 220, 221, 227, 229, 237, 250, 252, 253, 258, 260, 261, 264, 265, 267, 268, 273, 278, 282, 289, 296, 309, 310, 314–317
Japanese Army, 9, 98, 104
Japanese occupation of Manchuria (1931), 56
Japanese occupation of Nanjing, 98
Japanese tsunami, 317
Javanese, 188, 278
Jedi-ism, 235
Jerusalem, 23, 25, 75, 100, 120, 121
Jesus, 232, 233, 245

Jevons, Stanley, 189
Jewish emigration to Palestine, 23
Jewish–Arab tensions, 24
jihad polities, 232
jihadism, 296, 300, 301, 303, 306
Jin, Ba, 220
Jinnah, Muhammad Ali, 202, 280
Joan of Arc, 234
Jobbik Party, 308
Jobs, Steve, 141
John Paul II, Pope, 167
Johnson, Lyndon B., 141
Jordan, 119, 120
Joseph, Keith, 174
Judt, Tony, 252
Jules Ferry Laws (1881), 206
July 14th Revolution (1958)
Jung, Carl, 197
Junkers, 13, 60, 130
Jutland, Battle of (1916), 19

Kafka, Franz, 217
Kagame, Paul, 255
Kahlo, Frida, 41
Kai-shek, Chiang, 52
Kai-shek, Madame Chiang, 200
Kakuzo, Okakura, 217
Kandinsky, Wassily, 216, 219, 224
Kandy, kingdom of, 254
Kanji, Ishiwara, 57
Kapila, Shruti, 172
Karbala and Najaf, holy cities of, 24
Karen, Kachin and Shan ethnic tensions, 108
Kashmir, 108, 119, 121, 161, 172, 254, 301, 302
Katyn massacre (1945), 251
Kazakhstan, 63, 129, 236
Kennedy, Jacqueline, 202
Kennedy, John F., 130, 142
Kenya, 31, 76, 89, 100, 105, 123, 127, 153, 156, 186, 223, 252, 273, 281, 301, 312
Kenyatta University, 223
Kenyatta, Jomo, 186
Keynes, John Maynard, 45, 273, 295
Keynesianism, 95, 101
Khilafat, 22, 26, 27, 33, 34, 54, 245, 249, 264, 267, 303
Khmer Rouge, 148, 207, 254
Khomeini, Ayatollah Ruhollah, 168

Khrushchev, Nikita, 64, 128, 129, 133, 140, 143–146, 148, 165
Kikuyu (language), 76, 90, 127, 128, 153, 187, 248, 273, 278, 282
Kikuyu Central Association, 281
Killing, 8, 12, 17, 20, 97, 98, 101, 106, 148, 156, 199, 218, 247–262, 299, 300
Kindleberger, Charles, 95
King Faisal I, 54
Kirchner, Cristina, 313
Kirghizstan, 16
Kissinger, Henry, 159
Knossos, 184
Konfrontasi, 149
Korea, 7, 37, 57, 99, 107, 110, 125, 126, 133, 135–137, 143, 145, 146, 149, 155, 161, 165, 169, 170, 209, 228, 236, 237, 245, 260, 296, 310, 321
Korean War (1950–1953), 107
Korekiyo, Takahashi, 93
Kosovo, 300
K-pop, 209
Krugman, Paul, 95
Ku Klux Klan, 72
kulaks, dissolution of, 63, 128, 236, 250
Kurds, 8, 22, 27, 33, 53, 257, 303, 304
Kursk, Battle of (1943), 105–106
Kusama, Yayoi, 229
Kut al-Amara, Battle of (1915–1916), 23
Kuwait, 164, 300
Kwantung Army, 99

labour camps, 63, 128, 199, 209, 222
Labour Party (UK), 69
labour strikes, 69, 71
Lacan, Jacques, 197, 262
Laden, Osama Bin, 301
landlordism, 65
Lang, Fritz, 218
language politics, 30
Lascaux, cave paintings, 183
Lashkar-e Taiba, 301
Laski, Harold, 68
latifundia, 60, 61
Latin America, 5–9, 16, 41, 49, 51, 53, 58, 59, 62, 63, 71, 81, 90, 109, 110, 135, 136, 151, 159–161, 166, 173, 187, 188, 199, 205, 211, 213, 225, 232, 235, 242, 243, 258, 261, 269, 271, 274, 291, 305, 306, 310, 312–314, 319, 320
Latvia, 129, 307

Lawrence, T. E., 26
Le Corbusier, 226
Le Duan, 145, 170
Leach, Edmund, 188
League of Nations, 5, 8, 20, 23, 25, 39, 53, 71, 80, 98, 101, 111, 155, 207, 263, 266
League of Nations Official Journal, 266
Leakey family, 183
Lebanon, 22, 25, 120, 202, 207, 239, 245, 254
lebensraum, 11, 287, 294
Lega Nord, 308
Lehman Brothers, 192, 314, 316
Lenin, Vladimir, 9
Leningrad, siege of, 103
Leninism, 267, 306
Leopold, King, 31
Leow, Rachel, 259
Levi, Primo, 117
Lévi-Strauss, Claude, 187
Lewis, Sinclair, 219
Leyland, 182
Leyte Gulf, Battle of (1944), 106
Liberal Democratic Party, 137, 170
liberalism, 40, 46, 51, 141, 146, 166, 167, 172, 177, 195, 309, 312
liberation theology, 214
Liberia, 255
Libya, 21, 24, 26, 98, 131, 240, 299, 304
Liebknecht, Karl, 46, 79
Linguistics, 187
Lissitzky, El, 221
literacy, 205, 206, 223, 284
Lithuania, 129
Llosa, Mario Vargas, 225
Lockerbie bombing (1984), 304
Lombroso, Cesare, 262
London bombings (2005), 301
London riots (2012), 213
London School of Economics, 186, 191
Long March (1934–1935), 99
longue durée, 5, 6
Louis, William Roger, 323–4
Lowry, L. S., 224
Ludendorff, Erich, 46
Lugard, Lord (Frederick), 75
Lumumba, Patrice, 145
Luo and Kikuyu relations, 76, 282
Luther King, Martin, 142, 143
Luxemburg, Rosa, 46, 79, 251

Lynching, 272
Lysenko, T. D., 180

Maastricht Treaty (1992), 175
MacArthur, General Douglas, 72, 106,
　109, 126, 133, 135, 136, 237
Macaulay, T. B., 276
MacDonald, Ramsay, 69
machine guns, 247–248
Macmillan, Harold, 155
Macmillan, Margaret, 96
Madagascar, 127
Madero, Francisco, 40
madrassas, 168, 235
Mafia, 71, 261
Mahalanobis, P. C., 285
Maharaja of Bikaner, 265
Mahathir Mohamad, 285
Mahdi, the, 15
Mailer, Norman, 117
Maine, Henry, 283
Maji Maji rebellion (1905–1907), 31
Makerere University, 223
Malabar rebellion (1921)
Malagasy revolt (1947–48), 127
Malaka, Tan, 124
Malaya, 30, 75, 90, 100, 104, 106, 112,
　119, 122, 126–128, 137, 153, 161, 252,
　259, 267, 271
Malaysia, 149, 153, 169, 267, 276, 277,
　285, 292, 315
Malevich, Kazimir, 221, 222
Malinowski, Bronisław, 186, 187
Manchukuo, 57, 99
Manchuria, 9, 11, 37, 56, 57, 93, 95, 97,
　99, 125, 136, 231, 232, 264, 265
Mandal Commission, 171, 311
Mandarin Chinese, 274
Mandela, Nelson, 176, 177, 312
Mandler, Peter, 5
Manhattan Project, 181
Mann, Michael, 185
Mann, Thomas, 15
Mansfield, Katherine, 220
Maoism, 140, 305, 306, 309
Maori language, 275
Maoris, 115
Mappila, 33
Mapuche Indians, 306
March on Rome (1922), 59
Marconi, Guglielmo, 181

Marcos, Ferdinand, 170
Marcuse, Herbert, 201
Marinetti, F. T., 216
Maronite Christians, 25
Márquez, Gabriel García, 225
Marsh Arabs, 229
Marshall Plan, 111
Marshall, Alfred, 190
Martinique, 77
Marx, Karl, 10, 187, 196
Marxism, 131, 168, 180, 187, 266
mass killing, 12, 156, 247–250, 253, 255,
　256, 300
mass production, 113, 134, 141
Matisse, Henri, 219, 225
Matteotti, Giacomo, 59
Mau Mau insurrection (1952–1960), 153
May 1968 protests, 158
May Fourth Movement (1919), 35, 44,
　220
Mazowiecki, Tadeusz, 167
Mazzinians, 58
Mbembe, Achille, 188
McCarthy, Joseph, 110
McMeekin, Sean, 96
Mead, Margaret, 187
Medicaid, 142
Medicare, 142
Meiji Restoration (1868), 41
Meir, Golda, 200
Menshevik Party, 16
Menzies, Robert, 109
Mexican Liberal Party, 40
Mexican Revolution (1911–1917), 13,
　40, 159, 242, 306
Mexico, 15, 40–42, 51, 65, 82, 135, 141,
　217, 223, 242, 258, 260, 288, 291, 313
MI5, 139
Microsoft, 141, 173, 316
middle class, 8, 15, 32, 33, 37, 40, 53, 55,
　56, 59, 61, 65, 66, 71, 79, 81, 102, 103,
　114, 120, 123, 130, 131, 137, 150, 159,
　162, 169, 173, 177, 202, 209, 210, 213,
　224, 238, 240, 242, 245, 260, 291, 292,
　311–314, 320, 321
Middle East, 2, 9, 13, 15, 16, 21, 23, 27,
　34, 39, 41, 42, 51, 53, 55, 57, 75, 97,
　110, 111, 120–122, 127, 129, 184, 195,
　238, 239, 244, 254, 256, 264, 269, 280,
　299, 302, 305, 306, 308, 311, 313
Mill, James, 283

Mill, John Stuart, 189, 283
miners' strike (UK), 174
miracolo economico, il, 131
missionary activity, 112, 207, 241
Misuratis, 299
Mitterrand, François, 167, 175
Modi, Narendra, 245, 311, 319
Modigliani, Amedeo, 216
Mohenjo-daro, 184
Mokujiki Movement, 220
Molotov, Vyacheslav, 128
monarchy, 53–55, 60, 82, 120, 131
monetarism, 94, 95
Mongolia, 236
Monkey Trials, 206, 241
Montagu–Chelmsford Reforms
    (1919), 34
Monti, Mario, 318
Moore, Henry, 224
Moral Re-Armament, 242, 267
Morgan, T. H., 180
Mormonism, 234
Morocco; Rif rebellion (1920–1926), 250
Mosley, Oswald, 59, 67, 70, 101
Mossadegh, Mohammad, 134
Mountbatten, Louis, 108, 122, 253
Moyn, Samuel, 5
Mubarak, Hosni, 304
Mufti of Jerusalem, 100
Mugabe, Robert, 312
Mughal Empire, 185
Muhammad, the Prophet, 234
mui tsai, 259
mujahidin, 300
Mukerjee, Radhakamal, 295
Mumbai attacks (2008), 302
Munich agreement (1938) Murderous
    Outrages Act (1867), 259
mushairas, 228, 281
Muslim Brotherhood, 2, 55, 78, 110,
    168, 239, 244, 245, 267, 279, 281,
    299, 304
Muslim extremism, 2
Mussolini, Benito, 58
Myanmar, 256
Myint-U, Thant, 226

Nagas, 115, 232, 251
Nagasaki, 30, 106, 136, 139, 181, 248,
    251
Nanjing massacre (1937), 252

Naoroji, Dadabhai, 190, 284
Napoleonic Wars, 95
Narasimha Rao, P. V., 310
Nasser, Gamal Abdel, 110
National Algerian Movement, 90
National Congress of British West
    Africa, 75, 77
National Development and Reform
    Commission, 293
National Health Service (UK), 109
National Housing Act (Canada), 73
National Liberation Front, 90
National Party (South Africa), 127
National Rifle Association, 173, 317
National Socialism
nationalisation of banks, 93, 151, 154,
    159, 175
nationalism, 199, 220, 236, 237
NATO, 300, 307
Nazi Party, 78, 80
Nazism, 8, 27, 50, 52, 58, 60, 61, 64,
    68, 94, 130, 132, 138, 144, 198,
    242, 243
Negri, Antonio, 6, 10
Nehru, Jawaharlal, 34, 78, 238, 282, 285
neo-Buddhism, 127, 234
neo-Confucianism, 56
neoliberalism, 40, 134, 141, 172, 175,
    307, 309, 312, 313
Netanyahu, Benjamin, 304
Netherlands, 67, 78, 82, 103, 112, 199,
    266, 284, 292
Networks, 4, 6, 11, 65, 71, 187, 267, 306,
    310
New Deal, 61, 72, 93, 94, 102, 109, 110,
    142, 173, 241, 318
New Economic Policy, 54, 63, 86, 93,
    165, 196
new imperialism, 13, 21, 30, 31, 35, 75,
    95, 98, 99, 233, 305
New Life Movement, 52
New Zealand, 13, 23, 38, 73, 74, 155,
    161, 174, 199, 211, 231, 232, 272, 275,
    287
Newman, Barnett, 224
Nguyen Ai Quoc. See Ho Chi Minh
Nietzsche, Friedrich, 52
Nigeria, 75, 77, 89, 154, 176, 229, 244,
    255, 259, 301, 307, 312
Nigerian civil war (1967–1970), 255
Nigerian Youth Movement, 76

Nippon Kaigi, 309
Nivedita, Sister, 217
Nixon, Richard, 140, 146, 159, 172, 191
Nkrumah, Kwame, 78, 154
Non-Aligned Movement, 111
North Korea, 126, 161, 165, 209, 236, 310, 321
North Vietnam, 108
Northern Ireland, 70, 257
Northwest Frontier Province, 121, 259
Nozick, Robert, 198
Nu, U, 122
nuclear power, 8, 140, 179, 181, 302
nuclear weapons, 8, 10, 106
Nuremberg trials, 252
Nyerere, Julius, 283

O'Brien, P. K., 5
Oakeshott, Michael, 195
Obama, Barack, 3, 274, 309, 318, 319
obesity, 292, 293
Occupy Movement, 306
oil, 10, 26, 32, 54, 55, 90, 103, 104, 106, 134, 155, 164–167, 240, 260, 269, 303–305, 307, 312, 313
oligarchs, 10, 40, 192, 307, 308, 310
Olympic Games, 210
One-Child Policy (China), 202, 258, 291
opera, 108
Oppenheimer, Robert, 101
Opus Dei, 267
Organisation of African Unity, 268
organised crime, 209, 261
Orthodox Church, 2, 62, 83, 205, 308
Orwell, George, 101, 117
Osterhammel, Jürgen, 1, 5
Ostpolitik, 175
Ottoman Empire, 13, 15, 18, 20–22, 25, 30, 32–33, 41, 42, 53, 120, 218, 232, 238, 248, 249, 299
Ottoman Turkish, 22, 274
Overy, Richard, 97
Owen, Wilfred, 218

Pacific Islands, 13, 115
Padmore, George, 77, 186
Pahlavi, Reza Shah, 32, 55
Pakhtunistan, 121
Pakistan, 26, 108, 119, 121, 151, 155, 161, 168, 184, 196, 202, 203, 208, 229, 238, 253, 254, 256, 259, 276, 280, 293, 299, 301, 302, 304, 306, 310, 311, 319
Pakistani Taliban, 302
Palatinate, 60
Palestine, 22–25, 33, 100, 119, 120, 138, 160, 207, 239, 278, 303, 304
Pan-African Congress, 265
Pan-Asianism, 103
panchayats, 34
Pandey, Gyanendra, 253
Pandit, Vijaya Lakshmi, 268
Pan-European Union, 265
Pan-Islamism, 18
Pan-Slavism, 243
Pant, G. B., 88
Pan-Turanism, 243
Paraguay, 160
Paris Assembly, 68
Parsons, Talcott, 192
Parti colonial, 25
Partition of India, 253
Pasternak, Boris, 229
Patton, George, 72
Peace Corps, 188
Peace Treaties (1919), 27, 101
Peacekeeping, 300
Pearl Harbor, 103–106
Pearson, Karl, 295–296
peasant insurgencies, 124
Pende Revolt (1931), 90
Peng, Chin, 267
Pentecostalism, 7, 203, 245, 246
People's Republic of China, 126
perestroika, 165, 166, 290
Perón, Eva, 200
Perón, Juan, 58
Perry, Grayson, 224
Persia, 13, 15, 16, 24, 32, 41, 51, 54, 55, 164, 185, 276
Persian Cossack Brigade, 55
Persian Revolution (1905–1911), 15
Pétain, Marshal Philippe, 102
Peter the Great, 64
Philby, Harry St John, 26
Philippines; -Japanese WWII massacres (1945), 106; -US occupation of, 113; democracy, 205; -Catholic Church in, 205
Piaf, Edith, 227
Picasso, Pablo, 101
pieds noirs, 76, 152, 156

Piketty, Thomas, 3
Piłsudski, General Józef, 62
Pink Wave, 159
Pinochet, Augusto, 159
piracy, 260
Pius XI, Pope, 51
Pius XII, Pope, 51
Plath, Sylvia, 200
pogroms, anti-Jewish, 25
Poland, 27, 62, 68, 102, 106, 107, 112, 129, 130, 164–167, 237, 264
Politburo, 63, 144, 165
Pollock, Jackson, 117, 224
pollution, 182, 293
Pomeranz, Kenneth, 5
Popper, Karl, 324
Popular Front, 75, 79, 81, 243
population growth, 11, 288–290, 295
population transfers; -in India, 120; -in Israel, 120; -in Ottoman Empire, 120
Portugal, 62, 109
Post-Structuralism, 225
Pot, Pol, 148, 207, 252
Potsdam, 106
Poverty, 5, 46, 70, 72, 89, 134, 151, 167, 170, 174, 181, 190, 204, 247, 269, 285, 289, 291, 307, 313, 314, 316
Premchand, Munshi, 220
Presley, Elvis, 227
Privatisation, 307
Progressive movement (USA), 320
Progressive Writers' Movement, 220, 229
Prohibition, 45, 71, 72
Prokofiev, Sergei, 222
prostitution, 259, 261
Protestant Unionism, 16
Proust, Marcel, 216
Provisional IRA, 174
Prussia, 60
Psy, 228
Pussy Riot, 308
Putin, Vladimir, 307, 319

al-Qaeda, 5, 153, 212, 244, 257, 301, 303
Qajar dynasty, 32
Qichao, Liang, 68, 190
Qing Empire, 15, 37
Quakers, 280
Quit India Movement, 104, 131

Qur'an, 22, 245, 279
Qutb, Sayyid, 78

Rabin, Yitzhak, 304
race, 3, 15, 43, 45, 51, 52, 60, 70–72, 79, 98, 107, 115, 125, 155, 180, 181, 183, 185, 186, 200, 271–273, 281, 285, 295, 296
race relations, 71
race riots, 273
race theory, 186, 251
race war, 51, 273, 295
Radcliffe-Brown, A. A., 186
Radhakrishnan, Sarvepalli, 112
radical theology, 196
RAF. See Royal Air Force
Rancière, Jacques, 321
Rand, Ayn, 219
Rangarajan, Mahesh, 294
Rathenau, Walther, 79
Rauschenberg, Robert, 224
Raw Materials Section (KRA), 43
Rawls, John, 198
Razakars, 253
Reagan, Ronald, 3, 140, 146, 156, 163, 164, 168, 172, 241
Red Army, 79, 128–130
Red Army of the Ruhr, 79
Red Brigades, 156
Red Crescent Society, 33, 264
Red Cross, 111, 264
Red Guards, 147, 148, 208
Red Menace, 74
Red Scare (1919–1920), 71
re-education, 209
Reich, Wilhelm, 201
Reichsbank, 91
religion, 6, 7, 10, 15, 27, 51, 53, 57, 59, 129, 148, 150, 172, 173, 179, 180, 184, 192, 195, 197–199, 205, 206, 208, 216, 231–246, 270, 271, 273, 278–281
Remarque, Erich Maria, 218
Representation of the People Act (1918), 69
Republican Party, 110, 314, 318
reunification of Vietnam, 148
Reynolds, Joshua, 225
Rhineland, 44, 46, 59, 61, 79, 80, 101, 265, 273
Rhodes, Cecil, 9
Ricardo, David, 189

Rida, Rashid, 239
Rivera, Diego, 41, 222
Rivers, W. H. R., 186
Robinson, Joan, 191
Rocco, Alfredo, 58
Rockefeller Foundation, 111
Rolling Stones, 141, 227
Roma gypsies, 308
Romania, 164
Rommel, General Erwin, 102
Roosevelt, Eleanor, 200
Roosevelt, Theodore, 13, 15, 16
Rorty, Richard, 198
Rosanvallon, Pierre, 198
Rosenberg, Emily, 1, 4
Rosenthal, Laurent, 6
Rothko, Mark, 224
Roy, M. N., 266
Royal Air Force (RAF), 102
Rushdie, Salman, 225
Russell, Bertrand, 68, 190, 198, 220
Russia, 25, 26, 30, 32, 33, 37, 40, 42, 43,
    45–48, 51, 52, 55, 56, 60, 62–64, 79–
    81, 96, 103, 104, 106, 112, 123, 128,
    141, 150, 153, 163–167, 170, 176, 191,
    205, 209, 211, 212, 216–219, 222, 228,
    244, , 249, 259, 261, 269, 277, 287,
    289, 290, 294, 298, 300, 302, 307, 308,
    310, 319
Russian Empire, 25
Russian Provisional Government
    (1917), 51
Russian revolution (1905), 216
Russian revolution, (1917), 42
Russo-Japanese War (1904–1905), 37
Rwanda, 255, 256, 299

al-Shaker, Bassim, 229
SA, 52, 61, 64, 251
Said, Edward, 188
al-Said, Nuri, 120
Salafism, 279
Salazar, Antonio de Oliveria, 156
Samurai, 13, 51, 57, 237
San, Aung, 103, 107, 122
sanctions, 144, 145, 195, 196, 209, 313
Sandberg, Sheryl, 201
Sanskrit, 276
Sanskritisation, 188
Sarikamish, Battle of (1914), 19
Sarkar, Jadunath, 185

Sarraut, Albert, 25
Sartre, Jean-Paul, 117, 158, 187, 225
Sassoon, Siegfried, 218
satyagraha, 34, 238
Saud, Abdulaziz Ibn, 21
Saudi Arabia, 26, 181, 196, 202, 240,
    301, 321
Savarkar, V. D., 171, 238, 267
Sayyid Ahmad of Rai Bareilly, 301
Scarcity, 150, 288, 292, 297
Schacht, Hjalmar, 91
Schmidt, Helmut, 175
Schmitt, Carl, 52, 198
Schoenberg, Arnold, 216
Schumpeter, Joseph, 13
Schuster, George, 87
Scientology, 234
Scotland, 174, 242, 304
Scots Gaelic, 275
Scott, James C., 188
Scottish National Party, 309
Scriabin, Alexander, 222
Second Anglo-Afghan War
    (1878–1880), 33
Second Republic (Spain), 82
Second World War, 84, 88, 89, 91, 93,
    94, 96, 105, 110, 113, 114, 119, 121,
    123, 126–128, 138, 140, 150, 152, 155,
    181, 187, 190, 200, 203, 226, 227, 240,
    242–244, 249–251, 253, 266, 267, 290,
    292, 295, 296
sectarianism, 167–169
secularism, 2, 6, 40, 55, 161, 195,
    205–207, 237–239, 241, 243
segregation, 155, 176
Selassie, Haile, 55, 98
Seligman, G. C., 186
Sen, Amartya, 191
Senate (US), 73, 133, 318
Senegal, 25, 76, 81
September 11th 2001. See 9/11
Serbia, 16, 17, 26, 27, 33, 42, 186,
    256, 300
sex, 115, 181, 183, 197, 199–201, 203,
    204, 208–212, 228, 244, 258, 259, 262,
    272, 293, 321
sex workers, 204
Sexton, Anne, 200
sexual equality, 115, 200
sexual revolution, 199
sexual violence, 199

al-Shabab, 257
Shakespeare, William, 272
Shanghai School, 217
Sharia Council, 100, 278
Sharia law, 202
Sharif Hussein of Mecca, 22, 25
Sharifian dynasty (Iraq), 53
Sharifian sultanate (Morocco), 30
Sharpeville Massacre (1960), 142
Sheffield, 330
Shia Islam, 168, 245
Shia Revolt (1936), 54
Shia triangle, 303
Shikai, Yuan, 36
Shintoism, 51, 57, 65, 83, 208, 237, 279
Shintoism, 261, 279
Shiv Sena, 311
Siberia, 13, 104, 113, 209, 231
Sierra Leone, 255
Sikhism, 208
Silicon Valley, 275
Singapore, 26, 33, 57, 104, 122, 165,
    169, 182, 226, 275–277, 285, 310, 315
Singh, B. P., 171
Singh, Manmohan, 172
single currency, 163, 175, 308
Sinn Fein, 16, 70
Sino-Soviet split, 145
Sino-Vietnam War, 145
slavery, 272, 274
Slim, General William, 106
Slovenia, 251, 300
Sluga, Glenda, 264
Smallholders Party (Hungary), 129
Smith, Adam, 189
Smuts, General Jan, 73
Sneevliet, Henk, 266
Snowden, Edward, 321
social Darwinism, 248, 271, 273
Social Democratic Party (Germany), 16,
    79
Social Revolutionary Party (Russia), 63
Social Security Act (1935), 72
socialism, 6, 9, 10, 19, 56, 60, 63, 68, 69,
    86, 98, 110, 112, 127, 133, 141, 148,
    149, 163, 165, 167, 172, 178, 196, 206,
    218, 219, 237, 241–243, 245, 283
Socialism in One Country, 9, 63
Socialist Party (Japan), 137, 175
Solidarity, 13, 58, 114, 135, 164, 167,
    237, 245, 261, 309

Solomon Islanders, 187
Somalia, 301, 307
Sonderweg, 50, 74
Soros, George, 192
South Africa, 13, 16, 31, 34, 39, 41, 73,
    89, 90, 127, 142, 155, 156, 163, 166,
    172, 174, 176, 177, 195, 210, 211, 223,
    233, 255, 268, 271–273, 279, 284, 285,
    296, 311
South African War (1899–1902), 31
South China Sea, 9, 10, 260, 269, 309
South Korea, 7, 107, 137, 143, 165, 169,
    170, 228, 245, 310
South Manchuria Railway Company, 9, 99
South Sudan, 256, 305
South Vietnam, 235, 261
Southeast Asia, 5, 6, 16, 20, 37, 76, 84,
    97, 100, 103, 106, 108, 111, 112, 115,
    122, 123, 127, 137, 141, 142, 145, 148,
    151, 170, 233, 237, 240, 266, 268, 269,
    277, 278, 280, 285, 296, 309, 319
Southern Rhodesia, 76, 157
Soviet aid, 126
Soviet invasion of Hungary (1956), 133
Soviet Young Pioneers, 52
Spain, 30, 46, 47, 51, 59–61, 81, 82, 101,
    109, 135, 156, 225, 235, 242, 243, 250,
    316, 318
Spanish, 8, 14, 16, 30, 47, 51, 61, 71,
    152, 206, 225, 242, 247, 250, 274, 275,
    278, 309
Spanish Civil War (1936–1940), 100
Spartacist revolt (1919), 20
Spengler, Oswald, 17, 319
sport, 8, 45, 59, 60, 177, 208–212, 292,
    294, 320
sputnik (satellite), 113, 144, 181, 294
squadristi, 56, 59, 70, 95
Sri Lanka, 254, 256, 278
Srinivas, M. N., 188
SS, 52, 251
St. Augustine of Hippo, 197, 198
stagflation, 173, 191
Stakhanov, Alexey, 64
Stakhanovite movements, 64
Stalin, 9, 41, 45, 49, 50, 52, 63, 64, 67,
    68, 93, 95, 100–104, 106, 107, 110,
    112, 128, 129, 133, 143–146, 148, 161,
    165, 196, 222, 225, 236, 250, 251, 268,
    290, 310
Stalingrad, Battle of, 105, 113, 128

Stallone, Sylvester, 228
Stasi, 130
state capitalism, 7, 91, 147, 169
Statute of Westminster (1931), 73
Stavisky Affair (1934), 81
Steinbeck, John, 219
Sterling, Donald, 211
Stern Gang, 119
Stevenson, David, 18
Stewart, Rory, 304
Stiglitz, Joseph, 3
Stilwell, General Joseph, 106, 125
Strachan, Hew, 18, 42
Straits Settlement, 259
Strauss, Leo, 80, 195
Stravinsky, Igor, 216, 226
Stresemann, Gustav, 80
Structuralism, 185, 187, 188
Subaltern Studies, 5, 188
sub-Saharan Africa, 31, 142, 233, 269, 320
Sudan, 8, 15, 76, 102, 202, 232, 240,
    256, 259, 299, 305
Suez Canal, 23, 78, 119, 120
Suez Crisis, 23, 78
Suffragette movement, 39, 71, 200
Suffragettes, 16, 39, 71, 200
Sufism, 195, 232, 233, 236, 240, 245,
    285
Sukarno, Achmad, 124
Sullivan, Michael, 220
Sumatra, 124, 260
Sunni Islam, 10, 22, 25, 27, 53, 54, 120,
    122, 128, 168, 245, 280, 303, 304
Supreme Court, 135, 173
Surrealist movement, 219
Swadeshi, 16, 217, 218
Swahili, 278
Sweden, 67, 86, 273
Swettenham, Frank, 284
Switzerland, 19, 218
Sykes–Picot Agreement (1916), 2, 23
Sylvester, 203, 228
Syria, 8–10, 21–25, 27, 100, 207, 239,
    255–257, 269, 277, 280, 288, 299, 303,
    304
Syrian civil war (2011–2013), 304

Tablighi Jamaat, 267
Taft, William, 15
Tagore, Abanindranath, 217
Tagore, Rabindranath, 217, 220

Taiping rebellion, 97, 234
Taiwan, 37, 99, 103, 126, 169, 170, 241
Taliban, 8, 100, 148, 164, 168, 172, 196,
    202, 276, 301, 302
Tambo, Oliver, 176
Tamil Tigers, 254
Tanganyika, 31
Tanganyika Groundnut Scheme, 127
Tanzania, 312
Tanzimât reforms, 239
Tawney, R. H., 69
Taylor, A. J. P., 96
Taylor, Charles, 194, 255
Tea Party movement, 212, 317,
    318, 321
technological developments, 129
Telang, K. T., 190
Telangana Movement, 121
Telangana revolt, 253
Tendulkar, Sachin, 211
Tennessee Valley Scheme, 72
Territorial Army, 114
Terrorism, 44, 245, 262, 314
Tet Offensive (1968), 145
Thailand, 169, 273, 315, 319
Thatcher, Margaret, 3, 156, 163, 174,
    191, 268
Theosophy, 83, 216, 234
Third Anglo-Afghan War (1919–
    1920), 33
Third Reich, 17, 130, 265
Third World, 93, 145
Thompson, E. P., 5
Tiananmen Square (1989), 169
Tito, Josip Broz, 62
Toda people, 186
Tokyo earthquake, 92
Tolstoy, Leo, 197
Tooze, Adam, 18, 21, 42
tourism, 131, 261, 312
Toynbee, Arnold, 185
Trabant, 144
Transavantgarde movement, 225
Trans-Jordan, 22, 23, 55, 304
Trans-Siberian railway, 9
Treaty of Berlin (1885), 31
Treaty of Lausanne (1923), 27
Treaty of Rapallo (1922), 79
Treaty of Waitangi (1840), 74
Tribal Civil and Criminal Disputes
    Regulation, 24

tribal people, 40, 115, 136, 232, 245, 271, 282
Triple Entente, 19
Tripoli, 24, 240
Trobriand islanders, 186
Trocki, Carl, 259
Trotsky, Leon, 63, 64, 221, 223
Troubles, the, 157
Truman, Harry, 106, 109, 126, 133, 134, 268
Truth and Reconciliation Commission (South Africa), 177
Tunisia, 279
Turkey, 23, 26, 27, 53, 55, 238, 239, 245, 249, 250, 319
Turkification, 22, 26, 249
Turkish War of Independence, 47
Tutsi, 248, 255, 300
Twitter, 213, 313

U-2 Incident, 133
Uganda, 76, 127, 155, 204, 223, 255
Uighurs, 305
Ujamaa, 283
UK Independence Party (UKIP), 274
UK Treasury, 88
Ukraine, 2, 63, 64, 106, 129, 144, 166, 211, 251, 256, 299, 308
ulama, 24, 30, 236, 239, 245
Ulster, 70, 242
UN Convention on Weapons, 257
UN Security Council, 269
UNESCO, 9, 188, 198, 267–269, 296
Ungaretti, Giuseppe, 218
Union Minière, 90
Union of American States, 155
Union of South Africa (1910), 73
United Fruit Conglomerate, 136
United Kingdom, see Britain
United Nations (UN), 98, 111, 121, 124, 138, 154, 155, 188, 268, 272, 296, 300
United States, 2, 3, 13, 15, 16, 18, 19, 20, 36, 38, 39, 41, 43, 45, 48, 50, 57, 62, 67, 68, 69, 70, 71, 72, 73, 74, 79, 82, 84–87, 90, 91, 93–94, 97, 98, 102, 103, 104, 106, 108, 109, 110, 113, 124, 129, 132, 133–138, 139–158, 163, 164, 165, 166, 168, 169, 170, 172, 175, 180, 181, 183, 186, 187, 193, 194, 195, 196, 199, 200, 204, 206, 208, 209, 210, 211, 212, 213, 217, 219, 220, 222, 223, 227, 241,

242, 246, 249, 251, 252, 253, 258, 262, 264, 265, 268, 269, 272, 273, 274, 275, 277, 279, 290, 291, 292, 296, 298, 302, 303, 304, 306, 309, 310, 311, 312, 313, 315, 316, 318, 319, 320, 321, 323, 324, 325, 326, 329, 330
United States of America, 323
Universal Declaration of Human Rights (1948), 268
Universal Races Congress (1911), 273
universal suffrage, 68, 77, 79, 155
University of Cambridge, 2
Upper Silesia, 61, 264
Urabi rebellion (1881), 22
urbanisation, 11, 43, 51, 92, 110, 147, 167, 241, 258, 282, 286, 289, 293
Urdu, 220, 254, 274, 278
Uruguay, 159, 160, 313
USSR, 2, 9, 23, 41, 45, 47, 48, 50, 62–64, 68, 80, 86, 91, 93, 95, 97, 99, 103, 105–108, 110, 112, 113, 123, 127–130, 133–135, 139, 140, 143–146, 148, 151–155, 157–161, 164–170, 172–174, 176, 178, 180, 181, 189, 193, 200, 206, 208, 213, 218–220, 222, 225, 229, 236, 265, 266, 268, 277, 290, 300, 307–310
US–Vietnam War (1962–1973), 162, 224
Uzbekistan, 166

V2 rockets, 257
van Dyck, Anthony, 225
Vargas, Getulio, 92
Varma, Raja Ravi, 217
Vatican, 237, 242
Velvet Revolution, 164
Venezuela, 306, 312, 313
Venice Film Festival, 219
Vespasian, Emperor, 310
Victoria, Queen, 199
Viet Minh, 108, 123, 124, 145, 207, 267, 277
Viet Nam Quoc Dan Dang (VNQDD), 81
Vietnam, 6, 108, 112, 115, 122–126, 137, 138, 140, 141, 143, 145, 146, 148, 149, 152, 158, 160, 165, 170, 186, 191, 200, 206, 208, 209, 222–225, 228, 234, 235, 237, 244, 248, 252–254, 260, 261, 266, 273, 275, 277, 298, 307

Vietnamese invasion of Cambodia (1978), 148
Villa, Francisco, 40
Vivekananda, Swami, 233
Volcker, Paul, 173
Volkswagen, 144, 182
von Bethmann-Hollweg, Theobald, 42
von Moltke, Helmuth, 17
von Papen, Franz, 91
von Sternberg, Josef, 219
Voting Rights Act (1965), 142

Wafd Party, 24, 27, 55, 78, 110, 239, 281
Wahhab, Abdul, 240
Wahhabism, 195, 244
Wailing Wall Riots, 25
Wales, 174
Wałęsa, Lech, 167
Wall Street Crash, 69, 91
Walloons, 309
War Communism, 63
War in the Pacific, 181
war reparations, 59, 85, 90
Warhol, Andy, 224
warlordism, 48
wars of fragmentation, 7, 9, 11, 214, 256, 269, 298, 299, 304–306, 309, 313
Warsaw Pact, 166
Washington Naval Treaty (1922), 38
water tables, 4, 289
Watergate scandal, 140
wealth redistribution, 313
Weber, Max, 7, 80, 180, 186, 192, 233, 279
Webern, Anton, 226
Weimar Republic, 46, 49, 51, 59, 60, 68, 79, 80, 83, 91, 132, 200, 218
Weiwei, Ai, 229
Welfare State, 8, 9, 70, 79, 86, 94, 97, 131, 132, 134, 153, , 161, 192, 290, 315
Wellesley, Lord, 247
Wells, H. G., 48
Werner, Michael, 1
Wessel, Horst, 61
West Bank; -Jewish settlements in, 304
West Germany (Federal Republic of Germany), 132, 157, 158
whaling, 260
White Army, 13
White Dominions, 39, 72
Wikileaks, 213

Wilde, Oscar, 203
Wilhelm II, Kaiser, 50
Wilhelmina of the Netherlands, Queen, 199
Wilson, Harold, 157
Wilson, Woodrow, 38, 264, 265
Win, Ne, 122
Winter Olympic Games, 211
Wittgenstein, Ludwig, 198
Wojtyła, Karol (see Pope John Paul II)
women's rights, 71, 265
Wong, R. Bin, 6
Workers' Party (Brazil), 313
working class, 5, 8, 20, 23, 40, 51, 59, 63–65, 68, 70, 82, 88, 91, 116, 123, 130, 146, 160, 190, 211, 269, 306, 314, 316
Works Progress Administration, 72, 94
World Bank, 8, 190, 192. 269, 315, 317
World Health Organization (WHO), 269, 293
World Parliament of Religions (1893), 15, 232
Wozniak, Stephen, 141

Xiaoping, Deng, 147, 148, 169, 309
Xiaotong, Fei, 186

Yakuza, 261
Yalta, 106
Yat-sen, Sun, 36, 51, 55
Yazidis, 10
Yeltsin, Boris, 166, 307
Yemen, 303
Yew, Lee Kuan, 276, 285
Yiddish, 252
Young Communist Pioneers, 206
Young Turk revolution (1908), 15, 21–23, 249
Yousafzai, Malala, 202, 276
youth culture, 137, 140–143
Yugoslavia, 27, 62, 65, 68, 107, 108, 130, 166, 299, 300, 308
Yutang, Lin, 329

Zaibatsu, 9
Zamindari Abolition Acts (1949–1951), 150
Zapata, Emiliano, 40
Zapatista movement, 40, 306, 313
Zedong, Mao, 6, 37, 56, 118, 125, 146, 236, 267

Zhenhua, Xie, 293
Zhijie, Qiu, 222
Zhimo, Xu, 220
Zia-ul-Haq, General Muhammad, 168
Zimbabwe, 157, 273, 312

Zimmermann, Bénédicte, 1, 6
Zinoman, Peter, 267
Zinoviev, Grigory, 64
Zintanis, 299
Zionism, 11, 21, 198
Žižek, Slavoj, 10, 50, 222, 321